A Political and Economic Dictionary of Eastern Europe

A Political and Economic Dictionary of Eastern Europe

Alan J Day, Roger East and Richard Thomas

First Edition

Europa Publications
Taylor & Francis Group

First Edition 2002

© **Cambridge International Reference on Current Affairs (CIRCA) Ltd 2002**
Compiled and typeset by Cambridge International Reference on Current Affairs (CIRCA) Ltd, Cambridge, England

All rights reserved. No part of this publication may be
photocopied, recorded, or otherwise reproduced, stored in a
retrieval system or transmitted in any form or by any electronic
or mechanical means without the prior permission of the copyright owner.

ISBN   1-85743-063-8

Printed and bound by TJ International Ltd, Padstow, Cornwall

Foreword

A POLITICAL AND ECONOMIC DICTIONARY OF EASTERN EUROPE is being published for the first time in 2002. The structure and organization of government, politics, production, international relations and trade across this whole region has been reshaped so dramatically in the past decade and a half that the landscape is only just beginning to become familiar in its current configuration.

The likelihood of further major changes, foreseeable and otherwise, remains as a formidable challenge to the publishers of any reference work such as the present volume. There can be no 'ideal time' to try to capture the shape of the contemporary political and economic situation. There is, nevertheless, a powerful case for trying to establish an overview based on up-to-date information, and this is an objective that this book seeks to serve.

Eastern Europe, for the purposes of this book, is taken to encompass all the countries which once formed part of the Soviet Union with the exception of the five Central Asian republics (but including the whole of the Russian Federation, much of which is obviously Asian rather than European), and to extend westwards as far as Poland, the Czech Republic, Slovakia, Hungary and the former Yugoslavia, notwithstanding that for several of those countries the term Central Europe is both more historically appropriate and geographically accurate.

Entries in the dictionary are designed to stand on their own in providing definitions and essential facts, with coverage of recent developments and, where appropriate, full contact details. The broad scope of the dictionary includes political groups, institutions, main government leaders and prominent individuals, trade unions, financial and trade bodies, religious organizations, ethnic groups, regions, geographical areas and principal cities, as well as essential terms and concepts, flashpoints, and other entries as appropriate. There is extensive cross-referencing between entries, indicated by the simple and widely familiar device of using a bold typeface for those words or entities which have their own coverage. There is also a listing, by country, of the entries relevant to that country (Appendix, p. 627), and a comprehensive index of personal names (p. 637).

The longest individual entries in this book are those for the region's 22 individual countries, giving a succinct structural description and historical survey to place recent events in context. The country entries are followed in each case by entries on that country's economy, again combining up-to-date basic data with a short overview and a focus on recent issues and developments.

Cambridge, April 2002

Acknowledgements

The editors gratefully acknowledge the assistance received in the compilation of this book from many of the organizations listed in it. We are also greatly indebted to the staff of Cambridge International Reference on Current Affairs (CIRCA) Ltd for their painstaking work in collecting and revising data, and to two publications in particular, the *Europa World Year Book* and the *International Who's Who*, which have both been used extensively for the cross-checking of detailed factual information.

We also wish to acknowledge the assistance of national statistical offices, government departments and diplomatic missions, as well as the following publications as invaluable sources of statistical information for the present volume: the United Nations Population Fund's *The State of World Population 2001*, the World Bank's *World Bank Atlas 2001* and *World Development Indicators 2001*, the International Monetary Fund's *Direction of Trade Statistics Yearbook 2001*, the Inter-Parliamentary Union's Parline Database and CIRCA's *People in Power*.

Contents

International Telephone Codes	*viii*
Abbreviations	*ix*
The Dictionary	1
Appendix: Country-by-Country Listing	*627*
Index of Personal Names	*637*

International Telephone Codes

Eastern Europe
Albania	+355
Armenia	+374
Azerbaijan	+994
Belarus	+375
Bosnia and Herzegovina	+387
Bulgaria	+359
Croatia	+385
Czech Republic	+420
Estonia	+372
Georgia	+995
Hungary	+36
Latvia	+371
Lithuania	+370
Macedonia	+389
Moldova	+373
Poland	+48
Romania	+40
Russian Federation	+7
Slovakia	+421
Slovenia	+386
Ukraine	+380
Yugoslavia	+381

Other countries hosting relevant international organizations
Austria	+43
Belgium	+32
Finland	+358
France	+33
Germany	+49
Iran	+98
Italy	+39
Netherlands	+31
Saudi Arabia	+966
Sweden	+46
Switzerland	+41
Turkey	+90
United Kingdom	+44
United States of America	+1

Abbreviations

Used in addresses
Al.   Aleja (Alley, Avenue)
bd, Blvd, Bul., bulv.   Boulevard (Avenue)
BP   Boite Postale (Post Box)
Cad.   Caddesi (Street)
c/o   care of
CP   Case Postale (Post Box)
nábř.   nábřeží/nábřežíe (wharf/embankment)
nám.   námesti/námestie (square)
pall.   pallati (building)
per.   pereulok (lane/alley)
pl.   place (square)
POB   Post Office Box
pr.   prospect (avenue)
pst.   puiestee (avenue)
rkp.   rakpárt (wharf/embankment)
Rr.   Rruga (street)
Str.   strada (street)
sv.   Saint
u., ut.   utca (street)
ul.   ulica/ulitsa (street)
vul.   vulitsa (street)

Miscellaneous
ASSR   Autonomous Soviet Socialist Republic
b/d   barrels per day
c.   circa
GDP   Gross Domestic Product
GNP   Gross National Product
m.   million
PPP   Purchasing Power Parity
SSR   Soviet Socialist Republic
UN   United Nations

AB *see* Braghis Alliance.

Abaza

A north Caucasian people situated in **Karachai-Cherkessia**, in the extreme south of **European Russia**. Closely related to the **Abkhaz,** the Abaza migrated north of the **Caucasus** in the 13th century, having converted to Islam. In their new home they became vassals of the local Karachai princes. During the imperial battle for the region between the **Russian** and Ottoman Empires, Abaza communities were often deported *en masse* to Russia or Turkey to quell rebellion. By the end of the 19th century many tens of thousands of Abaza had migrated to Turkey, where their religious affiliations were better suited to the prevailing society. The Abaza left in Russia sided with both the Bolsheviks and White Russian forces during the civil war (1918–20), with famed Abaza horses serving as prestigious cavalry. After the war the Abaza lands were divided between the Karachai and **Cherkess** lands, but were rejoined when the two larger regions were amalgamated in 1957.

Traditional animal husbandry and small-scale farming were forcibly swapped for collectivized agriculture in the 1930s and Abaza culture was heavily slavicized. The Abaz language, originally transcribed using a Latin-based script from 1923, has used the **Cyrillic alphabet** since a decree from the **Soviet** authorities in 1938.

Abkhazia

A nominally autonomous republic within **Georgia** on the eastern coast of the Black Sea . The Abkhaz defeated Georgian forces in a war of secession between 1992 and 1994 and declared independance, which remains unrecognized. *Population*: 516,600 (1993 estimate). The general region was first colonized by the ancient Greeks in the 8th century BC and known as Colchis. The descendants of these first colonists are represented today by the **Pontic Greeks**. The indigenous Caucasian Abkhaz (known to themselves as Apswa) were converted to Christianity in the 6th century AD and became vassals of the Byzantine Empire. A later independent kingdom was absorbed into Georgia until the entire area came under Turkic Ottoman control in the 16th century. Under the Ottomans, some Abkhaz converted to Islam, and today the two religions coexist in relative peace.

The ethnic balance in Abkhazia was permanently undermined in the late 19th century when the new **Russian** masters (since 1810) rejected ideas of autonomy, and fiercely repressed a local uprising. Thousands of Abkhaz fled to Turkey and their land was appropriated by Russian colonists. The strong identity of Abkhaz culture (most closely related to that of the **Abaza** to the north) and the great difference of the language from Georgian or Russian ensured the region's separate status under the Bolshevik/**Soviet** regime after 1917. An Abkhazian republic was declared in 1921 but was lost in 1931 when it was reabsorbed into Georgia. In the 1930s a wave of **Georgian** colonists further diluted the Abkhaz population. However, Abkhaz culture and language were protected and promoted under the Soviet regime.

The growth of Georgian nationalism approaching independence in the late 1980s prompted calls for greater autonomy for Abkhazia. Tensions were exacerbated by Georgian attempts to establish a branch of Tbilisi University in the Abkhaz capital, Sukhumi. This was viewed by the Abkhaz authorities as an attempt to repress Abkhaz culture. Conflict was provoked in 1992 when Georgian troops were despatched to Sukhumi after the restoration of the autonomous Abkhaz 1925 Constitution. In the ensuing war Abkhazian forces, tactically supported by the Russian military and north Caucasian mercenaries, pushed back Georgian troops by October 1993. Independence, declared in 1994, remains unrecognized.

Georgians, the previous majority population in Abkhazia, fled the republic, and their homes and land were occupied by Abkhaz forces. The displaced Georgians have formed a powerful pressure group in Georgia, calling for an immediate restoration of their property. Abkhaz remain the minority in Abkhazia, with Russians and **Armenians** constituting the rest of the population. Travel to Georgia is banned and the border Gali district has become a dangerous region controlled by rival guerrillas and smugglers. Passage to the Russian Federation, which maintains peacekeeping soldiers in Abkhazia, was severely restricted after conflict in **Chechnya** in the early 1990s for fear of experienced Abkhaz soldiers aiding the Chechen separatists. Moves to overcome the political situation have foundered on both sides. Vladislav Ardzinba has been President of Abkhazia since 1994.

Economic activity is centred on the major urban centres of Sukhumi and Ochamchire, both on the coast, although restrictions on international commerce have increased the importance of agricultural production. Tobacco, nut oil, silk and fruits are major exports. The Soviet-era tourist industry has greatly diminished.

Abrene question

An unresolved territorial dispute between the **Russian Federation** and **Latvia** over the Abrene region along their common border. In the border reconstruction undertaken by the **Soviet** authorities towards the end of the Second World War, the Latvian district of Abrene and its environs was absorbed wholesale into Russia. Although dissent was muted by the totalitarian Soviet state, the independent Latvian authorities have never officially dropped their claim to the district and set out their case in a 1992 resolution. However, nominally cordial relations between the two countries have held back action on the question.

ACDU *see* **Armenian Christian Democratic Union**.

Adamkus, Valdas

President of **Lithuania**.

Valdas Adamkus is a member of the right-wing **Homeland Union–Lithuanian Conservatives** (TS–LK). Having spent most of his adult life in the USA, where he worked for the Environmental Protection Agency (EPA), he was inaugurated as President in February 1998.

Born in Kaunas on 3 November 1926, he joined the nationalist resistance as a teenager, opposing both his country's forcible absorption into the **Soviet Union** in 1940 and its subsequent wartime occupation by Nazi Germany. During the Nazi occupation he ran an underground newspaper, but as Soviet troops advanced he joined an anti-Soviet detachment supplied by the Nazis. When the Red Army took control of the country in 1944, he left Lithuania and fled to Germany where he attended the University of Munich.

He emigrated to the USA in 1949 and taught languages before moving to Chicago (where there is the largest **Lithuanian** community outside Lithuania). He joined the Republican Party in the USA and campaigned to prevent US recognition of the Soviet annexation of Lithuania, but had to cease party political activity when he started working for the US Environmental Protection Agency (EPA) in 1971. His work with the agency enabled him to travel throughout eastern Europe, including Lithuania. In 1981 he was promoted within the EPA to District Administrator for the Mid-West region of the USA. During his time in the USA he was a vocal promoter of Lithuanian-American ties.

Having been nominated as a presidential candidate by the TS–LK in July 1997, he returned to Lithuania that October. He was elected President in January 1998 after three rounds of voting, securing just 50.6% of the vote in the final round. Although as President he carries little political power, he has been openly critical of Lithuanian party politics. However, he openly sided with the right when he overlooked the victorious left in 2000 and gave the mandate instead to a right-wing coalition.

Valdas Adamkus is married to Alma, they have no children.

Address: Office of the President, S. Daukanto a. 3/8, Vilnius 2026.

Telephone: (26) 28986 [(526) 28986 from September 2002].

Adygeya

Fax: (521) 25382.
E-mail: info@president.lt
Internet: www.president.lt

ADS *see* Democratic Alliance of Albania.

Adygeya

A constituent republic of the **Russian Federation** situated to the north-east of the Black Sea in southern **European Russia**, north of the **Caucasus region**. *Population*: 432,046 (1997 estimate). The republic is dominated by the Circassian Adygei people, closely related to the **Cherkess** and Kabards (*see* **Kabardino-Balkaria**) and distinguished from them as a separate ethnic group only in the 1920s. The region was included as an autonomous *oblast* (region) in the Krasnodar district by the Bolsheviks in 1922 but separated as a full autonomous republic in 1934. After the collapse of the **Soviet Union**, Adygeya was declared a sovereign republic within the Federation in 1991. Economist Aslan Dzharimov was elected President of the republic in that year.

Economic activity is based on food production and exporting. The ancient Adygei were famed for their excellence in horse breeding, and efforts have been made to resurrect this traditional activity in the capital, Maikop.

Adzharia
(or Ajaria)

An autonomous republic within **Georgia** dominated by the **Muslim** Adzharians. *Population*: 381,500 (1991 estimate). The Adzharians were ethnic **Georgians** who converted to Sunni Islam while their homeland was under Turkish dominion between the 17th and 19th centuries. They came under **Russian** control in 1878 and were attached to the Georgian **Soviet** republic in 1922. Recognition as a separate ethnic group was ended after widespread unrest in Adzharia over religious intolerance and enforced collectivization. Large numbers of Adzharians were subsequently deported to central Asia. Since that time they have officially been considered to be Georgians, although their autonomous status was retained.

The rise of Georgian nationalism in the early 1990s prompted authorities in the Adzharian capital Batumi to prepare for the armed protection of their autonomy, should it be revoked. Open conflict in Adzharia has been avoided. Adzharian President Aslan Abashidze has reportedly reverted to increasingly authoritarian means to maintain his hold on power. Hostilities in **Abkhazia** and South **Ossetia** have put off a serious debate about the future of Adzharia within Georgia.

Agency for Reconstruction and Privatization (Slovenia)

Government agency in **Slovenia**.
Director: Mira Puc.
Address: Kotnikova 28, 1000 Ljubljana.
Telephone: (1) 1326030.
Fax: (1) 1316011.
Internet: www.arspip.si

AGPB *see* **United Civil Party of Belarus**.

Agrarian Party of Belarus
Agrarnaya Partiya Belarusi (APB)

A party in **Belarus** representing those agrarian interests which derived from the Soviet-era agricultural system, and opposing the restoration of individual peasant ownership of the land. Established in 1994, the APB emerged as the most powerful agrarian party in the 1995 legislative elections, winning 33 seats. In January 1996 APB leader Syamyon Sharetski was elected Chairman of the then unicameral legislature. The 2000 legislative elections were dominated by pro-**Lukashenka** candidates running either as independents or part of the **Belarusian People's Patriotic Union**, and candidates from the APB only won five seats.
Leadership: Syamyon Sharetski (Chair.).
Address: 86/2 Kazintsa Street, Minsk 220050.
Telephone: (17) 2203829.
Fax: (17) 2495018.

Agrarian Party of Ukraine
Ahrarna Partiya Ukrainy (APU)

A small peasant-based formation in **Ukraine** favouring the decollectivization of the agricultural sector. The APU was launched in 1996 as an alternative to the pro-collectivization **Peasants' Party of Ukraine** (SelPU) and was promoted by the presidency of Leonid **Kuchma**, thus obtaining some support in the agriculture bureaucracy. In the 1998 **Parliament** elections, the APU failed to surmount the 4% proportional threshold but won eight seats in the constituency section.
Leadership: Kateryna Vashchuk (Chair.).
Address: c/o Verkhovna Rada, M. Grushevskogo St 5, Kiev 01008.

AHIK *see* **Confederation of Azerbaijan Trade Unions**.

AIDS
(Acquired Immuno-deficiency Syndrome)

Discussion of the impact of AIDS in **eastern Europe** has generally focused on the poorer sections of society, and particularly on drug users. The prevalence of HIV (Human Immuno-deficiency Virus, the virus responsible for AIDS) varies across the region but the explosion of numbers in some countries is considered an epidemic. The situation is worst in **Ukraine**, where UN figures for 2000 recorded that 1% of all adults were infected with HIV, a total of over 300,000 people. Also badly affected are the **Russian Federation** (0.18%), **Azerbaijan** (0.23%) and **Moldova** (0.2%). The situation in other countries is an increasing problem, but one which is often not fully appreciated. The fact that the epidemic has its roots among the socially excluded—drug users, sex workers and homosexuals—has made raising awareness, and prompting government action, disproportionately difficult.

Ajaria *see* **Adzharia**.

AKC *see* **Azerbaijan Popular Front**.

AKP *see* **Azerbaijan Communist Party**.

Alania *see* **Ossetia question**.

Albania
Republika e Shqipërisë

An independent republic located on the western coast of the **Balkan** peninsula, bounded by Federal Republic of Yugoslavia to the north (Montenegro) and northeast (Kosovo), Macedonia to the east and Greece to the south. Albania is divided administratively into 36 districts (rrethe) and one municipality (**Tirana**).

Area: 28,750 sq km; *capital*: Tirana; *population*: 3.1m. (2001 estimate), comprising ethnic **Albanians** c.95%, Greeks c.3%, others c.2%; *official language*: Albanian; *religion*: Muslim c.70%, Albanian **Orthodox** c.20%, **Roman Catholic** c.10%.

The supreme organ of government is the unicameral **People's Assembly** (Kuvendi Popullor) of at least 140 members elected for a four-year term (100 directly in two rounds of voting, and at least 40 by proportional representation from party lists obtaining at least 3% of the vote). The Assembly elects the President as Head of State for a five-year term (once renewable) and also approves the Prime Minister designated by the President.

History: Albania was under Ottoman Turkish rule for five centuries from c.1400. Following an early revolt, conversion to Islam, often enforced, produced a majority Muslim population by the 18th century. Turkish repression and Albania's mountain-enclosed isolation inhibited the emergence of a nationalist movement until the 1870s. Independence was declared in November 1912 during the Balkan Wars and recognized internationally under the 1913 Treaty of Bucharest virtually within Albania's present-day borders. Thus Epirus was divided between Albania and Greece (*see* **Epirus question**), Albanian-majority **Kosovo** was confirmed as part of **Serbia**, and both **Macedonia** and **Montenegro** obtained a substantial ethnic Albanian population.

A brief period of democratic rule after the First World War was ended in 1924 by a conservative Albanian chieftain who proclaimed himself King Zog in 1928 (*see* **Albanian royal family**). King Zog was deposed by the Italian invasion of April 1939. Italian occupation was followed during the Second World War by the launching of an abortive Italian attack on Greece, German military intervention in 1941 and the creation of a **Greater Albania** entity under Italian protection. Following Italy's exit from the war in 1943, communist-led Albanian partisans backed by the Allies expelled the Germans in mid-1944.

A People's Republic was established in January 1946 under the leadership of what became the Albanian Party of Labour (PPS). Over the next four decades Albania pursued a rigidly Stalinist line. It was aligned with the **Soviet Union** until the early 1960s and then with China until the late 1970s, after which it maintained an isolationist stance. Long-term PPS leader Enver **Hoxha** died in April 1985 and was succeeded by Ramiz **Alia**, who had been Head of State since November 1982. A limited improvement in relations with the West included the ending of the technical state of war between Albania and Greece in 1987.

Although Albania was to some extent insulated from the turbulent events of 1989 as communist regimes collapsed elsewhere in **eastern Europe**, the Alia regime agreed to the formation of opposition parties in December 1990. Multi-party elections in March–April 1991 were won by the PPS, which in June was renamed the **Socialist Party of Albania** (PSS). A coalition Government headed by the PSS gave way in December 1991 to Albania's first non-Marxist administration since the Second World War. Further elections in March 1992 were won by the centrist **Democratic Party of Albania** (PDS), whereupon Alia resigned as President and was succeeded by Sali Berisha. The latter appointed Aleksander Meksi (PDS) as Prime Minister, heading a coalition which included two smaller parties.

Under a controversial law barring former communists from public life until 2002, some 70 opposition candidates, mostly PSS members, were excluded from legislative elections held in May–June 1996, with the result that the opposition boycotted the second round of voting. In polling adjudged by international observers to have been riddled with malpractice, the PDS obtained a large majority but nevertheless brought two smaller parties into the new Government. Opposition protest actions were compounded from early 1997 by popular outrage at the collapse of several **'pyramid' investment schemes**, amid allegations of government connivance in the frauds. Widespread anarchy and the establishment of rebel control in the south continued despite the declaration of a state of emergency and the formation in March 1997 of a broad-based 'Government of Reconciliation' under Bashkim Fino of the PSS. From April, on the initiative of the **Organization for Security and Co-operation in Europe** (OSCE), a 6,000-strong Italian-led multinational protection force was deployed in Albania with UN approval. The force helped to restore a measure of public order before it withdrew in August 1997, although without reducing the exodus of large numbers of Albanians seeking illegal entry to Italy and other west European countries.

Assembly elections in June–July 1997, described as relatively fair by observers, resulted in a heavy defeat for the PDS and the return to government of the PSS, which won 101 seats with 52.8% of the vote. The PDS was the second-largest party but with only 29 seats. Berisha resigned as President immediately after the elections, whereupon the Assembly elected Rexhep **Meidani** (PSS) as his successor unopposed. The new President appointed a coalition headed by Fatos **Nano** (PSS) and including four smaller parties, the **Social Democratic Party of Albania** (PSDS), the **Human Rights Union Party** (PBDNj), the **Democratic Alliance of Albania** (ADS) and the **Albanian Agrarian Party** (PAS).

Further instability in September 1998 resulted in Nano being replaced as Prime Minister by Pandeli Majko (PSS), who at 31 became Europe's youngest Head of Government, heading a coalition of the same five parties. The country's first post-communist Constitution was approved by 93.5% of those voting in a referendum held on 22 November 1998, although the PDS rejected the new text and claimed that the turnout had been well below the official figure of just over 50%.

Having failed to dislodge Nano's grip on the PSS leadership, Majko resigned as Prime Minister in October 1999 and was succeeded by Ilir **Meta** (PSS), who continued the existing five-party coalition. Controversial cabinet changes in July 2000 provoked a further temporary boycott of parliament by the PDS, which accused the Meta Government of fostering corruption and smuggling. Nevertheless, in local elections in October the PSS made major advances, notably by winning control of Tirana, hitherto a PDS stronghold.

Latest elections: Legislative elections held on 24 June 2001 resulted in another clear majority for the PSS, which won 73 of the 140 seats with 42% of the vote. The **Union for Victory** coalition, headed by the PDS, won 46 (36.8% of the vote), the **Democrat Party** (PD) 6 (5.1%), the PSDS 4 (3.6%), the PBDNj 3 (2.6%), the PAS 3 (2.6%), the ADS 3 (2.5%), non-partisans 2.

Recent developments: Despite relative approval for the 2001 poll from international election observers, the PDS condemned it as 'farcical'. From the opening of the new legislature in September 2001 until the end of the year, the party and its coalition partners refused to take up their seats.

Meta was re-elected Prime Minister at the head of a 'non-partisan' Cabinet. However, the PSS Government soon ran into internal difficulties. Party Chairman Nano blocked the appointment of Cabinet Ministers in a reshuffle in late 2001, accusing Meta and his team of corruption and ultimately forcing the resignation of four Ministers in December. Tensions between Meta and Nano remained high.

International relations and defence: Albania's transition to multi-party democracy in 1990–91 facilitated a transformation of its external relations. Admitted to what became the OSCE in 1991, Albania joined NATO's **Partnership for Peace** in 1994 and the **Council of Europe** in 1995. It is also a member of the **Organization of the Black Sea Economic Co-operation** and the **Central European Initiative**. As a predominantly Muslim country, Albania joined the **Organization of the Islamic Conference** (OIC) in 1992, confirming its membership in December 1998 after some uncertainty earlier in the year.

Relations with **Yugoslavia** deteriorated from mid-1998 over the treatment of ethnic Albanians in the Serbian-ruled province of Kosovo. The Albanian Government accordingly gave full support to the air-strikes launched against Yugoslavia by the **North Atlantic Treaty Organization** (NATO) in March 1999 and welcomed the agreement in June under which Yugoslav forces were obliged to withdraw from Kosovo and the province placed under an effective NATO protectorate. NATO subsequently deployed Albania Force (AFOR) to help Albania cope with the influx of refugees from Kosovo, this mission being succeeded by an Italian-led force in September 1999. Signalling its European aspirations, Albania in April 2000 signed Council of Europe instruments confirming the country's formal abolition of the death penalty.

A reconstruction of the armed forces, begun in 1998 and called 'Plan 2000', was still in progress at the end of 2000, when the Albanian armed forces were believed to number some 50,000 personnel. The plan was being implemented with assistance from Italy, Greece, Turkey and the USA. Defence expenditure in 1999 was estimated at about US $140m., or around 3.5% of GDP.

Albania, economy

The least-developed economy in Europe, generating the lowest income per head in a largely mountainous country with poor communications and infrastructure.

GNP: US $3,767m. (2000); *GNP per capita*: $1,100 (2000); *GDP at PPP*: $5,600m. (1999); *GDP per capita at PPP*: $1,650 (1999); *exports*: $261m. (2000); *imports*: $1065m. (2000); *currency*: lek (plural: lekë; US $1=L136.8 at the end of December 2001).

In 1998 agriculture and forestry contributed 54% of GDP, industry 25% and services 21%. Nearly half of the 1.7 million workforce are engaged in agriculture (often subsistence farming), 28% in state industry and 22% in the private sector. Some 21% of the land is arable, 20% permanent pasture and crops, and 38% forest or woodland. The main crops are cereals, sugar beet, tobacco, potatoes, fruit and vegetables; livestock raising, dairy farming and forestry are also important. The main mineral resources are chromium ore (of which Albania is the world's seventh-largest producer), hydrocarbons, lignite, copper and nickel. The main industries are food-processing, textiles, metal-working, building materials, wood processing and oil refining. The main energy sources are hydroelectric power and fossil fuels.

Albania's main exports by value are chromium, oil and other minerals and metals (47% of the total) and agricultural produce (20%). Principal imports are machinery and transport equipment, foodstuffs and miscellaneous manufactures. In 2000 Italy took 61% of Albanian exports, Greece 17% and Germany 7%; the main sources of imports are Italy (35%), Greece (26%), Germany and Turkey (6% each). Remittances from Albanians abroad make an important contribution to GNP, as does financial and other aid from overseas donors.

The end of communist rule in 1990 and the subsequent efforts to convert to a market economy caused severe dislocation and virtual economic collapse in 1991–92, when GDP fell by 40% a year and hyperinflation became a real threat. Assisted by extensive financial and technical aid from the West, aggregate growth resumed in 1993 (from a very low base), averaging 9% a year in 1993–96, and industrial production grew in 1995 (by 7%) for the first time since the collapse of communism. However, in the election year of 1996 the Government lacked sufficient resolve to maintain stabilization policies, and inflationary pressures were renewed as a result. The problems were compounded in 1997 by the collapse of **'pyramid' investment schemes** in which large numbers of Albanians had invested their savings. The resultant panic, popular uprising and anarchy contributed to an 8% fall in GDP in 1997. This was recovered in 1998 on the strength of a new economic restructuring programme. The Government's budget for 1999 projected GDP growth of 8% and a budget deficit of 5.2% of GDP (on expenditure of US $1,178m. against revenue of $793m.). The hostilities over **Kosovo** in 1999, however, and the resultant influx of ethnic **Albanian** refugees, caused particular economic problems. International aid helped to defray the resultant costs, and by the end of 1999 inflation and the budget deficit were under control, with economic growth of 8% being forecast for 2000. However, unemployment remained high at 17% officially (and probably over 30% actually) and was expected to become higher.

Most agricultural land was privatized in 1992, followed by small and medium-sized industrial concerns from 1993–94 and, theoretically, by large enterprises from 1995. A new banking law introduced in 1996 ended state control of the banks and redefined the role of the central **Bank of Albania**, while legislation was also introduced to protect foreign investors. However, in the late 1990s the privatization process was marked by erratic timetabling, pervasive corruption and chronic mismanagement. Thus, by 2001, many large enterprises still remained under state ownership.

Albanian Agrarian Party
Partia Agrar Shqiptare (PAS)

A small political party based in **Albania**'s large rural population. Founded in 1991, the PAS made slow headway advocating assistance for those disadvantaged by the

privatization of most agricultural land in 1992, failing to win representation in the 1992 and 1996 **People's Assembly** elections. In the mid-1997 polling, however, it won one seat and was subsequently included in the coalition Government headed by the **Socialist Party of Albania**. It increased its representation in June 2001, winning three seats with 2.6% of the vote.
Leadership: Lufter Xhuveli (Chair.).
Address: Rruga Budi 6, Tirana.
Telephone and Fax: (4) 227481.

Albanian Centre for Foreign Investment Promotion

Government-sponsored body founded in 1993, charged with promoting foreign investment in **Albania** and providing practical assistance to investors.
Director: Genc Gjoka.
Address: Bul. Zhan d'Ark, Tirana.
Telephone: (4) 230133.
Fax: (4) 228439.

Albanian Republican Party
Partia Republikane Shqiptare (PRS)

A conservative political party in **Albania** with little popular support. Founded in 1991 with backing from the Italian Republican Party, the PRS failed to gain representation in the 1991 **People's Assembly** elections but nevertheless joined the resultant 'non-partisan' Government. It won one seat in the 1992 Assembly elections, becoming a member of a coalition headed by the **Democratic Party of Albania** (PDS). Dissension at the June 1992 PRS congress resulted in the formation of at least three breakaway formations by centrist and right-wing dissidents. The party left the coalition in December 1994, criticizing the Government's 'shortcomings' but continuing to give general support.

The PRS was allocated three Assembly seats in the controversial 1996 elections (even though it joined the opposition boycott of the second round) and became a member of the resultant PDS-led coalition. Amidst resurgent social disorder, however, it left the Government in February 1997, becoming highly critical of the PDS. It was reduced to one Assembly seat in the mid-1997 elections, but nevertheless continued to aspire to lead a unification of conservative forces and remained cool to PDS approaches for a merger. In November 1997 the PRS leadership passed from Sabri Godo to the 32-year-old Fatmir Mediu.

For the June 2001 elections the PRS joined the **Union for Victory** coalition headed by the PDS. The coalition won 46 seats in the People's Assembly but strongly contested the legality of the poll and boycotted the new parliamentary session.

Leadership: Fatmir Mediu (Chair.).
Address: Bul. Dëshmorët e Kombit, Tirana.
Telephone: (4) 232511.
Fax: (4) 228361.

Albanian royal family

A short-lived monarchy of the period between the two World Wars, deposed in 1939 but six decades later still seeking a restoration. Albanian chieftain Ahmet Zogu ended a brief post-First World War period of democracy in 1924, declaring himself King Zog in 1928. He was ousted by the Italian invasion in April 1939, the crown passing to King Victor Emmanuel of Italy. Although Zog nominally resumed the throne in 1944, the post-Second World War communist regime proclaimed a People's Republic in 1946, whereupon Zog lived in exile until his death in April 1961. His only son, Leka Zogu, settled in South Africa in the 1970s, being given diplomatic immunity by the apartheid-era Government. He maintained a claim to the Albanian throne, backed by the small **Movement of Legality Party** (PLL).

Following the end of communist rule, Leka Zogu briefly attended the PLL's 50th anniversary celebrations in Albania in November 1993, before being asked to leave by the authorities. He returned in April 1997 'to share the suffering' of the Albanian people, successfully calling for a referendum on whether the monarchy should be restored. This took place simultaneously with the July 1997 parliamentary elections, and produced a 66.7% majority in favour of continued republican status, but the PLL claimed that the vote had been rigged. During the campaign Leka Zogu held a rally of armed supporters, and he was later convicted *in absentia* of trying to organize a coup attempt. In February 1999 Leka Zogu was arrested in South Africa (which had rescinded his diplomatic immunity) and charged with illegal possession of a large quantity of weaponry. The arms had been purchased in 1979 for an assault on the then communist regime which had never materialized.

Albanian Telegraphic Agency (ATA)

Albania's sole news agency, government-owned but professing an independent editorial line, with correspondents in most main Albanian towns and also in **Kosovo**. Originally founded in 1912, ATA is proud of its role in reporting to the world about anti-fascist resistance during the Second World War, but less proud that, together with Radio Tirana, it was one of the sole sources of information about Albania in the communist era, with coverage notorious for its promotion of the cult of personality surrounding Enver **Hoxha**.

Director-General: Frrok Cupi.
Address: Bul. Zhan D'Ark 23, Tirana.

Telephone: (4) 222929.
Fax: (4) 234230.
E-mail: hola@ata.tirana.al
Internet: www.ata-al.net

Albanians

An Indo-European people living within, and dispersed in significant numbers beyond, the present-day borders of **Albania**. The Albanians migrated to the **Balkans** in about 1000 BC to the region later named Illyria (Illyricum) and annexed by the Romans. Albanians therefore claim descent from the ancient Illyrians and stress that their history as a distinct ethnic group long predates that of the surrounding **Slavic peoples**. Their regional distinctness was accentuated by five centuries of Ottoman Turkish rule from c.1400, during which most Albanians were converted to Islam, whereas the Slavs and Greeks remained Christian. All religious observance in Albania was banned under communist rule, but in the post-communist era many ethnic Albanians have rediscovered their Muslim heritage. Although the Albanians are essentially a homogeneous people, there have been periodic strains between two distinct dialect groups, the dominant Tosk in the south and lowlands and the Gheg in the north.

The borders of independent Albania established in 1913 left substantial numbers of ethnic Albanians in other countries, notably in the **Kosovo** region of **Serbia**, in **Macedonia** and **Montenegro**, and in the **Epirus** region of Greece. The creation of a **Greater Albania** has therefore been a feature of Albanian nationalist aspirations, the aim being to acquire adjoining areas containing an ethnic Albanian majority.

Figures for the numbers of ethnic Albanians outside present-day Albanian borders are mostly speculative, except that the Albanian community in the USA is reliably estimated at some 600,000. At the end of 1999 there were an estimated 350,000 Albanian emigrants in Greece, 150,000 in Italy and 50,000 in other Western countries. The majority ethnic Albanian population of neighbouring Kosovo is usually put at 1.3 million, while 400,000 ethnic Albanians are thought to reside in Macedonia and 100,000 in Montenegro.

Alekperov, Avaz

Minister of Finance, **Azerbaijan**. Avaz Akbar oglu Alekperov is a trained economist who worked within the Economics Department of the former Soviet Azeri apparatus. He was appointed Minister of Finance on 11 July 1999.

Born in 1952, he graduated from the Azerbaijan National Economics Institute in 1973. He served on the Council of Ministers of the then Soviet Socialist Republic of Azerbaijan from 1981, rising to Deputy Head of the Economics Department.

Following Azeri independence in 1991 he was appointed Chairman of the country's new Social Security Fund. Amidst continuing economic problems, President Heydar **Aliyev** dismissed the incumbent Finance Minister on 11 July 1999 and appointed Alekperov to the Cabinet in his place.

Avaz Alekperov is married and has two children.
Address: Ministry of Finance, Samad Vurghun St 6, 370000 Baku.
Telephone: (12) 933012.
Fax: (12) 937691.
E-mail: adalet-ferd@artel.net.az

Aleph *see* **Aum Shinrikyo**.

Alfa-Bank

Rapidly growing independent bank network in the **Russian Federation**, founded in 1991. Capital: US $9.5m.; reserves: $249.2m.; deposits: $810.9m. (Dec. 1999); 30 branches.
President: Petr Aven.
Chief Executive: Aleksandr Knastr.
Address: ul. Novatorov 7, 117421 Moscow.
Telephone: (095) 9292515.
Fax: (095) 9137182.
Internet: www.alfabank.ru

Alia, Ramiz

The last communist leader of **Albania**, successor to Enver **Hoxha** in 1985, and President until 1992. Alia was born in 1925 in Shkodër to poor **Muslim** parents. In his late teens, with Albania under German occupation, Alia joined the communist Partisans. His war record and responsibilities led to a prominent position in the party youth movement; he was a leading proponent of Albania's 'cultural revolution' in the 1960s, and became Hoxha's chosen successor after the death of Mehmet Shehu. A full member of the Politburo from 1961 and Head of State from 1982, he assumed real power as First Secretary of the Party of Labour of Albania (PPS) after Hoxha's death in 1985. His approach was initially to proceed with cautious reforms, while preserving the Hoxha cult. Persuaded only in the course of 1990 that a desperate economic situation and growing popular protest required more rapid change, he effectively marginalized the hardline elements in the party, and took the gamble of allowing other parties to contest the 1991 elections. The PPS's overall success in those polls in March–April, securing a two-thirds majority in a **People's Assembly** which duly re-elected him as President, disguised a collapse of support in the towns (Alia himself lost humiliatingly in a **Tirana** constituency). As

President, he was debarred under the new interim Constitution from holding party leadership posts, which he duly resigned in early May. The PPS went on to re-form itself under the leadership of Fatos **Nano**, renaming itself the **Socialist Party of Albania** (PSS). On 1 January 1992 Alia survived a heart attack. After the defeat of the PSS in March legislative elections, he resigned the presidency, and by September 1992 he had been placed under house arrest. Alia denounced the proceedings against him as a politically-motivated show trial, but in July 1994 he was convicted of sanctioning a variety of crimes whilst President, including the killing of Albanians illegally crossing the border, the use of summary executions, and the embezzlement of state funds. Despite his ill health, he began a nine-year prison sentence in September 1994, but was released in July 1995 under amnesty. Charges of genocide were subsequently made against him, but were dropped in October 1997.

Aliyev, Heydar

Leading ex-communist and President of **Azerbaijan** since 1993. Born in May 1923 in the Azeri enclave of **Nakhichevan**, Heydar Alirza oglu Aliyev went to university in **Baku** to study architecture, but his studies were interrupted when the **Soviet Union** entered the Second World War in 1941. He later successfully completed a history degree. A member of the **Communist Party of the Soviet Union** (KPSS) from 1945 to 1991, he was Vice-Chairman and then Chairman of the Azerbaijan **KGB** between 1967 and 1969, when he was elected First Secretary of the Party Central Committee at republican level. In 1982 he became a member of the Politburo of the KPSS and also First Deputy Chairman in charge of transport in the Soviet Council of Ministers. However, in 1987 he retired from the KPSS Politburo following disagreements with Mikhail **Gorbachev**, who was implementing a controversial reform programme as KPSS General Secretary. In 1991, the year of Azerbaijan's declaration of independence, Aliyev resigned outright from the KPSS. The following year he founded the **New Azerbaijan Party** (YAP) and became its Chairman.

On 15 June 1993, after a rebellion had forced the incumbent President Abulfaz Elchibey to flee the capital, the *Milli Majlis* (**National Assembly**) elected Aliyev as its Chairman and he assumed the duties of State President. Following an August referendum supporting the removal of Elchibey, presidential elections were held on 3 October 1993. Aliyev was recorded as having won 98.8% of votes in a turnout of 97%. However, no major opposition candidates had stood for election, while human rights monitors described the poll as undemocratic and said that the media had been closely controlled by Aliyev.

The YAP, closely aligned with Aliyev, has continued to dominate the legislature, while Aliyev himself secured a second term at the October 1998 presidential elections. On this occasion, although many opposition parties boycotted the poll, there were at least real rival candidates. Aliyev's recorded share of the vote—

78%—was widely regarded as having been inflated by 'irregularities' in the conduct of the election, although it was at least generally recognized as more credible than the 1993 poll. Crucially, 78% was above the necessary two-thirds majority required to have Aliyev declared the outright victor rather than have to face a second round run-off. The cult of personality built up around Aliyev presents him as a father of the Azeri nation, whose portrait is omnipresent and whose sayings are prominently displayed on posters in public places. He has groomed his son, Ilham, for the succession and in November 2001 the YAP voted to give its backing to Ilham as his father's eventual successor. The state propaganda machine also emphasizes the image of Aliyev as a major international statesman, exploiting to the full his foreign visits—to the USA in particular.

Address: Office of the President, Istiklal St 19, 370066 Baku.
Telephone: (12) 927906.
Fax: (12) 980822.
E-mail: root@lider.baku.az
Internet: www.president.az

All-Georgian Union for Revival
Sruliad Sakartvelos Aghordzinebis Kavshiri (SSAK)

A predominantly Muslim political party based in the autonomous republic of **Adzharia,** which became part of the principal opposition formation in **Georgia**'s 1999 elections, in alliance with non-Muslim groups.

Founded in 1992, the SSAK contested the elections that year within the broad-based Peace Bloc (which won a narrow plurality). Standing on its own, the party came in third place in the 1995 parliamentary elections, winning a 6.8% vote share and a total of 31 seats. Thereafter the party advocated the creation of a free economic zone in Batumi, the capital of Adzharia, of which SSAK leader Aslan Abashidze was President.

In July 1999 the SSAK established the so-called Batumi Alliance with the Union of Georgian Traditionalists (KTK), the Socialist Party of Georgia (SSP), the 21st Century group of supporters of former President Zviad Gamsakhurdia and a faction descended from the former ruling Georgian Communist Party (GCP) led by Dzhumber Patiashvili. A former GCP First Secretary, Patiashvili had come second in the 1995 presidential election with 19.5% of the vote. In the October–November 1999 parliamentary elections, the SSAK and allied parties came in second place with 64 seats on a 25.2% vote share and so became the principal opposition to the ruling **Citizens' Union of Georgia** (SMK).

Abashidze opted not to run against incumbent Eduard **Shevardnadze** in the April 2000 presidential election, in which the main opposition mantle was again taken by Patiashvili. With the dubious benefit of endorsement by Stalin's grandson Yevgenii Dzhughashvili, leader of the People's Patriotic Union of Georgia, Patiashvili again came a poor second with 16.7% of the vote.

Leadership: Aslan Abashidze (Chair.).
Address: Gogebashvili 7, Batumi.
Telephone: (200) 76500.

All-Poland Alliance of Trade Unions
Ogólnopolskie Porozumienie Związków Zawodowych (OPZZ)

A left-leaning trade union centre, competitor to the larger **Solidarity**. The OPZZ was founded in November 1984 to head the then communist regime's attempt to create a new union structure after the banning of Solidarity in 1981. Following the collapse of communism and the relegalization of Solidarity in 1989, the OPZZ sought with some success to establish a new identity as an authentic trade union centre, benefiting from the speedy disenchantment of many workers with the pro-market policies of the post-communist Government and the attendant fall in wage and employment levels. The OPZZ was closely identified with the 1993–97 Government of the (ex-communist) **Democratic Left Alliance** (SLD), experiencing some rank-and-file discontent as previous economic restructuring policies were largely continued. It reverted to opposition in September 1997 on the election of a centre-right Government headed by **Solidarity Electoral Action**, although it supports Poland's application to join the **European Union**.

The OPZZ claims to represent over three million workers in some 11,000 enterprise-based branches, but its actual individual membership is estimated at around 750,000. The centre has no international affiliations, although it regards itself as part of mainstream European trade unionism.

President: Maciej Manicki.
Address: 36–40 Kopernika St, Warsaw 00924.
Telephone: (22) 8269241.
Fax: (22) 8265102.
E-mail: opzz@opzz.org.pl
Internet: www.opzz.org.pl

All-Russian Confederation of Labour (VKT)

One of the **Russian Federation**'s independent trade union centres, much smaller than the dominant **Federation of Independent Trade Unions of Russia** (FNPR). The VKT was established in 1995 principally on the initiative of the powerful Independent Miners' Union (NPG) and in 1999 became a member of the official Tripartite Commission for the regulation of labour relations. Claiming a membership of 1.27 million, the VKT became an affiliate of the International Confederation of Free Trade Unions (ICFTU) in November 2000 and at ICFTU prompting entered into talks on a merger with the **Confederation of Labour of Russia** (KTR).

President: Aleksandr Bugayev.

Alliance of Free Democrats

Address: 5/7 Rozhdestvenka St, Moscow 103031.
Telephone: (095) 7852131.
Fax: (095) 9158367.
E-mail: vkt@vkt.org.ru
Internet: www.vkt.org.ru

Alliance of Free Democrats
Szabad Demokraták Szövetsége (SzDSz)

A centrist political party in **Hungary**, affiliated to the **Liberal International**. The SzDSz began life in March 1988 as the opposition Network of Free Initiatives and was reorganized as a political party in November 1988. It won 91 **National Assembly** seats in 1990 on a vote share of 21.4%, becoming the leading opposition party of the post-communist era. Factional strife between 'pragmatists' and 'ideologues', many of the latter being ex-Marxists, subsided following the election in November 1992 of Iván Peto as Party Chairman.

Despite initial hopes of a major breakthrough, the party slipped to 70 seats in the May 1994 National Assembly elections, its first-round voting share falling to 19.8%. It decided to enter a centre-left coalition with the **Hungarian Socialist Party**, following which its nominee, Árpád **Göncz**, was elected President of Hungary by the National Assembly in June 1995. Tarnished by corruption allegations, Peto resigned as SzDSz Chairman in April and was succeeded the following month by Gabor Kuncze, then Interior Minister and Deputy Prime Minister.

The SzDSz suffered the most in the defeat of the ruling parties in the May 1998 National Assembly elections, slumping to 24 seats (with only 7.6% of the vote) and going into opposition. Kuncze was quickly replaced by Bálint Magyar, who was in turn replaced in December 2000 by Gábor Demszky, the Mayor of **Budapest**, while István Szent-Iványi became SzDSz parliamentary group leader.

Leadership: Gábor Demszky (Chair.).
Address: Mérleg utca 6, 1051 Budapest.
Telephone: (1) 1176911.
Fax: (1) 1187944.
E-mail: szdsz@szdsz.hu
Internet: www.szdsz.hu

Alpha Cartel National Trade Union Confederation
Confederatia Nationala Sindicala Cartel Alfa (CNS–Carta Alfa)

One of many competing union centres in post-communist **Romania**. Founded in 1990, the Alpha Cartel is affiliated to the World Confederation of Labour (WCL).
Leader: Bogdan Hossu.
Address: 202A Splaiul Independentei, Floor 2/3, Bucharest 77208.

Telephone: (1) 2126638.
Fax: (1) 3133481.
E-mail: alfa@cartel-alfa.ro
Internet: www.cartel-alfa.ro

AMIP *see* **Azerbaijan National Independence Party**.

Angjeli, Anastas

Minister of Finance, **Albania**.

Anastas Angjeli is a member of the **Socialist Party of Albania** (PSS). Coming from a respected academic career, he entered government in 1991 as Deputy Minister of Finance. He was appointed full Finance Minister in 1998.

Born on 6 May 1956, he graduated in economics from the University of Tirana in 1980. He went on to become a professor in the subject in 1998. In his 18-year academic career he taught at the university and also furthered his own education with visits to other universities around the world. He joined the Executive Committee of the PSS in 1991 and for six months that year he served as Deputy Finance Minister. He was elected to the **People's Assembly** in 1992, 1997 and 2001. At the beginning of his second term in the chamber he headed a parliamentary economic commission before being promoted to the Cabinet in 1998 as Minister for Labour and Social Affairs. He switched to the Finance Ministry later that year and was reconfirmed in the role in September 2001.

Anastas Angjeli is married and has two children.
Address: Ministria e Financave, Bul. Dëshmorët e Kombit, Tirana.
Telephone: (4) 228405.
Fax: (4) 228362.
E-mail: phida@yahoo.com

Antall, József

Prime Minister who headed the first democratically-elected Government of **Hungary** in the post-communist era. Born in 1932, he was the son of a founding leader of the original Independent Smallholders' Party. Active in youth organizations supporting the 1956 Hungarian uprising, he was consequently banned from teaching history and instead became an archivist and later a museum director. He was a founder member of the **Hungarian Democratic Forum** (MDF) in September 1987, regarded as on the liberal democratic wing of that broad centre-right movement. As MDF President from October 1989, he was charged with forming a governing coalition after the party's success in the April–May 1990 elections, and became the dominant figure in Hungarian politics for the next three years, despite the increasingly debilitating symptoms of lymph gland cancer. Antall's style was serious and reserved rather than charismatic. He was sometimes accused of a donnish aloofness which failed to communicate government policy to the Hungarian electorate. He nevertheless had the political skill to mould the MDF into a centre-right conservative party, and brought relative stability to Hungary over the period until his early death (in office) in December 1993. His political objective was to oversee fundamental changes with minimum upheaval; he therefore favoured a social market approach rather than economic '**shock therapy**'.

APB *see* **Agrarian Party of Belarus.**

APU *see* **Agrarian Party of Ukraine.**

ÁPVRt *see* **Hungarian Privatization and State Holding Company.**

Archangel

A major city and region in the north of **European Russia**, 50 km south of the frozen White Sea. *Population*: 428,200 (1991 estimate). The city was founded as a fortified monastery dedicated to the Archangel Michael in 1584 at the start of **Russia**'s great expansion into the Eurasian wilderness. As the Russian Empire established itself as an important European power in the 17th century, Archangel ('Arkangelsk' in Russian) became a vitally important trading port. It was the base for the first trade with Britain, supplying vital timber for the shipbuilding industry. Archangel's fortunes declined with the opening of **St Petersburg** in 1703 and the introduction of heavy tariffs to favour Peter the Great's new city. It regained its place as Russia's major centre for timber exporting after the completion of a railway in 1898. This role was preserved throughout the **Soviet** period until the present day. The local Bolsheviks took control of the city in February 1918, only to be temporarily ousted by Allied forces in the opening years of the Russian Civil War. Industrialization in the 1930s brought a wave of migration from further south, swelling the population by more than 150,000 by 1939. Archangel's working population has long been at the forefront of industrial action and held the greatest number of strikes in European Russia in 1998 with 374 separate recorded actions.

Arctic Council

A body in which the **Russian Federation** co-operates with Scandinavian and North American countries on Arctic issues. It was founded in 1996, and concentrates mainly on education, development and environmental protection.
 Members: Canada, Denmark, Finland, Iceland, Norway, Russian Federation, Sweden, USA.

Address: c/o Ministry of Foreign Affairs, Unit for Northern Dimension, POB 176, 00161 Helsinki, Finland.
Telephone: (9) 13416187.
Fax: (9) 13416120.
E-mail: johanna.lammi@formin.fi
Internet: www.arctic-council.org

Armenia
Hayastany Hanrapetoutioun

A landlocked republic in the south-western **Caucasus region**, bounded by Turkey to the west, Iran to the south, Azerbaijan to the east and Georgia to the north. The country is divided administratively into 11 regions (*marzer*).

Area: 29,800 sq km; *capital*: **Yerevan**; *population*: 3.8m. (2001 estimate), comprising ethnic **Armenians** 93%, **Azeris** 3%, **Russians** 2%, others 2%; *official language*: Armenian; *religion*: **Armenian Apostolic Church** 94%.

A new Constitution approved in July 1995 established a democratic presidential system, with an executive President as Head of State elected by popular vote for a term of five years, renewable once. The President appoints the Prime Minister and Cabinet subject to approval by the **National Assembly** (Azgayin Joghov), which the President may dissolve. Legislative authority is vested in the unicameral Assembly of 131 members elected for a four-year term by universal adult suffrage, 75 by majority voting in single-member constituencies and 56 by proportional representation from party lists obtaining at least 5% of the vote.

History: Settled in ancient times by Indo-European tribes, and claiming to have been the first state to adopt Christianity as its official religion (in 301), Armenia was dominated for centuries by conflicts between larger neighbouring powers. Once a Roman province, it was caught in the struggle between the Byzantine and Persian Empires, before being conquered by the Seljuk Turks in the 11th century, overrun by the Mongols in the 13th and incorporated into the Ottoman Empire in the 16th. In 1639 Armenia was partitioned, the Ottoman Turks retaining the larger, western region while the eastern region (the present-day republic) became part of the Persian Empire. In 1828 Persia ceded eastern Armenia to **Russia** and in 1878 the Congress of Berlin transferred the Kars province, a large territory in western Armenia, to Russian control. From the late 19th century the Ottoman Turks persecuted their Armenian subjects, and in 1915 over a million people were murdered or deported (*see* **Armenian question**). In 1918, following the 1917 Bolshevik revolution in Russia, Armenia declared its independence, but this was short-lived in the wake of subsequent Turkish and Soviet occupation. In 1920 the area under Bolshevik control was proclaimed a Soviet Republic and in 1922 became a member (with **Azerbaijan** and **Georgia**) of the Transcaucasian Soviet Federative Socialist Republic (TSFSR). The TSFSR was dissolved in 1936 and Armenia became a full union republic of the **Soviet Union**.

In the late 1980s the influence of the *glasnost* (openness) initiative in the Soviet Union and the nationalist tensions caused by the military conflict in **Nagorno-Karabakh** (an ethnic Armenian enclave ceded to Azerbaijan in the early 1920s) gave expression to Armenian historical and political grievances. In mid-1990 the pro-independence **Pan-Armenian National Movement** (HHSh) achieved the largest number of seats in the elections to the then Armenian Supreme Soviet. This legislature made a declaration of sovereignty, renamed the country the Republic of Armenia and in 1991 refused to participate in negotiations to renew the union treaty of the Soviet Union. Alleged Soviet support for Azerbaijan in the worsening Nagorno-Karabakh conflict, and the effects of political disintegration in Moscow, led to a huge majority in favour of full secession from the Soviet Union in a referendum on independence in September 1991. Levon Ter-Petrossian, the incumbent candidate of the HHSh, was elected President the following month with overwhelming support. In December 1991 Armenia became a fully sovereign member of the **Commonwealth of Independent States** (CIS).

In the first post-Soviet legislative elections in July 1995 the Republican Bloc, an alliance of six groups led by the HHSh, won 119 of the 190 seats and accordingly dominated subsequent Governments. In presidential elections in September 1996 Ter-Petrossian was re-elected outright in the first round with 51.8% of the vote. Robert **Kocharian**, who had been President of the 'independent' republic of Nagorno-Karabakh proclaimed unilaterally a year earlier, was appointed Prime Minister in March 1997. Ter-Petrossian's willingness to consider an agreement for the enclave which recognized Azerbaijan's sovereignty brought him into increasing conflict with Kocharian and the Armenian military, the outcome being the President's resignation in February 1998.

Latest elections: New presidential elections in March 1998 resulted in a victory for Kocharian, standing as a non-party candidate. He was elected in the second round with 59.5% of the vote, against 40.5% for Karen Demirchian, who later founded the **People's Party of Armenia** (HZhK). Assembly elections in May 1999 produced a relative victory for the Unity Bloc (Miasnutiun) of the HZhK and the **Republican Party of Armenia** (HHK), which won 55 of the 131 seats with 41.7% of the vote. Other seats and vote shares were won as follows: **Communist Party of Armenia** (HKK) 11 (12.1%), **Armenian Revolutionary Federation** (Dashnak) 9 (7.8%), **Justice and Accord Bloc** 6 (8.0%), **Country of Law Party** (OE) 6 (5.3%), **National Democratic Union of Armenia** (AZhM) 6 (5.2%), HHSh 1 (1.2%), **Democratic Party of Armenia** (HDK) 1 (1.0%), **Mission** 1 (0.8%), 'National Concord' Party 1 (0.4%), independents 32, invalid contests 2.

Recent developments: In June 1999 Kocharian appointed Vazgen Sarkissian of the HHK to head a new Government which also included the HZhK and several smaller parties. In October 1999, however, the Prime Minister and new Assembly President Demirchian were among eight political leaders shot dead by gunmen who invaded the legislative chamber. Subsequent investigation of the shootings made little progress, amidst persistent reports that they were an attempt by hardliners to sabotage a prospective peace agreement on Nagorno-Karabakh (see below). Sarkissian was succeeded by his younger brother, Aram Sarkissian, who was dismissed by Kocharian in May 2000 and replaced by the new HHK Chairman, Andranik **Markarian**. The latter faced growing dissidence from anti-Kocharian elements of the HHK as well as serious strains with the HZhK which by early 2001 had rendered the Miasnutiun alliance a virtual dead letter.

International relations and defence: Having joined the CIS at independence in December 1991, Armenia was admitted to the **Organization for Security and Co-operation in Europe** (OSCE) and the United Nations early in 1992. It also became a member of the **Organization of the Black Sea Economic Co-operation** and obtained observer status in the **Non-Aligned Movement**. In 1994 it became a member of NATO's **Partnership for Peace** programme, while an agreement on partnership and co-operation with the **European Union** was signed in 1996 (also covering Azerbaijan and Georgia). A Treaty of Friendship, Co-operation and Mutual Understanding signed with the Russian Federation in August 1997 highlighted a continuing close security relationship, reflecting in part Armenia's ancestral antagonisms with Turkey, aggravated by the recent success of the Armenian diaspora in persuading the USA and other Western legislatures to issue condemnations of the 1915 Armenian massacres. In January 2001 the **Council of Europe**'s Ministerial Committee voted unanimously to admit Armenia (and Azerbaijan) to membership.

Armenia's military successes against Azerbaijan in the Nagorno-Karabakh conflict in the mid-1990s failed to produce a peace agreement on the disputed enclave, despite the efforts of the OSCE's **Minsk Group** and other bodies. A series of meetings between Kocharian and President Heydar **Aliyev** of Azerbaijan in 1999–2000 gave some impetus to the deadlocked negotiations, possibly on the basis of an exchange of territory under which Azerbaijan would obtain a corridor to its **Nakhichevan** enclave in return for making concessions on the status of Nagorno-Karabakh. As of late 2001, however, no substantive progress had been reported.

Armenia's defence budget totalled the equivalent of some US $96m. in 2000, equivalent to about 4.5% of GDP. Total armed forces at the end of 2000 were some 42,000, including those drafted under compulsory conscription of 24 months, while reservists numbered an estimated 210,000.

Armenia, economy

A small, impoverished and still largely agricultural economy, afflicted in the 1990s with familiar post-Soviet difficulties but showing signs of recovery by 2000, helped by financial inflows from **Armenians** abroad. The main transport and communications links between landlocked Armenia and the outside world are currently confined to those through **Georgia** and Iran, since Turkey maintains a closed border with its eastern neighbour and Armenia remains effectively at war with **Azerbaijan** over **Nagorno-Karabakh**.

GNP: US $1,932m. (2000); *GNP per capita*: $520 (2000); *GDP at PPP*: $9,900m. (1999); *GDP per capita at PPP*: $2,900 (1999); *exports*: $300m. (2000); *imports*: $885m. (2000); *currency*: dram (plural: drams; US $1=D562.2 at the end of December 2001).

In 1999 agriculture accounted for 40% of GDP, services 35% and industry 25%. In 1999 some 55% of the 1.5 million workforce were engaged in agriculture, 25% in services and 20% in industry (manufacturing, mining and construction). About 17% of the land is arable, 3% under permanent crops, 24% permanent pasture and 15% forests and woodlands. The main crops are grapes and other fruit and vegetables, with animal husbandry in the upland areas. Mineral resources include small deposits of gold, copper, molybdenum, zinc and alumina. The main industries are relatively small-scale manufacturing and textiles, with computer software becoming important by 2000. Energy sources include hydroelectric power and energy from a reopened nuclear power plant at Medzamor, while petroleum and gas are imported from the **Russian Federation**, Iran and Turkmenistan.

Armenia's main exports by value are jewellery (about 30% of the total), electrical, transport and other equipment (19%), aluminium and other base metals (11%), and mineral products (10%). The principal imports are oil and gas (over 30%) and food and agricultural products (20%). About a quarter of Armenia's exports go to Belgium, 15% to the Russian Federation and 13% to the USA. The main sources of imports are the Russian Federation (15%), the USA (12%) and Belgium and Iran (9% each).

Prior to the dissolution of the **Soviet Union** in 1991, Armenia supplied a range of manufactured goods and textiles to the rest of the Soviet Union in exchange for raw materials, but this arrangement fell away after the end of 1991 and the external balance deteriorated sharply. The economic situation at that time had already been made more serious by the repercussions of the severe earthquake of December 1988, while further difficulties were experienced as a result of the ongoing conflict with Azerbaijan over Nagorno-Karabakh. As a result, output dropped drastically and there was a huge wave of emigration from Armenia in the 1990s, although this latter factor resulted in an increased flow of remittances from Armenians working abroad. In the early 1990s GDP fell by an average of around 10% annually and there was massive inflation.

From 1995 there was improvement on many fronts as Armenia began implementing a comprehensive programme of macroeconomic reform with the support of international financial institutions and donors. In 1996 GDP showed an annual growth of 5.8%, and by 1997 inflation had fallen to 13.2%. Nevertheless, in 1998–99 Armenia felt the effects of the Russian economic crisis (*see* **Russian Federation, economy**), with delays in flows of financing from Russia, reductions in net transfers from Armenian workers in Russia and cancellation of some private investment. The problems were compounded by a severe trade and balance-of-payments deficit, huge external debt service requirements, high rates of interest and persistent depreciation of the dram. Real GDP growth slowed to 3.3% in 1999, during which the average officially-registered rate of unemployment was 10.9%, although large numbers were effectively underemployed. The Government responded with new plans for avoiding over-dependence on the Russian Federation and the other former Soviet republics, and by seeking inward investment to help modernize its industry and other sectors of the economy.

The Government's budget for 1999 anticipated a deficit of some 5.3% of GDP, most of which would be financed through the use of foreign loans. In 2000 GDP growth slowed further to around 2% and the inflation rate to 2.5%, as the projected budget deficit was cut to 4.3% of GDP. The 2001 budget provided for expenditure of D247,200m. and revenue of D193,400m., to produce a deficit of 4.8% of projected GDP.

The privatization of arable land, instituted immediately after independence in 1991, was almost complete by the end of 1996, so that private farms accounted for some 95% of agricultural production in 1997. By 1998 most small enterprises had also been privatized, as were some 90% of medium and larger enterprises (after a slower start), following the launch of a major new programme in 1995. In July 2000 legislative approval was given to the controversial privatization of the four main energy distribution networks.

Armenian Apostolic Church

A Christian denomination of the 'Lesser' or 'Oriental' Orthodox Church adhering closely to **Orthodox Christianity** and intrinsically linked to the state of **Armenia**. Christianity was brought to Armenia by Sts Thaddeus and Bartholomew in the 1st century AD, and the apparent adherence to their tradition lends the Church its 'Apostolic' title. Armenia became the first Christian state in the world in 301 and the history of the Church and the country have since been interwoven. The unique Armenian script was devised in the early years of the 5th century by St Mesrob as a means of religious instruction. Ties between the Church and Armenian culture remain strong and in 2001 the country celebrated 700 years of Christianity. Karekin I has been Supreme Patriarch and Catholicos since 5 April 1995.

Armenian Christian Democratic Union (ACDU)

A party founded in **Armenia** in 1990 and supportive of the post-communist Government of the **Pan-Armenian National Movement**. It formed part of the victorious Republican Bloc in the 1995 legislative elections. Advocating Christian democracy on the west European model but adapted to Armenian conditions, the ACDU is affiliated to the **Christian Democrat International**.
Leadership: Azad Arshakian (Chair.).
Address: 8 Abovian Street, Yerevan.

Telephone: (1) 561067.
Fax: (1) 561963.

Armenian question

The issue of whether the massacres of **Armenians** in the last years of the Ottoman Empire should be recognized as genocide. Turkey strongly resists this. It regards the deaths as part of a general loss of life arising from the collapse of the Ottoman Empire, and emphasizes that many Turks were also killed by Armenian groups at this time. **Armenia**, as an independent State since 1991, has lobbied persistently for 'the Armenian genocide' (Armenians use the term 'metz yeghern', meaning great crime or great evil) to become an internationally-accepted part of the historical record. The Armenian case is that the treatment of the Armenian minority in areas under Ottoman control, in a period beginning with the Russo-Turkish war in the 1870s and including the large-scale massacres of 1894–96 and 1915, represented an attempt at their extermination. Armenia wants an apology from Turkey, in particular for the events of 1915, when the Armenians were accused of aiding the **Russian** invaders during the First World War, and many hundreds of thousands of Armenians (1.5 million is a commonly-cited estimate) were killed by Turkish soldiers or died of starvation during their forced deportation from eastern Turkey to Syria and Mesopotamia. Resolutions proposing the explicit recognition of 'the Armenian genocide' are debated frequently in legislatures in Europe and North America. Turkey is particularly sensitive to the possibility of such a resolution being passed by the European Parliament, because of the implications for its efforts to gain membership of the **European Union**.

Armenian Revolutionary Federation
Hai Heghapokhakan Dashnaktsutyun (HHD/Dashnak)

The historic Armenian nationalist political movement/party originally founded in 1890, which was the governing party in pre-Soviet independent **Armenia** (1918–20) and retained a large following in the **Armenian** diaspora after being proscribed by the Bolsheviks in 1920. Dashnak is affiliated to the **Socialist International**, having been a member of the pre-First World War Second International.

Re-established in 1990 as a nationalist opposition party of socialist orientation, Dashnak strongly criticized the conduct of the **Nagorno-Karabakh** war by the Government of the **Pan-Armenian National Movement** (HHSh), which claimed in response that Dashnak leaders in exile had co-operated with the Soviet security authorities. At the end of 1994 the party was suspended by presidential decree, on the grounds that it had engaged in terrorism and drug-trafficking. It therefore did not participate as a party in the July 1995 **National Assembly** elections. Some 30 Dashnak activists were put on trial in March 1996 charged with involvement in an alleged coup attempt during the elections, those receiving prison sentences including the then Chairman Vahan Hovhanissian. However, all were released in February 1998 when the ban on the party was lifted, a week after the resignation of President Ter-Petrossian (HHSh).

Dashnak backed the successful candidacy of Robert **Kocharian** (non-party) in the March 1998 presidential elections, following which Hovhanissian became a presidential adviser and the party obtained two ministerial portfolios in the new Government. In the May 1999 Assembly elections Dashnak achieved third place with nine of the 131 seats and 7.8% of the proportional vote, subsequently obtaining one portfolio in the new government coalition.

In February 2000 Dashnak held its 28th world congress in Tsaghkadzor (its first in Armenia since 1919), deciding to establish the party's head office in Yerevan. The Armenian executive subsequently appointed Armen Rustamyan as the party's principal representative in Armenia.

Leadership: Hrand Margaryan (Chair. of World Bureau); Armen Rustamyan (Leader of Armenian Executive); Davit Lokyan (Parliamentary Group Chair.); Giro Manoyan (Executive Director).
Address: Miasniak Ave 2, Yerevan 375025; POB 123, Yerevan 375010.
Telephone: (1) 535623.
Fax: (1) 531362.
Internet: www.arf.am

Armenian State Foreign Economic and Trade Association
(or Armenintorg)

Deals with the import and export of all types of goods, marketing, consultancy, auditing and other services. Armenintorg also conducts training programmes and arranges international exhibitions and trade fairs. Founded in 1987.
General Director: Dr Armen R. Darbinian.
Address: Hr. Kochar St 25, 375012 Yerevan.
Telephone: (1) 224310.
Fax: (1) 220034.

Armenians

An Indo-European people concentrated in the modern republic of **Armenia** but spread throughout neighbouring states. The name Armenian is derived from the Greek and Persian names—Armenioi and Armina respectively—given to a people known to themselves as the Hayq (singular: Hay). The Armenian language is Indo-European but has many phonetic and grammatical similarities to the neighbouring **Caucasian** tongues. Armenians pride themselves that their country was the first to adopt Christianity officially as a state religion (in 301) and modern Armenians are mostly either of the **Armenian Apostolic Church** or part of the Catholic Church of Armenia.

Armenians dominated their historic region—now mostly occupied by modern Turkey—until Muslim conquerors gained ascendancy from the 7th century AD. In the 19th century historic Armenia was divided between the Ottoman Turks and the **Russian** Empire. The division prompted a mass migration of Armenians from Turkey, including many to Europe and the USA as well as to Russian Armenia. Those remaining in Turkey faced mass persecution in 1915 as the Ottoman Empire viewed them as a potential 'fifth column'. Many were deported to areas further south. The Armenians claim many hundreds of thousands were killed and consider this episode a purposeful genocide (*see* **Armenian question**).

The Armenians in Russia were concentrated (a) in what is now the Armenian Republic, (b) in what is now the disputed enclave of **Nagorno-Karabakh** in neighbouring **Azerbaijan**, and (c) to a lesser extent in parts of what is now **Georgia**. In the Soviet era they largely abandoned their traditional agricultural lifestyle and became urbanized through industrialization drives. Those who live in what is now Georgia, estimated to number some 500,000, have no separate representation and the Georgian authorities are not keen to develop this, although there are Armenian-language facilities throughout the country. The Armenians live mainly in urban centres, where they have been greatly russified, but there are also significant rural communities in southern Georgia, particularly **Javakheti**, and the coastal regions of **Abkhazia** and **Adzharia**.

Armenintorg *see* **Armenian State Foreign Economic and Trade Association**.

Armenpress

Armenia's main and oldest-established news agency, which was restructured as a joint stock company in 1997 but remains in state ownership. It was originally founded in 1920, and holds a large photographic archive on Armenian history. Armenpress provides a daily news service in Armenian, English and Russian.

Director: Hrayr Zoryan.
Address: 4th Floor, Isaahakian St 28, 375009 Yerevan.
Telephone: (1) 526702.
Fax: (1) 151738.
E-mail: contact@armenpress.am
Internet: www.armenpress.am

Assembly (Croatia)
Sabor

The unicameral legislature of **Croatia**, the Chamber being known as the House of Representatives (Zastupnički Dom). It currently has 151 members (increased from 127 to at most 160 under a law of October 1999), directly elected for a four-year term. In the enlarged House, 140 deputies are elected in 10 constituencies, five elected by ethnic minorities, and a variable number (not more than 15) chosen to represent Croatians abroad (six in the 2000 elections). The Assembly was formerly bicameral, with an upper House of Counties (Županijski Dom). The then lower House of Representatives voted in late March 2001, however, to abolish the House of Counties after the expiry of its mandate in May 2001. The last elections were held on 3 January 2000.
 Address: Zastupnički Dom, Hrvatski Sabor, Trg sv. Marka 6–7, 10000 Zagreb.
 Telephone: (1) 4569420.
 Fax: (1) 6303010.
 Internet: www.sabor.hr

Assembly of the Republic (Macedonia)
Sobranie

The unicameral legislature of **Macedonia**. It has 120 members, directly elected for a four-year term. The last elections were held between 18 October and 1 November 1998.
 Address: Sobranie, 11 Oktomvri b.b., 91000 Skopje.
 Telephone: (2) 112255.
 Fax: (2) 111675.
 E-mail: sobranie@assembly.gov.mk
 Internet: www.assembly.gov.mk/sobranie

Association of Autonomous Trade Unions of Croatia
Savez Samostalnih Sindikata Hrvatske (SSSH)

The main trade union centre in **Croatia**, founded in May 1990 as effectively the successor to the communist-era organization. Having elected a former communist as its first Chairman, the SSSH quickly experienced internal divisions, leading to the formation of the breakaway **Confederation of Independent Trade Unions of Croatia** and the **Croatian Association of Trade Unions**. In 1999 the SSSH joined with the other union organizations in signing a compromise agreement with the Government on the distribution of the assets of the communist-era trade unions. However, its relations with the regime were generally strained, and in the January 2000 **Assembly** elections it strongly backed the opposition alliance which defeated the **Croatian Democratic Union** (HDZ). Affiliated to the International

Confederation of Free Trade Unions (ICFTU), the SSSH claims to represent about 500,000 workers.
   President: Davor Jurić.
   Address: 2 Kresimirov Trg, Zagreb 10000.
   Telephone: (1) 4655111.
   Fax: (1) 4655040.
   E-mail: sssh@sssh.hr
   Internet: www.sssh.hr

Association of Estonian Trade Unions
Eesti Ametiuhingute Keskliit (EAKL)

Estonia's principal trade union centre, founded in 1990 as successor to the Soviet-era union organization. The EAKL has backed privatization, while claiming that state assets have been disposed of too cheaply and without protecting the rights of former state employees. It also supports Estonia's application for **European Union** membership. An affiliate of the International Confederation of Free Trade Unions (ICFTU), the EAKL links unions which represent some 65,000 workers (as compared with the 800,000 membership total of the Soviet-era union federation).
   Chair.: Kadi Parnits.
   Address: 4 Rävala Boulevard, Tallinn 10143.
   Telephone: 6612383.
   Fax: 6612542.

Association of Free Trade Unions of Slovenia
Zveza Svobodnih Sindikatov Slovenije (ZSSS)

One of several competing union centres in **Slovenia**, founded on the country's achievement of independence in 1991.
   President: Dušan Semolič.
   Address: 4 Dalmatinova St, Ljubljana 1000.
   Telephone: (1) 4341200.
   Fax: (1) 2326982.
   E-mail: info@sindikat-zsss.si
   Internet: www.sindikat-zsss.si

Association of Independent Workers of Azerbaijan

An independent trade union centre in **Azerbaijan**, seeking to challenge the dominance of the **Confederation of Azerbaijan Trade Unions**.
   Chair.: Neymat Panakhli.
   Address: Baku.

Association of Lithuanian Chambers of Commerce, Industry and Crafts

The principal organization in **Lithuania** for promoting business contacts, both internally and externally, in the post-communist era. Founded in 1992.
Director-General: Rimas Varkulevičius
Address: J-Tumo Vaižganto 9/1–63a, Vilnius 2001.
Telephone: (26) 12102 [(526) 12102 from September 2002].
Fax: (26) 12112 [(526) 12112 from September 2002].
E-mail: lppra@post.omnitel.net.lt
Internet: www.lithuaniachambers.lt

Astrakhan

A historic city—and a similarly-named *oblast* (region)—at the mouth of the **Volga** river in south-eastern **European Russia**. *Population*: 509,000 (1987 estimate). The original settlement became a key trading city in the Mongol Golden Horde in the 14th century and was the capital of the **Tatar** Astrakhan khanate until it was conquered by the Russian Tsar, Ivan the Terrible, in 1556. It has been an integral part of **Russia** ever since.

Economic activity centres on the use of the Volga as access for goods flowing in and out of the Russia's industrial heartland and the bountiful products of the Caspian Sea. However, the shallow depths of the sea's northern waters means that seagoing vessels cannot reach the city's main port. Astrakhan is home to a large fishing fleet and fish processing and **caviar**-preserving are major activities.

ASzSz *see* **Autonomous Trade Union Confederation**.

ATA *see* **Albanian Telegraphic Agency**.

August coup

In the **Soviet Union**, the attempted coup d'état of 19–21 August 1991 to oust President Mikhail **Gorbachev** and install a hardline communist regime. The hardliners were seeking to prevent the continuation of the reform and devolution policies which they saw as destroying the Soviet communist system. A new Union treaty for the Soviet Union was about to be signed the following day, when members of the Politburo of the **Communist Party of the Soviet Union** (KPSS) and the heads of the Soviet military and security services detained Gorbachev at his villa in the **Crimea**. Announcing Gorbachev's removal on health grounds, they set up a Committee of the State of Emergency, but were met by strong popular resistance in Moscow, spearheaded by the then Russian President Boris **Yeltsin** who took a public stand with demonstrators outside the Russian Parliament building (the **White House**). Soldiers sent in with tanks either switched sides or turned back, and without full military backing the August coup quickly collapsed. It marked a critical moment, however, in the passing of effective power from Gorbachev to Yeltsin and, ironically, precipitated the rapid disintegration of the Soviet Union and the banning of the KPSS.

Aum Shinrikyo
(or Aleph)

A Japan-based religious cult, notoriously responsible for the 1995 sarin nerve-gas attack in Tokyo, which at its peak claimed around 30,000 followers in the **Russian Federation**. The cult is based loosely on **Buddhism** and Hinduism and teaches enlightenment through meditation and austerity. It changed its name to Aleph in January 2000 as part of its efforts to distance itself from its founder Shoko Asahara, who, it admits, was responsible for the 1995 attack. The political/violent nature of the sect has led to close monitoring of its adherents. Since 1995 it has lost support worldwide and has dwindled in numbers.

Auschwitz-Birkenau
Oświęcim-Brzezinka

The infamous Nazi concentration camp near the city of Katowice in south-west **Poland**. A memorial to the Holocaust, known as the Museum of Martyrdom, was established in 1946 on the site of the Auschwitz camp and the much larger Birkenau site where the majority of people were gassed. Most of Birkenau, including the gas chambers, was destroyed by German troops before they fled in 1945.

As one of the largest of the many concentration camps, Auschwitz-Birkenau is perhaps the most potent symbol of the genocide of European **Jews**. However, the Polish authorities have stressed that the memorial should not be seen as solely commemorating the Jewish victims. The first inmates of the camp, established in 1940 initially for the detention of political prisoners, were Polish political opponents of the Nazi regime. There was a long controversy from the mid-1980s over the establishment of a Polish Carmelite convent, in a building that was once a storehouse for the poisonous Zyklon B gas. Jewish groups protested that the 'Christianization' of the site was inappropriate and insulting to the memory of the camp's overwhelmingly more numerous Jewish victims. (It has been estimated that 1.6 million people died there, of whom 1.35 million were Jews.) The last nuns left the convent in the mid-1990s but there was renewed controversy over the erection of a number of wooden crosses for Christian victims of the Nazis, near the museum and visible from within the compound.

Autonomous Trade Union Confederation
Autonóm Szakszervezetek Szövetsége (ASzSz)

One of several trade union centres in **Hungary** formed after the end of communist rule, competing in particular with the dominant **National Confederation of Hungarian Trade Unions**. The ASzSz is one of three Hungarian affiliates to the International Confederation of Free Trade Unions (ICFTU).
President: Lajos Főcze.
Address: 45 út Benczúr, Budapest 1046.
Telephone: (1) 3421774.
Fax: (1) 3429975.

Avars

A Caucasian people who make up the largest group in the ethnically diverse **Russian** republic of **Dagestan**. Numbering around 500,000 the Avars account for about 28% of the republic's population. Unconnected to the historic Avars of central Asia who invaded **central Europe** from the 7th century, the Dagestani Avars were effectively created from an assortment of local groups in the 1930s. They were employed by the Russian and **Soviet** authorities as the ruling elite in Dagestan, but the introduction of a democratic system in 1992 has diluted this dominance. In 1993 ethnic Avars clashed with **Chechens** and Laks over land rights. Like most Dagestanis they are Sunni **Muslims**, and mainly absorbed in agricultural activity. The cultural predominance of the Turkic **Kumyk** group in the region has seen some Avars assimilated.

AWS *see* **Solidarity Electoral Action**.

Azerbaijan
Azarbaycan Respublikasi

An independent republic in the eastern **Caucasus**, bordering Iran to the south, Georgia and the Russian republic of Dagestan to the north, Armenia to the west and the Caspian Sea to the east. Administratively, the country is divided into 59 districts (rayons), 11 cities and two autonomous republics. One of the autonomous republics, Azeri-populated **Nakhichevan** is separated geographically from the rest of Azerbaijan by Armenian territory. The other, the mainly **Armenian**-populated enclave of **Nagorno-Karabakh**, has been the focus of lengthy conflict with **Armenia** (see below).
Area: 86,600 sq km; *capital*: **Baku**; *population*: 8.1m. (2001 estimate), comprising ethnic **Azeris** 90%, **Dagestani** peoples 3.2%, **Russians** 2.5%, Armenians

2.3%, others 2%; *official language*: Azeri; *religion*: **Muslims** 93.4%, **Russian Orthodox** 2.5%, **Armenian Apostolic Church** 2.3%, others 1.8% (1995 estimate).

Under a new Constitution adopted in November 1995, legislative authority is vested in the **National Assembly** (Milli Majlis), which has 125 members elected for a five-year term (100 returned from single-member constituencies and 25 by proportional representation according to party lists). Executive power rests with the President, who is directly elected by universal adult suffrage for a five-year term, and who appoints the Cabinet of Ministers, subject to approval by the Assembly.

History: Having from ancient times experienced rule by the Medes, Greeks and Persians, Azerbaijan came under Arab control in the 7th century, heralding the rise of Islam as the principal religion. Penetration by **Turkic** tribes from the 11th century onwards had a significant impact on the ethnic evolution of the population before the region fell again under Persian control in the 1500s. In the second half of the 18th century political fragmentation and internecine conflicts encouraged Russian encroachment. Two Russo-Persian wars followed, in 1804–13 and 1826–28, resulting in the division of the territory; the northern part (now independent Azerbaijan) was integrated into the Russian Empire while the southern area remained in Persian (subsequently Iranian) hands.

After the Russian Revolution of October 1917, there was a brief period of pro-Bolshevik rule in Azerbaijan before an anti-Soviet nationalist Government took power and declared the country an independent state in May 1918. However, Azerbaijan was reconquered by the Red Army in 1920 and joined the **Soviet Union** in 1922 as part of the Transcaucasian Soviet Federative Socialist Republic (together with Armenia and **Georgia**). In 1936 it became the Azerbaijan Soviet Socialist Republic with full union republic status. During this period religious intolerance was severe (reflecting Soviet efforts to reduce the influence of Islam in the republic), collectivization of agriculture led to peasant uprisings and their suppression, and political purges of perceived opponents of Stalin's regime took a heavy toll.

During the Second World War Soviet troops occupied Iranian Azerbaijan, rekindling pan-Azerbaijani sentiments. However, they were forced to withdraw under pressure from the USA and the UK in 1946, in one of the first confrontations of what became the **Cold War** between the Soviet Union and the West.

Since the 1960s Azerbaijan's political course has revolved around the fortunes of its most influential figure, Heydar **Aliyev**, and the longstanding ethnic tension with neighbouring Armenia, particularly over the disputed territory of Nagorno-Karabakh.

Aliyev, installed as First Secretary of the **Azerbaijan Communist Party** (AKP) in 1969, was appointed to the Politburo in **Moscow** from 1982, the highest position ever reached by an Azeri in the Soviet Union. In 1987, however, he was removed by the then leader Mikhail **Gorbachev** for alleged corruption. The following year fighting escalated in Nagorno-Karabakh between Azerbaijani forces and ethnic Armenian separatists.

The ensuing protracted military conflict took place against the backdrop of the collapse of the Soviet Union and the re-establishment, in 1991, of Azerbaijani independence under President Ayaz Mutalibov (the last AKP First Secretary).

Mutalibov was re-elected President unopposed in September 1991. However, unrest in Azerbaijan over defeats by Armenia in Nagorno-Karabakh led to his resignation in March 1992. His successor Abulfaz Elchibey of the nationalist **Azerbaijan Popular Front** (AKC), elected in June 1992, was in turn forced to resign a year later. At this point Aliyev, now leading the **New Azerbaijan Party** (YAP), again took up the political reins, claiming a conclusive victory in the presidential election of October 1993. A cease-fire agreement with Armenia, brokered by the Russian Federation, was reached in May 1994, although Azerbaijan by this time had lost control of almost 20% of its territory and was facing a serious refugee problem.

Restrictive registration requirements for the first post-Soviet elections to the National Assembly in November 1995 meant that only eight parties were allowed to take part. Official results (after further polling in February 1996) gave the YAP and independent candidates supporting President Aliyev an overwhelming majority, but international observers declared that the elections had not been conducted fairly, while opposition groups demanded fresh balloting.

Latest elections: In further presidential elections held in October 1998, Aliyev secured 76.1% of the votes cast to win on the first ballot, following which Artur **Rasizade** was reappointed Prime Minister of a YAP-dominated Government. The President's son, Ilham Aliyev, headed the YAP list in National Assembly elections held in November 2000, for which registration rules were relaxed at the last minute to allow 12 other parties to stand. Including reruns for 11 seats in early January 2001, the official results for the 124 seats filled (out of 125) gave the YAP 75 (with 62.3% of the proportional vote), the AKC 6 (10.9%), the **Civil Unity Party** 3 (6.4%), the AKP 2 (6.3%), the **New Muslim Democratic Party** (Musavat) 2 (4.9%), the **Azerbaijan National Independence Party** 2 (3.9%), five other parties 5 and independents 29. The conduct and outcome of the polling again attracted censure from the opposition parties and international observers.

International relations and defence: Since independence, Azerbaijan has been admitted to the United Nations, the **Organization for Security and Co-operation in Europe** (OSCE), the **Commonwealth of Independent States** (CIS), the **Organization of the Islamic Conference** (OIC), the **Economic Co-operation Organization** (ECO), the **Non-Aligned Movement** (as an observer) and the **Organization of the Black Sea Economic Co-operation**. It is also a member of NATO's **Partnership for Peace** and in 1996 signed a partnership and co-operation agreement with the **European Union** (together with Armenia and Georgia). In February 1999 Foreign Minister Tofik Zulfagarov stated that integration into European and trans-Atlantic institutions was a priority for Azerbaijan. In January

2001 the **Council of Europe**'s Ministerial Committee voted unanimously to admit Azerbaijan (and Armenia) to membership.

At regional level, Azerbaijan entered into a 10-year friendship and co-operation agreement with Turkey in 1994 and has pursued the delimitation of Caspian Sea boundaries with the other littoral states (Iran, Kazakhstan, Russian Federation and Turkmenistan) with a view to determining the ownership of the rich oil and gas resources in the area (*see* **Azerbaijan, economy**).

Although the cease-fire declared in Nagorno-Karabakh in 1994 generally held, no real progress was made thereafter on a settlement, despite continuing negotiations between Azerbaijan and Armenia under the aegis of the OSCE's **Minsk Group**. A series of meetings in 1999–2000 between President Aliyev and his Armenian counterpart, Robert **Kocharian**, gave some impetus to the quest for an agreement. A suggested possibility of an exchange of territory under which Azerbaijan would obtain a corridor to its Nakhichevan enclave in return for concessions on the status of Nagorno-Karabakh has been rejected. As of the end of 2001, no substantive progress had been reported.

Azerbaijan's defence budget totalled some US $120m. in 2000, equivalent to about 3% of GDP. Total armed forces at the end of 1999 were some 72,000, including those drafted under compulsory conscription of 17 months, while reservists numbered an estimated 576,000.

Azerbaijan, economy

An economy until recently relatively undeveloped, which shrank dramatically in the first half of the 1990s, and whose future is heavily based on exploitation of the rich hydrocarbon reserves beneath the Caspian Sea, the prospects for which have begun to alleviate the familiar post-**Soviet** transition problems.

GNP: US $4,829m. (2000); *GNP per capita*: $610 (2000); *GDP at PPP*: $14,000m. (1999); *GDP per capita at PPP*: $1,770 (1999); *exports*: $1,745m. (2000); *imports*: $1,172m. (1999); *currency*: manat (plural: manats; US $1=M4,775 at the end of December 2001).

In 1999 industry accounted for 35.4% of GDP, agriculture 23.3% and services 41.3%. Some 33% of the 2.8m workforce were engaged in agriculture and fisheries, 17% in industry and construction and 50% in other sectors. About 18% of the land is arable, 5% under permanent crops, 25% permanent pasture and 11% forests and woodland. The main crops are grain, grapes and other fruit, vegetables and cotton. Mineral resources include petroleum, natural gas, iron ore, non-ferrous metals and alumina. The main industries include petrochemicals, iron and steel, aluminium and glass and ceramics, while the traditional textiles and clothing sector has declined in the face of external competition. In 1998 about 10% of domestic electricity generation was produced from hydroelectricity and the other 85% from thermal power stations

Azerbaijan, economy

Azerbaijan's main exports by value in 1999 were petroleum products (almost 80% of the total), foodstuffs (6%) and machinery and transport equipment (5%). The principal imports were machinery and transport equipment (45%), food and agricultural products (18%) and metals and metal products (11%). In 2000 44% of Azerbaijan's exports went to Italy, 12% to France and 8% to Israel. The main sources of imports were the **Russian Federation** (21%), Turkey (11%) and the USA (10%).

Azerbaijan has long exploited its oil and gas resources in the Caspian Sea, with the result that the Apsheron peninsula (including **Baku**) is regarded by experts as the most polluted land area in the world. Production fell sharply in the 1980s, but following independence in 1991 major agreements were concluded for development of Caspian Sea reserves, notably the US $8,000m. 'deal of the century' signed by the Azerbaijan International Operating Company (AIOC) in September 1994. Although some exploring consortia achieved disappointing results, oil production rose to 260,000 barrels per day (b/d) in 1999, of which about half was exported, and was expected to reach around 1m. b/d by 2010. By 2000 Azerbaijan's oil reserves were put at between 3,600m. and 12,500m. barrels, depending in part on the still-unresolved issue of delimitation of littoral states' rights in the Caspian. A critical factor for future exploitation is a final decision on a main export pipeline (MEP), for which Azerbaijan favours a 1,730-km link between Baku and the Turkish Black Sea port of Ceyhan via **Georgia**.

Azerbaijan emerged from Soviet rule with an economy relatively less developed than those of neighbouring **Armenia** or Georgia and with its trade closely tied to the other Soviet republics. Economic difficulties were aggravated by the ongoing conflict with Armenia over **Nagorno-Karabakh**, which adversely affected agricultural production and caused huge refugee flows. At the same time, transport communications through Georgia and the southern Russian republics of **Dagestan** and **Chechnya** were disrupted by conflict in those areas. Accordingly, officially recorded GDP contracted by nearly 60% in 1990–95 and in 1996 was only half that of 1990.

Assisted by a cease-fire in Nagorno-Karabakh and large foreign investment in the oil sector, the economy showed substantial improvement from 1997 on the basis of a comprehensive stabilization programme drawn up by the Government and backed by the **International Monetary Fund**. Inflation was reduced to around zero by the end of 1997, during which real GDP expanded by 5.8%, followed by growth of 10% in 1998 (including 23% growth in the oil sector). Azerbaijan was little affected by the 1998 Russian financial crisis (*see* **Russian Federation, economy**), although the decline in world oil prices in 1998–99 and sharply reduced oil investment resulted in GDP growth slowing to 7.4% in 1999 and to around 6% in 2000. Growth in the agriculture sector was around 7% in 1999, but non-oil industrial output continued to decline, with previously dominant sectors such as metallurgy and machine building having come to a virtual standstill. The unemployment rate was given as 14% in 1999 but it was unofficially estimated to be considerably higher, reaching at least 20%. The 2001 budget provided for total expenditure of M4,590,000m. and revenue of M4,170,000m., with the deficit to be financed by a **World Bank** loan and privatization receipts. GDP growth of an ambitious 8.5% was projected for 2001.

Privatization effectively began only in 1995, with many shops and small enterprises passing into the private sector in 1996–97 and more medium-sized businesses in 1997–99 mainly through an auction process; however, the Government intended to keep certain major strategic businesses within the public sector, including the state oil company SOCAR.

Azerbaijan Communist Party
Azerbaycan Kommunist Partiyasi (AKP)

A **Soviet**-era ruling party which has retained some influence in independent **Azerbaijan**.

Under the hardline leadership of Ayaz Mutalibov the AKP won three-quarters of the seats in the first multi-party elections to the then Supreme Soviet in autumn 1990, following which Mutalibov was re-elected President unopposed in September 1991, the opposition parties having boycotted the contest. In March 1992 military setbacks in **Nagorno-Karabakh** forced the resignation of Mutalibov. He fled to the **Russian Federation** after a short-lived return to power in May which was claimed by the opposition to have been an attempted coup. The AKP was suspended under the subsequent Government of the **Azerbaijan Popular Front** (AKC), which replaced the Supreme Soviet with an interim 50-member **National Assembly** dominated by AKC members. Nevertheless, AKP members remained preponderant in the state bureaucracy and former AKP deputies continued to regard the 1990 Supreme Soviet as the legitimate legislative body.

In November 1993 an attempt was made to relaunch the party as the Azerbaijan United Communist Party (AVKP), the aim being to rally the opposition to the new Government of Heydar **Aliyev** of the **New Azerbaijan Party** (YAP). In early September 1995 the Supreme Court banned the AVKP in light of Justice Ministry allegations that the party had engaged in anti-State activities. Later in the month, however, the Court reversed its decision, thus enabling the party to contest legislative elections in November 1995, although it failed to win representation.

Divisions in communist ranks resulted in the relaunching of the AKP in the late 1990s. Along with the main AKP, there are now also three other smaller Communist Parties. The most prominent, and only registered version, is headed by Ramiz Ahmadov, who led the party to just surmount the 6% barrier to representation in the proportional section of elections in November 2000: it was allocated two seats in the National Assembly. The main splinter, AKP (2), is led by Firudin Hasanov, who received only 0.9% of the vote in presidential elections in October 1998.

Leadership: Ramiz Ahmadov (Chair.).

Address: 29 Hussein Javid Prospekti, Room 637te, Baku.
Telephone: (12) 380151.

Azerbaijan National Independence Party
Azerbaycan Milli Istiqlal Partiyasi (AMIP–Istiqlal)

A right-wing formation in **Azerbaijan** founded in July 1992 by Etibar Mamedov, hitherto a leader of the then ruling **Azerbaijan Popular Front** (AKC).

Mamedov's defection from the AKC was prompted by opposition within that party to hardline approach to the **Nagorno-Karabakh** conflict with **Armenia**. He had initially presented himself as a candidate for the June 1992 presidential election but had withdrawn, claiming that the AKC candidate had an unfair advantage.

After Heydar **Aliyev** of the **New Azerbaijan Party** (YAP) came to power in June 1993, Mamedov refused a ministerial post. He subsequently condemned the Government's willingness to accept the deployment of **Russian** forces in Azerbaijan to guarantee a Nagorno-Karabakh peace agreement.

The AMIP was officially stated to have won three seats in the November 1995 **National Assembly** elections on the basis of a national vote share of 9%. The party thereafter adopted an outright opposition stance, highlighted by Mamedov's candidacy in the controversial October 1998 presidential elections, in which he was runner-up to President Aliyev with 11.8% of the vote.

Registered for the November 2000 legislative elections, the AMIP was stated to have polled only 3.9% in the proportional section, but won two constituency seats, one in reruns in early January 2001. Mamedov joined in opposition demands for the elections to be annulled because of widespread gerrymandering by the Government.

Leadership: Etibar Mamedov (Chair.).
Address: 179 Azadlig Street, Baku 370087.
Telephone: (12) 627576.

Azerbaijan Popular Front
Azerbaycan Khalq Cabhasi (AKC)

A broad-based political party in **Azerbaijan** founded in 1989 under the leadership of Abulfaz Elchibey, which opposes the Government of Heydar **Aliyev** of the **New Azerbaijan Party** (YAP).

The AKC originally came into being to demand reform of the then communist-run system. It took a **pan-Turkic** line, supporting nationalist calls for the acquisition of **Azeri**-populated areas of northern Iran, and in January 1990 AKC members were among 150 people killed by the security forces in **Baku** and elsewhere in disturbances arising from AKC-led anti-**Armenia** demonstrations.

Allowed to contest the Supreme Soviet elections of autumn 1990, the AKC-led opposition won only 45 of the 360 seats (with a vote share of 12.5%). Together with other opposition parties, the AKC boycotted the direct presidential election held in September 1991 but subsequently brought about the resignation of President Mutalibov of the **Azerbaijan Communist Party** (AKP) in March 1992. In a further presidential election in June 1992, Elchibey was victorious with 59.4% of the vote against four other candidates.

The AKC-led Government blocked ratification of Azerbaijan's membership of the **Commonwealth of Independent States** but came under increasing pressure from opposition groups, notably Aliyev's recently-formed YAP. Replaced as Head of State by Aliyev in June 1993, Elchibey fled to **Nakhichevan** and disputed the official results of an August referendum (boycotted by the AKC) in which only 2% of voters were said to have expressed confidence in Elchibey. Aliyev secured popular endorsement as President in September 1993, in direct elections which were also boycotted by the AKC. The authorities subsequently launched a crackdown on the AKC, raiding its headquarters in Baku in February 1994 and arresting 100 AKC activists. Nevertheless, the AKC was able in 1994–95 to command substantial popular support for its opposition to the Aliyev Government's policy of seeking a **Nagorno-Karabakh** settlement through the mediation of the **Russian Federation**.

In May 1995 Elchibey repeated the AKC's call for the creation of a 'greater Azerbaijan', to include the estimated 15 million ethnic Azeris inhabiting northern Iran. In the same month Shahmerdan Jafarov, an AKC deputy, was stripped of his parliamentary immunity and accused of setting up illegal armed groups in Nakhichevan, where Elchibey's residence was reportedly surrounded by government troops. In June 1995 Jafarov was shot in a clash in the enclave, later dying of his injuries.

In the November 1995 **National Assembly** elections the AKC was officially credited with winning three proportional seats on the basis of a national vote share of 10%, and it took a fourth seat in balloting for unfilled seats in February 1996. Proceedings against AKC members early in 1996 included the sentencing to death in absentia of former Defence Minister Rakhim Gaziyev for treason, although his sentence was commuted to life imprisonment on his extradition from **Moscow** to Baku in April. Some AKC leaders were released under a presidential amnesty in July 1996, while in October 1997 Elchibey returned to Baku after four years in internal exile.

The AKC also boycotted the October 1998 presidential election, following which Elchibey was put on trial for insulting the Head of State. That the proceedings were called off in February 1999 on the initiative of President Aliyev was widely attributed to international pressure. Thereafter the AKC continued to be the leading component in various opposition fronts. However, increasing internal divisions led to an open split in August 2000, coinciding with the death of Elchibey in Turkey from cancer. A 'reformist' faction led by former AKC Deputy Chairman

Ali Kerimov advocated accommodation with the regime, while the 'conservative' wing led by Murmahmud Fattayev maintained an uncompromising opposition line.

The Fattayev faction of the AKC was barred from presenting candidates in the November 2000 Assembly elections, instead forming an alliance with the **New Muslim Democratic Party** (Musavat). The Kerimov faction of the AKC was allowed to stand, however. It was credited with 10.9% of the vote in the proportional section and six seats, including one won in reruns in early January 2001. In the wake of the balloting both factions joined in opposition condemnations of its validity. In mid-January 2001 the Kerimov AKC announced jointly with the **Civil Unity Party** that its deputies would participate in the work of the new Assembly, but in order to campaign for new elections.

Leadership: Ali Kerimov (Chair. of 'reformist' faction); Murmahmud Fattayev
 (Chair. of 'conservative' faction).
Address: 1 Injasanat Street, Baku 370000.
Telephone: (12) 921483.
Fax: (12) 989004.

Azerbintorg

Imports and exports a wide range of goods from **Azerbaijan**—90.4% of exports in 1995.

Director: E. M. Hureynov.
Address: Nekrasov St 7, 370004 Baku.
Telephone: (12) 937169.
Fax: (12) 983292.

Azeris

A **Turkic people** concentrated in **Azerbaijan**, descended from Seljuq Turks who invaded the region in the 11th century and incorporated the ethnic Iranian and **Caucasian** groups around the southern shores of the Caspian Sea. Their language belongs to the Turkmen or Oguz group of Turkic languages, similar to that spoken by Turkic people throughout the region. Until the 20th century Azeri was transcribed using Arabic script. Under **Soviet** domination, between 1939 and 1992, the **Cyrillic alphabet** was used but since independence Azeri has been written with the Latin alphabet. The 15–20 million Azari Turks living in northern Iran, ethnically identical to Azeris, have embraced Shi'a Islam and are well integrated into Iranian society.

AzerTAJ

The state news agency in **Azerbaijan**, originally founded in 1919.

AzerTAJ

Director-General: Shamil Mammad oglu Shahmammadov.
Address: Bul-Bul Ave 18, 370000 Baku.
Telephone: (12) 935929.
Fax: (12) 936265.
E-mail: office@azertac.baku.az
Internet: www.azertag.com

Azgayin Joghov *see* **National Assembly (Armenia)**.

AZhM *see* **National Democratic Union of Armenia**.

B

Baku

The capital city and major urban centre of **Azerbaijan**. *Population*: 1.7m. (estimate). The natural Baku harbour provides the best port on the Caspian Sea. Settlement at the site dates back to several centuries BC but the first historical reference dates from 885 AD. Long dominated by the Persian Empire, Baku became an important economic and administrative centre. **Russian** rule first came in a 12-year spell from 1723 and was finally established permanently in 1806. After the Russian Revolution Baku was made the capital of the Azeri republic, a role it maintained after the country's independence in 1991.

The oil industry has long dominated Baku's economy. Surface wells have been exploited for fuel since the 15th century. Modern commercial collection began in 1872, the second such venture in the world (after that in Ploieşti in **Romania**). Although the city's surrounding sources have largely dried up, Azerbaijan's claims in the Caspian remain bountiful and there are other sites inland. Along with extraction Baku has specialized in associated manufacture, producing equipment and machinery for the oil and chemical industries.

Baku Interbank Currency Exchange (BICEX)

The stock exchange for **Azerbaijan**, based in **Baku**. Originally established in 1886 BICEX was re-formed in June 1993 and trading began in August 1994. BICEX performs chiefly as a currency market, regulating exchange rates, but also trades in securities.
Address: Ingilab St 57, Baku 370110.
Telephone: (12) 906309.
Fax: (12) 906516.
E-mail: root@bicex.baku.az
Internet: www.az/bicex

Balcerowicz, Leszek

Central banker and former Minister of Finance in **Poland**, famous as the architect of the Balcerowicz Plan, the first and most radical pro-market reform programme in post-communist **central** and **eastern Europe**. Born in 1947, Balcerowicz had left the communist party during the 1981 crisis to work as an economic consultant to the **Solidarity** free trade union movement. In government after the fall of communism in 1989, as Deputy Prime Minister and Finance Minister, he was a leading advocate of '**shock therapy**', planning a rapid transition to a free-market economy despite the political risks this entailed. He believed the consequent short term social costs would be ameliorated by the revival of the economy in the medium term. He was sacrificed for political reasons with the appointment of a new Government in 1991. Balcerowicz joined the **Freedom Union** (UW), the principal post-Solidarity party, on its formation in 1994 and in April 1995 he was elected UW leader, a position he retained until 2000 when he became President of the **National Bank of Poland**. In the intervening period, having won election to the *Sejm* (lower house of the **National Assembly**) in 1997, he held his former post of Deputy Prime Minister and Finance Minister until 1999.

Balkan Stability Pact *see* **Stability Pact for South-Eastern Europe**.

Balkans

The south-east peninsula of Europe. The name derives from the Turkish for mountain and the area is traversed by various mountain chains, particularly in the west. The Balkans stretch south from the Pannonian plain (mainly in **Hungary**) to the northern highlands of Greece, and from the Italian Alps in the west to the Ukrainian plain in the east. Politically, the name Balkans is commonly used as a collective term for the countries of the region: **Albania, Bosnia and Herzegovina, Bulgaria, Croatia,** Greece, **Macedonia, Moldova, Romania, Slovenia** and **Yugoslavia**. The region's collective history has often set these countries apart from the rest of Europe, from the Ottoman domination of the 14th to 19th centuries, at least until the communist-dominated post-1945 period. More recently the Balkans have suffered some of the continent's most bitter wars, pitting diverse yet often closely-related ethnic groups and various religions against one another. The fragmentation of previously homogenous groups, particularly the south **Slavs**, has spawned the concept of Balkanization.

Balkars *see* **Kabardino-Balkaria**.

Baltic Council (BC)

An institution for facilitating co-operation between the Governments of **Estonia**, **Latvia** and **Lithuania**. It was formally established in its present structure, as an intergovernmental ministerial body, in June 1994, following an initiative by the Council of the Baltic States (an organization set up in 1990 which dissolved itself after handing over its mission to the Baltic Council and the interparliamentary Baltic Assembly). The Baltic Council's main areas of activity are foreign policy, justice, the environment, education and science.
Internet: www.bcmvs.net/bcm

Baltic Marine Environment Protection Commission
(or Helsinki Commission, HELCOM)

The main regional organization co-ordinating environmental protection efforts in the Baltic and seeking to combat pollution of the Baltic. Its original Helsinki Convention, signed in 1974 by the then seven Baltic coastal states and entering into force on 3 May 1980, marked the first time ever that all the sources of pollution around an entire sea were made subject to a single convention. In the light of political changes, and developments in international environmental and maritime law, a new convention was signed in 1992 by all the states bordering on the Baltic Sea and the European Community. After ratification this new convention entered into force on 17 January 2000. It covers the whole of the Baltic Sea area, including inland water, and also commits its signatories to take measures in the whole catchment area of the Baltic Sea to reduce land-based pollution.

Members: Denmark, **Estonia**, **European Union**, Finland, Germany, **Latvia**, **Lithuania**, **Poland**, **Russian Federation** and Sweden.
Leadership: Peter Ehlers (Chair.).
Address: Katajanokanlaituri 6 B, 00160 Helsinki, Finland.
Telephone: (9) 62202235.
Fax: (9) 62202239.
E-mail: helcom@helcom.fi
Internet: www.helcom.fi

Baltic States

The three countries—**Estonia**, **Latvia** and **Lithuania**—along the eastern shore of the Baltic Sea. Although ethnically, linguistically and culturally very distinct, these three territories have had a common history facing **German**, Swedish and ultimately Russian encroachment. In particular the Baltic States were grouped together as the first three countries to break free from the **Soviet Union** in 1991 and the only three to emerge with relatively stable and prosperous economies. As such they occupy a unique place on the European political map, squashed between the aspirations of **central Europe**, the political hegemony of the **Russian Federation**, and the economic success of Scandinavia. All three have pressed for greater ties with the West including membership of the **North Atlantic Treaty Organization** and the **European Union**—thereby causing concern in the neighbouring Russian Federation and straining regional relations.

Banja Luka

A city in the north of **Bosnia and Herzegovina** and the capital of the **Serb Republic** (RS). *Population*: 200,000 (2001 estimate). An ancient settlement dating from pre-Roman times, Banja Luka rose to significance during the Ottoman occupation of Bosnia from the 14th century. When an international conference placed Bosnia and Herzegovina under Austro-Hungarian rule from 1878, the **Hungarians** made the city a regional administrative centre. Rebuilt after massive destruction in an earthquake on 27 October 1969, it was home to an evenly-mixed population of **Serbs**, **Croats** and **Bosniaks** before the Bosnian Civil War (1992–95) and had one of Bosnia's largest communities of those who preferred to define their nationality as **Yugoslav**. However, in the very first year of fighting Banja Luka became a focus for Serbian nationalists and the Bosniak population was driven out wholesale, their properties seized and given to ethnic Serbs. In 1993 the Croats became the subject of Serbian aggression and were also 'encouraged' to leave, swapping homes in many cases with ethnic Serbs driven out of the **Krajina** region of **Croatia**. Finally in 1995, during the climax of the Croatian–Bosnian Serb conflict, the remaining Croats were forcibly exiled. Completing the city's **'ethnic cleansing'**, the empty homes were soon filled with ethnic Serbs from the Krajina and areas of Bosnia under control of the **Muslim-Croat Federation**. Now 90% of the city's people are ethnically Serb. Tensions remained high in 2001, as was shown when an international delegation attending a ceremony to rebuild the city's mosques was trapped in a community centre by violent Serb demonstrators.

The surrounding region is home to almost half of the population of the RS and is an important centre for the republic's economy. The major activities in the city are the metallurgy and electrical industries while production of timber products is vital to the nearby rural districts.

Bank for Foreign Trade (Russian Federation)
Vneshtorgbank

Founded in 1990. Capital: US $1,432m. (Dec. 1999); reserves: $318m. (Dec. 1996); deposits: $2,146m. (Dec. 1999); 32 branches.
   Chair. and Chief Executive: Yurii V. Ponomarev.
   Address: Kuznetskii most 16, 103778 Moscow.
   Telephone: (095) 1011880.

Fax: (095) 2584781.
E-mail: vneshtorgbank@infotel.ru
Internet: www.vtb.ru

Bank for International Settlements (BIS)

One of the institutions of the international financial and monetary system, originally founded pursuant to the Hague Agreements of 1930 to promote co-operation among national Central Banks and to provide additional facilities for international finance operations. As of January 2002 the Central Banks of 48 countries and Hong Kong, together with the European Central Bank, were entitled to attend and vote at general meetings, held annually in June. Of the countries of eastern Europe, Bosnia and Herzegovina, Bulgaria, Croatia, the Czech Republic, Estonia, Hungary, Latvia, Lithuania, Macedonia, Poland, Romania, the Russian Federation, Slovakia, Slovenia and Yugoslavia all participate and hold shares in the BIS.

The Yugoslav issue of the Bank's share capital had been in suspense between 1992 and June 2001, new shares having been issued on an interim basis in 1997 to the Central Banks of four of the successor states—Bosnia and Herzegovina, Croatia, Macedonia and Slovenia. In April–May 2001, however, these four and the Federal Republic of Yugoslavia reached agreement on the division of the original Yugoslav holding. On 11 June the BIS accordingly decided to cancel the shares of the original Yugoslav issue, and the interim shares, and to issue an equivalent number of new shares, divided between the Central Banks of the five successor states.

Leadership: Nout Wellink (President and Chair. of the Board);
Andrew Crockett (General Manager).
Address: Centralbahnplatz 2, 4002 Basel, Switzerland.
Telephone: (61) 2808080.
Fax: (61) 2809100.
E-mail: emailmaster@bis.org
Internet: www.bis.org

Bank of Albania
Banka e Shqipërisë

The Central Bank founded in 1992 in the context of the post-communist Government's commitment to the creation of a market economy. The Bank's principal statutory objective is to achieve and maintain price stability, its basic tasks being (i) to run the country's monetary and exchange-rate policies; (ii) to supervise and regulate the banking system; (iii) to hold and manage official foreign reserves; (iv) to act as banker to the Government; and (v) to promote the smooth operation of the payments system. The Bank's independence came under challenge during the presidency of Sali Berisha of the **Democratic Party of Albania**, who in April 1997 dismissed the Governor and imposed his own nominee in the post. However, following Berisha's resignation in July, his appointee was replaced by Shkëlqim Cani, who reaffirmed the Bank's independence with government backing. The Bank's total assets at the end of 1998 were 198,424m. lekë.

Governor: Shkëlqim Cani.
Address: Sheshi Skënderbeu 1, Tirana.
Telephone: (4) 222752.
Fax: (4) 223558.
E-mail: public@bankofalbania.org
Internet: www.bankofalbania.org

Bank of Estonia
Eesti Pank

The Central Bank in **Estonia**, originally founded in 1919 by the Provisional Government. It was restructured in 1927 to implement League of Nations monetary reforms. The kroon, declared sole legal tender in 1928, was devalued by 35% in 1933 and fixed to sterling. The Bank was nationalized in 1940 as the Estonian Republican Office of the State Bank of the **Soviet Union**, occupied as the Gemeinschaftsbank Estland in 1941 and returned to the Soviet monetary system in 1944. Re-established in 1990 by the Estonian SSR, the Bank was fully recognized in 1991 under the presidency of Siim **Kallas**. Under legislation in 1993, the board consists of the President and eight members appointed by the **State Assembly** for a five-year term. The 1998 board fixed the kroon against the euro. In March 2000 Vello Vensel, a professor of statistics at Tallinn Technical University, replaced Vahur Kraft as President. However, Vensel resigned the following month owing to ill health and Kraft was reappointed in June.

President: Vahur Kraft.
Address: Estonia pst. 13, Tallinn 15095.
Telephone: 6680719.
Fax: 6680954.
E-mail: info@epbe.ee
Internet: www.ee/epbe

Bank of Latvia
Lativijas Banka

The Central Bank of **Latvia**, originally founded in 1922. Nationalized in 1940 as the Latvian Republican Office of the State Bank of the **Soviet Union**, it was transferred to the jurisdiction of the German Riga State Credit Bank from 1941 until its return to the Soviet monetary system in 1944. The Bank was re-established in

1990 by the Latvian SSR and restored to Central Bank status after independence in 1991. The Governor, appointed by **Parliament**, chairs the six-member board.
Governor: Ilmars Rimsevics.
Address: K. Valdemara iela 2a, Riga 1050.
Telephone: 7022300.
Fax: 7022420.

Bank of Lithuania
Lietuvos Bankas

The Central Bank of **Lithuania**, originally established in 1922, following Lithuania's independence. It was nationalized in 1940, under the authority of the **Soviet Union** Gosbank. The Bank was re-established by the Lithuanian SSR in 1990 and restored to Central Bank status after independence in 1991.
Chair. of Board: Reinoldijus Šarkinas.
Address: Gedimino pr. 6, Vilnius 2001.
Telephone: (26) 80001 [(526) 80001 from September 2002].
Fax: (521) 21501.
E-mail: lb_spauda@lbank.lt
Internet: www.lbank.lt

Bank of Slovenia
Banka Slovenije

The Central Bank of **Slovenia**. The Bank was established from the remains of the **Yugoslav**-era republican National Bank of Slovenia in June 1991 as one of the institutions needed by a state in the process of becoming independent. As a modern Central Bank it controls monetary policy and regulates the banking industry. It is independent of the Government. The Bank introduced payment notes in October 1991 and these remain legal tender alongside the tolar, which was first issued in January 1992. As at December 1999 the Bank had reserves of 89,484m. tolars.
Governor: Mitja Gaspari.
Address: Slovenska 35, 1505 Ljubljana.
Telephone: (1) 4719000.
Fax: (1) 2515516.
E-mail: bsl@bsi.si
Internet: www.bsi.si

Barents Euro-Arctic Council (BEAC)

A regional grouping officially established in January 1993 in Kirkenes, Norway, which convenes once per year as a forum for co-operation between the central

Governments of the member countries. Its existence testifies to the notion of a common history of the peoples of northern Scandinavia and north-western **Russia** (the Barents region), interrupted by the closed borders regime of the 1917–91 era. The Kirkenes Declaration set out five principal objectives, relating to peace and stability, cultural ties, better bilateral and multilateral inter-state relations, sustainable economic, social and environmental development, and active participation by indigenous peoples of the region.

Members: Denmark, Finland, Iceland, Norway, Sweden and the Russian Federation.
Address: Barents Regional Council Secretariat, House of Soviet, Lenin Prospekt 75, 183006 Murmansk, Russian Federation.
E-mail: postmast@comimm.murmansk.su
Internet: finnbarents.urova.fi/barentsinfo

Bashkirs *see* **Bashkortostan**.

Bashkortostan

A heavily-industrialized constituent republic of the **Russian Federation** situated at the southern end of the Ural mountain chain. Bashkortostan, with a population of 3.9m. (1997 estimate), is the most heavily populated of the non-Russian republics in **European Russia**. The Bashkir people are ethnically **Turkic** and similar to the **Tatars** (who outnumber Bashkirs in the republic), but are differentiated by the assimilation of local **Finno-Ugric peoples**. Like the Tatars they are largely **Muslim** in religion.

The lands of the Bashkirs came under the suzerainty of the Russian Empire in 1552 after the collapse of the Kazan khanate. Along with the Tatars the Bashkir population largely supported the 'Whites' during the Russian Civil War. Bashkortostan (known to the Russians as Bashkiria) was granted the status of an Autonomous Republic by the Bolsheviks in 1919 after attempts to merge it with **Tatarstan** were defeated. The Sovereign Republic of Bashkortostan was declared in October 1990, and secured a favourable federal treaty with Russia in August 1994. Heavily industrialized, the republic now accounts for around 3% of the Federation's total industrial output.

The 1.3 million Bashkirs are only the third-largest ethnic group, outnumbered by both **Russians** and Tatars. Their political dominance, and the official promotion of the Bashkir language over Tatar, has led to tensions. Murtaza Rakhimov has been President of Bashkortostan since December 1993, and before that was the Chairman of the Bashkir Supreme Council from April 1992.

Basic Agreement *see* **Erdut Agreement**.

BC *see* **Baltic Council**.

BEAC *see* **Barents Euro-Arctic Council**.

Behman, Alija

Prime Minister of the **Muslim-Croat Federation**.

Alija Behman is a member of the moderate **Social Democratic Party of Bosnia and Herzegovina** (SDPBiH). He was a successful businessman before entering politics in 1998. He was appointed Prime Minister of the Muslim-Croat Federation on 12 March 2001.

Born on 25 December 1940 in Split, he is a member of the tiny **Croatian** Muslim minority. He graduated in economics from the University of Sarajevo in 1969. From 1970 he worked for the ŽTO railway company in **Sarajevo** and by 1978 he had become President of the company's Executive Board. He then headed the freight company INTERŠPED until 1980 when he returned to academia after receiving an associate professorship. He was first elected to public office in 1998, as a candidate for the SDPBiH. He represents the Sarajevo Canton in the Parliament of the Muslim-Croat Federation. He was appointed Prime Minister of the Federation in March 2001 after months of negotiations.

Alija Behman is married and has two sons.
Address: Office of the Prime Minister, Alipašina 41, 71000 Sarajevo.
Telephone: (33) 663649.
Fax: (33) 444718.
E-mail: abehman@fbihvlada.gov.ba

Belarus
Respublika Byelarus

A landlocked independent republic in north-eastern Europe, bounded by Lithuania and Latvia to the north-west, Ukraine to the south, the Russian Federation to the east and Poland to the west. The country is divided administratively into six *oblasts* (regions) and one municipality.

Area: 207,600 sq km; *capital*: **Minsk**; *population*: 10.1m. (2001 estimate), comprising ethnic **Belarusians** 78%, **Russians** 13%, **Poles** 4%, **Ukrainians** 3%, others 2%; *official languages*: Belarusian and Russian; *religion*: **Orthodox Christianity** 80%, others (including **Roman Catholic**, **Protestant**, **Jewish** and **Muslim**) 20% (1997 estimate).

Under the Constitution adopted in March 1994 and amended in November 1996, legislative power is vested in the bicameral **National Assembly** (Natsionalnoye Sobranie). This consists of a 110-member lower chamber, the House of Representatives (Palata Predstaviteley), elected by universal adult suffrage for a four-year term, and a 64-member upper chamber, the Council of the Republic (Soviet

Respubliki). Eight members of the upper house are appointed by the President and 56 are indirectly elected by local administrative bodies. The executive President, directly elected for a five-year term, is Head of State and appoints the Prime Minister and Cabinet of Ministers.

History: Settled by east **Slavic** tribes in the 5th century, Belarus was controlled by the Princes of **Kiev** from the 9th to 12th centuries. Following the Mongol invasion in the 1200s, the territory was absorbed into **Lithuania** before coming under Polish rule in the mid-16th century. Between 1772 and 1795 **Poland** suffered three successive partitions between **Russia, Prussia** and Austria, resulting in the integration of Belarus into the Russian Empire under Catherine the Great. A battleground in the Napoleonic invasion of Russia in 1812, Belarus suffered this fate again in both World Wars. At the time of the Russian Revolution of 1917, much of the country was under **German** control. The withdrawal of German forces was followed by the declaration of the Byelorussian Soviet Socialist Republic in 1919. The western part of the region, ceded to Poland in 1921 after Soviet defeat in the Polish–Soviet war of 1919–20, was retaken by Soviet forces in 1939, but the republic as a whole was subsequently devastated by German invasion and occupation. In 1945, at the end of the Second World War, the Byelorussian SSR was restored. Part of the **Soviet Union**, it was also given membership of the United Nations in its own right.

Post-war reconstruction needs led to a rise in Russian immigration into the republic. As the process of 'russification' continued in the 1960s and 1970s, there was decreasing use of the Belarusian language. The republic did, however, enjoy relative economic prosperity within the Soviet Union.

With the imminent collapse of the Soviet Union, the republic declared its sovereignty in July 1990, and then its independence in August 1991 after the failed coup by hardliners in **Moscow** (*see* **August coup**). In September 1991 the official name of the new nation was changed to the Republic of Belarus. A reformist, Stanislau Shushkevich, assumed the leadership of the country as Chairman of the Supreme Council (parliament) elected in March 1990. However, conflict with the communist-dominated Council led to Shushkevich's resignation in January 1994 and his replacement by Mechislau Gryb, a hardliner. Following the adoption of a new presidential Constitution in March 1994, elections for the Presidency were held in June and July. Alyaksandr **Lukashenka**, an independent campaigning against corruption, won on the second ballot, taking 85% of the vote.

Against a background of ongoing confrontation between the new President and the Supreme Council over constitutional issues, a referendum on four policy questions was held in May 1995. Voters expressed strong support for an extension of presidential powers, closer integration with the Russian Federation, equal status for Russian and Belarusian as official languages, and the introduction of a new flag. At the same time as the referendum, Belarus's first post-Soviet legislative elections were held. Under half of the 260 seats in the Supreme Council were filled owing to the stringent electoral regulations and, since this failed to produce the necessary two-thirds quorum, further rounds of voting took place in November and December 1995 (although 62 seats still remained unfilled).

Tensions between Lukashenka on the one hand and the Supreme Council and Constitutional Court on the other escalated in 1996. In a further controversial referendum held on 24 November, 70.5% of voters backed changes to the 1994 Constitution that significantly strengthened Lukashenka's presidential authority. In addition to lengthening his term of office from 1999 to 2001, the amendments also granted him extensive powers of appointment and provided for a new bicameral National Assembly to replace the Supreme Council. At the end of November a majority of parliamentary deputies supporting Lukashenka (mainly independents) adopted legislation reconstituting themselves as the House of Representatives, or lower chamber of the new Assembly, and abolishing the Supreme Council. A new upper chamber, the Council of the Republic, was convened in January 1997. Doubts about the legitimacy of the November 1996 referendum were expressed by international organizations, including the **Council of Europe** (which suspended Belarus's 'guest status') and the **Organization for Security and Co-operation in Europe** (OSCE). Opposition to the constitutional changes and to the authoritarian nature of the Lukashenka regime has since been repressed, giving rise to widespread international concern about the observance of human rights in Belarus.

Latest elections: Elections to the House of Representatives, once again highly controversial in the manner of their conduct, were held in October 2000. They were boycotted by most of the opposition parties on grounds of their perceived fraudulence, which was confirmed by international observers. The official results gave pro-Lukashenka candidates all but three of the 110 seats (independents and candidates of the **Belarusian People's Patriotic Union** with 102 seats, **Agrarian Party of Belarus** with 5). The three remaining seats were won by the **Social Democratic Party of Popular Accord** (SDPNZ) and the Republican Party of Labour and Justice. The result was not altered by the holding of rerun elections in 13 of the seats in March–April 2001. Indirect elections for the Council of the Republic in December 2000 also confirmed the entrenched power of the 'presidential' parties.

In a presidential election held in September 2001, Lukashenka was credited with winning 75.6% of the vote. The opposition parties continued to protest that he had no legitimate mandate, but their failure to mount an effective challenge left their own credibility somewhat diminished.

International relations and defence: On the demise of the Soviet Union in 1991, Belarus retained close links with other former constituent republics through its accession to the **Commonwealth of Independent States** (CIS). In particular, Belarus under Lukashenka has pursued greater economic, political and military integration with the Russian Federation. In April 1996 and April–May 1997 the two countries signed initial union treaties and a charter establishing a structure for the co-ordination of joint affairs. This was followed in December 1998 by agreements envisaging a staged convergence of their economic and political systems, leading to the signature in December 1999 of a full **Belarus-Russia Union** treaty. Belarus's pursuit of formal links with the Russian Federation, together with the question marks over its commitment to democratic processes, soured relations with the West, notwithstanding its post-Soviet admission to European structures such as the OSCE, the **Central European Initiative** and NATO's **Partnership for Peace** programme.

Belarus's official defence budget totalled some US $75m. in 2000, less than 1% of GDP. The armed forces at the end of 2000 were estimated to total about 83,000, including those drafted under compulsory conscription of 18 months, while reservists numbered an estimated 290,000. Under the Belarus-Russia Union it was envisaged that a joint military force would be created, although the Russian side ruled out a joint military command.

Belarus, economy

An economy operating in a landlocked country which has close political and economic links with the neighbouring **Russian Federation**.

GNP: US $35,952m. (2000); *GNP per capita*: $2,990 (2000); *GDP at PPP*: $55,200m. (1999); *GDP per capita at PPP*: $5,300 (1999); *exports*: $7,342m. (2000); *imports*: $8,489m. (2000); *currency*: Belarus rouble; US $1=BR1,603 at the end of December 2001).

In 1999 industry contributed 44.2% of GDP, agriculture 13.5% and services 42.3%. Of the workforce of 4.3 million, industry and construction accounted for 35%, agriculture and forestry for 17% and services for 48%. 29% of land is arable, 1% under permanent crops, 15% permanent pasture and 34% forests and woodland. The main agricultural products are grain, potatoes, vegetables, meat and milk. There are small identified reserves of oil and natural gas, while other principal natural resources include forests and peat. (Since the 1986 **Chernobyl** nuclear reactor disaster just over the border in **Ukraine**, peat cannot be used for fuel in Belarus for fear of dispersal of contaminated ash.) The principal industries include machine-building, chemicals, power generation and textiles. In view of the lack of mineral resources, most of Belarus's energy requirements are met through imports of petroleum and natural gas (the latter in particular from the Russian Federation).

Belarus's main exports by value (1999) are machinery and transport equipment (33%), chemicals and petroleum products (21%) and light industrial goods (9%). Principal imports include petroleum and natural gas (24%), machinery and transport equipment (22%), chemical and petroleum products (17%) and ferrous metals (10%). In 2000 about 50% of Belarus's exports, and 65% of its imports, were to/from the Russian Federation.

As part of the **Soviet Union**, Belarus had a relatively prosperous economy, with a substantial engineering basis linked to the military-industrial complex. After the 1991 dissolution of the Soviet Union, however, the economy declined sharply, with political instability aggravating the situation and with little outside investment. In the five years to 1996 GDP fell by an annual average of over 6%, while inflation escalated to around 2,000% in both 1993 and 1994.

The advent to power of President **Lukashenka** in 1994 led to the readoption of centralist policies of regulatory 'market socialism' and a slowing-down of market-related reforms in the interests of preserving jobs and minimizing social problems. A stabilization plan agreed with the **International Monetary Fund** (IMF) in September 1995 was quickly suspended when performance criteria were not met. Inflation was initially curbed but resumed an upward path from 1996, rising to 182% in 1998 and 250% in 1999. In 1998 Belarus's currency came under severe pressure as a result of financial crisis in the Russian Federation, again worsening the general economic position. A further attempt by the IMF to agree a contingency facility with Belarus broke down in May 1999.

Although GDP was officially stated to have risen by 8.5% in 1998 (and industrial output by 11%), growth slowed in 1999 to 3.5%, before recovering to around 6% in 2000, in which year the high inflation rate was somewhat reduced, to just over 100%. The Government's budget for 2001 provided for revenue equivalent to US $5,500m. and a deficit of 1.5% of GDP (as against about 2.5% in 2000), the projected GDP growth rate being 3.5% and the planned inflation rate 2.5%. At the end of 2000 the official unemployment rate was 2.1%, although there was also large-scale under-employment of workers.

In January 2000 new banknotes were issued converting 1,000 roubles into one new currency unit, while in September 2000 the official rate of the rouble against the US dollar was set at close to the unofficial market rate. In February 2001 President Lukashenka claimed that in the period 1996–2000 GDP had increased by 36%, industrial production by 60% and real incomes by 70%, although there was no independent confirmation of such figures.

Certain industries and enterprises were privatized after 1991, but progress was limited because of rampant corruption combined with a preference after the 1994 change of government for maintaining a dominant state sector. Even the privatization of smaller enterprises was suspended in 1996, so that by the end of the 1990s only about 10% of all enterprises under central control had been privatized. In April 2000 President Lukashenka declared that the collective farm system would 'always' be the basis for the country's agricultural production.

Belarus's already close economic links with the Russian Federation were solidified by the 1996 **Commonwealth of Independent States** (CIS) customs union agreement (together with Kazakhstan, Kyrgyzstan and subsequently also Tajikistan). Subsequent bilateral agreements and treaties, culminating in the signature of the **Belarus-Russia Union** treaty in December 1999, envisaged full-scale economic and monetary union by 2005, although many details remained to be elaborated. In November 2000 Belarus and the Russian Federation signed an agreement providing for a single currency, while as from January 2001 the Belarus rouble was tied to the Russian rouble within a 3% permitted fluctuation band. The 2001 Union budget amounted to the equivalent of US $82m., of which Belarus was expected to contribute 35% and the Russian Federation 65%.

Belarus-Russia Union

The structure under which **Belarus** and the **Russian Federation** are supposedly to merge eventually into a single confederal entity. The Belarus-Russia Union is based in **Minsk**. Belarus has been independent since the collapse of the **Soviet Union** in 1991. However, from the earliest days of its independence the idea of returning to the Russian fold has been popular among the ruling elite. Under the guidance of Belarusian President Alyaksandr **Lukashenka** and the then Russian President Boris **Yeltsin**, the two countries signed a preliminary Union agreement on 2 April 1996, and a second agreement a year later. The basis of the Union lies in the relative weakness of the independent **Belarusian economy**, the country's long historical connection to Russia and the ethnic similarity between the two dominant east **Slavic peoples**. Under the agreement, the two countries would retain their nominal independence—with separate representation at the United Nations—after entering into a confederal Union with each other, but would share government policy in all fields.

The agreement was refined at the end of the Yeltsin presidency through the signing of a draft Union Treaty on 8 December 1999. This finalized the eventual structure of the Union and set a deadline, 2005, for the harmonization of currencies, legislatures, tax policies, border security, customs and defence policies. A Supreme State Council was established to form Union agencies. Eventually it is envisaged that the Union will have an upper House of Union, with delegates from the National Assemblies of both Belarus and the Russian Federation, a directly-elected lower House of Representatives and an executive Council of Ministers whose role remains undefined.

Since the election of Vladimir **Putin** as Russian President in May 2000, however, the pace of the Union preparations has been considerably reduced. Putin has expressed doubts as to the 2005 deadline and has taken the emphasis away from the Union in matters of regional policy. As late as December 2001, Belarusian Prime Minister Gennadz **Novitski** was reported as suggesting that the Russian Federation was not ready to fulfil the terms of the 1999 Treaty, and that Putin had even unofficially requested the Treaty's revision. Nonetheless in April 2001 the upper house of the Belarusian **National Assembly** approved plans to introduce the Russian rouble in Belarus on 1 January 2005, and the proposed Union currency in 2008.

Couched in Article Seven of the 1996 Agreement was also an invitation for other countries to join the proposed Union. The offer has not been taken up by any Governments, but has been seriously mooted by **Ukraine** and, since the election of a communist Government there, by **Moldova**. The possibility of extending the Union was boosted in late 2001 when the Russian Government passed laws allowing the theoretical membership of new Republics to the Russian Federation itself—a proposition welcomed in particular by the Georgian Republics of **Abkhazia** and South Ossetia (*see* **Ossetia question**).

Belarusian Chamber of Commerce and Industry

The principal organization in **Belarus** for promoting business contacts, both internally and externally, in the post-communist era. Originally founded in 1953.
President: Uladzimir K. Lesun.
Address: pr. Masherava 14, 220035 Minsk.
Telephone: (17) 2269127.
Fax: (17) 2269860.
E-mail: ggp@cci.belpak.minsk.by
Internet: www.cci.by

Belarusian Congress of Democratic Trade Unions (BKDP)

An independent federation founded in **Belarus** in 1993 as an alternative to the 'official' **Belarusian Federation of Trade Unions** (FPB). Registered in 1997 and claiming to represent some 20,000 workers, the BKDP embraces the Free Trade Union of Belarus and the Independent Trade Union of Belarus (both founded in 1992). From 1999 the BKDP joined with the FPB in protesting against falling living standards and government moves to end collective bargaining.
Chair.: Alyaksandr Lysenka.
Address: 24 Zaharova St, Minsk 220005.
Telephone: (17) 2333182.
Fax: (17) 2101500.

Belarusian Currency and Stock Exchange

The exchange in **Belarus** created by the merger in 1998 of the Belarusian Stock Exchange (BSE) and the Interbank Currency Exchange (ICE). The BSE had been 40% owned by the Ministry of State Property but had a total of 490 stockholders, while the ICE was a department of the **National Bank of Belarus**.
General Director: Vyacheslav A. Kasak.
Address: vul. Melnikaite 2, 220004 Minsk.
Telephone: (17) 2769121.
Fax: (17) 2292566.

Belarusian Federation of Trade Unions (FPB)

The little-changed successor to the Soviet-era trade union organization in **Belarus**. The FPB claims to represent 4.2 million members (including pensioners), almost all of the 92% of workers who are organized. Although it is closely connected with the post-Soviet government structure, from 1999 the FPB joined with independent trade union bodies in protesting against falling living standards and government moves to end collective bargaining. Chairman Uladzimir Gancharyk also aspired to a directly political role by announcing his willingness to run in the 2001 presidential election, although the Government contended that his candidacy would be a breach of the FPB's charter. As the main opposition candidate to incumbent President Alyaksandr **Lukashenka**, he polled 15.4% of the vote.

Chair.: Uladzimir Gancharyk.
Address: Minsk.

Belarusian Peasants' Party
Belaruskaya Syalanskaya Partiya (BSP)

A party founded in **Belarus** in 1990 as successor to the pre-Soviet agrarian movement, advocating the restoration of peasant land ownership, and associated with the opposition **Belarusian Popular Front–Renaissance** (NFB–A). The BSP nominated Alyaksandr Dubko (Chairman of the Belarus Agrarian Union) in the 1994 presidential elections, in which he won 6% of the first-round vote. In the 1995 legislative elections the BSP was heavily outpolled by the pro-collectivism **Agrarian Party of Belarus**, winning only one seat. The NFB–A boycotted the October 2000 legislative elections on the grounds that there was no prospect of their being free and fair.

Leadership: Yaugen Lugin (Chair.).
Address: 38/1 Gaya Street, Minsk 220068.
Telephone: (17) 2771905.
Fax: (17) 2779651.

Belarusian People's Patriotic Union
Belaruski Narodna Patryatychny Soyuz (BNPS)

A grouping in **Belarus** created in 1998 as a political alliance of some 30 conservative parties supportive of President Alyaksandr **Lukashenka**, and in particular of the imminent **Belarus-Russia Union** treaty. The alliance succeeded the Popular Movement of Belarus (NDB), formed in 1992 by parties resistant to the reforms demanded by the pro-democracy **Belarusian Popular Front–Renaissance** (NFB–A).

The NDB had embraced both the conservative left and the **pan-Slavic** right on a platform advocating the maintenance of close relations with the **Russian Federation** and resistance to Western capitalism. Many of its leaders had prospered under the Soviet-era rule of the republican Communist Party, whose suspension in August 1991 had not affected the predominance of former communists in the Government and in the Supreme Soviet elected in 1990. The NDB included the **Communist Party of Belarus** (KPB) following its return to legality in 1993, as well as the right-wing **Liberal Democratic Party of Belarus** (LDPB) and the Slavic Assembly of Belarus.

The advent of Mechislau Gryb as President in January 1994 strengthened the position of the NDB hardliners, who backed the introduction of a new presidential Constitution in March 1994, the signature the following month of a monetary union treaty with the Russian Federation and moves to participate in the collective security arrangements of the **Commonwealth of Independent States** (CIS). In the mid-1994 presidential elections, however, the hardliners were outmanoeuvred by the NDB's more moderate wing, which supported the successful independent candidacy of Lukashenka, who won 85% of the vote in the second round.

The factionalism which surrounded this election left the NDB in disarray. Four years later, however, the newly-formed pro-Lukashenka BNPS included the main elements of the old NDB alliance, namely the KPB (whose leader Viktar Chykin was elected as its first Executive Secretary), the right-wing LDPB, and the pan-Slavic **White Rus Slavonic Council**. In elections to the House of Representatives (the lower house of the **National Assembly**) in October 2000 the BNPS and its allies obtained near-total ascendancy, amidst opposition and external claims of electoral manipulation and fraud.

Leadership: Viktar Chykin (Executive Secretary).

Address: c/o Palata Predstaviteley, Natsionalnoye Sobranie, Sovetskaya St 11, 220010 Minsk.

Belarusian Popular Front–Renaissance
Narodni Front Belarusi–Adradzhennie (NFB–A)

A major political movement in **Belarus** with a strong Christian democratic current, seeking post-Soviet reform, which has opposed the Government of President Alyaksandr **Lukashenka** since 1994.

What became the NFB–A was launched in June 1989 at a conference of pro-independence groups in **Vilnius** (Lithuania), after the communist authorities had refused to allow it to be held in the republic and had denounced its organizers as 'extremists'. Founding or subsequent NFB–A participating parties included the **Belarusian Peasants' Party**, the **Belarusian Social Democratic Party**, the **National Democratic Party of Belarus**, the Belarusian Christian Democratic Union, the Movement for Democratic Reforms and the United Democratic Party of Belarus.

Elected leader at the Vilnius session was Zyanon Paznyak, an archaeologist who in 1988 had published evidence of mass graves found near **Minsk** on the site of a detention camp established on Stalin's orders in 1937. As European communism began to crumble from late 1989, the new movement had some impact in Belarus, where opposition candidates were allowed to run in the April 1990 Supreme Soviet elections. However, the entrenched position of the **Communist Party of Belarus** (KPB) enabled it to win a large majority, the NFB–A winning only 34 seats in the 360-member legislature. In August 1991 the NFB–A was strongly critical of the Government's initial support for the attempted coup by hardliners in **Moscow** (*see* **August coup**). It therefore welcomed the resultant downfall of the

Minsk conservatives and the accession of the Shushkevich Government, supporting the latter's declaration of Belarus's independence in late August.

Remaining in opposition, the NFB–A in 1992 and 1993 twice collected the requisite 350,000 signatures for a referendum on early multi-party elections, but neither petition was accepted by a legislature dominated by conservative elements. The NFB–A opposed the new presidential Constitution introduced in March 1994, on the grounds that a democratic parliament had not yet been elected. It also opposed the treaty on monetary union with the **Russian Federation**, signed by the Government in April, and Belarus's participation in the security arm of the **Commonwealth of Independent States** (CIS). In the direct presidential elections of June–July 1994, Paznyak stood as the NFB–A candidate but received only 13.5% of the first-round vote and was eliminated. In the second round, NFB–A support swung overwhelmingly behind Lukashenka as being the more reformist candidate.

By the time of the 1995 parliamentary elections, the NFB–A was as clearly opposed to President Lukashenka's Government as it had been to the predecessor, the main issue being once again the President's policy of close integration with the Russian Federation. The NFB–A won no seats in the 1995 elections, following which Paznyak went into exile in the USA. Following the signature of an initial **Belarus-Russia Union** treaty in April 1996, NFB–A leaders came under pressure from the authorities for organizing protests against constitutional amendments tabled by the Government to replace the unicameral Supreme Council with a bicameral legislature. The approval of the amendments in a referendum in November 1996 was rejected as invalid by the NFB–A.

The political impasse continued in the late 1990s, during which the NFB–A mounted regular opposition demonstrations. In May 1999 the NFB–A was a principal organizer of 'alternative' presidential elections, which according to the opposition attracted over 60% voter participation and which, they further claimed, yielded a two-thirds majority for Paznyak. Thereafter the Government combined repression of NFB–A leaders and other opponents with periodic attempts, under pressure from Western Governments, to initiate a dialogue with the opposition, although little progress was made.

The sixth NFB–A congress held in Minsk in August 1999 precipitated a split between critics of Paznyak's leadership in exile and his supporters. The following month the pro-Paznyak (minority) faction broke away to form the **Conservative Christian Party**, of which Paznyak was declared leader, while Vintsuk Vyachorka was elected NFB–A Chairman. The NFB–A boycotted the October 2000 legislative elections on the grounds that there was no prospect of their being free and fair.

Leadership: Vintsuk Vyachorka (Chair.).
Address: 8 Varvasheni Street, Minsk 220005.
Telephone: (17) 2314893.
Fax: (17) 2395869.

Belarusian Social Democratic Party
Satsiyal-Demokratychnaya Partiya Belarusi—Narodnaya Hramada (SDPB/Hramada)

A party prominent in the opposition to the **Lukashenka** regime in **Belarus**, first established in 1991 as successor to the Revolutionary *Hramada* (Assembly) Party (founded in 1903), which had spearheaded the early movement for the creation of a Belarusian state but had been outlawed following the declaration of the Soviet Socialist Republic in January 1919. The present-day SDPB/Hramada is an observer member of the **Socialist International**.

The revived SDPB/Hramada participated in the opposition **Belarusian Popular Front**, supporting the latter's unsuccessful candidate in the first round of the June–July 1994 presidential elections. In the 1995 legislative elections the SDPB/Hramada won two seats and later formed a 15-strong parliamentary group which included the **Social Democratic Party of Popular Accord**.

The SDPB/Hramada was prominent in the opposition to the Lukashenka presidency in the late 1990s, its Chairman being prosecuted several times for alleged public order offences. In September 2000 the party's head office in **Minsk** was attacked by a gang whose affiliation was unclear. Unlike most of the opposition, the SDPB participated in the October 2000 legislative elections, but failed to win representation.

Leadership: Nikolai Statkevich (Chair.).
Address: pr. F. Skaryny 153–2–107, Minsk 220114.
Telephone and Fax: (17) 2633748.
E-mail: bsdp@tut.by

Belarusian Socialist Party
Belaruskaya Satsyalistychnaya Partiya (SPB)

A conservative formation in **Belarus** favouring the retention or restoration of the Soviet-era economic and social system. The SPB was founded at a **Minsk** congress in the wake of the mid-1994 presidential elections, its first leader being the then Deputy Chairman of the Belarus legislature, Vyacheslau Kuznyatsow. The party called for the political union of the members of the **Commonwealth of Independent States** (CIS) and strongly supported President **Lukashenka**'s signature of an initial **Belarus-Russia Union** treaty in April 1996.

Leadership: Michail Padgainy (Chair.).
Address: 25 pr. F. Skaryny, Minsk.
Telephone: (17) 2293738.

Belarusians
(literally, White Russians)

A **Slavic people** dominant in **Belarus** (White Russia) and known as White Russians (not to be confused with the anti-Red, i.e. anti-Bolshevik, '*White* Russian' forces of the Russian Civil War, 1918–20). Ethnically Belarusians are very closely related to the other east Slavs, namely **Russians** and **Ukrainians**. During the 20th century the political domination of the former led to intense russification of the Belarusians. The Belarusian language is central to the notion of Belarusian nationalism. It was revived after the country's independence in 1990 and became the official state language (although most Belarusians are fluent in Russian). It is written using the **Cyrillic alphabet** and contains many loan words from Polish (reflecting the region's history). Like other east Slavs most Belarusians embrace **Orthodox Christianity** although some follow the **Roman Catholic Church** (*see* **Uniate Churh**). Around 1.2 million Belarusians live in the **Russian Federation**.

Belgrade

The capital of **Yugoslavia** and **Serbia**, situated at the confluence of the Danube and Sava rivers. *Population*: 1.6m. (1996 estimate). The name *Beograd* literally means white fortress in Serbian, a reference to the ancient fortified settlement on the site, and testimony to the city's strategic importance. Belgrade changed hands between various groups in the **Balkans** until 1284 when came under the control of the **Serbs**, who made it their capital in 1440.

As Serbia emerged from centuries under Ottoman rule, Belgrade began growing rapidly, particularly after 1920 when it was made the capital of the new Yugoslav kingdom. A process of industrialization and the increase in the city's importance drew thousands of people from the surrounding rural areas. Under communist rule Belgrade was established as a major centre for mechanical engineering and light industry. It was the largest commercial centre for Yugoslavia and the focal point of that country's transport connections, a regional role which it is seeking to re-establish after the upheavals of the 1990s during which the Yugoslav state was dismembered by conflict. Damage caused to the city during the 1999 **North Atlantic Treaty Organization** (NATO) bombing campaign seriously affected the local economy but work has been under way to reconstruct the battered infrastructure since the fall of Slobodan **Milošević** in 2000.

The population is mainly ethnically Serb although there are significant numbers of **Croats** and Montenegrins (*see* **Montenegro**). The city is also home to one of the biggest Chinese communities in the Balkans, encouraged by close ties between Yugoslavia and China during the Milošević era.

Belgrade Stock Exchange
Beogradska berza (BB)

The principal stock exchange in **Yugoslavia**, based in **Belgrade**. The original bourse was established in 1894 but was closed down in the 1950s by the communist regime. It reopened as the Yugoslav Capital Market in 1989 and was transformed into the BB in 1992. Total turnover for 2000 equalled US $128m. As at 1 December 2001 there were 44 members trading on the BB.
Chair.: Bozidar Djelić.
Address: Omladinskih Brigada 1, POB 214, 11070 Belgrade.
Telephone: (11) 3117410.
Fax: (11) 3117304.
E-mail: marketing@belex.co.yu
Internet: www.belex.co.yu

Belka, Marek

Deputy Prime Minister and Minister of Finance, **Poland**. An independent economist, Belka first worked in government after the fall of communism, as an adviser in the Ministry of Finance in 1990. He has twice been economic adviser to President Aleksander **Kwaśniewski** (in 1996–97 and again from November 1997 to October 2001), was Deputy Prime Minister and Finance Minister between February and November 1997, and was appointed to these posts for the second time on 19 October 2001 in the incoming new left-of-centre Government headed by Leszek **Miller**.

Born on 9 January 1952, Marek Belka graduated in economics from the University of Łódź in 1972 and received his doctorate from the same institution in 1978. From 1973 until 1996 he worked at the university's economics faculty, first as an assistant professor and finally as a full professor from 1994. He also taught at the Polish Academy of Science's Institute of Economics from 1986 to 1997, acting as its Director from 1993 until 1996.
Address: Ministry of Finance, ul. Świętokrzyska 12, 00916 Warsaw.
Telephone: (22) 6945555.
Fax: (22) 8266352.
E-mail: biuro.prasowe@mofnet.gov.pl
Internet: www.mofnet.gov.pl

Belkić, Beriz

Member of the Presidency (Bosniak), **Bosnia and Herzegovina**.

Beriz Belkić is a senior member of the multi-ethnic, pro-Western **Social Democratic Party of Bosnia and Herzegovina** (SDPBiH). He was appointed to the tripartite Presidency on 30 March 2001.

Born in **Sarajevo** in 1946, he graduated in economics from the city's university and has politically represented the Muslim **Bosniak** community there throughout his career. He was Minister for Labour, Refugees and Displaced Persons for the Sarajevo Canton from 1997 to 1998, overseeing efforts to attract Bosniaks and **Croats** back to the war-ravaged capital. He was the Canton's Prime Minister from 1998 until his election to the Bosnian Presidency in 2001. He has been particularly outspoken about the continuing effort to resettle the internally displaced, and over the issue of suspected war criminals in the **Serb Republic**.

Beriz Belkić is married with one child.
Address: Office of the Presidency, Musala 5, 71000 Sarajevo.
Telephone: (33) 664941.
Fax: (33) 472491.

BelTa

The state news agency in **Belarus**. Originally founded in 1921, it was overshadowed throughout the Soviet era by the Telegraph Agency of the Soviet Union (TASS—*see* **ITAR-TASS**). It is owned, controlled and run by the Government.

Director: Yakov Aleksejchik.
Address: vul. Kirava 26, 220600 Minsk.
Telephone: (17) 2223040.
Fax: (17) 2271346.
Internet: belta.press.net.by

Berzinš, Andris

Prime Minister of **Latvia**.

Andris Berzinš leads the centrist **Latvia's Way** (LC). Formerly Mayor of **Riga**, he was appointed Prime Minister on 5 May 2000.

Born on 4 August 1951 in Riga, he graduated in history and philosophy from the Latvian State University in 1979. He continued his pre-university work in the Soviet education system before entering the Welfare Department of the Economy Ministry in 1990. Following Latvian independence he was appointed Deputy Welfare Minister in 1992 and Labour Minister in 1993, after the electoral success of LC. He returned to the Ministry of Welfare in 1994 as a full minister and his reform of the pension system is still hailed as an ideal model by the **World Bank**. However, he had been shuffled back to the Labour Ministry by the end of the year.

He left the Cabinet in 1997, having been elected Mayor of Riga. Through this high-profile role he earned himself a reputation as a capable administrator and was consistently voted in polls as one of the country's most popular politicians. He was called on by President Vaira **Vike-Freiberga** to take over as Prime Minister following the resignation in April 2000 of the unpopular Andris Škele. Vike-Freiberga noted on his appointment that his first priority should be merely to stay in power long enough to provide a sense of stability for the country.

Andris Berzinš is married with two children.

Address: Office of the Prime Minister (Chancery), Brivibas bulv. 36, Riga 1520.
Telephone: 7332232.
Fax: 7286598.
Internet: www.mk.gov.lv

Berzinš, Gundars

Minister of Finance, **Latvia**.

Gundars Berzinš is a member of the centre-right **People's Party** (TP). His political career began in 1986 at the Soviet-era Transport Ministry. He was appointed Finance Minister on 5 May 2000.

Born in Jekabpils on 26 September 1959, he graduated in mechanical engineering from the Riga Polytechnic Institute in 1983. After working at the Institute of Motor Transport he began service at the Transport Ministry in 1986. He took four years out of active politics to concentrate on his newly-acquired farm near Jekabpils from 1989, but returned as a Political Secretary at the Agriculture Ministry in 1993, having been elected to **Parliament**. Despite not being re-elected in 1995 he was appointed adviser to Prime Minister Andris Škele. After a year as a consultant to a private company he was re-elected to Parliament in November 1998 and led the TP's parliamentary faction. He was appointed Finance Minister in the new Government formed by Andris **Berzinš** (no relation) in May 2000. He has encouraged government transparency, famously installing a webcam in his office in October 2000.

Address: Ministry of Finance, Smilšu iela 1, Riga 1932.
Telephone: 7226672.
Fax: 7227220.
Internet: www.fm.gov.lv

Berzinš, Indulis

Minister of Foreign Affairs, **Latvia**.

Indulis Berzinš is a member of the centrist **Latvia's Way** (LC). He was a university lecturer before joining the Latvian Supreme Soviet in 1990. He was appointed Foreign Minister in July 1999.

Born on 4 December 1957 in the eastern town of Madona, he graduated in history and philosophy from the Latvian State University in 1981. He went on to pursue a postgraduate qualification before teaching and lecturing at the university until 1990 when he became a member of the Latvian Supreme Soviet. He established himself in Latvian political culture by founding the pro-independence People's Front of Latvia in 1989, and gained notoriety as a television broadcaster from 1988 to 1989. He switched to the LC when he was elected to **Parliament** in 1993. He sat on various parliamentary commissions and was a member of numerous governmental delegations to the West, particularly to the **North Atlantic Treaty Organization** (NATO) and the **European Union** (EU), before becoming Foreign Minister in the Government of Prime Minister Andris Škele in 1999. He retained this post in the new Government formed by Andris **Berzinš** (no relation) in May 2000.

Indulis Berzinš is married to Inese and they have one son and one daughter.
Address: Ministry of Foreign Affairs, Brivibas bulv. 36, Riga 1395.
Telephone: 7223307.
Fax: 7227755.
E-mail: info@mfa.gov.lv
Internet: www.mfa.gov.lv

Bessarabia question

A historical territorial dispute between **Romania** and **Russia**, arising from the artificial division of the Romanian principality of Moldavia between Romania and Russia in the 1812 Treaty of Bucharest. Resurrecting the mediaeval title Bessarabia for the eastern half of Moldavia, between the Rivers Prut and Dnester, the Tsarist authorities attempted to distance the ethnic **Romanian** population from their connections with the state of Romania, and thus foster a separate sense of Bessarabian identity. The division, however, laid the foundation for Romanian claims to the area, and for conflict with future Russian Governments.

With the rise of the **Soviet Union** the Bessarabia question was aggressively revisited. The temporary reunification of Bessarabia and Romania during the inter-war years (1918–39) flew in the face of Soviet insistence that Bessarabia remained an integral part of the Soviet Union. With the onset of hostilities at the start of the Second World War the Romanian Government conceded the Soviet annexation of Bessarabia. The Moldavian Soviet Socialist Republic (already created east of the Dnester to substantiate Russia's claims) was redrawn to include part of Bessarabia and thus to cover the area of what is now **Moldova**. On the other hand southern and northern Bessarabia, known as Bukovina (*see* **Bukovina question**), were ceded to the Ukrainian Soviet Socialist Republic. A program of russification of the Bessarabian Romanians resulted in the creation of a **Moldovan** identity, based on communist social policies and the use of the **Cyrillic alphabet**. The authorities also encouraged the influx of non-Romanians.

The collapse of the Soviet Union in 1991 unleashed a wave of pro-Romanian sentiment in Moldova and reignited the Bessarabia question, which the pre-1989 Romanian communist regime had preferred to leave dormant. Political parties on both sides of the Prut called for the reunification of the Moldavian lands, despite initial hesitation in Romania. Claims to the southern and northern districts were not included. However, attempts to move towards unification led to uprisings in the non-Romanian/Moldovan areas of Moldova, known as **Transdnestria** and **Gagauzia**, in the same year. By the mid-1990s the concept of unification was irrevocably entwined with the idea of the division of Moldova and was thus popularly rejected by the Moldovan people. Aspirations for unification remain dormant for the time being and the notion of Bessarabia seems dead and buried.

Bessarabian Church

A Church of the **Orthodox Christian** denomination in **Moldova** which is subordinate to the **Romanian Orthodox Church** and involved in a legal dispute with the Moldovan Government. The Bessarabian Church was formed in 1992 when priests broke away from the Autonomous Moldovan Church (which is subordinate to the **Russian Orthodox Church**) and claimed lineage from the pre-Second World War Romanian Church in **Bessarabia**. Issues of Moldovan national identity, and more specifically the close relationship between the Government and the Moldovan Church, led to the Government's refusal to register the Bessarabian Church. It has subsequently refused recognition three further times, claiming unresolved property issues and branding the new Church as 'schismatic'. The Bessarabian priests have appealed, first to the **Chişinau** court in 1997 and then to the European Court of Human Rights in 1998. Both courts ruled in their favour, with the latter reaching its verdict in late 2001. However, the Moldovan Government responded that it was an internal matter and would not consider itself bound by the courts' decisions. The Bessarabian Church claims to have around 400,000 adherents. Bishop Petru Paduraru is the current Metropolitan.

BF *see* **Union for Victory**.

BH Press

The official news agency of **Bosnia and Herzegovina**, originally founded in April 1992, and providing news services in Bosnian and English.
  Address: Branilaca grada 21/II, 71000 Sarajevo.
  Telephone: (33) 445336.
  Fax: (33) 445312.
  E-mail: bhpres@bih.net.ba
  Internet: www.bihpress.ba

BIS *see* **Bank for International Settlements**.

BK see **National Front**.

BKDP see **Belarusian Congress of Democratic Trade Unions**.

Black Sea Fleet

The Russian naval fleet based in the Black Sea and harboured in the Ukrainian port of **Sevastopol**. The housing of the Fleet (BSF) in the Crimean port made it the focus of strained relations between **Ukraine** and the **Russian Federation** in the early 1990s despite its dilapidated state and crippling maintenance costs. The newly independent Ukraine was eager to assert its separation from the Russian Federation and its sovereignty over **Crimea**, which had been transferred to Ukraine as a goodwill gesture in 1954. However, it could not afford the upkeep of even half of the cumbersome Fleet or the potential economic costs of losing its associated Russian sailors and their families from Sevastopol. For the Russians, the BSF has historical significance in maintaining strategic dominance across the country's southern flank and also in upholding its image as an international power.

From 1991 to 1994 a series of potentially serious incidents involving the BSF and its bases in Sevastopol threatened to bring the two countries into direct conflict. Tensions were invariably cooled, however, by the intervention of the two Governments. Draft agreements regarding the BSF in 1992 placed it first under the auspices of the newly-created **Commonwealth of Independent States** and later under joint Ukrainian-Russian control.

A definitive solution was agreed between the then Ukrainian Prime Minister Pavlo Lazarenko and his then Russian counterpart Viktor Chernomyrdin on 28 May 1997. This consolidated proposals to split the BSF nominally 50–50 between the two countries, but granted the Russian Federation the facility to 'buy' an extra third from Ukraine in return for debt relaxation. It also agreed to grant the Russian Federation a 20-year lease on the port and surrounding areas of Sevastopol at a cost of US $97.75m. a year, and secured the recognition by both countries of Ukraine's inalienable sovereignty over Crimea. The remaining one-sixth of the Fleet, left in Ukrainian hands and to be housed in alternative Crimean harbours, was redesignated as the new Ukrainian navy.

BLD see **Liberal Democratic Union**.

BNPS see **Belarusian People's Patriotic Union**.

BNS see **National Trade Union Bloc**.

Bohemia

One of the two ancient states which in combination form the modern **Czech Republic**, the other being **Moravia**. Making up the north-western two-thirds of the republic, with its traditional capital in **Prague**, Bohemia has long been a vital **central European** state. Bismarck, the architect of **German** unification in the 19th century, famously summed up the state's strategic importance when he said 'He who controls Bohemia, controls Europe'.

Bohemia takes its name from the ancient Celtic tribe of the Boii, which inhabited the region before the arrival of the **Czechs** in the 5th and 6th centuries. The Bohemian kingdom became a powerful regional force under the aegis of the Holy Roman Empire between the 12th and 13th centuries. After sporadic revolts inspired by **Protestant** Hussite or nationalistic sentiments, the region was fully absorbed into the Habsburg Empire in 1620. Within the empire it was stripped of its authority over the surrounding territory and obliged to convert to Catholicism. By the time of the creation of **Czechoslovakia** in 1918, the industrial development concentrated in Bohemia had made it the country's economic as well as political centre. In 1949 the communist authorities stripped Bohemia of its separate administrative status.

Bosnia and Herzegovina

An independent republic in south-eastern Europe, bounded by Croatia to the north and west and by the Federal Republic of Yugoslavia to the east (Serbia) and south (Montenegro), with a narrow land corridor to the Adriatic Sea. The country is divided within its recognized international borders into two entities—a joint **Muslim-Croat Federation** (covering about 51% of the territory) and a **Serb Republic** (about 49%).

Area: 51,233 sq km; *capital*: **Sarajevo**; *population*: 4.1m. (2001 estimate), comprising **Muslims/Bosniaks** 44%, **Serbs** 32%, **Croats** 17%, others 7%; *official language*: Serbo-Croat (also known as Bosnian); *religion*: Muslim 40%, **Orthodox** 31%, **Roman Catholic** 15%, other 14%.

Bosnia and Herzegovina's current government structures were created by the 1995 **Dayton Agreement** which ended three years of civil war (see below). The National Government is responsible for foreign, economic and fiscal policy. Executive power lies with an elected three-member rotating presidency (one representative from each of the Muslim, Serb and Croat communities) and a Council of Ministers headed by a Prime Minister (who may not be from the same community as the Chairman of the Presidency). Legislative authority rests with a bicameral **Parliamentary Assembly** (Skupština), consisting of a 42-member House of Representatives (Predstavnički Dom) directly elected for a four-year term (28 from the Muslim-Croat Federation and 14 from the Serb Republic) and a 15-member House of Peoples (Dom Naroda), elected indirectly by the legislatures of the two entities

Bosnia and Herzegovina

(10 from the Federation and five from the Serb Republic). Under changes introduced for the 2000 legislative elections aimed at decreasing the power of nationalist parties, election to the House of Representatives became dependent upon having support in both the Federation and the Serb Republic, while voters were required to vote for individual candidates rather than party lists.

Within the Muslim-Croat Federation, there is an indirectly-elected House of Peoples and a directly-elected 140-member House of Representatives, which chooses the President and Vice-President, who nominate the Council of Ministers for endorsement by the legislature. There are also 10 cantonal assemblies. The Serb Republic has a directly-elected President as well as an 83-member unicameral People's Assembly.

History: Once a part of the Roman Empire, Bosnia and Herzegovina was settled by **Slavic** tribes during the 7th century. In the 11th–12th centuries it was under **Hungarian** authority, before gaining independence around 1200. In 1463 the territory was conquered by the Turks; it remained a province of the Islamic Ottoman Empire for over 400 years, during which a distinctive Bosnian Muslim culture took form within a multi-ethnic population. At an international congress in 1878, Bosnia and Herzegovina was placed under Austro-Hungarian administration. Formal annexation by Austria-Hungary in 1908 embittered **Serbia** (which had aspirations towards a **Greater Serbia** in the **Balkans**); this hostility climaxed in the assassination in 1914 of the heir to the Austro-Hungarian throne by a Serb nationalist, precipitating the start of the First World War. In 1918 Bosnia and Herzegovina became part of the newly-formed 'Kingdom of Serbs, Croats and Slovenes' (known as **Yugoslavia** from 1929).

During 1941–45 the territory was under Nazi occupation, within a fascist-controlled puppet-state of **Croatia**. At the end of the Second World War it came under communist rule as one of six constituent republics (with Serbia, Croatia, **Montenegro, Macedonia** and **Slovenia**) of the **Socialist Federal Republic of Yugoslavia**, under Marshal **Tito** until his death in 1980.

On the collapse of communism in **eastern Europe** from 1989, Yugoslavia's political structure could not contain increasing nationalism and rivalry among the republics. Slovenia and Croatia seceded in 1991, provoking conflict with Serbia. In March 1992, following a referendum, the republican Government of Bosnia and Herzegovina also declared independence. Despite international recognition, this was opposed vehemently by Bosnian Serb nationalists, precipitating a savage civil war between the ethnic communities in which Croatia and rump Yugoslavia (Serbia and Montenegro) were also closely involved. During 1992 Serb nationalist forces, with the help of the largely Serbian Yugoslav army, gained control of about 70% of Bosnian territory. Under the leadership of Radovan **Karadžić**, they declared their own Serb Republic (Republika Srpska, RS) in Serb-controlled areas and pursued a campaign of **'ethnic cleansing'**. Bosnian Croats, aided by Croatia, similarly declared a new republic in the Croat-controlled area of the country, before joining the mainly Muslim government forces in a new Muslim-Croat Federation in March 1994 (under a power-sharing agreement brokered by the USA). Fighting between Muslim-Croat forces and Bosnian Serbs continued through 1994 and 1995, galvanizing international efforts through the **Contact Group** (**Russian Federation**, USA, UK, France and Germany), the United Nations and **NATO** to bring about a settlement. An estimated 250,000 people were killed in the conflict, over 200,000 injured and 13,000 permanently disabled.

The **Dayton Agreement**, a US-sponsored peace accord between the warring parties, was agreed in Dayton, Ohio, in November 1995. This preserved Bosnia and Herzegovina as a sovereign state, with a central republican Government and bicameral Parliamentary Assembly, while dividing it territorially between the Muslim-Croat Federation and the Serb Republic. NATO-led peacekeeping forces have since overseen the implementation of the military requirements of the agreement, initially as the Implementation Force (IFOR) and from December 1996 as the **Stabilization Force** (SFOR), while an **Office of the High Representative** created by the UN Security Council has supervised the civilian aspects of the accord.

The first pan-Bosnian presidential and Assembly elections, held in September 1996 under the terms of the Dayton accord, were dominated by three main nationalist parties—the (Muslim) **Party of Democratic Action** (SDA), the **Serbian Democratic Party** (SDS) and the **Croatian Democratic Union** (HDZ)—mirroring the ethnic divisions in the country. At the executive level, Alija **Izetbegović** of the SDA became the first Chairman of the new rotating Presidency following his election together with Momčilo Krajišnik (SDS) and Kresimir Zubak (HDZ), while the two posts of Co-Prime Minister went to Haris Silajdžić of the moderate Muslim **Party for Bosnia and Herzegovina** (SBiH) and Boro Bosić (SDS). In the RS, Biljana Plavšić of the SDS was re-elected President (having replaced indicted war criminal Karadžić in 1995). The Western-backed Plavšić quickly came into conflict with Karadžić, who secured her expulsion from the SDS in July 1997 after she had dissolved the SDS-dominated RS Assembly. In further RS elections in November 1997, SDS strength was eroded by Plavšić's new **Serbian People's Alliance** (SNS). As a result Plavšić was able to appoint a 'non-partisan' Government headed by Milorad Dodik of the moderate **Party of Independent Social Democrats** (SNSD).

In nationwide elections in September 1998, Izetbegović was re-elected as the Muslim candidate for the union presidency with 86.8% of the Muslim vote (and 31% nationally), along with hardline Croat nationalist Ante Jelavić of the HDZ, who took 52.9% of the Croat vote (and 11.5% nationally) and moderate Serb Zivko **Radišić** of the **Socialist Party of the Serb Republic** (SPRS), who won 51.2% of the Serb vote (and 21.8% nationally) standing for the Sloga ('Unity') alliance. At the legislative level, there was a decrease in support for nationalist parties in the all-Bosnia and Federation lower houses, so that moderate Serb Svetozar Mihajlović of the SNS joined Silajdžić as union Co-Prime Minister. Polling in the RS, in contrast, resulted in Plavšić being defeated in the presidential contest by Nikola

Poplasen of the ultra-nationalist **Serbian Radical Party** (SRS) with the backing of the SDS. Poplasen then tried to replace Dodik as RS Prime Minister, but was himself dismissed in March 1999 by the UN High Representative (the chief overseer of the Dayton accords) for 'abuse of power'. At the same time, an international arbitration tribunal ruled that the disputed town of **Brčko** (strategically linking the eastern and western sections of the Serb entity) should become a neutral district shared by Bosnia's two halves, further enflaming Serb opinion.

While the political impasse continued in the RS, further progress towards depoliticization at the union level was made in June 2000 with the appointment of Spasoje Tusevljak (a non-party Serb) as sole Prime Minister, although with misgivings in the SDA and HDZ and among Western Governments because of his former links with Karadžić and rump Yugoslavia. In October 2000 Izetbegović retired from the collective presidency on grounds of age and was succeeded by Halid Genjac of the SDA. The chairmanship of the collective presidency then passed to Radišić, meaning that—under the Dayton rule that this post and the union prime ministership could not be held by the same ethnic group—Martin Raguz of the HDZ was installed as union Prime Minister in place of Tusevljak.

Latest elections: Further elections in November 2000 produced a major advance for the multi-ethnic **Social Democratic Party of Bosnia and Herzegovina** (SDPBiH) in the all-Bosnia and Federation legislatures, although Serb nationalist parties remained dominant in the RS. In the all-Bosnia lower house the SDPBiH won 9 seats (with 19.0% of the vote nationally), the SDA 8 (18.8%), the SDS 6 (17.8%), the HDZ 5 (11.4%), the SBiH 5 (11.4%), the moderate Serb **Party of Democratic Progress** (PDP) 2 (6.4%) and seven other parties one seat each.

The results for the Federation lower house were: SDA 38 seats (26.8% of the vote), SDPBiH 37 (26.1%), HDZ 25 (17.5%), SBiH 21 (14.9%), **Democratic People's Union** (DNZ) 3 (2.1%), **Bosnian-Herzegovinan Patriotic Party** (BPS) 2 (1.7%), **New Croatian Initiative** (NHI) 2 (1.6%), Pensioners' Party 2 (1.3%), Bosnian Party 2 (1.1%), eight other parties one seat each. The nationalist parties boycotted the presidential elections which followed in February 2001.These resulted in the election of two moderates to the bi-partisan body, President Karlo **Filipović** (SDPBiH and Croat) and Vice-President Safet Halilović (SBiH and Bosniak).

In the November 2000 elections for the RS presidency, incumbent Vice-President Mirko **Sarović** of the SRS, who had remained in office despite the dismissal of Poplasen in March 1999, dismayed Western Governments by achieving a comfortable victory over Dodik of the SNSD, taking 53% of the vote with backing from the SDS. In the RS Assembly elections the SDS received reciprocal SRS backing, enabling the party to recover its numerical dominance by winning 31 of the 83 seats on a 36.1% vote share. The SNSD took 11 seats (with 13% of the vote), the PDP 11 (12.2%), the SDA 6 (7.6%), the SBiH 4 (5.2%), the SDPBiH 4 (5%), the SPRS 4 (4.9%), the **Democratic Socialist Party** 4 (4.2%), the **Democratic People's Alliance** 3 (3.5%), the SNS 2 (2.3%) and three other parties one seat each.

Recent developments: The November 2000 electoral advance of the moderate parties in the all-Bosnia and Federation legislatures resulted in tension between the new Alliance for Change (of moderate parties) and union Prime Minister Raguz (of the Croat nationalist HDZ). The outcome was the replacement of Raguz in February 2001 by Bozidar Matić (a Croat member of the SDPBiH), heading the first all-Bosnia Government not dominated by nationalists.

In the RS, hardline President Sarović sought to accommodate moderate forces by appointing eminent economist Mladen **Ivanić** of the PDP as Prime Minister in January 2001, heading a 'non-partisan' coalition Government which included the SPRS, a Muslim and a representative of the SDS. Ivanić responded to Western criticism by arguing that political stability required the inclusion of the SDS and by decreeing that his Ministers should not act as party representatives.

Meanwhile in the Muslim-Croat Federation, three months passed between the elections and the final approval of a moderate Government headed by Alija **Behman** of the SDPBiH on 12 March. His administration immediately faced a major new crisis when the HDZ reacted to the loss of the union premiership by declaring a revived separate Croat state based in **Mostar** and led by Jelavić and Raguz. The UN High Representative thereupon used his powers to dismiss Jelavić from the union collective presidency, amidst urgent UN and other efforts to preserve the structure created under the Dayton Agreement.

The departure of Jelavić from the union presidency broke the stranglehold of the ethnic-nationalist parties; the moderate Alliance for Change provided two new members—who joined Radišić, the incumbent Chair—Jozo **Križanović** (SDPBiH and Croat; assumed the rotating chairmanship of the presidency in June) and Beriz **Belkić** (SBiH and Bosniak).

In June, the failure of the union parliament to adopt key electoral laws, necessary to conduct polls independent of the UN, prompted union Prime Minister Matić to resign. He was replaced the following month by Foreign Minister Zlatko **Lagumdžija**. The electoral laws were finally passed in August, and were widely praised although the **Organization for Security and Co-operation in Europe** (OSCE) condemned a clause banning voters from electing candidates from outside their own ethnic group in presidential elections. Tensions with the HDZ had calmed sufficiently by November for the party to end its eight-month boycott of the legislature.

International relations and defence: Bosnia and Herzegovina was recognized as an independent state by the **European Union** and the USA in April 1992 and admitted to UN membership in May 1992. It is a member of the OSCE (which has supervised the country's post-Dayton elections to date) and the **Central European Initiative**, and has guest status at the **Council of Europe** and the **Non-Aligned Movement**. It also has observer status at the **Organization of the Islamic Conference**.

The defence budget of the all-Bosnia Government (excluding expenditure by the RS) was US $163m. in 2000, equivalent to about 3.5% of GDP. At the end of

2000 the armed forces remained divided between the ethnic communities, the (mainly Muslim) Bosnian army numbering 30,000, the Croatian Defence Council (HVO) commanding 10,000 and RS forces numbering 30,000. Plans for the merging of the Bosnian and Croatian forces remained to be implemented.

Bosnia and Herzegovina, economy

An economy hugely damaged by three years of civil war following independence in 1992, although some progress has been made towards recovery under post-war reconstruction programmes largely financed by the international community.

GNP: US $4,556m. (2000); *GNP per capita*: $1,260 (2000); *GDP at PPP*: $6,200m. (1999); *GDP per capita at PPP*: $1,770 (1999); *exports*: $683m. (2000); *imports*: $2,645m. (2000); *currency*: convertible marka pegged to Deutsche Mark/euro (plural: maraka; US $1=BKM2.197 at the end of December 2001).

Within a virtually landlocked territory, Bosnia and Herzegovina as a republic in the **Socialist Federal Republic of Yugoslavia** was relatively less developed than the other republics, with inefficient agriculture (almost all in private hands on small farms) and a stagnant, though diversified, state-owned industrial sector. In normal times about 14% of land is arable, 5% under permanent crops, 20% permanent pasture and 39% forests and woodlands; the main crops are wheat, maize, fruit and vegetables, and there is some animal husbandry. Mineral resources include copper, zinc, lead and gold, as well as some coal (lignite) and iron ore. Prior to 1992 the main industries were concentrated on military construction and armaments manufacturing as well as other branches of metallurgical and electrical/engineering industries.

The civil war destroyed much of the country's infrastructure and severely disrupted economic life. Whereas total GDP in 1990 had been US $11,000m. and annual per head income $2,400, by 1995 GDP had plummeted to $2,000m. and per head income to an estimated $500, with much economic activity taking place in the 'black' market. Whereas in 1991 industry accounted for over 40% of GDP, this had shrunk by 1996 to 23% (with an estimated 80% fall in production and with unemployment reaching 80%). In 1996 agriculture contributed 19% of GDP and services 58%, but in each case there were considerable differences as between the **Muslim-Croat Federation** and the **Serb Republic** (RS), whose economies had become separate in many respects. Whereas prior to 1991 Bosnia and Herzegovina enjoyed a substantial trade surplus, since 1996 there has been a huge deficit. The main exports are wood and paper products and iron and steel, while the principal imports are food products and electric power. Bosnia and Herzegovina's deficit is met principally through foreign aid and remittances from overseas. Italy takes 31% of Bosnia and Herzegovina's exports, the other main destinations being Germany (14%) and **Croatia** (10%). The main sources of imports are Croatia (20%), **Slovenia** (16%), Germany (14%) and Italy (13%).

Since 1995 major reconstruction progress has been achieved (although almost entirely in the Federation), with the **World Bank** putting real growth in GDP at 69% in 1996, 35% in 1997, 13% in 1998 and 10% in 1999 (the slow-down in 1999 being partly attributable to the crisis in **Kosovo**). A major step was taken in June 1998 when a new currency went into circulation, with a currency board arrangement and with the external value for the new marka guaranteed through being pegged to the German currency (and from 1999 the euro) for an initial six-year period. By the end of 2000 transport, telecommunications, power, water and education services had been restored to close to pre-war levels of availability and unemployment had been reduced to around 40%. Fiscal discipline has also been imposed, with the budget deficit falling from 5% of GDP in 1998 to 1.3% in 1999 and inflation from 5% to zero. Nevertheless, the economic situation remained precarious (especially in the RS), in view of continued reliance on external support and slow progress on achieving structural reforms and market liberalization.

Because of the civil war no privatization took place in the first three years of independence, and since then progress in that direction has been slow. Although in April 1999 the first **voucher privatization** was undertaken (mainly in the Federation), rigid labour laws and corruption have slowed the process.

Bosniaks

A title adopted by the Muslim **Slav** population, proportionately the largest, of **Bosnia and Herzegovina** to distinguish themselves from the ethnically identical, but Christian, **Croat** and **Serb** populations. The Bosniaks are the descendants of south Slavs, mostly originally **Orthodox Christians**, who converted to **Islam** during Bosnia's incorporation into the Ottoman Empire (1463–1878). Sharing their overlords' religious faith gave the Bosniaks an opportunity to attain positions of responsibility in the Ottoman administration. After 1918, once included in what was to become **Yugoslavia**, the Muslim community in Bosnia failed to identify itself as a separate ethnic group until the late 1960s. Eventually the Muslims were granted 'nation' status by the communist authorities. By the 1970s they were the rebublic's largest ethnic group and a clear separate identity appeared.

This fuelled tensions in Bosnia which exploded in the country's civil war in 1992–95. Whereas Bosniaks had once occupied areas across the country, after 1995 they were concentrated in the **Muslim-Croat Federation**, having been all but wiped out of Serb- and Croat-dominated areas through deliberate campaigns of '**ethnic cleansing**'. Mosques were destroyed and Muslims forced from their homes in these areas. Although work was undertaken from 2000 to rebuild the mosques and invite Bosniaks back to their original homes, the process has progressed little.

The persecution served to strengthen the Bosnian Muslims' identity, and the adoption of the Bosniak title legitimized the idea of a distinct ethnic group. Bosnian is recognized as one of the country's three official languages despite its great similarity with Serbian and Croatian. Like the latter it uses the Latin alphabet. Bosniak 'nationalist' interests are represented by the **Party of Democratic Action**, although Muslims have led the way in voting for the multi-ethnic **Social Democratic Party of Bosnia and Herzegovina** which, from March 2001, controlled both the union Government and that of the Muslim-Croat entity.

Bosnian-Herzegovinan Patriotic Party
Bosanskohercegovaćka Patriotska Stranka (BPS)

A small **Muslim**-based formation in **Bosnia and Herzegovina**, whose Chairman won 5.7% of the Muslim vote in the September 1998 elections to the three-member collective presidency, while his newly-formed party took two of the 140 seats in the **Muslim-Croat Federation** lower house. In the November 2000 elections the BPS won one of the 42 seats in the union lower house and two out of 140 in the Federation lower house.
Leadership: Sefer Halilović (President).
Address: 9 Hakije Kulenovića, Sarajevo.
Telephone and Fax: (33) 216881.

BPS *see* **Bosnian-Herzegovinan Patriotic Party**.

Braghis Alliance
Alianţa Braghis (AB)

A centre-left bloc in **Moldova** formed for the 2001 **Parliament** elections. The AB was launched in January 2001 under the leadership of Dumitru **Braghis**, who had been Prime Minister of a largely technocratic Government since December 1999, and reflected general disillusion with the factionalism of the centre-right parties which had been dominant since the 1998 elections. Members of the Alliance included the New Force Social-Political Movement (MSPFN), the Speranţa Movement of Professionals, the Centrist Union of Moldova (UCM), the 'Ant' Social Democratic Party (PDSF), the Socialist Party of Moldova (PSM) and the Labour Union (UM).

In the February 2001 elections, in which the **Communist Party of the Moldovan Republic** (PCRM) won an overall majority, the AB took second place with 19 of the 101 seats and 13.4% of the vote. It subsequently rejected a PCRM proposal that it should join a new Government, Braghis stating that the grouping would advocate its policies from a stance of opposition to the communists.
Leadership: Dumitru Braghis (Chair.).
Address: c/o Parlamentul, Blvd Ştefan cel Mare 105, 2073 Chişinau.

Braghis, Dumitru

Former Prime Minister of **Moldova**, appointed on 21 December 1999 but replaced following the February 2001 elections, and leader of the centre-left **Braghis Alliance** (AB).

Dumitru Braghis was born in a peasant family in Gratieşti, just north of **Chişinau**, on 28 December 1957, in what was then the Moldovan Soviet Socialist Republic. He graduated from the Chişinau Polytechnic Institute as an electrical engineer in 1980 and began work in the city's tractor company. In 1981 he took up his first position within the communist youth organization, the *Komsomol*. From 1987 he began to rise within the party administration with a post on the Central Committee of the Moldavian Communist Party. (The name was not changed to the less russified version, Moldova, until 1990.) In 1988 he was appointed as First Secretary of the *Komsomol*. His period in office overlapped with the tenure of future President Petru Lucinschi as First Secretary of the Moldavian Communist Party.

In late 1991 the country split away from the disintegrating **Soviet Union**, and in the new Moldovan Republic Braghis turned to the world of commerce for his first post-Soviet role. Until 1995 he was Deputy Director of Moldova–EXIM, a firm dealing in foreign trade. This position prepared him for a return to government administration as Director-General, and ultimately First Deputy Minister, at the Economics and Reform Ministry, where he stayed until his appointment as Prime Minister. While at the Ministry he co-chaired the Moldova-**European Union** Co-operation Committee, while also overseeing negotiations for membership of the **World Trade Organization** (WTO).

In November 1999 the then Prime Minister was forced to step down after a vote of no confidence. Braghis was the last of three replacements proposed by President Lucinschi, the first two having been rejected by the Parliament in a confrontation which came close to causing the calling of fresh elections. As Prime Minister, Braghis represented a break with the old agronomic order, and the rise of economy-oriented politicians with a keen interest in greater involvement in the global economy. At first he recognized the need to meet **International Monetary Fund** (IMF) demands for greater privatization of the economy, as a passport to WTO membership. In early 2000, however, he backed away from further IMF demands. Braghis turned against President Lucinschi in November 2000 when he backed parliamentary calls for the scrapping of the nationwide presidential election, a step intended to reduce the power of the presidency. Following the victory of the **Communist Party of the Moldovan Republic** (PCRM) in the February 2001 elections, Braghis took his newly-formed AB into opposition.

Bratislava

The capital city of **Slovakia**, situated in the far west of the country on the banks of the River Danube. *Population*: 440,000 (1991 estimate). The city was known as

Pozsony under its prolonged domination by the neighbouring kingdom of **Hungary**, for which it served as the capital from 1526 until 1784. Its dominating castle also served until 1811 as the residence of the Habsburg royal family, to whom the city was known by its German name of Pressburg. The city's infrastructure and economic importance made it the natural choice for the capital of the Slovak Republic within **Czechoslovakia** in 1919 and it remained in this role when an independent **Slovakia** emerged in 1993. Bratislava's modest community of **Jews** was completely destroyed in the Holocaust and the Jewish quarter was bulldozed to make way for the Bridge of the Slovak National Uprising.

Bratislava Stock Exchange
Burza cenných papierov v Bratislave a.s. (BCPB)

Officially founded in **Slovakia** in 1991, the BCPB first began trading in April 1993. Trading in foreign securities began in July 1997. The exchange trades mainly in government bonds, with only a total of eight share issues listed on its main market and three more on the parallel market. At the end of the first half of 2001 it had 42 members and a total market capitalization equivalent to US $8,200m.

General Secretary: Juraj Lazový.
Address: Vysoká 17, POB 151, 81499 Bratislava.
Telephone: (2) 49236111.
Fax: (2) 49236103.
E-mail: info@bsse.sk
Internet: www.bsse.sk

Brazauskas, Algirdas

Prime Minister of **Lithuania**.

Algirdas Mykolas Brazauskas is Chairman of the left-wing **Lithuanian Social Democratic Party** (LSDP). He became a member of the Soviet-era Government in 1965 and went on to become Lithuania's last Soviet ruler, and its first democratically-elected President. He was appointed Prime Minister on 29 June 2001.

Born in Rokiškis on 22 September 1932, he graduated from the Soviet Kaunas Polytechnic Institute in 1956, having specialized in hydrotechnology. He spent eight years as Chairman of the Energy Building Trust Board, before shifting directly into the Soviet administration, as Minister for the Building Material Industry, in 1965. Two years later he was made Deputy Chairman of the State Planning Committee, and effectively a potential member of the ruling Politburo. He was appointed Secretary for Economic Affairs to the Central Committee of the Communist Party of Lithuania (CPL) in 1977. He was in the Politburo for a further 10 years, and in 1988 was elected First Secretary of the CPL, during a decisive party split.

He helped lead the country towards independence, as a prominent figure in the broad-based **Lithuanian Reform Movement** (Sajudis). In 1990 he transformed the CPL into the Lithuanian Democratic Labour Party (LDDP) and was appointed Deputy Prime Minister of Lithuania. After winning 60% in elections, he was inaugurated as President on 25 February 1993. He did not stand for re-election in 1998 and returned to **Parliament** to lead the LDDP. He united the political left behind the A. Brazauskas Social Democratic Coalition, which went on to electoral success in October 2000. Although his claims to the right to try and form a government were overlooked by President Valdas **Adamkus**, the subsequently-formed right-wing coalition collapsed in June 2001. Brazauskas, now Chairman of the new LSDP party (formed by the merger in January of his LDDP with the existing party bearing the historic LSDP name), was called upon to form a Government.

Algirdas Brazauskas married Julia Styraite, a medical doctor, in 1958 and they have two daughters and five grandchildren.

Address: Office of the Prime Minister, Gedimino pr. 11, Vilnius 2039.
Telephone: (26) 29039 [(526) 29039 from September 2002].
Fax: (521) 27452.
E-mail: kanceliarija@lrvk.lt
Internet: www.lrvk.lt

Brčko

Town in north-eastern **Bosnia and Herzegovina**, on the Sava river which runs along the border with **Croatia**. At the end of the Bosnian war, following the **Dayton Agreement** of November 1995, control of the town was divided between the different Bosnian ethnic groups. However, owing to the strategic sensitivity of its geographical position—as both a part of the narrow corridor between the eastern and northern sections of the **Serb Republic** (RS), and an important north-south link between the **Muslim-Croat Federation** and north-eastern Croatia—the final status and governance of the town became the subject of arbitration by an international tribunal. Both the Federation and the RS pressed for exclusive control of the area, but the international tribunal decided in March 1999 that the pre-war Brčko municipality would become a self-governing 'neutral district', subject to Bosnian sovereignty and the authority of the Bosnian central institutions.

BSDP *see* **Bulgarian Social Democratic Party**.

BSEC *see* **Organization of the Black Sea Economic Co-operation**.

BSP *see* **Belarusian Peasants' Party**.

BSP *see* **Bulgarian Socialist Party**.

BSPSh *see* Union of Independent Trade Unions of Albania.

BTA *see* Bulgarian News Agency.

Bucharest

The capital city of **Romania**, situated in the centre of the Wallachian plain north of the Danube river. *Population*: 2m. (1987 estimate). The city was first fortified by the infamous Romanian prince Vlad the Impaler (believed to be the historical figure behind Count Dracula) in 1459. However, it was under Ottoman suzerainty that Bucharest gained in importance. It was made the administrative centre of **Wallachia** in 1659. During the 19th century it functioned as the focus for Romanian nationalism. Bucharest-based movements helped topple the Greek Phanariote dynasty in 1821 and led to the unification of Wallachia and Moldavia (*see* **Bessarabia question**) in 1859. Three years later the city was proclaimed the capital of the unified Romanian state.

The growth of Romania after independence in 1878 was reflected in the expansion of Bucharest. Under communist rule its architecture was dominated by prestige projects. The dictator Nicolae **Ceauşescu** left particularly drastic marks upon it, most notoriously by tearing down 10,000 hectares of the old city to make way for his grandiose House of the People. Economic activity is varied including production of consumer goods and vehicles.

Bucharest Stock Exchange
Bursa de Valori Bucureşti (BVB)

The principal stock exchange in **Romania**, trading mainly in government bonds. Reopened officially in July 1995 after the communist period, it began trading in November that year. It is managed by its members and 24 securities companies that form the Stock Exchange Association. In 2001 there were 59 members, of whom 39 are trading on the exchange. There are 86 companies with shares listed on the BVB, compared with over 4,000 listed on the less stringently-regulated RASDAQ market, which began operations in October 1995, to give all companies from the Mass Privatization Programme the possibility of being listed on an organized market.

President: Sergiu Oprescu.
Address: Str. Doamnei 8, 70421 Bucharest.
Telephone: (1) 3158209.
Fax: (1) 3158149.
E-mail: bvb@bvb.ro
Internet: www.bvb.ro

Budapest

The capital city of **Hungary** situated in the north of the country on the River Danube, which divides the historically separate entities of Buda and Pest. *Population*: 2m. (1993 estimate). Budapest as a single city only came about in 1873 when the fortified town of Buda, located on the river's west bank, was amalgamated with the economically vibrant Pest to the east. Since then it has been the capital of Hungary and as such has become the economic and cultural heart of the country, with good transport connections to the rest of **central Europe** and the **Balkans**. It was also the central stage for the country's major political events in the 20th century including the invasion of Soviet tanks in 1956 and the re-emergence of democracy in 1989.

Economic activity centres on heavy industry in the city itself as lighter industries have gradually spread out around the country. The services sector is also significant.

Budapest Stock Exchange
Budapesti Értéktőzsde (BSE)

Originally founded in **Hungary** in 1864, the exchange reopened after the communist period on 21 June 1990. As at 31 December 2000 it had 42 members and there were a total of 58 share listings in addition to trading in bonds.

President: András Simor.
Address: Deák Ferenc u. 5, 1052 Budapest.
Telephone: (1) 4296700.
Fax: (1) 4296800.
E-mail: info@bse.hu
Internet: www.bse.hu

Buddhism

The fourth-biggest religion in the world based almost entirely in Asia. The **Russian** republic of **Kalmykia** is the only Buddhist state in Europe. The followers of Buddhism venerate the founder, Buddha, his teachings and his relics. It is more a philosophy than a religion in the Western sense, with no God and no concept of Heaven or Hell, but instead Buddhists believe in successive reincarnation, until enlightenment brings the faithful to *Nirvana*. Buddhism is divided into three main branches and the Kalmyks follow the Tibetan strain which has been headed by the Dalai Lama since 1940. The religion was persecuted along with other creeds by the **Soviet Union** and the Kalmyks, in particular, were targeted by Stalin. They were deported *en masse* to **Siberia** in 1943 (*see* **Deported Nationalities**). They were rehabilitated in the 1950s and the first Buddhist temple was rebuilt in the republic in 1988. Like other religions Buddhism has undergone a revival in the post-Soviet period.

Bukovina question

A dispute between **Romania** and **Ukraine** over the division of the Bukovina region, which was rather arbitrarily divided between the two at the end of the Second World War. The northern part of Bukovina had, under Austrian suzerainty, become home to a large **Ukrainian (Ruthenian)** population and is contiguous with the similarly-populated regions of **Transcarpathia** and eastern **Galicia**. At the end of the Second World War the **Soviet** authorities incorporated it into the Ukrainian Soviet Socialist Republic. Owing to unclear instructions at the time, the cession included the principally Romanian town of Herta. The region is now known as the Chernovtsy *oblast* (region). The southern region of Bukovina is traditionally the cradle of Moldavian civilization (*see* **Bessarabia question**) and was consequently incorporated into Romania's Moldavian region. Romanian nationalists have long cherished the aspiration of obtaining the return of northern Bukovina, especially Herta. However, since the normalization of relations between Romania and Ukraine after 1991 the claim has not been pursued.

Bulgaria
Republika Bulgaria

An independent republic located in south-eastern Europe, bounded by Romania to the north, Serbia and the Former Yugoslav Republic of Macedonia to the west, Greece and Turkey to the south, and the Black Sea to the east. Administratively, Bulgaria is divided into 28 regions (obruzi).

Area: 110,910 sq km; *capital*: **Sofia**; *population*: 7.9m (2001 estimate), comprising **Bulgarians** 85.3%, **Turks** 8.5%, **Roma** 2.6%, **Macedonians** 2.5%, **Armenians** 0.3%, **Russians** 0.2%, other 0.6%; *official language*: Bulgarian; *religion*: **Bulgarian Orthodox** 85%, **Muslim** 13%, **Jewish** 0.8%, **Roman Catholic** 0.5%, **Uniate Church** 0.2%, **Protestant**, Gregorian-Armenian, other 0.5%.

Executive power rests with the President who is directly elected (with a Vice-President) for a five-year term and nominates the Prime Minister and Council of Ministers. Legislative authority is vested in the unicameral **National Assembly** (Narodno Sobranie) whose 240 members are elected for a four-year term by universal adult suffrage under a system of proportional representation from party lists, subject to a minimum requirement of 4% of votes cast.

History: The Bulgars founded their first state in the 7th century and were a powerful nation until subjugated by the Byzantine Empire in the 11th century. A second Bulgarian state was established in the 12th century, but was conquered by the Ottoman Turks towards the end of the 14th century and remained a province of

Bulgaria

the Ottoman Empire for the next 500 years. The 1878 Congress of Berlin, concluding a Russo-Turkish war, recognized an autonomous principality of Bulgaria under Turkish sovereignty. In 1908 the Government adopted the Constitution of a monarchy and Bulgaria was proclaimed an independent kingdom under Tsar Ferdinand I (*see* **Bulgarian royal family**). Ferdinand abdicated in 1918 following Bulgaria's defeat alongside Germany in the First World War, as a result of which Bulgaria was obliged to cede the Black Sea coastal region of Southern **Dobruja** to **Romania** under the 1919 Treaty of **Neuilly**. Ferdinand's successor, Boris III, reigned until his death in 1943, establishing a virtual dictatorship from 1934. He was succeeded by his infant son, Simeon II (*see* Simeon **Saxecoburggotski**). During the Second World War Bulgaria was again allied with Germany before it was occupied by Soviet forces in September 1944 and a coalition Fatherland Front Government, dominated by the Communist Party of Bulgaria (BKP), set up. A referendum held in 1946 formally deposed the Tsar and the following year a new Soviet-style Constitution abolished all opposition parties and established a People's Republic. The 1947 Treaty of Paris formally restored Southern Dobruja to Bulgaria.

The post-war period was dominated by the BKP under the leadership of Todor **Zhivkov**, who maintained Bulgaria as one of the **Soviet Union**'s most loyal satellites. After 35 years in power, Zhivkov was eventually forced to resign in November 1989 in the face of mounting economic problems and the influence of the democratization movements sweeping other **east European** countries. Under his immediate successor, Petur Mladenov, the BKP was obliged to relinquish its constitutional monopoly of power and to hold multi-party elections, prior to which it renamed itself the **Bulgarian Socialist Party** (BSP). Against the odds and amidst allegations of corruption, the BSP narrowly won the elections in June 1990. Political instability ensued, with mass demonstrations and strikes, until the formation the following December of a multi-party administration which undertook to implement a programme of economic and political reform. A new Constitution was adopted in July 1991, enshrining democracy and commitment to a free-market economy. In the October 1991 legislative elections the right-of-centre **Union of Democratic Forces** (SDS) defeated the BSP by a narrow four-seat margin to form the first non-communist Government, with Filip Dimitrov as Prime Minister. In January 1992 the incumbent President, Zhelyu Zhelev (SDS), was re-elected for five years in the country's first popular presidential election.

The immediate post-communist years were marked by political fragility in Bulgaria. No single party held a clear mandate to govern, nor was there any obvious consensus between them about how to tackle the mounting economic problems because of the pressure of vested interests. Prime Minister Dimitrov's administration collapsed at the end of 1992, and the subsequent Government of non-party technocrats led by Lyuben Berov resigned in September 1994. Early legislative elections held in December 1994 returned a BSP-led alliance with an overall majority of seats in the National Assembly, capitalizing on the economic discontent in the country. Zhan Videnov of the BSP was appointed Prime Minister. This

Bulgaria

Government dismissed the heads of state television and radio within six months of taking office, creating intense suspicion of the BSP's political agenda. However, it was the inability to manage the extreme crisis in the financial sector in 1996, caused by the collapse in the banking system and in the value of the currency, which did most to undermine public confidence in the administration. Zhelev was defeated in the October–November 1996 presidential election by Petar **Stoyanov** of the SDS. Videnov resigned as Prime Minister and BSP party leader in December 1996, and in February 1997 the new President overcame BSP resistance to the installation of a caretaker Government and the calling of early legislative elections for April. This poll was won by the SDS-led United Democratic Forces (ODS) alliance which gained an overall majority of 137 seats in the National Assembly, leaving the BSP once again in opposition, with only 58 seats for their Democratic Left alliance. The Union for National Salvation, headed by the mainly ethnic Turkish **Movement for Rights and Freedoms** (DPS), won 19 seats, the **Euro-Left Coalition** 14 and the Bulgarian Business Bloc (subsequently renamed the Georgi Ganchev Bloc) 12.

Installed as SDS Prime Minister in May 1997, Ivan Kostov headed a strongly-mandated Government which moved quickly to restore economic and social stability after the crisis of 1996 and early 1997 (*see* **Bulgaria, economy**). In December 1998 Bulgaria formally abolished capital punishment. Despite periodic tensions in the ruling ODS alliance and the surfacing of corruption allegations against certain Ministers in 2000, the Government retained its command of the Assembly for the four-year parliamentary term, largely untroubled by various efforts by the BSP to construct a viable opposition alliance for the 2001 elections.

However, more opposition materialized from a somewhat unexpected quarter. The former child-king, Simeon II, now a successful businessman based in Spain, had made a number of attempts to return to Bulgaria and was finally able to take up residence in early 2001 after which he formed the **National Movement Simeon II** (NDS II). The non-party movement rapidly gained popularity, drawing support from voters weary of the established party system, and from disaffected members of the ruling SDS. By the time of legislative elections in June the NDS II posed a very credible threat to the Government.

Latest elections: In the June 2001 National Assembly elections the NDS II won exactly half of the 240 seats, securing 42.7% of the popular vote. The ODS (including the SDS, the **Bulgarian Agrarian People's Union** (BZNS), the **Bulgarian Social Democratic Party** (BSDP), the **Democratic Party** (DP) and the National Movement for Rights and Freedoms) won 51 seats (with 18.2% of the vote), the Coalition for Bulgaria (headed by the BSP and including the Communist Party of Bulgaria among other factions) won 48 (17.1%) and the DPS 21 (7.5%).

Recent developments: Despite initially suggesting he would remain outside the Cabinet, ex-Tsar Simeon II, now known as Simeon Saxecoburggotski, was appointed Prime Minister on 15 July 2001. He turned to the DPS to create a working majority in the Assembly—marking the first time the DPS had been given a role in government. Saxecoburggotski's popularity rating, although gradually falling from the record levels in mid-2001, remains high. However, his personal endorsement of the candidacy of incumbent President Stoyanov in presidential elections in November 2001 was insufficient to save the SDS stalwart. Stoyanov was defeated in the second round by the BSP candidate Georgi **Purvanov**, who garnered 54% of the vote against Stoyanov's 45.9%, suggesting a trend back towards the left among the electorate.

International relations and defence: Bulgaria is a member of the United Nations, the **Organization for Security and Co-operation in Europe**, the **Council of Europe**, the **Central European Initiative**, the **Central European Free Trade Area**, the **Danube Commission** and the **Organization of the Black Sea Economic Co-operation**. It participates in **NATO**'s **Partnership for Peace** programme, the Kirov Government confirming Bulgaria's aim of full membership of the Alliance and in 1999 allowing NATO warplanes to use Bulgarian airspace during the **Kosovo** conflict with **Yugoslavia**. The Government also pledged to work towards membership of the **European Union**, which in December 1999 placed Bulgaria on its official list of prospective new members.

At the regional level, Bulgaria in February 1999 signed a declaration with **Macedonia** settling a longstanding language dispute that arose when Bulgaria refused to recognize Macedonian as a language separate from Bulgarian. The agreement also resolved potential territorial disputes that had threatened to prevent both countries from joining NATO. Bulgaria's relations with Turkey also improved in the late 1990s, following the sharp tensions caused by the programme of 'Bulgarianization' (forced assimilation) in the last months of the communist regime in 1989 and the resultant mass exodus of ethnic Turks to Turkey. In March 1999 Bulgaria, Turkey and Romania agreed to set up a free-trade zone.

Bulgaria's defence budget for 2001 amounted to some US $390m., equivalent to about 3% of GDP. The size of the armed forces at the end of 2000 was some 80,000 personnel, including those serving under compulsory conscription of nine months, while reservists numbered an estimated 300,000. In March 1999 the Government approved a controversial plan to reduce the size of the armed forces to 45,000 within five years.

Bulgaria, economy

A formerly centrally-planned economy whose initially halting transition to a market system has been accelerated since 1997. Although traditionally an agricultural country, Bulgaria underwent a considerable programme of industrialization after the Second World War.

GNP: US $11,734m. (2000); *GNP per capita*: $1,510 (2000); *GDP at PPP*: $34,900m. (1999); *GDP per capita at PPP*: $4,300 (1999); *exports*: $4,760m. (2000); *imports*: $6,362m. (2000); *currency*: lev, pegged to Deutsche Mark/euro (US $1=L2.187 at the end of December 2001).

Bulgaria, economy

In 1999 industry accounted for 29% of GDP, agriculture for 21% and services for 50%. Some 37% of the land is arable, 2% under permanent crops, 16% permanent pasture and 35% forests and woodland. The main crops are grain, oilseed, vegetables, fruit (including grapes for wine) and tobacco, and there is also animal husbandry. The principal mineral resources are bauxite, copper, lead, zinc and coal (mostly lignite and brown coal). The main industries are machine-building and metal-working, food processing, chemicals, textiles, construction materials, and ferrous and non-ferrous metals. Bulgaria's own resources account for rather less than half of its energy requirements (including substantial generation of electricity by nuclear power, accounting for 40% of consumption, and some hydroelectricity generation) and there are small hydrocarbon reserves.

Bulgaria's main exports by value are textiles, clothing and footwear (19% in 2000), iron, steel and other metals (18%), mineral fuels, oil and electricity (14%), machinery and equipment (12%), and agricultural and food products (6%). Principal imports are non-energy raw materials (33%), mineral fuels, oil and electricity (27%), machinery and equipment (25%), and consumer goods (15%). In 2000 the **European Union** (EU) countries took 52% of exports (headed by Italy with 15%) and supplied 44% of imports (headed by Germany with 14%), while the former Soviet-bloc countries supplied 27% of imports (headed by the **Russian Federation** with 24%) but took only 6% of exports.

Having already been in decline prior to the end of communist rule in 1989–90, the Bulgarian economy continued to suffer in the early 1990s, as lack of political stability meant that necessary decisions were frequently postponed. Industrial and agricultural output dropped sharply, serious trade and balance-of-payments deficits were experienced, and by 1996 foreign exchange reserves had fallen to US $446m. (covering only one month's imports). The problems were exacerbated by the reluctance of the post-1994 Government headed by the (ex-communist) **Bulgarian Socialist Party** to pursue pro-market and liberalization reforms, in the interests of preserving social stability. The result in late 1996 was a major banking and financial crisis, featuring a massive depreciation of the external value of the lev and hyperinflation which spiralled to over 200% a month in early 1997 and to 580% for the full year. GDP contracted by some 10% in 1996, with devastating effects on social conditions.

The situation was retrieved by the centre-right Government of the **Union of Democratic Forces** elected in April 1997, following which structural and other economic reforms were vigorously reactivated and macroeconomic discipline was imposed. With the support of the **International Monetary Fund** (IMF) and other international donors, a currency board was established in July 1997 and the lev was pegged to the Deutsche Mark (and to the euro from the beginning of 1999). Real GDP growth of 3.5% was achieved in 1998, while the inflation rate was dramatically reduced to only 1%. Further recovery in 1999 was hampered by the damaging economic impact of the **Kosovo** crisis on Bulgaria; GDP growth fell back to 2.4% and inflation revived to 6%. The reform programme was continued, however, and was boosted in December 1999 when the Government achieved its aim of securing acceptance of Bulgaria as a designated candidate for EU membership, to assist which it had joined the **Central European Free Trade Area** (CEFTA) at the beginning of the year. GDP growth recovered to around 5% in 2000, although inflation rose to 10% and unemployment increased to 18% at the end of 2000 from 15% a year earlier. The Government's 2001 budget projected further GDP growth of 5%, inflation of 6% and a budget deficit of only 1.5% of GDP.

The post-1997 Government completed the privatization of nearly all agricultural land (mostly restored to former owners) and also introduced a free-market structure by abolishing food price subsidies and by privatizing most of the food industry. Having been approached spasmodically and with rampant corruption in the early 1990s, privatization of the industrial sector was relaunched with urgency in 1998, resulting in the sell-off of 80% of former state-owned asset value by the end of 1999. The Government also instituted a programme of isolation and liquidation of unviable industrial enterprises. By the end of 2000 well over 90% of the former state-owned industrial sector was actually or imminently under private ownership.

Bulgarian Agrarian People's Union
Bulgarski Zemedelski Naroden Sayuz (BZNS)

A party in **Bulgaria** which claims direct descent from one of the world's oldest peasant parties, but which has split into several factions since the collapse of communism. The historic BZNS was founded in 1899 to represent what then constituted 80% of the Bulgarian population. After the First World War a BZNS Government was in power from 1920 under Aleksandur Stamboliyski, until being overthrown by a right-wing coup in 1923, in which Stamboliyski was killed. During the Second World War left-wing BZNS elements participated in the Fatherland Front led by the Bulgarian Communist Party (BKP), which came to power in 1944 following the ejection of German forces by the Red Army. The anti-communist wing of the party, led by Nikola Petkov, refused to participate in the obligatory Front list for the October 1946 elections, which entrenched the BZNS pro-communists. Petkov was hanged for alleged treason in September 1947. Under the People's Republic, the BZNS was always represented in the **National Assembly** as well as in successive Governments, usually holding the agriculture portfolio.

As east European communism crumbled in late 1989, the BZNS asserted its independence of the BKP by replacing its long-time leader, Deputy Premier Petur Tanchev, and by refusing to participate in the Government formed in February 1990. Meanwhile, the party's anti-communist faction had formed the separate Bulgarian Agrarian People's Union–Nikola Petkov (BZNS–NP). Advocating full political democracy and a market economy based on private agriculture, the BZNS–NP became a component of the pro-democracy **Union of Democratic Forces** (SDS) and featured in the SDS list of candidates for the June 1990 Assembly elections, while the rump BZNS won 16 of the 400 seats in its own right and in December 1990 joined a national unity coalition with the **Bulgarian Socialist Party** (BSP, successor to the BKP). In early 1991 a faction of the BZNS–NP reunited with the parent party to form BZNS–United for the October 1991 elections, while the bulk of the remaining BZNS–NP opted to stand independently of the SDS. Neither list surmounted the 4% threshold for representation.

In February 1992 the BZNS–NP leadership passed to Anastasia Moser, who advocated co-operation with the SDS minority Government by then in office. The following month the BZNS–NP faction which had remained in the SDS opted to set up its own organization within the SDS, while most of the BZNS–United became the Bulgarian Agrarian People's Union–Aleksandur Stamboliyski (BZNS–AS). Moser's faction contested the December 1994 Assembly elections within the People's Union (NS) alliance with the **Democratic Party** (DP), which won 18 of the 240 seats, while the remainder of the BZNS–NP participated in the defeated SDS electoral front and the BNZS–AS was part of the victorious BSP-led alliance.

The BZNS–NS and the rump BZNS–NP backed the successful SDS candidacy of Petar **Stoyanov** in the autumn 1996 presidential elections, in which Todor Kavaldzhiev of the BZNS–NS was elected Vice-President, while the BZNS–AS endorsed the defeated BSP candidate. The NS then returned to the SDS umbrella, with the result that the two anti-BSP Agrarian factions, now called the BZNS–NS and simply the BZNS, were part of the victorious United Democratic Forces (ODS) alliance headed by the SDS in the April 1997 Assembly elections, whereas the BZNS–AS was part of the losing alliance headed by the BSP. In mid-2000 the bulk of the BZNS–AS withdrew from the BSP alliance in opposition to its support for membership of **NATO** and the **European Union**.

The remaining BZNS factions stayed loyal to the ODS, and followed it into opposition in legislative elections in June 2001 which were decisively won by the newly-formed **National Movement Simeon II**.

Leadership: Petko Iliev (Chair. of main BZNS–SDS faction); Anastasia Moser (Chair. of BZNS–NS); Svetoslav Shivarov (Chair. of independent BZNS–AS faction); Dragomir Shopov (Chair of pro-BSP BZNS–AS faction).

Address: c/o Narodno Sobranie, 1 Aleksandur Battenberg Sq., 1169 Sofia.

Bulgarian Chamber of Commerce and Industry

The principal organization in **Bulgaria** for promoting business contacts, both internally and externally, in the post-communist era. Originally founded in 1895.

President: Bojidar Bojinov.
Address: Parchevich St 42, 1000 Sofia.
Telephone: (2) 9872631.
Fax: (2) 9873209.

E-mail: bcci@bcci.org
Internet: www.bcci.bg

Bulgarian Industrial Association (BISA)

BISA assists economic enterprises in **Bulgaria** with promotion and foreign contacts, analyses the economic situation, formulates policies for legislative and commercial projects, assists the development of small and medium-sized firms and organizes privatization and investment operations. Founded in 1980.
Chair. and President: Bojidar Danev.
Address: Alabin St 16–20, 1000 Sofia.
Telephone: (2) 9809914.
Fax: (2) 872604.
E-mail: office@bia.bol.bg
Internet: www.bia-bg.com

Bulgarian National Bank
Bulgarska Narodna Banka (BNB)

The Central Bank of **Bulgaria**. A Bulgarian Central Bank was first created in 1879 after the country's emergence from rule under the Ottoman Empire, and the Bulgarian lev was first put into circulation in note form by the Bank in 1885. In 1991 a two-tier banking system was enforced, remodelling the BNB as an independent, modern Central Bank in the post-communist era. The country was struck by hyperinflation in the winter of 1996–97 before the BNB fixed the lev to the Deutsche Mark. In 1998 the Bank began issuing its own lev notes for the first time since 1948 and the currency was devalued by a factor of 1000 the following year. As at December 1999 the BNB had reserves of 865,538m. lev.
Governor: Svetoslav Gavriyski.
Address: Aleksandur Battenberg Sq. 1, 1000 Sofia.
Telephone: (2) 91451203.
Fax: (2) 9802425.
E-mail: press_office@bnbank.org
Internet: www.bnb.bg

Bulgarian News Agency
Bulgarska Telegrafna Agentsia (BTA)

Bulgaria's main and official news agency, originally set up in 1898. BTA is now regulated under legislation dating from June 1994 which designates it as an 'autonomous national news organization' with a Director-General elected by the

Bulgarian **National Assembly**. It has its own network of reporters in major towns throughout the country.
Director-General: Panayot Denev.
Address: Blvd Tzarigradsko Chaussee 49, 1124 Sofia.
Telephone: (2) 926242.
Fax: (2) 802488.
E-mail: bta@bta.bg
Internet: www.bta.bg

Bulgarian Orthodox Church

An autocephalous branch of the **Orthodox Christian** Church based in **Bulgaria**. Christianity was preached in the plains and hills of modern Bulgaria in the first few centuries AD. However, it was not officially adopted by the **Slavic** Bulgars until 865. Since then it has been the majority religion in Bulgaria. After a break of some 600 years under the **Muslim** Ottoman Empire, the Autocephalous Bulgarian Patriarchate was restored on 10 May 1953. Patriarch Maxim was elected on 4 July 1971.

Bulgarian royal family—Saxe-Coburg-Gotha dynasty

The family which gave rise to the hereditary monarchs of **Bulgaria** from 1908 to 1946. Drawn from the German Duchy of Saxe-Coburg-Gotha, the dynasty was founded by Prince Ferdinand of Bulgaria who proclaimed himself King (Tsar) Ferdinand I in 1908. The last reigning monarch was Simeon II who succeeded as King in 1943 at the age of six, and who was forced to abdicate three years later after a dubious communist-organized referendum ruled in favour of a republic. He made a dramatic return to political prominence in 2001 as the inspiration behind a newly-formed **National Movement Simeon II** which achieved a striking victory in legislative elections in June of that year. Under the name Simeon **Saxecoburggotski**, the ex-King was appointed Prime Minister of Bulgaria on 15 July 2001. He has never dropped his claim to the throne but maintains that his current political agenda does not include a return to monarchy. The heir apparent is his eldest son Kardam, Prince of Tirnovo.

Bulgarian Social Democratic Party
Bulgarska Sotsialdemokraticheska Partiya (BSDP)

A party of the non-communist left in **Bulgaria**, descended from the historic BSDP founded in 1891, which was re-established in 1989 but split apart in 1998. During the Second World War left-wing Social Democrats joined the communist-dominated Fatherland Front, which came to power in 1944 on Bulgaria's liberation by

Bulgarian Social Democratic Party

the Red Army. The party's anti-communist wing was powerless to resist the post-war consolidation of communist power. Following the declaration of a People's Republic in December 1947, the BSDP was merged with the Bulgarian Communist Party (BKP) in 1948. Over the next four decades exiles kept the party alive as the Socialist Party, which was re-established in Bulgaria in 1989 under the leadership of Petur Dertliev, a veteran of the pre-1948 party.

In March 1990 the party reverted to the historic BSDP title in view of the imminent decision of the BKP to rename itself the **Bulgarian Socialist Party** (BSP). As a component of the pro-democracy **Union of Democratic Forces** (SDS), the BSDP took 29 of the 144 seats won by the SDS in the June 1990 **National Assembly** elections. The following month Dertliev was the initial SDS candidate for the presidency but withdrew to allow the then SDS Chairman Zhelyu Zhelev to be elected unopposed in the sixth round of Assembly voting. The BSDP supported the decision of some SDS elements to enter a BSP-dominated coalition Government in December 1990 but thereafter came into increasing conflict with the SDS pro-market wing. Whereas the latter advocated full-scale economic liberalization, the BSDP favoured a welfare market economy and argued that privatized industries should become co-operatives where possible. In the October 1991 Assembly elections the BSDP headed a separate SDS–Centre list, which failed to surmount the 4% threshold.

The BSDP backed Zhelev's successful candidacy in the January 1992 direct presidential elections and thereafter sided with the President in his developing conflict with the SDS minority Government. Following the appointment of a non-party 'Government of experts' in December 1992, the BSDP warned that it marked a reassertion of communist influence. Alliance-building by the BSDP culminated in the formation of the Democratic Alternative for the Republic (which included the Green Party) for the December 1994 Assembly elections, but its vote share of 3.8% was again below the 4% threshold. In the autumn 1996 presidential elections the BSDP backed the successful candidacy of Petar **Stoyanov** of the SDS, thereafter contesting the April 1997 Assembly elections as a component of the victorious SDS-led United Democratic Forces (ODS).

In late 1998, however, the BSDP split into a pro-SDS faction and a majority rump led by Dertliev, who was soon succeeded by Petar Agov. Agov's rump entered a Coalition for Bulgaria alliance headed by the BSP in January 2001. The result was effectively two separate parties, both of which claimed the right to use the BSDP name.

The pro-ODS faction was kept in opposition after legislative elections in June 2001, while the group affiliated with the BSP was drawn into the governmental sphere following the BSP alliance with the victorious **National Movement Simeon II**. This faction, the 'Dertliev' BSDP, is considered the direct heir to the historic BSDP and is a full member party of the **Socialist International**.

Leadership: Petar Agov (Chair. of pro-BSP faction);
Yordan Nihrizov (Chair. of pro-ODS faction).

Bulgarian Socialist Party

Address: 37 Ekzarch Yossif Street, 1504 Sofia.
Telephone: (2) 801584.
Fax: (2) 390086.
E-mail: biltd@vt.bia-bg.com

Bulgarian Socialist Party
Bulgarska Sotsialisticheska Partiya (BSP)

The successor to the former ruling Bulgarian Communist Party (BKP), dating from April 1990 when the BKP changed its name and embraced democratic socialism. The BKP had traced its descent from the **Bulgarian Social Democratic Party** (BSDP), founded in 1891, but really dated from 1919, when the pro-Bolshevik BSDP faction became a founder member of the Third International (Comintern). It later organized armed opposition to right-wing regimes of the inter-war period and renamed itself the Workers' Party in 1927, before it was banned in 1934. For the following decade the party was based in **Moscow**, where many of its exiled leaders were executed in Stalin's purges. During the Second World War the party played a leading role in resistance to the pro-German Bulgarian regime in power until 1944, its activities being directed by Georgi Dimitrov, Bulgarian Secretary-General of the Comintern. In September 1944 the communist-dominated Fatherland Front, including left-wing agrarians and social democrats, took power in Sofia, assisted by the advancing Red Army. In the post-war period the communists consolidated their position, Dimitrov becoming Prime Minister after the October 1946 elections and a People's Republic being declared in December 1947. In 1948 the rump of the old BSDP was merged with the Workers' Party, the resultant formation adopting the BKP rubric and effectively becoming the sole ruling party, although the **Bulgarian Agrarian People's Union** (BZNS) remained a nominally independent component of the Front.

On Dimitrov's death in 1949 the BKP leadership passed to Vulko Chervenkov, but he was replaced in 1954 by Todor **Zhivkov** after being accused of fostering a personality cult. Under Zhivkov's long rule Bulgaria remained closely aligned with the **Soviet Union** and participated in the 1968 Soviet-led intervention in **Czechoslovakia** (*see* **Prague Spring**). At the 13th BKP congress in April 1986 Zhivkov announced a reform programme reflecting the **Gorbachev** *glasnost* and *perestroika* initiatives in the Soviet Union; but reform proved difficult to accomplish because of party in-fighting. Amidst the rapid collapse of European communism in late 1989, Zhivkov was replaced as BKP leader and Head of State by Petur Mladenov, who initiated a purge of Zhivkov supporters. The BKP's 'leading role' in society and the state was terminated under constitutional amendments enacted in January 1990, following which an extraordinary party congress renounced 'democratic centralism' and opted for a 'socially-oriented market economy'. The party leadership passed to Aleksandur Lilov (a prominent BKP reformer of the Zhivkov era), with Mladenov remaining Head of State.

Paradoxically, the BKP was obliged to form the first openly all-communist Government in Bulgaria's history in February 1990, when the BZNS opted to go into opposition and the new pro-democracy **Union of Democratic Forces** (SDS) refused to join a national unity coalition. In April 1990, following a ballot of party members, the BKP officially renamed itself the BSP, which in multi-party elections in June resisted the post-communist east European trend by being returned to power with 211 of the then 400 **National Assembly** seats. In July 1990, however, Mladenov resigned as Head of State, after disclosures about his role in the suppression of anti-Government demonstrations in December 1989. He was succeeded by SDS leader Zhelyu Zhelev in August, while in December 1990 the BSP also vacated the premiership, although it remained the largest component in an uneasy coalition with the SDS and the BZNS.

The adoption of a new democratic Constitution in July 1991 was followed by political dissension over the BSP's attitude to the **August coup** attempt by hardliners in **Moscow**, seen by many as initially supportive. In further elections in October 1991 the BSP was allied with eight small parties and organizations on a platform of preserving the 'Bulgarian spirit and culture', but was narrowly defeated by the SDS. It therefore went into opposition for the first time since 1944. At a party congress in December 1991, Lilov was replaced as leader by Zhan Videnov, who advocated a 'modern left socialist party' and easily defeated the candidate of the reformist social democrats, Georgi Pirinski. The BSP also suffered a narrow defeat in the direct presidential election held in January 1992, its preferred candidate securing 46.5% of the second-round vote.

In September 1992 the decision of the (ethnic Turkish) **Movement for Rights and Freedoms** (DPS) to withdraw support from the SDS minority Government enabled the BSP to reassert its influence. A 'Government of experts' headed by Lyuben Berov (non-party), appointed in December, was backed by most BSP deputies. Thereafter, as the Government achieved a degree of stability by not hurrying privatization and deregulation of the economy, the BSP was content to avoid direct governmental responsibility during a period of transition, while relying on its establishment network and the party's strength in the Assembly to influence decision-making. By mid-1993 the BSP was again the largest Assembly party, owing to the steady erosion of SDS affiliation, although the BSP also experienced defections in this period.

On the resignation of the Berov Government in September 1994, the BSP declined the opportunity to form a new administration, preferring early elections. These were held in December, the BSP being allied principally with factions of the BZNS and the **Ecoglasnost Political Club**. The outcome was an overall Assembly majority of 125 seats for the BSP-led list and the formation of a coalition Government in January 1995 under the premiership of Videnov, committed to a socially-oriented market economy and integration into European institutions. It made little progress on either front, however, and so faced a renewed challenge from the SDS in the 1996 presidential elections. Aiming to attract centrist support, the BSP nominated Pirinski (by now Foreign Minister) as its candidate, but he was ruled ineligible because he had been born in the USA. The BSP replacement was Culture Minister Ivan Marazov, who ran under the 'Together for Bulgaria' label but who was defeated by Petar **Stoyanov** (SDS) in the second voting round in early November on a 60–40 split.

Videnov quickly resigned as both Prime Minister and BSP Chairman, being replaced in the latter capacity by Georgi **Purvanov** in December 1996. After initial resistance by the BSP, Stoyanov was able to install a caretaker administration and to call early Assembly elections in April 1997. The BSP ran as leader of the Democratic Left alliance (again including BZNS and Ecoglasnost factions) but was heavily defeated by the SDS-led United Democratic Forces, the BSP alliance being reduced to 58 seats.

In opposition, the BSP in December 1998 formed the Social Democracy Union with other left-wing forces, while also establishing an alliance with the **Euro-Left Coalition** with a view to broadening its popular base for the 2001 Assembly elections. In mid-2000 the pro-BSP faction of the BZNS broke into two groups, the main one withdrawing from the alliance in opposition to the BSP's support for membership of **NATO** and the **European Union**. In January 2001 the BSP launched yet another alliance of left-wing parties, this time called the New Left, which was committed to 'the values of modern social democracy and the European left'.

Heading into the 2001 elections the BSP formed the Coalition For Bulgaria, uniting left-of-centre parties in the face of dwindling support for the ruling SDS-led coalition, but also up against the overwhelmingly popular **National Movement Simeon II** (NDS II). The Coalition gained just 17% of the vote but was invited into a broad-based coalition by the NDS II Prime Minister, Simeon **Saxecoburggotski**, along with the DPS. The BSP was awarded two Cabinet positions in the initial Government. Purvanov proved the party's continuing political effectiveness when he surprised political analysts by winning presidential elections in November 2001. He was inaugurated on 22 January 2002, having already stepped down as party leader.

Leadership: Sergei Stanishev (Chair.).
Address: 20 Pozitano Street, 1000 Sofia.
Telephone: (2) 9894010.
Fax: (2) 9805219.
E-mail: bsp@bsp.bg
Internet: www.bsp.bg

Bulgarian Stock Exchange (BSE)

The successor, launched in October 1997, to the suspended First Bulgarian Stock Exchange (FBSE). The FBSE had been inaugurated in November 1991 but was suspended in October 1996 owing to new regulations from the Securities and Stock Exchange Commission. By the end of 1999 there were 32 companies listed on the

BSE's official market while over 800 companies were being traded in the free market. Total market capitalization is close to US $1,000m. The BSE is managed by a Board of Directors and the Chief Executive Officer.
Chair.: Apostol Apostolov.
Address: Makedonia Sq. 1, 1040 Sofia.
Telephone: (2) 9865863.
Fax: (2) 9865566.
E-mail: bse@bse-sofia.bg
Internet: www.bse-sofia.bg

Bulgarian Turks

A community of around 800,000 ethnic Turks (1992 estimate) in **Bulgaria**, concentrated in the traditional tobacco-growing regions in the southern Arda basin and north-eastern **Dobruja**. In 1992 they constituted 9.4% of the total population. It is largely accepted that the Bulgarian Turks arrived in Bulgaria during the era of the Ottoman Empire, between the 14th and 19th centuries. However, some scholars have attempted to prove that they were either ethnic **Bulgarians** who adopted the Turkish language and Islam under Ottoman suzerainty, or the descendants of much earlier **Turkic** migrants from central Asia.

After Bulgaria became autonomous under Turkish sovereignty in 1878, the Bulgarian Turks had their own Turkish-language schools and retained their own cultural identity. This situation continued within the independent Bulgaria to the extent that even in 1946 half of all Bulgarian Turks could not understand Bulgarian. Although initially this situation was tolerated by the post-war communist authorities, a strenuous policy of Bulgarianization was implemented after 1958. Over the next 30 years Turkish schools were shut, Turkish was dropped from the curriculum and Turkish newspapers were closed down; by 1985 the Government forced the adoption of **Slavic** names and outlawed the use of Turkish in public. The policy led to violent resistance, imprisonments and killings. A mass exodus of Turks to Turkey began in June 1989, actively encouraged through intimidation and confiscation of property. Although 350,000 fled within two months, 130,000 had returned by January 1990 as the Bulgarian communist regime liberalized.

Between 1990 and 1992 Bulgarian Turks were rehabilitated into Bulgarian society. Arabic and Islamic names were readmitted and Turkish-language media flourished. However, the decline of the country's tobacco industry has hit the Turkish community particularly badly and large numbers continue to emigrate to Turkey. This demographic downturn has eroded the traditional support base of the **Movement for Rights and Freedoms** (DPS), forcing it to seek greater links with the minority **Pomak** community.

Bulgarians

A modern people of south-eastern Europe, usually considered south **Slavic**. The Bulgars, from whom their name is derived, actually originated as a **Turkic** tribe from central Asia, who settled in the 7th century in what is now **Ukraine**, where they established a Great Bulgarian Empire. On the disintegration of this empire a group of Bulgars migrated south and west into the southern **Balkans** where they merged with the earlier immigrant Slavs, and to a lesser extent with local **Vlachs**, to form the modern Bulgarian people. As such they are considered most closely related to the neighbouring **Macedonians**; indeed it is sometimes said there is no discernible ethnic difference between Bulgarians and Macedonians. The further advance of the Bulgarians into what is now **Macedonia** in the 9th century led to their adoption of Christianity, the spread of the Slavic Macedonian language, and ultimately the spread of the **Cyrillic** alphabet.

Outside Bulgaria itself, there are some 234,000 Bulgarians concentrated in the Odessa region of Ukraine, with whom the Bulgarian Government has striven to forge links. The second-largest group outside Bulgaria consists of 88,000 who live in the rural southern **Taraclia** district of **Moldova**, where they have sought some regional autonomy. 25,000 reside in **Serbia** and another 10,000 in the **Dobruja** area of **Romania**.

Buzek, Jerzy

Former activist in the **Solidarity** movement and Prime Minister of **Poland** 1997–2001.

Born in 1940, he is by religion a Protestant in an overwhelmingly Catholic country. Buzek studied chemical engineering and became a professor in technical sciences, developing an interest in environmental issues which would later lead to his involvement in an international research programme on tackling problems of global warming. He was active in the Solidarity trade union from its inception at the beginning of the 1980s, having helped found a branch of the union at the Polish Academy of Science, and earned a national reputation as President of the first Solidarity national summit in 1981. His skill in handling this emotional meeting led to his being asked to preside subsequently at the fourth, fifth and sixth Solidarity summits. When the free trade union movement was outlawed and Poland placed under martial law between 1981 and 1985, Buzek led the clandestine regional Solidarity movement in Silesia and was a member of the union's national body.

Faced with the fragmentation of Solidarity in the post-communist era, Buzek continued to focus on the original trade union issues with which the movement concerned itself. Before the September 1997 general election he acted as economic adviser to Marian Krzaklewski, the head of both the **Solidarity Electoral Action** alliance (AWS) and the Solidarity trade union. At that election, Buzek (who co-wrote the AWS economic programme) was unanimously chosen to head the AWS electoral list. It recorded an unexpectedly strong performance, becoming by far the largest grouping by winning 201 out of 460 seats in the *Sejm* (the lower house of the **National Assembly**). This left Buzek, who was appointed Prime Minister on 17 October, with the task of forming a coalition with the liberal **Freedom Union** (UW) to secure an overall parliamentary majority. The resulting Government held together, under increasing tension, only until June 2000, when the withdrawal of the UW left Buzek at the head of a minority AWS Government with diminishing parliamentary and popular support. The poor showing of its candidate (Krzaklewski) in presidential elections in October 2000 was a clear indicator of problems ahead for the AWS in the parliamentary contest due the following autumn. Buzek himself took over the AWS leadership from Krzaklewski in January 2001, initiating moves to convert it from a fractious alliance into a cohesive political movement. His uphill struggle was compounded by Solidarity's withdrawal of all support for the AWS in May 2001, and by corruption scandals, undermining its credibility with the electorate to the extent that the September 2001 election saw its complete elimination from the legislature. Buzek had been, nevertheless, the only Polish Prime Minister in the post-communist era to complete a full term in office.

BZNS *see* **Bulgarian Agrarian People's Union**.

C

Camera Deputaţilor
(Chamber of Deputies)

The lower house of the **Parliament of Romania**.

Carpatho-Ukraine *see* **Transcarpathia**.

Casule, Slobodan

Minister of Foreign Affairs, **Macedonia**.

Slobodan Casule is a member of the small right-wing **New Democracy** (ND) party and was a celebrated journalist and political commentator before being drafted into government service as an adviser in March 2000. He was appointed Foreign Minister on 29 November 2001.

Born on 27 September 1945 in **Skopje**, he excelled at languages and began work in 1965 as an interpreter and journalist with Skopje Television. His command of Spanish was put to use from 1967 when he was posted to South America to act as the company's Chile and Peru correspondent. He remained in the region for 13 years and graduated in philology from the Pontifical Catholic University in Lima, Peru, in 1972. After seven years with Skopje Television he switched to the Yugoslav TANJUG news agency in 1974 and was moved to Rio de Janeiro, Brazil, to cover all of Latin America.

He returned to **Yugoslavia** in 1980 to become Chief Editor of TANJUG in Macedonia. He held this position for 10 years before becoming Director and Chief Editor at Macedonian Radio. In the newly independent Macedonia he continued to work at the radio station, as editor/commentator from 1994. For four months in 1999 he was Director General of the *Nova Makedonija* daily newspaper. The following year he was appointed Republic Adviser to the Government. In November 2001, when Prime Minister Ljubčo **Georgievski** turned to small parliamentary allies such as the recently established ND to form a new coalition, Casule, one of two ND Ministers, was elevated to the post of Fereign Minister.

Slobodan Casule is a member of many internationalist organizations which seek to promote ties between **eastern Europe** and the West, as well as more specific groups looking to improve regional relations.

Address: Ministry of Foreign Affairs, Dame Gruev 4–6, 91000 Skopje.
Telephone: (2) 119190.
Fax: (2) 115790.
E-mail: mailmnr@mnr.gov.mk
Internet: www.mnr.gov.mk

Catholicism *see* **Roman Catholic Church**.

Caucasus region

The mountainous and ethnically diverse region at the extreme south of **European Russia** which forms a natural and political boundary between Europe and Asia. The Greater and Lesser Caucasus ranges rise sharply from the southern Russian steppe and plunge precipitously into the Black and Caspian Seas to the west and east, slicing the land and people into different cultural, linguistic and religious pockets. The region has had a rich and varied history. It has often been overrun by regional powers, only to shake off centuries of domination time and again. It serves effectively as a volatile buffer between the Middle East and Europe, and particularly between Christianity and Islam.

The region can be usefully divided into two. The northern Caucasus lies within the **Russian Federation**, while the southern areas (known collectively as Transcaucasia) are split between the **Soviet** successor states of **Armenia**, **Azerbaijan** and **Georgia**. Within the Russian north Caucasus lie the republics of (from west to east) **Adygeya**, **Karachai-Cherkessia**, **Kabardino-Balkaria**, North **Ossetia** (Alania), **Ingushetia, Chechnya** and **Dagestan**. Two crossover regions—**Abkhazia** and South Ossetia—are within Georgia.

The most recent overlords, the **Russians**, first attempted to stake their imperial claim to the 'land of mountains' in the late 18th century, having beaten back rival claims from the Ottoman Turks and the Persians. Many of the **Muslim people's** of the north Caucasus took a prominent part in a rebellion against Russian rule in the mid-19th century. At first they succeeded while Russian forces were preoccupied in the **Crimea**, but the revolt was crushed in 1864 and Russian rule was secured. Attempts by the region's larger ethnic groups to assert autonomy after the fall of the Russian Empire in 1917 were crushed by the new Soviet authorities, particularly under the Commissar for Nationalities, and future Soviet leader, Josef Stalin (a Georgian himself). The various republics of today were established after the failure of Stalin's pet Transcaucasian and Mountain Peoples' Republic projects.

The collapse of the Soviet Union in 1991 opened a Pandora's box of nationalist aspirations and religious fervour. The war in Chechnya has threatened to destabilize the entire north Caucasus while Georgia has lost effective control of Abkhazia and South Ossetia. Armenia and Azerbaijan, traditional enemies held together under communism, soon fell dramatically apart with open conflict in **Nagorno-Karabakh** remaining unresolved.

The autochthonous Caucasian peoples (Abaza, Abkhaz, Adygei, Adzharians, Avars, Chechens, Cherkess, Dargins, Georgians, Ingush, Kabardins, Lezghins, Meskhetians, Ossetes and Tabasarans, to name the ones covered in this dictionary) form the dominant ethnic group although their many languages are, in varying degrees, mutually unintelligible and transcribed using various scripts. There are also large communities of **Turkic** origin (Azeris, Balkars and Kumyks) and other non-indigenous Armenian and Iranian peoples.

Caviar

The eggs of the sturgeon fish, highly prized as a gourmet delicacy, commanding prices which have made the trade in top quality caviar from the Caspian Sea especially lucrative. Over-exploitation, particularly in the Caspian region, has led to a severe drop in sturgeon numbers. Both **Azerbaijan** and the **Russian Federation** have borders on the Caspian Sea, along with three other central Asian states, and 90% of the world's caviar supply originates from that body of water, with Russian fishermen harvesting 32%. Extreme overfishing led to action within the terms of the Convention on International Trade in Endangered Species (CITES). Regulations imposed on the industry from 1998, enforceable in all Caspian Sea countries, did have some impact on the trade but proved insufficient to protect the sturgeon, particularly because of the existence of a flourishing illegal smuggling network via the Middle East. A six-month moratorium on all sturgeon fishing in the Caspian and associated rivers was introduced in 2001.

CBSS *see* **Council of Baltic Sea States**.

CDI *see* **Christian Democrat International**.

Ceauşescu, Nicolae

Communist leader in **Romania** from 1965 until the violent overthrow of his dictatorial regime in December 1989, and Head of State for all but two of those years. Born in 1918, he began his political life as a teenage communist activist from a peasant family, and was imprisoned under King Carol and again by the pro-Nazi Iron Guard during the war. Associated closely with Gheorghe Gheorghiu-Dej's nationalist group in the communist party, he succeeded his mentor as General Secretary in 1965, and played the patriotic card riskily but successfully. Besides maintaining contacts with China and Israel, he condemned the **Warsaw Pact**'s

1968 invasion of **Czechoslovakia**, and declared all-out resistance against the threat of Romania suffering the same fate. Although he kept Romania within the Warsaw Pact, he offered Western Governments the possibility of an intermediary, and enjoyed the attention and foreign honours which he (and his high-profile wife Elena) received in return. His economic schemes were geared to notions of Romania's grandeur, and a pride in what modern man could do to his environment, but his lifestyle was remote from the hardship which such policies entailed for ordinary people. The Ceauşescu nepotism was unpopular in the upper echelons of the party, but strict censorship and a pervasive personality cult stifled dissenting voices as he proclaimed his rule to be the 'golden age'. He seemed genuinely astonished to encounter protest and even hatred from his people in December 1989, when he and Elena were overthrown, captured and shot. Some national-communist politicians have since called for Ceauşescu's rehabilitation as a national hero who protected Romania from Soviet domination.

CEFTA *see* **Central European Free Trade Area**.

CEI *see* **Central European Initiative**.

Central Bank of Armenia

The **Yerevan** branch of the Russian State Bank was redesignated the People's Bank of the Soviet Socialist Republic of **Armenia** in December 1920. With the collapse of the **Soviet Union** in 1991 the Bank was transformed into the National Bank of Armenia. For two years Armenia continued to use Soviet roubles despite their withdrawal across the **Commonwealth of Independent States** (CIS). The situation was rectified when the bank was renamed the Central Bank in March 1993 and the dram was introduced in note form: coins followed in January 1994. As at November 1998 the Bank had reserves of 162m. drams.
  Governor: Tigran Sarkissian.
  Address: Nalbandian St 6, 375010 Yerevan.
  Telephone: (1) 583841.
  Fax: (1) 151107.
  E-mail: cba@mbox.amilink.net
  Internet: www.cba.am

Central Bank of Bosnia and Herzegovina
Centralna Banka Bosne i Hercegovine

The Central Bank of **Bosnia and Herzegovina** with sole authority for the country's currency and monetary policy since it began operations in 1997. It replaced the National Bank of Bosnia and Herzegovina and the National Bank of the

Republika Srpska. It does not grant credits, or lend capital to private or governmental concerns, and is not a lender of last resort to the banking system.
Governor: Peter Nicholl.
Address: 25 Maršala Tita, 71000 Sarajevo.
Telephone: (33) 278100.
Fax: (33) 278299.
E-mail: contact@cbbh.ba
Internet: www.cbbh.gov.ba

Central Bank of the Russian Federation
Bank Rossiya

An imperial State Bank was first created in 1860 as part of the emerging capitalist system and effectively remained in place until 1920 when the renamed People's Bank was finally dissolved. The Soviet-era *Gosbank* or State Bank was created in 1921 under Lenin's New Economic Policy (NEP). From then until 1987 it served within a single-tier system, financing the planned economy of the **Soviet Union**. A two-tier system was reintroduced in 1987–88 and the *Gosbank* was transformed into the CBR in 1990—it was restricted to the **Russian Federation** after the collapse of the Soviet Union in 1991. In 1993 the CBR was given regulatory control of the country's banking system. It has struggled to contain the ailing **Russian economy** in its return to capitalism and the rouble was revalued in 1997. The Bank undertook a major revision of the banking sector in 1998–2001 to recover from the crippling financial collapse of the mid-1990s. As at December 1997 the bank had reserves of 50,546,438m. (old) roubles.
Governor: Viktor Gerashchenko.
Address: ul. Neglinnaya 12, 103016 Moscow.
Telephone: (095) 9243465.
Fax: (095) 9219147.
E-mail: webmaster@www.cbr.ru
Internet: www.cbr.ru

Central Europe

An ill-defined term used generally of the countries between the Baltic and Adriatic seas, and in its adjectival form to describe historic cities such as Prague and Vienna. Changing borders and geopolitical configurations in the area have confused the usage of terms such as central Europe, and indeed eastern and western Europe. Eastern Europe would have been generally taken to include East Germany during the communist period, whereas reunified Germany after 1990 would now be considered an integral part of western Europe. In intellectual terms central Europe now exists as a transitional zone somewhere between the liberal economies of the

'West', with their apparent security, prosperity and established democratic pluralism, and the largely authoritarian and struggling states of the 'East'—the former **Soviet Union** and the **Balkans**—with their so-called 'economies in transition'. In this sense, to become 'central European' is an aspiration, and suggests a greater suitability for entry into the western-dominated world economy, particularly the **European Union**. This loose use of the term is most frequently applied to a group consisting of the **Baltic States, Poland,** the **Czech Republic, Hungary,** and **Slovenia**. However, this is by no means definitive, and by varying political, cultural and geographic criteria **Croatia, Slovakia,** Austria, and even parts of Germany and Italy could be considered central European.

Central European Free Trade Area (CEFTA)

A grouping founded in 1992, which became effective in 1993, to promote trade and co-operation, originally between the **Czech Republic, Hungary, Poland** and **Slovakia**. A fifth member, **Slovenia**, joined from the beginning of 1997, followed in July 1997 by **Romania** and in January 1999 by **Bulgaria**. Of the three **Baltic States, Estonia** and **Latvia** are no longer actively pursuing CEFTA membership, although joining the organization is still one of the declared objectives of **Lithuania**'s policy. **Croatia** is also a candidate but does not yet satisfy the preconditions, which include having free trade agreements in place with all existing members.By 1997 duties on intra-CEFTA trade in industrial products had been abolished apart from specified 'sensitive items'. All CEFTA countries have submitted a request for full **European Union** membership. CEFTA does not have a Secretariat or Head Office. Decisions are adopted within the Joint Committee, whose members are the Ministers of CEFTA countries with jurisdiction over foreign economic relations.
Internet: www.cefta.org

Central European Initiative (CEI)

A sub-regional co-operation initiative in **central** and **eastern Europe**, which originated in 1989 as the 'Pentagonale' group (Austria, **Czechoslovakia**, Italy, **Hungary, Yugoslavia**). It became 'Hexagonale' with the admission of **Poland** in July 1991, and adopted its present name in March 1992. It aims to encourage regional and bilateral co-operation, working within the **Organization for Security and Co-operation in Europe** (OSCE).
Members: 17 eastern and central European countries: **Albania**, Austria, **Belarus, Bosnia and Herzegovina, Bulgaria, Croatia, Czech Republic**, Hungary, Italy, **Macedonia, Moldova**, Poland, **Romania, Slovakia, Slovenia, Ukraine**, Yugoslavia.
Leadership: Harald Kreid (Director-General).

Centre for the Prevention of Conflict (CPC)

Address: CEI Executive Secretariat, Via Genova 9, 34132 Trieste, Italy.
Telephone: (040) 7786777.
Fax: (040) 360640.
E-mail: cei-es@cei-es.org
Internet: www.ceinet.org

Centre for the Prevention of Conflict (CPC)

One of the two main departments of the **Organization for Security and Co-operation in Europe** (OSCE). The Centre was established in Vienna, Austria, in March 1991, following the decision of a summit meeting the previous November. Its main function is to support the OSCE Chairman-in-Office in the implementation of OSCE policies, in particular the monitoring of field activities and co-operation with other international bodies.

CERN *see* **European Organization for Nuclear Research**.

CFE *see* **Conventional Forces in Europe**.

CFTUU *see* **Confederation of Free Trade Unions of Ukraine**.

Chamber of Citizens (Yugoslavia)
Veće Gradjana

The lower house of the **Federal Assembly** of **Yugoslavia**.

Chamber of Commerce and Industry of Azerbaijan

The principal organization in **Azerbaijan** for promoting business contacts, both internally and externally, in the post-communist era.
President: Suleyman Bayram oglu Tatliyev.
Address: Istiglaliyat St 31/33, 370601 Baku.
Telephone: (12) 928912.
Fax: (12) 989324.
E-mail: expo@chamber.baku.az
Internet: www.exhibition.azeri.com

Chamber of Commerce and Industry of Georgia

The principal organization in **Georgia** for promoting business contacts, both internally and externally, in the post-communist era.

Chair.: Guram D. Akhvlediani.
Address: Chavchavadze 11, 380079 Tbilisi.
Telephone: (32) 293375.
Fax: (32) 235760.
E-mail: ktm@ean.kheta.ge
Internet: www.gcci.org.ge

Chamber of Commerce and Industry of Romania and the Municipality of Bucharest

The principal organization in **Romania** for promoting business contacts, both internally and externally, in the post-communist era. Originally founded in 1868.
President: George Cojocaru.
Address: Blvd Octavian Goga 2, Sector 3, Bucharest.
Telephone: (1) 3229516.
Fax: (1) 3229517.
E-mail: ccir@ccir.ro

Chamber of Commerce and Industry of Slovenia

The principal organization in **Slovenia** for promoting business contacts, both internally and externally, in the post-communist era.
President: Jožko Čuk.
Address: Dimičeva 13, 1504 Ljubljana.
Telephone: (1) 5898000.
Fax: (1) 5898100.
E-mail: infolink@hq.gzs.si
Internet: www.gzs.si

Chamber of Commerce and Industry of the Republic of Armenia

The principal organization in **Armenia** for promoting business contacts, both internally and externally, in the post-communist era.
Chair.: Ashot Sarkissian.
Address: Hanrapetoutian St 39, 375033 Yerevan.
Telephone: (1) 565438.
Fax: (1) 565071.

Chamber of Commerce and Industry of the Republic of Moldova

The principal organization in **Moldova** for promoting business contacts, both internally and externally, in the post-communist era. Originally founded in 1969.

Chamber of Commerce and Industry of the Russian Federation

Chair.: Gheorghe Cucu.
Address: Str. M. Eminescu 28, 2012 Chişinau.
Telephone: (2) 221552.
Fax: (2) 241453.
E-mail: inform@chamber.md
Internet: www.chamber.md

Chamber of Commerce and Industry of the Russian Federation

The principal organization in the **Russian Federation** for promoting business contacts, both internally and externally, in the post-communist era. Founded in 1991.
President: Stanislav A. Smirnov.
Address: ul. Ilinka 6, 103684 Moscow.
Telephone: (095) 9290934.
Fax: (095) 9290355.
E-mail: tpprf@tpprf.ru
Internet: www.rbcnet.ru

Chamber of Deputies (Czech Republic)
Poslanecká Sněmovna

The lower house of **Parliament** of the **Czech Republic**.

Chamber of Deputies (Romania)
Camera Deputaţilor

The lower house of the **Parliament of Romania**.

Chamber of Economy of Bosnia and Herzegovina

The principal organization in **Bosnia and Herzegovina** for promoting business contacts, both internally and externally, in the post-communist era.
President: Mensur Smajlović.
Address: Branislava Durdeva 10, 71000 Sarajevo.
Telephone: (33) 663370.
Fax: (33) 663635.
E-mail: cis@komorabih.com
Internet: www.komorabih.com

Chamber of Industry and Trade for Foreign Investors
Izba Przemysłowo-Handlowa Inwestorów Zagranicznych

A private-sector body promoting economic and business contacts; effectively **Poland**'s main externally-oriented Chamber of Commerce.
  Address: ul. Krakowskie Przedmieście 47/51, 00071 Warsaw.
  Telephone: (22) 8261822.
  Fax: (22) 8268593.

Chamber of Republics (Yugoslavia)
Veće Republika

The upper house of the **Federal Assembly** of **Yugoslavia**.

Charter 77

A document drawn up by dissidents in **Czechoslovakia** in 1977, which called for the liberalization and democratization of the communist regime, and spawned a human rights movement by the same name. Charter 77 served as a focal point for the intellectual opposition in Czechoslovakia, and several of its signatories, including Václav **Havel**, emerged as leading political figures in and after the '**velvet revolution**' of 1989. Charter 77 was disbanded in 1992, having 'completed its historical role'.

Charter of Paris for a New Europe

An agreement signed in November 1990 by Heads of Government of the member states of the Conference on Security and Co-operation in Europe (CSCE—*see* **Organization for Security and Co-operation in Europe**) which undertook to strengthen pluralist democracy and observance of human rights, and to settle disputes between participating states by peaceful means.

Chavash Republic

A constituent republic of the **Russian Federation** situated on the west bank of the Volga river in central **European Russia**. It was renamed the Chavash Republic in June 2001, having been previously known as Chuvashia. *Population*: 1.3m. (1997 estimate). The region was incorporated into the Russian Empire in the 16th century. Unlike in other ethnic republics, **Russians** form only a small minority, less than 30%, and the republic is dominated by the agriculturalist Chavash people, a mixed ethnic group combining Bolgars, **Turkic peoples**, and **Finno-Ugric** groups. The Chavash language is of the Uralo-Altaic branch of Turkic, and is renowned as

107

the only surviving dialect of the ancient language of the Bolgars. Alone among Europe's Turkic peoples the Chavash follow Eastern **Orthodox Christianity**. Outside the Chavash Republic there are significant Chavash minorities notably in **Tatarstan** (130,000) and **Bashkortostan** (119,000).

Chavashia became an autonomous *oblast* (region) within the **Soviet Union** in 1920 and achieved full republic status in 1925. The republic escaped the excesses of industrialization as visited upon some of the other **Volga region** states but its urban areas did undergo considerable development. However, the economy is still largely based on exploitation of key natural resources, particularly the abundant forest, which covers one-third of the land area, and mineral deposits such as phosphorites and carbonates. The revival of Chavash culture in the 19th century was suppressed by the Soviet regime and only revived during *glasnost* in the late 1980s. A Chavash sovereign republic within the Russian Federation was declared on 31 March 1992. The capital is Cheboksary. Nikolay Vasilyevich Fyodorov was re-elected for a third four-year term as President of Chavashia in December 2001.

Chechnya
Ichkeria

A constituent republic of the **Russian Federation** situated in the north-east **Caucasus** region, and the scene of two protracted wars with **Russian** forces from 1994. Known in Chechen as Ichkeria. *Population*: 1.2m. (1989 estimate including **Ingushetia**).

Dominated by the Caucasian and **Muslim** Chechen people (known to themselves as the Nokhchuo), the region resisted Russian control in the mid-19th century and again in the Russian Civil War (1918–20), but succumbed to the Bolshevik victory and was constituted as an autonomous *oblast* (region) in 1922, before being amalgamated with neighbouring **Ingushetia** in 1934. The two remained joined as a Checheno-Ingush republic from 1936 until 1992. Chechens and Ingush were deported *en masse* by Stalin in 1944 but rehabilitated under Khrushchev in 1956 (*see* **Deported Nationalities**).

A Chechen nationalist movement arose in the late 1980s. In 1991, in the face of nationalist opposition led by former **Soviet** air force general Dzhokhar Dudayev, the communist Government of Checheno-Ingushetia collapsed and a separate Chechen republic, known as Ichkeria, was declared. Plans by Russian President Boris **Yeltsin** to despatch forces to restore 'order' in the republic were undermined by the strongly independent Supreme Soviet, which refused to endorse the strategy. Tensions between Chechens and Ingush in the republic led to the creation of a separate Ingush republic in 1992.

Dudayev's increasingly authoritarian rule provoked strong internal division in Chechnya. His dissolution of the Chechen Parliament in 1993 led to a full-scale civil war. The anti-Dudayev forces received covert support from the Russian Federation, but by December 1994 the campaign to oust Dudayev had failed. Yeltsin, his leadership in Russia re-energized by the defeat of an attempted hardline coup, was not held back from ordering a full-scale invasion of the breakaway republic by the newly-resurrected **Duma**. Despite very heavy losses on both sides, the Russian army emerged ostensibly victorious, having effectively levelled the Chechen capital Grozny in a prolonged siege. A cease-fire was signed in 1996 and by early 1997 Russian forces had been largely withdrawn. Later that year Aslan Maskhadov was elected as the new President of Chechnya.

By 1999 the situation had deteriorated once again. The declaration of an Islamic state in Chechnya, the lending of Chechen tactical support to Islamic insurgents in nearby **Dagestan**, and terrorist attacks in the Russian Federation blamed on Chechen extremists, prompted Yeltsin's new Prime Minister (and future successor) Vladimir **Putin** to order another full-scale invasion that winter. By early 2000 Russian forces again proclaimed victory but intense Chechen guerrilla activity subsequently told another story. It was estimated in mid-2000 that an average of 160 Russian soldiers were being killed every day by Chechen guerrillas. Direct rule of the republic was imposed from Moscow and the pro-Russian Mufti Akhmed Kadyrov was appointed as administrator. Putin capitalized on the Russian nationalism generated by the rapid 'success' of his invasion, securing his own election as President in March 2000, but by the end of the year he was suffering the same negative press as had Yeltsin in 1995–96. By January 2001 the security situation had worsened to the stage where Putin handed over control of Chechnya's security to the **Federal Security Service** (FSB), under its Director Nikolai Patrushev. Human rights campaigners and the international community joined to condemn the 1999–2000 invasion.

From 1996 the pro-Russian administration has been based in the town of Gudermes, east of the ruined Grozny. Economic activity has traditionally focused on oil refining, for which Grozny's facilities had been among the largest in the **Soviet Union**.

Cherkess
(also known as Circassians)

A **Muslim** Caucasian people closely related to other north Caucasian groups, particularly the Adygei (*see* **Adygeya**) and Kabards (*see* **Kabardino-Balkaria**), and concentrated in the **Russian** republic of **Karachai-Cherkessia**. 'Circassian' is a term originally used to describe all related north-west Caucasians, but later limited to these related three, and finally just the Cherkess. They are considered indigenous to the region and have a long chronicled history of interaction with local powerbrokers. When the Russian Empire exerted its influence over the entire region the Cherkess were among the peoples who resisted. By 1864 the Caucasian rebellion was suppressed and the Cherkess became Russian vassals. Thousands fled to Muslim countries to the south. Under **Soviet** rule the Cherkess were classified as a distinct ethnic group and given the opportunity to develop their language and culture within the repressive bounds of the regime. The Cherkess of Karachai-Cherkessia have led calls for the unification of the 'Circassian' peoples.

Chernobyl

A now defunct nuclear power station in northern **Ukraine** which was the scene of the world's worst nuclear accident in 1986. Human error and poor design (Chernobyl used RBMK water-cooled graphite-moderated reactors of a **Soviet** design) led to two explosions during a safety test at the plant's No. 4 reactor on 25 April 1986. The resultant release of radioactive material contaminated the atmosphere, sent a cloud of pollution across northern Europe, and led to the eventual evacuation of over 200 villages in the surrounding area. Neighbouring **Belarus** was particularly badly affected by radioactive contamination and loss of agricultural land. In dealing with the emergency, containing and extinguishing the fire and conducting a clean-up operation, over 600,000 'liquidators' were exposed to high levels of radiation, leading to at least 31 deaths. Estimates of longer-term casualties from exposure to radiation varied widely. Incidences of treatable thyroid cancer among 1,750 local children appear to have been a direct effect of the disaster, and scientists reported in October 2000 an alarmingly high number of genetic mutations among plant life in the region. While the remains of the No. 4 reactor were encased in a concrete shell, the other reactors at Chernobyl continued to operate, providing much needed energy to Ukraine. A timetable for the plant's complete closure was not agreed until April 2000 and the last operational reactor was finally shut down on 15 December 2000. International donors have pledged US $768m. to help safeguard the plant, and the **European Union** has provided funding for the construction of new nuclear power plants to make up the shortfall in the energy supply.

Chetniks

The name originally given to the **Serb** nationalist and royalist guerrillas, led by Draza Mihailovic, who fought in **Yugoslavia** during the Second World War both against the German/Italian occupation forces and against the rival communist **Yugoslav** Partisans led by **Tito**. The term, which carries associations from this period of Serb atrocities against other Yugoslav nationalities, has more recently been applied to Serb militias fighting **Bosniaks** and **Croats** in the Bosnian civil war in the first half of the 1990s.

Chişinău

Capital city of **Moldova,** situated on a tributary of the Dnester river. *Population*: 667,100 (1992 estimate). The city was sacked during the retreat of German and

Romanian troops at the end of the Second World War. Like many industrialized centres in the country it attracted a large population of ethnic **Russians** during the period of **Soviet** rule.

Christian Democrat International (CDI)

An organization founded in 1961 as a platform for the co-operation of political parties of Christian Social inspiration.
Members: Parties in 64 countries.
Leadership: José María Aznar (President).
Address: rue d'Arlon 67, B-1040 Brussels, Belgium.
Telephone: (2) 2854160.
Fax: (2) 2854166.
E-mail: idc@idc-cdi.org
Internet: www.idc-cdi.org

Christian Democratic National Peasants' Party
Partidul Național Țaranesc Creștin Democrat (PNȚCD)

The leading party in the centre-right coalition which held power in **Romania** from 1996 to 2000, affiliated to the **Christian Democrat International**. The PNȚCD is descended from the National Peasants' Party (PNȚ) founded in 1869, which was of political importance in the inter-war period and was banned by the communists in 1947. Revived in December 1989 under veteran leader Ion Puiu, the PNȚ refused to co-operate with the post-communist National Salvation Front (FSN) because it was dominated by former communists. Prior to the May 1990 elections the bulk of the historic PNȚ merged with a Christian democratic peasant faction to form the PNȚCD on a pro-market platform which also favoured the restoration of the monarchy and the recovery of **Romanian**-populated territories lost during the Second World War. The new party's first leader was Corneliu Coposu, another veteran peasant leader who had served 17 years in prison under the communist regime before becoming Prime Minister in its final phase.

Having won 12 seats in the Chamber of Deputies (lower house of **Parliament**) in 1990, the PNȚCD, as a leading component of the broad centre-right Democratic Convention of Romania (CDR), advanced to 42 seats in September 1992. Coposu died in November 1995 and was succeeded by Ion Diaconescu, who led the PNȚCD and the CDR to a relative victory in the November 1996 elections, in which CDR candidate Emil Constantinescu was elected President with 54.4% of the second-round vote and the PNȚCD won 88 of the CDR's 122 Chamber seats. Victor Ciorbea of the PNȚCD became Prime Minister of a centre-right coalition, which included the **Democratic Party**, the **National Liberal Party** and the

Hungarian Democratic Union of Romania (UDMR), but inter-party feuding resulted in his replacement by Radu Vasile of the PNȚCD in March 1998.

Ciorbea reacted to being ousted by launching the breakaway Christian Democratic National Alliance (ANCD) in April 1999, as the PNȚCD-led Government descended into increasing disarray amidst accelerating economic and social deterioration. In August 2000 the PNȚCD and four other parties relaunched the CDR, but in the November elections the so-called 'CDR 2000' and its allies failed to surmount the 5% threshold for representation, while PNȚCD-backed independent presidential candidate Mugur Isarescu came a poor fourth with 9.5% of the first-round vote. In January 2001 Diaconescu was succeeded as PNȚCD Chairman by former Education Minister Andrei Marga, who quickly secured the return of Ciorbea's ANCD (also now unrepresented) into the party as part of his aim of uniting peasant forces in opposition to the new Government of the **Social Democratic Pole of Romania**. However, tensions within the PNȚCD led to Marga's resignation and his replacement by former Prime Minister Ciorbea in July 2001. Marga went on to form the separate Popular Christian Party in October.

Leadership: Victor Ciorbea (Chair.).
Address: Blvd Carol I 34, Bucharest 73231.
Telephone: (1) 3143277.
Fax: (1) 3121303.
E-mail: secretariat@pntcd.ro
Internet: www.pntcd.ro

Christian Democratic People's Party
Partidul Popular Creștin și Democrat (PPCD)

A centre-right party in **Moldova** which originally favoured unification with **Romania** but now accepts the post-Soviet status quo. The party was founded in 1992 as the Christian Democratic People's Front (FPCD) and the successor of the radical pan-Romanian wing of the Popular Front of Moldova, which had been the dominant political grouping during the collapse of Soviet communist rule in mid-1991. Preferring to call Moldova by the historic name **Bessarabia**, the FPCD saw independence as the first step towards the 'sacred goal' of reunification with Romania. Under the new leadership of Iurie Roșca, the FPCD shared in the defeat of pro-Romanian parties in the first multi-party **Parliament** elections in February 1994, winning nine seats on a vote share of 7.5%.

Having backed the unsuccessful re-election bid of Mircea Snegur in the late 1996 presidential elections, the FPCD was in June 1997 a founder component of the Democratic Convention of Moldova (CDM), which included Snegur's Party of Revival and Accord of Moldova (PRCM). In the March 1998 legislative elections the CDM won only 26 seats with 19.2% of the vote and was outpolled by the revived **Communist Party of the Moldovan Republic** (PCRM); but the CDM and other centre-right formations were able to form a coalition Government which included FPCD representation.

The FPCD broke with the CDM and the centre-right coalition in March 1999 when it joined the PCRM in voting against the installation of Ion Sturza as Prime Minister. In opposition, the FPCD in December 1999 changed its name to Christian Democratic People's Party (PPCD) and adopted a new basic programme calling for 'integration within a Europe of nations and the fulfilment of national unity' (instead of its previous advocacy of 'the national unity of all Romanians in Romania and Moldova'). In early parliamentary elections in February 2001, in which the PCRM obtained a landslide majority, the PPCD was one of only two other parties to gain representation, winning 11 seats with 8.3% of the vote.

Leadership: Iurie Roşca (Chair.).
Address: Str. Nicolae Iorga 5, Chişinau.
Telephone: (2) 234547.
Fax: (2) 234480.
E-mail: magic@cni.md
Internet: ppcd.dnt.md/romana/titlu.htm

Christian Democratic Union–Czechoslovak People's Party
Křestánská a Demokratická Uniei–Československá Strana Lidová
(KDU–ČSL)

A Catholic-oriented centrist party in the **Czech Republic**, affiliated to the **Christian Democrat International** and the **International Democrat Union**. The KDU–ČSL is descended from the main inter-war Catholic party, which was represented in several Governments in **Czechoslovakia** until its dissolution in late 1938. Revived as a component of the communist-dominated National Front in 1945, the then Czechoslovak People's Party (ČSL) was allowed to continue in existence as a Front party after the communists took sole power in 1948. On the collapse of communist rule in late 1989, the ČSL became an independent pro-democracy formation and joined a broad-based coalition Government appointed in December 1989. The party contested the elections of June 1990 in an alliance called the Christian Democratic Union (KDU), which won nine of the 101 Czech seats in the federal lower house and was included in the post-1990 Czech coalition Government. Following the departure of the Christian Democratic Party (KDS) to form an alliance with the new **Civic Democratic Party** (ODS), in April 1992 the remaining constituents officially became the KDU–ČSL, which in the June 1992 elections won 15 seats in the Czech National Council (with 6.3% of the vote). The party became a member of the ODS-led Czech coalition Government which took the Republic to separate independence in January 1993. However, the party's residual preference for the federation with Slovakia was apparent in the retention of 'Czechoslovak' in its combined title.

Following the separation, the KDU–ČSL came out in favour of a free enterprise system and Czech membership of Western economic and security structures. In late 1995 its parliamentary party was strengthened by the defection to it of five KDS deputies opposed to their party's decision to merge with the ODS. In the mid-1996 elections to the lower house of **Parliament** the KDU–ČSL won 18 seats on a vote share of 8.1% and was included in another ODS-led Government, now with minority status. Growing political and economic troubles in 1997 impelled the KDU–ČSL and the other junior coalition party to withdraw in November 1997, causing the Government's resignation, following which the party was represented in a transitional administration pending new elections.

In the early lower house elections in June 1998 the KDU–ČSL improved to 20 lower house seats and 9% of the vote, but went into opposition to a minority Government headed by the **Czech Social Democratic Party**. In June 1999 long-time Party Chairman Josef Lux was succeeded by Jan Kasal, who took the KDU–ČSL into an opposition Coalition of Four with the **Freedom Union** and two other centrist parties. The Coalition of Four planned to present a joint list of candidates and prospective ministerial team in the 2002 elections. In the November 2000 partial Senate elections the KDU–ČSL advanced strongly within the opposition alliance, becoming the second-largest party with 21 of the 81 seats. In January 2001 KDU–ČSL Deputy Chairman Cyril Svoboda was unexpectedly elected leader of the Coalition of Four, ahead of the party's official candidate Jaroslav Kopriva, and went on to take the chairmanship of KDU–ČSL in May 2001.

Leadership: Cyril Svoboda (Chair.).
Address: Karlovo nám. 5, 12801 Prague 2.
Telephone: (2) 24914826.
Fax: (2) 24917630.
Internet: www.kdu.cz

Christian Labour Confederation
Křestanská Odborova Koalice (KOK)

A Christian democratic-oriented trade union centre in the **Czech Republic**, affiliated to the World Confederation of Labour (WCL). KOK has remained much smaller than the mainstream **Czech-Moravian Confederation of Trade Unions** (ČMKOS).

Chair.: Anton Alois.
Address: 24 nám. Senovážné, 11000 Prague 3.
Telephone: (2) 24102450.
E-mail: KokAnton@Telecom.cz

Chuvash Republic (Chuvashia) *see* **Chavash Republic**.

Cimoszewicz, Włodzimierz

Minister of Foreign Affairs, **Poland**.

Włodzimierz Cimoszewicz is a member of the **Democratic Left Alliance** (SLD). He held many posts within the Soviet-era administration and was an active member of the Polish United Workers' Party (PZPR). He entered government as Deputy Prime Minister and Minister of Justice in 1993, and was Prime Minister in 1996–97. He was appointed Foreign Minister on 19 October 2001.

Born on 13 September 1950 in **Warsaw**, he graduated in law from Warsaw University in 1972 and went on to receive a doctorate from the same institution in 1978. He had joined communist student organizations in 1968, and graduated to membership of the PZPR in 1971. Having fulfilled a scholarship to the USA in 1981, he returned to Poland to work as an assistant professor, but left academia altogether in 1985 to become a farmer. He returned to the political scene in 1989 as a parliamentary deputy for the PZPR, and joined its successor, Social Democracy of the Republic of Poland, in 1990. He stood, unsuccessfully, as the party's candidate in presidential elections that year against the victorious Lech **Wałęsa**. After electoral victory for the left in 1993 he was appointed to the Cabinet as Deputy Prime Minister and Minister of Justice, but dropped his official party affiliations when elected Deputy Speaker of the **National Assembly** in 1995. He retained his nominal political independence when appointed Prime Minister on 7 February 1996. His Government was defeated in elections in late 1997, but when the SLD (of which he was now a member) achieved its landslide win in elections in September 2001 he was appointed Foreign Minister.

Address: Ministry of Foreign Affairs, Al. Szucha 23, 00580 Warsaw.
Telephone: (22) 5239000.
Fax: (22) 6298635.
E-mail: poland@mfa.gov.pl
Internet: www.msz.gov.pl

Circassians *see* **Cherkess**.

CIS *see* **Commonwealth of Independent States**.

Citizens' Platform
Platforma Obywatelska (PO)

A centrist political formation in **Poland** launched in January 2001. The principal founders of the PO were Maciej Plazyński, Speaker of the *Sejm* (lower house of the **National Assembly**) and hitherto a member of the then ruling **Solidarity Electoral Action** (AWS); Donald Tusk, Deputy Speaker of the *Senat* (upper house) and hitherto a member of the **Freedom Union** (UW); and independent politician Andrzej Olechowski, who had come second in the 2000 presidential election with 17.3% of the vote. Declaring its basic aim as being to prevent the **Democratic Left Alliance** (SLD) from regaining power in the autumn 2001 parliamentary elections, the new formation quickly attracted substantial support from within both the UW and the AWS. The PO was the second-placed party in the Sejm elections, winning 65 seats (and 12.7% of the vote), but a long way behind the SLD-led coalition. In the Senat elections PO candidates stood as part of the Blok Senat 2001, which won 15 seats.

Leadership: Andrzej Olechowski, Donald Tusk and Maciej Plazyński.
Address: c/o Zgromadzenie Narodowe, ul. Wiejska 6/8, Warsaw 00902.

Citizens' Union of Georgia
Sakartvelos Mokalaketa Kavshiri (SMK)

Georgia's ruling party for most of the post-independence period, essentially a **nomenklatura**-based formation although it is an observer member of the **Socialist International**.

The SMK was established in November 1993 by Head of State Eduard **Shevardnadze**. Initially an umbrella organization, it quickly attracted support from other pro-democracy and pro-market formations. In November 1995, when Shevardnadze was re-elected President by an overwhelming popular majority, the concurrent legislative elections gave the SMK the dominant position in the new Parliament with approximately half of the seats. It increased its advantage in the 1999 parliamentary elections, winning 130 of the 227 seats filled (with 41.7% of the vote) on a platform promising an improvement in economic conditions, increased wages and prompt payment of pensions.

In the April 2000 presidential election, which was boycotted by the main opposition leader, Shevardnadze also set the improvement of economic and social conditions as a primary goal and was re-elected with an overwhelming 78.8% of the vote. It was confirmed that in the external sphere the key objectives of a new SMK Government headed by Giorgi Arsenishvili would be admittance to the **European Union** and the **North Atlantic Treaty Organization**. Following the presidential contest, a number of SMK and allied members of Parliament, including the 12-strong Abkhazeti Bloc representing ethnic **Georgian** refugees from **Abkhazia**, resigned from the SMK parliamentary group in protest against various decisions by the leadership. In December 2001 Arsenishvili was dismissed as State Minister, along with the rest of the Cabinet, over a much-criticized raid on the 'tax-evading' television station Rustavi-2. He was replaced by an independent.

Leadership: Eduard Shevardnadze (Chair.).
Address: Marshal Gelovani 4, Tbilisi.
Telephone: (32) 959825.
Fax: (32) 958325.
E-mail: cug@access.sanet.ge

CITUC *see* **Confederation of Independent Trade Unions of Croatia**.

Civic Alliance of Serbia
Gradjanski Savez Srbije (GSS)

A radical liberal party in **Yugoslavia** forming part of the **Democratic Opposition of Serbia** (DOS). The GSS was created in 1992 by peace campaigner Vesna Pešić, who was elected to the Serbian Assembly in 1993 within the DEPOS opposition coalition. It subsequently joined the Zajedno (Together) alliance with the **Democratic Party** (DS), the **Democratic Party of Serbia** (DSS) and the **Serbian Renewal Movement** (SPO), which won 22 lower house seats in the November 1996 **Federal Assembly** elections, but boycotted the Serbian Assembly elections in September 1997 in protest against media manipulation by the **Milošević** regime. In late 1998 the GSS joined a new opposition grouping called the Alliance for Change, which formed the core of the anti-Milošević DOS alliance launched in January 2000, by which time Pešić had left the country and had been succeeded as GSS President by Goran **Svilanović**. When the DOS alliance came to power in October 2000, Svilanović was appointed Foreign Minister in the Federal Government.

Leadership: Goran Svilanović (President).
Address: Terazije 3/8, Belgrade 11000.
Telephone: (11) 3341696.
Fax: (11) 3341478.
E-mail: infocentar@gradjanskisavez.org.yu
Internet: www.gradjanskisavez.org.yu

Civic Democratic Party
Občanská Demokratická Strana (ODS)

The leading centre-right political formation in the **Czech Republic**, affiliated to the **International Democrat Union**, and founded in February 1991 as a result of a split in the original pro-democracy **Civic Forum**.

Under the leadership of Federal Finance Minister Václav **Klaus** the ODS quickly built a strong organization and concluded an electoral alliance with the Christian Democratic Party (KDS). In the June 1992 elections the ODS/KDS combination became the leading formation both at federal level and in the Czech National Council. The resultant Czech-Slovak federal coalition was headed by Jan Stráský (ODS), while Klaus preferred to take the Czech premiership at the head of a coalition which included the KDS and the **Christian Democratic Union–Czechoslovak People's Party** (KDU–ČSL).

The ODS-led Government moved swiftly to implement the party's economic reform programme, including wholesale privatization of the state sector, especially in the Czech Lands. However, the party's main immediate concern was the constitutional question and, in particular, the gulf between the Slovak demand for sovereignty within a federation and the Czech Government's view that preservation of the federation only made sense if it had a real role. The failure of Václav **Havel** to secure re-election as President in July 1992, owing to Slovak opposition in the Federal Assembly, served to harden attitudes. The outcome was a formal separation as from the beginning of 1993, when the Czech coalition headed by the ODS became the Government of the independent Czech Republic, with Klaus as Prime Minister. In January 1993 Havel was elected President of the new Republic on the proposal of the ODS and its government allies.

In November 1995 the ODS voted in favour of a formal merger with the KDS (under the ODS party name), although the decision of half of the 10-strong KDS parliamentary party to join the KDU–ČSL rather than the ODS reduced the impact of the merger. The ODS lost ground in the mid-1996 elections to the lower house of the **Parliament**, winning only 68 seats on a 29.6% vote share. Klaus was nevertheless reappointed Prime Minister of a further centre-right coalition, now with minority status and dependent on the qualified external support of the **Czech Social Democratic Party** (ČSSD). Mounting difficulties in 1997, including a major financial crisis in May and allegations that the ODS had accepted illegal funding, led to the resignation of the Klaus Government in November.

Although Havel secured parliamentary re-election as President in January 1998 on the proposal of the ODS, divisions in the party resulted in the creation of the breakaway **Freedom Union** (US) and a sharp decline in ODS membership. In early lower house elections in June 1998 the ODS slipped to 63 seats and 27.7% of the vote, being overtaken by the ČSSD. It opted thereafter to give external support to the resultant ČSSD minority Government, thus ending its previous centre-right alliance. In partial Senate elections in November 2000 the ODS won eight seats (its representation in the 81-member upper chamber falling to 22), while in simultaneous regional elections its vote share fell to 23.8%. In January 2001 Klaus dismissed as 'nonsense' reports that the ODS was preparing to terminate the so-called 'opposition agreement' with the ruling ČSSD.

Leadership: Václav Klaus (Chair.).
Address: Sněmovní 3, 11800 Prague 1.
Telephone: (2) 3114800.
Fax: (2) 3118273.
E-mail: info@ods.cz
Internet: www.ods.cz

Civic Forum
Občanská Fórum (OF)

The Czech-dominated pro-democracy movement launched in **Czechoslovakia** in November 1989 by various anti-communist groups, notably the **Charter 77** movement, under the acknowledged leadership of dissident playwright Václav **Havel**.

Together with its Slovak counterpart **Public Against Violence**, it brought about the '**velvet revolution**', quickly forcing the then regime to give up sole state power. In December 1989 Havel was elected President by a Federal Assembly still dominated by communists, while the OF itself triumphed in the Czech Lands in the June 1990 Czechoslovak elections. It then entered a federal coalition Government with other pro-democracy parties and headed the Czech Government. In October 1990 Federal Finance Minister Václav **Klaus** was elected as the first official Chairman of the OF, but internal divisions resulted in February 1991 in Klaus and his supporters formally launching the **Civic Democratic Party**.

Civil Unity Party
Ventendash Birliyi Partiyasi (VBP)

A political party in **Azerbaijan** relaunched in April 2000 as the vehicle of ex-President Ayaz Mutalibov, the hardline leader of the **Soviet**-era **Azerbaijan Communist Party** who had lived in exile in Moscow since May 1992.

The VBP was among the first parties to be registered for the November 2000 **National Assembly** elections, which it contested as the leading component of the Democratic Azerbaijan bloc. It was officially stated to have just surmounted the 6% barrier to representation in the proportional section of the balloting, winning three seats.

Mutalibov was formally elected Chairman at the party's second congress in December 2000 and declared his intention to contest the presidential elections due in 2003. In mid-January 2001 the VBP announced jointly with the 'reformist' wing of the **Azerbaijan Popular Front** that its three deputies would participate in the work of the new Assembly, but in order to campaign for new elections.

Leadership: Ayaz Mutalibov (Chair.).
Address: c/o Milli Majlis, 1 Parliamentary Avenue, Baku 370152.
E-mail: office@vbp-az.org
Internet: www.vbp-az.org

CMEA *see* **Council for Mutual Economic Assistance**.

ČMKOS *see* **Czech-Moravian Confederation of Trade Unions**.

CNS–Carta Alfa *see* **Alpha Cartel National Trade Union Confederation**

CNSLR–Fratia *see* **Fratia National Confederation of Free Trade Unions of Romania**.

Cold War

A phrase in common usage from 1947, describing the protracted period of post-war antagonism between the communist bloc, particularly the **Soviet Union**, and the West, led by the USA. Sir Winston Churchill's March 1946 speech at Fulton in Missouri, USA, when he warned of the threat of Soviet expansion and of an 'iron curtain' falling across Europe, and the subsequent Soviet imposition of communism in east-central Europe, are usually offered as starting points of the Cold War. The two blocs fought a vigorous propaganda battle in which each sought to discredit its rival and to gain prestige for itself. The balance of terror which followed the Soviet Union's development of the atomic bomb led the blocs to avoid direct military conflict, although there were several dangerous confrontations. Much conflict took place by proxy: one bloc funded and trained indigenous military groups to engage opposing forces when it appeared that the rival bloc was likely to extend its sphere of influence, for instance in Afghanistan. The Cold War forced the two blocs to maintain their readiness for a possible 'hot war'; the expense of the resulting arms race eventually helped to bankrupt the Soviet Union. The appointment in 1985 of Mikhail **Gorbachev** as General Secretary of the **Communist Party of the Soviet Union** marked the beginning of a rapprochement with the West, which was confirmed with the Soviet decision in 1989 not to intervene when the communist regimes in eastern Europe were collapsing. Three of the clearest symbols of the ending of the Cold War were the beginning of work on 2 May 1989 to dismantle the 'iron curtain' barrier between **Hungary** and Austria, the opening in November 1989 of the Berlin Wall, and the final dissolution in 1991 of the **Warsaw Pact**—the military alliance between the former communist bloc countries.

Comecon *see* **Council for Mutual Economic Assistance**.

Commonwealth of Independent States (CIS)

The Commonwealth of Independent States is a voluntary association of 12 (originally 11) states, established at their independence at the time of the collapse of the **Soviet Union** on 21 December 1991, and joined by a 12th, **Georgia**, in December 1993. Its Charter was adopted formally by the Council of Heads of States on 22 January 1993. Preoccupied initially with arms control and collective security issues, the CIS developed institutionally with the signature of treaties on Collective Security (Tashkent, May 1992) and on Economic Union (Moscow, September 1993). CIS peacekeeping forces operated in Tajikistan until the end of the 1990s and also in **Abkhazia**. A programme on combating terrorism was adopted at the CIS's Moscow summit in June 2000, including the establishment of a CIS anti-terrorism centre.

Members: **Armenia**, **Azerbaijan**, **Belarus**, Georgia, Kazakhstan, Kyrgyzstan, **Moldova**, **Russian Federation**, Tajikistan, Turkmenistan, **Ukraine** and Uzbekistan.
Leadership: Yurii Yarov (Executive Secretary).
Address: Kirava 17, 220000 Minsk, Belarus.
Telephone: (17) 2223517.
Fax: (17) 2272339.
E-mail: postmaster@www.cis.minsk.by
Internet: www.cis.minsk.by

Communist Party of Armenia
Hayastani Komunistakan Kusaktsutyun (HKK)

Armenia's sole ruling party in the **Soviet** era, still influential, although many of its former members in the state bureaucracy have joined other parties.

The HKK managed only second place in multi-party legislative elections in 1990 and was suspended in September 1991. Relegalized in 1994, it came a poor third in the 1995 **National Assembly** elections. In the 1996 presidential elections the then party leader Sergei Badalian also came third, with 6.3% of the vote. He stood again in the 1998 presidential contest, winning 11% in the first round but coming only fourth.

The HKK's call for Armenia's accession to the new **Belarus-Russia Union** was an important plank in its platform for the May 1999 Assembly elections, in which it took second place with 12.1% of the proportional vote and 11 of the 131 seats. Badalian died of a heart attack in Moscow in November 1999 and was succeeded in January 2000 by Vladimir Darbinian, who had been Armenian SSR Interior Minister in the 1970s. The following month the HKK joined the Government (headed by the **Republican Party of Armenia**) for the first time since losing power in 1990.

Leadership: Vladimir Darbinian (First Secretary);
    Hrant Voskanian (Chairman of Parliamentary Group).
Address: 22 Khorenatsi Street, Yerevan.
Telephone: (1) 567933.
Fax: (1) 523506.

Communist Party of Belarus
Kommunisticheskaya Partiya Belarusi (KPB)

The largest party in **Belarus** since 1995, directly descended from the Soviet-era ruling party. The KPB had originated as a regional committee of the Russian Social Democratic Labour Party (formed in 1904) covering both Belarus and **Lithuania**. Established as the ruling Communist Party of the Soviet Socialist

Republic of Byelorussia in 1920, the party suffered greatly during Stalin's purges of the 1930s, when almost all of its leaders were liquidated and party membership fell by more than half. Enlarged by Soviet territorial acquisitions from **Poland** in the Second World War, the Byelorussian SSR was given UN membership in 1945, but its ruling party and Government remained wholly subservient to Moscow.

From mid-1989 the republican leadership came under official Soviet criticism for not being ready to make compromises with the pro-democracy movement. It therefore allowed candidates of what became the **Belarusian Popular Front–Renaissance** (NFB–A) to contest the April 1990 Supreme Soviet elections, while ensuring that a decisive KPB victory was recorded. The conservative Minsk leadership, however, then unwisely backed the abortive **August coup** by hardliners in Moscow in 1991, following which the hardline republican Head of State, Mikalay Dzemyantsei, was replaced by the reformist Stanislau Shushkevich, who declared independence from the Soviet Union. The KPB itself was suspended and its property was nationalized.

The party remained under suspension for 18 months, although the government structure and the legislature continued to be under the control of persons appointed or elected as communists. At government level, Shushkevich came into increasingly bitter dispute with the hardline Prime Minister, Vyacheslau Kebich, who commanded majority support from the so-called Belarus Group of conservative deputies for his resistance to political and economic reform. The relegalization of the KPB in February 1993 did little to clarify political allegiances, in part because government members preferred to retain the 'independent' label. Moreover, a KPB leadership dispute led to the creation by Viktar Chykin in October 1993 of the Movement for Democracy, Social Progress and Justice as a merger of seven hardline communist groups. At the same time, the various KPB factions came under the umbrella of the Popular Movement of Belarus (NDB), a loose alliance of conservative parties which backed the ousting of Shushkevich as Head of State in January 1994 and his replacement by hardliner Mechislau Gryb.

Having embraced multi-partyism, the mainstream KPB contested the June–July 1994 presidential elections in its own right. Its candidate was the then Chairman Vasil Novikau, who was placed last of six contenders in the first round, winning only 4.5% of the vote. However, forecasts that **'nomenklatura** power' would ensure victory for Kebich (standing as an independent) proved to be badly mistaken: relegated to a poor second place in the first round, he was heavily defeated in the second by another independent, Alyaksandr **Lukashenka**, a moderate but increasingly authoritarian conservative who as anti-corruption supremo had played a key role in the ousting of Shushkevich.

The KPB's organizational strength enabled it to become the largest formal party in the 1995 legislative elections, in which it won 42 seats. Having established his leadership of the rump KPB, Chykin in September 1998 became Executive Secretary of the pro-Lukashenka **Belarusian People's Patriotic Union** (BNPS), grouping some 30 conservative parties which backed the **Belarus-Russia Union** treaty.

In elections to the House of Representatives (the lower house of the **National Assembly**) in October 2000 the BNPS and its allies obtained near-total ascendancy, amidst opposition and external claims of electoral manipulation and fraud.
Leadership: Viktar Chykin (Chair.).
Address: 52 Varanyanskaga Street, Minsk 22007.
Telephone: (17) 2266422.
Fax: (17) 2323123.

Communist Party of Bohemia and Moravia
Komunistická Strana Čech a Moravy (KSČM)

A party in the **Czech Republic**, founded under its present name in March 1990, which is directly descended from the former ruling Communist Party of Czechoslovakia (KSČ).

The KSČ was founded in 1921 by the pro-Bolshevik wing of the **Czech Social Democratic Party** (ČSSD) and was the only east European communist party to retain legal status in the 1930s, under the leadership of Klement Gottwald. It was eventually banned, as a gesture of appeasement to Nazi Germany, its leaders mostly taking refuge in Moscow. They returned at the end of the Second World War in the wake of the Red Army as the dominant element of a National Front of democratic parties and in the 1946 elections became the largest party in the Czech Lands and the second strongest in **Slovakia**. Gottwald became Prime Minister and a government crisis of February 1948 enabled the KSČ to assume sole power, although most other Front parties were allowed to remain in existence in a subservient role throughout the subsequent 40 years of communist rule.

Purges of the KSČ leadership in 1951 in the wake of the Soviet–Yugoslav breach led to show trials and the execution of 11 prominent communists in 1952. Among the victims was Rudolf Slánský, who had succeeded Gottwald as party leader when the latter became President in 1948. Following Gottwald's sudden death in 1953, Antonín Novotný was elected to the revived post of party leader and later became President. Nikita Khrushchev's denunciation of Stalin in 1956 resulted in the rehabilitation of most of those executed in **Czechoslovakia** in 1952 and also of those imprisoned in that era, including Gustáv **Husák**. Pressure for political reform grew in the 1960s within and outside the party. In January 1968 Novotný was replaced as KSČ leader by Alexander **Dubček**, hitherto Slovak party leader, and as President by Gen. Ludvík Svoboda.

In the short-lived '**Prague Spring**', the KSČ central committee in April 1968 elected a new presidium dominated by reformers and promised democratization of the government system (although not multi-partyism), freedom of assembly, the press, foreign travel and religion, curbs on the security police (**StB**), rehabilitation of previous purge victims, and autonomy for Slovakia. This 'socialism with a human face' alarmed the Soviet leadership and its **Warsaw Pact** satellites. Increasing pressure on the Prague reformers culminated in the military occupation of

Czechoslovakia in August 1968 by forces of the **Soviet Union**, East Germany, **Poland**, **Hungary** and **Bulgaria**, on the grounds that they had been invited in by KSČ leaders, including Husák, who believed that the reform movement was out of control. Dubček and his immediate supporters were taken to Moscow as prisoners. They were quickly released on the insistence of President Svoboda, but the reform movement was effectively over. After anti-Soviet riots in early 1969, Husák replaced Dubček as party leader and initiated a major purge of reformist elements, those expelled from the party including Dubček himself.

Over the following two decades Husák combined rigorous pro-Soviet orthodoxy with a measure of economic liberalization. Having become President in 1975, Husák held both this post and his party position until in December 1987 he surrendered the party leadership to Miloš **Jakeš**, another political hardliner. Meanwhile, the impact of the post-1985 **Gorbachev** reform programme in the Soviet Union was beginning to be felt in Czechoslovakia. In the event, the communist regime crumbled with remarkable rapidity following the opening of the Berlin Wall in early November 1989, amidst an upsurge of massive popular protest. At the end of November Jakeš was replaced as KSČ leader by Karel Urbánek and the following month Husák resigned as President. Shortly before he stepped down he had attempted to assuage the demand for far-reaching change by swearing in the first Government with a non-communist majority for over four decades, although it was led by a KSČ member.

The Federal Assembly, still dominated by KSČ deputies, elected Dubček as its new Chairman and went on to vote in the dissident playwright Václav **Havel** as State President in succession to Husák. In late December 1989 an extraordinary KSČ congress elected Ladislav Adamec to the new post of Party Chairman and issued a public apology for the party's past actions.

The Czech component of the KSČ responded to events by relaunching itself as the KSČM in March 1990, with Jiří Svoboda as leader and with a socialist rather than a Marxist-Leninist orientation. In the June 1990 multi-party elections, the Czech communists took second place in the Czech National Council, winning 32 of the 200 seats, and were also runners-up in the Czech balloting for the Federal Assembly, winning 15 of the 101 Czech lower house seats. The communists then went into opposition for the first time since 1945, amidst a continuing exodus of party members.

In October 1990 the KSČM declared itself independent of the federal KSČ, shortly before the passage of a law requiring the KSČ to surrender its assets to the Government. In mid-1991 the KSČ was officially dissolved, but both the KSČM and its Slovak counterpart remained 'Czechoslovak' in orientation, i.e. opposing the break-up of the federation.

In the June 1992 elections the KSČM headed the Left Bloc, which won 35 of the 200 Czech National Council seats (with 14.1% of the vote) as well as 19 of the 99 Czech seats in the federal lower house and 15 of the 75 Czech seats in the upper house. Still in opposition, the KSČM mounted ultimately abortive resistance to the dissolution of the federation. Following the creation of the independent Czech Republic in January 1993, the party experienced much internal strife, including the resignation of Svoboda as leader over the rejection of his proposal to drop 'Communist' from the title. He was replaced in June 1993 by the conservative Miroslav Grebeníček, whose election precipitated the creation of two breakaway parties by the end of the year, to which the KSČM lost the majority of its deputies elected in 1992.

The KSČM nevertheless retained substantial core membership and organizational strength, as well as significant support for its advocacy of a 'socialist market economy' based on economic democracy and co-operatives, and for its opposition to membership of the **North Atlantic Treaty Organization** (NATO) and to absorption into the 'German sphere of influence'. In the mid-1996 elections to the **Parliament** it took 10.3% of the national vote and 22 lower house seats, effectively becoming the main opposition to a further coalition headed by the centre-right **Civic Democratic Party**, given that the Social Democrats (ČSSD) gave the new Government qualified support. In April 1998 the KSČM joined the far-right Republicans in voting 'against' in the decisive parliamentary vote in favour of NATO membership. In the early June 1998 elections the KSČM advanced marginally to 24 lower house seats on an 11% vote share, remaining in opposition, now to a minority Government of the ČSSD. In regional elections in November 2000 the KSČM advanced strongly to take 21% of the vote.

Leadership: Miroslav Grebeníček (Chair.).
Address: Politických vězňů 9, 11121 Prague 1.
Telephone: (2) 22897111.
Fax: (2) 22897207.
E-mail: leftnews@kscm.cz
Internet: www.kscm.cz

Communist Party of the Moldovan Republic
Partidul Comunistilor din Republica Moldova (PCRM)

One of the few parties of central/eastern Europe which has retained the communist designation and been electorally successful. The PCRM obtained registration in 1994 as effectively the successor to the Soviet-era Communist Party, which had been banned in August 1991. Although not legalized in time for the 1994 **Parliament** elections, the PCRM subsequently attracted defectors from other parties and formed the 'Popular Patriotic Forces' front to support the candidacy of party leader Vladimir **Voronin** in the 1996 presidential elections. He came third in the first round with 10.3% of the vote, whereupon the party backed the victorious Petru Lucinschi in the second and was rewarded with two ministerial posts in the resultant coalition Government.

In its first parliamentary elections in March 1998 the PCRM advocated 'the rebirth of a socialist society' and became the strongest single party, with 40 seats and 30.1% of the vote, but went into opposition to a centre-right coalition. In one of a series of subsequent government crises, Voronin was in late 1999 nominated by President Lucinschi to take over the premiership, but he failed to obtain sufficient parliamentary support.

Voronin obtained his revenge in early legislative elections in February 2001, when the PCRM swept to a landslide victory by winning 71 of the 101 seats with 49.9% of the vote. In early April Moldova became the first former communist country to democratically elect a communist as Head of State, when Voronin was elected President by the new Parliament. Vasile Tarlev became Prime Minister of a PCRM Government committed to a strong state role in the economy and the re-establishment of close ties with the Russian Federation. Later in April the new President was re-elected PCRM Chairman, after the Constitutional Court had ruled that the two posts were not incompatible.

Leadership: Vladimir Voronin (Chair.).
Address: Str. M. Dosoftei 118, Chişinău 2073.
Telephone: (2) 248384.
Fax: (2) 233673.

Communist Party of the Russian Federation
Kommunisticheskaya Partiya Rossiiskoi Federatisii (KPRF)

The successor to the Soviet-era ruling communist party, in opposition in the post-Soviet period but remaining the **Russian Federation**'s largest single party until a spate of mergers in the period after the 1999 elections. The KPRF was registered in March 1993 following a Constitutional Court ruling in December 1992 that the banning in November 1991 of the Communist Party of the Soviet Union (KPSS) had been illegal. The KPSS was directly descended from Lenin's majority (Bolshevik) wing of the Russian Social Democratic Labour Party founded in 1898, which at the party's second congress held in London in 1903 out-voted the minority (Menshevik) wing on Lenin's proposal that the party should become a tightly-disciplined vanguard of professional revolutionaries.

In 1912 the Bolshevik wing became a separate party, which achieved legal status following the overthrow of the Tsar in February 1917. Under Lenin's leadership, the Bolsheviks seized power in October 1917 and eventually established themselves in sole power in the new Union of Soviet Socialist Republics (USSR or **Soviet Union**).

The party changed its name to Russian Communist Party (Bolsheviks) in 1918, to All-Union Communist Party (Bolsheviks) in 1925 and to the KPSS title in 1952. Following Lenin's death in 1924, the party was led by Josef Stalin (until his death in 1953), Nikita Khrushchev (until he was ousted in 1964), Leonid Brezhnev (until his death in 1982), Yurii Andropov (who died after a year in office), Konstantin Chernenko (who did likewise) and Mikhail **Gorbachev** (1984–91). From 1985 Gorbachev embarked upon a radical reform programme which was to lead to the collapse of communist rule in the Soviet-bloc countries in 1989 and ultimately to the demise of the Soviet Union itself at the end of 1991.

The leader of the revived KPRF, elected at a congress in Klyazm, near Moscow, in February 1993, was Gennadii **Zyuganov**, a former Soviet apparatchik who had been Co-Chairman of the National Salvation Front formed the previous year by communists and Russian nationalists who deplored the passing of the Soviet empire. The KPRF was thus placed in uneasy alliance with the nationalist right, in opposition to the reformist pro-market forces in power in Moscow under the presidency of Boris **Yeltsin**. The manifest negative effects of rapid economic transition, including unemployment, inflation, rampant corruption and organized crime, provided the KPRF with powerful ammunition in the unfamiliar task of seeking electoral support in a democratic system.

In the elections of December 1993 to the State Duma (lower house of the **Federal Assembly**) the KPRF took third place with 65 seats and 12.4% of the proportional vote, thereafter becoming the principal focus of opposition to the Yeltsin administration. Despite the appointment in January 1995 of an acknowledged communist as Justice Minister, the KPRF continued to be essentially an opposition party, its platform for the December 1995 State Duma elections promising the restoration of 'social justice'. Its reward was 157 seats (with 22.3% of the proportional vote), making it the largest single party in the chamber.

Remaining in opposition (although welcoming Yeltsin's shift to a more conservative line), the KPRF nominated Zyuganov as its candidate for the mid-1996 presidential election, on a platform condemning the destruction of the Russian Federation's industrial base by **IMF**-dictated policies and promising to restore economic sovereignty. Zyuganov came a close second to Yeltsin in the first round, winning 32% of the vote, but lost to the incumbent in the second, in which his tally was 40.4%. The KPRF then launched the Popular-Patriotic Union of Russia (NPSR) to rally anti-Yeltsin forces, Zyuganov being elected as its leader.

In the late 1990s the KPRF sought to distance itself from the nationalist right, while continuing to articulate a Russian nationalism harking back to the Soviet era. The party urged a return to centralized government and the transfer of presidential powers to the Government and the legislature, as well as the creation of a 'Slavic union' of the Russian Federation, **Ukraine** and **Belarus**, arguing that only a KPRF Government could restore Russia's status as a great power. However, the KPRF's opposition to the war in **Chechnya** cost it some support, so that the party slipped to 113 seats in the December 1999 State Duma elections, although its share of the proportional vote increased to 24.3%, making it still the largest single party.

Yeltsin's unexpected resignation at the end of 1999 presented a new challenge to the KPRF in that his designated successor, Vladimir **Putin**, was popularly perceived as having impeccable nationalist and pro-authority credentials. In presidential elections in March 2000, Zyuganov was again the KPRF candidate but was soundly defeated by Putin in the first round, receiving only 29.2% of the vote. The KPRF subsequently declared its readiness to provide 'constructive opposition' to the new Government, although following the re-election of Zyuganov as Chairman at the 7th party congress in December 2000 the KPRF embarked upon 'active opposition' to what it described as the 'anti-people' Putin administration. In January 2001 Zyuganov was elected Chairman of the Council of Communist Parties in the former Soviet republics.

Leadership: Gennadii Zyuganov (Chair.).
Address: B. Komsomolskii per. 8/7, Moscow 101000.
Telephone and Fax: (095) 2068751.

Communist Party of the Soviet Union
Kommunisticheskaya Partiya Sovetskogo Soyuza (KPSS)

The former single ruling party of the **Soviet Union** until 1991. The Bolshevik (literally, majority) branch of the left-wing Russian Social Democratic Labour Party (RSDRP) was in the ascendant from 1903 and went on to call for socialist revolution in **Russia** along Marxist lines. Led by Vladimir Lenin, the Bolsheviks capitalized on mass discontent and the failure of the new Government to withdraw Russia from the disastrous First World War to increase their popularity and to agitate for revolution. In October–November 1917 the Bolsheviks seized power in the second Russian Revolution, and instigated a one-party-state system based on Lenin's interpretation of Marxism. Facing opposition from democrats and royalists, as well as from the foreign powers still involved in the war, the Bolsheviks were able to consolidate their control through their victory in the Russian Civil War (1918–21). The Bolsheviks renamed their party the All-Russian Communist Party (Bolsheviks) in 1918, and the later Soviet leader Josef Stalin changed its title to the KPSS in 1952. The KPSS totally dominated Soviet life as the sole political movement, with control over all areas of society. Beneath the Politburo (political bureau) and its leader, the General Secretary, was the Party Secretariat and the Central Committee which ran the party between congresses. At the five-yearly congresses, party members from the regional divisions of the party would meet, theoretically to debate party/Government policy. However, under the totalitarian regime they were used merely to endorse the wishes of the General Secretary. At the base of the party were regional cells of at least three party members who would theoretically implement party policy at the local level.

Used by Stalin to promote his own cult of personality, the KPSS was from the beginning entwined with the communist State and served as a model for other communist parties around the world. On his climb towards dominance of the party following Lenin's death in 1924, Stalin had opposition groups high up in the party 'liquidated' in various purges, leaving him unassailable by 1929. His paranoia continued, however, into the 1930s culminating in the terrible *Yezovshchina* of 1937, which saw many 'dissident' party members executed or exiled to **Siberia**. The party membership was reduced from a high of 3.5 million in 1933 to just 1.9 million in 1938.

The Second World War, known in the Soviet Union as the Great Patriotic War, galvanized the party's popularity, aided hugely by the Government's propaganda efforts. The death of Stalin in 1953, and the process of 'de-Stalinization' under his successor Nikita Khrushchev, briefly eased the grip of the KPSS in the early 1960s, prompting easier international relations and encouraging low-level liberalization in the Soviet Union. However, Khrushchev's successors from 1964 to 1985 reasserted the party's dominance and increased the control of the state machinery. The last General Secretary of the KPSS, Mikhail **Gorbachev**, initiated the reform processes (*see **glasnost*** and ***perestroika***) which ultimately saw the undoing of the Soviet Union in 1991 following attempts by hardline members of the KPSS to halt the changes (*see* **August coup**). Following the defeat of the August coup the new Russian President Boris **Yeltsin** banned the KPSS on 23 August 1991 and seized all of its assets as state property. The **Communist Party of the Russian Federation** claims descent from the KPSS.

Communist Party of Ukraine
Komunistychna Partiya Ukrainy (KPU)

The successor to the Soviet-era ruling party, and **Ukraine**'s largest single political formation. The Soviet-era KPU was banned in August 1991, but was revived in mid-1993 under the leadership of Petro Symonenko on a platform calling for the restoration of state control over the economy and a confederative union with the **Russian Federation**. The KPU attracted particular support in the economically-troubled industrial areas of eastern Ukraine, especially in the Donbass mining region, where Symonenko had been a senior party official in the Soviet era. The party gave decisive backing to Leonid **Kuchma** in the mid-1994 presidential elections, while in the 1994 **Parliament** elections it emerged as substantially the largest single party, with a total of over 90 seats (nearly all in eastern and southern Ukraine).

The KPU quickly came into conflict with Kuchma, leading opposition in 1995–96 to the 'presidential' Constitution favoured by him. Following the final adoption of the new text in June 1996, the party accepted its legitimacy but mounted a campaign for early presidential and parliamentary elections, combined with mass industrial action in protest against government economic policy. The KPU confirmed its position as the largest party in the March 1998 parliamentary elections, advancing to 115 seats on a vote share of 26% and subsequently being joined by some independent deputies.

Standing as the KPU candidate in the autumn 1999 presidential elections, Symonenko came second to the incumbent Kuchma in the first round with 22.2% of the vote, and was defeated in the second round despite increasing his support to 37.8% on the strength of backing from other left-wing parties. The KPU leader complained that the polling had been rigged, as did international observers, and in March 2000 the KPU's headquarters in **Kiev** were briefly occupied by nationalist militants, who accused the party of promoting the colonization of Ukraine by the Russian Federation.

In the major crisis which overtook the Kuchma administration in early 2001, the KPU claimed credit for securing the dismissal of 'pro-US' Prime Minister Viktor Yushchenko in April and declared itself ready to form a Government, although it held back from joining moves to impeach Kuchma. At a May Day rally Symonenko asserted that 'nationalists and oligarchic capitalists', assisted by the West, were seeking to divide Ukraine into three parts and to detach the country from 'fraternal **Slavic peoples**'. Earlier in the year the KPU had signed a cooperation agreement with the **Communist Party of the Russian Federation** and declared its support for Ukrainian membership of the **Belarus-Russia Union**.

Leadership: Petro Symonenko (First Secretary).
Address: Vinohradniy 1/11, Kiev 252024.
Telephone: (44) 2934044.

Confederation of Albanian Trade Unions
Konfederata e Sindikatave të Shqipërisë (KSSh)

The organization founded in 1991 in **Albania** as successor to the official Central Council of Trade Unions of the communist era. The KSSh links 17 union federations in various sectors of the economy with an estimated membership of 80,000. It lost ground in the late 1990s to the alternative **Union of Independent Trade Unions of Albania** (BSPSh).

Chair. of Man. Council: Kastriot Muço.
Address: Bul. Dëshmorët e Kombit, Pallati Ali Kelmendi, Tirana.
Fax: (4) 222956.

Confederation of Autonomous Trade Unions of Yugoslavia
Savez Samostalnih Sindikata Jugoslavije (SSSJ)

The main union centre in **Yugoslavia**, descended from the communist-era structure. Dating from 1990, the SSSJ inherited the assets of the previous official trade union organization and has retained substantial membership in the state sector, but faces competition from the **Independence Trade Union Confederation**.

President: Radoslav Ilić.
Address: Trg Nikole Pašića 5, Belgrade 11000.
Telephone: (11) 3230922.
Fax: (11) 3241911.

Confederation of Azerbaijan Trade Unions (AHIK)

The main trade union centre in **Azerbaijan**, little changed from the Soviet-era. Dominant in the formal economy, the AHIK has not been seriously challenged by the post-independence **Association of Independent Workers of Azerbaijan**. Although closely connected with the Government, the AHIK was admitted into membership of the International Confederation of Free Trade Unions (ICFTU) in 2000.
Chair.: Sattar Mehbaliyev.
Address: 3 Youth Square, Baku.
Telephone: (12) 926659.
Fax: (12) 927268.

Confederation of Democratic Trade Unions of Romania
Confédération des Syndicats Démocratiques de Roumanie (CSDR)

One of many competing union centres in post-communist **Romania**, of Christian democratic orientation. Founded in 1994, the CSDR is affiliated to the World Confederation of Labour (WCL) and claims to represent some 650,000 members in over 30 branch federations.
Leader: Iacob Baciu.
Address: 1–3 place Walter Maracineauunu, BP 1-788, Bucharest.
Telephone and Fax: (1) 3102080.
E-mail: csdrdri@fx.ro

Confederation of Free Trade Unions of Ukraine (CFTUU)

The principal independent union centre in **Ukraine**, although far smaller than the (ex-communist) **Federation of Trade Unions of Ukraine** (FPU). The CFTUU on 27 August 2001 decided to join the antipresidential National Salvation Forum, an electoral bloc of the democratic opposition led by former Deputy Premier Yuliya Tymoshenko.
Chair.: Mikhail Volynets.

Confederation of Independent Trade Unions of Bulgaria (KNSB)

The largest trade union centre in **Bulgaria**. The KNSB was launched in February 1990 as successor to the communist-era Central Council of Trade Unions, declaring itself to be politically non-partisan with industrial rather than political priorities. It has supported the transition to a market economy, while frequently complaining that privatization has principally benefited 'old and new profiteers'. Affiliated to the International Confederation of Free Trade Unions (ICFTU), the KNSB embraces about 75 federations and individual unions, with a combined membership of three million.

Confederation of Independent Trade Unions of Croatia (CITUC)

Chair.: Jeliazko Hristov.
Address: 1 Makedonia Sq., Sofia 1040.
Telephone: (2) 9170479.
Fax: (2) 9885969.
E-mail: knsb@mbox.cit.bg

Confederation of Independent Trade Unions of Croatia (CITUC)

The confederation founded in June 1990 in **Croatia** by unions opposed to the choice of a former communist as leader of the **Association of Autonomous Trade Unions of Croatia** (SSSH). CITUC claims to represent about 50,000 workers, but has not been able to challenge the dominance of the SSSH.
President: Mladen Mesić.
Address: Zagreb 10000.

Confederation of Labour of Russia (KTR)

One of the **Russian Federation**'s independent trade union centres, much smaller than the dominant **Federation of Independent Trade Unions of Russia** (FNPR). The KTR was created in 1995 by unions representing railway workers, seamen, air traffic controllers and doctors. Claiming a membership of 1.25 million, the KTR became an affiliate of the International Confederation of Free Trade Unions (ICFTU) in November 2000 and at ICFTU prompting entered into talks on a merger with the **All-Russian Confederation of Labour** (VKT).
President: Vladimir Konusenko.
Address: 42 Lenin Prospect, Moscow 117119.
Telephone and Fax: (095) 9388270.

Confederation of the Peoples of the Caucasus (KNK)

A loose grouping of national movements which emerged at the end of the 1980s representing the various ethnic groups of the north **Caucasus**, and building on the idea of an independent north Caucasian republic as realized briefly in 1918. An Assembly of the Mountain Peoples of the Caucasus, established in August 1989, was transformed into a Confederation in November 1991, and the word Mountain was dropped from its title in October 1992. A non-official body, the Confederation was supported mostly by **Abkhazia** and **Chechnya**, with few **Turkic** representatives. Although it outwardly espoused peaceful integration and regional stability, its volunteer defence force became actively involved in the Abkhazia conflict, playing a sizeable role in **Georgia**'s defeat. It was badly split by attempts by Chechnya to use the Confederation as a staging post for full independence, and KNK fighters did not take part in the Chechen conflict, leading to the organization's effective marginalization in regional politics.

Confederation of Trade Unions of Macedonia
Sojuzot na Sindikatite na Makedonija (SSM)

Macedonia's principal union centre, successor to the Macedonian wing of the former federal Yugoslav structure.
President: Zhivko Tolevski.
Address: 12, Udarna Brigada 2, Skopje 91000.
Telephone: (2) 231374.
Fax: (2) 115787.

Confederation of Trade Unions of the Republic of Moldova
Confederatia Sindicatelor din Republica Moldova (CSRM)

The larger trade union confederation formed from the split in 2000 of the General Federation of Trade Unions of Moldova (FGSRM), previously the sole trade union centre in **Moldova**. The FGSRM was the reformed successor to the Soviet-era structure, whose assets it inherited. It benefited from almost universal union membership in the employed labour force.

In late 2000 the union broke into two separate unions—the CSRM and **Solidaritate** (Solidarity), a new organization. The CSRM retained the previous federation's affiliation to the International Confederation of Free Trade Unions and kept about 80 percent of all union members in Moldova, mainly from the agriculture and agricultural-processing sectors, public services, radio electronics, medicine, education and culture.
President: Petru Chiriac.
Address: 129 rue 31 Aout, Chișinau 277012.
Telephone: (2) 232789.
Fax: (2) 237698.
E-mail: cfsind@cni.md
Internet: www.csrm.md

Confederation of Trade Unions of the Serb Republic

The umbrella organization of trade unions in one of the two territorial/ethnic components of **Bosnia and Herzegovina**.
Chair.: Cedo Volas.
Address: Srpska 32, Banja Luka.

Confederation of Trade Unions of the Slovak Republic
Konfederácia Odborových Zväzov Slovenskej Republiky (KOZSR)

The principal union centre in **Slovakia**, directly descended from the communist-era structure. The KOZSR itself dates from the separation of **Czechoslovakia** into Czech and Slovak states at the beginning of 1993, the previous Czechoslovakian confederation having unsuccessfully opposed this so-called '**velvet divorce**'. Though ideologically close to the (ex-communist) **Party of the Democratic Left** (SDĽ), the KOZSR is politically independent and has strongly opposed the austerity programme of the post-1998 coalition Government including the SDĽ. Affiliated to the International Confederation of Free Trade Unions (ICFTU), the KOZSR claims total membership of 750,000 in 39 affiliated unions.
Chair.: Ivan Saktor.
Address: 3 Odborárské St, Bratislava 81570.
Telephone: (2) 50239109.
Fax: (2) 55561956.
E-mail: internat.dep@kozsr.sk
Internet: www.internet.sk/kozsr

Conservative Christian Party
Konservativnaya Khrystsiyanska Partiya (KKP)

An anti-**Lukashenka** party launched in **Belarus** in September 1999 by supporters of 1994 presidential election candidate Zyanon Paznyak, who had been ousted the previous month as leader in exile of the **Belarusian Popular Front–Renaissance**. Strongly opposed to the **Belarus-Russia Union** treaty, the party joined the general opposition boycott of the October 2000 legislative elections.
Leadership: Zyanon Paznyak (Chair.).

Contact Group (for the former Yugoslavia)

An unofficial collection of six countries (France, Germany, Italy, **Russian Federation**, UK and USA). It was formed in April 1994 (at which point it comprised five countries—Italy joining in 1996) to co-ordinate US-**European Union**-Russian policy regarding the warring nations of the former **Socialist Federal Republic of Yugoslavia**. Following the signing of the final **Dayton Agreement**, which ended the war in **Bosnia and Herzegovina** in 1995, the Contact Group assumed responsibilities for overseeing the implementation of the Agreement. The Group has continued to apply international pressure in the region to secure security, most notably calling for sanctions and paving the way for airstrikes by **North Atlantic Treaty Organization** forces against **Yugoslavia** over the crisis in **Kosovo** in 1999, and raising concern over the ethnic crisis in **Macedonia** in 2001.

Conventional Forces in Europe
(or CFE Treaty)

A key disarmament agreement at the end of the **Cold War**, signed in November 1990 by the member states of the **North Atlantic Treaty Organization** and of the **Warsaw Pact**. The Treaty limits non-nuclear air and ground armaments in the signatory countries. It was negotiated within the framework of the Conference on Security and Co-operation in Europe (CSCE—*see* **Organization for Security and Co-operation in Europe**) and signed at a CSCE summit meeting in Paris.

Cossacks

A culturally distinct ethnically mixed **Russian** and **Ukranian** group of around 80,000 people (1997 estimate) spread across southern **European Russia**. Formed from bands of freed and escapee serfs in the 16th century, the Cossack *hosts* established a fierce reputation as horse-borne warriors. This was put to good use by the Russian Empire which employed them as frontier guards in exchange for land tenure. Cossack military units were thus used effectively throughout the empire, but particularly in the **Don basin** and the north **Caucasus**.

Following the Russian Revolution of 1917 the Cossacks of the Don region were instrumental in leading the anti-Bolshevik 'White' resistance in the south. Their defeat by the Bolshevik forces led to mass persecution, and deportations under Stalin. Under **Soviet** rule the Cossacks were denied their separate cultural status and officially classed as either Russians or Ukrainians.

A re-emergence of Cossack nationalist sentiment in the late 1980s led to the formation of the Association of Cossacks in 1990. Cossack troops played a key role in the conflict in the breakaway Moldovan republic of **Transdnestria** in 1992. Former Russian President Boris **Yeltsin** rehabilitated the Cossacks in 1991 and granted them state support from 1993. These moves strengthened Cossack resolve and have lent weight to calls for an ethnically-based autonomous territory, spearheaded by the Don Cossacks.

Council for Mutual Economic Assistance (CMEA or Comecon)

The now defunct structure (known more colloquially as Comecon) established in 1949 during the Stalin era, within which the centrally-planned economies of the so-called Soviet-bloc countries were co-ordinated. In 1971 the organization moved on from its co-ordination phase to a so-called integration phase, with the adoption of a Comprehensive Program for the Further Extension and Improvement of Co-operation and the Further Development of Socialist Economic Integration.

Significant growth in mutual trade among member countries was recorded until a generalized slump in the 1980s. Following the collapse of communism in Europe in 1989–91 the CMEA was disbanded, leaving a legacy of problems for member countries. Their economies, having been structured over decades to fulfil specific roles within the CMEA, could suddenly count on neither the resources on which they had come to depend from other member countries (such as gas from the **Soviet Union**, at costs not reflecting the world market) nor the market for their output, particularly in heavy industry.

Members of the CMEA at the time it was disbanded in 1991 were **Bulgaria**, Cuba, **Czechoslovakia**, East Germany, **Hungary**, Mongolia, **Poland**, **Romania**, Soviet Union and Vietnam. A form of associate status in the organization was specified for **Yugoslavia** in a 1964 agreement. **Albania** was a member until 1961 (when it ceased participating, although without formally revoking its membership). China and to some extent North Korea also participated with observer status until 1961.

Council of Baltic Sea States (CBSS)

A regional forum meeting at the level of Foreign Ministers (with summit meetings also being held from time to time, totalling three to date) with a broad remit to promote democracy, greater regional unity and economic development. The Council was established in 1992 under the Copenhagen Declaration, the outcome of a meeting held in the Danish capital in March of that year. A small permanent International Secretariat was inaugurated on 20 October 1998 and is located in Stockholm, Sweden.

Members: Denmark, **Estonia**, Finland, Germany, Iceland, **Latvia**, **Lithuania**, Norway, **Poland**, **Russian Federation** and Sweden. The European Commission (of the **European Union**) is also represented in its own right.
Leadership: Jacek Starosciak (Secretary-General).
Address: CBSS Secretariat, Strömsborg, POB 2010, 103 11 Stockholm, Sweden.
Telephone: (8) 4401920.
Fax: (8) 4401944.
E-mail: cbss@cbss.org
Internet: www.baltinfo.org

Council of Europe

A regional organization originally founded in May 1949 with 10 members in western Europe, which has now been expanded continent-wide. Its objectives are promoting regional unity and social progress, and upholding the principles of parliamentary democracy, respect for human rights and the rule of law. It has a Committee of Ministers and a Parliamentary Assembly, which elects its Secretary-General. The European Court of Human Rights, established in 1959 in Strasbourg, is part of the activities of the Council of Europe, overseeing the implementation of the Convention for the Protection of Human Rights and Fundamental Freedoms (usually known as the European Convention on Human Rights). Council member countries are required to adhere to the Convention, which should entail amongst other things the abolition of the death penalty.

Members: 43 European countries, including Albania, Armenia, Azerbaijan, Bulgaria, Croatia, Czech Republic, Estonia, Georgia, Hungary, Latvia, Lithuania, Macedonia, Moldova, Poland, Romania, Russian Federation, Slovakia, Slovenia and Ukraine. Bosnia and Herzegovina and Yugoslavia have applied for full membership. Belarus has applied for membership, but as at January 2002 no progress had been made on its application, owing to its domestic political situation.

Leadership: Dr Walter Schwimmer (Secretary-General).
Address: 67075 Strasbourg Cédex, France.
Telephone: (3) 88412000.
Fax: (3) 88412781.
E-mail: point_i@coe.int
Internet: www.coe.int

Council of the Baltic States *see* **Baltic Council**.

Council of the Federation (Russian Federation)
Soviet Federatsii

The upper house of the **Federal Assembly** of the **Russian Federation**.

Council of the Republic (Belarus)
Soviet Respubliki

The upper house of the **National Assembly** of **Belarus**.

Country of Law Party
Orinats Erkir (OE)

A small right-wing political party in **Armenia** advocating the rule of law. The OE gave important support to the successful presidential candidacy of Robert **Kocharian** (non-party) in March 1998, subsequently forming part of the presidential coalition. The party achieved fifth place in the May 1999 **National Assembly** elections, winning 5.3% of the vote and six out of 131 seats.

Leadership: Artur Bagdasarian (Chair.);
Sergo Yeritssian (Parliamentary leader).

Crimea

Address: 2 Arshakuniatis Street, Yerevan.
Telephone: (1) 563584.

Cour permanente d'arbitrage *see* **Permanent Court of Arbitration**.

CPA *see* **Permanent Court of Arbitration**.

CPC *see* **Centre for the Prevention of Conflict**.

CPSU *see* **Communist Party of the Soviet Union**.

Crimea

An overcrowded and impoverished peninsula and administrative region in the south of **Ukraine**. Surrounded by the Black Sea and the Sea of Azov, Crimea is connected to Ukraine proper via the thin Perekop land bridge. Since the arrival of Greek colonists in the 6th century BC, Crimea has had a separate history from Ukraine, but in 1954 it was ceded from the **Russian** to the Ukrainian republic as a 'symbol of friendship between the Russian and Ukrainian peoples'.

The Mongol invasion of **eastern Europe** in the 13th century AD brought ethnic **Tatars** to the peninsula and in 1443 the Khanate of Crimea was established in the wake of the Golden Horde. This state, which gave rise to the ethnically distinct **Crimean Tatars**, was eventually absorbed into the Russian Empire in 1783. Russian suzerainty permanently altered Crimea. The Tatars were persecuted and replaced by ethnic **Russians** and the region was developed as a key base in the Black Sea, its strategic significance attested by the Crimean War in the 1850s. After the Bolshevik Revolution of 1917 the aspirations of the Tatars were to some extent realized when a Crimean Autonomous Republic was created in 1921. The region was heavily developed, particularly the port of **Sevastopol**. This phase in Crimea's history ended abruptly, however, after a three-year period of German occupation during the Second World War (1941–43). Stalin, already responsible for the wholesale suppression of Tatar culture, had the Tatars deported in 1944 (*see* **Deported Nationalities**). They have not been effectively rehabilitated. In 1945 the region was stripped of its republic status and in 1954 it was ceded to Ukraine, while a determined policy was undertaken to slavicize the region, both culturally and demographically.

Following the collapse of the **Soviet Union** in 1991 Crimea voted in favour of returning to its republic status, this time within Ukraine. The campaign for greater autonomy, led by the majority Russian community, climaxed with a short-lived declaration of independence in May 1992. Since then the Russian nationalist movement has been divided and undermined by the Russian Federation's diplomatic support for Ukraine. Ethnic tensions on the peninsula are high. The returning

Crimean Tatars (around 10% of the population by 1994) are marginalized and suffer disproportionately from unemployment. **Ukrainians** (25%) are also disadvantaged by the use of Russian in the peninsula. The general economic situation is of grave concern to the Ukrainian authorities. Privatization on the peninsula is slow in proceeding and wage arrears are near to unserviceable. The regional authorities are frequently stalemated by disagreements between the pro-Ukrainian executive and the pro-autonomy legislature.

Crimean Tatars

An ethnic **Turkic people** originally from the **Crimean** peninsula in **Ukraine** but now scattered throughout the former **Soviet Union**. The Crimean Tatars developed separately from other Russian-based **Tatars** from as early as the 15th century. In 1445 the Khanate of Crimea was established on the peninsula from the remnants of the Mongol Golden Horde. The Tatar state was an important regional power for the next 300 years, establishing strong links with ethnically-related Turkey across the Black Sea. However, it was destroyed in 1783 after Crimea was annexed by **Russia** at the conclusion of the latest in a sequence of Russo-Turkish wars.

The Tatars were immediately demoted from the ruling class in Crimea and their language and culture were suppressed amidst attempts to russify the region. During the Crimean War in the 1850s they came under wholesale persecution and even deportation. Ethnic **Russians** were relocated to the region in their stead. Although a Crimean Republic was established under Bolshevik rule in 1921 the Tatars fell foul of Stalin's policy on nationalities from as early as 1928. The Turkic language and culture were again suppressed. However, the worst was yet to come. Following a three-year occupation by German forces between 1941 and 1943, the reinstated **Soviet** regime identified the Tatars as collaborators. Stalin ordered the deportation of all 183,000 Tatars. Almost half of the Tatars removed to central Asia died during their transportation. Unlike most **deported nationalities** the Tatars were not physically rehabilitated in the 1950s. Their rights were returned in 1956 and they were legally absolved of collusion with the invading Nazis in 1967. However, the failure of the Soviet regime to acknowledge a separate ethnic identity for the Crimean Tatars blocked their repatriation to Crimea. Instead, nominally autonomous regions were created in the central Asian states they now occupied.

Finally in 1987 plans were drawn up to repatriate the Crimean Tatars to Crimea. Since then some 200,000 have returned to the peninsula. Population pressures and institutionalized discrimination have forced many of the returnees to take land in the less fertile south of the peninsula. Tatar groups remain resilient in demanding full compensation and the return of confiscated land and property, but there is little hope of a favourable response. The Crimean Tatar Congress (Kurultai) was constituted in the late 1980s to champion their cause.

Crkvenac, Mato

Minister of Finance, **Croatia**.

Mato Crkvenac is a member of the ruling **Social Democratic Party of Croatia** (SPH), and a celebrated academic economist. Appointed Finance Minister on 27 January 2000, he has attempted to contain and reduce budget expenditure through cuts and austerity reforms in order to stabilize the economy (*see* **Croatia, economy**).

Born in 1945 in Donja Petrička, near Bjelovar in northern Croatia, in what was then a constituent republic of the **Socialist Federal Republic of Yugoslavia** (SFRY), he graduated in economics from the University of Zagreb in 1968. He stayed with the university, pursuing an academic career which has spanned over 30 years. He received his doctorate in 1979, and his professorship in 1991. Throughout the 1970s and 1980s he aided the Government's State Planning Institute, and went on to specialize in macroeconomics and economic policies. He has been a member of various scientific and economic boards and councils. He was appointed Finance Minister in January 2000 and has attempted to gradually reduce the country's budget. His offer to resign in September 2000, over an unpopular bid to limit duty-free imports, was rejected by President Stipe **Mesić**.

Address: Ministry of Finance, Katančićeva 5, 10000 Zagreb.
Telephone: (1) 4591333.
Fax: (1) 4922583.
E-mail: kabinet@mfin.hr
Internet: www.mfin.hr

Croatia
Republika Hrvatska

An independent republic in south-eastern Europe, bordered by Slovenia and Hungary to the north, the Federal Republic of Yugoslavia (FRY) to the east (Serbia) and south (Montenegro), Bosnia and Herzegovina to the south-east, and the Adriatic Sea to the west. The country is divided administratively into 21 counties.

Area: 56,538 sq km; *capital*: **Zagreb**; *population*: 4.7m. (2001 estimate), comprising roughly **Croats** 78%, **Serbs** 12%, **Bosniaks** 1%, others 9% (based on 1991 census); *official language*: Croatian; *religion*: **Roman Catholic** 76.5%, **Orthodox** 11.1%, Muslim 1.2%, **Protestant** 0.4%, others 10.8%.

Whereas the 1990 Constitution provided for a presidential form of government, with a President as head of the executive branch, under amendments which obtained parliamentary approval in November 2000, Croatia moved to a form of full parliamentary democracy under which the Prime Minister and Cabinet became accountable solely to the legislature, which could only be dissolved by the President on its recommendation. The President retained substantial powers in the spheres of foreign and security policy and continued to be directly elected. Legislative authority is vested in a unicameral **Assembly** (Sabor), containing a Chamber of

Representatives (Zastupnički Dom), elected for a four-year term. It has up to 160 members (currently 151), of whom 140 are elected by proportional representation from multi-member constituencies, up to 15 (currently six) elected to represent Croatians abroad and five to represent ethnic minorities whose share of the population is at least 8%. Until 2001 there was also an upper house, the Chamber of Districts (Županijski Dom) with 63 elective members, plus a further five appointed by the President.

History: Croatia was part of the Roman Empire for several centuries before settlement of the area by **Slavic** migrations beginning in the 6th century (the original home of the Slavic Croats is generally believed to be present-day **Ukraine**). By the 10th century, an independent and Christian Croat kingdom (including parts of modern **Bosnia and Herzegovina**) had been established. In 1102 Croatia, retaining its autonomy, entered into an enduring dynastic union with the kingdom of **Hungary**. The Hungarians were defeated by the invading Turks in 1526, after which much of Croatia fell under Ottoman rule. The rest of the territory was absorbed into the Habsburg Empire, and a military frontier, peopled largely by ethnic Serbs, developed along the border between the Habsburg and Turkish dominions. By the end of the 17th century all of present-day Croatia was under Habsburg rule, becoming in 1867 part of the Hungarian-ruled half of the empire.

Following Austria-Hungary's disintegration at the end of the First World War, Croatia joined other south Slav territories in an uneasy union within the Kingdom of Serbs, Croats and Slovenes (renamed **Yugoslavia** in 1929). In 1941 Germany invaded Yugoslavia and created a separate Croatian state (including Bosnia and Herzegovina and part of present-day **Serbia**) controlled by a fascist dictatorship sympathetic to the Nazis. At the end of the Second World War, Croatia came under communist rule as one of six constituent republics (with Bosnia and Herzegovina, Serbia, **Slovenia, Macedonia** and **Montenegro**) of the **Socialist Federal Republic of Yugoslavia**. However, it consistently sought greater autonomy within a federal structure that became increasingly dysfunctional after the death of President **Tito** in 1980.

The collapse of communism at the end of the 1980s led to the election in 1990 of a nationalist Croatian Government under Franjo **Tudjman** of the **Croatian Democratic Union** (HDZ). This Government's declaration of independence in June 1991 sparked insurrection by the ethnic Serb minority within the Croatian republic, who carved out autonomous regions with the military help of the Serb-dominated Federal Yugoslav Army. A six-month war subsided in January 1992 with a UN-brokered cease-fire and the deployment of UN peacekeeping forces in the Serb-controlled areas (**Krajina** and **Slavonia**). Croatian policy towards the concurrent eruption of ethnic conflict in neighbouring Bosnia and Herzegovina veered from an initial alliance with the Muslim-dominated Government against Bosnian Serb nationalism, to military support (from early 1993) for Bosnian Croat separatism, and then to acceptance in March 1994, under pressure from the USA, of a **Muslim-Croat Federation**. In mid-1995 most Serb-held territory in Croatia, with the exception

Croatia

of eastern Slavonia, was recovered in an advance by Croatian forces (leading to a mass exodus of ethnic Serbs). Under the **Erdut Agreement** of November 1995 (complementing the **Dayton Agreement** for Bosnia and Herzegovina), a transitional UN administration was established in eastern Slavonia, leading to the eventual reintegration of the enclave into Croatia in January 1998.

Meanwhile, the HDZ had retained an overall majority in parliamentary elections in October 1995 and Tudjman had been re-elected as President in June 1997 with 61.4% of the vote, although the ballot was criticized as unfair by the **Organization for Security and Co-operation in Europe** (OSCE). In April 1997 the HDZ won a majority of 42 seats in elections to the 63-member Chamber of Districts. In November 1997 the legislature approved constitutional amendments which prohibited the re-establishment of a union of **Yugoslav** states.

In the late 1990s growing popular discontent with economic and social conditions was accompanied by increasing disarray within the ruling HDZ, as Tudjman slowly succumbed to cancer. His death in December 1999 precipitated parliamentary and presidential elections which marked the end of a decade of HDZ supremacy.

Latest elections: Elections to the Chamber of Representatives in early January 2000 resulted in a centre-left alliance of the **Social Democratic Party of Croatia** (SPH), the **Croatian Social-Liberal Party** (HSLS) and two small regional parties winning 71 of the 151 seats with 38.7% of the vote, while the HDZ retained only 46 seats (with 26.7%). The United List alliance of the **Croatian Peasants' Party** (HSS), the **Istrian Democratic Assembly** (IDS), the **Croatian People's Party** (HNS) and the **Liberal Party** (LS) won 25 seats (14.7%), an alliance headed by the **Croatian Party of Rights** (HSP) 5 (5.2%) and ethnic minority communities 4.

In presidential elections in late January and early February 2000, the HNS candidate, Stipe **Mesić**, headed the first round with 41.1%, against 27.7% for Dražen Budiša of the HSLS (also backed by the SPH) and 22.5% for Mate Granić of the HDZ, who was therefore eliminated. In the second round Mesić easily defeated Budiša by 56% to 44%.

Recent developments: As leader of the dominant party within the victorious centre-left alliance, Ivica **Račan** of the SPH became Prime Minister in January 2000, heading a six-party coalition which also included the HSLS, the HSS, the IDS, the HNS and the LS. He set as his two main policy goals the reduction of unemployment and the integration of Croatia into European/Western institutions. Under a compromise accord between the Government and President Mesić, the Assembly in November 2000 adopted constitutional amendments curtailing presidential powers and establishing Croatia as a parliamentary democracy. In March 2001 the Assembly voted to abolish the upper Chamber of Districts, which took effect on the expiry of that house's term in May. The IDS left the ruling coalition in June in protest over the Government's revocation of a law adopting Italian as an official language in **Istria**. Further defections came the following month when four members of the HSLS abandoned the Cabinet over the Government's continued co-operation with the **International Criminal Tribunal for the former**

Yugoslavia. Račan's position regarding the Tribunal has persistently prompted opposition from rightist parties, but his administration managed to survive a vote of no confidence in July 2001.

International relations and defence: Croatia's independent status received international recognition in early 1992 and the country was admitted to the United Nations in May of that year. It is a member of the **Council of Europe**, the OSCE and the **Central European Initiative**, and has observer status at the **Non-Aligned Movement**. Aspirations towards integration in Western institutions, such as the **European Union** (EU) and the **North Atlantic Treaty Organization** (NATO), were boosted by the end of HDZ rule in January 2000, following which Croatia joined NATO's **Partnership for Peace** programme in May 2000 and was admitted to the **World Trade Organization** in July. In November 2000 Croatia hosted the first summit conference of the EU and **Balkan** states in Zagreb. Some progress has been made in normalizing relations with rump Yugoslavia, although the issue of sovereignty over the **Prevlaka peninsula** on the Croatia–Montenegro border (currently under UN military observation) remains unresolved.

Croatia's defence budget for 2000 amounted to some US $600m., equivalent to about 3% of GDP. The size of the armed forces at the end of 2000 was some 60,000 personnel, including those serving under compulsory conscription of nine months, while reservists numbered an estimated 220,000.

Croatia, economy

Once one of the two most prosperous former federal republics of the **Socialist Federal Republic of Yugoslavia** (with **Slovenia**), subsequently beset by post-communist transition problems compounded by involvement in regional conflict.

GNP: US $18,765m. (2000); *GNP per capita*: $4,510 (2000); *GDP at PPP*: $23,900m. (1999); *GDP per capita at PPP*: $5,100 (1999); *exports*: $4,071m. (2000); *imports*: $7,688m. (2000); *currency*: kuna (plural: kuna; US $1=K8.254 at the end of December 2001).

In 1999 industry accounted for 32% of GDP, agriculture for 9% and services for 59%. Some 21% of the land is arable (though much was severely affected during the 1991–95 hostilities), 2% is under permanent crops, 20% permanent pasture and 38% forests and woodland. The main crops are wheat, corn, sugar beet, sunflower seed, alfalfa, olive, citrus, grapes and vegetables, and there is animal husbandry and dairy farming as well as fishing on Croatia's lengthy Adriatic Sea coast. The main mineral resources are petroleum, coal, bauxite and low-grade iron ore. The principal industrial sectors are textiles, chemicals and plastics, machine tools, aluminium, shipbuilding and petroleum. A major industry which was almost eliminated by the post-independence fighting was tourism, although there was a considerable revival in the later 1990s as the political and security situations became more settled.

Croatia, economy

Croatia's main exports in 1999 were manufactures (13%), chemicals (8%) and capital goods (6%), while principal imports were capital goods (35%), fuel and energy (11%) and food items (7%). The main destinations of Croatia's exports in 2000 were Italy (22%), Germany (15%), **Bosnia and Herzegovina** (12%) and **Slovenia** (11%), while the main sources of imports were Italy (17%) and Germany (16%). In 1999 around 60% of Croatia's foreign trade was with **European Union** member states.

Prior to the dissolution of the former **Yugoslavia** in 1991–92, Croatia had an economic position within the federation well above average among the republics and was relatively industrialized. The ethnic and factional disturbances following secession caused severe material destruction, damage to arable land, communications disruption and the virtual suspension of the country's tourist industry, while the movement of refugees also resulted in serious economic problems. Over the period 1989–93 GDP declined in real terms at an average of just over 10% a year, while between 1990 and 1994 industrial GDP dropped by an annual average of 11.4% and production of machinery and equipment by over 20%. Inflation, which had fallen to about 120% in 1991, shot up in the following two years to over 1,500% in 1993, while unemployment rose officially to over 20% and probably higher.

In 1993 Croatia instituted a comprehensive economic stabilization plan, under which a new currency was introduced in 1994 and the inflation rate dropped sharply to around 4% per year in 1995–97, before rising to an estimated 6% in 1998 and then falling to 4.4% in 1999. The plan also yielded buoyant GDP growth rising to 6.5% in 1997, although a subsequent slow-down cut the growth rate to 2.5% in 1998 and to –0.3% in 1999, when confidence was damaged by a major bank corruption scandal. The centre-left Government elected in January 2000 declared its commitment to promoting growth and reducing unemployment (still running at 21% of the labour force) as well as to market-oriented structural reform and liberalization. GDP growth revived to around 3% in 2000, while the Government's 2001 budget envisaged balanced expenditure and revenue at K49,700m., to be achieved in particular by cuts in the state wage bill.

Legislation in 1991 providing for a degree of privatization was implemented only slowly. Although most of the 2,600 small and medium-sized state-owned companies had been transferred into the private sector by the end of 1998, little progress was made under the **Tudjman** regime in privatizing large enterprises in sectors such as oil, electricity, the railways and telecommunications. The succeeding Government relaunched the process, partly to assist with its aim of eliminating the fiscal deficit and also in the framework of Croatia's accession to the **World Trade Organization** in July 2000.

Croatian Association of Trade Unions (HUS)

The trade union centre founded in **Croatia** in December 1990 to support the then ruling **Croatian Democratic Union** (HDZ). Identified with the HDZ Government in the 1990s, the HUS remained much smaller than the **Association of Autonomous Trade Unions of Croatia** (SSSH). The defeat of the HDZ in the January 2000 legislative elections placed a question mark over the survival of the HUS.
President: Berislav Belec.
Address: Zagreb.

Croatian Chamber of Economy
Hrvatska Gospodarska Komora (HGK)

The principal organization in **Croatia** for promoting business contacts, both internally and externally, in the post-communist era.
President: Nadan Vidošević.
Address: Rooseveltov trg 2, 10000 Zagreb.
Telephone: (1) 4561555.
Fax: (1) 4828380.
E-mail: hgk@alf.hr
Internet: www.hgk.hr

Croatian Defence Force
Hrvatske Obrambene Snage (HOS)

A paramilitary group once active in **Croatia** and with connections to similar groups in neighbouring **Bosnia and Herzegovina**. The HOS, effectively the armed wing of the far-right **Croatian Party of Rights** (HSP), was founded along with its parent party in 1990. The guerrillas gained popularity among local **Croats** in the frontline areas (*see* **Krajina**) and were credited with putting up a more credible defence against local ethnic **Serb** militias than the regular Croatian army. Following the country's independence in 1991, the Government moved to dilute the HOS and began absorbing its armed units into the army under the pretext of not permitting the existence of private armies. Like the HSP, the group has lost popularity as the country edges towards permanent stability.

Croatian Democratic Union (Bosnia and Herzegovina)
Hrvatska Demokratska Zajednica (HDZ)

The dominant political party of the ethnic **Croat** population of **Bosnia and Herzegovina**, of nationalist orientation. The HDZ was launched in August 1990, partly on the initiative of the then ruling **Croatian Democratic Union of Croatia**. In the pre-independence Assembly elections of late 1990 it took most of the ethnic

Croatian Democratic Union (Bosnia and Herzegovina)

Croat vote, electing the two guaranteed Croat members of the then seven-member collegial presidency. It joined a post-election coalition Government with the main **Muslim** and **Serb** parties, but strains developed over the Bosnian Croats' ambivalence on whether there should be an independent state of Bosnia and Herzegovina.

The party effectively withdrew from the central Government in 1992 and in August 1993 spearheaded the proclamation of the Croatian Republic of **Herceg-Bosna** in the Croat-populated south-western region, with its own assembly at Grude. A change of policy in Zagreb, however, resulted in HDZ participation in the March 1994 agreement to set up a (**Muslim-Croat**) **Federation** of Bosnia and Herzegovina in the territory not under Bosnian Serb control, and in the replacement of hardliner Mate Boban as HDZ leader by the more moderate Kresimir Zubak, who became Federation President in May 1994. After long resistance by hardline Croats, Zubak in August 1996 signed an agreement for the abolition of Herceg-Bosna and full Croat participation in the Federation. In the first post-**Dayton** elections (September 1996), Zubak was elected as the Croat member of the union collective presidency with overwhelming support from Croat voters, while the HDZ won seven of 42 seats in the all-Bosnia House of Representatives (lower house of the **Parliamentary Assembly**) and 35 of 140 in the Federation lower house. In March 1997 Zubak was succeeded as Federation President by Vladimir Soljić of the HDZ.

The election of Croat nationalist Ante Jelavić as HDZ Chairman in May 1998 precipitated the exit of Zubak and his supporters, who formed the **New Croatian Initiative** (NHI), while the **Organization for Security and Co-operation in Europe** banned some HDZ candidates from running in the September 1998 elections because of their close links with Croatia. Nevertheless, the HDZ remained dominant among Croat voters, Jelavić being elected as the Croat member of the union collective presidency with 53% of the Croat vote (and 11.5% nationally), although the party's representation slipped to six seats in the all-Bosnia lower house and to 28 in the Federation lower house.

In June 1999 Jelavić began an eight-month term in the rotating chairmanship of the union collective presidency, declaring as his priorities Bosnia and Herzegovina's admission to the **European Union**, the **Council of Europe** and the **World Trade Organization**. However, a poor HDZ performance in local elections in April 2000 exacerbated internal divisions, which became public in July at an HDZ congress which re-elected Jelavić to the chairmanship, and also adopted new statutes making the party formally independent of the Croatian HDZ. In elections for five Vice-Chairmen, the congress declined to return moderate Foreign Minister Jadranko Prlić, who in September resigned from the party, claiming that Jelavić was wedded to 'obsolete political methods'.

In October 2000 Martin Raguz of the HDZ became union Prime Minister in succession to Spasoje Tusevljak, a non-party Serb (who could not remain in office because the accession of Zivko **Radišić** of the **Socialist Party of the Serb Republic** to the chairmanship of the union's collective presidency on the retirement of Alija **Izetbegović** of the (Muslim) **Party of Democratic Action** would have meant that the both posts were held by the same ethnic group, a situation not permitted under the Dayton Agreement). In the November 2000 legislative elections, the HDZ slipped to five seats in the union lower house and to 25 in the Federation lower house, while moderate parties gained ground in both legislatures. The consequence was the replacement of Raguz in February 2001 by a Croat member of the **Social Democratic Party of Bosnia and Herzegovina**, heading the first all-Bosnia Government not dominated by nationalists. The reaction of the HDZ the following month was the declaration of a revived separate Croat state based in Mostar, whereupon the UN **High Representative** dismissed Jelavić from the union collective presidency, amidst urgent UN and other efforts to preserve the structure created under the Dayton Agreement. The party eventually backed down and, in November, ended an eight-month boycott of the Parliamentary Assembly.

Leadership: Ante Jelavić (Chair.).
Address: bb Kneza Domagoja, Mostar Zapad.
Telephone: (36) 319478.
Fax: (36) 315024.
E-mail: hdzbih@hdzbih.org
Internet: www.hdzbih.org

Croatian Democratic Union (Croatia)
Hrvatska Demokratska Zajednica (HDZ)

A nationalist party of Christian orientation which took **Croatia** to independence in 1991 but lost power a month after the death of founder Franjo **Tudjman** in December 1999. Founded in mid-1989 in opposition to the then communist regime of the **Socialist Federal Republic of Yugoslavia**, the HDZ was joined by many of the elite of the Yugoslav regime, although Tudjman himself, a history professor with a military background, had been a prominent dissident in the 1970s and 1980s. Contesting the 1990 multi-party elections on a pro-autonomy platform, the HDZ won a landslide parliamentary majority, by virtue of which Tudjman was elected President in May 1990 by vote of the deputies. The HDZ Government secured a 94% pro-independence vote in a referendum in May 1991 and declared Croatia's independence the following month. In further elections in August 1992, the HDZ retained an overall parliamentary majority in the lower house of the **Assembly** and Tudjman was directly re-elected President with 56.7% of the popular vote.

Thereafter, the HDZ Government was riven by dissension about how to deal with the civil war in neighbouring **Bosnia and Herzegovina**. Also controversial was its maintenance of much of the panoply of central economic control. In October 1993 a special HDZ congress approved a new party programme espousing Christian democracy, describing the HDZ as the guarantor of Croatian independence and defining the liberation of **Serb**-held Croatian territory as the Government's most important task. In February 1994 President Tudjman publicly apologized for having, in an earlier book, doubted the veracity of received accounts of the Nazi extermination of **Jews** during the Second World War. The following month he also apologized for the role of the pro-German Ustaša regime in the extermination.

In April 1994 the HDZ was weakened by the breakaway of a moderate faction which favoured alliance with the **Muslims** of Bosnia and Herzegovina against the **Serbs** and also objected to Tudjman's dictatorial tendencies. Nevertheless, boosted by **Croat** military successes against the Serbs, the HDZ retained an overall majority in lower house elections in October 1995, winning 75 out of 127 seats with a vote share of 45.2%. The party also retained its majority in the upper house of the Assembly in April 1997, while in June 1997 Tudjman was re-elected President with 61.4% of the vote.

In the late 1990s the HDZ displayed evidence of internal dissension between hardliners and moderates as Tudjman became increasingly ill, amidst rising popular discontent with economic and social conditions. Following Tudjman's death in December 1999, the HDZ was heavily defeated in Assembly elections in early January 2000, retaining only 40 of the 151 seats (with 26.7% of the proportional vote) and going into opposition to a centre-left Government headed by the **Social Democratic Party of Croatia**. In subsequent presidential elections, moreover, outgoing Deputy Premier and Foreign Minister Mate Granić of the HDZ, despite resigning his party offices on the eve of polling, was eliminated in the first round in late January 2000, taking third place with 22.5% of the vote.

Ousted from government, the HDZ experienced an exodus of leading members, including Granić in March 2000, as new evidence emerged of corruption in the Tudjman regime. In April 2000 the party presidency was conferred on Ivo Sanader, a moderate, who declared his aim of restoring the HDZ's public image. In November 2000 HDZ deputies unsuccessfully opposed the conversion of Croatia into a parliamentary democracy.

Leadership: Ivo Sanader (Chair.).
Address: 4 Trg Hrvatskih Velikana 4, 10000 Zagreb.
Telephone: (1) 4553000.
Fax: (1) 4552600.
E-mail: hdz@hdz.hr
Internet: www.hdz.hr

Croatian National Bank
Hrvatska Narodna Banka (HNB)

The Central Bank of **Croatia**. The HNB was established as Croatia's central issuing bank in December 1990. The Yugoslav dinar was replaced by a Croatian dinar in 1991 and the Croatian kuna replaced the latter as the sole legal tender in May 1994. As of December 1999 the HNB had reserves of 2215m. kuna.

Governor: Zeljko Rohatinski.
Address: Trg Hrvatskih Velikana 3, 10002 Zagreb.

Telephone: (1) 4564555.
Fax: (1) 4610551.
E-mail: info@hnb.hr
Internet: www.hnb.hr

Croatian Party of Rights
Hrvatska Stranka Prava (HSP)

A far-right formation in **Croatia** descended indirectly from a nationalist party of the same name founded in 1861. The modern-day HSP was founded in February 1990 by Dobroslav Paraga, with support among **Croats** outside Croatia, on a platform of 'national-state sovereignty' for all of Croatia's 'historical and ethnic space', implying a territorial claim not just to the Croat-populated areas of **Bosnia and Herzegovina** but to the whole of that state. To these ends, the party formed a military wing called the **Croatian Defence Force** (HOS), which became heavily involved on the Croat side in inter-ethnic conflict in Bosnia. The party won five seats in the August 1992 elections to the lower house of the **Assembly** and Paraga came fourth in the concurrent presidential contest, winning 5.4% of the national vote. The party failed to win a seat in the February 1993 upper house elections, after which Paraga and three other HSP leaders were charged with terrorism and inciting forcible changes to the constitutional order.

In July 1993 police evicted the party from its headquarters in the capital, **Zagreb**, on the grounds that its occupation of the state-owned building since 1991 was illegal. Steps were also taken by the authorities to curtail the independence of the HOS by integrating its forces into units controlled by the Defence Ministry. Meanwhile, Paraga had been replaced as HSP leader by Boris Kandare at an extraordinary congress in September 1993, when a new main committee was elected as the party's governing body. Having been acquitted of the charges against him in November 1993, Paraga proceeded to form the breakaway Croatian Party of Rights 1861.

In the October 1995 lower house elections the HSP narrowly surmounted the 5% threshold, winning five seats. In the same year Kandare was replaced as party leader by Ante Djapić. In the January 2000 elections the HSP was allied with the small Croatian Christian Democratic Union (HKDU), the joint list winning 5.2% and five seats (including four for the HSP). In the presidential elections later the same month Djapić took only 1.8% of the first-round vote as the joint HKDU-HSP candidate.

Leadership: Ante Djapić (Chair.).
Address: 5 Primorska, 10000 Zagreb.
Telephone: (1) 3778016.
Fax: (1) 3778736.
Internet: www.hsp.hr

Croatian Peasants' Party (Bosnia and Herzegovina)
Hrvatska Seljacka Stranka (HSS)

The counterpart in **Bosnia and Herzegovina** of the **Croatian Peasants' Party of Croatia**. The moderate HSS contested the post-**Dayton** elections in September 1996 as part of the United List (ZL). The ZL candidate in the contest for the collective presidency, the then HSS Chairman Ivo Komsić, came second in the Croat section with 10% of the vote, while the ZL won three seats in the union lower house and 11 in the **Muslim-Croat Federation** lower house. Under the new leadership of Ilija Simić, the HSS won one seat in the Federation lower house in the September 1998 elections, retaining it in November 2000.

Leadership: Ilija Simić (Chair.).
Address: 4 Radićeva, Sarajevo.
Telephone: (33) 441987.
Fax: (33) 441897.

Croatian Peasants' Party (Croatia)
Hrvatska Seljačka Stranka (HSS)

A middle-ranking formation in **Croatia** which has participated in post-independence Governments. The HSS is descended from a co-operative party founded in 1904, which became a standard-bearer of **Croat** nationalism in inter-war **Yugoslavia** but was suppressed by the wartime pro-Nazi Ustaša regime in Croatia. Revived in November 1989 and committed to pacifism, local democracy, privatization and rural co-operatives, the HSS won three seats in the August 1992 elections to the lower house of the **Assembly** and five in the February 1993 upper house balloting. It then joined a coalition with the then ruling **Croatian Democratic Union** (HDZ) until the end of 1994.

In the October 1995 lower house elections the HSS won 10 seats as part of the opposition United List (ZL) alliance. For the January 2000 lower house elections it maintained the ZL, which then included the **Istrian Democratic Assembly**, the **Liberal Party** and the **Croatian People's Party** (HNS). The HSS took 16 of the 25 seats won by the alliance and obtained two portfolios (including agriculture) in the new centre-left coalition Government headed by the **Social Democratic Party of Croatia**. In presidential elections in January–February 2000 the HSS backed the successful candidacy of Stipe **Mesić** of the HNS.

Leadership: Zlatko Tomčić (President).
Address: 17 ul. Kralja Zvonimirova, 10000 Zagreb.
Telephone: (1) 4553627.
Fax: (1) 4553631.
E-mail: hss-sredisnjica@hss.hr
Internet: www.hss.hr

Croatian People's Party
Hrvatska Narodna Stranka (HNS)

A centrist formation whose candidate was elected President of **Croatia** in February 2000. The HNS was founded in 1990, although its core leadership had formed a dissident group since the attempt in 1970–71 to liberalize the then ruling **League of Communists** of Croatia within the **Socialist Federal Republic of Yugoslavia**. Drawing some support from ethnic **Serbs** as well as **Croats**, the party advocates 'modernity' in political and economic structures, private enterprise, regionalism and membership of the **European Union** and the **North Atlantic Treaty Organization**. In the August 1992 elections to the lower house of the **Assembly** it won six seats, while its Chairman came third in the concurrent presidential contest with 6% of the national vote. For the October 1995 lower house elections the HNS was part of the United List (ZL) alliance, winning two seats in its own right.

The HNS retained two lower house seats in the January 2000 Assembly elections, again standing as part of the ZL, which then included the **Croatian Peasants' Party**, the **Istrian Democratic Assembly** and the **Liberal Party**. One HNS Minister was appointed to the new centre-left Government headed by the **Social Democratic Party of Croatia**. The party also secured the election of its Vice-Chairman, Stipe **Mesić**, as President of Croatia in the January–February 2000 presidential elections, in which he stood as the HNS/ZL candidate. Against most initial forecasts, Mesić led in the first round with 41.1% of the vote and triumphed in the second with 56%.

Leadership: Vesna Pusić (Chair.).
Address: 2 Tomićeva, 10000 Zagreb.
Telephone: (1) 4846106.
Fax: (1) 4846109.
E-mail: webmaster@hns.hr
Internet: www.hns.hr

Croatian Privatization Fund

Founded in 1994 by a merger of the Croatian Fund for Development and the Restructuring and Development Agency.

President: Hrvoje Vojković.
Address: Ivana Lučića 6, 10000 Zagreb.
E-mail: hfp@hfp.hr
Internet: www.hfp.hr

Croatian Social-Liberal Party
Hrvatska Socijalno-Liberalna Stranka (HSLS)

A mainstream liberal party in **Croatia** founded in 1989, which came to government office in January 2000. Having made little impact in the 1990 pre-independence elections, the HSLS became the second-strongest party in the lower house elections to the **Assembly** in August 1992, winning 14 seats, while its Chairman took second place in the simultaneous presidential contest with 21.9% of the national vote. In the February 1993 upper house elections, the party won 16 of the 63 elective seats. Opposed to the Government of the **Croatian Democratic Union** (HDZ), the HSLS participated in an opposition boycott of the Assembly from May to September 1994. In the October 1995 lower house elections the party took 11.6% of the vote and 12 seats, confirming its status as the strongest single opposition party. In the June 1997 presidential elections, the then HSLP Chairman Vlado Gotovać came third with 17.6% of the vote (later leaving the HSLP to found the **Liberal Party**).

For the January 2000 Assembly elections, the HSLS was allied with the **Social Democratic Party of Croatia** (SPH), together with two small regional formations, and won 24 seats in the anti-HDZ victory. It took six portfolios in the resultant six-party coalition Government headed by the SPH. In the presidential elections three weeks later HSLS Chairman Dražen Budiša, backed by the SPH, took second place in the first round with 27.7% of the vote and therefore contested the second round in early February, when he won 44% but was defeated by the candidate of the **Croatian People's Party** (HNS).

In July 2001 four members of the HSLS withdrew from the Cabinet over the Government's continued co-operation with the **International Criminal Tribunal for the former Yugoslavia**.

Leadership: Dražen Budiša (President).
Address: 17/I Trg Nikole Šubića Zrinskog, 10000 Zagreb.
Telephone: (1) 4810403.
Fax: (1) 4810404.
E-mail: hsls@hsls.hr
Internet: www.hsls.hr

Croats

A south **Slavic people** dominant in **Croatia** and **Herzegovina**. Having arrived in the western **Balkans** in the Slavic migration of the 7th century, the Croats converted to **Roman Catholicism** under the suzerainty of the **Hungarian** kingdom. Ethnically and linguistically the Croats are almost identical to their neighbours the **Bosniaks** in **Bosnia and Herzegovina**, and the **Serbs** in **Yugoslavia** and Bosnia. The major distinction between the Croats and other south Slavs is their Catholic faith and the use of the Latin alphabet to transcribe their (Croatian) language.

Around 20% of Croatians, roughly 750,000, live in Bosnia and Herzegovina where they constitute around 17% of the total population, mostly in the southern Herzegovina region. Communities living in what became the **Serb Republic** within Bosnia were subject to discrimination and policies of **'ethnic cleansing'** during the Bosnian War (1992–95). Although calls for the union of Bosnian Croat communities with Croatia proper were effectively extinguished in the **Dayton Agreement** of November 1995, calls for greater ethnic autonomy have been close to the surface of Bosnian politics ever since, coming to the fore in a provocative, if short-lived, declaration of Croatian self-determination in March 2001 (*see* **Herceg-Bosna**).

Csángós

A minority **Roman Catholic** ethnic group resident in Moldavia (eastern **Romania**). The estimated 60–70,000 Csángós are generally accepted to be a community of ethnic **Hungarians** who arrived in modern Romania in the Middle Ages. However, the Romanian authorities are keen to see them as 'Hungarianized' Romanians. They have maintained a separate status owing to their strong adherence to Catholicism within their dominantly **Orthodox Christian** host country, and through the use of their language, which is seen as an ancient dialect of Hungarian. Csángó culture is proudly rooted in folk traditions but is perceived to be under threat as there is no established means of preserving the language and customs in Moldavia, unlike in neighbouring **Transylvania** where there is a well-established Hungarian community. As a result the European Council pledged in November 2001 to investigate and protect the minority.

CSDR *see* **Confederation of Democratic Trade Unions of Romania**.

CSRM *see* **Confederation of Trade Unions of the Republic of Moldova**.

ČSSD *see* **Czech Social Democratic Party**.

Cyrillic alphabet

The script used to transcribe eastern and southern **Slavic** languages as well as some non-Slavic tongues. It was first created in the 9th century by the Byzantine monks St Cyril and St Methodius, when they were dispatched to **Moravia** to help convert the local Slavic people to Christianity. The monks adapted their native Greek alphabet specifically for the use of the Slavic tribes, enabling the production of a Slavic liturgy. The script was reformed over the centuries with a final deletion of Greek-specific characters in 1918. The adoption of Cyrillic became linked to the **Orthodox Christian** Church, and its use remains a clear ethnic distinction between the **Roman Catholic** Slavs, who use Latin script, and their Orthodox neighbours. In the most significant cases, the difference has become the focus for nationalists in **Moldova** and has delineated major ethnic divisions in the former **Yugoslavia**. The alphabet was also exported by the Russian Empire to the conquered non-Slavic peoples. In recent years there have been specific moves to switch from Cyrillic to Latin script by some of these peoples, notably the **Tatars** and the **Azeris**. The reasons are various but include efforts to define non-Russian cultures more clearly and to increase potential trade with the West.

The countries in eastern Europe in which the Cyrillic script is used are: **Belarus, Bosnia and Herzegovina (Serbs), Bulgaria, Macedonia,** Moldova, the **Russian Federation, Ukraine** and Yugoslavia.

Czech-Moravian Confederation of Trade Unions
Českomoravská Konfederace Odborových Svazů (ČMKOS)

The principal trade union centre in the **Czech Republic**. The ČMKOS was established in November 1992 in anticipation of the separation of the Czech Republic from **Slovakia** from the beginning of 1993. The Czech union organization had previously been part of the Czechoslovak Confederation of Trade Unions (ČSKOS) founded in April 1990 (as the successor to the communist-era structure) and had shared the general ČSKOS opposition to the break-up of **Czechoslovakia**. The ČMKOS has no party affiliation, although its Chairman sits in the **Czech Social Democratic Party** group in the Senate. Affiliated to the International Confederation of Free Trade Unions (ICFTU), the ČMKOS groups together 29 unions representing 906,000 members.

President: Richard Falbr.
Address: 2 nám. Winston Churchilla, 11359 Prague 3.
Telephone: (2) 24461111.
Fax: (2) 22718994.

Czech National Bank
Česká národní banka (ČNB)

The Central Bank of the **Czech Republic**. The ČNB was formed in 1993 as a result of the need to divide the activities of the former State Bank of **Czechoslovakia** into its Czech and Slovak elements. It is independent of the Government and aims to control the national currency, the koruny. It is the central authority on monetary policy, legislation and foreign exchange permission. It also supervises the banking industry in general. As at December 1999 the ČNB had reserves of 8,935m. koruny.

Governor: Zdeněk Tůma.
Address: Na Příkopě 28, 11503 Prague 1.

Telephone: (2) 24411111.
Fax: (2) 24413708.
E-mail: info@cnb.cz
Internet: www.cnb.cz

Czech News Agency
Česká tisková kancelář (ČTK)

The national news agency of the **Czech Republic**, a public corporation with a supervisory council elected by the Chamber of Deputies. In its current form the ČTK was established in 1992, and has been required to finance itself without a budget from the Government since 1996.
General Director: Dr Milan Stibral.
Address: Opletalova 5–7, 11144 Prague 1.
Telephone: (2) 22098111.
Fax: (2) 24220553.
E-mail: ctk@mail.ctk.cz
Internet: www.ctk.cz

Czech Republic
Česká Republika

An independent republic in **central Europe**, bounded to the north-east by Poland, to the west and north-west by Germany, to the south by Austria and to the south-east by Slovakia. Administratively, the country is divided into 13 regions (kraje) and the district of **Prague**.

Area: 78,703 sq km; *capital*: Prague; *population*: 10.3m. (2001 estimate), comprising **Czechs** 94.4%, **Slovaks** 3%, **Poles** 0.6%, **Germans** 0.5%, **Roma** 0.3%, **Hungarians** 0.2%, others 1%; *official language*: Czech; *religion*: **Roman Catholic** 39.2%, **Protestant** 4.6%, **Orthodox** 3%, other 13.4%, atheist 39.8%.

Legislative authority is vested in the bicameral **Parliament**, consisting of an 81-member upper chamber, the Senate (Senát), and 200-member lower house, the Chamber of Deputies (Poslanecká Sněmovna). Senate members are elected for a six-year term by popular vote from single-member constituencies, with one-third coming up for renewal every two years (although all 81 were elected in the inaugural ballot in 1996). The Chamber of Deputies is elected for a four-year term by a system of proportional representation applied to party lists winning at least 5% of the popular vote. The Head of State is the President, who is elected for a five-year term (renewable once only) by both houses of the legislature jointly. Executive power is held by the Prime Minister, who is appointed by the President, and the Council of Ministers.

Czech Republic

History: The region was settled by **Slavic** tribes from the 5th century. In the 9th century the Great Moravian Empire (*see* **Bohemia, Moravia** *and* **Slovakia**) was established. Moravia was conquered by the Magyars (Hungarians) before becoming a fief of Bohemia in 1029 (Bohemia itself having become an independent margravate in the late 10th century). In 1526 Bohemia came under the rule of the Habsburg dynasty. It was fully integrated from 1620 into the Austrian (subsequently Austro-Hungarian) Empire. In September 1919 the Treaty of St Germain recognized the new Republic of **Czechoslovakia**, proclaimed in 1918 and consisting of Bohemia, Moravia, and Slovakia. The 'tail' of **Ruthenia** was added from **Hungary** under the 1920 Treaty of **Trianon**.

Presidents Tomás Masaryk (elected in 1918) and Edvard Beneš (elected in 1935) maintained the young democracy between the wars until ethnic tensions increased. The Slovaks resented the dominance of Czech power in the political life of the state, while, more importantly, the German minority, influenced by the rise of Nazism, embraced extreme nationalism. Under the 1938 Munich Agreement, Czechoslovakia was forced to accept the annexation by Germany of its (German-speaking) **Sudetenland** border territories. The following year Nazi forces invaded the weakened state, establishing Bohemia and Moravia as a German protectorate and Slovakia as a self-governing puppet state.

After Soviet forces had liberated the country in 1945, the pre-1938 Czechoslovak state was re-established, although Ruthenia was ceded to the **Soviet Union** and the ethnic German population of the Sudetenland was expelled. In legislative elections in 1946, the Communist Party of Czechoslovakia (KSČ) won 38% of the vote and became the dominant political party. Two years later the communists gained full control and declared a 'people's democracy' in the Soviet style of government. In 1968, following the political repression of the post-war years, KSČ leader Alexander **Dubček** introduced a programme of political and economic liberalization known as the '**Prague Spring**'. This was perceived by the Soviet Union as a threat to stability, and **Warsaw Pact** forces consequently invaded Czechoslovakia to restore the orthodox line. Czech dissidence continued, however, reflected most notably in the **Charter 77** human rights movement.

In 1989, encouraged by democratization movements elsewhere in central and **eastern Europe**, anti-Government demonstrations in Czechoslovakia forced the communists to relinquish their monopoly of power, in what was dubbed the '**velvet revolution**'. By the end of 1989 a new Government with a non-communist majority, including members of the **Civic Forum** (OF) coalition of Czech opposition groups, had been formed, and Gustáv **Husák** (KSČ leader in 1969–87) had been replaced as State President by Václav **Havel**, a prominent writer and long-time dissident. The historic KSČ was proscribed in mid-1991, but by then its Czech component had become the **Communist Party of Bohemia and Moravia** (KSČM).

Political liberalization in Czechoslovakia was paralleled by the emergence of a strong Slovak nationalist movement seeking independence for Slovakia as a sovereign state. The creation of separate Czech and Slovak entities was agreed during

1992 and took effect in January 1993 with the dissolution of the Czechoslovak federation (the so-called '**velvet divorce**'). Havel was subsequently elected President of the new Republic (having previously resigned as Head of State of Czechoslovakia in 1992).

In mid-1996, in the first post-separation elections to the Czech Chamber of Deputies, the incumbent centre-right Government headed by the **Civic Democratic Party** (ODS) under the leadership of Václav **Klaus** was returned to power but without an overall majority, having obtained a combined total of 99 of the 200 seats. It therefore concluded an external support arrangement with the **Czech Social Democratic Party** (ČSSD), which had won 61 seats. In 1997 the Klaus Government faced mounting difficulties, including a major financial crisis in May and allegations of illegal funding against the ODS. The withdrawal of the two small coalition parties impelled Klaus to resign in November 1997. A mainly 'technocratic' Government was installed under a non-party Prime Minister, after the ČSSD had secured an agreement that early elections would be held. In January 1998 Havel was re-elected as President for a second term (and subsequently underwent further surgery for a serious medical condition).

Latest elections: Polling in June 1998 for the Chamber of Deputies resulted in the ČSSD becoming the largest party with 74 seats (with 32.0% of the vote), followed by the ODS with 63 (27.7%), the KSČM (11.0%), the **Christian Democratic Union–Czechoslovak People's Party** (KDU–ČSL) with 20 (9.0%) and the **Freedom Union** (US) with 19 (8.6%). Partial elections to the Senate in November 1998 and November 2000 resulted in its composition becoming as follows: ODS 22 seats, KDU–ČSL 21, US 18, ČSSD 15, KSČM 3, independents 2.

Recent developments: In July 1998 a ČSSD minority Government was formed under the premiership of Miloš **Zeman**, who secured a pledge of external support from Klaus and the ODS. Zeman agreed to continue his predecessor's pro-market policies, but the presence of several former communists among his Ministers raised question marks about the Government's commitment to reform, as the economic situation deteriorated in 1999 and little progress was made against financial corruption. The so-called 'opposition agreement' between the ČSSD and the ODS continued to underpin the Government into 2001, but was increasingly questioned in both parties, especially after both suffered major reverses in the November 2000 partial Senate elections.

International relations and defence: The Czech Republic, as a new sovereign state, was admitted to the United Nations in 1993 and also joined the **Organization for Security and Co-operation in Europe**, the **Council of Europe**, the **Central European Initiative** and the **Central European Free Trade Area**, as well as the **Organization for Economic Co-operation and Development** and the **World Trade Organization**. Having acceded to the **Partnership for Peace** programme in 1994, the Czech Republic became a full member of **NATO** (together with **Hungary** and **Poland**) in March 1999. Following its 1996 application for membership of the **European Union** (EU), the Czech Republic opened formal accession negotiations with the EU in March 1998, after the contentious issue of compensation for expelled Sudetenland Germans had been put aside in March 1997. A lengthy dispute with Slovakia over the division of assets of the former federation was finally resolved in May 2000, while in December 2000 serious strains with Austria over a controversial new Czech nuclear plant at Temelín were eased, at least at government level, by an EU-mediated agreement that the plant would not be activated until an assessment of its safety had been completed.

The Czech Republic's defence budget for 2000 amounted to some US $1,200m., equivalent to about 2.3% of GDP. The size of the armed forces at the end of 2000 was some 58,000 personnel, including those serving under compulsory conscription of 12 months, while reservists numbered an estimated 240,000.

Czech Republic, economy

In gradual transition from communist-era state control to a free-market system, with many attendant difficulties. The 1993 division of **Czechoslovakia** and the resultant creation of the Czech Republic and **Slovakia** presented additional economic problems to the two new countries in view of the separation of their respective economic bases.

GNP: US $46,933m. (2000); *GNP per capita*: $4,920 (2000); *GDP at PPP*: $121,000m. (1999); *GDP per capita at PPP*: $11,700 (1999); *exports*: $28,941m. (2000); *imports*: $31,880m. (2000); *currency*: koruna (plural: koruny; US $1=K35.56 at the end of December 2001).

In the Czech Republic, industry contributed 42% of GDP in 1999, agriculture 5% and services 53%. Some 41% of the land is arable, 2% under permanent crops, 11% permanent pasture and 34% forests and woodland. The main crops are grain, potatoes, sugar beet, hops and fruit, while pigs, cattle and poultry are raised and forests are exploited. The main mineral resources include both hard coal and soft coal (lignite). The principal industries are ferrous metallurgy, machinery and equipment, coal, motor industries and armaments; tourism is an important asset. About 20% of energy requirements are provided through nuclear power generation.

Although landlocked, the Czech Republic is placed on a strategic trans-European communications crossroads, which has enabled it to become a major trading country. Its main exports by value in 1998 were machinery and transport equipment (41%), other manufactured goods (40%), chemicals (8%) and raw materials and fuel (8%). Principal imports in 1998 were machinery and transport equipment (39%), other manufactured goods (21%), chemicals (12%), raw materials and fuel (10%) and foodstuffs (5%). Germany is by far the largest purchaser of Czech exports (41% in 2000), followed by Slovakia (8%) and Austria (6%). Germany is also the largest supplier of Czech imports (33% in 2000), followed by the **Russian Federation** (7%) and Slovakia (6%). Trade with the **European Union** (EU) represents over 60% of both imports and exports.

The Czech Republic emerged from the division of Czechoslovakia stronger than Slovakia economically. Despite damaging new barriers to Czech-Slovak trade, by the end of 1995 the Czech economy was regarded as a success story of post-communist transition, with low inflation and unemployment rates combined with GDP growth of 6% in 1995 and apparent speedy progress towards a market economy. As a mark of the transformation, the Czech Republic in 1995 became the first post-communist state to be admitted to the **Organization for Economic Co-operation and Development** (OECD) of the rich developed countries.

However, macroeconomic performance began to falter in 1996, as Western investment and weak corporate governance fuelled inflation and undermined the current account, so that the existing fixed exchange rate system became unmanageable. A crisis in May 1997, partly brought on by the Asian financial collapse, forced the Government to adopt a managed float of the previously pegged koruna and effectively to devalue the currency by 10–12%. GDP growth was under 1% in 1997, when the position was worsened by massive floods over a third of the country, following which GDP contracted by 2.3% in 1998, as inflation rose to 13% and unemployment to over 8%.

The minority Government of the **Czech Social Democratic Party** elected in June 1998 committed itself to stabilization plans already in place and to pursuing transition to a market economy. Its central goal was accession to the EU, on which formal negotiations opened in November 1998.

GDP contracted further in 1999, by 0.5%, but inflation was reduced to 2.5%. Modest recovery began in 2000, with GDP growth of 2%, although unemployment remained high at around 9%. The Government's budget for 2001 provided for expenditure of K685,180m. and revenue of K636,200m., in line with the aim of reducing the fiscal deficit to meet EU criteria.

The post-1993 independent Czech Republic continued the privatization programme which had started under the Czechoslovak regime, using an innovative system under which vouchers for prospective share ownership were issued to citizens (*see* **voucher privatization**). Almost all small and medium-sized enterprises passed into private ownership, while in 1995 the Government announced that certain major enterprises were also to be privatized, although the state would retain holdings. Pervasive domestic corruption tarnished the privatization process, however, with the result that economic efficiency was by no means enhanced. The post-1998 Government relaunched the process, which was extended to the banking sector. In April 1999 the Government announced that a number of struggling Czech-owned companies would be taken back into temporary state control. A new restructuring agency would take over loans made by state-owned banks and seek foreign buyers for the companies.

Czech Social Democratic Party
Česká Strana Sociálně Demokratická (ČSSD)

The governing party in the **Czech Republic** since 1998, and a member party of the **Socialist International**. Founded in 1878 as an autonomous section of the Austrian labour movement, the ČSSD became an independent party in 1911. Following the creation of **Czechoslovakia** after the First World War, it won a quarter of the vote in the 1920 elections but was weakened by the exodus of its pro-Bolshevik wing in 1921. In 1938 the party was obliged to become part of the newly-created National Labour Party under the post-Munich system of 'authoritarian democracy'. When Hitler moved on to the further dismantling of Czechoslovakia in March 1939, the party went underground and was a member of the Government-in-exile in London during the Second World War. It participated in the post-war communist-dominated National Front but came under mounting pressure from the communists, who used the state security apparatus in a campaign to eliminate their main political rivals. In a political crisis in February 1948 the ČSSD was forced to merge with the Communist Party, and thereafter maintained its separate existence only in exile.

Following the collapse of communist rule in late 1989, the ČSSD was officially re-established in Czechoslovakia in March 1990, aspiring at that stage to be a 'Czechoslovak' party appealing to both **Czechs** and **Slovaks**. It failed to secure representation in the June 1990 elections, after which its Czech and Slovak wings in effect became separate parties, although 'Czechoslovak' remained its official descriptor. In the June 1992 elections the ČSSD won 16 seats in the 200-member Czech National Council and also secured representation in the Czech sections of both federal houses. It then mounted strong opposition to the proposed '**velvet divorce**' between Czechs and Slovaks, arguing in favour of a 'confederal union', but eventually accepting the inevitability of the separation. At its first post-separation congress in February 1993, the party formally renamed itself the 'Czech' SSD and elected a new leadership under Miloš **Zeman**, who declared his aim as being to provide a left-wing alternative to the neo-conservatism of the Government led by the **Civic Democratic Party** (ODS), while at the same time ruling out co-operation with the **Communist Party of Bohemia and Moravia**.

The ČSSD made a major advance in the 1996 Parliament elections, winning 61 of the 200 lower house seats on a 26.4% vote share and becoming the second-strongest party. It opted to give qualified external support to a new centre-right coalition headed by the ODS, on the basis that privatization of the transport and energy sectors would be halted and that a Social Democrat would become Chairman of the new lower house. Following the resignation of the Government in November 1997, the ČSSD became the largest party in early elections in June 1998, winning 74 of the lower house seats with 32.3% of the vote. Zeman therefore formed a minority ČSSD Government, which was given external support by the ODS under a so-called 'opposition agreement'.

In March 1999 the Zeman Government took the Czech Republic into the **North Atlantic Treaty Organization** (NATO) and in December secured official candidate status for **European Union** accession. It also continued the previous Government's pro-market liberalization policies, although a deteriorating economic situation eroded its support, as did allegations of illicit ČSSD funding. In partial Senate elections in November 2000 the ČSSD won only one seat (its representation in the 81-member upper chamber falling to 15), while in simultaneous regional elections its vote slumped to 14.7%. With Zeman having given notice that he would stand down as party leader before the elections due in 2002, his heir apparent, Deputy Chairman Vladimír Špidla, distanced himself from the accord with the ODS, advocating that the ČSSD should be 'free and without commitment' in the next electoral contest. Špidla was dutifully elected Chairman of the party on 7 April 2001.

Leadership: Vladimír Špidla (Chair.).
Address: Hybernská 7, 11000 Prague 1.
Telephone: (2) 24219911.
Fax: (2) 24222190.
E-mail: info@socdem.cz
Internet: www.cssd.cz

CzechInvest
Česká agentura pro zahraniční investice

Foreign investment agency in the **Czech Republic**. Founded in 1992.
Director: Martin Jahn.
Address: Štěpánská 15, 12000 Prague 2.
Telephone: (2) 96342500.
Fax: (2) 96342501.
E-mail: marketing@czechinvest.com
Internet: www.czechinvest.com

Czechoslovakia

A former unified state which divided formally into the **Czech Republic** and **Slovakia** on 1 January 1993. Czechoslovakia was first created as one of the successor states to the Habsburg Empire in November 1918 and was officially recognized by the international community in the Treaty of St Germain in September 1919. Containing the industrially important regions of **Bohemia** and **Moravia**, Czechoslovakia, with its capital at **Prague**, had an apparently bright future. However, ethnic tensions between the **Czechs**, **Slovaks** and other minorities (chiefly **Germans** and **Hungarians**) were exacerbated by the new centralized state. These rifts were successfully exploited by nationalist Governments in neighbouring Germany and

Hungary. Its integrity fatally compromised by the Munich Agreement in 1938 (*see* **Sudetenland**), whereby Germany was allowed to annexe swathes of its territory, Czechoslovakia was reduced to a rump entity before and during the Second World War, under Nazi rule apart from a nominally independent Slovak collaborationist regime.

In 1945 a reconstituted Czechoslovakia (minus the 'tail' of Ruthenia which had been added from Hungarian territory under the 1920 Treaty of **Trianon**) became one of the key frontier states between western and **eastern Europe** (*see* **Potsdam Agreements** and **Yalta Agreements**). Under communist government from 1947, it attempted an experiment in liberalization—the **Prague Spring** of 1968—which was crushed by **Soviet**-led military intervention, but in 1989 the old regime was swept aside by one of the more dramatic of that year's wave of pro-democracy movements, a democratic Czechoslovakia emerging from what became known as the '**velvet revolution**'. Despite a federal-style Constitution, tensions between the Czech Lands and Slovakia quickly emerged thereafter, leading to the so-called '**velvet divorce**' and the final separation of the two modern states.

Czechs

A west **Slavic people** dominant in the modern **Czech Republic**. The Czechs had replaced the local Celtic and **German** tribes of **Bohemia** and **Moravia** by the 5th to 6th century and established the two respective kingdoms in following centuries. Like the other neighbouring west Slavs (**Slovaks** and **Poles**) the Czechs are largely Catholic and use the Latin script to transcribe their language, which is very similar to Polish and almost identical to Slovak. As the most westerly of all Slavic states the Czechs have perhaps the most 'western' identity of all the Slavs, and consider themselves very much to be a **central European** people. Tensions between Czechs and Slovaks, with whom they shared the state of **Czechoslovakia** after 1919, gained free expression after the collapse of communism and prompted the '**velvet divorce**' which left each with a separate state in 1993. Small communities of ethnic Czechs live throughout **eastern Europe**.

D

DA *see* Democratic Alternative.

Dade, Arta

Minister of Foreign Affairs, **Albania**.

Arta Dade was a member of the **Socialist Party of Albania** (PSS) from its creation in 1991, and has been an active voice in centre-left politics ever since. She first entered government in 1997 and returned as Foreign Minister in September 2001.

Born on 15 March 1953 in **Tirana**, she graduated from the language department of the city's university in 1975 and taught languages to schoolchildren for 10 years. She returned to the university in 1985 as a professor of English, and achieved a postgraduate qualification in the UK in 1992. During this time she joined the PSS, which was founded in 1991 and from 1992 she was a member of the party's Presidency. She has also been a member of various socialist women's groups. She was first elected to the **People's Assembly** in 1997 and was appointed Minister of Culture, Youth and Sport that year. From 1998 until her reappointment to the Cabinet as Foreign Minister in 2001 she served on a number of parliamentary committees.

Arta Dade has two children and is fluent in English, French and Italian.
Address: Ministria e Punëve të Jashtme, Bul. Zhan d'Ark, Tirana.
Telephone: (4) 234600.
Fax: (4) 232971.
E-mail: dshtypi@abissnet.com.al
Internet: www.mfa.gov.al

Dagestan

A constituent republic of the **Russian Federation** stretching along the western shore of the Caspian Sea down to the **Caucasus** mountains. It is the most ethnically diverse state in Europe with more than 32 ethnic groups, only four of them numbering more than about 200,000. It is also the centre of Islam in the region.

Dalmatia

Population: 1.8m. (1997 estimate). Russian suzerainty was not officially established over Dagestan until 1877, although contact had been made as early as the 15th century. An autonomous Dagestani **Soviet** republic was created in January 1921. Despite the wide variety of peoples from varying ethnic backgrounds—Caucasians, Iranians, **Slavs** and **Turks**—tensions were kept in check during the Soviet era. Most people are at least bilingual, speaking their own dialect and usually one of the three major languages: Avar, Kumyk and Russian.

Although it was declared a full Soviet republic in May 1991, Dagestan did not become an independent state when the **Soviet Union** collapsed later that year, but instead became a sovereign republic within the Russian Federation in March 1992. Adherence to Islam is a major binding force, with **Muslim** brotherhoods regulating social life, but in 1999 an abortive Islamic uprising in the north was swiftly and severely crushed by Russian troops. Clashes over land rights and the campaigns of various nationalist movements have added to the volatility of the situation. A series of ethnic nationalist movements, among the mostly Sunni Muslim groups, have made calls ranging from greater ethnic autonomy to full regional separatism. There has been pressure for the establishment of a mini-federal system in the republic to try to reconcile these demands.

The main ethnic groups, which make up almost 80% of the population, are the **Avars** (the traditional ruling elite and, at around 28%, the largest single group in the republic), **Dargins, Lezghins, Kumyks** (whose Turkic language and culture serves as a *lingua franca* across the north Caucasus region), and **Russians**. Other groups include the Aguls, **Azeris, Chechens**, Laks, Nogai, Rutuls and **Tabasarans**. The smallest linguistic group are the c.5000 Hinukhs.

Economic activity is largely agricultural, centring on breeding sheep. Large potential reserves of oil, gas, coal, iron and other minerals have been mostly under-developed, due in part to the mountainous terrain. The republic's capital is at Makhachkala. Dagestan's Soviet-era ruler since 1987, Magomedali Magomedovich Magomedov, was appointed State Council Chairman in July 1994.

Dalmatia

The Adriatic coast of **Croatia** extending from Rijeka in the north to the **Prevlaka peninsula** in the south. The thin coastal strip, with its many nearby islands, is agriculturally rich and scenically beautiful. Separated from the **Balkan** hinterland by the Dinaric Alps, it has had a history distinct from that of the inland regions. Originally inhabited by Illyrians, Dalmatia felt the tread of over 30 different conquerors up to the 15th century when the area fell under the sway of the Venetian trading empire. It was part of the Habsburg Empire, apart from a nine-year period when it formed the coastal region of the Napoleonic Illyrian Provinces (1805–14), and was directly ruled from Vienna from 1879 to 1918. Under the post-1918 European peace settlement Dalmatia was reunited with the Croatian district of **Slavonia** and formed an integral part of Croatia within what was later named **Yugoslavia**.

Noted for the cultivation of vines and olives, Dalmatia also contains some rich deposits of bauxite and limestone, and the major tourist destinations of Split and **Dubrovnik** (although the vibrant tourist industry was greatly set back by the wars of the early 1990s). There are also some shipyards at Split and hydroelectric plants along the course of some of the fast-flowing Dalmatian rivers.

Danube Commission

A body set up in 1948 to supervise the implementation of the convention on the regime of navigation on the River Danube. The Commission holds annual sessions, approves projects for river maintenance, and supervises a uniform system of traffic regulations on the whole navigable portion of the Danube and on river inspection.

Members: Austria, **Bulgaria, Croatia,** Germany, **Hungary, Moldova, Romania, Russian Federation, Slovakia, Ukraine** and **Yugoslavia**.
Leadership: Dr H. Strasser (President).
Address: Benczúr utca 25, 1068 Budapest, Hungary.
Telephone: (1) 3521835.
Fax: (1) 3521839.
E-mail: dunacom@mail.matav.hu
Internet: www.dunacom.matav.hu

Danzig *see* **Gdańsk**.

Dargins

A Caucasian people who make up the second-largest group in the **Russian** republic of **Dagestan** after the **Avars**. Known in Dargin as *Dargan* or *Dargwa*. Numbering around 350,000 they constitute nearly 20% of the republic's population. They are concentrated in the south and central areas of the republic where they practise agriculture, particularly breeding sheep. Although most Dargins are Sunni **Muslim**, there is a Shi'ite minority. Tensions exist between Dargins and **Kumyks,** into which culturally dominant group some Dargins have been assimilated.

Dashnak *see* **Armenian Revolutionary Federation**.

Dayton Agreement

The November 1995 Agreement to end the conflict in **Bosnia and Herzegovina**. The Agreement, signed formally the following month in Paris, was named after the US town of Dayton, Ohio, where the so-called 'proximity talks' took place after the 5 October cease-fire. Its signatories were representatives of the Republic of Bosnia and Herzegovina (but not of the Bosnian **Serb** side in the war), the Republic of **Croatia** and the Federal Republic of **Yugoslavia** (FRY). It was witnessed by representatives of the **Contact Group** nations—the USA, the UK, France, Germany and the **Russian Federation**—and the **European Union** Special Negotiator.

The Dayton Peace Agreement consisted of a General Framework for Peace in Bosnia and Herzegovina (a brief document in which the signatories agreed to respect each other's sovereignty and to settle disputes by peaceful means, and under which the FRY and the Republic of Bosnia and Herzegovina recognized one another) and 11 annexes on the detailed issues. These included: the withdrawal of forces and the involvement of the multinational military Implementation Force (IFOR—*see* **Stabilization Force**); the definition of the boundary within Bosnia between the **Muslim-Croat Federation** and the **Serb Republic**; the arrangement of elections according to a prescribed timetable; the adoption of the new Constitution of Bosnia and Herzegovina; provisions on human rights and the right of return for refugees; and the creation of the **Office of High Representative** to co-ordinate and facilitate civilian aspects of the peace settlement.

Democrat Party
Partia Demokratike (PD)

A centre-right pro-market party in **Albania** formed in February 2001 as a splinter from the main opposition **Democratic Party of Albania** (PDS). Its leader Genc Pollo is a former General Secretary of the PDS. He represented the main opposition to PDS stalwart Sali Berisha and had challenged him for the party leadership in September 1999. Pollo had withdrawn from that contest claiming he had received threats against himself and his family. Consequently he led a 'reform' movement within the PDS, which entitled itself the Democratic Alternative, in direct opposition to Berisha's tenure and in favour of greater party democracy. Pollo and three other parliamentarians were subsequently dismissed from the PDS's parliamentary group in February 2000.

The Democratic Alternative continued to clash with Berisha, ignoring demands to boycott parliamentary sessions and frequently calling for Berisha's resignation as Party Chairman. Pollo and his supporters eventually split formally from the PDS to form the New Democratic Party (PD e Re) in February 2001. The new party absorbed the Movement for Democracy and the Right Democratic Party. Among its notable members was former Mayor of **Tirana** Albert Brojka. Eager to hold itself up as the rightful inheritor to the PDS legacy as the main opposition in post-communist Albania, PD e Re voted in April 2001 to change its name to the Democrat Party, taking the same initials in Albanian as the PDS (which is known within the country as just 'PD'). The new party only managed to garner 5% of the vote in legislative elections in June 2001, giving it just six seats in the **People's Assembly**.

Democratic Alliance of Albania
Aleanca Demokratike e Shqipërisë (ADS)

A small centre-right political party in **Albania**. The ADS was founded in October 1992 by a breakaway group of the then ruling **Democratic Party of Albania** (PDS) opposed to the alleged autocratic tendencies of President Berisha, who in turn accused the dissidents of having pro-**Serbian** inclinations. For the controversial mid-1996 **People's Assembly** elections the ADS was part of the 'Pole of the Centre' alliance with the **Social Democratic Party of Albania**. However, after several ADS candidates had been banned because of their communist past, the ADS joined an opposition boycott of the second round. In the 1997 Assembly elections the ADS presented its own list, winning two seats with 2.8% of the vote, and subsequently joined a centre-left coalition headed by the **Socialist Party of Albania**. It ran again in elections in June 2001 and won three seats in the Assembly.

Leadership: Neritan Çeka (Chair.).
Address: c/o Kuvendi Popullor, Tirana.
Internet: www.aleanca.org

Democratic Alternative
Demokratska Alternativa (DA)

A pro-business political party in **Macedonia**. The DA was launched in March 1998 by Vasil Tupurkovski, who had been the Macedonian member of the presidency of the former federal **Yugoslavia** in the last phase of communist rule, and espoused a pro-market platform seeking to appeal to all ethnic groups. The party formed the 'For Changes' alliance with the nationalist **Internal Macedonian Revolutionary Organization–Democratic Party for Macedonian National Unity** (VMRO–DPMNE) in the autumn 1998 **Assembly of the Republic** elections, contributing to the victory of the alliance by winning 13 seats and 11% of the vote itself. Five DA members were appointed to the resultant coalition Government headed by the VMRO–DPMNE and also including the ethnic Albanian **Democratic Party of Albanians** (DPA), the party being particularly associated with Macedonia's controversial decision in January 1999 to recognize Taiwan.

Initial plans that Tupurkovski would be the joint presidential candidate of the main ruling parties in late 1999 were thwarted by increasing divisions between the DA and the VMRO–DPMNE. Running under the DA banner, Tupurkovski managed only 16% of the first-round vote and was therefore eliminated. Strife in the ruling coalition intensified, resulting in the DA's withdrawal from the Government in November 2000, although some DA dissidents backed the successor administration.

An insurgency launched in February 2001 by ethnic Albanian rebels seeking greater rights for the Albanian community led to the formation of a Government of National Unity in May comprising parties from all sides of the Assembly, but not including the DA. However, following the implementation of a peace accord, the more nationalistic ethnic Macedonian parties left the Government in November and were replaced by **New Democracy** (ND), which had been formed in March from a small splinter of the DA.

Leadership: Vasil Tupurkovski (Chair.).
Address: c/o Sobranie, 11 Oktomvri b.b., Skopje 91000.
Telephone: (2) 362713.
Fax: (2) 363089.

Democratic League of Independent Trade Unions
Független Szakszervezetek Demokratikus Ligája (FSzDL/Liga)

An independent trade union centre in **Hungary** launched in early 1989, the first to challenge the then communist-dominated union structure. The Liga has remained smaller than the dominant **National Confederation of Hungarian Trade Unions**, but has established a strong second-ranking presence in elected works' councils. Claiming to represent some 100,000 workers, the Liga has links with the centre-left **Alliance of Free Democrats** and is one of three Hungarian affiliates to the International Confederation of Free Trade Unions (ICFTU).

President: István Gaskó.
Address: 156 út Thököly, Budapest 1146.
Telephone: (1) 2512300.
Fax: (1) 2512288.
E-mail: liga@telnet.hu

Democratic League of Kosovo
Lidhja Demokratike e Kosovës (LDK)

The principal party of **Yugoslavia**'s ethnic **Albanians**, advocating independent status for the province of **Kosovo**. It is the successor, since 2000, to the Democratic Alliance of Kosovo (DSK).

The DSK was formed in 1990 when the Government ended Kosovo's autonomous status, thus provoking widespread ethnic Albanian protest against **Serb** rule. Calling for a negotiated settlement and officially opposing armed struggle, the DSK won a majority of seats in provincial assembly elections organized by

Albanians in May 1992, with its leader Ibrahim Rugova being declared the 'President of Kosovo'. However, the elections were declared illegal by the Serbian and federal authorities and the Assembly was prevented from holding its inaugural session. Subsequent Serbian and federal elections were boycotted by the DSK.

Although Rugova and the DSK won large majorities in further presidential and assembly elections organized illegally in Kosovo in March 1998, he and his party appeared to be marginalized as conflict in the province intensified and the **Kosovo Liberation Army** (UCK) came to the fore. Rugova continued to support a negotiated settlement, attracting criticism from ethnic Albanians when he appeared on television with President Slobodan **Milošević** in April 1999 (possibly under duress), soon after the start of the **North Atlantic Treaty Organization** bombardment of **Serbia**. He was also censured for departing to Italy for the rest of the conflict.

Following the withdrawal of Serb forces from Kosovo in June 1999 and Rugova's return a month later, the DSK recovered its status as the principal political representative of Kosovar Albanians. In August 1999 it joined the Kosovo Transitional Council set up by the new UN administration, thereafter working with the UN to promote inter-ethnic peace and reconciliation. In October 2000 the LDK welcomed the ousting of the Milošević regime, although the successor Government of the **Democratic Opposition of Serbia** (DOS) was also resolutely opposed to independence for Kosovo. In municipal elections in Kosovo in the same month, the renamed LDK obtained 58% of the vote and won control of 21 of the 30 municipalities at issue. Its success, however, was not welcomed by pro-independence groups who launched a brief violent backlash which included the assassination of a close aide to Rugova in November 2000. Tensions were quickly calmed but the party registered a slight drop in support in elections for the UN-sponsored regional assembly a year later. It did nevertheless emerge as the largest single party, winning 46% of the vote. Rugova immediately angered the international community by making open calls after the LDK victory for the full independence of Kosovo. By the end of 2001 the party remained in a deadlock with other Albanian parties over the formation of a coalition Government.

Leadership: Ibrahim Rugova (Chair.).
Address: Priština.

Democratic Left Alliance
Sojusz Lewicy Demokratycznej (SLD)

The principal left-wing party in **Poland**, descended from communist-era formations but now of democratic socialist orientation and affiliated to the **Socialist International**. The SLD was created prior to the 1991 elections as an alliance of Social Democracy of the Polish Republic (SdRP), the direct successor of the former ruling (communist) Polish United Workers' Party, and the **All-Poland Alliance of Trade Unions** (OPZZ), which was derived from the official federation of the communist era. Having won 60 seats in the lower house of the **National Assembly** in 1991, the SLD became the largest party in the September 1993 elections, with 171 seats and 20.4% of the vote, and formed a coalition Government with the **Polish Peasant Party** (PSL).

The PSL held the premiership until February 1995, when Józef Oleksy of the SLD/SdRP took the post. The then SdRP leader, Aleksander **Kwaśniewski**, was the successful SLD candidate in the November 1995 presidential elections, narrowly defeating incumbent Lech **Wałęsa** with the support of over 30 other groupings. In February 1996 Oleksy was replaced as Prime Minister by Włodzimierz **Cimoszewicz**, an adherent of the SLD but not of any of its constituent parts.

In the September 1997 parliamentary elections the SLD increased its share of the vote to 27.1%, but its lower house representation fell to 164 seats, well below the total achieved by the new centre-right **Solidarity Electoral Action** (AWS). The SLD therefore went in opposition, taking some consolation from a strong performance in local elections in October 1998, when its 32% vote share gave it control of nine of the country's 16 voivodships.

Having supported Poland's accession to the **North Atlantic Treaty Organization** (NATO) in March 1999, the SLD formally established itself as a unitary party two months later, this being followed by the dissolution of the SdRP in June. At the first congress of the new SLD in December 1999, former Interior Minister Leszek **Miller** was elected Chairman and the party undertook to support pro-market reforms but in a way that would soften their impact on the population. The party also reiterated its strong support for Polish accession to the **European Union**.

Benefiting from the unpopularity of the AWS-led Government, the SLD secured the re-election of Kwaśniewski in presidential elections in October 2000, his outright first-round victory being achieved with 54% of the vote. The SLD went on to achieve a massive victory in legislative elections on 23 September 2001 in partnership with the **Labour Union** (UP), collectively securing 216 seats in the 460-seat lower house. Miller was nominated as Prime Minister and again formed a coalition Government with the PSL, along with the UP.

Leadership: Leszek Miller (Chair.).
Address: ul. Rozbrat 44A, Warsaw 00419.
Telephone: (22) 6210341.
Fax: (22) 6216657.

Democratic Opposition of Serbia
Demokratska Opozicija Srbije (DOS)

The broad alliance of parties in the **Yugoslav** republic of **Serbia** which defeated the **Milošević** regime in the 2000 elections.

The DOS was launched in early 2000 in the wake of the 1999 **Kosovo** crisis as a broad-based alliance of parties and groups seeking the removal of Slobodan Milošević from power and an end to the dominance of his **Socialist Party of**

Serbia (SPS). The alliance eventually embraced 19 parties and organizations, including the nationalist **Democratic Party** (DS) and **Democratic Party of Serbia** (DSS), the radical liberal **Civic Alliance of Serbia** (GSS), the pro-business **New Democracy** (ND), the centrist Christian Democratic Party of Serbia and Democratic Centre, the centre-left Social Democratic Union and Social Democracy, four parties representing ethnic **Hungarians** in **Vojvodina** and the **Muslim**/ethnic Albanian Party of Democratic Action (SDA).

The DOS candidate for the September 2000 federal presidential elections was Vojislav **Koštunica** of the DSS, regarded as the most right-wing of the alliance components. Despite widespread intimidation and vote-rigging, Koštunica was widely believed to have obtained an outright first-round victory over Milošević. Attempts by the regime to resist the democratic verdict prompted a DOS-orchestrated national uprising, which forced Milošević to hand over power in early October. Concurrent federal parliamentary elections, regarded by observers as equally flawed, resulted officially in the DOS alliance winning 58 of the 138 seats in the lower house of the **Federal Assembly**.

Inaugurated as Federal President, Koštunica appointed Zoran Zizić of the **Socialist People's Party of Montenegro** (SNPCG) as Federal Prime Minister, heading a transitional Government which consisted mainly of DOS representatives. In elections to the Serbian Assembly in December 2000, the DOS alliance displayed its true popular support by winning 176 of the 250 seats with a 64.1% vote share. A new Serbian Government appointed in January 2001 was headed by DS leader Zoran **Djindjić** and included representatives of all of the main DOS components.

The coming to power of the DOS and Koštunica was warmly welcomed by the international community, although the new President made it clear that his administration would be nationalist in orientation, notably in that it would resist any move to detach Kosovo from Serbia and would not co-operate with the **International Criminal Tribunal for the former Yugoslavia** in its pursuit of Yugoslavs indicted for alleged crimes, including Milošević. He also came out strongly in favour of maintenance of Serbia's federation with **Montenegro** and against the latter's moves towards independence.

Despite being in government, the alliance continued to use the DOS appellation pending a possible decision to adopt a more appropriate title and/or to create a unitary movement. Meanwhile, the component parties and organizations all maintained their individual identities and structures. This loose framework has proved increasingly fragile with clashes between the constitutionally weak Koštunica and the reform-minded Djindjić, sparked by the latter's unilateral decision to extradite Milošević in June 2001. The DOS only narrowly voted to remain intact at an internal vote held in August, but lost the support of the DSS, which withdrew from the Serbian Government on 17 August claiming disappointment at the Government's record on fighting crime.

Democratic Party (Bulgaria)

Leadership: Vojislav Koštunica (Chair.).
Address: Simina 41, Belgrade 11000.
Telephone: (11) 3340620.
Fax: (11) 3341924.
E-mail: info@dos.org.yu
Internet: www.dos.org.yu

Democratic Party (Bulgaria)
Demokraticheska Partiya (DP)

A political formation in **Bulgaria** descended from the conservative Christian party of the same name founded in 1896, affiliated to both the **Christian Democrat International** and the **International Democrat Union**. The DP was revived in 1989 and joined the opposition **Union of Democratic Forces** (SDS). Following the SDS victory in the October 1991 elections, the then DP Chairman Stefan Savov secured election as President of the **National Assembly**, but was forced to resign in September 1992 after being named in a censure motion tabled by the opposition **Bulgarian Socialist Party** and supported by some SDS deputies. For the December 1994 Assembly elections the DP broke with the SDS, forming the People's Union (NS) with a faction of the **Bulgarian Agrarian People's Union**, the alliance achieving third place with 18 of the 240 seats on a 6.5% vote share.

The DP/NS returned to the SDS fold, contesting the April 1997 Assembly elections as a component of the victorious SDS-led United Democratic Forces (ODS) and backing the successful candidacy of Petar **Stoyanov** of the SDS in the autumn 1997 presidential elections.

Savov died in January 2000. The DP remained in the ODS alliance for general elections in June 2001, when it was forced into opposition, along with the rest of the coalition, by the victory of the newly-created **National Movement Simeon II**.
Leadership: Aleksandur Pramatarski (Chair.).
Address: 8 Dondukov Blvd, 1000 Sofia.
Telephone: (2) 800187.
Fax: (2) 9813711.
E-mail: ful_bg@techno_link.com

Democratic Party (Romania)
Partidul Democrat (PD)

A centre-left political party in **Romania**, descended from the less successful of two factions which emerged within the National Salvation Front (FSN) after it assumed power following the overthrow of the **Ceauşescu** regime in December 1989. Most FSN leaders had previously been members of the communist **nomenklatura**. Having won landslide victories in the 1990 presidential and parliamentary elections, however, the FSN became divided between those favouring rapid transition to a market economy and President Ion **Iliescu**'s more cautious approach. In March 1991 an FSN conference, against the vote of the Iliescu faction, approved radical free-market reforms tabled by the then Prime Minister Petre Roman. When Roman was re-elected FSN leader in March 1992 (having vacated the premiership the previous October), the Iliescu faction broke away to form a new left-wing party which later became the core of the Social Democracy Party of Romania (PDSR). The rump pro-market FSN fared badly in the autumn 1992 presidential election, obtaining only 4.8% for its candidate, but in the simultaneous parliamentary elections it won 43 seats in the Chamber of Deputies (lower house of **Parliament**) on a vote share of over 10%. The following year it adopted 'Democratic Party' as a prefix in its title and quickly became known as the PD.

The PD contested the November 1996 elections within the Social Democratic Union (USD) alliance with the Romanian Social Democratic Party (PSDR), Roman coming third in the presidential contest with 20.5% of the vote and the PD again winning 43 Chamber seats in its own right. The PD joined the subsequent coalition Government headed by the centre-right **Christian Democratic National Peasants' Party** (PNȚCD) as the leading component of the Democratic Convention of Romania (CDR), left it in February 1998 and rejoined it two months later when a new Prime Minister was appointed, but continued thereafter to have strained relations with the other coalition parties.

Whereas the PSDR opted to join Iliescu's PDSR in the **Social Democratic Pole of Romania** for the November–December 2000 elections and was therefore on the winning side, the PD was damaged by its participation in a deeply unpopular Government. Roman sank to sixth place, winning less than 3% of the vote, in the first round of the presidential contest, whereupon the PD backed Iliescu in his second-round victory over the leader of the far-right **Greater Romania Party**. In the Chamber elections the PD avoided the wipe-out experienced by the CDR parties, but was reduced to 31 seats and 7% of the vote. It thereafter gave qualified external support to a PDSR minority Government, while becoming preoccupied with an internal power struggle between Roman and his would-be successors.

Leadership: Traian Basescu (President).
Address: Al. Modrogan 1, Bucharest 71274.
Telephone: (1) 2120343.
Fax: (1) 2121332.
E-mail: office@pd.ro
Internet: www.pd.ro

Democratic Party (Yugoslavia)
Demokratska Stranka (DS)

A right-wing although not ultra-nationalist **Serbian** party in **Yugoslavia** which came to power in late 2000 as a leading component of the **Democratic Opposition** of **Serbia** (DOS). Founded in 1990 as **Serbia**'s first opposition party under the leadership of prominent academic Dragoljub Mićunović, the DS adopted a nationalistic programme and advocated Serbian intervention in support of Serb separatists in **Bosnia and Herzegovina**. Nevertheless, its ultra-nationalist wing broke away in 1992 to form the **Democratic Party of Serbia** (DSS). Having won five lower house seats in the December 1992 **Federal Assembly** elections, the DS advanced to 29 seats in the Serbian Assembly elections in December 1993 and subsequently joined a coalition Government headed by Slobodan **Milošević**'s **Socialist Party of Serbia** (SPS), hoping to reform the system from within. In January 1994 Mićunović was succeeded as DS Chairman by Zoran **Djindjić**, then Mayor of **Belgrade**.

The DS reverted to opposition in 1996, joining the Zajedno (Together) alliance with the DSS, the **Serbian Renewal Movement** (SPO) and the **Civic Alliance of Serbia**, which won only 22 lower house seats in the November 1996 federal elections. The alliance collapsed in mid-1997 when Djindjić refused to back the SPO leader as opposition candidate for the Serbian presidency, the SPO retaliating by helping to eject the DS leader from the Belgrade mayorship. The DS then boycotted the Serbian Assembly elections in September 1997 in protest against media manipulation by the Milošević regime.

In late 1998 the DS joined a new opposition grouping called the Alliance for Change, which formed the core of the anti-Milošević DOS alliance launched in January 2000. The eventual victory of the DOS candidate, Vojislav **Koštunica** of the DSS, in the September 2000 federal presidential elections resulted in DS representatives joining the Federal Government. Moreover, following a landslide DOS victory in Serbian Assembly elections in December 2000, Djindjić was appointed Prime Minister of the Serbian Government in January 2001.

Leadership: Zoran **Djindjić** (Chair.).
Address: Krunska 69, Belgrade 11000.
Telephone: (11) 3443003.
Fax: (11) 3442946.
E-mail: info@ds.org.yu
Internet: www.ds.org.yu

Democratic Party of Albania
Partia Demokratike e Shqipërisë (PDS)

Centre-right pro-market political formation in **Albania** which was the first authorized opposition party to emerge in the post-communist era. Founded in December 1990 and based primarily in northern Albania, the PDS was descended from a movement of dissident intellectuals seeking to undermine communist rule from within. Led by cardiologist Sali Berisha, the PDS won 75 of 250 **People's Assembly** seats in the March–April 1991 elections, subsequently joining a 'non-partisan' Government with the **Socialist Party of Albania** (PSS). Complaining about the slow pace of reform, the PDS withdrew from this Government in December 1991. Its breakthrough to political dominance came shortly thereafter, when the party won 92 out of 140 Assembly seats in the March 1992 election, with 62.8% of the first-round vote. The following month Berisha was elected President of Albania (and was succeeded as PDS Chairman by Eduard Selami), whereupon Aleksander Meksi of the PDS became Prime Minister in a coalition with the small **Social Democratic Party of Albania** (PSDS).

The rejection in November 1994 of a draft Constitution proposed by the PDS-led coalition was accompanied by charges that Berisha was seeking to increase presidential powers at the expense of the Assembly. At a special PDS conference in March 1995 Selami was deposed from the chairmanship, having opposed Berisha's plan to hold another constitutional referendum. In March 1996 the pro-Berisha Tritan Shehu was appointed PDS Chairman, while a month later Selami and a group of supporters were ousted from the party's national council. In the controversial Assembly elections of May–June 1996 the PDS won 122 of the 140 seats, but the descent into near anarchy and north–south conflict early in 1997 forced the PDS to surrender the premiership to the PSS in March. In new Assembly elections in June–July 1997 the PDS slumped to 29 seats out of 155 (and 25.7% of the vote), whereupon Berisha vacated the presidency and the party went into opposition to a Government led by Fatos **Nano** of the PSS.

The shooting of a PDS deputy by a PSS member in September 1997 provoked a PDS boycott of the Assembly which was to last, with short intervals of participation, for nearly two years. The murder of prominent PDS deputy Azem Hajdari in September 1998 produced a new crisis in which Berisha and the PDS were accused of attempting a coup in **Tirana**. The resignation of Nano at the end of September was welcomed by Berisha, who gave qualified support to the new Government of Pandeli Majko (PSS). New strains developed over the PDS boycott of a constitutional referendum in November 1998 and its rejection of the result on the grounds of low turnout. However, from March 1999 the PDS gave general backing to the Government's line on the **NATO–Yugoslavia** hostilities over **Kosovo**, and in July it called off its latest boycott of the Assembly.

In September 1999 the then PDS parliamentary leader Genc Pollo called on the centre-right opposition parties to unite under PDS leadership. At a party congress the following month, however, Pollo failed to unseat Berisha, who was re-elected PDS Chairman unopposed following a purge of moderate members of the party executive. The moderates subsequently regrouped within the party as the Democratic Alternative, which attracted the support of eight PDS parliamentary deputies. Tensions within the party between Berisha and Pollo came to a head in February 2001 when Pollo created a splinter party, which became the **Democrat Party** (PD), and contested the June elections on a separate ticket.

The PDS had suffered major reverses in local elections in October 2000, winning only a third of the vote and losing control of Tirana to the PSS. It improved its share of the vote at the June 2001 elections, however, receiving 46 seats at the head

175

of the **Union for Victory** coalition, despite the existence of the splinter PD. The PDS hotly contested the final results, declaring them 'farcical' and beginning a four-month boycott of the People's Assembly.

Leadership: Sali Berisha (Chair.).
Address: Rruga Punetoret e Rilndjes, Tirana.
Telephone: (4) 223525.
Fax: (4) 234639.
E-mail: profsberisha@albaniaonline.net

Democratic Party of Albanians
Demokratska Partija na Albancite (DPA)

A moderate formation in **Macedonia**, one of several representing ethnic **Albanians**, who make up about a quarter of the country's population. The DPA was created in mid-1997 by a merger of splinter groups of the **Party for Democratic Prosperity** (PDP) which had opposed the PDP's participation in government. The new formation contested the autumn 1998 elections in partial alliance with the PDP, winning 11 seats (compared with 14 for the PDP), and then surprised many observers by joining a coalition Government headed by the **Slav** nationalist **Internal Macedonian Revolutionary Organization–Democratic Party for Macedonian National Unity** (VMRO–DPMNE), whereas the PDP went into opposition.

In the presidential election in late 1999, DPA candidate Muharem Nexipi came fourth in the first round with 14.9% of the vote, three times as many as the PDP nominee. Despite this apparent vote of confidence from ethnic Albanians, the DPA's government participation came under increasing criticism as Macedonia descended into inter-ethnic strife in February 2001. It admitted it had joined with the PDP in negotiating with the National Liberation Army (UCK) rebels, but nonetheless took part in the Government of National Unity, and remained in the ruling coalition after the departure from the Government of the more nationalistic ethnic **Macedonian** parties.

Leadership: Arben Xhaferi (Chair.).
Address: Maršal Tito 2, Tetovo 94000.
Telephone: (44) 31534.

Democratic Party of Armenia
Hayastani Demokratakan Kusaktsutyun (HDK)

A small party established in **Armenia** in late 1991 as the self-proclaimed successor to the former ruling **Communist Party of Armenia** (HKK), but which failed to attract many senior communists who switched allegiance instead to the ruling **Pan-Armenian National Movement** (HHSh). The HDK was also weakened by the revival of the HKK in 1994.

In the 1995 **National Assembly** elections the HDK won only 1.8% of the vote and failed to win representation. The resignation of President Ter-Petrossian (HHSh) in February 1998 triggered a partial recovery for the HDK, whose Chairman became a foreign policy adviser to the new non-party President, Robert **Kocharian**. In the May 1999 Assembly elections the HDK won one seat and 1% of the proportional vote.

Leadership: Aram Sarkissian (Chair.).
Address: 14 Koriun Street, Yerevan.
Telephone and Fax: (1) 525273.
Internet: dem_party.tripod.com

Democratic Party of Kosovo *see* **Kosovo Liberation Army**.

Democratic Party of Serbia
Demokratska Stranka Srbije (DSS)

A nationalist party which came to power in **Yugoslavia** in late 2000 as a leading component of the **Democratic Opposition of Serbia** (DOS). Founded in 1992 by a right-wing faction of the **Democratic Party** (DS), the DSS contested the December 1992 **Federal Assembly** elections as part of the DEPOS opposition alliance, which won 20 lower house seats. In the December 1993 Serbian Assembly elections, the DSS won seven seats in its own right, remaining in opposition. It subsequently joined the Zajedno (Together) alliance with the DS, the **Serbian Renewal Movement** (SPO) and the **Civic Alliance of Serbia**, which won 22 lower house seats in the November 1996 federal elections. The party joined the DS in boycotting the Serbian Assembly elections in September 1997 in protest against media manipulation by the **Milošević** regime.

In late 1998 the DSS joined a new opposition grouping called the Alliance for Change, which formed the core of the anti-Milošević DOS alliance launched in January 2000. The eventual victory of DSS founder and DOS candidate Vojislav **Koštunica** in the September 2000 federal presidential elections resulted in DSS representatives joining the Federal Government. Following a landslide DOS victory in Serbian Assembly elections in December 2000, the DSS was strongly represented in the resultant Serbian Government headed by the DS Chairman, Zoran **Djindjić**. However, clashes between Koštunica and Djindjić drove a wedge between the DSS and the DS, prompting the DSS to withdraw from the Serbian Government altogether on 17 August 2001, officially in protest at the Government's failure to tackle rising crime levels.

Leadership: Vojislav Koštunica (Chair.).
Address: Braće Jugovića 2a/I, Belgrade.
Telephone: (11) 3282886.
Fax: (11) 182535.

E-mail: info@dss.org.yu
Internet: www.dss.org.yu

Democratic Party of Slovenian Pensioners
Demokratska Stranka Upokojencev Slovenije (DeSUS)

A party in **Slovenia** which defends the rights of the elderly generally and pensioners in particular, and opposes any privatization of pension arrangements. Also known as the Grey Panthers, the DeSUS was part of the (ex-communist) **United List of Social Democrats** (ZLSD) in the 1992 **National Assembly** elections. It contested those of 1996 independently, winning five seats with 4.3% of the vote, and joining the subsequent coalition Government headed by **Liberal Democracy of Slovenia** (LDS). In the October 2000 elections, the party slipped to four seats (while improving to 5.2% of the vote), but was included in a new ruling coalition headed by the LDS and also including the ZLSD and the **Slovenian People's Party** (SLS+SKD).

Leadership: Janko Kušar (President).
Address: Kersnikova 6, Ljubljana 1000.
Telephone: (1) 4397350.
Fax: (1) 4314113.
Internet: www.desus.si

Democratic Party of Socialists of Montenegro
Demokratska Partija Socijalista Crne Gore (DPSCG)

The leading party in **Montenegro**, latterly favouring secession from the Federal Republic of **Yugoslavia**, and the direct successor to the **League of Communists** of Montenegro (SKCG).

The DPSCG, which changed its name from SKCG in 1991, was until the late 1990s in favour of the federation with **Serbia**. The party obtained an overall majority in the Montenegrin Assembly in December 1992, also winning 17 lower house seats in simultaneous **Federal Assembly** elections and joining a coalition Government led by the **Socialist Party of Serbia** (SPS) of Slobodan **Milošević**. The following month its then leader Momir Bulatović was elected President of Montenegro. The DPSCG retained its Montenegrin Assembly majority in November 1996, when it also advanced to 20 federal lower house seats.

Increasing internal opposition to Bulatović for his pro-Federation stance culminated in October 1997 in his narrow defeat by Prime Minister Milo **Djukanović** in Montenegrin presidential elections in which both ran as DPSCG candidates. Djukanović also became undisputed DPSCG Chairman, while Bulatović launched the breakaway **Socialist People's Party of Montenegro** (SNPCG). Advocating greater independence for Montenegro, the DPSCG contested the May 1998

Montenegrin Assembly elections at the head of the 'For a Better Life' alliance, which won 42 out of 78 seats and therefore formed a new Government with Filip **Vujanović** as Prime Minister.

Relations between the DPSCG and the Milošević regime deteriorated during the 1998–99 **Kosovo** crisis, with the Montenegrin Government receiving strong Western backing for its proposal for loose 'association' with Serbia. When Milošević enacted constitutional amendments in July 2000 which were seen as reducing Montenegrin powers in the Federation, the DPSCG came out in favour of full separation and boycotted the September 2000 federal elections, in which Milošević and the SPS were defeated by the **Democratic Opposition of Serbia** (DOS). The DPSCG then headed an alliance of pro-independence parties called 'The Victory is Montenegro's' in Montenegrin Assembly elections in April 2001, emerging as the largest bloc with 36 seats (and 42% of the vote) in a tight finish, in which the overall pro-separation vote was only 5,000 greater than the vote against.

Short of an overall majority and failing to reach a coalition agreement with the pro-independence **Liberal Alliance of Montenegro**, the DPSCG-led bloc opted to form a minority Government and to announce plans for a referendum on independence. However, the fact that the new Government in Belgrade was as opposed to the break-up of the Federation as its predecessor, and enjoyed Western support, raised major question marks over whether the DPSCG would pursue the independence objective.

Leadership: Milo **Djukanović** (Chair.).
Address: Tomaševića 66, Jovana, Podgorica 81000.
Telephone: (81) 243952.
Fax: (81) 243347.
E-mail: webmaster@dps.cg.yu
Internet: www.dps.cg.yu

Democratic People's Alliance
Demokratski Narodni Savez (DNS)

A moderate Serb political party in the **Serb Republic** (RS). The DNS was launched in July 2000 by former members of the **Serbian People's Alliance–Biljana Plavšić** after the ousting of former RS President Plavšić from the party leadership the previous month had been ruled to be illegal by a **Banja Luka** court. In the November 2000 elections for the RS People's Assembly, the DNS narrowly outpolled its parent party by winning three seats on a 3.5% vote share.

Leadership: Dragan Kostić (Chair.).
Address: 1 Jespejcka Street, Banja Luka.
Telephone: (51) 215542.
Fax: (51) 216951.
Internet: www.dnsrs.org

Democratic People's Union
Demokratska Narodna Zajednica (DNZ)

A political party in **Bosnia and Herzegovina** led by Fikret Abdić which draws its support mainly from within the north-western **Muslim**-populated enclave of Bihać. The DNZ was founded by Abdić in 1996 as the successor to his Muslim Democratic Party (MDS), which itself had originated from an autonomy declaration by Bihać, by then a UN-designated 'safe area', in September 1993.

A wealthy chicken farmer with a chequered history as an entrepreneur, Abdić had been elected to the collegial presidency in 1990 as a candidate of the **Party of Democratic Action** (SDA) but had later broken with the SDA leader, Alija **Izetbegović**, over the reluctance of the Izetbegović Government to sign a peace agreement with the **Serbs** and **Croats**. Following the Bihać breakaway, Abdić signed local 'treaties of lasting peace' with the Croat and Serbian leaders, his MDS forces subsequently acting as a deterrent to encroachment by the surrounding Serbs. By the end of 1994, however, they had succumbed to Bosnian government forces, and Abdić was forced to flee from his stronghold in the town of Velika Kladuša.

In the first post-**Dayton** elections in September 1996, Abdić took third place in the contest for the Muslim member of the Bosnian collective presidency, winning 3% of the Muslim vote. He improved to second place in the September 1998 contest, with 6.2% of the Muslim vote. In simultaneous legislative elections, the DNZ took one of the 42 seats in the union lower house and three out of 140 in the **Muslim-Croat Federation** lower house. In the November 2000 elections the DNZ retained the same representation in each house. Abdić was nominated by the DNZ to stand again in the collective presidency elections due in 2002, amidst doubts as to whether he was eligible because the Government had declared him to be a war criminal.

Leadership: Fikret Abdić (Chair.).
Address: 23 Pucara Starog, Velika Kladuša.
Telephone and Fax: (37) 770407.
E-mail: dnzbih@bih.net.ba

Democratic Socialist Party
Demokratska Socijalisticka Partija (DSP)

A moderate **Serb** formation in **Bosnia and Herzegovina**, launched in March 2000 by a breakaway faction of the **Socialist Party of the Serb Republic** (SPRS). The DSP opposed the SPRS's decision to leave the moderate coalition supporting the **Serb Republic** (RS) premiership headed by the **Party of Independent Social Democrats** (SNSD). In the November 2000 elections the DSP was allied with the SNSD for the all-Bosnia lower house elections, their joint list winning one seat. Standing on its own in the RS People's Assembly elections, the DSP drew on former SPRS support to win four seats, on a 4.2% vote share.

Leadership: Nebojsa Radmanović (Chair.).
Address: 9 Kralia Alfoesa, Banja Luka.
Telephone: (51) 212614.
Fax: (51) 211026.

Democratic Union of the Greek Minority–Concord
Bashkimia Demokratik i Minoritet Grek–Omonia

A political movement in **Albania** based amongst the country's 3% ethnic Greek population concentrated in Northern Epirus (*see* **Epirus question**). Commonly known as Omonia, the movement was founded in 1990 as successor to a clandestine ethnic Greek opposition movement of the communist era. It has accepted that any transfer of all or part of Northern Epirus from Albanian to Greek sovereignty could come only through negotiation, and has focused its efforts on securing improved conditions for ethnic Greeks in Albania. Omonia won five seats out of 250 in the 1991 **People's Assembly** elections, but in early 1992 it was the main target of a legislative ban on ethnically-based parties. It therefore contested subsequent Assembly elections within the **Human Rights Union Party**, which retained representation and entered the Government in 1997.

In the early 1990s Omonia agitation contributed to the flight of many ethnic Greeks from Albania to Greece, amidst increasingly serious border incidents and alleged ethnic Greek subversion within Albania. In May 1994 six Omonia activists, including Chairman Theodhori Bezhani, were among many ethnic Greeks arrested in a government crackdown, five of them being convicted and sentenced in September 1994 on treason and other charges, including 'carrying out the orders of a foreign secret service'. By early 1995, however, all five had been released, as the Albanian Government sought to accommodate ethnic Greek grievances and to improve its relations with Greece.

Leadership: Jorgo Labovitjadhi (Chair.).
Address: Tirana.

Deported Nationalities

Ethnic peoples persecuted by Stalin and deported *en masse* to central Asia and **Siberia**. There are two main groups of deported nationalities; those generally targeted by the Soviet regime, and those particularly accused by Stalin of collaborating with the invading Germans during the Second World War and transported across the **Soviet Union** in 1943 and 1944.

The first group consists of strong and traditionally powerful ethnic communities seen to represent an ongoing threat to the regime. These included Adzharians (*see* **Adzharia**), **Cossacks** and **Tatars**. An exception was the **Roma** who suffered simply at the hands of institutionalized racism. For these people their new homes in the extremities of the Soviet Union were essentially permanent.

For the second group the story was different. Following the end of the war and more specifically the death of Stalin, and with him Stalinism, these groups (almost exclusively from the north **Caucasus**) were rehabilitated under Khrushchev in 1956 and 1957. The groups affected included Balkars (*see* **Kabardino-Balkaria**), Chechens (*see* **Chechnya**), Volga **Germans**, Ingush (*see* **Ingushetia**), Kalmyks (*see* **Kalmykia**) and Muslim Ossetes (*see* **Ossetia question**). A special case were the **Meskhetians**, who were never rehabilitated and remain a permanent refugee population, often exposed to severe persecution.

For all groups the experience of being evicted from their homes and land and carted across thousands of miles of barren steppe was horrific and devastating. Up to 20% (some estimates suggest even 50%) of entire ethnic groups died during the decade-long exile, with thousands of people killed during the migration itself.

DeSUS *see* **Democratic Party of Slovenian Pensioners**.

Development Corporation of Slovenia

Corporation charged with promoting economic development in **Slovenia**.
Chair.: Marjan Rekar.
Address: Kotnikova 28, 1000 Ljubljana.
Telephone: (1) 1894880.
Fax: (1) 1894879.
E-mail: jana.bogdanovski@svd.si

Diet (Poland)
Sejm

The lower house of the **National Assembly** of **Poland**.

Djindjić, Zoran

Prime Minister of **Serbia**.

Zoran Djindjić is President of the right-wing **Democratic Party** (DS) and Prime Minister of Serbia in the first post-**Milošević** Government, in office since 25 January 2001. His efforts to exert his own constitutional power over the Federal Government have brought him into conflict with Federal President Vojislav **Koštunica**.

Born in Bosanski Samac, northern **Bosnia**, on 1 August 1952, he graduated in philosophy from the University of Belgrade in 1974. He has written many articles on philosophy and politics and received a doctorate from the University of Konstanz,

Germany. He was active in the student pro-democracy movement in **Yugoslavia** and was jailed for a year for his activities. He briefly taught philosophy at the University of Novi Sad before cofounding the DS in 1989. He was elected the party's President in 1994.

A prominent member of the DS, in the Serbian Parliament and since 1993 in the **Federal Assembly**, he was also the first non-communist Mayor of **Belgrade**, for seven months from February to September 1997. In June 2000 he was appointed Co-ordinator of the pro-democracy Alliance for Change and led the DS into the **Democratic Opposition of Serbia** (DOS) that year. The DOS swept to victory in the Serbian elections in December 2000 and he was appointed Prime Minister in January 2001. Of the many clashes between him and Koštunica, there have been none greater than when he exerted his power to overrule the Constitutional Court in order to have Slobodan Milošević extradited to the **International Criminal Tribunal for the former Yugoslavia** in The Hague in June 2001.

Address: Office of the Prime Minister, Nemanjina 11, 11000 Belgrade.
Telephone: (11) 685872.
Fax: (11) 659682.

Djorbenadze, Avtandil

State Minister, **Georgia**. Avtandil Djorbenadze is an independent with a background in medicine who was appointed State Minister on 21 December 2001 to head the right-of-centre Government under President Eduard **Shevardnadze**.

Born on 23 February 1951, he graduated as a doctor from the Tbilisi State Medical University in 1974. After completing a two-year stint of military service as an army doctor from 1976 he worked in the main hospital in **Tbilisi** for seven years. He first entered government service when he was appointed Deputy Head of the Tbilisi Health Department in 1985. After seven years in this position, he was elevated to Deputy Minister at the Ministry of Health in 1992, in what was now the independent state of Georgia. He was appointed to the office of the Head of the State Consultant in 1993. He re-entered the Cabinet in 2000 when he was made Minister for Labour, Health and Social Affairs. Dismissed along with the entire Cabinet on 1 November 2001, he was returned as State Minister on 21 December.

Address: Office of the Government, Ingorokva 7, 380018 Tbilisi.
Telephone: (32) 935907.
Fax: (32) 982354.

Djukanović, Milo

President of the Republic, **Montenegro**.

Milo Djukanović, Chairman of the centre-left **Democratic Party of Socialists of Montenegro** (DPSCG), was initially a supporter of former Yugoslav dictator

Slobodan **Milošević**, but latterly has distanced the DPSCG and **Montenegro** from their ties with **Serbia** and plans to hold a referendum on the Republic's future status. Only 29 when first appointed on 15 February 1991 as Prime Minister of Montenegro, he became the republic's President on 15 January 1998.

Born into a socially prominent Montenegrin family in Nikšić on 15 February 1962, he graduated in economics from the Titograd (now Podgorica) University in 1986. While at university he became active in politics and joined the **League of Communists of Yugoslavia** (SKJ) in 1979. After graduating he became a member of the SKJ's Central Committee. The party was transformed into the DPSCG in 1991. He was a keen supporter of Milošević and was rewarded in February 1991 with the post of Prime Minister of Montenegro. Over the course of the disintegration of the **Socialist Federal Republic of Yugoslavia** (SFRY) in the 1990s, he was a growing voice of discontent against Milošević's authoritarian regime, and in 1996 led the anti-Milošević faction within the DPSCG against the incumbent Montenegrin President Momir Bulatović. The party was split in two and Djukanović successfully campaigned for the rump DPSCG in presidential elections in late 1997. After a slim victory in the second round he finally replaced Bulatović in January 1998. As President he has consistently defied the Republic's Serbian partner in the new **Yugoslavia,** and Montenegro is effectively run as an independent country as a result. The two constituent Republics came close to conflict in mid-2000 as Djukanović increased his anti-Milošević rhetoric. The fall of the dictator in October 2000 did little to thaw relations with Serbia, but a very slim electoral victory for the DPSCG in April 2001 cut the party's pro-independence momentum.

Address: Office of the President, Podgorica.
Fax: (81) 42329.

Dnestr Republic *see* **Transdnestria**.

DNS *see* **Democratic People's Alliance**.

DNZ *see* **Democratic People's Union**.

Dobruja question

A dormant territorial dispute between **Bulgaria** and **Romania** concerning the fertile plain between the River Danube and the Black Sea. Dobruja has long been an ethnically diverse region and a vital economic centre for the south-west **Balkans**. Incorporation into the Ottoman Empire in 1419 ended rival Romanian and Bulgarian claims to the region. The dispute was renewed in 1878, however, when the Ottoman Empire's loss of control in the area was formalized in the Treaty of Berlin. This treaty awarded the larger northern part of Dobruja to the newly-emerged

Romanian state, and the smaller southern 'quadrilateral' to the Bulgarian principality.

After the Second Balkan War of 1913 all of Dobruja was assimilated into Romania, only to be redivided in 1940 under Nazi supervision. The modern border, similar to that of 1878, was drawn up in 1947 under the Treaty of Paris. Friendly cross-Danube relations since then have laid the dispute to rest. Bulgarian Dobruja is home to a large minority of **Bulgarian Turks,** who mostly farm tobacco there. In Romania the Dobruja has diversified its agricultural industry with heavy communist-era industrialization: the port of Constanţa is Romania's major Black Sea port.

Dom Naroda
(House of Peoples)

The upper house of the **Parliamentary Assembly** of **Bosnia and Herzegovina**.

Don Basin

The heavily-industrialized valley of the Don river in the south of **European Russia**. It first became an economic centre as early as the 2nd century BC and came under the authority of the Turkic **Tatars** in the 13th century AD. Settlements of freed and escapee **Russian** serfs in the Don region developed into the notorious **Cossack** frontier guards. Their descendants, the Don Cossacks, were a renowned military unit used to great effect to guard the borders of the Russian Empire, although they were later persecuted by Stalin. The Don basin was incorporated into the Russian Empire in the 16th century.

Heavy industrialization came under Soviet rule in the 1950s, including the construction of key dams, especially the creation of the Tsimlyansk reservoir. This and other reservoirs were used for irrigation of the surrounding land in a bid to increase its productivity. The Volga-Don Ship Canal connects the navigable Don with its eastern sister and caters for much waterborne traffic. However, the greater use of Don water has severely reduced the usual outflow at the river's mouth and so increased the salinity of the Sea of Azov which has damaged that region's ecosystem. The larger cities along the Don include Rostov and Voronezh.

Donbass Russians

A large ethnic **Russian** community concentrated in the Donbass (Donetsk) industrial region of eastern **Ukraine**. The majority of the 10 million Russians in the region are recent migrants, drafted in to carry out the industrial reconstruction of Ukraine after the Second World War. Fears that they might actively seek unification with **Russia** following Ukraine's independence in 1991 proved unfounded during the course of the 1990s. Initial agitation has given way to calls for autonomy within Ukraine.

DOS *see* **Democratic Opposition of Serbia**.

DP *see* **Democratic Party**.

DPA *see* **Democratic Party of Albanians**.

DPS *see* **Movement for Rights and Freedoms**.

DPSCG *see* **Democratic Party of Socialists of Montenegro**.

Drnovšek, Janez

Prime Minister of **Slovenia**.

Janez Drnovšek is Chairman of the centre-left **Liberal Democracy of Slovenia** (LDS). An economist by training, he was elected to the Slovenian parliament within the **Socialist Federal Republic of Yugoslavia** (SFRY) in 1986 and was President of the SFRY's collective presidency in 1989–90. After playing a prominent role in talks on Slovenia's independence, he was the country's Prime Minister for eight years from April 1992, then returned to office again on 14 November 2000 after just six months in opposition.

Born on 17 May 1950 in Celje, north-east of **Ljubljana**, he obtained a doctorate in economics from the University of Maribor in 1986. Having completed his education, he worked first with a construction company, then as Chief Executive of a branch of Ljubljanska Bank, and finally as adviser on economic affairs at the Yugoslav Embassy in Egypt. In 1989 he was elected as the Slovenian representative on the collective State Presidency of the SFRY, standing as an independent and defeating the communist candidate in the first such election to be genuinely contested. In May 1989 he took office for a year as President of the Presidency, on the principle of the rotation of this post among the SFRY's constituent republics, but with the distinction of being the first non-communist to hold this office. In October 1990, however, he withdrew from the SFRY presidency, protesting over its manipulation by its new Serbian President. As Slovenia moved to obtain its independence from the disintegrating SFRY the following year, he was the principal negotiator in efforts to halt the countervailing military action by the federal Yugoslav People's Army (JNA).

Also in 1991 Drnovšek cofounded and headed the Liberal Democratic Party, precursor of the LDS, which has dominated Slovenian politics since independence. He headed a coalition which took office, with himself as Prime Minister, in April 1992, while the first post-independence elections that December saw the

Liberal Democrats established as the largest grouping in the parliament. Drnovšek's broad left-of-centre coalition survived until April 2000, when he was ousted for a six-month period while Andrej Bajuk of the **Slovene People's Party** (SLS+SKD) held office in a shaky centre-right alliance. Drnovšek and the LDS were returned to office in November 2000.

Address: The Prime Minister's Office, Gregorčičeva 20, 1000 Ljubljana.
Telephone: (1) 4781000.
Fax: (1) 4781607.
E-mail: gp.upv@gov.si
Internet: www.gov.si/pv/en

Državni Zbor *see* National Assembly (Slovenia).

DS *see* Democratic Party.

DSP *see* Democratic Socialist Party.

DSS *see* Democratic Party of Serbia.

Dubček, Alexander

The communist party leader of **Czechoslovakia** during the 1968 '**Prague Spring**', who attempted to abandon Stalinism in favour of 'socialism with a human face'. When he replaced Antonín Novotný as leader of the Communist Party of Czechoslovakia (KSČ) in January 1968 the 47-year-old Dubček's name was not widely known, despite his role as leader of the **Slovak** communists. His appointment was regarded as a bid to placate disgruntled Slovaks in the party. The reforms introduced under Dubček's leadership won him wide popularity. When **Warsaw Pact** forces invaded in August 1968 Dubček was arrested but then released after effectively being pressured into abandoning his reform policies. By April 1969 he had been ousted as KSČ leader. After a brief spell as Ambassador to Turkey, Dubček was expelled from the KSČ in 1970. He returned to obscurity as an administrator in the Slovak Forestry Service. During the November 1989 '**velvet revolution**' Dubček was received ecstatically at mass pro-democracy rallies. Although suggested as a possible figurehead President, he stood aside in favour of Václav **Havel**, and instead became Speaker of the Federal Parliament. Dubček joined the **Public Against Violence** movement, switching to the **Movement for a Democratic Slovakia** in July 1991 but strongly opposing the dissolution of the Czechoslovak federation. In March 1992 he was elected as Chairman of the small Social Democratic Party in Slovakia. The party performed poorly in the 1992 elections and Dubček resigned as Speaker of the Federal Parliament. In September 1992 Dubček suffered grave injuries in a car crash and he died on 7 November 1992. Thousands of mourners attended his funeral.

Dubrovnik

A historic port on the southern **Dalmatian** coast, one of **Croatia**'s main cities, and the focus of international outrage when it was besieged by Yugoslav forces in 1991. *Population*: around 45,000. The south **Slav** settlement of Dubrovnik (from the Serbo-Croatian for 'grove') was incorporated by the Italian community on the nearby island of Ragusa into a city-state which for much of its history was known as Ragusa. Its connection with the Venetian trading empire ensured a distinctly west European feel to the city and enabled it to increase its influence along the Dalmatian coast.

Dubrovnik maintained a large amount of autonomy under the Ottomans but was finally subjugated by the Austro-Hungarian Empire in 1815. It was incorporated into the Croatian state within the Kingdom of Serbs, Croats and Slovenes in 1918. The city's splendid mediaeval architecture made it one of **Yugoslavia**'s main tourist attractions in the later 20th century. However, some of the historic buildings were severely damaged during the 1991 siege. Some of the tourist trade has since been regenerated. Other economic activity revolves around the city's port and the production of quality consumer goods.

Dudau, Nicolae

Minister of Foreign Affairs, **Moldova**.

Nicolae Dudau is an independent. Having held various posts within the Soviet-era communist administration, he later became an Ambassador to key former Soviet states. He first entered government as Deputy Chairman of the State Planning Committee in 1988, and was appointed Foreign Minister on 3 September 2001.

Born on 19 December 1945 in Grinauti-Moldova, in the far north of the country, he first found work in the Chișinau tractor factory in 1963. Apart from a three-year term of service in the Soviet army between 1964 and 1967, he stayed at the factory until 1975. From then until 1990 he fulfilled various posts within the administration of the Moldovan branch of the Communist Party, including First Secretary of the Chișinau Communist Party Committee (1990–91). Following the party's disappearance in 1991 he worked as the Executive Director of an international charities association until 1993 when he became a councillor at the Moldovan Embassy in the **Russian Federation**. He was appointed Ambassador to Uzbekistan in 1994, with responsibility also for Kyrgyzstan and Tajikistan. He returned to Moldova in 1997 to join the Cabinet as Deputy Foreign Minister. The next year he was posted to **Belarus** as Moldovan Ambassador, with responsibility also for the

Baltic States. He was recalled to Moldova once again in September 2001 to take up the position as full Foreign Minister.

Nicolae Dudau is married and has one daughter.

Address: Ministry of Foreign Affairs, Government House 3rd Floor, Piața Marii Adunari Nationale 1, 227033 Chișinau.
Telephone: (2) 233940.
Fax: (2) 232302.
Internet: www.moldova.md/ro/government/oll/FOREIGN/en/index_en.html

Duma

The lower house of the **Federal Assembly** of the **Russian Federation**; formally the State Duma (*Gossoudarstvennaya Duma*).

Dzurinda, Mikuláš

Prime Minister of **Slovakia**.

A Christian-democrat politician who has held office as Prime Minister since 30 October 1998, Mikuláš Dzurinda is an ardent advocate of European integration and free-market economics, who regards membership of the **European Union** and the **North Atlantic Treaty Organization** as top priorities for Slovakia. He currently heads the centrist Slovak Democratic and Christian Union (SDKU), a new party set up by him and as yet untested in elections, while still being Chairman of the ruling **Slovak Democratic Coalition** (SDK).

Born in Spišský Štvrtok, in the central mountain district of Spišská Nová Ves on 4 February 1955, he graduated from the University of Transport and Communications in Žilina and began work at the city's Transport Research Institute in 1979. After only a year he moved to **Bratislava** to work in the Information Technologies section of Czechoslovak State Transport, and from 1988 he headed the agency's Automated Controls section. After the fall of communism in 1991, he was appointed Deputy Transport Minister in the Government of the Slovak Republic, at that time still part of **Czechoslovakia**. As the Federal State fell apart he entered the newly-formed Slovak National Council in 1992 representing the Christian Democratic Movement (KDH), and was chosen to head the joint opposition SDK in 1997. He was appointed Prime Minister following the SDK's electoral success in October 1998. **European Union** membership is a stated priority and Dzurinda has striven to reform the economy to meet the Union's standards. When President Rudolf **Schuster** fell seriously ill in 2000, Dzurinda was roundly criticized by the opposition, and by Schuster himself, for quickly adopting executive powers (together with the Speaker of the National Council). Opposition to his fervently pro-Western stance has led to fractures in the ruling coalition and, in January 2000, he

Dzurinda, Mikuláš

formed the SDKU to contest elections due in 2002. He survived a vote of no confidence in April 2000.

Address: Office of the Government of the Slovak Republic, Nám. Slobody 1, 81370 Bratislava.
Telephone: (2) 57295111.
Fax: (2) 52497595.
E-mail: tio@government.gov.sk
Internet: www.government.gov.sk

E

EAKL *see* Association of Estonian Trade Unions.

EAPC *see* Euro-Atlantic Partnership Council.

Eastern Europe

The European region comprising states east of **central Europe**, extending south to the **Balkan** states of **Albania, Bulgaria, Romania** and the former **Yugoslavia**, and including the former Soviet Republics, except those of central Asia (which lie outside Europe's geographical borders). Following the post-war division of Europe along the 'iron curtain', the term eastern Europe gained a political connotation, being used to denote all communist (and more recently post-communist) states east of the **Oder-Neisse line**. In this usage it excluded two Balkan states, Greece and Turkey, and included, on political rather than geographical criteria, the communist states of central Europe.

Eastern Slavonia *see* Slavonia.

EBRD *see* European Bank for Reconstruction and Development.

ECE *see* Economic Commission for Europe.

ECO *see* Economic Co-operation Organization.

Ecoglasnost Political Club
Politicheski Klub Ekoglasnost (PKE)

A political/environmentalist movement in **Bulgaria** which played a key role in the overthrow of communism, following which it retained considerable influence, latterly with a left-wing orientation. Founded in April 1989, Ecoglasnost was the main organizer of the popular demonstrations which surrounded the downfall of

Todor **Zhivkov** in November 1989 and became a leading component of the opposition **Union of Democratic Forces** (SDS). Following the election of Zhelyu Zhelev of the SDS as President in July 1990, Filip Dimitrov of Ecoglasnost became SDS Chairman and led the alliance to a narrow victory in the October 1991 **National Assembly** elections, becoming Prime Minister of an SDS minority Government.

Following the fall of the Dimitrov Government in October 1992, Ecoglasnost activists became concerned at the rightward drift of the SDS but were divided about alternative strategies. The dominant PKE opted to join an alliance headed by the (ex-communist) **Bulgarian Socialist Party** (BSP) for the December 1994 Assembly elections, sharing in the alliance's victory and being allocated the environment portfolio in the resultant BSP-led Government. It maintained the alliance in the 1996 presidential and 1997 Assembly elections, sharing in its defeat on both occasions by a revived SDS. By the time of the 2001 elections PKE had little political impact.

Leadership: Edwin Sugarev (Chair.).
Address: 37 Ekzarch Yossif Street, 1054 Sofia.

Economic Chamber of Macedonia

The principal organization in **Macedonia** for promoting business contacts, both internally and externally, in the post-communist era. Originally founded in 1962.
President: Dušan Petreski.
Address: Dimitrie Čupovski 13, 1000 Skopje.
Telephone: (2) 118088.
Fax: (2) 116210.
E-mail: ic@ic.mchamber.org.mk
Internet: www.mchamber.org.mk

Economic Chamber of the Czech Republic
Hospodářská komora České republiky

The principal organization in **the Czech Republic** for promoting business contacts, both internally and externally, in the post-communist era. Originally founded in 1850.
Chair.: Dr Zdeněk Somr.
Address: Argentinská 38, 17005 Prague 7.
Telephone: (2) 66794939.
Fax: (2) 875438.

Economic Commission for Europe (ECE)

The UN Economic Commission for Europe was established in 1947. Representatives of all European countries, the USA, Canada, Israel and central Asian republics study the economic, environmental and technological problems of the region and recommend courses of action. ECE is also active in the formulation of international legal instruments and the setting of international standards.
Address: Palais des Nations, 1211 Geneva 10, Switzerland.
Telephone: (22) 9174444.
Fax: (22) 9170505.
E-mail: info.ece@unece.org
Internet: www.unece.org

Economic Co-operation Organization (ECO)

The Economic Co-operation Organization was established in 1985 as the successor to the Regional Co-operation for Development. Its focus is on western Asia rather than eastern Europe, with member countries from Turkey in the west to Pakistan and the former Soviet central Asian republics. **Azerbaijan**, however, with its traditional and Turkic language links with Turkey, is a member of the ECO, which aims at co-operation in economic, social and cultural affairs.
Members: Afghanistan, Azerbaijan, Iran, Kazakhstan, Kyrgyzstan, Pakistan, Tajikistan, Turkey, Turkmenistan and Uzbekistan.
The 'Turkish Republic of Northern Cyprus' has been granted special guest status.
Leadership: Dr Abdulrahim Gavahi (Secretary-General).
Address: 1 Golbou Alley, Kamranieh St, POB 14155-6176, Tehran, Iran.
Telephone: (21) 2831731.
Fax: (21) 2831732.
E-mail: registry@ecosecretariat.org
Internet: www.ecosecretariat.org

Edinstvo People's Trade Union

An independent trade union centre in **Bulgaria**, founded in 1990 as a splinter group of the **Confederation of Independent Trade Unions of Bulgaria** (KNSB). Principally representing professional workers, Edinstvo ('Unity') has been less prominent in industrial relations than the KNSB and the **Podkrepa Confederation of Labour**.
Chair.: Ognyan Bonev.
Address: 5 Moskovska St, Sofia 1000.
Telephone: (2) 879640.

EEC *see* **Eurasian Economic Community.**

EK *see* **Estonian Coalition Party.**

EKe *see* **Estonian Centre Party.**

ELTA
(Lithuanian News Agency)

The main news agency in **Lithuania**. Founded on 1 April 1920, ELTA was a source of regional information for major foreign news agencies until Soviet invasion in 1940. Thereafter it was subordinated to the Telegraph Agency of the Soviet Union (TASS—*see* **ITAR-TASS**) until 1990. In 1996 the agency was divorced from its direct links to the Lithuanian state and has become a joint stock company; it has also rebuilt its links with other international agencies.
    Director: Kęstutis Jankauskas.
    Address: Gedimino pr. 21/2, Vilnius 2600.
    Telephone: (26) 28864 [(526) 28864 from September 2002].
    Fax: (26) 19507 [(526) 19507 from September 2002].
    E-mail: eltar@elta.lt
    Internet: www.elta.lt

Enterprise Restructuring Agency (Albania)
Agjensia e Ristrukturimit te Ndermarrjeve (ARN)

Government body in **Albania** charged with assisting state-owned enterprises to become privately owned. It offers enterprise sector surveys, strategic plans, consultancy services and technical assistance.
    Director: Adriatik Bankja.
    Address: Rr. e Durrësit 83, Tirana.
    Telephone: (4) 227878.
    Fax: (4) 225730.

Epirus question

An issue arising from the division of the ancient **Balkan** province of Epirus between **Albania** and Greece in 1913, and residual (and non-official) Greek aspirations to unite Albanian-ruled northern Epirus with the Greek province of (southern) Epirus. Northward expansion of the independent Greek state established in 1830 focused on historic **Macedonia**, the Greek claim to which encompassed not only the whole of Epirus but also much of what is now Albania. In the Balkan Wars of 1912–13 most of Macedonia was partitioned between Greece, **Serbia** and

Bulgaria, but plans for Greece to acquire the whole of Epirus were thwarted by the declaration in November 1912 of an independent principality of Albania. Under the Treaty of Bucharest of August 1913, Albania's independence was internationally recognized within virtually its present-day borders, including northern Epirus (where ethnic **Albanians** outnumbered Greeks), while Greece acquired Greek-majority southern Epirus. Greece occupied northern Epirus soon after the outbreak of the First World War in 1914, but was eventually persuaded to accept a post-war settlement, signed in Paris in July 1926, under which northern Epirus was recognized as belonging to Albania.

Dominated by fascist Italy from 1926 and occupied by Italian forces in April 1939, Albania provided a springboard for Italy's attack on Greece in October 1940. The resounding victory of Greek forces brought them into occupation of southern Albania, where northern Epirus was declared 'liberated'. In 1941, however, German forces overran both **Yugoslavia** and Greece, whereupon **Greater Albania** was restored to Italian control. Following Italy's exit from the war in 1943, the Albanian communists gradually established control, their Government being recognized by the Allies in October 1945. The Paris peace conference in 1946 reaffirmed the independence of Albania within its 1926 borders.

With Albania under communist rule and Greece becoming a member of the **North Atlantic Treaty Organization** (NATO) in 1952, the Epirus question remained frozen during the **Cold War** era. In 1958 Albania expressed a desire to normalize relations with Greece, but rejected the Greek response that a termination of the technical state of war between the two countries should encompass negotiations on the status of northern Epirus. The establishment of diplomatic relations between Albania and Greece in 1971 was understood to imply Greek recognition of Albania's existing borders. However, not until 1987 did the Greek Government formally agree to ending the state of war with Albania, one aim being to encourage better treatment of the ethnic Greek minority in northern Epirus. The Albanian census of 1989 recorded 59,000 inhabitants as being of self-declared ethnic Greek origin, but Greek estimates continued to put the actual number at over 300,000.

The end of communist rule in Albania in 1991 and the relaxation of exit restrictions resulted in an accelerating exodus to Greece, at first mainly of ethnic Greeks but later also of ethnic Albanians in search of a better life. Anxious to reverse the tide, the Greek Government urged better treatment for ethnic Greeks within Albania, while also stressing that there was no territorial issue between the two countries. Nevertheless, as violence against ethnic Greeks in southern Albania increased in 1992, some on the Greek right called for a reopening of the territorial question, while the Albanian Government accused Greece of launching a new 'cold war' against Albania. Relations worsened in mid-1994 when activists of the **Democratic Union of the Greek Minority–Concord** (Omonia) were prosecuted in a government crackdown on alleged subversion in southern Albania.

Erdut Agreement

The release of the Omonia members facilitated an improvement in Albanian-Greek relations in 1995, assisted by Albanian moves to meet Greek demands for independent Greek-language schools in southern Albania. However, Albania's descent into virtual anarchy following the collapse of the country's **'pyramid' investment schemes** in 1997 produced particular instability in southern Albania. About 830 Greek troops returned to Albania (for the first time since 1941) as part of the multinational force sent in to restore order; with Tirana's agreement they remained deployed in southern Albania after the withdrawal of the main force. With stability restored in the border area, the remaining Greek forces were withdrawn in August 2000, except for about 85 military advisers who remained in Albania under a training programme.

ER *see* **Estonian Reform Party**.

Erdut Agreement
(or Basic Agreement)

A peace treaty signed on 12 November 1995 by ethnic **Croat** and **Serb** forces, following the conclusion of hostilities, concerning the eastern **Slavonia** region of **Croatia**. Under the terms of the Erdut (or Basic) Agreement the region of eastern Slavonia, Baranja and western Sirmium was placed under the mandate of a United Nations transitional administration (UNTAES) for a period of 12 months. UNTAES was charged with maintaining security in the region, which was to be demilitarized, and ensuring the peaceful return of refugees of all ethnic backgrounds. In the first years following the Erdut Agreement the UN administration noted that the right-wing regime of Franjo **Tudjman** was apparently unwilling to leave the region demilitarized following the departure of UNTAES, and that little progress had been made regarding the return of refugees. Nonetheless the 3,000-strong peacekeeping force, whose mandate had been extended for two six-month periods, finally wound up its operations in January 1998.

ERL *see* **Estonian People's Union**.

Estonia
Eesti Vabariik

An independent **Baltic State** in north-eastern Europe, bordered to the south by Latvia and to the east by the Russian Federation. The Gulf of Finland lies on its northern coastline, and the Baltic Sea to the west. The country is divided administratively into 15 districts (maakonnad).

Area: 45,226 sq km; *capital*: **Tallinn**; *population*: 1.4m. (2001 estimate), comprising **Estonians** 64.2%, **Russians** 28.7%, **Ukrainians** 2.7%, **Belarusians** 1.5%, Finns 1%, others 1.9%; *official language*: Estonian; *religion*: majority Evangelical Lutheran, Russian and Estonian **Orthodox Christianity**; others include Baptist, Methodist, Seventh Day Adventist, **Roman Catholic**, Pentecostal, Word of Life, Seventh Day Baptist.

Legislative authority is vested in the unicameral **State Assembly** (Riigikogu), which has 101 members directly elected for a four-year term by a system of proportional representation. The Head of State is the President who is elected for a five-year term by a two-thirds majority of the Riigikogu (or, if the required majority is not secured after three rounds of voting, by an electoral assembly composed of parliamentary deputies and local government representatives). Executive authority is vested in the Prime Minister, who is nominated by the President and appoints the Council of Ministers.

History: The first independent state of Estonia was conquered by the Vikings in the 9th century. By the 13th century the Teutonic Knights of Germany controlled southern Estonia; in the 14th century they purchased northern Estonia from Denmark. The country was partitioned in 1561 between Sweden (the north) and **Poland** (the south), and most of present-day Estonia had come under Swedish rule by the mid-17th century. The end of the Great Northern War between **Russia** and Sweden brought Estonia under Tsarist Russian rule from the early 1700s until the time of the Russian Revolution in 1917. Estonia was occupied by German and then Bolshevik forces in the First World War, but in 1918 declared its independence, which was recognized by the Treaty of **Tartu** with Soviet Russia in 1920 and by the League of Nations in 1921. An authoritarian regime seized power in 1934.

In 1940, shortly after the start of the Second World War, Soviet forces occupied Estonia (as had been agreed under the terms of the 1939 **Nazi-Soviet Pact**) and the country was incorporated into the **Soviet Union** as the Estonian Soviet Socialist Republic. German forces subsequently invaded and occupied Estonia from 1941 until the Soviet Union regained control in 1944. The 'Sovietization' of Estonia followed, including agricultural collectivization and the immigration of ethnic **Russians** and other groups.

In the late 1980s the influence of the ***glasnost*** (openness) initiative in the Soviet Union encouraged the growth of a popular movement in Estonia to campaign for democratization and independence. Close links with popular fronts in **Latvia** and **Lithuania** were also established. In 1988 the Estonian Supreme Soviet declared the sovereignty of the republic and a law was subsequently passed replacing Russian with Estonian as the state language. In late 1989 the Estonian Supreme Soviet denounced the 1940 Soviet incorporation of the Republic as illegal. In 1990 the communist monopoly of power was abolished, the broad-based Estonian Popular Front led by Edgar Savisaar secured a majority of seats in multi-party elections to the Estonian Supreme Soviet, and a pro-independence coalition Government was formed. A referendum held in 1991 returned a vote of 78% in favour

Estonia

of independence. Following the failure of the attempted **August coup** in the Soviet Union to remove President **Gorbachev**, Estonia declared its independence. This was recognized in September by the Soviet Union and by Western nations.

Presidential and legislative elections were held in 1992, following the approval of the new Constitution by referendum. As the presidential poll failed to produce a clear winner, the Riigikogu chose the former Foreign Minister, Lennart **Meri**, as the new President. The parliamentary elections returned a centre-right coalition Government led by Mart **Laar**, who embarked upon a radical policy of free-market reform and was widely credited with reviving Estonia's ailing post-communist economy. Laar's Government fell when it was voted out of office by the Riigikogu in 1994.

Following the March 1995 general election, Tiit Vähi, the leader of the **Estonian Coalition Party** (EK) and a caretaker Prime Minister in 1992, formed a centre-left coalition Government with Savisaar's **Estonian Centre Party** (EKe) and a rural party. This coalition collapsed (over a phone-tapping scandal) six months later, and Vähi formed a new coalition with the **Estonian Reform Party** (ER). President Meri was re-elected by an electoral assembly vote in September 1996. Vähi resigned (accused of corruption) in February 1997, having formed another minority Government a month before, and was replaced by Mart Siimann, also of the EK.

Latest elections: In the March 1999 parliamentary elections Savisaar's EKe became substantially the largest party on a populist platform, winning 28 seats with 23.4% of the vote. The centre-right **Fatherland Union** (IL) led by Laar won 18 seats (16.1%), the ER 18 (15.9%), the **Moderates** 17 (15.2%), the EK 7 (7.6%), the Estonian Rural People's Party (EME) 7 (7.3%) and the **United People's Party of Estonia** 6 (6.1%). The EME subsequently became the core of the new **Estonian People's Union** (ERL).

Recent developments: After Savisaar's hopes of forming an EKe-led coalition had been dashed, Laar returned to the premiership following the March 1999 elections. His centre-right coalition, between his own IL, the ER and the Moderates, had only a narrow majority of 53 of the 101 parliamentary seats. This led to periodic political crises, notably over the passage of a supplementary austerity budget for 1999. The Government nevertheless remained in office, buoyed by economic recovery in 2000 (*see* **Estonia, economy**). However, its privatization programme met with increasing opposition within the State Assembly, and it faced a number of no-confidence votes through the course of 2001. Divisions within the coalition itself became clear when the former transitional President Arnold **Rüütel**, now of the opposition ERL, was elected President on 21 September but only after successive rounds of voting in the Assembly. The pressure of dissent within the coalition eventually proved too much: first the Minister of Economics Mikhel Parnoja resigned in late September, and eventually Laar himself announced on 19 December that he would resign in the new year; effectively threatening to take the coalition Government with him.

International relations and defence: As a newly-recognized independent state, Estonia was admitted to the UN in 1991 and also joined the **Organization for Security and Co-operation in Europe**. The republic's prime objective is to integrate into Western institutions. It was admitted to the **Council of Europe** in 1993 and NATO's **Partnership for Peace** programme in 1994, and has associate partner status in the **Western European Union**. Further to its 1995 application for membership of the **European Union** (EU), Estonia opened formal accession negotiations with the EU in March 1998. In March 2001 the parliamentary parties agreed that, following the hoped-for completion of EU negotiations in 2002, a proposal for membership would be put to a referendum before an accession agreement was signed.

A central feature of Estonian foreign policy is close links with the other Baltic states within the framework of revived trilateral institutions dating from the interwar period. The **Council of the Baltic Sea States** provides the organizational framework for political, economic and other co-operation between Baltic littoral and adjacent countries. In 1998 the Presidents of Estonia, Latvia, Lithuania and the USA signed a US-Baltic Charter of Partnership.

Post-communist relations with the **Russian Federation** have not been smooth. Russian troops were not removed from Estonia until 1994. Against the backdrop of an unresolved border dispute (*see* **Petseri question**), the Russian Federation has opposed Estonia's attempts to join **NATO** (although Estonian membership is not imminent) and has criticized Estonian citizenship laws as being discriminatory against Estonia's Russian minority.

Estonia's defence budget for 2000 amounted to some US $80m., equivalent to about 2% of GDP. The size of the armed forces at the end of 2000 was some 5,000 personnel, including those serving under compulsory conscription of 12 months (which the Government agreed in July 2000 to reduce to eight months for the army and 11 months for other services). Reservists numbered an estimated 14,000.

Estonia, economy

An economy in generally successful transition from communist-era state control to a free-market system, assisted by its maritime traditions and links with the Nordic region.

GNP: US $4,611m. (2000); *GNP per capita*: $3,410 (2000); *GDP at PPP*: $7,900m. (1999); *GDP per capita at PPP*: $5,600 (1999); *exports*: $3,828m. (2000); *imports*: $5,055m. (2000); *currency*: kroon (plural: krooni; US $1=K17.58 at the end of December 2001).

In 1999 industry accounted for 27% of GDP, agriculture for 6% and services for 67%. About 22% of the land is arable, 11% permanent pasture and 31% forests and woodland. The main crops are potatoes, fruit and vegetables, although the principal agricultural activity is animal husbandry and the production of dairy products. There is fishing along the lengthy coastline and a major forestry indus-

Estonia, economy

try. The main mineral resource is oil-shale. There are also deposits of peat and phosphorite ore. The principal industries are machine building, electronics, electrical engineering and textiles and clothing, as well as the processing of oil-shale, the production of phosphates and some shipbuilding. However, the oil-shale and phosphate sectors are under considerable pressure on environmental and pollution grounds. The main energy source is oil-shale and gas produced from shale, while natural gas is imported from the **Russian Federation**.

Estonia's main exports by value in 1999 were machinery and transport equipment (19% of the total), forestry products (15%), textiles (13%), food products (12%), metals (10%) and chemicals (8%). Principal imports in 1999 were machinery and equipment (26%), foodstuffs (15%), chemical products (10%), metal products (9%) and textiles (8%). The principal purchasers of Estonian exports in 2000 were Finland (27%), Sweden (17%) and Germany (8%). The main suppliers of Estonia's imports in 2000 were Finland (24%), the Russian Federation (14%) and Germany and Sweden (9% each).

In the 1950s and 1960s, within the **Soviet Union**, Estonia moved away from its earlier largely agricultural base in an intense period of industrialization. When Estonia regained its independence in 1991, the country accelerated the moves towards a market economy which had already been taking place. The post-independence changes resulted in initial falls in GNP and real GDP, but successful stabilization measures yielded real GDP growth of 4% in 1995 and 1996, rising to a remarkable 10% in 1997. Inflation, which had been as high as 954% in 1992, dropped rapidly to 36% in 1993 and to around 10% in 1997. Measures introduced in the 1992–97 period to create a sound financial sector included the creation of an independent board to manage the currency and strict restraints on public expenditure, while much of the state-owned economy was privatized (see below).

The 1998 financial crisis in the Russian Federation (*see* **Russian Federation, economy**) had an adverse knock-on effect in Estonia. GDP growth dropped back to 4% in 1998, but the real impact was felt in 1999, when real GDP contracted by 1.4% and foreign trade volumes dropped sharply. However, austerity measures introduced by the new centre-right Government appointed in March 1999 had the desired effect, leading to renewed GDP growth of around 5% in 2000 and a budget deficit of only 1.2% of GDP. Inflation remained high by **Baltic** standards, at 5% in 2000, while unemployment continued at a stubborn 15%, many affected being long-term jobless. But the overall record since independence was positive, real GDP per head having risen by 40% and real wages by around 25%. The Government's budget for 2001, as adopted by the *Riigikogu* (**State Assembly**) in December 2000, provided for a balance between expenditure and revenue of K29,780m.

The privatization process was initially slow, but the pace later accelerated. By the end of 1996 almost all state-owned small enterprises and three-fifths of medium-sized businesses had been transferred to the private sector, largely through a version of the **voucher privatization** system. In 1997 a programme was launched for the privatization of some of the largest concerns, including the state shipping corporation and Estonia Telecoms, to which the post-1999 Government added the railways, the alcohol industry and the power grid. Conversely, only 30% of state-owned agricultural land had been privatized by the end of 1999, partly because of the entrenched position of communist-era functionaries.

The central focus of post-independence Estonian economic policy has been the almost universal aspiration to join the **European Union** (EU) and the need to meet the economic criteria for membership. As one of the original six 'fast-track' entry candidates, Estonia began formal accession negotiations with the EU in November 1998, with the result that harmonization of domestic policy with EU requirements was accelerated. The Government was therefore gratified when a European Commission report on enlargement issued in November 2000 identified Estonia as a front-runner for accession. Meanwhile, Estonia had become the 135th member of the **World Trade Organization** in November 1999.

Estonian Centre Party
Eesti Keskerakond (EKe)

A populist party in **Estonia**, the largest in the *Riigikogu* (**State Assembly**) since 1999, although in opposition. The EKe was founded in October 1991 as an offshoot of the Estonian Popular Front (ER), which had spearheaded the post-1988 independence movement but had split into various parties after independence was achieved. As ER Chairman, Edgar Savisaar had been Prime Minister from April 1990 to January 1992, having previously been Chairman of the Estonian branch of the Soviet-era Planning Committee (Gosplan). The EKe used the ER designation in the September 1992 **State Assembly** and presidential elections, winning 15 seats (with 12.2% of the vote) and achieving third place (with 23.7%) for its presidential candidate, Rein Taagepera. In the March 1995 parliamentary elections the EKe won 16 seats with 14.2% of the vote, following which it joined a coalition Government headed by the **Estonian Coalition Party** (EK), obtaining four portfolios, including that of internal affairs for Savisaar.

This Government collapsed in October 1995 over the dismissal of Savisaar for alleged involvement in a phone-tapping scandal. The EKe was not included in the succeeding coalition, even though Savisaar announced his retirement from politics and was replaced as EKe leader by Andra Veidemann. The following year Savisaar made his political comeback. Heading an anti-Veidemann group within the party, he regained the party leadership in March, and in July he was cleared of the allegations against him. Meanwhile, Veidemann and her supporters founded a breakaway Progress Party, whose political influence proved short-lived although it initially attracted seven of the 16 EKe deputies.

In opposition, the EKe absorbed the small Green Party in June 1998 and pursued plans for a prospective ruling alliance with the Estonian Rural People's Party (EME) (*see* **Estonian People's Union**). In the March 1999 parliamentary elections the EKe advanced strongly to become the largest party with 28 seats

(winning 23.4% of the vote), on a platform calculated to appeal to voters who were disenchanted with the free-market economy. However, the relatively poor performance of its prospective coalition party, the EME, which won only seven seats, meant that an EKe-EME Government was not feasible. The EKe instead continued in opposition, to a centre-right coalition led by the **Fatherland Union** (IL).
Leadership: Edgar Savisaar (Chair.).
Address: Toom-Rüütli 3/5, Tallinn 10130; POB 3737, Tallinn 10158.
Telephone: 6273460.
Fax: 6273461.
E-mail: keskerakond@keskerakond.ee
Internet: www.keskerakond.ee

Estonian Chamber of Commerce and Industry (ECCI)

The principal organization in **Estonia** for promoting business contacts, both internally and externally, in the post-communist era. Originally founded in 1925.
President: Toomas Luman.
General Director: Mart Relve.
Address: Toom-Kooli 17, Tallinn 10130.
Telephone: 6460244.
Fax: 6460245.
E-mail: koda@koda.ee
Internet: www.koda.ee

Estonian Coalition Party
Eesti Koonderakond (EK)

A centrist political formation in **Estonia** which headed the Government in 1995–99. The EK was founded in December 1991 and its then leader, Tiit Vähi, became caretaker Prime Minister in January 1992. In the September 1992 **State Assembly** elections the party was part of the nationalist Secure Home coalition, which formed the main parliamentary opposition until 1995. The EK headed the Coalition and Rural People's Union (KMÜ) in the March 1995 election, winning 18 of the 41 alliance seats in its own right. The following month Vähi was appointed Prime Minister of a coalition Government between the KMÜ and the **Estonian Centre Party** (EKe), the EK obtaining four portfolios in addition to the premiership.

A political crisis in October 1995 resulted in the exit of the EKe from the Government and its replacement by the **Estonian Reform Party** (ER), under the continued premiership of Vähi, who soldiered on after the ER left the ruling coalition in November 1996. Vähi finally resigned in February 1997 and was succeeded as Prime Minister and Party Chairman by Mart Siimann. In the March 1999 parliamentary elections, however, the EK slumped to only seven seats (with 7.6% of the

vote) and went into opposition, Siimann vacating the party chairmanship two months later.
Leadership: Märt Kubo (Chair.).
Address: Tulika 19, Tallinn 10613.
Telephone: 6505113.
Fax: 6505114.
E-mail: koondera@online.ee
Internet: www.koonderakond.ee

Estonian Investment Agency

Government agency to promote inward investment in **Estonia**.
Director: Mait Marran.
Address: Roosikrantsi 11, Tallinn 10119.
Telephone: 6279420.
Fax: 6279427.
E-mail: info@eia.ee
Internet: www.investinestonia.com

Estonian News Agency
Eesti Teadeteagentuur (ETA)

Estonia's main news agency, with a staff of some 40 local reporters. ETA describes itself as Estonia's national information agency since 1918 'with a brief interruption'—a reference to the period of Estonia's incorporation into the **Soviet Union** from 1940 until 1991.
Director: Tiit Lohmus.
Address: Pärnu mnt. 142, Tallinn 10134.
Telephone: 6300800.
Fax: 6300816.
E-mail: eta@eta.ee
Internet: www.eta.ee

Estonian People's Union
Eestimaa Rahvaliit (ERL)

The recently-launched successor to the Estonian Rural People's Party (EME), which had been **Estonia**'s largest agrarian formation. The EME was founded in September 1994 on the initiative of Arnold **Rüütel**, a former Chairman of the Estonian Supreme Soviet, who had supported moves to throw off Soviet rule and who became independent **Estonia**'s first Head of State. Rüütel had subsequently headed the popular poll in the September 1992 presidential elections as the Secure Home candidate, winning 42.2% of the vote, but lost in the decisive legislative balloting. The EME formed an alliance with the **Estonian Coalition Party** (EK) for the March 1995 **State Assembly** elections, winning nine seats, and joined the resultant coalition Government headed by the EK.

In government, the EME was weakened by two defections from its parliamentary group in February 1996, but made its presence felt by opposing key legislation. In the run-up to the March 1999 parliamentary polling the EME and the opposition **Estonian Centre Party** (EKe) announced plans to form a post-election Government. However, despite the EKe's major advance, the EME retained only seven seats (with 7.3% of the vote), so that an EKe-EME coalition was not feasible. In opposition, the EME sought to broaden its base by absorbing the small Rural Union and the Pensioners' and Families' Party into a new Estonian People's Union (ERL), which was formally launched in June 2000. Rüütel was elected President of Estonia on 21 September 2001 after successive rounds of voting in the Assembly.

Leadership: Arnold Rüütel (Chair.).
Address: Marja 4/D, Tallinn 10617.
Telephone: 6112909.
Fax: 6112908.
E-mail: erl@erl.ee
Internet: www.erl.ee

Estonian Privatization Agency (EPA)
Eesti Erastamisagentuur

A state-funded entity in **Estonia** established by the Privatization Act 1993, charged with all aspects of the privatization of state-owned assets. Until August 1993, privatization (already accepted in principle before independence) was the responsibility of two separate organizations: the Privatization Enterprise, established in 1992, using Treuhand, a German consultancy, to manage the sale of large enterprises, and the State Property Department, required under the Basis of Property Reform Act 1991 to handle the sale of small businesses by auction.

Reporting to the Ministry of Finance, the Minister of Economic Affairs chairs the 11-member Board, which includes the Minister of Finance, currently Siim **Kallas**, and a representative of the **Bank of Estonia**. Between 1991 and 1997 the number of smaller privatized businesses increased from 10,000 to 60,000 (all sold by auction for cash), while over 400 of the 500 larger companies were sold by tender, many to foreign bidders. Since 1998, the EPA has been working on the privatization of the major infrastructure companies in the transport, communications and energy sectors.

Director-General: Väino Sarnet.
Address: Rävala 6, Tallinn 0105.
Telephone: 6305600.

Fax: 6305699.
E-mail: eea@eea.ee
Internet: www.eea.ee

Estonian Reform Party
Eesti Reformierakond (ER)

A 'liberal-rightist' pro-market formation in **Estonia**, affiliated to the **Liberal International**. The ER was launched in 1994 by **Bank of Estonia** Governor Siim **Kallas**, who had made an unsuccessful bid for the premiership after being instrumental in the downfall of a Government headed by what became the **Fatherland Union** (IL). Using the unofficial designation 'Liberals', the ER took second place in the March 1995 **State Assembly** elections, winning 19 seats and 16.2% of the vote. Having thus effectively become leader of the opposition, Kallas resigned from his post at the Bank of Estonia. Six months later, in November 1995, he became Deputy Premier and Foreign Minister when the ER joined a new coalition Government headed by the **Estonian Coalition Party** (EK). However, in late 1996 the ER left the Government, while continuing to give it qualified external support.

In the March 1999 parliamentary elections the ER slipped to 18 seats with 15.9% of the vote. It nevertheless joined a centre-right coalition headed by the IL in which Kallas obtained the finance portfolio and four other ER Ministers were appointed. Despite an ongoing court case against him over alleged financial impropriety, Kallas was re-elected ER Chairman in May 1999. In January 2001 the ER issued a manifesto calling for income tax to be cut to 20% and for state spending to be reduced in various areas.

Internal dissent within the coalition led to the announcement by Prime Minister Mart **Laar** in December 2001 that he would resign in January, casting doubt over the future of the IL-led coalition itself.

Leadership: Siim **Kallas** (Chair.).
Address: Tonismägi 3A/15, Tallinn 10119.
Telephone: 6408740.
Fax: 6408741.
E-mail: info@reform.ee
Internet: www.reform.ee

Estonians

An Indo-European people, the name 'Estonian' deriving from the ancient **German** word 'Aisti', first recorded by the Roman historian Tacitus.

The Estonian language belongs to the Baltic-Finnic group of **Finno-Ugric** languages, and is closely related to Finnish. It replaced Russian as the official language in **Estonia** in 1989. Written in the Latin script, it dates back to the 16th century. The proportion of ethnic Estonians decreased from 1940 following the 'Sovietization' policies, but the people retain the cultural and religious legacy of German and Scandinavian rule, adhering to the Evangelical Lutheran Church (*see* **Protestantism**).

ETA *see* **Estonian News Agency**.

Ethnic cleansing

A euphemism for the use of terror by one ethnic group to expel another from an ethnically-mixed community. The phrase was first widely used in war-torn **Bosnia and Herzegovina** in the summer of 1992, when Bosnian **Serbs** systematically drove many **Bosniaks** (Bosnian Muslims) from their homes. Their property was often then seized by Serb families. Serb ethnic cleansing was allegedly part of a plan to create an ethnically homogeneous **Greater Serbia** from the ruins of **Yugoslavia**. The Bosnian Serb tactics allegedly included systematic murder and rape, siege and starvation. By the spring of 1993 there were allegations that all three parties in the conflict in Bosnia and Herzegovina had perpetrated ethnic cleansing. These allegations led to the establishment by the UN Security Council in May 1993 of the **International Criminal Tribunal for the former Yugoslavia**, which began its investigations in November 1993.

EU *see* **European Union**.

EUR *see* **United People's Party of Estonia**.

Eurasian Economic Community (EEC)

A grouping which came into existence in 2001 to co-ordinate regional trade. The EEC's founding agreement was signed in Astana, the capital of Kazakhstan, in October 2000. It grew out of the joint commitment expressed by its five members to observe the provisions of the **Commonwealth of Independent States**' agreements on economic integration, starting with the Economic Union Treaty in September 1993, which had proven to have little substantive content. The workings of the new organization were to be based on existing customs union agreements, but it was designed as the logical next step in an incremental process of policy harmonization. Its decision-making is based on a weighted voting system in which the **Russian Federation**, with 40% of the votes, can block any major policy decision, for which a two-thirds majority is required. **Belarus** and Kazakhstan each have 20% of the votes and Kyrgyzstan and Tajikistan each 10%.

The EEC consists of an Inter-state Council (Presidents, meeting for annual summits, and Prime Ministers of member Governments, meeting twice yearly), an Integration Committee (Deputy Premiers, meeting every three months) and an Inter-parliamentary Assembly.

Members: Belarus, Kazakhstan, Kyrgyzstan, Russian Federation, Tajikistan.

Leadership: Annual rotating chairmanship, held in the first year (until 30 June 2002) by Kazakh President Nursultan Nazarbayev.

Euro-Atlantic Partnership Council (EAPC)

A partnership of the **North Atlantic Treaty Organization**. The EAPC was inaugurated in May 1997 as a successor to the North Atlantic Co-operation Council (NACC), which had itself been established in December 1991 to provide a forum for consultation on political and security matters with the countries of central and eastern Europe, including the former Soviet republics. It meets on a regular basis to discuss political and security-related issues. As of January 2002 there were 46 members: the 19 NATO member countries and 27 partner countries. All EAPC members are members of the **Partnership for Peace** programme.

Euro-Left Coalition
Koalicija Evrolevica (KEL)

A political formation in **Bulgaria** of left-wing pro-European orientation. The KEL was launched in February 1997 by two left-leaning parties, including the Civic Union of the Republic (Tomov), and some dissident deputies of the **Bulgarian Socialist Party** (BSP). The Civic Union Chairman, Aleksandur Tomov, became leader of the new grouping, which in the April 1997 **National Assembly** elections won 14 seats with 5.6% of the vote. Also known as the Bulgarian Euro-Left, the grouping in December 1998 reached agreement with the BSP on the creation of a broad left-wing front for the 2001 elections. However, the KEL received only 1% of the popular vote and was therefore not allocated any seats after the poll.

Leadership: Aleksandur Tomov (Chair.).

Address: c/o Narodno Sobranie, 1 Aleksandur Battenberg Sq., 1169 Sofia.

European Bank for Reconstruction and Development (EBRD)

A multilateral financial institution founded in May 1990 and inaugurated in April 1991 with the objective of providing loan capital and project support in **central and eastern Europe**, to contribute to the progress and the economic reconstruction of the region. Participant countries must undertake to respect and put into practice the principles of multi-party democracy, pluralism, the rule of law, respect for human rights and a market economy.

Members: 59 countries, including Albania, Armenia, Azerbaijan, Belarus, Bosnia and Herzegovina, Bulgaria, Croatia, Czech Republic, Estonia, Georgia, Hungary, Latvia, Lithuania, Macedonia, Moldova, Poland, Romania, Russian Federation, Slovakia, Slovenia, Ukraine and Yugoslavia.
Leadership: Jean Lemierre (President).
Address: One Exchange Square, 175 Bishopsgate, London, EC2A 2EH, United Kingdom.
Telephone: (20) 73386000.
Fax: (20) 73386100.
Internet: www.ebrd.com

European Court of Human Rights

Part of the activities of the **Council of Europe**.
President: Luzius Wildhaber.

European Organization for Nuclear Research

Organisation européenne pour la recherche nucléaire (CERN)

A scientific organization founded in 1954 (initially with 12 member countries) to provide for collaboration among European states in nuclear research of a pure scientific and fundamental character. The work of CERN is for peaceful purposes only and concerns subnuclear, high-energy and elementary particle physics. Its membership amounts to 20 European countries, including **Hungary** (joined in 1991), **Poland** (1992), **Czech Republic** and **Slovakia** (1993) and **Bulgaria** (1999). The five countries with observer status include the **Russian Federation**.
Leadership: Luciano Maiani (Director-General).
Address: European Laboratory for Particle Physics, 1211 Geneva 23, Switzerland.
Telephone: (22) 7676111.
Fax: (22) 7676555.
Internet: www.cern.ch

European Russia

The western portion of the **Russian Federation**, considered to be the eastern edge of Europe. European Russia stretches from the **Kola peninsula** in the north-west to the Ural mountains in the far east, the **Caucasus** mountains to the south and the historically mobile political borders of eastern Europe in the west. The vast region encompasses Arctic tundra, temperate grassland, boggy marshes, steep mountains, enormous river networks, broad steppe and even desert. It is the traditional home of the **Slavs**. The early Russian state of Muscovy, centred on **Moscow**, was the first political entity that could be described as European Russia.

As Russian power grew, the country took in ever greater swathes of the region and other non-Slavic peoples, including in particular the **Finno-Ugric** peoples now concentrated to the west of the Urals, and the many Caucasian peoples. Although control of European Russia happened in tandem with the conquest of **Siberia**, the former has always been the demographic and economic heart of the Russian state. Its integration with the rest of Europe has been determined by the changing foreign policy aims of Russian Governments. The **pan-Slavic** movement of the early 19th century was tempered by the imperialist expansion towards the century's close. Similarly the revolutionary evangelism of Lenin was toned down by the isolationism of Stalin and the **Cold War**. In the early 21st century the dominance of the 'West' and the expansion of the **North Atlantic Treaty Organization** (NATO) and the **European Union** (EU) have refocused international attention on the relationship between the Russian Federation and Europe.

Soviet-era industrialization and collectivization changed the landscape permanently, giving rise to enormous cities on the **Volga** and **Don** rivers, and forcing nomadic herders into settled communities. With the collapse of the **Soviet Union**, European Russia effectively shrank back as a political entity, with the creation of successor buffer states between it and the rest of Europe and Asia. The integrity of modern European Russia has been tested by nationalist aspirations, particularly in **Chechnya** and **Tatarstan**, but has remained intact. Control from Moscow was reasserted in 2000–01 under the centralizing policies of President Vladimir **Putin**.

European Stability Initiative (ESI)

A non-profit research and policy institute, established in 1999 to assist international efforts to promote stability and prosperity in south-eastern Europe.
Leadership: Gerald Knaus (Executive Director).
Address: Kiefholzstrasse 402, D-12435, Berlin, Germany.
Telephone: (30) 53214455.
Fax: (30) 53214457.
E-mail: esiweb@t-online.de, esi@operamail.com
Internet: www.esiweb.org

European Union (EU)

The principal organization of European integration, which 10 of the former communist countries of **central** and **eastern Europe** have applied to join. For these countries, EU membership represents a means of cementing the process of transition to free-market economies and pluralist democracies. The EU is also a major

European Union (EU)

source of funding and expertise for their economic reform and development programmes.

Based on the 1951 Treaty setting up what was then the six-member European Coal and Steel Community (ECSC), and the 1957 Treaties of Rome setting up the European Economic Community (EEC) and Euratom, the European Union today has expanded to 15 member countries (Austria, Belgium, Denmark, Finland, France, Germany, Greece, Ireland, Italy, Luxembourg, Netherlands, Portugal, Spain, Sweden and the UK) and has developed substantially in the economic, monetary, social and (to a lesser extent) political spheres. It is currently preparing for enlargement to include up to 13 more countries (10 of them in central and eastern Europe, plus Cyprus, Malta and Turkey).

The dates of formal application for EU membership by central and eastern European applicants were:

Hungary 31 March 1994
Poland 5 April 1994
Romania 22 June 1995
Slovakia 27 June 1995
Latvia 13 October 1995
Estonia 24 November 1995
Lithuania 8 December 1995
Bulgaria 14 December 1995
Czech Republic 17 January 1996
Slovenia 10 June 1996

When the EU formally launched its accession process in March 1998, covering these 10 states and Cyprus, it opened accession negotiations simultaneously with five of them (and Cyprus), generally identified as 'first wave' candidates for admission, namely the Czech Republic, Estonia, Hungary, Poland and Slovenia. In October 1999 the EU Commission recommended that member states open accession negotiations with the other five (and Malta), but the member states have yet to approve this recommendation.

The EU's timetable envisages concluding the accession negotiations by the end of 2002 with those countries which fulfil the accession criteria (as set out originally at the EU's Copenhagen summit meeting in 1993, covering a comprehensive set of political and economic issues). On this basis these countries would be ready to become members of the EU in 2004.

According to the EU Commission's assessment on the economic criteria, published in November 2001, the Czech Republic, Estonia, Hungary, Latvia, Lithuania, Poland, Slovakia and Slovenia are functioning market economies which, provided they continue with various specified measures, should be able to cope with competitive pressure and market forces within the Union in the near term. Bulgaria is assessed as 'close to being a functioning market economy' and, 'provided it continues implementing reforms and intensifies the reform effort to remove persistent difficulties, it should be able to cope with competitive pressure and

European Union (EU)

market forces within the Union in the medium term'. Romania, however, 'does not yet meet either criterion but has, for the first time, made decisive progress towards this objective'.

When the EU enlarges it will acquire new neighbours, and it has developed specific policies for each neighbouring region. In eastern Europe this process is known as the Partnership and Co-operation framework for the Russian Federation, Ukraine and other Newly Independent States (NIS). At an EU-Russia summit in October 2001 agreement was reached on a High Level Group to develop a concept for a Common European Economic Space. The EU has Partnership and Co-operation Agreements (PCAs) in place with the Russian Federation, Ukraine and Moldova, although not with Belarus, relations with that country being limited on account of its poor record on democracy, human rights and the rule of law.

In respect of what it terms the western Balkans (Albania, Bosnia and Herzegovina, Croatia, Macedonia and the Federal Republic of Yugoslavia), the EU has established a Stabilization and Association Process (SAP). This is the framework within which it sees its relationships, and the assistance programmes it provides, helping each country to progress at its own pace as a potential candidate for EU membership. The EU also considers that all the countries in the region need to be assisted in their attempts to synchronize regional co-operation efforts with the requirements of EU integration.

Internet: europa.eu.int (*European Union website*)
europa.eu.int/comm/enlargement/index.htm (*enlargement issues: press releases and progress reports on individual candidate countries*)
europa.eu.int/pol/enlarg/index_en.html (*framework documents on enlargement and other links*)

Address of European Commission: 200 rue de la Loi, 1049 Brussels, Belgium.
Telephone: (2) 2991111.
Fax: (2) 2950138.
Internet: www.europa.eu.int/comm

F

Fatherland
Batkivshchyna

A moderate conservative political party in **Ukraine**. Fatherland was launched in 1999 by a faction of the **Hromada All-Ukrainian Association** after Hromada leader Pavlo Lazarenko had fled to the USA to escape charges of financial corruption when he was Prime Minister in 1996–97. In January 2000 Fatherland leader Yuliya Tymoshenko was appointed Deputy Prime Minister and put in charge of the energy sector. In August 2000 her husband was among several state energy officials arrested on embezzlement charges and was later also accused of paying large bribes to Lazarenko when he was Prime Minister. Tymoshenko was then herself charged with corruption when she had been a state energy official, and was dismissed from the Government in January 2001. Fatherland thereupon joined the parliamentary opposition to President Leonid **Kuchma**, who was concurrently under intense pressure to resign over his alleged involvement in the murder of a journalist. The arrest of Tymoshenko in mid-February was condemned by Fatherland as punishment for her anti-Kuchma activities and her attempts to reform the energy sector.

Leadership: Yuliya Tymoshenko (Chair.).
Address: c/o Verkhovna Rada, M. Grushevskogo St 5, Kiev 01008.

Fatherland–All Russia
Otechestvo–Vsya Rossiya (OVR)

A conservative nationalist political grouping in the **Russian Federation**. Fatherland was launched in November 1998 by Yurii Luzhkov, the popular Mayor of **Moscow**, to rally opposition to the increasingly troubled presidency of Boris **Yeltsin**, attracting considerable support from regional Governors and business leaders for its call for a better balance between the free market and state economic control. In April 1999 it formed the OVR bloc with the regionalist All Russia movement, but from September 1999 faced strong competition on the right from the new **Unity Inter-regional Movement** (Medved) backing the then Prime Minister Vladimir **Putin**.

The OVR took third place in the December 1999 elections to the State Duma (lower house of the **Federal Assembly**), winning 66 seats with a proportional vote share of 13.3%. Yeltsin's surprise resignation after the elections and the elevation of Putin as his designated successor resulted in Luzhkov abandoning his own presidential ambitions and swinging the OVR behind Putin in the March 2000 presidential elections. The OVR group subsequently formed part of the pro-Government parliamentary majority and entered into negotiations for a merger with Medved.

Leadership: Yurii Luzhkov (Chair.).
Address: c/o Gossoudarstvennaya Duma, Okhotnyi Ryad 1, Moscow 103265.
Internet: www.kprf.ru

Fatherland and Freedom–Latvian National Conservative Party
Tevzemei un Brivibai–Latvijas Nacionala Konservativa Partija (TB–LNNK)

A right-wing political formation in **Latvia**, resulting from the merger in June 1997 of the TB and the LNNK, which were both then part of a broad centre-right coalition Government. Of these two components, the TB had emerged during the independence struggle as an alliance of ultra-nationalist groups and had won six seats in the 1993 elections, rising to 14 in 1995, when it was part of the National Bloc of right-wing parties and its leader Maris Grinblats became a Deputy Prime Minister. The right-wing LNNK was originally founded in 1988 as the Latvian National Independence Movement (*Latvijas Nacionalas Neatkaribas Kustiba*—from which the party still retains its LNNK initials). It had won 15 seats in the 1993 elections, but its image had been tarnished by the campaign rhetoric of a far-right member of German origin, Joahims Zigerists, who was later expelled from the party. Renamed and allied with the Latvian Greens in the 1995 elections, the LNNK dropped to eight seats.

After the TB–LNNK merger, the party in August 1997 successfully nominated Guntars Krasts as Prime Minister of a reconstituted centre-right coalition. In the October 1998 parliamentary elections, however, the TB–LNNK won only 17 of the 100 seats on a 14.7% vote share, well below its aggregate performance in 1995. The party also failed to get popular endorsement in a simultaneous referendum for its attempt to block recent legislation liberalizing Latvia's naturalization laws. It nevertheless joined a new centre-right coalition headed by **Latvia's Way** (LC), continuing in government when the **People's Party** obtained the premiership in July 1999 and also when the premiership reverted to the LC in April 2000.

Leadership: Maris Grinblats (Chair.).
Address: 10 Kaleju iela, Riga 1050.
Telephone: 7220131.
Fax: 7216762.
E-mail: tb@tb.lv
Internet: www.tb.lv

Fatherland Union
Isamaaliit (IL)

The major centre-right party in **Estonia**, affiliated to the **International Democrat Union**. The IL was created in December 1995 by the merger of the Fatherland (or Pro Patria) National Coalition (RKI) and the Estonian National Independence Party (ERSP). These two parties had contested the March 1995 elections in alliance but had retained only eight seats with 7.9% of the vote, thereafter going into opposition.

Of the IL components, the RKI had been formed in early 1992 as an alliance of several Christian Democratic and other centre-right parties seeking to make a decisive break with the Soviet era. Led by Mart **Laar**, it had won an indecisive plurality of 29 seats in the September 1992 **State Assembly** elections, its deputies combining the following month with those of the ERSP and others to elect Lennart **Meri** as President despite his having come second in the popular balloting. Laar had then become Prime Minister in a coalition Government, until being ousted in September 1994, in part because of his self-confessed 'dictatorial' methods.

The ERSP had been founded in August 1988, being then the only organized non-communist party in the **Soviet Union**. Although centrist in orientation, it was consistently more anti-communist than other pro-independence formations, declining to participate in the 1990 Estonian Supreme Soviet elections and instead organizing the alternative 'Congress of Estonia'. Following independence in 1991, the ERSP had emerged as Estonia's strongest party, but had been eclipsed by the RKI in the September 1992 elections, becoming a junior coalition partner in the Government headed by the RKI.

In the March 1999 parliamentary elections the IL took second place, winning 18 seats on a 16.1% vote share, whereupon Laar was able to form a three-party centre-right coalition with the **Moderates** and the **Estonian Reform Party**. However, the Government was soon facing strong opposition within the State Assembly, and dissent within the coalition itself led to the election of opposition **Estonian People's Union** candidate Arnold **Rüütel** as President in 2001. By the end of the year the cracks had widened; Laar announced that he would resign in January, leaving the future of the coalition itself in doubt.

Leadership: Mart Laar (Chair.).
Address: Endla 4A, Tallinn 10142.
Telephone: 6263325.
Fax: 6263324.
E-mail: info@isamaaliit.ee
Internet: www.isamaaliit.ee

Federal Assembly (Russian Federation)
Federalnoye Sobraniye

The bicameral legislature of the **Russian Federation**, comprising the State Duma (Gossoudarstvennaya Duma) and the Council of the Federation (Soviet Federatsii). The lower State Duma has 450 members, directly elected for a four-year term. The upper Council of the Federation has 178 members (two representatives from each of the constituent federal administrative units of the Russian Federation). The individual members' terms vary according to the electing region. The last elections to the State Duma were held on 19 December 1999.

Address of lower house: Gossoudarstvennaya Duma, Okhotnyi Ryad 1, 103265 Moscow.
Telephone: (095) 2923057.
Fax: (095) 2925358.
E-mail: www@duma.ru
Internet: www.duma.ru
Address of upper house: Soviet Federatsii, Bolshaya Dmitrovka 26, Moscow.
Telephone: (095) 2925969.
Fax: (095) 2925967.
E-mail: post_sf@gov.ru
Internet: www.council.gov.ru

Federal Assembly (Yugoslavia)
Savezna Skupština

The bicameral legislature of the Federal Republic of **Yugoslavia**, comprising the Chamber of Citizens (Veće Gradjana) and the Chamber of Republics (Veće Republika). The lower Chamber of Citizens has 138 members (108 members from **Serbia** and 30 from **Montenegro**), directly elected for a four-year term. The upper Chamber of Republics has 40 members (20 from Serbia and 20 from Montenegro). Under the 2000 amendments to the Constitution, the Chamber of Republics is directly elected for a four-year term. The last elections were held on 24 September 2000. Serbia and Montenegro both have separate parliamentary chambers, namely the 250-member Serbian Assembly (Skupština Srbije) and the 78-member Montenegrin Assembly (Skupština Republika Crne Gore), also elected for four-year terms. The Serbian National Assembly was last elected on 24 December 2000, and the Montenegrin Republican Assembly on 22 April 2001.

Address: Savezna Skupština, Trg Nikole Pašića 13, Belgrade 11000.
Telephone: (11) 3229687.
Fax: (11) 3227099.
Internet: www.gov.yu/institutions/assembly/assembly.html

Federal Republic of Yugoslavia (FRY) *see* Yugoslavia.

Federal Security Service
Federal'naya Sluzhba Bezopasnosti (FSB)

The secret service and security agency of the **Russian Federation**. The FSB is the direct descendant of the infamous Soviet-era secret service, the KGB (*Komitet Gossoudarstvennoy Bezopasnosti*—Committee for State Security), and was formed from its ashes in 1993—initially as the Federal Counterintelligence Service (*Federal'naya Sluzhba Kontrrazvedky*, FSK) from 1993 to 1995. The FSB continues to be based in the home of the KGB in Lubyanka Square, Moscow. The KGB was the result of Soviet efforts to create an all-powerful intelligence-gathering network which began with the creation of the All-Russian Extraordinary Commission for the Suppression of Counterrevolution and Sabotage (Cheka) in 1917. The Cheka was used to suppress opposition to the newly-formed communist State. Through many transformations and purges the KGB emerged in 1953, with strong links to the Interior Ministry of the **Soviet Union**. The KGB persisted as the main tool of intelligence and counterintelligence work and was closely tied, as were all organs of the communist State, with the **Communist Party of the Soviet Union**. Its workings were demystified by Khrushchev in the late 1950s and the emphasis on the use of terror was somewhat lessened. This process was furthered under Soviet leader Mikhail **Gorbachev** in the late 1980s. In reaction many senior members of the KGB were involved in the hardline **August coup** in 1991, prompting Gorbachev to overhaul the service completely. Internal security matters were initially transferred to a new Security Ministry before the creation of the FSK/FSB. In February 2000 the then Acting President Vladimir **Putin** granted the service control over military intelligence.

Putin's relationship with the FSB has brought the agency to the forefront of Russian politics in recent years. Putin himself was a former KGB agent and was appointed head of the FSB in July 1998. He only relinquished the position five months after he had been elected President in March 2000. Consequently his own past is shrouded in mystery and many of the people he has promoted to positions of authority in his administration have had links with the agency or its predecessors in the past. The FSB has also had administrative control over the breakaway republic of **Chechnya** since January 2001.

Director: Nikolai Patrushev.
Address: 1/3 Bolshaya, Lubyanka Ul., 101000 Moscow.
Telephone: (095) 9143908.
Fax: (095) 9752470.
E-mail: fsb@fsb.ru
Internet: www.fsb.ru

Federalnoye Sobraniye *see* Federal Assembly (Russian Federation).

Federation of Bosnia and Herzegovina *see* Muslim-Croat Federation.

Federation of Independent Trade Unions of Russia
Federatsiya Nezavisimykh Profsoyuzov Rossii (FNPR)

The main union centre in the **Russian Federation**, successor to the Soviet-era structure and much larger than independent centres of more recent creation. The FNPR retained some of the assets of the previous All-Union Central Council of Trade Unions (AUCCTU) and also much of the universal trade union membership of the Soviet era. In 2000 it still claimed to represent 80% of Russian workers and to have 28 million members, although its active membership is a fraction of this number and the centre has rarely been able to mobilize protest actions against plummeting real incomes and unpaid wages. The FNPR is one of three Russian affiliates of the International Confederation of Free Trade Unions (IFCTU), the other two being the **All-Russian Confederation of Labour** (VKT) and the **Confederation of Labour of Russia** (KTR).

President: Mikhail Shmakov.
Address: 42 Lenin Prospect, Moscow 117119.
Telephone: (095) 9308984.
Fax: (095) 9382293.
E-mail: korneev@fnpr.ru
Internet: www.fnpr.ru

Federation of Trade Unions of Ukraine (FPU)

Ukraine's largest union centre, relaunched in 1990 as the direct successor to the Soviet-era structure. It claims 20 million members among a workforce still highly unionized, especially in the still-dominant state sector.

Chair.: Oleksandr Stoyan.
Address: 2 Maydan Nezalezhnosti St, Kiev 252012.
Telephone: (44) 2288788.
Fax: (44) 2290087.

Federation of Young Democrats–Hungarian Civic Party
Fiatal Demokraták Szövetsége–Magyar Polgári Párt (FIDESz–MPP)

A conservative political party in **Hungary**, affiliated to the **Christian Democrat International**, which headed the Government after May 1998. Originally known simply as the Federation of Young Democrats, the grouping finished no better than fifth in the 1990 **National Assembly** elections, winning 22 of 378 elective seats on a 9% vote share. Later that year it won mayoral elections in nine of the country's largest cities, but in the May 1994 general elections its national representation declined further, to 20 seats, and it remained in opposition. A 35-year-old age limit on membership was abandoned in April 1993, paving the way for the adoption of the FIDESz–MPP designation two years later.

The FIDESz–MPP was strengthened in 1997 and early 1998 by its absorption of part of the Christian Democratic People's Party (KDNP), which had won 22 seats in 1994. Benefiting from public disenchantment with the ruling centre-left coalition, the FIDESz–MPP achieved a major advance in the May 1998 National Assembly elections, winning 147 seats on a 29.5% vote share. As Chairman of the largest party, its leader Viktor **Orbán** formed a centre-right coalition with the **Independent Smallholders' and Civic Party** (FKgP) and the **Hungarian Democratic Forum** (MDF), in which the FIDESz–MPP took 12 of the 17 ministerial posts. The new Government took Hungary into the **North Atlantic Treaty Organization** in March 1999 and set accession to the **European Union** as its key objective.

In January 2000 a FIDESz congress decided to split the posts of Party Chairman and Premier and elected László Kövér to the party post. However, having come under criticism for his aggressive style, Kövér stood down in March 2001 and was replaced by Zoltán Pokorni, the Interior Minister.

Leadership: Viktor Orbán (political leader); Zoltán Pokorni (Chair.).
Address: Lendvay utca 28, 1062 Budapest.
Telephone: (1) 2695353.
Fax: (1) 2695343.
E-mail: sajto@fidesz.parlament.hu
Internet: www.fidesz.hu

FIDESz–MPP *see* **Federation of Young Democrats–Hungarian Civic Party**.

Filipović, Karlo

President of the **Muslim-Croat Federation**.

Karlo Filipović is Secretary-General of the moderate **Social Democratic Party of Bosnia and Herzegovina** (SDPBiH). He was appointed President of the Muslim-Croat Federation on 27 February 2001, to remain in the post for one year before switching places with his **Bosniak** Vice-President, Safet Halilović.

Born in 1954 in Solakovici, near Ilijas, Filipović is an ethnic **Croat**. He was an engineer by training before entering politics. He was elected to the Muslim-Croat Federation's House of Representatives (lower house) in 1998 where he led the parliamentary section of the SDPBiH before his appointment as President.

Address: Office of the President, 71000 Sarajevo.
Telephone and Fax: (33) 472618.

Finlandization

A term used when the affairs—particularly the foreign policy—of a small state are heavily influenced by a neighbouring major international power. Finland from 1945 remained an independent state with a pluralist democratic system, but until the collapse of communism in Europe its leaders consulted frequently with their Soviet neighbours, and attuned their policies in tacit acknowledgement that they should not cut across vital Soviet interests. For former Soviet Republics in the 1990s, **Russia**'s concept of its **near abroad** is a reminder of the delicate balances implied by the notion of Finlandization.

Finno-Ugric peoples

An ethnic group, thought to have originated in the west Kazakh steppe but now inhabiting areas from **Hungary** to the River **Volga**. From the original Uralic group there arose four main descendant groups (in order of separation from original community): the Magyars (see **Hungarians**) in **central Europe** and **Siberia**; the Permians in the centre of **European Russia**—Udmurts (see **Udmurtia**) and Komi (see **Komi Republic**); the Volga Finns around the River Volga—**Mordvins** (see **Mordova**) and **Mari** (see **Mari El Republic**); and the Baltic Finns in the Baltic and Scandinavian areas—**Estonians**, Finns, **Karelians** (see **Karelia question**) and **Sami**.

This wide geographic spread, and the influence of the other European peoples, has emphasized the differences between the various Finno-Ugric peoples. The Volga Finns have largely embraced the **Muslim** faith, while the European Magyars converted to Catholicism (see **Roman Catholic Church**) in 1000. Some isolated Finno-Ugric people in the far north still practise a form of the original Uralic animist religion. There are strong linguistic connections between the Finno-Ugric languages, with varying degrees of borrowing from neighbouring tongues.

FKgP see **Independent Smallholders' and Civic Party**.

FNPR see **Federation of Independent Trade Unions of Russia**.

Foreign Trade Institute
Institut za Spoljnu Trgovinu

Government agency in the Federal Republic of **Yugoslavia**.
   Director: Dr Slobodan Mrkša.
   Address: Moše Pijade 8, 11000 Belgrade.
   Telephone: (11) 339041.

Former Yugoslav Republic of Macedonia (FYROM) *see* **Macedonia.**

Forum for the Co-operation of Trade Unions
Szakszervezetek Együttműködési Fóruma (SzEF)

A trade union centre in **Hungary** representing public sector workers such as teachers, social and health service workers and local government employees. Dating from 1990, the SzEF was relaunched as a national federation in 1995 in response to deteriorating conditions in the public sector. Independent of political parties but frequently co-operating with the dominant **National Confederation of Hungarian Trade Unions**, it claims to represent some 450,000 employees.
President: Dr Endre Szabó.
Address: 4 u. Puskin, Budapest 1088.
Telephone: (1) 3382651.
Fax: (1) 3187360.

FPB *see* **Belarusian Federation of Trade Unions.**

FPU *see* **Federation of Trade Unions of Ukraine.**

Fratia National Confederation of Free Trade Unions of Romania
Confederatia Nationala a Sindicatelor Libere din România–Fratia (CNSLR–Fratia).

The largest of the many competing union centres in post-communist **Romania**, of social democratic orientation. The CNSLR was the successor to the communist-era union organization, inheriting most of its membership and assets. In 1993 it merged with the rival Fratia centre to establish a fully independent identity, the merged organization becoming an affiliate of the International Confederation of Free Trade Unions. The CNSLR–Fratia claims to represent 1.2 million members in 47 sectoral federations and 41 regional branches.
President: Marius Petcu.
Address: 1–3 Ministerului St, Bucharest 70109.
Telephone: (1) 3134179.
Fax: (1) 3126206.
E-mail: presedinte@cnslr-fratia.ro
Internet: www.cnslr-fratia.ro

Freedom Union (Czech Republic)
Unie Svobody (US)

A centrist political party in the **Czech Republic** formed in early 1998 by a dissident faction of the **Civic Democratic Party** (ODS). The US resulted from deepening divisions in the ODS following the resignation in November 1997 of the Government led by Václav **Klaus**, whose leadership style so offended a faction led by former Interior Minister Jan Ruml that it formed a new party in January 1998. The new party attracted the support of 30 of the 69 ODS lower house deputies, including two of the ODS Ministers in the post-Klaus interim Government, who had accepted portfolios in defiance of a party decision not to participate.

In early lower house elections in June 1998 the US returned only 19 candidates, with an 8.6% vote share, and went into opposition to a minority Government of the **Czech Social Democratic Party** backed externally by the ODS. In opposition, the US formed a 'Coalition of Four' with the **Christian Democratic Union–Czechoslovak People's Party** and two other centrist parties. This coalition planned to present a joint list of candidates and prospective ministerial team in the 2002 elections.

In February 2000 Ruml was succeeded as Party Chairman by Karel Kühnl, a former Trade and Industry Minister. In the November 2000 partial Senate elections the US advanced strongly within the opposition alliance, becoming the third-largest party with 18 of the 81 seats.

Leadership: Karel Kühnl (Chair.).
Address: Malostranské nám. 266/5, 11800 Prague 1.
Telephone: (2) 57011411.
Fax: (2) 57530102.
E-mail: info@unie.cz
Internet: www.uniesvobody.cz

Freedom Union (Poland)
Unia Wolności (UW)

A liberal centrist political party in **Poland** which has often played a pivotal role between the stronger forces of left and right. Founded in 1994 by the merger of the Democratic Union (UD) and the smaller Liberal Democratic Congress (KLD), the UW declared itself to be of the democratic social centre, favouring market-oriented reforms combined with sensitivity to resultant social problems.

As the larger of the UW components, the UD had been created to support the unsuccessful presidential candidacy of the then Prime Minister Tadeusz Mazowiecki in 1990 and was later joined by other centrist groups. Although identified with the **'shock therapy'** economic programme of the then Finance Minister Leszek **Balcerowicz** (later to become leader of the UW), the UD urged that more consideration should be given to the social consequences. In the October 1991 **National**

Freedom Union (Poland)

Assembly elections the UD won 62 seats on a 12.3% vote share, more than any of the other 28 parties which gained representation. Its then leader, Bronislaw Geremek, tried but failed to form a Government, so that the UD became the main opposition to the 1991–92 Olszewski Government. Upon its fall in June 1992, Hanna Suchocka of the UD formed a seven-party coalition, becoming Poland's first female Prime Minister, but her Government fell in May 1993. In the September 1993 elections the UD improved its representation to 74 seats, but fell back to 10.6% of the vote and third place in the parliamentary order, becoming the principal opposition to a left-dominated Government.

The pro-privatization KLD had been founded in 1990 under the leadership of journalist Donald Tusk and had won 37 seats in 1991, but had failed to reach the 5% threshold for representation in the 1993 elections.

The UW candidate in the 1995 presidential elections was Jacek Kuron, who achieved a creditable third place in the first round with 9.2% of the national vote. In the September 1997 parliamentary elections the UW advanced to 13.4% and 60 seats and opted, after some hesitation, to join a centre-right coalition Government headed by **Solidarity Electoral Action** (AWS) in which Balcerowicz returned to the Finance Ministry and Geremek became Foreign Minister. Both Ministers won international plaudits, Geremek for piloting Poland into the **North Atlantic Treaty Organization** in 1999 and both for advancing the cause of Polish membership of the **European Union**. However, opposition to Balcerowicz's further economic reform proposals on the populist wing of the AWS resulted in the UW leaving the Government in June 2000. The UW did not present a candidate in the October 2000 presidential election.

In December 2000 Balcerowicz was appointed as President of the **National Bank of Poland** and was succeeded as UW Chairman by Geremek. In January 2001 the UW was weakened when Tusk and other prominent centrist politicians formed the **Citizens' Platform** (PO), which was joined by a substantial number of UW members. The UW's fortunes slipped further as the PO soaked up its electoral support. The UW received only 3.1% of the vote in the September legislative elections, failing to breach the 5% barrier for representation and therefore gaining no seats in the *Sejm* (lower house). The party contested seats for the *Senat* (upper house) as part of the Blok Senat 2001 coalition (which included the PO, **Law and Justice**, the AWS and the **Movement for the Reconstruction of Poland**), which won 15 seats. Geremek resigned as UW Chairman soon after the defeat and was replaced by Władysław Frasyniuk.

Leadership: Władysław Frasyniuk (Chair.).
Address: Al. Jerozolimskie 30, Warsaw 00024.
Telephone: (22) 8275047.
Fax: (22) 8277851.
E-mail: uw@uw.org.pl
Internet: www.uw.org.pl

FRY

The Federal Republic of Yugoslavia, *see* **Yugoslavia**.

FSB *see* **Federal Security Service**

FSzDL *see* **Democratic League of Independent Trade Unions**.

FYRM *or* FYROM

The Former Yugoslav Republic of Macedonia, *see* **Macedonia**.

G

G8 *see* Group of Eight.

Gabčíkovo-Nagymaros Dam

A controversial hydroelectric dam on the River Danube in southern **Slovakia**, at the point where the Danube forms the border with **Hungary**. It was originally conceived in 1977 as a joint project between Hungary and **Czechoslovakia**. By 1989 Hungary had pulled out, on economic, ecological and domestic grounds, but Czechoslovakia (and later Slovakia) chose to complete its part of the project, which had become a symbol of national pride. The main loser in Slovakia was the Magyar (**Hungarian**) community, which had historically lived on land which was to be partially inundated by dammed water.

Gagauzia
Gagauz Yeri

An autonomous region in the southernmost tip of **Moldova**. The regional capital is Comrat. The *Baskan*, a directly-elected President, answers to the 35-seat Gagauz Popular Assembly (Halk Toplusu). Gagauzia is dominated by the ethnic Gagauzi, a Christian Turkic-language speaking people of either Turkish or Bulgarian ethnicity (*see* **Turkic peoples** and **Bulgarian Turks**) who are popularly thought to have settled in the area during the period of Turkish Ottoman rule in the late 18th–early 19th century. Almost three-quarters of Gagauzi consider Russian to be their second language, which tied them closely to the dominant ethnic **Russian** regime established under Soviet rule.

Largely ignored by the Soviet authorities, Gagauzia did not emerge as a defined area until the rise of **Romanian**-centred nationalism in Moldova in the late 1980s. A law designating Moldovan as the country's main official language in 1989 prompted calls for autonomy led by the Gagauz Halki (Gagauz People), the region's most prominent political group. An independent Gagauz Soviet Socialist Republic was declared in 1991 in response to the declaration of Moldovan independence from the **Soviet Union**. The Gaugauzi avoided direct involvement in the conflict between the Moldovan authorities and the separatist struggle in **Transdnestria**, but their demands for autonomy gained ground among moderates in **Chişinau**, and in return for dropping their separatist claims they were granted some autonomy within Moldova from December 1994.

Galicia

A historic region stretching from southern **Poland** into western **Ukraine**. The concept of Galicia was effectively invented by the Habsburg Empire in 1772 when it was awarded the region at the first partition of Poland. It comprised a western and Polish half known as Malopolska (literally 'little Poland'), and an eastern and Ukrainian (or **Ruthenian**) half (*see* **Transcarpathia**) consisting roughly of the ancient duchy of Halychina-Wolyn, from which the name Galicia was derived. Briefly during the Revolutionary–Napoleonic period Galicia stretched to include **Warsaw** but its reduced borders were finally established when the semi-autonomous Republic of Kraków was added in 1846.

Following the dismemberment of the Habsburg Empire after the First World War, Galicia was included in the new Polish Republic. It was briefly redivided into east and west at the start of the Second World War in 1939 before it was swallowed *en masse* into the Nazi General Government district in 1941. During the Nazi occupation the large **Jewish** population of Galicia, the centre of the Hasidic branch of Orthodox Judaism, was all but wiped out. Under the Polish-Soviet Treaty of 1945 Galicia ceased to exist, with east and west becoming integral parts of Poland and Ukraine respectively. The ethnic **Polish** and **Ukrainian** populations were redistributed to fall within their new states, although traditionally they had been largely restricted to their respective halves in any case.

The main urban centres of the region are Kraków in Poland and Lvov in Ukraine. The area is rich in oil and gas deposits as well as other minerals, and the two halves have become important economic centres in their respective countries.

Gazprom

A partially state-run gas monopoly in the **Russian Federation**, founded in 1989 as part of the **Soviet Union**'s Gas Ministry. Gazprom is now the largest commercial producer in the world, accounting for 23% of global gas output and 94% of the Russian Federation's output. Its activities provide 8% of the country's GDP and 25% of tax revenues. It employs 300,000 people and boasts that 500,000 Russians are shareholders, the company having been part privatized in 1993. Gazprom controls all aspects of gas prospecting, mining, production, refining and supply. It also has a massive commercial interest in other economic areas, most notably in the country's media industry.

Opponents of President Vladimir **Putin**'s centralizing tendencies view Gazprom as an arm of the State which has been used to mount financial attacks on the **Yeltsin**-era 'oligarchs'. In September 2000 the Chairman of the Media-MOST press empire, Vladimir Gusinsky, denounced Gazprom's bid to purchase a controlling share in his own company as politically motivated. By January 2001 the seizure of Media-MOST's assets by the State as punishment for Gusinsky's alleged corruption left Gazprom as the single largest shareholder in the country's only private news station, NTV, which had been notably critical of the Putin administration. A matter of months later, the television station was entirely controlled by Gazprom, prompting mass domestic criticism and leading international media watchdogs to warn of the growing threat to press freedom in the Russian Federation. Indeed, in April that year Gazprom helped to close down the Media-MOST-run liberal newspaper *Segodnya*, claiming it was running at a loss.

In October 2000 Prime Minister Mikhail **Kasyanov** outlined proposals to reform the country's large state monopolies. However, he specifically set Gazprom aside, suggesting that investigations into its reconstruction would wait until late 2001 at the earliest. By then, however, the press was suggesting that Putin had put the brakes on the reform of Gazprom for fear of the economic and political repercussions of rapid change in such a large and powerful company.

Chair. of the Board of Directors: Rem I. Vyakhirev.
Chair. of the Management Committee: Alexei B. Miller.
Address: 16 Ul. Nametkina, Moscow.
Telephone: (095) 7193001.
Fax: (095) 7198333.
Internet: www.gazprom.ru

Gdańsk

A major port on the Baltic Sea in northern **Poland**. *Population*: 465,400 (1991 estimate). Gdańsk was a prosperous northern port for much of the mediaeval period, declining after its separation from Poland and incorporation into **Prussia** in 1772. It re-emerged as a free city in 1919 but its **German** population made it a target for Nazi territorial demands, a contributing factor to the German invasion of Poland in 1939 which marked the beginning of the Second World War in Europe. As Danzig the city was thoroughly destroyed in the war and reconstructed by the Polish communist regime along industrial designs. In 1980 labour unrest at the Lenin shipyards led to the formation of the **Solidarity** movement, led by locally born Lech **Wałęsa**, and the authorization of free trade unions in Poland. The city remains of significant economic value to the country.

General Confederation of Armenian Trade Unions

The successor to the Soviet-era trade union organization in **Armenia**. The collapse of state enterprises and high unemployment have severely restricted its scope of operations.
Chair.: Martin Haroutunian.
Address: Hanrapetoutian St, Yerevan 375010.
Telephone: (1) 583682.
Fax: (1) 566033.

Geoana, Mircea

Minister of Foreign Affairs, **Romania**.

Mircea Geoana is an independent. He is a career diplomat and an expert on international relations. He was appointed Foreign Minister in December 2000.

Born on 14 July 1958 in **Bucharest**, he studied law at the Romanian Polytechnic Institute and the University of Bucharest. He joined the Foreign Service in 1990 and rose rapidly to become Director of European Affairs. From 1993 to 1995 he served as Spokesman for the Foreign Ministry and was Director-General of its Asia, Latin America, Middle East and Africa department from 1994, adding Europe and North America after 1995. In 1996, at the age of 37, he became Ambassador to the USA, but was recalled to Romania to serve as Foreign Minister in December 2000.

Having continued his education in tandem with his diplomatic career, Geoana obtained postgraduate degrees from the École Nationale d'Administration in Paris in 1992 and the Harvard Business School in 1999, and has worked for a doctorate in global economics from the Academy for Economic Sciences in Bucharest.
Address: Ministry of Foreign Affairs, Al. Alexandru 31, 71274 Bucharest.
Telephone: (1) 2302071.
Fax: (1) 2307489.
E-mail: mae@mae.ro
Internet: www.mae.ro

Geoimpex *see* **Georgian Import Export**.

Georgi Ganchev Bloc
Georgi Ganchev Blok (GGB)

A radical pro-market political grouping in **Bulgaria** launched in March 2000 as successor to the Bulgarian Business Bloc (BBB). The BBB had been founded in 1990 by leading businessman Valentin Mollov as a right-wing, pro-market formation advocating the conversion of Bulgaria into a tariff- and tax-free zone so that it could become the conduit for trade between the former Soviet republics and the West. It failed to win representation in the 1991 **National Assembly** elections but support grew under the new leadership of Georgi Ganchev, a charismatic former fencing champion whose colourful past attracted much media publicity. In the December 1994 Assembly elections the BBB achieved a breakthrough, winning 4.7% of the vote and 13 of the 240 seats, while in the autumn 1996 presidential elections Ganchev attracted an impressive 21.9% in taking third place in the first voting round.

In the April 1997 Assembly elections the BBB improved slightly to 4.9% of the vote but its representation fell to 12 seats. By September 1997 two expulsions and a resignation from the BBB Assembly group had reduced its size to below the 10 deputies required to qualify for group status. Subsequent uncertainty about the formation's future was eventually clarified by the launching of the GGB in March 2000 as the effective successor to the BBB. However, the GGB failed to win representation in the 2001 elections.

Leadership: Georgi Ganchev (President).
Address: Shipka 13, 1505 Sofia.
Telephone: (2) 446128.

Georgia
Sakartvelos Respublika

An independent republic in the north-western **Caucasus region** of the former **Soviet Union**, bounded by the Russian Federation to the north, Armenia and Turkey to the south, Azerbaijan to the south-east and the Black Sea to the west. The country includes the two autonomous republics of **Abkhazia** and **Adzharia** and the autonomous region of South Ossetia (*see* **Ossetia question**).

Area: 69,700 sq km; *capital*: **Tbilisi**; *population*: 5.2m. (2001 estimate), comprising ethnic **Georgians** 70.1%, **Armenians** 8.1%, **Russians** 6.3%, **Azeris** 5.7%, Ossetians 3%, Abkhaz 1.8%, others 5%; *official language*: Georgian; *religion*: **Georgian Orthodox** 65%, **Russian Orthodox** 10%, Armenian Orthodox 8%, **Muslim** 11%, other 6%.

Under the 1995 Constitution, the Head of State and Government is the executive President, who is directly elected for a five-year term by universal adult suffrage and who appoints the State Minister and the Council of Ministers. Legislative authority is currently vested in a 235-member unicameral **Parliament**, elected for a four-year term. It comprises 150 deputies returned by a system of proportional representation subject to a 7% threshold, and a further 85 elected from single-member constituencies by majority voting. The Constitution states that the Parliament will be transformed into a bicameral body upon the restoration of Georgia's territorial integrity (see below).

History: Georgia flourished as an independent kingdom in the 12th and early 13th centuries, its territory expanding to encompass the whole of what is now known as the Caucasus region. Subsequently devastated by Mongol and other invasions, Georgia then struggled against Ottoman and Persian incursion, before turning gradually to the Russian Empire (in the 18th century) for protection as a vassal state. After the Russian Revolution of 1917, a nationalist Government came to power in Georgia, declaring independence in 1918. However, occupation by Bolshevik forces in 1921 led the following year to the territory's incorporation in the Transcaucasian Soviet Federative Socialist Republic (with Armenia and Azerbaijan). In 1936 Georgia became a separate republic within the **Soviet Union**.

Upon the abolition of the communist monopoly on power, the Georgian Soviet Socialist Republic was dissolved in August 1990. Subsequent multi-party elections resulted in the assumption of the Presidency by nationalist leader Zviad Gamsakhurdia, following which Georgia declared its independence from the Soviet Union in April 1991. At the same time, the country subsided into serious ethnic and civil strife. Accused of dictatorial tendencies, Gamsakhurdia's regime was confronted by armed opposition and overthrown in January 1992. In March a new State Council was established with Eduard **Shevardnadze** as Chairman. Shevardnadze had long been Georgia's most widely known political figure. He had been First Secretary of the Georgian Communist Party from 1972, gaining prominence on an anti-corruption platform, and had become Soviet Foreign Minister and Politburo member in 1985 as a key player in the reformist **Gorbachev** regime.

Shevardnadze obtained electoral endorsement as Head of State in October 1992. However, by September 1993 rebellion by **Zviadists** (supporters of Gamsakhurdia), separatist military advances in the autonomous republics and general economic chaos had rendered the country seemingly ungovernable. Shevardnadze was forced to seek Russian military support to re-establish his Government's authority, in return for which Georgia agreed (and in March 1994 ratified) its accession to the **Commonwealth of Independent States** (CIS), which it had resisted since the establishment of the CIS in 1991.

Separatist tensions in Georgia had revived in 1989 as South Ossetia (seeking reunification with North Ossetia in the Russian Federation) and Abkhazia aspired to independence. Bitter armed conflict with Georgian government forces ensued before cease-fires were declared in South Ossetia (in 1992) and Abkhazia (in 1994), reinforced by the deployment of (largely Russian) peacekeeping forces in both regions and the operation of a UN Observer Mission in Abkhazia. Both territories declared their secession from Georgia, and negotiations on their future status have since continued under UN and other auspices. However, an enduring political settlement remains an elusive goal.

In October 1995 Georgia adopted its present Constitution, maintaining the autonomous status under Georgian sovereignty of Abkhazia, South Ossetia and Adzharia (although this provision has been rejected by Abkhazia). Presidential and legislative elections in November 1995 resulted in victory for Shevardnadze and for his new **Citizens' Union of Georgia** (SMK), Shevardnadze being re-elected with around 75% of the votes cast. In the legislative elections, 107 of the 231 seats filled were won by the SMK. In February 1998 there was another in a series of unsuccessful assassination attempts against Shevardnadze, while in May 1999 the authorities foiled a coup plot against the President.

Latest elections: Parliamentary elections in October–November 1999 confirmed the dominance of the SMK, which won an overall majority of 130 of the 227 seats filled with 41.7% of the popular vote. The opposition **All-Georgian Union for Revival** took 64 seats (and 25.2% of the vote), **Industry Will Save Georgia** 15 (7.1%) and independents and others 18 seats. In presidential elections in April 2000 Shevardnadze was re-elected with 78.8% of the vote.

Recent developments: Following his re-election in April 2000, Shevardnadze appointed a new SMK Government headed by Giorgi Arsenishvili, charged in particular with overcoming the country's chronic economic problems and combating corruption. A series of variously-motivated defections from the SMK parliamentary group later in 2000 posed no real threat to the President's position, although the Government became less certain of being able to command a parliamentary majority. The fragile internal security situation was highlighted by the mass escape from a Tbilisi prison in October 2000 of Gamsakhurdia supporters awaiting trial on conspiracy charges.

In May 2001 Shevardnadze floated the idea of reforming the government system with the introduction of a full Cabinet under a Prime Minister as Head of Government. However, his proposals were quickly overshadowed by renewed tensions with Abkhazia (prompted by the attack, apparently by **Chechen** and Georgian irregulars, on a UN helicopter over the **Kodori Gorge**), and by potentially more threatening domestic disturbances. Mass demonstrations in Tbilisi calling for Shevardnadze's resignation in October followed a heavy-handed police raid on the tax-evading television station Rustavi-2. In response to the public outcry Shevardnadze dismissed the entire Council of Ministers on 1 November. Opposition to the President was set to grow further when opposition-backed candidate Nino Burdzhanadze was elected President of Parliament—the first woman to ever hold the post—nine days later. By the end of 2001 tensions had calmed somewhat on both fronts and a new Council had been appointed (in late December), headed by Avtandil **Djorbenadze**.

International relations and defence: Georgia was admitted as an independent state to the United Nations and to the **Organization for Security and Co-operation in Europe** in 1992 and was a founder member of the **Organization of the Black Sea Economic Co-operation**. Full membership of both the **North Atlantic Treaty Organization** (NATO) and the **European Union** (EU) being central foreign policy goals, Georgia became a member of NATO's **Partnership for Peace** programme (launched in 1994) and in 1996 signed a partnership and co-operation agreement with the European Union (EU). Georgia was admitted to the **Council of Europe** in February 1999 and to the **World Trade Organization** in June 2000.

The **Russian Federation** has retained a significant influence over Georgia's affairs since the latter's reluctant agreement to join the CIS. With the Russian Federation providing military assistance, the two countries signed a 10-year treaty of friendship and co-operation in 1994, under which the Russian Federation secured the right to maintain military bases in Georgia. Relations continued to be strained by the unresolved problem of Abkhazia and Georgian suspicions about Russian regional ambitions, especially when negotiations on the withdrawal of Russian troops from Georgia became bogged down in 2000. Troops finally began to leave their bases in the course of 2001, pulling out of the Guduata base in Abkhazia in October (four months over schedule and amidst increasing regional tensions—see above).

To counter Russian regional influence, Georgia was a founder member in 1998 of what became the **GUUAM group** (with **Ukraine**, **Uzbekistan**, **Azerbaijan** and **Moldova**) within the CIS. In May 1999 Georgia effectively withdrew from the CIS Collective Security Treaty, having entered into military co-operation with the USA with the aim of preparing for eventual membership of NATO. It has also established military co-operation arrangements with neighbouring Turkey, a NATO member.

Georgia's defence budget for 2000 amounted to some US $22m., equivalent to about 1% of GDP. The size of the armed forces at the end of 2000 was some 27,000 personnel, including those serving under compulsory conscription of two years, while reservists numbered an estimated 250,000.

Georgia, economy

In transition from state control to a free-market system but severely affected by political disorder since independence in 1991.

GNP: US $3,176m. (2000); *GNP per capita*: $590 (2000); *GDP at PPP*: $11,700m. (1999); *GDP per capita at PPP*: $2,300 (1999); *exports*: $330m. (2000); *imports*: $704m. (2000); *currency*: lari (plural: lari; US $1=L2.06 at the end of December 2001).

In 1999 industry accounted for 23% of GDP, agriculture for 32% and services for 45%. Only some 9% of land is arable, 4% under permanent crops, 25% permanent pasture and 34% forests and woodland. The main crops are citrus and other fruit, grapes, tea and vegetables, and there is a small animal husbandry sector. The principal mineral resources are deposits of manganese ore (although these are becoming increasingly depleted) and of iron ore, together with small quantities of coal and hydrocarbons. The main industries are machine building, construction of transport and other mechanical equipment, textiles and the production of wine. Georgia's former dependence on tourism on its Black Sea coast has been almost wholly undermined by the loss of central government control in **Abkhazia** and by internal disorder and armed conflict. Georgia's only substantial existing energy source is hydroelectricity; much of the energy requirement is met through imports,

Georgia, economy

but financial constraints have reduced oil imports from the **Russian Federation** and halted imports of natural gas from Turkmenistan, while the continuation of Russian gas supplies has continually been subject to both financial and political factors.

Georgia's main exports in 1999 by value were ferrous and non-ferrous metals (36%), citrus fruit, tea, wine and other agricultural products and foodstuffs (25%) and mineral products (14%). Principal imports were fuel products (52%) and foodstuffs and vegetable products (26%). The main purchasers of Georgian exports in 2000 were Turkey (22%), the Russian Federation (21%), and Germany (9%); the principal sources of Georgia's imports were Turkey (15%), Russian Federation (13%) and the USA (10%).

For the first four years after Georgia achieved independence in 1991, the country was riven by armed disturbance, especially in Abkhazia and South Ossetia (*see* **Ossetia question**). When the main conflicts ended the devastated economy had to cope with the repercussions. Moreover, the close economic links which had existed between Georgia and the other Republics of the **Soviet Union** were disrupted after 1991. The resultant deterioration of the Georgian economy was characterized by massive inflation (of some 8,000% in 1993 and 1994), a 70% contraction of GDP in 1990–95 arising from huge falls in agricultural and industrial production, and difficulties in the purchase of oil and natural gas from the Russian Federation and Turkmenistan. A flourishing black market, estimated to account for about 50% of economic activity by the late 1990s, distorted the real economic position.

From 1995, however, the Government embarked on a major structural adjustment programme with support from the **International Monetary Fund** (IMF) and **World Bank**, introducing a new currency, the lari, in September 1995 and instituting fiscal and other reforms. As a result, real GDP growth resumed and averaged about 10–11% in 1996–97, while annual inflation fell to around 7% in 1997 and the fiscal deficit was brought down from 20% of GDP in 1994 to 4.6% in 1997. The Russian financial crisis (*see* **Russian Federation, economy**) in mid-1998 then adversely affected Georgia, where the external value of the lari depreciated sharply, GDP growth fell back to some 2% in 1998 and the budget deficit came in at 5% of GDP. Modest recovery began in 1999, with annual growth of around 3% in 1999 and 2000 projected to continue in 2001 and to rise to 4.5% from 2002. The state budget for 2001 provided for expenditure of L1,120m. and revenues of L839.7m., the anticipated deficit representing some 4% of GDP.

Confidence in the economy's future was boosted by the opening in April 1999 of the Georgian section of the pipeline from **Baku** in **Azerbaijan** to Supsa on the Georgian Black Sea for the transport of oil from the Azerbaijani Caspian fields; this represented a partial realization of the **EU**-funded Transport Corridor Europe-Caucasus-Asia (**TRACECA**), or the 'Great Silk Road project', initiated in 1993. In the longer term, Georgia expected to benefit substantially from the planned main export pipeline (MEP) for Caspian oil from Baku via Georgia to the Turkish

Mediterranean port of Ceyhan, although at the end of 2001 many issues remained to be resolved on this project.

The privatization of state-owned enterprises, which was barely on the agenda in the first few years of independence, accelerated from 1995. By 1999 most small and medium-sized enterprises had passed to the private sector, and the Government appointed in April 2000 declared its commitment to the privatization of key infrastructure industries, including telecommunications, the power sector and the ports.

Georgian Import Export
(Geoimpex)

Trade association in **Georgia**.
General Director: T. A. Gogoberidze.
Address: Giorgiashvili 12, 380008 Tbilisi.
Telephone: (32) 997090.
Fax: (32) 982541.

Georgian Orthodox Church

An autocephalous branch of the **Orthodox Christian** Church based in **Georgia**. By tradition Georgia was placed under the spiritual guidance of Mary, the mother of Jesus Christ, and Christianity was first brought to the region on her behalf by the Apostle St Andrew in the 1st century. Christian missionaries succeeded in converting the Georgian Princes in 326. From then the religion became closely tied to the concept of an independent Georgian state, bounded as it was by **Muslim** countries to the south and the **Slavs** to the north. After the absorption of Georgia into the **Russian** Empire, the autocephalous Georgian Church was abolished in 1811 and subjugated to the **Russian Orthodox Church**. Its independence was reinstated in 1917 but the Church suffered at the hands of the **Soviet** authorities along with fellow Orthodox Christians in Russia. The autocephalous Georgian Church was recognized by the ecumenical Constantinople Patriarch in 1989. Cathilicos-Patriarch Illya II was elected in 1977.

Georgian paramilitaries *see* **Mkhedrioni**.

Georgian Stock Exchange

The first self-regulated exchange in **Georgia**. Established in January 1999, the GSE was licensed as a stock exchange in January 2000. It was founded by

brokerage companies, banks and insurance firms. As at 1 December 2001 there were 40 brokerage companies operating on the exchange.
Chair.: George Loladze.
Address: 74a Chavchavadze Ave, Tbilisi 380062.
Telephone: (32) 227319.
Fax: (32) 251876.
E-mail: info@gse.ge
Internet: www.gse.ge

Georgian Trade Union Amalgamation
Sakartvelos Profesiuli Kavshirebis Gaertianaba (GTUA)

The principal trade union centre in **Georgia**. The GTUA was created in December 1992 as the successor to the Confederation of Trade Unions of Georgia, which had replaced the Soviet-era trade union federation in 1990 but had been abolished by President Gamsakhurdia in August 1991 because it had supported the democratic opposition.

A decree issued by President **Shevardnadze** in January 1999 enjoining state agencies to consult with trade unions had little effect. In 1999–2000 the GTUA backed public sector strikes called in protest against non-payment of wages, but its influence remained minimal and its affiliated membership is believed to be considerably lower than the claimed 850,000 in 31 branches and two territorial committees (as at January 2001). The GTUA was admitted to the International Confederation of Free Trade Unions (ICFTU) in November 2000.
Chair.: Irakli Tugushi.
Address: 7 Shartava St, Tbilisi 380122.
Telephone: (32) 382995.
Fax: (32) 224663.

Georgians

A Caucasian people dominant in **Georgia**. Georgians are considered autochthonous to the **Caucasus** region and constitute a diverse people renowned for their nationalist pride. The Kartli dialect, spoken around the capital **Tblisi**, is the basis of the literary language, which uses its own unique script. Other distinct dialects exist among the related Mingrelians and Svans (who both live in the region bordering **Abkhazia**), and the Laz who live in Turkey. Almost all Georgians practise **Orthodox Christianity**, and the autocephalous **Georgian Orthodox Church** promotes itself as the final frontier of European Christianity. There are some 80,000 **Muslim** Georgians resident in Turkey.

Georgievski, Ljubčo

Prime Minister of **Macedonia**.

Ljubiša 'Ljubčo' Georgievski heads the right-of-centre **Internal Macedonian Revolutionary Organization–Democratic Party for Macedonian National Unity** (VMRO–DPMNE). A prominent figure in the Macedonian independence movement from 1990, he was appointed Vice-President of the newly independent state in 1991. He was elected Prime Minister in November 1998.

Born in the central town of Štip in 1966, he graduated with a degree in literature from Skopje University and has produced two volumes of poetry and a collection of short stories since 1988. He was prominent in the Macedonian independence movement from 1990 and was appointed as the country's first Vice-President in 1991. However, after only eight months in the post, he resigned and took the VMRO–DPMNE out of government with him. In 1993 he was nominated to be the Chair of the VMRO–DPMNE and led the party in opposition until electoral success won him the premiership in 1998. His tenure has been greatly troubled—from **NATO**'s bombing campaign in neighbouring **Yugoslavia**, to a violent insurgency by ethnic **Albanians**.

Address: Office of the Prime Minister, Ilindenska b.b., 91000 Skopje.
Telephone: (2) 115389.
Fax: (2) 112561.
Internet: www.gov.mk

Germans

An ethnic group concentrated in **central Europe** but spread in small communities throughout **eastern Europe**, and sharing a common language (although regional variations can be extreme). Thought to have originated on the shores of the Baltic Sea, the Germans spread south to occupy much of the north European plain. Several mini-states flourished in this region in the mediaeval period, rather than one contiguous German state, with **Prussia** and Austria the most powerful of many German entities. A unified Germany, stretching as far south as Bavaria, did not emerge until the mid-19th century (with Austria even then remaining separate, bound up as it was with the Habsburg Empire).

Meanwhile, steady eastward migration created German communities whose presence in the central European states of the 20th century was to prove a source of conflict. Many Germans were despatched specifically as frontier settlers, notably the Saxons in Northern **Transylvania**. Penetration of the east by German settlers extended as far as the River Volga where they settled under the invitation of Catherine the Great from 1763. In the Soviet era a German autonomous republic (ASSR) was even created within the **Soviet Union**, although it was disbanded during the Second World War and the so-called 'Volga' Germans deported *en masse* to internment camps in **Siberia**. The survivors were later allowed to return to the

Volga region where they consider themselves to be among **Russia**'s repressed peoples.

The irredentist ambitions of Hitler and the Nazi regime were briefly realized in the creation of the so-called Third Reich in the 1930s. Defeat in the Second World War, however, was followed by the forcible movement of thousands of Germans across eastern Europe to the new reduced German state, devastating areas of previous German settlement. A similar, this time voluntary, movement occurred in the 1990s following the collapse of communism in the east. Thousands of ethnic Germans migrated to Germany away from the economic uncertainty of the emerging post-Soviet states.

Officially, the largest ethnic German population in eastern Europe is the 842,000-strong Volga community. Between 750,000 and one million Germans live in modern **Poland** where they are largely considered autochthonous, and where the pursuit of their ethnic identity has only recently been encouraged. The size of this population was greatly affected by the forced post-war migrations (*see* **Yalta Agreements** and **Potsdam Agreements**). The same is true of the once large German population in the **Czech Republic** which was expelled after 1945 (*see* **Sudetenland**). An original community of 750,000 Germans in Transylvania has been cut down to just 119,000 through voluntary and forced migration. Some 75,000 were deported to the Soviet Union after 1945. Representation in **Romania** is plagued by a lack of resources. Around 30,000 Germans are scattered throughout **Hungary,** where there is some German-language schooling, but where assimilation has reduced German to a 'grandmother language'. In an attempt to accommodate the many Germans stranded throughout the former Soviet Union, Germany and **Ukraine** agreed in 1992 to assist 400,000 to settle in the south of Ukraine, although many chose to emigrate to Germany instead.

GGB *see* **Georgi Ganchev Bloc**.

Glasnost

The slogan, meaning 'openness' in Russian, adopted by Soviet leader Mikhail **Gorbachev** in 1985 to cover a package of political reforms improving freedom of speech and information. After the **Chernobyl** disaster of April 1986, which was poorly reported, glasnost became more radical, featuring a critical reappraisal of the past, including revelations of repression under Stalin, the toleration of press criticism, the publication of works of literature long banned as subversive, and the release of dissidents. Glasnost was accompanied by the policy of *perestroika*.

Gligorov, Kiro

The pre-eminent political figure in **Macedonia**'s transition to independence, and the country's President until 1999. Gligorov was born in May 1917 in Štip, Macedonia, in a family with a history of activity in the nationalist movement against Ottoman rule. A student of law and later of economics, which he taught at Belgrade University in the late 1940s, he was – like most **Yugoslav** political figures of the latter part of the 20th century – an active member of Tito's Partisan resistance against German wartime occupation.

Making a career in federal government service, he rose to be Minister of Finance (1962–67), a Vice-President of the Federal Executive Council (federal government), and President of the Federal Assembly for four years in the 1970s. His main distinction was in leading the team which initiated the **Socialist Federal Republic of Yugoslavia**'s unique experiment in market-based economic reforms. The suspension of the reform programme in the 1970s led to a hiatus in Gligorov's political career until the late 1980s, when he was brought back to join a government team responsible for tackling Yugoslavia's financial crisis. Gligorov became increasingly involved from 1989 onwards with developments in Macedonia, where a three-way split between nationalists, reform communists and **Albanian** groups led a newly-elected **Assembly of the Republic** to turn to him as a compromise presidential candidate after its declaration of Macedonian sovereignty on 25 January 1991. Nominated by the ex-communist Social Democratic Union of Macedonia (SDSM) and elected to office on 27 January 1991, he successfully negotiated the removal of the Yugoslav National Army from Macedonian territory in 1992, and prevented the outbreak of open conflict between rival nationalist and ethnic Albanian groups. Gligorov was re-elected President in October 1994 for a five-year term, this time as candidate of a broad Union of Macedonia (SM) alliance, winning over 78% of the vote in a poll marred by allegations of vote rigging. He survived an assassination attempt on 3 October 1995, in which two people died and six others were injured, but became less actively involved in political life, retiring ahead of the December 1999 presidential elections in which the voters swung away from the broad left-of-centre alliance he had helped to build.

Göncz, Árpád

Post-communist President of **Hungary**, 1990–2000. Born on 10 February 1922 in **Budapest**, he completed a degree in law in 1944 and worked briefly with the National Land Credit Institute while becoming involved in resistance to German occupation. After the end of the war he was Private Secretary to a leader of the **Independent Smallholders' Party** and edited a periodical, but the party was broken up in 1948 as the communists moved to establish single-party rule. Göncz worked as a welder and pipe fitter, then turned to soil conservation, returning to university in 1952 to study agricultural sciences. His involvement in the 1956

Hungarian uprising, resisting the arrival of Soviet troops, led to his arrest and a sentence of life imprisonment, but he was released under a 1963 amnesty. Having learnt English in prison, he then made his name as a literary translator and writer, becoming President of the Writer's Union in 1988–89 and of the Hungarian Writer's Association in 1989–90. As Hungary's political system began to open up to the possibility of pluralism, Göncz and other intellectuals became involved in the liberal **Alliance of Free Democrats** (SzDSz), which was founded in November 1988. He was elected in April 1990 as an SzDSz member in the first post-communist legislature, and was chosen at the inaugural session on 2 May as Speaker, thereby becoming interim President pending a decision on the method of election of the Head of State. He was formally elected President by the legislature, unopposed, on 3 August 1990, and re-elected (overwhelmingly defeating one other candidate) on 19 June 1995, holding office until June 2000. As President he was formally independent of any political party, but during his first term he clashed with the centre-right coalition Government led by the **Hungarian Democratic Forum** (MDF), notably over the MDF's attempt to appoint new Directors of the state broadcast media. His nomination in 1995 was put forward by the then governing coalition of the **Hungarian Socialist Party** (MSzP) and SzDSz.

Goražde

A town on the River Drina in eastern **Bosnia and Herzegovina**, deep into Bosnian Serb territory (*see* **Serb Republic**). The town and surrounding region was traditionally home to a **Bosniak** majority and a large **Serb** minority. It was declared a UN 'safe haven' in May 1993 during the Bosnian Civil War. Unlike other safe havens, such as **Srebrenica** and Žepa, Goražde did not permanently fall to Bosnian Serb forces and was spared the atrocities of '**ethnic cleansing**'. The surrounding hills were the target of the first **NATO** air-strikes against Bosnian Serb forces in April 1994, signalling the beginning of direct international military involvement in the war.

Gorbachev, Mikhail

Last President of the **Soviet Union**, from 1988, and reformist leader of the ruling **Communist Party of the Soviet Union** (KPSS) from 1985. Gorbachev is credited internationally with engineering his country's peaceful retreat from the **Cold War**, and accepting the end of the 'iron curtain' division of Europe. Most Russians resented, however, the economic dislocation and instability they suffered through the demise of Soviet communism itself—the outcome which Gorbachev had unsuccessfully sought to avert by reforming the system.

Mikhail Sergeyevich Gorbachev was born on 2 March 1931 in the Stavropol region of the north **Caucasus**. He was working as a tractor driver at the age of 14,

Gorbachev, Mikhail

but subsequently gained a place to study law at Moscow University, where he was active in the Komsomol youth movement and joined the KPSS in 1952. He also met Raisa Maksimovna Titarenko, a philosophy student, whom he married in 1953; they have one daughter, Irina.

Upon graduation he returned to Stavropol in 1955, working as a Komsomol official, then for the KPSS. He became party's First Secretary for Stavropol in 1966 and First Secretary of the Regional Party Committee in 1970. He also studied by correspondence for an agriculture degree which he completed in 1967.

A member of the KPSS Central Committee from 1971, Gorbachev moved to Moscow in November 1978 to work as its Secretary for Agriculture. He became a candidate member of the Politburo a year later and a full member from October 1980. His chief mentor Yurii Andropov, who also came from the north Caucasus, became KPSS General Secretary after Leonid Brezhnev's death in 1982. Andropov was succeeded in turn by the elderly Konstantin Chernenko as stopgap leader, but Chernenko's death in March 1985 opened the way for Gorbachev to become General Secretary. The position of Chairman of the Supreme Soviet (Head of State) was given to veteran Foreign Minister Andrei Gromyko, but Gorbachev succeeded to this office too in October 1988.

Once in power, Gorbachev initiated the twin processes of **perestroika** (restructuring) and **glasnost** (openness). The plans to transform the Soviet system into a 'socialist pluralist democracy' resulted in 1989 in competitive elections to a new Congress of People's Deputies. In early 1990 Gorbachev even accepted the recognition of other parties, removing the Constitution's reference to the 'leading role' of the KPSS.

Abroad, he sought relations with the West which would spare the failing economy from the demands of the arms race. A sequence of US-Soviet summits, and the signature in 1987 of the Intermediate Nuclear Forces (INF) treaty, opened the way to strategic arms reductions talks (**START**). The disarmament process ran in parallel with major changes on the diplomatic front, the withdrawal of Soviet troops from Afghanistan, and disengagement from **eastern Europe**, as Gorbachev made it known among the leaders of the **Warsaw Pact** member countries in 1989 that there would be no armed intervention to prevent internal change.

1989–90 marked the high water mark of Gorbachev's global popularity. Acclaimed for his statesmanship and honoured by the Nobel Peace Prize judges in 1990, he faced sustained criticism, however, at home. The conservatives saw compromise as fatally weakening the Soviet system, while radicals pressed impatiently for faster change. The Soviet Union itself, in chronic economic crisis, was torn by nationalist and secessionist demands. Gorbachev, having taken on the title of State President in March 1990 as part of a restructuring of Soviet leadership posts, began in April 1991 the so-called 'nine-plus-one' talks with other Soviet Republics on a new Union treaty. He was continually outflanked, however, by demands from the Russian republican leadership and others for more radical reform—and unable to claim the democratic mandate which the popular Russian leader Boris **Yeltsin** was able to evoke as Republican President after direct elections in June 1991.

The pace of change, and especially the new draft Union treaty which envisaged a reduction in central powers, provoked leading army generals and their conservative allies to attempt to halt the process by force. Gorbachev, unable to harness to his own reformist objectives the more radical demands which had been unleashed within the Soviet Union, now suffered a double ignominy. His powerlessness was exposed, as the conservatives briefly took over in the **August coup** in Moscow in 1991. Gorbachev, absent from Moscow on an ill-timed holiday, dissociated himself from the coup, but his role was the subject of much speculation, and his position was fatally weakened. Yeltsin, his 'rescuer' in the August coup, called the tune thereafter. Gorbachev, having resigned as General Secretary of the KPSS on 24 August 1991, stepped down as President of the Soviet Union on 25 December 1991, handing over to Yeltsin the command of the armed forces and control of nuclear weapons. By the end of the year the Soviet Union was no more, its successor states more or less loosely associated through a new **Commonwealth of Independent States**.

Gorbachev largely disappeared from domestic view after stepping down. When he stood in the **Russian Federation**'s June 1996 presidential election he came seventh, with a derisory 386,000 votes or 0.51% of the poll. He does still make occasional appearances in the Western media, giving his perspective on events such as the accession of three former Warsaw Pact member countries to membership of the **NATO** alliance in March 1999. Author of numerous publications, he is also propounding a global environmental charter drawn up by Green Cross International, an organization which he founded in 1993. He heads a Moscow-based International Foundation for Socio-Economic and Political Studies (the 'Gorbachev Fund'), in which he invested some of his own money.

Grabovac, Nikola

Deputy Prime Minister and Minister of Finance, **Muslim-Croat Federation**.

Nikola Grabovac is a member of the moderate **New Croatian Initiative** (NHI). He was first appointed to public office in June 1994 when he was made Minister for Trade in the joint Cabinet of **Bosnia and Herzegovina** and the fledgling Muslim-Croat Federation. He was appointed Deputy Prime Minister and Minister of Finance on 12 March 2001.

Born on 11 May 1943 in Bugojno in central Bosnia, then a part of the Nazi-era **Croatia**, he earned a degree in economics from the University of Zagreb, continuing his studies at the University of Sarajevo in Bosnia and Herzegovina. He eventually received a professorship in the subject. He also worked as Director of a textile factory before joining the civil service as Manager for Commercial Issues, and later, Director of External Trade. As the Bosnian civil conflict came towards a close he joined the newly-established joint Cabinet of the Muslim-Croat

Federation and an independent Bosnia and Herzegovina as Minister for Trade in June 1994. He held this position until the Cabinets were separated in January 1996. From then until his reappointment to the Muslim-Croat Federation's Cabinet in 2001, he worked behind the scenes for the Bosnian Council of Ministers.
Address: Ministry of Finance, Mehmeda Spahe 5, 71000 Sarajevo.
Telephone and Fax: (33) 663314.
E-mail: ngrabovac@fbihvlada.gov.ba

Greater Albania

Term designating the present-day territory of **Albania** and adjoining areas with an ethnic **Albanian** majority population. The independent state of Albania, declared in November 1912 during the First Balkan War, encompassed the whole of the area with an ethnic Albanian majority. However, under the 1913 Treaty of Bucharest and a final demarcation agreement signed in 1926, independent Albania was recognized within borders which excluded Albanian-majority **Kosovo** as well as smaller areas of **Macedonia** and **Montenegro** with a dominant Albanian population and southern **Epirus**. Albania's aspiration to acquire these areas was a constant theme of inter-war regional politics and impelled some Albanian nationalists to see fascist Italy as the potential deliverer of a Greater Albania, on the basis of Mussolini's recognition of the 'Illyrian' Albanians as an ancient Mediterranean people.

The Italian occupation of Albania in April 1939 was followed in the autumn by a joint Italian-Albanian assault on Greece, whose forces quickly repelled the attackers and themselves invaded and occupied southern Albania. The German defeat of Greece and **Yugoslavia** in 1941 enabled a Greater Albania to be created under Italian protection, including Kosovo and other parts of Yugoslavia as well as the whole of Epirus. However, Italy's exit from the war in 1943 was followed by the gradual establishment of communist control, the communist Government being recognized by the Allies in October 1945 on the understanding that Greater Albania aims had been abandoned. At the 1946 Paris Peace Conference Albania's independence was reaffirmed within its 1926 borders.

The post-war communist regime disavowed any territorial ambitions, a line followed by Governments of the post-communist era. In 1991 Albania joined the **Organization for Security and Co-operation in Europe**, acceding to its requirement that existing borders should be regarded as inviolable. Nevertheless, the break-up of the old **Socialist Federal Republic of Yugoslavia**, and in particular the Kosovo crisis of the late 1990s, appeared to some Albanians to reopen the possibility of territorial change, while fuelling fears of Albanian ambitions among **Serbs**.

Greater Croatia

A concept involving the territorial expansion of **Croatia** into neighbouring, and largely ethnic **Croat**, regions, which is popular among nationalists. The modern State of Croatia was formed from the former **Yugoslav** Republic of the same name and covers an area which has been considered 'Croatian' for centuries. However, millions of ethnic Croats are to be found in adjoining regions of **Bosnia and Herzegovina**, particularly in the south-eastern region of **Herzegovina** itself. During the Second World War Croat irredentist ambitions were realized briefly with the creation of the enlarged Croatian puppet State by the invading Nazis, which swallowed modern-day Bosnia and Herzegovina and regions of western **Serbia**. The short-lived State's fascist Government persecuted ethnic **Serbs** and **Muslims** (**Bosniaks**) and so the concept of a Greater Croatia became entwined, in Serbian eyes in particular, with the concept of racial discrimination.

The possibility of a Greater Croatia was raised again at the time of the violent disintegration of the **Socialist Federal Republic of Yugoslavia** in the early 1990s, as nationalist Croat factions in Croatia and Bosnia called for the unification of all ethnic Croats in the region. The division of Bosnia and Herzegovina between Croatia and Serbia (*see* **Greater Serbia**) was even mooted as a viable option to end the Bosnian civil war. A particularly strong proponent of the Greater Croatia idea was former Croatian President Franjo **Tudjman**, who championed the so-called 'Greater Greater Croatia' which involved annexing not only Herzegovina but also the entire western half of Bosnia, including the modern Bosnian Serb capital **Banja Luka**, in an uneasy reminder of the earlier Nazi State. The creation of an intact Bosnia and Herzegovina under the 1995 **Dayton Agreement**, and the death of Tudjman, have since lessened the influence of the 'Greater Greater Croatia' faction. However, nationalist parties continue to pursue the idea of uniting Croatia with Herzegovina (in a so-called 'Lesser Greater Croatia'), and have lent support to Croat nationalists in Bosnia and Herzegovina (*see* **Herceg-Bosna**).

Greater Hungary

A nationalist concept of an enlarged **Hungarian** State based on that country's historical domination of the surrounding area. **Hungary** was a major regional power from early mediaeval times until the disintegration of the Habsburg Empire in 1918. From a very early period, and at various stages from then on, it covered the entire Pannonian Plain, which is still dominated by the modern State, and adjoining territories in modern southern **Slovakia**, **Transylvania**, **Vojvodina** and **Croatia**. The restructuring of this inland Empire was completed at the conclusion of the First World War under the points of the 1920 Treaty of **Trianon** which left Hungary's borders much as they are today. Consequently the idea of a Greater Hungary has been created to match nationalist and romantic resentment at the country's reduction at the hands of the Allied powers. The concept is not seriously championed by mainstream parties, although relations with the Hungarian minorities in the historic Hungarian lands are a major concern for the Government and a source of regional tension.

Greater Romania

A nationalist concept of an enlarged **Romania** covering regions inhabited by ethnic **Romanians** (and **Moldovans**) and lands historically connected to the Romanian State. Ethnically isolated among **Slavic** neighbours, Romanian nationalists held tight to the idea of uniting all Romanian peoples in a single state. This goal was practically achieved following the First World War when Romania was rewarded with the annexation of **Transylvania**, **Bukovina**, southern **Dobruja** and all of historic Moldavia (*see* **Bessarabia question**). However, this Greater Romania was short-lived and was greatly reduced after the Second World War, losing Dobruja, northern Bukovina, and most importantly eastern Moldavia.

The possibility of the unification of Moldova and Romania was immediately raised following the collapse of the **Soviet Union**, of which Moldova had been a part, in 1991. However, it was soon rejected in the following years and is now only championed by nationalist Romanian parties and some fringe Moldovan parties.

Greater Romania Party
Partidul România Mare (PRM)

An influential far-right nationalist party in **Romania** whose leader obtained a third of the popular vote in the 2000 presidential election. The PRM was founded in 1991 as the political wing of the **Greater Romania** movement, which advocates strong government in pursuit of Romanian national interests and the recovery of **Romanian**-populated territories lost during the Second World War. The party won 16 Chamber of Deputies seats and six Senate seats in the 1992 **Parliament** elections, on a vote share of 3.9%, and became one of the parties giving external support to the Government of the (ex-communist) Social Democracy Party of Romania (PDSR). In 1995 party leader Corneliu Vadim Tudor repeatedly urged the Government to institute a clamp-down on the **Hungarian Democratic Union of Romania** (UDMR), which he accused of planning the break-up of Romania. This and other differences resulted in the PRM withdrawing its support from the Government in October 1995.

In April 1996 a party congress approved a programme which promised that a PRM Government would ban the UDMR and place restrictions on foreign investment in Romania. In the November 1996 elections Tudor came fifth in the presidential contest with 4.7% of the vote and the party won 19 Chamber seats with 4.5%. In late 1998 the PRM was strengthened by the adhesion to it of Gheorghe Funar, former leader of the Romanian National Unity Party (PUNR). In the

November–December 2000 elections the PRM benefited from the deep unpopularity of the centre-right Government, sufficient for Tudor to come second in the first round of the presidential contest with 28.3% of the vote and therefore to go forward to the second round, in which he obtained 33.2% against 66.8% for Ion **Iliescu** of the **Social Democratic Pole of Romania** (PDSR-led coalition). In the parliamentary contest the PRM became the second-largest party with 84 of the 346 Chamber seats on a vote share of 19.5%. It thereafter mounted strenuous opposition to a bill granting certain language rights to ethnic **Hungarians** and other minorities.

Leadership: Corneliu Vadim Tudor (Chair.).
Address: Str. G. Clemenceau 8–10, Bucharest 70101.
Telephone: (1) 6130967.
Fax: (1) 3126182.
E-mail: prm@romare.ro
Internet: www.romare.ro

Greater Russia

A nationalist concept of a dominant **Russian** State which would export Russian language and culture to regions within and near to the modern **Russian Federation**. Unlike other 'Greater' nationalist ideas, Greater Russia has less to do with territorial expansion (Russia is after all the largest country in the world), and more to do with straightforward cultural imperialism. The notion relies on the supposed superiority of Russian culture, including adherence to the doctrine of the **Russian Orthodox Church**. Its champions look to the further centralization of the Russian Federation, the impending Union with **Belarus** (*see* **Belarus-Russia Union**) and possible future unions with the fellow east **Slavic** State of **Ukraine** and even **Moldova**. On a broader, but less popular, scale the concept of Greater Russia has links with notions of **pan-Slavism**, Russia being the largest and most powerful Slavic state in the world. The imposition of centralized control from **Moscow** and the fearsome response to separatist claimants among the constituent republics could be seen as directed towards the maintenance of such a Greater Russia as already exists, but beyond this the aspiration for a Greater Russia does not have serious political proponents.

Greater Serbia

A nationalist concept of an enlarged **Serbia** covering regions inhabited by ethnic **Serbs** and lands historically connected to the Serbian state. Greater Serbia is perhaps the strongest of such irredentist ideas in **eastern Europe** and is still openly discussed in **Belgrade**. Serbia reached its territorial zenith under the stewardship of the Emperor Stephen Dushan in the mid-14th century, and stretched to incorporate **Herzegovina** (modern-day south-east **Bosnia and Herzegovina**), **Montenegro**, **Macedonia**, **Albania** and much of northern Greece. This short-lived Empire has gone on to form the basis of the concept of a Greater Serbia, although it did not include the **Vojvodina**, the Bosnian **Serb Republic** or even the modern Serb capital Belgrade. Conquered by the Ottoman Turks, the Serbian State was buried for over 500 years until it regained autonomy in the late 19th century. By this time ethnic Serbs had been spread by their **Muslim** rulers across lands to the north and west, and many had fled into neighbouring, Christian, states (*see* **Krajina** *and* Vojvodina), laying the basis for a more northerly Greater Serbian idea. In Bosnia in particular a large Serb community was now established.

Under the **Socialist Federal Republic of Yugoslavia** Serbia came to dominate the eastern half of the country and, with its capital serving as the Federal centre as well, it also dominated the bureaucracy of the Yugoslav State. Towards the end of the 1980s, as the Federation began to splinter, Serbian nationalist movements began to equate Yugoslavism with the idea of a Greater Serbia, and the territorial integrity of the Serbian lands led to the quashing of regional autonomy in the Vojvodina and **Kosovo**. In the later war in neighbouring Bosnia and Herzegovina, Bosnian Serb nationalists looked to the Yugoslav state as their protector and openly called for a Greater Serbia. The division of Bosnia and Herzegovina between Serbia and **Croatia** (*see* **Greater Croatia**) was even mooted as a possible solution to the war there. However, as the violent excesses of the Bosnian Serb campaign became clear, and as the Yugoslav authorities began considering a post-war reality, the idea of a Greater Serbia was dropped from the political mainstream.

Green Party of Ukraine
Partiya Zelenykh Ukrainy (PZU)

One of the more electorally successful environmentalist parties in **eastern Europe**. Founded in 1990 by groups which had emerged in the wake of the 1986 **Chernobyl** nuclear accident, the PZU argued for radical action on the huge environmental problems faced by independent **Ukraine** arising from Soviet-era industrialization. It had early links with the **Communist Party of Ukraine** (KPU) and backed the presidency of Leonid Kravchuk (1991–94), but usually opposed the successor administration of Leonid **Kuchma**. Having failed to achieve representation in 1994, the PZU won 19 seats in the 1998 **Parliament** elections on a vote share of 5.3%, becoming part of a highly fluid parliamentary majority defined by its opposition to the KPU-led left and broadly supportive of the Government, although without any enthusiasm for Kuchma. In the 1999 presidential elections, however, PZU leader Vitaliy Kononov obtained only 0.3% of the first-round vote, while by early 2001 the Green parliamentary group had declined to 17 members.

Leadership: Vitaliy Kononov (Leader).
Address: Shota Rustaveli 38, Kiev 01021.
Telephone: (44) 2205080.

Fax: (44) 2206694.
E-mail: office@greenparty.org.ua
Internet: www.greenparty.org.ua

Group of Eight (G8)

The grouping created by the decision in the 1990s that the Group of Seven (G7) principal industrialized countries, which had been meeting regularly at summit level since 1976, should also include the **Russian Federation** in their discussions on international affairs. The then Soviet President Mikhail **Gorbachev** attended a meeting in the margins of the London G7 Summit in 1991, and Russian President Boris **Yeltsin** was invited to annual G7 summits from 1992 onwards, initially to discuss the terms of financial assistance to the Russian Federation, and subsequently (beginning in 1994) also to participate in foreign policy discussions. The summit meeting in Denver in 1997 was called the 'Summit of the Eight', in recognition of fuller Russian involvement, while the 1998 Birmingham Summit was the first full G8 Summit.

Members: Canada, France, Germany, Italy, Japan, Russian Federation, UK, USA.

Gruevski, Nikola

Minister of Finance, **Macedonia**.

Nikola Gruevski is a member of the right-of-centre **Internal Macedonian Revolutionary Organization–Democratic Party for Macedonian National Unity** (VMRO–DPMNE). He joined the Government in November 1998 and was appointed Finance Minister on 27 December 1999.

Born on 31 August 1970 in **Skopje**, he graduated from the Economics Faculty in Prilep in 1994. He began his career at the Balkanska Banka in 1995 as Director for securities, planning and analysis, before being drafted into the Cabinet as Minister without Portfolio on 30 November 1998. He was switched to the Ministry of Trade in January 1999 before arriving in the Finance Ministry in December that year. He was among a number of senior officials who discovered in early 2001 that they had been the subject of wiretapping by the secret service.

Address: Ministry of Finance, Dame Gruev 14, 91000 Skopje.
Telephone: (2) 117288.
Fax: (2) 117280.
E-mail: finance@finance.gov.mk
Internet: www.finance.gov.mk

Grybauskaite, Dalia

Minister of Finance, **Lithuania**.

Dalia Grybauskaite is an independent. Although she was nominated to the Cabinet by the left-wing **Lithuanian Social Democratic Party** (LSDP), she is considered to be politically right of centre. She entered politics as a Programme Director in the Prime Minister's Office in 1991 and was appointed Finance Minister on 5 July 2001.

Born on 1 March 1956 in **Vilnius**, she graduated in economics from the Leningrad (now St Petersburg) University in 1983. She continued her academic career with a doctorate from the Moscow Academy of Public Sciences in 1988 and a specialized course at the School of Foreign Service at Georgetown University, USA, in 1991. She returned to Lithuania to work as a Programme Director in the Prime Minister's Office and later as Director of the European Department of the Ministry of International Economic Relations. From 1993 to 1994 she was Director of the Economic Relations Department in the Foreign Ministry, in which role she acted as chief negotiator for the free trade agreement with the **European Union** (EU). She expanded this role as Extraordinary Envoy and Plenipotentiary Minister at the Lithuanian Mission to the EU from 1994 to 1995 and travelled back to the USA in 1996 to act as Plenipotentiary Minister at the Lithuanian Embassy there. On returning to Lithuania in 1999 she was appointed Deputy Finance Minister and was chief negotiator in talks with the **International Monetary Fund** (IMF) and the **World Bank**. In a reshuffle in 2000 she switched to Deputy Foreign Minister. She was brought into the forefront of the Cabinet as Finance Minister by Prime Minister Algirdas **Brazauskas** in July 2001.

Address: Ministry of Finance, J. Tumo-Vaižganto 8A/2, Vilnius 2600.
Telephone: (23) 90005 [(523) 90005 from September 2002].
Fax: (27) 91481 [(527) 91481 from September 2002].
E-mail: finmin@finmin.lt
Internet: www.finmin.lt

GSS *see* **Civic Alliance of Serbia**.

GTUA *see* **Georgian Trade Union Amalgamation**.

GUUAM group

The GUUAM (**Georgia**, **Ukraine**, Uzbekistan, **Azerbaijan** and **Moldova**) group is designed to encourage broad political, economic and strategic co-operation so as to strengthen the independence and sovereignty of these former Soviet Republics. Its major focus has been the development of a Europe-Caucasus-Asia transport corridor (**TRACECA**).

GUUAM group

The GUUAM group took on its current form in April 1999, when Uzbekistan joined what had hitherto been a four-member group at a summit meeting held in Washington, D.C., on the margin of the **NATO** summit there. They decided the following year to convene regular summits at the level of Heads of State at least once a year, and meetings at the level of Ministers for Foreign Affairs at least twice a year. The original framework of co-operation between Azerbaijan, Georgia, Moldova and Ukraine first came into being in 1996 at the **Conventional Forces in Europe** (CFE) Treaty Conference in Vienna, followed up by a presidential-level meeting in Strasbourg in October 1997.

The dissemination of information about the activities of the GUUAM group is co-ordinated primarily by the Embassies of the member countries in Washington, D.C.

Internet: www.guuam.org

Gypsies *see* **Roma**.

H

Havel, Václav

The former dissident playwright who became leader of **Czechoslovakia**'s '**velvet revolution**' in 1989 and thereafter President first of Czechoslovakia, then (from 1993) of the **Czech Republic**.

Born on 5 October 1936 in **Prague**, he was initially denied a university place under the post-war communist regime because he had a bourgeois family background. A career in the theatre in the 1960s, and increasingly as a successful playwright with an international reputation, ensured him a high profile as an enthusiastic supporter of new ideas of liberal communism in the so-called '**Prague Spring**' of 1968. Havel chaired the Circle of Independent Writers, and was a fierce opponent of the invasion by **Warsaw Pact** forces that August. The subsequent period of repression saw his work banned in Czechoslovakia, although it circulated as *samizdat* (illegal 'self-published' manuscripts) and was published in the West. As spokesperson for a small group of dissident intellectuals, he was a founding signatory on 1 January 1977 of what became the rallying call of the human rights movement, **Charter 77**. He spent four years in prison from 1979 to 1983 on a charge of sedition, and in January 1989 was again arrested, with a group of human rights demonstrators, and sentenced to nine months' imprisonment for incitement and obstruction. This aroused a major international protest, which embarrassed the regime into releasing him in May.

The astonishingly rapid collapse of communist rule in late 1989 propelled Havel into a national leadership role. Heading the **Civic Forum** which he helped set up in November, he was at the forefront of the protest movement and the massive popular demonstrations which swept the old regime from power. On 29 December he was elected by the legislature as interim President, pending the holding of general elections the following June. The new Federal Assembly, meeting on 5 July 1990, then confirmed him in office for two years. During this period his relations with **Slovak** nationalist leader Vladimír **Mečiar** were often difficult, while it was common knowledge that he differed with the Finance Minister and later Czech Prime Minister Václav **Klaus** over the speed and uncompromising radicalism of the switchover to a free-market economy.

Havel stood down as Czechoslovakia's President in July 1992, after his federalist constitutional proposals were rejected, and it was becoming increasingly unlikely that any form of Czech and Slovak Federation would survive the pull of Slovak separatism. When the separation of the two States had been formalized, the Parliament of the Czech Republic elected him unopposed to the presidency on 26 January 1993. Although the presidency is required to be non-partisan, Havel's moral stature gave him considerable weight in Czech public life and in promoting the country's interests in integration within a democratic Europe. It nevertheless took two rounds of voting among members of Parliament for him to win re-election for a further five-year term of office in January 1998—mainly because supporters of Klaus resented Havel's role in relegating him to a period in opposition after his Government collapsed in late 1997. Havel took the opportunity of his inaugural speech to rededicate himself to the development of democracy and civic society and to combating the growth of nationalism and xenophobia. On several occasions since then he has decried prejudice and discrimination against the **Roma** minority, calling for greater tolerance and the renewal of the 'spirit of 1989'.

Havel's first wife Olga died in January 1996. A year later he married the acclaimed Czech actress Dagmar Veskrnova. His health has on several occasions caused serious alarm. A heavy smoker, he had surgery for lung cancer in December 1996, and he has undergone a succession of subsequent health crises and hospitalizations.

Address: Office of the President of the Republic, Prazsky Hrad, 11908 Prague 1.
Telephone: (2) 24371111.
Fax: (2) 24373300.
E-mail: president@hrad.cz
Internet: www.hrad.cz

HDK *see* **Democratic Party of Armenia**.

HDZ (Bosnia and Herzegovina)
see **Croatian Democratic Union (Bosnia and Herzegovina)**.

HDZ (Croatia) *see* **Croatian Democratic Union (Croatia)**.

HELCOM *or* **Helsinki Commission**
see **Baltic Marine Environment Protection Commission**.

Helsinki Final Act

The diplomatic agreement signed in Helsinki on 1 August 1975 at the end of the first Conference on Security and Co-operation in Europe (*see* **Organization for Security and Co-operation in Europe**). The 35 participants, including the members of the **North Atlantic Treaty Organization** and the **Warsaw Pact** and 13 neutral and non-aligned European countries, effectively accepted the post-1945 status quo in Europe. Four 'baskets' of agreement in the Final Act (also known as the Helsinki Accord) covered, respectively, security and confidence-building; co-operation on economic, scientific and environmental issues; human rights and freedoms; and the holding of follow-up conferences.

Helsinki process

The continuing round of negotiations and follow-up conferences set in train by the 1973–75 Helsinki conference. The Helsinki process was officially known as the Conference on Security and Co-operation in Europe (CSCE). Over a period of 25 years, the CSCE and its successor the **Organization for Security and Co-operation in Europe** (OSCE) became a significant element in the architecture of European dialogue and ultimately co-operation during and after the **Cold War**. The so-called 'Basket One' of the Helsinki Accord of 1975 set up the process which led ultimately to the conclusion of the landmark multilateral arms reduction treaty on **Conventional Forces in Europe** (CFE) in 1990. 'Basket Two' dealt with co-operation in science, technology and environmental protection. 'Basket Three', in which the participant States made commitments on human rights and freedoms, had a special significance for the emergence of movements pressing for greater respect for civil liberties within communist countries. Notable among these were the Moscow Helsinki Group founded in 1976 by a group including Yuri Orlov, Yelena Bonner and Anatoly Shcharansky; **Charter 77** in **Czechoslovakia**; and the Helsinki Watch group founded in **Poland** in 1979. These initiatives were supported by 'Helsinki Watch' committees across western Europe, Canada and the USA, leading to the holding of a conference in 1982 and the creation in 1983 of the International Helsinki Federation for Human Rights (IHF).

Herceg-Bosna

The self-declared **Croat** entity in south **Bosnia and Herzegovina**, founded by Croat nationalists in July 1992 during the early phase of the Bosnian Civil War and proclaimed as a separate republic on 28 August 1993. The declaration by nationalist leader Mate Boban prompted the widening of the conflict in Bosnia, drawing the **Bosniak** Muslims and the Croat populations into open hostility and encouraging the military intervention of **Croatia** in 1993. The entity was governed by the Croatian Defence Council (HVO) which successfully gained ground in the region and captured the city of **Mostar**, which became the entity's capital, in October 1992. Mostar became the centre for some of the war's most ferocious fighting between Muslims and Croats.

Herzegovina

Herceg-Bosna was effectively absorbed into the Muslim-Croat Federation in March 1994 at the start of the alliance between the two groups. The region today contains a majority of Bosnia's c.700,000-strong Croat population and is the centre for their aspirations to self-rule.

Herzegovina

The south-eastern corner of **Bosnia and Herzegovina**. Historically the region stretches with indeterminate reach into **Montenegro** and south-eastern **Croatia** and is renowned as the first home of the **Serbs**. It draws its name from the *Herceg*, local leaders who resisted the encroachment of Ottoman rule in the Middle Ages. Now Herzegovina is dominated by ethnic **Croats** (*see* **Herceg-Bosna**). The main urban area is **Mostar** which serves as a regional administrative centre. The region is blocked from the Adriatic Sea by a Croatian coastal strip, apart from a small port at Neum.

Hexagonale

A sub-regional co-operation initiative in **central** and **eastern Europe**, which was formed in July 1991 following the expansion of the former **Pentagonale** to include **Poland**, and went on to form the basis of the **Central European Intiative** in 1992. The Hexagonale consisted of Austria, **Czechoslovakia**, Italy, **Hungary**, Poland and the **Socialist Federal Republic of Yugoslavia**.

HHD *see* **Armenian Revolutionary Federation**.

HHK *see* **Republican Party of Armenia**.

HHSh *see* **Pan-Armenian National Movement**.

High Representative of the International Community *see* **Office of the High Representative**.

HINA news agency

Croatia's main news agency, founded in 1990, which also produces an electronic news service online known as Hina News Line and a news database, EVA.
Manager: Mirko Bolfek.
Address: Marulićev trg 16, 10000 Zagreb.
Telephone: (1) 4808700.
Fax: (1) 4808820.

E-mail: newsline@hina.hr
Internet: www.hina.hr

HIV—Human Immuno-deficiency Virus *see* AIDS.

HKK *see* Communist Party of Armenia.

HNS *see* Croatian People's Party.

Homeland Union–Lithuanian Conservatives
Tevynes Sanjunga–Lietuvos Konservatoriai (TS–LK)

A centre-right political party which has played a leading role in **Lithuania**. The Homeland Union was launched in May 1993 as successor to the remnants of the Lithuanian Reform Movement (**Sąjudis**), which had spearheaded the independence campaign. Under the leadership of Vytautas Landsbergis, the broadly-based Sąjudis had been the leading formation in the 1990 elections, but in the face of economic adversity had suffered a heavy defeat in the 1992 contest, winning only 20.5% of the popular vote. The new Homeland Union proclaimed a centre-right orientation, while announcing that its ranks were open to former communists.

Profiting from the unpopularity of the post-1992 left-wing Government, the TS–LK swept to an overall majority of 70 seats in the autumn 1996 parliamentary elections, opting to form a centre-right coalition with the **Lithuanian Christian Democratic Party** (LKDP) and the **Lithuanian Centre Union** (LCS) under the premiership of Gediminas Vagnorius. In direct presidential elections in late 1997 and early 1998, Landsbergis came a poor third in the first round with only 15.7%, but the party then gave crucial backing to the narrow second-round victor, Valdas **Adamkus** (non-party).

Vagnorius was succeeded as Prime Minister in May 1999 by Rolandas Paksas, then the TS–LK Mayor of **Vilnius**, but growing divisions between the coalition partners resulted in his replacement in October 1999 by Andrius Kubilius. Splits within the TS–LK followed, so that in parliamentary elections in October 2000 the rump party was heavily punished, slumping to only nine seats and 8.6% of the vote. It has remained in opposition since.

Leadership: Vytautas Landsbergis (Chair.).
Address: Gedimino pr. 15, Vilnius 2001.
Telephone and Fax: (23) 96450 [(523) 96450 from September 2002].
E-mail: info@tslk.lt
Internet: www.tslk.lt

Horn, Gyula

Hungary's former communist-era Foreign Minister, who led the ex-communist **Hungarian Socialist Party** (MSzP) back to power in 1994 and was Prime Minister from 1994 to 1998. He was born in a working class district of **Budapest** on 5 July 1932, in a strongly communist family—his father was executed by the Gestapo during the Second World War and his brother later died fighting on the Soviet side to suppress the Hungarian uprising in 1956 (during which Gyula Horn was himself in the Interior Ministry militia assisting the Soviet forces). Having left school originally at 11, he subsequently completed his education in the **Soviet Union**, returning to Hungary in 1954 with an accountancy degree. In his career as a government and party official he rose to be Permanent Secretary at the ministry of Foreign Affairs from 1985 to 1989. He then became Minister of Foreign Affairs, which involved him in a series of momentous decisions on the dismantling of the 'iron curtain' (*see* **Cold War**). On 27 June 1989 he and the then Austrian Foreign Minister, Alois Mock, symbolically cut the barbed wire on the Austro-Hungarian border. In September he suspended a bilateral agreement with East Germany under which East Germans without valid travel documents had hitherto been returned to East Germany, effectively opening a route for them to flee via Hungary to the West. He also completed preparations for, and later signed, the agreement on the withdrawal of Soviet troops from Hungary.

A leading voice in the reform communist movement within the ruling party, Horn helped refound it as the Hungarian Socialist Party (MSzP) in 1989. He became a parliamentary deputy in 1990 and Party Chairman in May 1990. In the May 1994 parliamentary elections Horn's MSzP secured an absolute majority of seats. Asked to form a Government, he brought the **Alliance of Free Democrats** into coalition and was sworn in as Prime Minister on 15 July 1994. His Government's handling of the economy and international relations reassured many in the West who had doubted whether former communists could be trusted to pursue a process of transition. Horn promoted Hungarian membership of both the **North Atlantic Treaty Organization** (NATO) and the **European Union**. In 1995 and 1996 he concluded agreements with Slovakia and Romania accepting current borders and undertaking to protect the rights of respective minorities. The MSzP was relegated to opposition once more at the May 1998 elections, however, and in September of that year Horn gave up the party chairmanship.

HOS *see* **Croatian Defence Force**.

House of Peoples (Bosnia and Herzegovina)
Dom Naroda

The upper house of the **Parliamentary Assembly** of **Bosnia and Herzegovina**.

House of Representatives (Belarus)
Palata Predstaviteley

The lower house of the **National Assembly** of **Belarus**.

House of Representatives (Bosnia and Herzegovina)
Predstavnički Dom

The lower house of the **Parliamentary Assembly** of **Bosnia and Herzegovina**.

Hoxha, Enver

The dictatorial head of the communist regime in **Albania** from 1944 until his death in office in 1985. A southern Albanian from Gjirokastër, Hoxha (born in 1908) joined the communist party in the 1930s while at university in France. Returning to Albania in 1936 as a French teacher after abandoning his studies in law, he joined a Marxist group in Korçë to organize against the regime of King Zog. In 1941 Hoxha was chosen as first Secretary-General of the newly-constituted Albanian Communist Party. The resistance struggle brought this small group to prominence, thanks in part to Hoxha's charismatic leadership and ruthlessness. In power from 1944, he formally relinquished in 1954 his government post as Prime Minister, but retained the first secretaryship of the renamed Party of Labour of Albania (PPS). He consolidated his personal supremacy in a series of purges beginning with the 'pro-Yugoslav' faction (Hoxha himself having always been associated with the rival Albanian nationalist standpoint). Hoxha oversaw the creation of a Stalinist centralized power structure and command economy, but fell out with the Soviet leadership over the Sino-Soviet split in 1960–61, whereupon Khrushchev denounced the 'bloody atrocities' of his purges. Ever more xenophobic in the cocoon of his personality cult after the break with China in the late 1970s, Hoxha in 1982 denounced his long-time associate Mehmet Shehu (who had died in mysterious circumstances the previous December) for having been a US, Yugoslav and Soviet agent since the war. Further purges followed. When Hoxha died in April 1985 his personality cult remained intact. His widow Nexhmije continued to wield much influence as a hardliner in the Party Central Committee, chairing the umbrella Democratic Front until December 1990. The violence of attacks on the statues and symbols of Hoxha all over Albania in 1991 underlined the extent to which the communist period had been defined by his omnipresence.

Hromada All-Ukrainian Association
Vseukrayinske Obyednannya Hromada

A pro-business political party whose fortunes declined after its founder was charged with financial corruption. Hromada ('Community') was relaunched in late 1997 under the leadership of Pavlo Lazarenko, who had been dismissed as Prime Minister by President Leonid **Kuchma** in June because of corruption allegations against him. Based in Dnipropetrovsk (where Lazarenko has been Governor), the party became part of the anti-Kuchma opposition and won 20 seats in the 1998 **Parliament** elections with a vote share of 4.5%. In February 1999, however, Lazarenko fled to the USA after Parliament had removed his immunity from prosecution, whereupon a substantial section of Hromada broke away to form the **Fatherland** grouping. By late 2000 Lazarenko was in custody in the USA facing money-laundering charges.

Leadership: Pavlo Lazarenko (Chair.).
Address: c/o Verkhovna Rada, M. Grushevskogo St 5, Kiev 01008.
E-mail: admin@hromada.kiev.ua
Internet: www.hromada.kiev.ua

HSLS *see* **Croatian Social-Liberal Party**.

HSP *see* **Croatian Party of Rights**.

HSS (Bosnia and Herzegovina)
see **Croatian Peasants' Party (Bosnia and Herzegovina)**.

HSS (Croatia) *see* **Croatian Peasants' Party (Croatia)**.

Human Rights Union Party
Partia për Mbrojtjen e te Drejtave te Njeriut (PBDNj)

A political party representing **Albania**'s 3% ethnic Greek population concentrated in Northern Epirus (*see* **Epirus question**).

The PBDNj was inaugurated in February 1992. It came into being primarily because a new law had banned ethnically-based parties. This measure was targeted at the **Democratic Union of the Greek Minority–Concord** (Omonia), founded in 1990 as successor to a clandestine ethnic Greek organization of the communist era, which had won five seats out of 250 in the 1991 **People's Assembly** elections. In the 1992 elections the PBDNj, advocating 'full democratization of the social order', a market economy and peasant ownership of the land, won two of the 140 seats. In the disputed 1996 Assembly elections the PBDNj was awarded three seats out of 140, while in further Assembly polling in mid-1997 it advanced to four seats out of 155 with 2.8% of the vote. The PBDNj was then allocated one portfolio in a coalition headed by the **Socialist Party of Albania** and strongly backed the Government's efforts to improve relations with Greece. Despite mending its strained relations with Omonia in time for the June 2001 elections, the PBDNj failed to win

the five seats necessary to form a separate parliamentary group, receiving only three seats with a reduced 2.4% share of the vote.
Leadership: Vasil Melo (Chair.).
Address: c/o Kuvendi Popullor, Tirana.

Hungarian Chamber of Commerce and Industry
Magyar Kereskedelmi és Iparkamara

The principal organization in **Hungary** for promoting business contacts, both internally and externally, in the post-communist era. Originally founded in 1850.
President: Dr Lajos Tolnay.
Secretary-General: Peter Dunal.
Address: POB 452, 1372 Budapest V.
Telephone: (1) 3686890.
Fax: (1) 2505138.
E-mail: mkik@mail.mkik.hu

Hungarian Coalition Party
Strana Mad'arskej Koalície (SMK)

A party in **Slovakia** which is the main political representative of the ethnic **Hungarian** minority population. In Hungarian its name is Magyar Koalíció Pártja (MKP).

The SMK was launched in January 1998 as a merger of three ethnic Hungarian parties in Slovakia, namely: (i) Coexistence (ESWS), an alliance of Hungarian and other ethnic minority parties which was founded in 1990 and which won nine seats in the 1994 **National Council** elections; (ii) the Hungarian Christian Democratic Movement (MKdH/MKdM), which was founded in 1990 and which won seven seats in 1994; and (iii) the Hungarian Civic Party (MOS), which obtained one seat in 1994. In July 1998 the SMK registered as a single party, in light of new electoral rules specifying that each component of an alliance must surmount the 5% threshold to obtain representation.

In the September 1998 parliamentary elections the SMK lost ground slightly, returning 15 deputies on a vote share of 9.1%. It opted to join a centre-left coalition Government headed by the **Slovak Democratic Coalition** (SDK), receiving three ministerial portfolios.
Leadership: Béla Bugár (Chair.).
Address: Zabotova 2, Bratislava 81104.
Telephone: (2) 52497684.
Fax: (2) 52495791.
E-mail: smk@smk.sk
Internet: www.mkp.sk

Hungarian Democratic Forum
Magyar Demokrata Fórum (MDF)

A party of populist/nationalist orientation, affiliated to the **International Democrat Union**, which headed **Hungary**'s first post-communist Government. Founded in September 1988, the MDF held its first national conference in **Budapest** in March 1989, when it demanded that Hungary should again become 'an independent democratic country'. In the April 1990 **National Assembly** elections the party achieved first place with 165 of 378 elective seats. Its leader József **Antall** became Prime Minister, in a coalition Government also including the **Independent Smallholders' and Civic Party**.

In January 1993 Antall survived a challenge to his leadership by the MDF's nationalist right, led by István Csurka. In early June Csurka and three parliamentary colleagues were expelled from the party, promptly forming the **Hungarian Justice and Life Party**. Antall died in December 1993 and was succeeded by the then Defence Minister, Lajos Für.

In the May 1994 National Assembly elections the MDF slumped to 37 seats on a vote share of only 11.7% and went into opposition. Internal divisions ensued, the confirmation of right-winger Sándor Lezsák as Chairman in early 1996 precipitating the defection of several MDF deputies.

Allied with the **Federation of Young Democrats–Hungarian Civic Party** (FIDESz–MPP) in the May 1998 elections, the MDF declined further to 18 seats and 3.1% of the vote, but was nevertheless included in the new three-party centre-right Government headed by the FIDESz–MPP. In January 1999 Lezsák was ousted as MDF leader by Ibolya Dávid, the Justice Minister, who in February 2000 launched the 'Right Hand of Peace 2000' alliance of assorted right-wing groups with the aim of recovering lost support for the MDF.

Leadership: Ibolya Dávid (Chair.).
Address: 3 Bem József tér, 1027 Budapest; POB 579, 1539 Budapest.
Telephone: (1) 2124601.
Fax: (1) 1568522.
Internet: www.mdf.hu

Hungarian Democratic Union of Romania
Uniunea Democrata Maghiara din România (UDMR)
or *Romániai Magyar Demokrata Szövetség* (MDSz)

The principal party of the ethnic **Hungarian** minority in **Romania**, affiliated to the **Christian Democrat International** and the **International Democrat Union**. The UDMR was registered in 1990 with the aim of furthering ethnic Hungarian rights within the framework of a democratic Romania. It took 7.2% of the vote in the May 1990 **Parliament** elections, winning 29 Chamber of Deputies seats and becoming the largest single opposition formation. Despite then being affiliated to the broad centre-right Democratic Convention of Romania (CDR), the UDMR contested the September 1992 elections separately, winning 7.5% of the vote and 27 Chamber seats.

Following the resignation of Géza Domokos as UDMR President, the moderate Béla Markó was elected as his successor at a party congress in January 1993, after the more radical Bishop László Tökés (hero of anti-**Ceauşescu** protest actions in Timişoara, Northern **Transylvania**, in the late 1980s) had withdrawn his candidacy and accepted appointment as Honorary President. The same congress urged the Government to assist with the preservation of Hungarian language and culture, while calling for self-administration of majority Hungarian districts (rather than full autonomy, as demanded by some radicals). In mid-1995 the UDMR was rebuffed in its efforts to re-establish political co-operation with the CDR parties, whose spokesmen contended that it had become a party of extreme nationalism.

In 1996 the UDMR came under increasingly fierce attack by the extreme nationalist **Greater Romania Party** (PRM), which called openly for the UDMR to be banned. In the November 1996 presidential election UDMR candidate György Frunda came fourth with 6% of the first-round vote, while in the simultaneous Chamber elections the UDMR slipped to 25 seats with 6.6% of the vote. It then opted to join a coalition Government headed by the CDR.

Despite frequent strains with CDR parties over Hungarian language rights, the UDMR's participation government survived until the November–December 2000 elections, in which Frunda came fifth in the presidential contest with 6.2% of the vote, while in the parliamentary contest the UDMR improved slightly to 27 seats, with 6.8%. It thereafter gave qualified external support to a minority Government of the **Social Democratic Pole of Romania** on the understanding that legislation would be enacted granting more language rights to ethnic Hungarians.

Leadership: Béla Markó (Chair.).
Address: Str. Herastrau 13, Bucharest 71297.
Telephone: (1) 2305877.
Fax: (1) 2306570.
E-mail: office@rmdsz.ro
Internet: www.rmdsz.ro

Hungarian Justice and Life Party
Magyar Igazság és Élet Párt (MIEP)

A far-right grouping which aspires to a **greater Hungary**. The MIEP was launched in June 1993 by dissidents of the then ruling **Hungarian Democratic Forum** (MDF) after István Csurka had unsuccessfully challenged József **Antall** for the MDF leadership. Overtly antisemitic, the party contends that national revival is being thwarted by a 'Jewish-Bolshevik-liberal conspiracy'. It advocates the recovery of **Hungary**'s pre-1914 borders. Its original **National Assembly** contingent of about 10 fell to zero when it secured only 1.6% of the vote in the May 1994 Assembly elections, but it bounced back in the May 1998 contest, winning 14 seats with 5.5% of the vote.

In February 1999 the MIEP was the only parliamentary party to vote against Hungary's accession to the **North Atlantic Treaty Organization**. In September 2000 Csurka demanded that a referendum should be held before Hungary joined the **European Union**.
Leadership: István Csurka (Chair.).
Address: 3 Akadémia utca, 1054 Budapest.
Telephone: (1) 2685199.
Fax: (1) 2685197.
Internet: www.miep.hu

Hungarian News Agency
Magyar Távirati Iroda (MTI)

The national news agency of **Hungary** which was founded in 1880 and continues to provide news and analysis from around the world from a 'Hungarian perspective'. It also provides foreign news services with information and photographs relating to Hungarian news items.
Director-General: Károly Alexa.
Address: Naphegy tér 8, 1016 Budapest.
Telephone: (1) 3756722.
Fax: (1) 3188297.
Internet: hirek.mti.hu

Hungarian Privatization and State Holding Company (ÁPVRt)

Founded in 1995 by a merger of the State Property Agency and the State Holding Company.
Chair.: Gyula Gansperger.
Address: Pozsonyi út 56, 1133 Budapest.
Telephone: (1) 2374400.
Fax: (1) 2374100.
E-mail: apvrt@apvrt.hu

Hungarian Socialist Party
Magyar Szocialista Párt (MSzP)

The successor to the former ruling (communist) Hungarian Socialist Workers' Party (MSzMP), now of social democratic orientation and affiliated to the **Socialist International**.

Hungarian Socialist Party

Founded in November 1918, the original Hungarian Communist Party was outlawed under the inter-war Horthy dictatorship but in 1945 joined a Soviet-backed provisional Government with the Smallholders, Social Democrats and Agrarians. Having become the largest single party in the 1947 elections, the communists then eliminated their coalition partners as independent parties, forcing a merger with the Social Democrats in June 1948 and thereafter exercising complete power, although the façade of a front was preserved. The drama of the abortive Hungarian Uprising in 1956, in which an attempt to throw off Moscow's yoke was brutally crushed by Soviet tanks, was followed by the reassertion of communist rule under János **Kádár**. It was at this time that the party adopted the MSzMP designation. Economic and cultural liberalization from the 1960s was followed in the 1980s by partial democratization, although within the framework of MSzMP supremacy.

Responding to the rapid collapse of east European communism, an MSzMP extraordinary congress in October 1989 renounced Marxism in favour of democratic socialism and adopted the MSzP title. This did not prevent the party's defeat in the April 1990 multi-party elections. Gyula **Horn**, who then became MSzP leader, rebuilt the party in opposition and led it to an overall majority in the May 1994 National Assembly elections, with a tally of 209 seats on a 32.6% first-round vote share. Mainly for purposes of international respectability, the centrist **Alliance of Free Democrats** was brought into the resultant Horn Government as junior coalition partner.

Quickly unpopular for its economic austerity measures, the post-1994 MSzP Government was also troubled by various corruption scandals and by dissent within the party. In the May 1998 National Assembly elections it fell back to second place with 134 seats, although its share of the proportional vote increased to 32.9%. The party went into opposition and in September 1998 Horn was succeeded as its Chairman by former Foreign Minister László Kovács.

MSzP deputies backed the accession of Hungary to the **North Atlantic Treaty Organization** in March 1999 and also formed part of the consensus in favour of accession to the **European Union**. A party congress in November 2000 re-elected Kovács as Chairman and elected Katalin Szili to the new post of Deputy Chairman, while in December Sándor Nagy succeeded Kovács as MSzP parliamentary group leader.

Leadership: László Kovács (Chair.).
Address: 26 Köztársaság tér, 1081 Budapest.
Telephone: (1) 2100081.
Fax: (1) 2100011.
Internet: www.mszp.hu

Hungarians
Magyars

A **Finno-Ugric** people, the majority population in **Hungary** and sizeable minorities in neighbouring countries. Their language, quite different from the neighbouring Slavic, Romance and German tongues, has its closest modern European relatives in Finnish and Estonian. Originating in central Asia, the Magyars/Hungarians arrived in **central Europe** in the late 9th century and established a Magyar kingdom across the eastern Pannonian plain including the southern Tatras (modern-day **Slovakia**) and **Transylvania**. This kingdom quickly became a significant force in European politics and a part of Christendom after the conversion to **Roman Catholicism** under King (Saint) Stephen in 1000. Defeated by the Turks at Mohács in 1526, Hungary elected a Habsburg as its new king, and Hungarians spread out to fill the furthest reaches of the Habsburg Empire. As part of the ruling elite, Hungarians filled high positions in the imperial system. Their elevated and separate status, along with their use of the Hungarian language, made integration with the local people extremely difficult. The existence of well-established Hungarian communities, with distinct identity, created problems in several of the successor states to the Habsburg Empire after 1918, providing fuel for Hungarian nationalists eager to reassert Hungary's former territorial glory under the concept of a **Greater Hungary**.

The most significant of these communities is in Transylvania, in **Romania**, where roughly 1.5 million Hungarians live today. Another 500,000 live in Slovakia, and 300,000 in the **Vojvodina** region of northern **Yugoslavia**. In all three cases there are moves to achieve greater autonomy for the communities, with varying success and backed in all instances by the Hungarian Government. The use of the Hungarian language in schools was eventually given support by the Slovak and Romanian Governments in early 2001. In the Vojvodina, Hungarians were promised a return to 'territorial autonomy' in March 2001.

Hungary
Magyar Köztársaság

An independent landlocked republic in **central Europe**, bounded by Slovakia to the north, the Federal Republic of Yugoslavia (Serbia) and Croatia to the south, Romania to the east, Ukraine to the north-east, and Austria and Slovenia to the west.

Area: 93,030 sq km; *capital*: **Budapest**; *population*: 9.9m. (2001 estimate), comprising ethnic **Hungarians** 89.9%, **Roma** 4%, **Germans** 2.6%, **Serbs** 2%, **Slovaks** 0.8%, **Romanians** 0.7%; *official language*: Hungarian; *religion*: **Roman Catholic** 67.5%, **Protestant** 25%, other 7.5%.

The President of the Republic, elected by the unicameral **National Assembly** (Országgyűlés) for a five-year term, is the Head of State. The Head of Government is the Prime Minister, who is elected by the National Assembly on the recommendation of the President. Constitutionally, supreme power is vested in the legislature, which has 386 members elected by popular vote for a four-year term. The complex electoral system involves 210 proportionally-allocated seats and 176 single-member constituencies.

History: The original **Hungarians** were Magyar tribes who invaded the region in 896 and settled the territory, driving out or absorbing the existing population mix and founding a kingdom. Christianity was accepted during the reign of King Stephen I (997–1038) of the Arpad dynasty, who was canonized after his death. Hungary was devastated in 1241 by Mongol invaders, recovering to achieve its peak of mediaeval power during the reign of King Louis I (1342–82). A protracted struggle against the advancing Ottoman Turks began in the late 14th century. When the Turks crushed the Hungarian army at Mohács in 1526, western and northern Hungary accepted Habsburg rule to escape Ottoman occupation. Intermittent hostilities between the Habsburg and Turkish dominions continued until the close of the 17th century, when the Turks were driven out.

Oppressive Habsburg rule bred Hungarian resentment, culminating in an armed rebellion in 1848–49 led by Louis Kossuth, which was put down with the help of the Russian army. In 1867 the Hungarians concluded a compromise (Ausgleich) with the Habsburgs, whereby the dual monarchy of Austria-Hungary was set up. This disintegrated in 1918 upon the defeat of the central European powers in the First World War. The Austro-Hungarian Empire was dismembered. The Hungarian State created under the 1920 Treaty of **Trianon** was divested of two-thirds of Hungary's pre-war territory. The subsequent declaration of a Republic and brief period of communist rule ended in 1920 with the reconstitution of Hungary as a kingdom and the proclamation of Admiral Nikolaus Horthy as regent. Under his authoritarian rule Hungary entered the Second World War on the side of Germany in 1941, but was itself occupied by the Nazis in 1944. Liberation by Soviet troops led to the formation of a provisional Government which signed an armistice in early 1945. A Republic was proclaimed the following year. By 1949 the communist Hungarian Workers' Party, with Soviet support, had gained a monopoly of power and Hungary was declared a People's Republic under a new Constitution.

In October 1956 a popular revolt against the Stalinist system broke out in Budapest, but the uprising was crushed by Soviet military intervention the following month and a new Hungarian Socialist Workers' Party (HSWP) regime led by János **Kádár** was installed. Under Kádár's leadership (until 1988), Hungary remained within the communist camp but became the most liberal of the Soviet-bloc nations of **eastern Europe**.

The HSWP voluntarily abandoned its monopoly on power in 1989, and the Constitution was amended in October of that year to allow for a multi-party democracy. Free elections in April and May 1990 led to the formation of a centre-right coalition Government led by the **Hungarian Democratic Forum** (MDF). The following August, acting Head of State Árpád **Göncz** of the liberal **Alliance of**

Free Democrats (SzDSz) was elected President by the National Assembly. The last Soviet troops left Hungary in 1991.

In legislative elections in May 1994 the MDF suffered a heavy defeat. The **Hungarian Socialist Party** (MSzP, the renamed former communist party) won an overall majority of seats in the National Assembly and formed a new coalition Government with the SzDSz under the premiership of Gyula **Horn**. President Göncz was re-elected President for a second term in June 1995.

Latest elections: After four years of Socialist-led Government, elections to the National Assembly in May 1998 resulted in the centre-right **Federation of Young Democrats–Hungarian Civic Party** (FIDESz–MPP) becoming the largest party with 147 seats on a 29.5% vote share. The MSzP won only 134 seats (32.9%), the **Independent Smallholders' and Civic Party** (FKgP) 48 (13.2%), the SzDSz 24 (7.6%), the MDF 18 (3.1%), the far-right **Hungarian Justice and Life Party** (MIEP) 14 (5.5%) and one other 1. In July 1998 a new centre-right coalition was formed under the premiership of Viktor **Orbán** of the FIDESz–MPP, also including MDF and FKgP representation.

Recent developments: Although commanding a relatively small National Assembly majority, the Orbán coalition remained securely in power in 1999–2000, the principal threat to its stability being bitter factional dissension within the FKgP. In June 2000 non-party candidate Ferenc **Mádl** was elected President in succession to Göncz and took the opportunity of stressing the importance of good relations with neighbouring countries containing ethnic Hungarian minorities, notably **Romania**. Domestically, legislative measures continued to be implemented to protect the cultural, civil and political rights of the various minority groups in Hungary. At the same time, increasingly overt nationalism on the right, including within the ruling coalition, focused Hungary's territorial grievances and the perceived mistreatment of ethnic Hungarians abroad.

International relations and defence: In the post-Soviet era, as Hungary has restructured itself as a market economy, the country has pursued twin goals of membership of the **European Union** (EU) and of the **North Atlantic Treaty Organization** (NATO). A recipient of the EU's **PHARE programme** of economic aid since 1989, Hungary signed an association agreement with the EU in 1991. Its application for full EU membership was made in 1994 and, in March 1998, formal accession negotiations opened. Hungary joined NATO's **Partnership for Peace** programme in 1994 and formally joined the Alliance in March 1999 (together with the Czech Republic and Poland). Hungary's other multilateral links include membership of the United Nations, the **Organization for Security and Co-operation in Europe**, the **Council of Europe**, the **Central European Initiative**, the **Central European Free Trade Area** and the **Danube Commission**. It has also been admitted to the **Organization for Economic Co-operation and Development** and the **World Trade Organization**.

Bilaterally, relations with Romania and **Slovakia** have been strained over issues arising from the treatment of sizeable ethnic Hungarian communities in these countries, although recent treaties include minority protection provisions. There has also been friction with Slovakia over the **Gabčíkovo-Nagymaros Dam**, a hydroelectric construction project on the River Danube, initiated jointly by Hungary and Czechoslovakia in 1977 but suspended controversially at the end of the 1980s. The issue was the subject of a ruling by the **International Court of Justice** in 1997, following which Hungary and Slovakia agreed in March 1998 to resume negotiations to complete the disputed project.

Hungary's defence budget for 2000 amounted to some US $790m., equivalent to about 2% of GDP. The size of the armed forces at the end of 2000 was some 44,000 personnel, including those serving under compulsory conscription of nine months, while reservists numbered an estimated 90,000.

Hungary, economy

In transition, in the main successfully, from state command to a free-market system.

GNP: US $44,140m. (2000); *GNP per capita*: $4,740 (2000); *GDP at PPP*: $79,400m. (1999); *GDP per capita at PPP*: $7,800 (1999); *exports*: $28,087m. (2000); *imports*: $32,187m. (2000); *currency*: forint (plural: forint; US $1=F274.8 at the end of December 2001).

In 1999 industry contributed 30% of GDP, agriculture 5% and services 65%. Some 51% of land is arable, 2% under permanent crops, 13% permanent pasture and 19% forests and woodland. The main crops are wheat, maize, other grains, sunflower seed, sugar beet and vegetables, while there are important vineyards and there is a developed dairy industry. The main mineral resources are bauxite, lignite, hard and brown coal, and some oil and considerable natural gas reserves. The main industries are food, beverages and tobacco, chemicals (especially pharmaceuticals), petroleum and plastics, and metallurgy and engineering. Over 40% of Hungary's domestic energy requirements are met from nuclear power.

Hungary's main exports by value in 1999 were machinery and transport equipment (52%), basic and miscellaneous manufactures (33%), agricultural and food products (11%), raw materials (3%) and fuels and electricity (2%). The principal imports in 1999 were machinery and transport equipment (47%), other manufactures (40%), fuels and electricity (7%), agricultural and food products (4%) and raw materials (2%). In 2000 Germany was the largest purchaser of Hungarian exports (37%), followed by Austria (9%) and Italy (6%). Germany was also the principal supplier of Hungarian imports (26%), followed by the **Russian Federation** (8%) and Austria and Italy (7% each). Around 60% of Hungary's trade is with **European Union** (EU) member countries.

After communist rule ended in 1989–90, successive Governments pursued the creation of a free-market economic system and the dismantling of the previous centralized industrial structure, assisted by the relative economic freedom permitted in non-industrial sectors under the previous regime. A four-year restructuring programme initiated in 1991 had an initial adverse effect on GDP, which contracted by nearly 20% in 1991–93, while unemployment rose to around 12% in 1994 and inflation to over 20% in 1995. As GDP began to recover in 1994–95, a comprehensive stabilization programme introduced in March 1995, including a currency devaluation, produced modest GDP growth in 1996 and then an acceleration to annual expansion of around 5% in each of the four years of 1997 to 2000, assisted by large inflows of foreign direct investment. Over the same period, unemployment showed a marked fall, to an estimated 7% in 2000, while the inflation rate also came down, although it remained relatively high at around 10% in both 1999 and 2000.

The Government took particular satisfaction in a GDP growth rate of 5.3% in 2000, the highest since the end of communism. Growth in that year was officially stated to have restored output and living standards to 1990 levels, thus marking the completion of the transition phase. Initial projections for 2001 were for continued growth of around 5%, although in early 2001 the worst floods for a century imposed a huge unexpected cost on the economy.

In 1991 legislation was approved authorizing the partial compensation of former owners of expropriated land and property, through the issue of vouchers (*see* **voucher privatization**) which could then be used to purchase state assets; this measure applied not only to property seized during the communist era but was backdated to May 1939. An accompanying privatization programme resulted in the transfer to the private sector by 1995 of some 80% of the hitherto state-owned assets, and the sale of most state farms. Privatization of the major utilities and the commercial banks followed, so that by 1999 the private sector accounted for over 80% of Hungary's GDP and over two-thirds of employment. In December 2000 the Prime Minister declared that the privatization process had been completed and that the extent of private ownership in Hungary was now similar to western European levels.

A central goal of the economic reform programme has been to prepare for accession to the European Union (EU). The EU has accepted Hungary as one of the first six 'fast-track' central and eastern European candidates for entry. As a staging post to EU membership, Hungary was in 1993 a founder member of the **Central European Free Trade Area** (CEFTA) of EU aspirant countries. Formal EU-Hungary negotiations opened in November 1998 and made steady progress, such that a European Commission report on enlargement published in November 2000 praised Hungary as being among the most advanced of the ex-communist states towards meeting membership requirements. In 1996 Hungary had become the second ex-communist state to join the **Organization for Economic Co-operation and Development** (OECD); it was also among the first members of the **World Trade Organization** (WTO) inaugurated in 1995.

HUS *see* **Croatian Association of Trade Unions**.

Husák, Gustáv

Hardline communist party leader in **Czechoslovakia** until he was forced to resign by the '**velvet revolution**' of November–December 1989. Born in 1913, he first made his name in the Communist Party of Slovakia and helped to lead the 1944 **Slovak** uprising against the German occupation. The victim of one of the party purges of the 1950s, he was imprisoned by Czechoslovakia's hardline Stalinist regime in 1954 as a Slovak 'bourgeois nationalist' and not released until 1960. He then rose to become part of the leadership group in the Communist Party of Czechoslovakia (KSČ) and Czechoslovak Government, and was initially associated with the 1968 '**Prague Spring**' liberalization headed by Alexander **Dubček**. When that experiment was crushed by the tanks of invading **Warsaw Pact** forces, the Soviet leadership turned to Husák to take charge of 'normalizing' Czechoslovakia and he became known principally for establishing a neo-Stalinist regime. He replaced Dubček as KSČ leader in April 1969 and held that office until his replacement by Miloš **Jakeš** in 1987. He was also Head of State from 1975 until he was forced to resign by mass pro-democracy rallies on 10 December 1989, a moment which marked the triumph of the 'velvet revolution'. Expelled from the KSČ in February 1990, he died on 18 November 1991.

HZDS *see* **Movement for a Democratic Slovakia**.

HZhK *see* **People's Party of Armenia**.

I

IAEA *see* International Atomic Energy Agency.

IBRD

The International Bank for Reconstruction and Development, generally known as the **World Bank**.

IBSFC *see* International Baltic Sea Fisheries Commission.

Ichkeria *see* Chechnya.

ICJ *see* International Court of Justice.

ICTY *see* International Criminal Tribunal for the former Yugoslavia.

Idel-Ural

A collective term for the non-**Russian**, and largely **Muslim**, republics between the River Volga (Idel in Tatar) and the southern Ural mountains. The region is inhabited by various **Tatar** and **Finno-Ugric peoples** and came under the dominion of the Russian Empire after the fall of the Kazan khanate in 1552. The connections between the subjugated people led to episodes of collective action against their Russian overlords, culminating in the formation of a Tatar-led Idel-Ural Federation in 1917 in opposition to the Bolsheviks. The success of the Bolsheviks over their adversaries in the Russian Civil War led to the conspicuous division of the Idel-Ural state and the foundation in its place of five ethnically-based successor regions (roughly from west to east, **Mordova**, **Mari El**, the **Chavash Republic**, **Tatarstan** and **Bashkortostan**) between 1918 and 1930. Today these republics cover the important Volga-Ural oilfield and are largely industrialized. There are no serious aims to recreate the Idel-Ural unit.

IDS *see* Istrian Democratic Assembly.

IDU *see* International Democrat Union.

IeM *see* Justice and Accord Bloc.

IFOR *see* Stabilization Force.

IL *see* Fatherland Union.

Iliescu, Ion

The first President of **Romania** after the overthrow of the **Ceauşescu** regime in 1989, who dominated Romanian politics for the next seven years, and made a comeback after four years in opposition to win the Presidency again in December 2000.

A railway worker's son born on 3 March 1930 in the rural town of Oltenita, near the border with **Bulgaria**, Iliescu was active in communist youth groups and completed his engineering degree at the Energy Institute in **Moscow**. Working thereafter in **Bucharest**, he rose within the Romanian Communist Party to full membership of the Central Committee by 1968 and a seat on the Politburo in 1971, but lost this position one year later owing to his open opposition to Ceauşescu's proposed 'cultural revolution'. Shunted into remote regional posts and put under close surveillance by Ceauşescu's secret police, the Securitate, he was one of the few people with the political experience to take the helm when public discontent at the communist regime spiralled into open revolution in December 1989. The emerging National Salvation Front, a collection of generals, artists, and outcast party members from the previous regime, nominated him as Interim President the following January, and in May 1990 he won the presidential election with a convincing 80% of the vote.

His two terms in office—he won re-election in October 1992—were blighted by economic chaos and political confrontation. Iliescu manoeuvred to avoid incurring blame for the pain inflicted by supposed free-market reforms, drawing his support opportunistically from a range of groups including intimidatingly violent miners and even the ultra-nationalist **Greater Romania Party** (PRM). His own party, a former faction of the National Salvation Front which he renamed in 1993 as the Social Democracy Party of Romania (PDSR), was defeated in the November 1996 elections, and he himself was also rejected by the voters, losing the second round of the presidential contest in December to Emil Constantinescu. Iliescu held on to a seat in the Senate (upper house of **Parliament**), however, and was a vocal critic of the increasingly unpopular Constantinescu Government. His dramatic comeback in the November–December 2000 presidential elections, after four years in opposition, was based on a toned-down version of his former leftist politics, while he also embraced European integration. In winning the election, Iliescu withstood an initially strong showing by an opponent representing the far right, Corneliu Vadim Tudor. The PDSR campaigned as part of a new alliance, the Social Democratic Pole of Romania, in the legislative elections held at the same time. This alliance recovered some of the ground lost four years previously by the centre-left, and ended up in a position to form a minority Government with enough external support to keep the far right out of power. The fundamental aims of the new Iliescu presidency and new Prime Minister Adrian **Nastase** were to bring a greater degree of social concern to the pursuit of free-market reforms and eventual membership of the **European Union**.

Address: Office of the President, Cotroceni Palace, Blvd Geniului 1, 76238 Bucharest.
Telephone: (1) 4100581.
Fax: (1) 3121179.
Internet: www.presidency.ro

Ilves, Toomas Hendrik

Minister of Foreign Affairs, **Estonia**.

Toomas Hendrik Ilves is deputy leader of the **Moderates** (Moodukad). Educated in the USA, he had an academic career and worked for Radio Free Europe before becoming an ambassador for the newly independent Estonia in 1993. He was first appointed Foreign Minister in 1996 and was reappointed to the post on 30 March 1999.

Born in Stockholm, Sweden, on 26 December 1953, he graduated from Columbia University, USA, in 1976 and received his Master's Degree in psychology in 1978. His academic career began as an English teacher in 1979 and went on to include administrative roles in Canadian universities from 1981 to 1984. He joined the Munich-based Radio Free Europe as a research analyst in 1984, working there until 1993 and rising to be Director of its Estonian service. He returned to the USA in 1993 as Estonia's ambassador, with additional remit over Canada and Mexico. He was recalled to Estonia and served as Foreign Minister from 1996 to 1998. He was elected deputy head of the Moderates in 1999 and was appointed to the coalition Cabinet of Prime Minister Mart **Laar** in March that year.

Toomas Hendrik Ilves is married to Merry Bullock and they have two children.
Address: Ministry of Foreign Affairs, Islandi Väljak 1, Tallinn 15049.
Telephone: 6317000.
Fax: 6317099.
E-mail: vminfo@vm.ee
Internet: www.vm.ee

IMF *see* **International Monetary Fund**.

Implementation Force see **Stabilization Force**.

Independence–Confederation of New Trade Unions of Slovenia
Konfederacija Novih Sindikatov Slovenije Neodvisnost (KNSS-Neodvisnost)

One of several competing union centres in **Slovenia**, founded on the country's achievement of independence in 1991.
President: Drago Lombar.
Address: 13 Linhartova St, Ljubljana 1000.
Telephone: (1) 3061000.
Fax: (1) 2302868.

Independence Trade Union Confederation
Nezavisnost

An independent union centre in **Yugoslavia**, founded in 1991 to challenge the dominance of the **Confederation of Autonomous Trade Unions of Yugoslavia**. It has organized strikes in protest against low wages, and participated in the opposition movement which ousted Slobodan **Milošević** from power in October 2000. Affiliated to the International Confederation of Free Trade Unions (ICFTU), Nezavisnost has 13 affiliated unions with a total membership of some 180,000.
President: Branislav Čanak.
Address: 4/V Nušićeva St, Belgrade 11000.
Telephone: (11) 3238226.
Fax: (11) 3244118.
E-mail: nezavisn@eunet.yu
Internet: www.nezavisnost.org.yu

Independent Christian Trade Union of Slovakia
Nezávislé Kresťanské Odbory Slovenska (NKOS)

A Christian-oriented union centre in **Slovakia**, with some influence though much smaller than the dominant **Confederation of Trade Unions of the Slovak Republic**. Affiliated to the World Confederation of Labour (WCL), the NKOS embraces three federations with a total membership of 12,000.
Chair.: Peter Novovesky.
Address: 1 Predstaničné St, Bratislava 81104.
Telephone and Fax: (2) 52444480.
E-mail: centrum@nkos.sk
Internet: www.nkos.sk

Independent Smallholders' and Civic Party
Független Kisgazda-, Földmunkás- és Polgári Párt (FKgP)

An influential agrarian formation in **Hungary** which has favoured the return of collectivized land to former owners. It is affiliated to the **Christian Democrat International**.

The FKgP was founded in November 1989 as a revival of Hungary's strongest post-Second World War party, which had been eliminated as an independent formation by 1948. It won 44 seats and 11.7% of the vote in the 1990 **National Assembly** elections and joined a centre-right coalition Government headed by the **Hungarian Democratic Forum** (MDF). Riven by internal dissension and splits, however, the FKgP withdrew from the Government in February 1992, because the MDF had denied it an opportunity to influence policy. This decision provoked the immediate breakaway of a majority of the FKgP deputies, who continued to support the MDF-led Government.

The rump FKgP recovered somewhat by winning 26 seats on an 8.9% vote share in the May 1994 general elections, remaining in opposition. The party then became embroiled in fierce conflict over government moves to produce a new Constitution to replace the much-amended communist-era text. One FKgP proposal was that the President should be directly elected, with enhanced powers. Seeking to force a referendum, the FKgP collected well over the number of signatures required for a popular consultation, but the ruling MSzP contended that such a change would generate political instability.

Allied with the rump Christian Democratic People's Party (KDNP) in the May 1998 National Assembly elections, the FKgP advanced strongly to 48 seats (with 13.2% of the vote) and joined the subsequent centre-right Government headed by the **Federation of Young Democrats–Hungarian Civic Party** (FIDESz–MPP). By 2000 the party was again beset by chronic internal dissension, which led to the formation of the breakaway Hungarian Reform Movement in January 2001 and the election of Zsolt Lányi as FKgP Chairman in May. Lányi replaced the party's controversial long-term leader and former Agriculture Minister, József Torgyán.

Leadership: Zsolt Lányi (Chair.).
Address: 24 Belgrád rakpárt, 1056 Budapest.
Telephone: (1) 1182855.
Fax: (1) 1181824.
E-mail: fkgp@fkgp.hu
Internet: www.fkgp.hu

Independent Trade Union Association of Bosnia and Herzegovina

A trade union federation seeking to replace the communist-era structure which effectively collapsed during **Bosnia and Herzegovina**'s post-independence civil

war (1992–95). Its aspiration to be a countrywide federation has been thwarted by the emergence of ethnically-based union organizations such as the **Confederation of Trade Unions of the Serb Republic**.
Chair.: Sulejman Hrle.
Address: Obala Kulina Bana 1, Sarajevo.
Telephone and Fax: (33) 664872.

Industry Will Save Georgia
Mretsveloba Gadaarchens Sakartvelos (IWSG)

A pro-business political movement in **Georgia**, known by the initials of its English title. IWSG was launched in advance of the 1999 parliamentary elections by brewery owner Giorgi Topadze. Arguing that the Government's tax policies were damaging Georgian business and forcing dependence on foreign aid, Topadze called for tax breaks and import controls until a stable economy was established. The IWSG, allied in the elections with the ultra-nationalist Georgia First movement and the Movement for Georgian Statehood, won 15 seats with a 7.1% vote share. Its group of deputies adopted the name Entrepreneurs.
Leadership: Giorgi Topadze (Chair.).
Address: Barnovi 69, Tbilisi.
Telephone: (32) 235335.

Information Telegraphic Agency of Russia *see* **ITAR-TASS**.

Infotag News Agency (Moldova)

The main private news agency in **Moldova**. Created in 1993, Infotag rivals the official agency Moldpres (*see* **National News Agency**) in providing news about Moldova to domestic and international clients in Romanian, Russian and English.
Address: Blvd B. Bodoni 57/114, 2012 Chişinau.
Telephone: (2) 234875.
Fax: (2) 233717.
E-mail: office@infotag.net.md

Ingushetia

A constituent republic of the **Russian Federation** situated in the north **Caucasus region**, which was joined to nearby **Chechnya** from 1934 to 1992. *Population*: 170,000 (1997 est.). The Ingush people (known to themselves as Galgai) are ethnically similar to the Chechens, and were only recognized as a separate ethnic group in the late 19th century after they opposed the Chechens and sided with **Russian** forces in their war against an Islamic uprising in the north Caucasus. The Ingush only converted to **Islam** during this period. They were isolated again in the early 20th century when they did join the local resistance to Bolshevik rule. After the success of the Bolsheviks in the Russian Civil War (1918–20) the Ingush were granted a position within the autonomous 'Mountain Republic' and were given their own *oblast* (region) in 1924. In 1934 Ingushetia was joined to Chechnya. During the Second World War the previous loyalty of the Ingush was quickly forgotten and they, the Chechens and many other Caucasian peoples were accused by Stalin of collaborating with the invading German forces and were deported *en masse* to central Asia in 1944 (*see* **Deported Nationalities**). They were rehabilitated in 1956 and returned to Ingushetia.

Tensions between Chechens and Ingush escalated rapidly in the early 1990s following the declaration of independence by the nationalist regime in Chechnya in 1991. Supported by the Russian authorities, who were opposed to the Chechen regime, Ingushetia declared its sovereignty within the Russian Federation in June 1992. The borders of the new republic in theory followed the 1934 demarcation. However, disputes with neighbouring North **Ossetia** over the Prigorodni region, ceded to the Ossetes in 1944, descended into armed conflict in 1992. Thousands of Ingush fled the fighting and they now constitute a large refugee population, along with Chechens, in Ingushetia. A cease-fire was agreed in 1995 with the help of supervising Russian forces.

A traditionally pastoral economy was converted in the Soviet era into one focused on the petroleum industry. The capital, Nazran, is the centre of industrial activity. The republic was badly hit by the war with North Ossetia and the influx of Chechen refugees from 1994 onwards. It remains impoverished and unproductive, but has been helped by the creation of a free economic zone across the republic to encourage trade. It is also attempting to market its breathtaking Caucasian mountain scenery for tourism. Ruslan Sultanovich Aushev was elected President of Ingushetia in March 1993.

Interlatvija

Seeks to promote exports, imports and the establishment of joint ventures in **Latvia**. Founded in 1987.
Director-General: Maris Forsts.
Address: Kalpaka bulv. 1, Riga 1010.
Telephone: 7333602.

Internal Macedonian Revolutionary Organization–Democratic Party for Macedonian National Unity
Vnatrešno-Makedonska Revolucionerna Organizacija–Demokratska Partija za Makedonsko Nacionalno Edinstvo (VMRO–DPMNE)

A nationalist party in **Macedonia** claiming descent from the historic VMRO, which had fought for independence from the Turks before the First World War. In 1990 the revived VMRO merged with the DPMNE (originally founded by **Macedonian** migrant workers in Sweden) to create a party seeking to promote the revival of Macedonian **Slavic** cultural identity. The merged party became the largest single formation in the 1990 **Assembly of the Republic** elections (with 38 seats) and formed the core of the resultant 'Government of experts' which asserted Macedonia's independence. However, a mid-1992 government crisis resulted in the VMRO–DPMNE going into opposition, from where it failed to gain representation in the controversial October 1994 elections. Party leader Ljubčo **Georgievski** was the runner-up in simultaneous presidential polling, receiving 21.6% of the vote.

The VMRO–DPMNE staged a revival in opposition to the post-1994 Government headed by the **Social Democratic Union of Macedonia** (SDSM), forming an alliance with the new pro-business **Democratic Alternative** (DA) for the autumn 1998 legislative elections. The alliance emerged as substantially the largest grouping, with 59 of the 120 seats, and formed a coalition Government under Georgievski which, to the surprise of many observers, also included the (ethnic **Albanian**) **Democratic Party of Albanians** (DPA). The VMRO–DPMNE consolidated its authority in the late 1999 presidential elections, in which party candidate Boris **Trajkovski** was elected with 53% of the second-round vote.

The VMRO–DPMNE was weakened in March 2000 by the formation of a breakaway VMRO led by former Finance Minister Boris Zmejkovski, while at the end of the year the withdrawal of the DA from the Government left the remaining VMRO–DPMNE/DPA coalition dependent on DA dissidents and the small Liberal-Democratic Party for a parliamentary majority. The reconstituted Government faced its greatest challenge, however, from an insurgency launched in February 2001 by ethnic Albanian rebels seeking greater rights for the Albanian community.

Under intense international pressure a Government of National Unity was established in May, still headed by Georgievski but comprising parties from all sides of the Assembly, including the opposition PDP and SDSM. The alliance was volatile as the struggle for greater Albanian autonomy was largely backed by the Albanian parties and had prompted a powerful nationalist backlash among their ethnic Macedonian counterparts. However, peace initiatives gradually gained ground in July and a final agreement was signed between the Government and the **Kosovo Liberation Army** (UCK) at Ohrid on 13 August 2001.

The process of approving the various key elements of the peace deal—providing limited autonomy and social equalization for the Albanian community—was complex and frequently delayed. At its conclusion in November, the SDSM and the Liberals withdrew from the grand coalition. **New Democracy** (ND), which

International Atomic Energy Agency (IAEA)

had been formed in March from a small splinter of the DA, was drafted in to take their place.
Leadership: Prof. Ljubčo Georgievski (Chair.).
Address: Macedonia 17A, Skopje 91000.
Telephone: (2) 124244.
Fax: (2) 124336.

International Atomic Energy Agency (IAEA)

The UN organization founded in 1957 to promote and monitor peaceful use of atomic energy.
Members: 132 countries, including Albania, Armenia, Azerbaijan, Belarus, Bosnia and Herzegovina, Bulgaria, Croatia, Czech Republic, Estonia, Georgia, Hungary, Latvia, Lithuania, Macedonia, Moldova, Poland, Romania, Russian Federation, Slovakia, Slovenia, Ukraine and Yugoslavia.
Leadership: Dr Mohammad el-Baradei (Director-General).
Address: POB 100, Wagramerstrasse 5, 1400 Vienna, Austria.
Telephone: (1) 26000.
Fax: (1) 26007.
E-mail: official.mail@iaea.org
Internet: www.iaea.org/worldatom

International Baltic Sea Fisheries Commission (IBSFC)

A fisheries management body established in 1974 after the signing of the Gdańsk Convention the previous year. Its main purpose is the fixing of fish catch quotas for the different species (herring, sprats, cod and salmon).
Members: **European Union** (representing Denmark, Germany, Finland and Sweden), **Estonia**, **Latvia**, **Lithuania**, **Poland** and the **Russian Federation**.
Leadership: Lauri Vaarja (Chair.).
Address: International Baltic Sea Fisheries Commission (IBSFC), 20 Hosa St, 00950 Warsaw, Poland.
Telephone: (22) 6288647.
Fax: (22) 6253372.
E-mail: ibsfc@polbox.pl
Internet: www.ibsfc.org

International Bank for Reconstruction and Development (IBRD)

Generally known as the **World Bank**.

International Court of Justice (ICJ)

The principal judicial organ of the United Nations, founded in 1945.
Leadership: Gilbert Guillaume (President).
Address: Peace Palace, Carnegieplein 2, 2517 KJ The Hague, Netherlands.
Telephone: (70) 3022323.
Fax: (70) 3649928.
E-mail: information@icj-cij.org
Internet: www.icj-cij.org

International Criminal Tribunal for the former Yugoslavia (ICTY)

The UN Tribunal established in The Hague, Netherlands, by Security Council Resolution 827 on 25 May 1993, to try cases relating to war crimes committed in the former **Yugoslavia** since 1991. The ICTY covers charges relating to breaches of the Geneva Convention, violations of the laws or customs of war, genocide and crimes against humanity. It consists of 16 permanent Judges and a maximum of nine *ad litem* Judges, all of whom are elected by the UN General Assembly.

One of the ICTY's most significant rulings was made on 22 February 2001 when Zambian Judge Florence Ndepele Mwachande Mumba ruled that rape was to be considered as an 'instrument of terror' and a war crime. The sentences passed for this crime on three Bosnian **Serb** defendants ranged from 12 to 28 years in prison, and ranked second only to those for genocide in severity.

The most celebrated spectacle was the pre-trial of Slobodan **Milošević** in October 2001—the first former Head of State ever to face such proceedings. The former President denounced the Court's legitimacy and refused to enter a plea against charges including genocide and relating to the wars in **Croatia** and **Bosnia and Herzegovina**, and Yugoslavia's actions in **Kosovo**. The trial proper, at which Milošević was to defend himself, having refused legal counsel, began on 12 February 2002 and was expected to last a number of years. The case is being heard by Presiding UK Judge Richard George May.

As at 31 December 2001 11 people had been released by the Court after either completing their sentences (3), being transferred to other courts (3) or having been acquitted (5). Six had been provisionally released and two more were awaiting provisional release. Eleven people were in the process of serving their sentence and one was still awaiting a sentence, having been found guilty. Eight people were currently on trial and 21 were awaiting trial, including Milošević. Three indictments against detainees had been withdrawn and nine people had died before facing trial (three in custody at the ICTY). 30 people were wanted by the Court but were still at large, including Bosnian Serb warlord Radovan **Karadžić**, while 17 indictments had been withdrawn before the suspects had been apprehended. According to the Court's rules undisclosed indictments may also have been confirmed.

Leadership: Claude Jorda (President).

International Democrat Union (IDU)

Addresses: Churchillplein 1, 2517 JW The Hague, Netherlands;
POB 13888, 2501 EW The Hague, Netherlands.
Internet: www.un.org/icty/index.html

International Democrat Union (IDU)

An international grouping of centre-right political parties founded in 1983, which holds conferences every six months. Its membership includes the member parties of the European Democrat Union (EDU) and other political parties in 36 countries.

Leadership: Richard Normington (Executive Secretary).
Address: 32 Smith Sq., London, SW1P 3HH, United Kingdom.
Telephone: (20) 79848052.
Fax: (20) 79760486.
E-mail: rnormington@idu.org
Internet: www.idu.org

International Monetary Fund (IMF)

The principal organization of the international monetary system, founded in December 1945 to promote international monetary co-operation, the balanced growth of trade, and exchange rate stability. A critical role of the IMF has been to provide credit resources to members, on condition that specified (and sometimes domestically highly controversial) conditions are met for management of the economy and attainment of monetary targets.

The IMF's 183 member countries now include all the countries of **central** and **eastern Europe**. Czechoslovakia and Poland were both early members but withdrew in the 1950s. Yugoslavia was a founder member and remained one throughout the communist era. Romania joined in 1972, Hungary in 1982 and Poland in 1986, but none of the other states of the region joined until after the collapse of communism. The years in which each country joined were:

1972 Romania.
1982 Hungary.
1986 Poland (rejoined).
1990 Bulgaria; Czech Republic/Slovakia (both rejoining as Czechoslovakia).
1991 Albania.
1992 Armenia; Azerbaijan; Belarus; Bosnia and Herzegovina; Croatia; Estonia; Georgia; Latvia; Lithuania; Macedonia; Moldova; Russian Federation; Slovenia; Ukraine.
2000 Yugoslavia (readmitted in December as the FRY, the membership of the former SFRY (dating originally from 1945) having been suspended since December 1992.

Leadership: Horst Köhler (Managing Director).
Address: 700 19th St, NW, Washington, DC 20431, USA.
Telephone: (202) 6237300.
Fax: (202) 6236220.
Email: publicaffairs@imf.org
Internet: www.imf.org

International Organization for Migration (IOM)

Founded as the International Committee for Migration (ICM) in 1951, the organization changed its name in 1989.

Members: 91 countries, including Albania, Armenia, Azerbaijan, Bulgaria, Croatia, Czech Republic, Georgia, Hungary, Latvia, Lithuania, Poland, Romania, Slovakia, Slovenia, Ukraine and Yugoslavia. Observers include Belarus, Bosnia and Herzegovina, Estonia, Macedonia, Moldova and the Russian Federation.
Leadership: Brunson McKinley (Director General).
Address: 17 route des Morillons, CP 71, 1211 Geneva 19, Switzerland.
Telephone: (22) 7179111.
Fax: (22) 7986150.
E-mail: uinfo@iom.int
Internet: www.iom.int

International Whaling Commission (IWC)

The organization which reviews the conduct of whaling throughout the world, and co-ordinates and funds whale research. Its 43 member countries include the **Russian Federation**. Traditionally a whaling nation, the Russian Federation observes the international moratorium on commercial whaling introduced by the IWC amidst mounting concern that continued hunting had become unsustainable owing to declining whale numbers.

Leadership: Prof. Bo Fernholm (Chair.).
Address: The Red House, 135 Station Road, Impington, Cambridge, CB4 9NP, United Kingdom.
Telephone: (1223) 233971.
Fax: (1223) 232876.
E-mail: iwc@iwcoffice.org
Internet: www.iwcoffice.org

IOM *see* **International Organization for Migration**.

Islam *see* **Muslim peoples**.

Islamic fundamentalism

An extreme interpretation of Islam which promotes *jihad* (holy war) against non-Muslims, and aims to implement strict *sharia* (Islamic) law. Since the terrorist attacks in the USA on 11 September 2001 by the fundamentalist al-Qaida group, Islamic fundamentalism has taken on a renewed political importance in **eastern Europe**. Although the small size of **Muslim** communities in the region and their largely peaceful coexistence with Christian neighbours has somewhat negated its threat, the rapid growth of Islamic fundamentalism, fuelled by Arab nationalism and the success of such Islamic states as Iran, has seen it take on an almost evangelic-revolutionary tinge. It is often linked to nationalist causes in separatist regions to further polarize the antagonists. In particular Islamic fundamentalism has influenced separatist struggles in **Chechnya** and **Dagestan**. It was also somewhat invoked during the civil war in **Bosnia and Herzegovina** in the 1990s to draw Islamic mercenaries to fight alongside fellow Muslim **Bosniaks**. However, in all cases the major motivation for conflict has been ethno-political, rather than religious.

Istiqlal *see* **Azerbaijan National Independence Party**.

Istria

A small peninsula at the northern end of the Adriatic Sea, divided politically between **Slovenia** and **Croatia**, but with the area around its principal city, **Trieste**, under the administration of adjacent Italy. While the north and interior of the peninsula are hilly and dry, the coasts provide fertile land for agricultural production. Along with cultivation and grazing, Istria also produces anthracite coal and bauxite.

The region has had a long history of conquest and domination by the various regional powers. After a reasonably prolonged period of peace under Austrian control, Istria was ceded to Italy in 1919. However, the peninsula was overrun by Allied and Yugoslav forces at the end of the Second World War, and was absorbed, bar the region around Trieste, into the newly-formed **Yugoslavia** in 1947. Tensions over sovereignty of the area, particularly the municipality of Trieste, continued for years, but did not flare up as some predicted when both Slovenia and Croatia proclaimed independence in 1991. Italians form minorities in the Istrian regions of both countries.

Istrian Democratic Assembly
Istarski Demokratski Sabor (IDS) / *Sieta Democratica Istriana* (SDI)

A centrist party representing ethnic Italians and other minorities in the Istrian region of **Croatia**. Advocating the creation of a 'trans-border' **Istria** encompassing areas of Croatia, **Slovenia** and Italy, the IDS has been especially exercised by the Croatian–Italian dispute over compensation for Italians who left **Yugoslavia** in the wake of the latter country's territorial gains after the Second World War. In the August 1992 elections to the lower house of the **Assembly**, the IDS stood as part of a regionalist front, winning four of the six seats taken by the alliance. In the February 1993 upper house elections the IDS won one elective seat and was allocated two more under the President's prerogative. In the same month it won 72% of the Istrian vote in local elections.

In the October 1995 lower house elections the IDS formed part of the centre-right United List (ZL), winning four seats within the alliance. It maintained its ZL alignment in the January 2000 Assembly elections, winning four of the ZL's 25 seats. The party subsequently joined the new Government headed by the **Social Democratic Party of Croatia** (SPH), with the IDS President becoming Minister for European Integration. However, the failure of the Government to introduce Italian as an official language in Istria prompted the IDS to withdraw from the ruling coalition in June 2001.

Leadership: Ivan Jakovčić (President).
Address: 3 Splitska, 52100 Pula.
Telephone: (52) 223316.
Fax: (52) 213702.
E-mail: ids-ssi@pu.tel.hr
Internet: www.ids-ddi.com

ITAR-TASS
Informatsionnoye Telegrafnoye Agentstvo Rossii
(Information Telegraphic Agency of Russia)

The main state news agency in the **Russian Federation**, focusing originally on the domestic market as opposed to supplying information abroad (*see* **Novosti**). ITAR-TASS traces its ancestry back to the formation in 1904 of the St Petersburg Telegraph Agency (SPTA), as the Russian Empire's official news service. In 1925 the SPTA was transformed by the **Soviet** authorities into the Telegraph Agency of the Soviet Union (TASS) and was mobilized in the Government's propaganda efforts. From 1987 it began storing its information electronically in the INFO-TASS department. In 1992, following the collapse of the Soviet Union, TASS was reorganized as an open and independent institution, and was renamed as the Information Telegraphic Agency of Russia (ITAR), although it retains the 'TASS' suffix. ITAR now has 74 offices around the Russian Federation and other **Commonwealth of Independent States** countries, and 65 further afield. It has links with most other news agencies around **eastern Europe** and many more beyond. Its photo service is the largest of its kind in the Russian Federation.

Director-General: Vitalii N. Ignatenko.
Address: Tverskoi blvd 10/12, 103009 Moscow.

Ivanić, Mladen

Telephone: (095) 2906070.
Fax: (095) 2033180.
E-mail: dms@itar-tass.com
Internet: www.itar-tass.com

Ivanić, Mladen

Prime Minister of the **Serb Republic**.

Mladen Ivanić heads the centrist **Party of Democratic Progress** (PDP). An economics professor, he was nominated as Prime Minister on 23 December 2000.

Born on 1 September 1958 in Sanski Most, in north-western **Bosnia**, he graduated in economics from the University of Banja Luka in 1981, going on to the University of Belgrade to complete a master's degree in 1984 and a doctorate in 1988. He returned to Bosnia and is a professor at the University of Banja Luka. He stood, unsuccessfully, as a moderate non-party Serb candidate in elections for the Bosnian tripartite presidency in 1996. He formed the PDP in September 1999, and it went on to perform well in elections within the Serb Republic in November 2000. After months of deliberation he was chosen to head a centrist coalition as Prime Minister from 16 January 2001. His appointment of Fuad Turalić as the first ever **Muslim** Minister for the Serb Republic was overshadowed by the nomination of seven members of the ultra-nationalist **Serbian Democratic Party** (SDS).

Address: 78000 Banja Luka.

Ivanov, Igor

Minister of Foreign Affairs, **Russian Federation**.

Igor Sergeyevich Ivanov is an independent. He has worked in the Russian diplomatic departments and Foreign Ministry since 1973. He was appointed to the Cabinet as Deputy Minister of Foreign Affairs in January 1994 and was made full Foreign Minister on 11 September 1998.

Born on 23 September 1945 in Moscow, he graduated from the State Pedagogical Institute of Foreign Languages in 1969 before starting work as a researcher at the Soviet Academy of Sciences. He was Counsellor at the Soviet Trade Agency in Madrid from 1973 and was appointed First Secretary and adviser to the Ambassador when the agency was upgraded to a full embassy in 1977. He returned to the Soviet Union in 1983, working on European affairs in the Ministry of Foreign Affairs. In 1986 he was made a Deputy Chief of the Ministry's General Secretariat and was promoted to head the executive body three years later. In 1991, in the last days of the Soviet Union, he was sent back to Spain, this time as Ambassador, and remained in this capacity on behalf of the newly-formed Russian Federation. He was recalled to Russia in December 1993 and was appointed Deputy Foreign Minister. He was elevated to full Minister in September 1998 in one of President Boris

Yeltsin's frequent cabinet changes. Despite the turbulent politics of the Yeltsin era, he was one of the few survivors in the subsequent reshuffles and was retained in post by President Vladimir **Putin** in 2000.

Address: Ministry of Foreign Affairs, Smolenskaya-Sennaya pl. 32/34, 121200 Moscow.
Telephone: (095) 2443448.
Fax: (095) 9243233.
Internet: www.mid.ru

IWC *see* **International Whaling Commission**.

IWSG *see* **Industry Will Save Georgia**.

Izetbegović, Alija

Former President of **Bosnia and Herzegovina**, holding that post for 15 months before the country's 1992 declaration of independence amidst the disintegration of the **Socialist Federal Republic of Yugoslavia**, and throughout the Bosnian conflict of 1992–95, when he was, in practice, the leader only of the **Bosniaks** (Bosnian Muslims).

Alija Izetbegović was born on 8 August 1925 in Bosanski Samac in northern Bosnia. He studied law in **Sarajevo**, but was sent to prison for three years by the post-war communist Government of Yugoslavia in 1946 when his writing for a Muslim newspaper was denounced as pan-Islamic activity. After his release he completed his studies and worked as a legal consultant. An 'Islamic declaration' which he published in the late 1970s led to his arrest once again in 1983 and a conviction for disseminating Islamic propaganda. He had served five years of his 14-year sentence when he was released in 1988. In May 1990 he founded the **Party of Democratic Action** (SDA), a Muslim nationalist organization which became the largest party in the Bosnian Republic's legislature in the November 1990 elections. He was elected to the seven-member republican collective presidency, and chosen in December as its President. For most of the next 15 months he sought some formula for Bosnia to remain a multi-ethnic Republic in a wider Yugoslav context. However, the March 1992 referendum on Bosnian independence was boycotted by **Serbs**, while both Bosnian Muslims and Bosnian **Croats** voted heavily in favour. Left with little option but to declare independence, Izetbegović then saw the State of which he was President torn three ways by civil war.

Izetbegović stood down as SDA President in December 1992, trying to show that the State President could stand apart from ethnically-based politics, but he resumed the party leadership in March 1994. Throughout three years of bitter fighting he insisted repeatedly that his position be respected as the lawful Head of

State, rather than as leader of one of the warring parties. In reality, however, he commanded the allegiance only of the Muslim community, even this being challenged at one stage by his old rival in the north-west, Fikret Abdić.

Izetbegović was a signatory of the eventual **Dayton Agreement** in November 1995, under which the fighting was halted after **NATO** intervention, and the task of rebuilding national institutions resumed. This opened the way for elections on 14 September 1996 for the various state institutions, including the three-member collective presidency. Izetbegović topped the poll for the Bosniak (Muslim) representative by a huge margin, winning 80% of the vote against seven other candidates. Despite a recent history of heart problems, he was formally sworn in on 5 October 1996 to take the first two-year term as Chairman of the Presidency, at a ceremony boycotted by the Bosnian Serbs. He remained in office (with a further period as President of the Presidency under the revolving formula) until October 2000.

J

Jaanilinn question

A border dispute between **Estonia** and the **Russian Federation** over the division by their Soviet-era border of the historic town of **Narva**. The town itself is divided by the River Narva which, from 1945, came to serve as the border between the two countries, leaving the eastern Jaanilinn—in Russian, Ivangorod—district of the town in the Leningrad (**St Petersburg**) Oblast. The incorporation of Estonia into the **Soviet Union** made this distinction somewhat arbitrary and the two halves of the town continued to interact as one. In particular, factories in Narva employed almost half of the residents of Jaanilinn. In this way the district acted to draw Russian migrants into eastern Estonia, in line with Soviet efforts to reduce the ethnic homogeneity of its constituent republics.

With the collapse of the Soviet Union in 1991 and the independence of Estonia that summer, the question of the sovereignty of Jaanilinn was raised. However, the town is inhabited by an overwhelming ethnic **Russian** majority, negating Estonian claims to the suburb. The dispute has been muted since initial attempts to redraw the border were resolved in 1995 with grudging recognition of the Soviet-era division.

Jakeš, Miloš

A major figure in the hardline post-1968 communist regime in **Czechoslovakia** until its overthrow in the '**velvet revolution**' of November–December 1989. Born in 1922, Jakeš was a friend and contemporary of Alexander **Dubček** from the 1950s, when both had attended the Higher Party School in Moscow. He joined the Dubček reform communist leadership in March 1968 as Chairman of the Central Control and Auditing Commission of the Communist Party of Czechoslovakia (KSČ), but turned against the '**Prague Spring**' experiment, under Soviet pressure, and after the **Warsaw Pact** invasion he became, with Gustáv **Husák**, one of the key leaders of the repressive Soviet-inspired process of 'normalization'. In December 1987 Jakeš succeeded Husák as Party General Secretary. Jakeš' harsh rule made him the most despised of the communist leaders. His resignation on

24 November 1989 was received ecstatically by pro-democracy demonstrators. The KSČ expelled him on 7 December, and he was subsequently detained for criminal investigation. Over a decade later, however, in 2001, prosecutors finally succeeded in bringing charges against him and two fellow members of the 1968 Government. They were accused of signing the document which invited the Warsaw Pact armies into Czechoslovakia, the first time anyone had been brought to trial over this key event in the history of **east European** communist rule. Jakeš was indicted on the charge of treason on 19 December 2001.

Jaruzelski, Gen. Wojciech

The last leader of communist-era **Poland**. Jaruzelski was Head of both Government and party from the time of the regime's crisis in dealing with the **Solidarity** movement in 1981, until the partially free elections of mid-1989. He was born in 1923 in a minor aristocratic family, in part of eastern Poland which was annexed by the **Soviet Union** in 1939. After fighting the Nazis with the Polish Army in the Soviet Union in 1943–45, he combined his post-war military career with party and government posts, becoming Defence Minister in 1968 and gaining a place two years later on the Politburo of the ruling Polish United Workers' Party (PZPR). Named Prime Minister in February 1981, he also took over as PZPR First Secretary in October. His decision to introduce martial law in December 1981, for which his opponents would never forgive him, was an act he always insisted was justified as the only way of averting a Soviet invasion to crush the Solidarity movement. In November 1985 he took the post of President, while remaining party First Secretary. When he took the party into round-table negotiations in 1989, to work out **eastern Europe**'s first pluralist system, the gamble did not succeed for the PZPR, which was comprehensively rejected by the electorate at the June 1989 partially free parliamentary elections. He himself, however, stood for the restyled post of President and was narrowly elected by the parliament, thanks to key Solidarity votes cast in his favour for the sake of stability. As President, Jaruzelski briefly enjoyed high approval ratings, peaking at 74% in September 1989, as measured by opinion polls. Accepting ultimately that he would always symbolize the old regime, and taking note of the revolutionary changes across eastern Europe, Jaruzelski was persuaded within little over a year to step down and make way for the direct election of his successor, Lech **Wałęsa**. Efforts to have him brought to trial over the imposition of martial law proved inconclusive, although it was deemed a criminal act by the legislature in 1992. Another case against him, however, did eventually come to trial in 2001, after repeated postponements owing to his ill health. He was charged with ordering troops to fire on striking shipyard workers in **Gdańsk** in December 1970 (while he was Defence Minister), suppressing the protest at the cost of at least 44 lives.

Javakheti

A predominantly **Armenian** enclave in south-western **Georgia** bordering **Armenia** and adjoining **Meskheti**. Situated high up in the Lesser Caucasus mountains, Javakheti has a harsh climate which has earned it the nickname 'Georgia's **Siberia**'. Tensions between the 90% Armenian population (around 200,000) and the Georgian Government have so far not escalated into armed conflict. The Armenian nationalists (represented by the Javakhk movement) stop short of separatism, pressing instead for greater autonomy within Georgia. Conflict is also kept at bay by the Georgian authority's fear of sparking another major conflagration (as in **Abkhazia**, where an Armenian minority sided with the separatists, and in South **Ossetia**), and the Armenian Government's reluctance to be drawn into another situation like that in **Nagorno-Karabakh**. The existence of **Russian** military bases is another factor in the security equation. However, the possibility of a future conflict is high, as demands for autonomy remain largely unanswered and Armenian militia such as the *Parvents* are well armed and experienced from combat in Nagorno-Karabakh.

Javakheti's infrastructure is poor. A lack of Soviet-era investment, along what was then its heavily-restricted border with Turkey, has been exacerbated by economic difficulties in Georgia and the absence of effective Georgian administration. However, unemployment is officially low. Much commerce is generated by the presence of the Russian military bases.

Jehovah's Witnesses

A religion based on Christianity with some 500,000 adherents in **eastern Europe**. Founded in the USA in the late 19th century, it has been spread across the world by 'publishers', who are encouraged to canvass their neighbours door-to-door. The largest communities in eastern Europe are found in **Poland** (125,000), the **Russian Federation** (114,000) and **Ukraine** (113,000). Jehovah's Witnesses believe in a strict interpretation of the Bible, and the essential humanity of Jesus Christ, and they reject the symbol of the cross. Their religion, which isolates its followers from other religious groups, is often vilified by mainstream Christian denominations as a cult. One of its greatest areas of conflict with modern states is its prohibition on members fulfilling military service. In countries where there is no civilian alternative to the draft, Jehovah's Witnesses often end up being prosecuted. The situation is particularly severe in **Armenia** and **Belarus**, where prison sentences with hard labour are often passed on Jehovah's Witnesses who conscientiously object to enforced military service, and where the religion has been refused official registration.

Jews

A religious group once found in large communities in many parts of **eastern Europe**, including especially **Belarus, Poland** and regions of **European Russia,** but now greatly reduced in numbers as a result of the Second World War, the Holocaust and large-scale emigration. **Eastern Europe** was home to the greatest proportion of the world's Jews for many centuries. Sidelined by mainstream society for their religion, Jews often took up industries deemed unfit for Christians, such as money-lending, and promoted their own educational institutions through close-knit communities. Their successes bred resentment and they were the targets of various attacks, early instances of which were the Crusades which began in the 11th century. Antisemitism is now officially condemned but low-level discrimination continues across the region, with Jews particularly targeted by far-right nationalist groups.

Most of the Jews from eastern Europe are known as *Ashkenazi*. The Yiddish language, widely spoken among *Ashkenazi* Jews, is a hybrid of Hebrew and German. Jewish communities in **Bulgaria,** however, tend to be *Sephardic*, i.e. Hispanic, in origin. All of **Albania**'s 300 Sephardic Jews migrated on invitation of the Israeli Government in 1990–91.

The liberalization of the **Soviet Union** from the 1980s opened up a new mass migration of Jews to Israel. Between 1989 and 1998 over 768,000 Jews made *aliyah* (migrated to Israel) from the former Soviet Union, with 375,000 departing in 1990–91 alone. Today the largest populations of Jews in eastern Europe are found in urban centres in the **Russian Federation** (around 500,000) and among the ethnic **Russian** communities in **Ukraine** (c.240,000, down from 486,000 in 1989). A few thousand remain on Russia's border with China in the far east of **Siberia**, where a special Jewish Autonomous *Oblast* (AO) was established in the Soviet era, although very few Jews ever migrated there.

JKP *see* **New Christian Party**.

John Paul II, Pope

The first Polish pope in history, in office since 1978 (s*ee* **Roman Catholic Church**).

Born Karol Jozef Wojtyła on 18 May 1920 in Wadowice, the son of an army officer, he was reputedly active in Christian underground wartime activities, and was ordained to the priesthood on 1 November 1946. Gaining a reputation as a theologian with conservative views on marriage, he rose to become Archbishop of Kraków in 1964 and a Cardinal in June 1967. He was elected as Pope on 16 October 1978. He was treated by many in his native **Poland** as a symbol of freedom against the power of the communist state, and his visits to Poland in the ensuing years accordingly took on a special significance. He has become better known worldwide than any of his predecessors, making over 80 foreign trips and clearly revelling in the acclamation he receives. Retaining his conservative orientation on Catholic moral doctrine, he has sought to stem the growing acceptance of more liberal ideas on such issues as birth control, abortion, homosexuality and the ordination of women. A convinced anti-communist, he has nevertheless also developed in recent years a critique of global capitalism and the operation of the free market, concerned that it fails to guarantee the global good and the exercise of economic and social rights.

JUL *see* **Yugoslav United Left**.

Justice and Accord Bloc
Iravunk yev Miabanutyun (IeM)

A left-wing political alliance in **Armenia** created in March 1998 by seven nationalist parties to back the candidacy of Robert **Kocharian** (non-party) in that month's presidential elections. Following Kocharian's victory, however, the IeM was reduced to, principally, National Accord (*Miabanutyun*) led by Artashes Geghamian and the small Union of Constitutional Rights (*Sahmanadrakan Iravunqi Miutyun*, SIM). In the May 1999 **National Assembly** elections the bloc achieved third place in the proportional section with just under 8% of the vote and fourth place overall with six seats out of 131.

After the 1999 elections Geghamian became increasingly critical of successive Governments headed by the centre-right **Republican Party of Armenia**. At a Miabanutyun congress in May 2000 Geghamian argued that much greater state involvement was needed to overcome Armenia's economic crisis (*see* **Armenia, economy**). In September 2000 Geghamian launched a national campaign for new elections, but received little support from the SIM.

Leadership: Artashes Geghamian (Chair.).
Address: 50A Eznik Koghbatsi Street, Yerevan.
Telephone: (1) 532725.
Fax: (1) 532676.

K

Kabardino-Balkaria

A constituent republic of the **Russian Federation**, formed by the amalgamation of the autonomous regions of the Caucasian Kabards and the **Turkic** Balkars. Situated in the centre of the north **Caucasus region**, in the extreme south of **European Russia**, the republic extends from the peaks of the Greater Caucasus mountains down to the Kabardin plain and the Terek river system. *Population*: 753,531 (1997 estimate).

The Kabards, considered closely related to the **Cherkess** and speaking a language similar to that of the **Abaza** and **Abkhaz**, were one of the last in the north Caucasus to convert to Islam. They allied themselves to the Terek **Cossacks** as early as 1557, which drew their allegiance north to Russia. The Balkars, traditionally concentrated in the mountains and more closely related to the neighbouring Karachai, long resisted **Russian** domination. Both peoples were absorbed into the Russian Empire in the 19th century and were lumped together by the **Soviet** authorities in 1922, first in the Kabardino-Balkar autonomous *oblast* (region), and then in 1936, in a full republic.

The Balkars were persecuted like many other Caucasian peoples during the Second World War after being accused of collaborating with the Germans. Stalin had them deported *en masse* to central Asia and **Siberia** in 1944 (*see* **Deported Nationalities**). Balkaria was reorganized as part of the Georgian republic until the Balkars were politically rehabilitated in 1956 and returned from exile. However, although the Kabardino-Balkar republic was reconstituted the Balkars were prevented from settling in their original homeland and were scattered throughout the republic. This dispersal caused ethnic tensions later when the republic declared its sovereignty within the Russian Federation in March 1992.

The Balkars have pressed for the return of confiscated property and the restitution of a separate Balkar region. A referendum in December 1991 confirmed the desire to form a Balkar republic and for 13 days in November 1996 Balkaria declared itself independent from Kabardinia. Although the move failed there are residual calls to redivide Kabardino-Balkaria and neighbouring Karachai-Cherkessia into more ethnically homogenous Kabardino-Cherkessian and Karachai-Balkarian entities.

Economic activity is focused on mining of heavy metals and gold. Agriculture is confined mostly to the Kabardin plain and light manufacturing is concentrated in the capital, Nalchik, and the second city, Prokhladny. Valery Mukhamedovich Kokov has been President since January 1992, and was Chair of the republic's Supreme Soviet from March 1990.

Kádár, János

Leading figure in communist-era **Hungary**, First Secretary of the party for over three decades (1956–88) and the dominant figure of what became known as the 'Kádár era'. Born in 1912, he was active in clandestine communist youth movements and as a wartime resistance leader, and emerged after the liberation as Party Secretary in **Budapest**. In 1948–50 he was Minister of the Interior. In the party's factional disputes he turned against his close friend László Rajk, who was executed in 1949, but was himself purged in turn in 1950, and then imprisoned from 1951 to 1954. Rehabilitated in 1954, he was soon identified with Imre **Nagy** and the reformism of 1956, but swiftly changed horses when Soviet troops moved to crush the Hungarian uprising. The Soviet authorities left Kádár in charge—as Prime Minister (1956–58) as well as party leader—of pursuing the repressive process of 'normalization'. In the 1960s Kádár launched a new experiment: 'whoever is not against us is with us' on the ideological front, and the 'new economic mechanism' (introduced in 1968) which encouraged a 'regulated market' to deliver material benefits which would win public support. It was only in the 1980s, when Hungary's economic situation deteriorated, that Kádár came seriously under challenge, and he became entrenched in a sterile defensiveness against calls for 'reform of the reform'. The May 1988 party conference provided the occasion for the reformers to oust him, designating him as President of the party but without a Politburo seat. Seriously ill, he died in hospital on 6 July 1989.

Kaliningrad

A city and **Russian** enclave in the south-western corner of the Baltic Sea. *Population*: 886,900 (1991 estimate). The Kaliningrad *oblast* (region), roughly rectangular in shape, extends 88 miles (140 km) inland from the city of the same name. It was formed from the northern half of the **German** territory of East **Prussia,** which had been occupied by advancing Soviet troops at the end of the Second World War (1945). Bordering **Poland** to the south, it is separated from the rest of the Russian Federation by territory belonging to **Lithuania** (which borders Kaliningrad to the north and east) and by the entire width of **Belarus**.

Germanized since the era of the mediaeval Teutonic Order, the region around the city of Königsberg (literally 'king's mountain'), the administrative capital of East Prussia, was the centre for the reawakening of German nationalism during the Napoleonic Wars. It was incorporated into the Prussian-dominated unified Germany in 1871. It experienced 20 years as a German enclave from 1919 to 1939, cut off from the rest of Germany by Polish territory under the territorial settlement imposed on defeated Germany at the end of the First World War (*see* Treaty of **Versailles**). Rejoined to Germany by the Nazi military advance eastwards in the Second World War, East Prussia was then split in two by the **Potsdam Agreements** in 1945. The northern half was annexed to Russia and the southern half ceded to the reorganized state of Poland, while the German population left to seek new homes in the rump Germany. For the next 46 years Kaliningrad was merely the edge of the vast **Soviet Union**, abutting only Soviet-dominated eastern Europe and repopulated with Russian colonists.

The collapse of the Soviet Union and the emergence of independent **Baltic states** in 1991 turned administrative isolation into a real political distance. With the admission of Poland into the **North Atlantic Treaty Organization** in 1999, Lithuania's stated intention to follow suit, and the inclusion of both in the next wave of potential **European Union** (EU) member states, Kaliningrad's position has become of even greater diplomatic significance. Civil authorities in the *oblast* have toyed with and ultimately rejected independence from Russia, but have been forced to take a decidedly more Western view than their masters in Moscow, calling for EU investment to help solve their dire socio-economic problems. Kaliningrad was made a free economic zone soon after the fall of the Soviet Union, with the intention of creating a 'Baltic Hong Kong'. However, prosperity has been elusive and unemployment, violence, poverty and environmental degradation have set in. In early 2001 rumours of the Russian Federation's intention of using the *oblast* as a base for nuclear missiles caused uproar among its neighbours. There has also been friction over the freedom of movement from Kaliningrad to Russia proper. The introduction of border checks and visa requirements by Lithuania and Poland seriously strained regional relations. A new rail line bypassing Lithuania altogether was proposed in 2001.

The city of Kaliningrad is home to almost half of the *oblast*'s population— 408,100 (1991 estimate). Built on the ruined north-western suburbs of Königsberg, Kaliningrad underwent heavy industrialization under Soviet rule and economic activity now centres on engineering and metalworking, although the traditional amber industry is still active. For their size the city and *oblast* provide a large amount of the Russian Federation's industrial output—around 0.3%—and draw a similar proportion of aid.

Kallas, Siim

Minister of Finance, **Estonia**.

Siim Kallas is Chairman of the **Estonian Reform Party** (ER) and a career economist. After four years as the President of the **Bank of Estonia** he first entered the Cabinet as Foreign Minister in 1995. He was appointed Finance Minister on 25 March 1999.

Born in **Tallinn** on 2 October 1948, in what was then the Estonian Soviet Socialist Republic, he graduated in economics from the Tartu State University in 1972. After postgraduate studies he entered the Estonian Soviet Finance Ministry in 1975 and was made Director of the Estonian Central Board of Savings Banks in 1979. He supported the growing Estonian pro-democracy movement as Deputy Editor of the *Rahva Hääl* (People's Voice) newspaper from 1986 to 1989. Following the country's independence from the **Soviet Union** in 1991 he was appointed President of the Bank of Estonia. He served as Foreign Minister from 1995 to 1996 and founded and led the ER in the **State Assembly** from 1995. He was appointed Finance Minister by Prime Minister Mart **Laar** on 30 March 1999.

Siim Kallas married Kristi Kartus, now a doctor, in 1972, and they have one son and one daughter.

Address: Ministry of Finance, Suur-Ameerika 1, Tallinn 15006.
Telephone: 6113558.
Fax: 6966810.
E-mail: info@fin.ee
Internet: www.fin.ee

Kalmykia

A constituent republic in south-western **European Russia**, formally known as Kalmykia-Khalmg-Tangch, which stretches southwards to a small shoreline on the Caspian Sea. It has an arm of territory that extends west towards Stavropol along the ancient salt beds that once linked the Caspian and Black Seas. It is unique as the only **Buddhist** state in Europe. *Population*: 322,579 (1996 estimate).

Absorbed into the **Russian** Empire after the collapse of the khanate of Astrakhan in 1556, the region was inhabited in the early 17th century by the Kalmyks, a nomadic, ethnically Mongolian people who had migrated westwards from what is now Xinjiang province in China. Welcomed by Peter the Great and given Russian citizenship, they established a Kalmyk khanate in the region under the aegis of the Tsar. This kingdom stretched from Stavropol to Astrakhan. However, incursions on Kalmyk lands by Russian and **German** colonists prompted a mass exodus back to Mongolia in 1771. Some fled west and joined the Don **Cossacks**.

With the fall of the Tsarist state a Kalmyk *oblast* (region) was established in 1920 and converted to a full republic in 1936. However, the Kalmyks suffered greatly at the hands of Stalin. They were forced to abandon their nomadic lifestyle for collective farms and industrialized cities, while Buddhist preachers were persecuted and temples destroyed. With the outbreak of the Second World War Stalin accused them of collaborating with their ethnic German neighbours and had all Kalmyks deported *en masse* to **Siberia** in 1943 (*see* **Deported Nationalities**).

A fifth of the deportees are thought to have died on the way and in exile. The end of wholesale Stalinist repression after the dictator's death in 1956 enabled the rehabilitation of the Kalmyks in 1957 and a Kalmyk republic was reinstated. The population did not recover in numbers until 1970.

Perestroika in the late 1980s encouraged Kalmyk political parties to form and a Declaration of Sovereignty was adopted by the authorities in the capital, Elista, in 1990. The modern Republic of Kalmykia-Khalmg-Tangeh was declared on 31 March. Claims have been made for the return of the territory ceded to neighbouring regions after 1943. The charismatic Kirsan Nikolayevich Ilyumzhinov has been President since April 1993. Opposition parties aim to block his quest for a third term in 2002 but face stiff and often violent action by the state authorities.

The Kalmyks are most closely related to the western, *Oyrat* Mongols. As well as a Mongolian language, transcribed using the **Cyrillic alphabet** since 1938, the original Kalmyk settlers also brought with them the Buddhist faith. Adherence to the Tibetan creed is widespread and Kalmyk culture remains devoted to the Dalai Lama, who dispatched Telo Rinpoche, a US-educated Kalmyk held to be the reincarnation of an Indian holy man, to serve as the Kalmyk *Shaddin* (High) Lama.

Karachai-Cherkessia

A constituent republic of the **Russian Federation** situated in the north-west **Caucasus region**. *Population*: 414,970 (1997 estimate). The region came under Russian imperial rule in the 19th century. The republic is dominated by two ethnically dissimilar peoples, the **Turkic** Karachai and the Caucasian **Cherkess**. The Karachai are most closely related to the neighbouring Balkars (*see* **Kabardino-Balkaria**) and suffered deportation at the hands of Stalin in 1944 (*see* **deported nationalities**).

Briefly a part of the abortive Mountain People's Republic in 1921, the Karachai-Cherkess autonomous *oblast* (region) was first created in 1922. The two peoples were given their own administrative regions in 1924, but the whole *oblast* was abolished and incorporated into **Georgia** following the deportation of the Karachai in 1944. It was reconstituted in 1957 when the Karachai were rehabilitated under First Secretary Nikita Khrushchev. In 1990 the *oblast* was upgraded to a full republic and on 31 March 1992 a sovereign republic was declared. Vladimir Semyonev has been head of the republic's Executive Committee since 14 September 1999.

While the Karachai have called for the return of land and property confiscated in 1944, and for possible union with the Balkars, the Cherkess have led the way for calls to reunify the Circassian people (Cherkess, **Adygei** and Kabards). Tensions between Karachai and Cherkess, however, have been kept to a minimum. Relations with the republic's minority **Cossack** community, on the other hand, have been tense. In February 1991 the Zelenchuk-Urup *okrug* (district) was established in the predominantly Cossack areas.

Karadžić, Radovan

Former **Serb** leader during the 1992–95 war in **Bosnia and Herzegovina**, now wanted to face war crimes charges at the **International Criminal Tribunal for the former Yugoslavia**.

Radovan Karadžić was born on 19 June 1945 in the village of Petnjica in Montenegro. His father fought with the **Chetniks** against the wartime Nazi occupation and against **Tito**'s Partisans, the rival communist resistance movement, and later served a prison sentence under the Tito regime for these activities. When Radovan Karadžić was 15, the family moved to **Sarajevo**, where he was a university student in the 1960s, studying medicine and psychiatry, writing poetry, and doing a one-year placement at Columbia University, New York. After qualifying as a psychiatrist he worked in various Sarajevo hospitals, but spent several months in prison in the mid-1980s on charges related to alleged involvement in corruption rackets such as selling prescriptions and false medical certificates and misusing government materials and funds.

In 1990, as the **Socialist Federal Republic of Yugoslavia** (SFRY) moved towards multi-party elections along increasingly nationalistic lines, Karadžić entered politics, cofounding the radical Serb nationalist **Serbian Democratic Party** (SDS) of which he was elected President. The SDS won 72 seats in November–December 1990 in a reorganized 240-seat Assembly in Bosnia and Herzegovina, when the ruling communists were heavily defeated.

With the SFRY fast fragmenting, Karadžić opposed the creation of an independent Bosnia and Herzegovina, in which ethnic Serbs would be outnumbered. Allying himself closely at this stage with Serbian President Slobodan **Milošević**, he successfully urged Bosnian Serb voters to boycott the referendum on independence, held in February–March 1992, and warned **Bosniaks** (Bosnian Muslims) the following month that a declaration of Bosnian sovereignty could result in their annihilation. With the outbreak of war he moved the Bosnian Serb administration to Pale and in December 1992 was elected President of the self-proclaimed **Serb Republic** of Bosnia and Herzegovina, or Republika Srpska.

The Bosnian Serb army held the upper hand until the latter stages of the 1992–95 war, conducting a brutal campaign and committing atrocities which led to Karadžić and others being charged with war crimes. Although he attended a series of abortive peace negotiations in London, Geneva and New York, pretending a willingness to negotiate, he was never prepared to deliver any settlement in practice, until the **Croatian** offensive of mid-1995 turned the military tide decisively against the Serbs. Remaining obdurate under growing international pressure even when Milošević had begun to want a settlement, Karadžić was strongly critical of the late-1995 **Dayton Agreement**. Unable to attend the Dayton talks himself because of the war crimes indictment issued against him in July 1995, he eventually had no choice but to accept the accord under pressure from Milošević.

The indictment against Karadžić related to the crime of genocide, crimes against humanity, and crimes against the civilian population and places of worship throughout Bosnia and Herzegovina between April 1992 and July 1995. In particular they relate to the unlawful detention, murder, rape, sexual assault, torture, beating, robbery and inhumane treatment of thousands of Bosniak and Bosnian Croat civilians, as part of a programme of '**ethnic cleansing**', the killing of civilians in sniper attacks during the siege of Sarajevo and other towns, and the taking as hostages of UN peacekeepers in mid-1995. In November 1995 he was further indicted over the mass killings of Bosniaks after Bosnian Serb forces overran the so-called 'safe area' of **Srebrenica** in July that year.

In July 1996, as stipulated by the Dayton Agreement, Karadžić was obliged formally to resign as Bosnian Serb leader and was replaced by his deputy and former ally, Biljana Plavšić. He also resigned as President of the SDS, although he continued to play an influential role behind the scenes, and to be regarded as a symbol of resistance by many Bosnian Serbs resentful of the Dayton settlement. An international warrant for his arrest was issued in July 1996, but despite the offer of a large bounty for his capture, he remained at large as of the end of 2001, believed to be somewhere in hiding in the Pale area in the Serb Republic.

Karelia question

A long-dormant territorial dispute between the **Russian Federation** and Finland, stemming from the annexation of the western half of Karelia by the **Soviet Union** in 1940. Historically Karelia comprises the lands to the east of southern Finland, east of the Gulf of Finland and around the north of Lake Ladoga. As a modern Russian region it also encompasses much of the land to the north of this region as well.

The basis for the Finnish claim to the lands is partly the presence of the Karelians—ethnic Finns (a **Finno-Ugric people**) who converted to **Orthodox Christianity** and have been greatly russified in society and language. There are approximately 125,000 in the Karelian Republic. The political part of the claim relates to western Karelia and was established from the 14th century. At this time the west fell under Swedish rule and was joined to Finland, while the east came under Russian dominion. The two halves were both under Russian suzerainty from 1721 but remained seperate administrative regions, even when the whole of Finland was annexed by the Russian Empire in 1809 and ruled as a Grand Duchy including western Karelia. This political situation was then formalized in 1917 when Finland became an independent country, recognized in 1920 by the new communist authorities in Russia.

Russia's claim to western Karelia was laid down in 1940 when, after the Russo-Finnish 'Winter War', the region was absorbed into the Soviet Union and the border redrawn to reflect the Soviet military victory. A Karelian ASSR was created in 1956. On the collapse of centralized communist rule in the Soviet Union in 1990, Karelia was the first region to declare its sovereignty and is now an integral republic in the Russian Federation. Sergei Katanandov has been Head of the Karelian Republic since May 1998.

Under the firm yoke of Soviet rule and during the nervous diplomacy of the **Cold War**, the Karelia question was effectively buried. However, the post-1991 era released aspirations from sections of the minority Karelian population, and elements of the Finnish right, to return to the pre-1940 border. Some extremists even called for the full annexation by Finland of the whole Karelian Republic. In December 1991, however, the Finnish authorities officially relinquished their claim to any part of Karelia.

Kasyanov, Mikhail

Chairman of the Government (Prime Minister) of the **Russian Federation** since 17 May 2000, and before that the Minister of Finance who played a major part in negotiating a crucial debt write-off deal. A political independent, he spent nine years in the Soviet era in the economic planning agency, Gosplan, and worked in government (in the Economics Ministry and then the Finance Ministry) throughout the 1990s.

Mikhail Mikhailovich Kasyanov was born in Solntsevo, near Moscow, on 8 December 1957. After service in the army from 1976 to 1978, he became Senior Technician and Engineer at the Soviet Research Institute of Industrial Transport, then joined Gosplan in 1981 and completed his education while working there. In 1990 he transferred to the new Russian Economics Ministry before crossing over to the Finance Ministry in 1993. He quickly worked his way up to become Deputy Minister, then First Deputy Minister before being appointed to the Cabinet as Minister for Finance in May 1999. Following President Boris **Yeltsin**'s dramatic resignation on 31 December 1999, he was promoted to Deputy Chairman of the Council of Ministers, effectively heading the Government since the titular Chairman, Vladimir **Putin**, was serving as Interim President. Kasyanov also maintained his position as Minister of Finance, and in February 2000 achieved his greatest triumph when he successfully negotiated with the 'London Club' of private international investors to overhaul Russia's Soviet-era debts, getting US $10,000m. written off entirely. For this achievement he has become known as 'Mr Debt'.

He was appointed Chairman of the Government just 10 days after Putin's inauguration as President in May 2000. He has faced increasing opposition in the **Duma** over his sometimes unsuccessful attempts to further reduce the country's debts, and the **Communist Party of the Russian Federation** has led calls for his resignation amidst persistent rumours that he would be a prominent victim of Putin's first cabinet reshuffle.

Address: Office of Government (Prime Minister), Krasnopresnenskaya 2, Moscow.
Telephone: (095) 9253581.

Kavan, Jan

Fax: (095) 2054219.
Internet: www.gov.ru

Kavan, Jan

Deputy Prime Minister and Minister of Foreign Affairs, **Czech Republic**.

Jan Michael Kavan is a respected writer and political activist, and a leading member of the **Czech Social Democratic Party** (ČSSD). Having spent 20 years in exile in the UK, he returned to **Czechoslovakia** in 1989 and was elected to the Federal Assembly in 1990. Elected a Senator in 1996, he was appointed Foreign Minister in June 1998 and Deputy Prime Minister in December 1999.

Born in London on 17 October 1946, he was the son of a Czech diplomat and an English schoolteacher, giving him the dual citizenship which enabled him to escape communist persecution in later life. His family returned to **Prague** in 1950 and he established himself as a prominent pro-democracy student activist in the 1960s. He was expelled from Charles University in 1968 by the reactionary Government installed after the crushing of that year's '**Prague Spring**'. He fled to the UK in 1969 and began studying international relations at the London School of Economics. After further study at other UK universities he began a career as an outspoken journalist and active supporter of pro-democracy movements, most notably the **Charter 77** group. He was a member of the British Labour Party from 1982 to 1990. He returned to Prague in November 1989 to participate in the '**velvet revolution**' and joined the **Civic Forum** (OF). He was a member of the Czechoslovak Federal Assembly in the early 1990s, where he aligned himself with social democrats, and he joined the ČSSD in 1993. In 1996 he was acquitted of charges of collaborating with the communist authorities in the 1960s, and later that year won election to the Czech Senate (upper house of **Parliament**). Prime Minister Miloš **Zeman** appointed him to his Cabinet as Foreign Minister in June 1998 and he was promoted to Deputy Prime Minister for Foreign and Security Policy in December 1999.

Jan Kavan married Lenka Mázlová in 1991 and they have one son and three daughters.

Address: Ministry of Foreign Affairs, Loretánské nám. 5, 11800 Prague 1.
Telephone: (2) 24181111.
Fax: (2) 24310017.
Internet: www.czech.cz

Kazakhs

A **Turkic** people dominant in Kazakhstan and forming a small minority of around 600,000 within the **Russian Federation**. The nomadic Kazakhs came under Russian dominion in the 19th century, at the same time that they adopted Islam. Once within the Russian Empire, and particularly the **Soviet Union**, some Kazakhs migrated into Russia in search of work, having been forced to abandon their nomadic lifestyle for collectivization and industrialization.

At the collapse of the Soviet Union in 1991 and the creation of an independent Kazakhstan, the Russian Federation effectively abandoned its Kazakh minority. Leaving it for their own homeland, Kazakhstan, to look after their cultural and linguistic needs, the Russian state has been in no hurry to provide education in Kazakh or support for Kazakh cultural aspirations and the community is expected to fund its own programmes. Caught in this situation many Kazakhs have migrated to Kazakhstan, although this has in no way matched the exodus of ethnic **Russians** from Kazakhstan.

KDU–ČSL see **Christian Democratic Union–Czechoslovak People's Party**.

KEL see **Euro-Left Coalition**.

KFOR
(Kosovo Force)

A UN-mandated multinational peacekeeping force, led by the **North Atlantic Treaty Organization** (NATO), which maintains security in **Kosovo**. KFOR entered the Yugoslav province of Kosovo on 12 June 1999 following the successful conclusion of NATO's bombing campaign against **Yugoslavia** under the terms of UN Resolution 1244. Dividing the province into five sectors controlled by Italian, French, British, US and, later, non-NATO **Russian** troops, KFOR oversees the military aspects of the enforced peace in Kosovo and protects the UN administration there (UNMIK). At full strength KFOR totals 50,000 personnel drawn from over 30 countries including obviously many non-NATO countries. Although sectors are effectively run by the five original forces, all troops obey a single command structure, headed by French Lt-Gen. Marcel Valentin since 3 October 2001.

Address: Priština, Kosovo.
E-mail: pio@main.kfor.nato.int
Internet: www.nato.int/kfor

KGB see **Federal Security Service**.

Khachatrian, Vartan

Minister of Finance and Economy, **Armenia**. Vartan Khachatrian has no official party affiliation and has been a member of the Armenian Government since his appointment as Minister of Finance and Economy on 14 November 2000.

Born on 4 April 1959, in Jermuk in the south of the then Soviet Socialist Republic of Armenia, he attended the Yerevan Polytechnic Institute from 1975 to 1980 before studying as a doctoral student at the Technical University of E. Bauman in Moscow between 1982 and 1985. He went on to pursue a career as a manager in the food and water industry in Armenia. Following the country's independence in 1991, he entered the Commission of Privatization and Denationalization. He was first elected to the **National Assembly** (Azgayin Joghov) in 1995 and was re-elected in 1999. Until his appointment to the Cabinet in November 2000 he had served on various parliamentary and ministerial budget committees.

Vartan Khachatrian is married and has two children.

Address: Ministry of Finance and the Economy, Melik-Adamian St 1, 375010 Yerevan.
Telephone: (1) 527082.
Fax: (1) 523745.
E-mail: staff@mf.gov.am

Khvastow, Mikhail

Minister of Foreign Affairs, **Belarus**.

Mikhail M. Khvastow is a career diplomat and a key supporter of President Alyaksandr **Lukashenka**. He has been Foreign Minster since 27 November 2000.

Born on 27 June 1949 in the Vitebsk region of the then Belarusian Soviet Socialist Republic, he graduated from the Minsk State Institute of Foreign Languages in 1975 and began work in the Belarusian Ministry of Foreign Affairs in 1982. After 18 years in the diplomatic service—including three years spent in the USA, after Belarusian independence, at the new country's Permanent Mission to the UN and its US Embassy, and three years (from 1997 to 2000) as Belarusian Ambassador to Canada—he was recalled to Belarus to act as Presidential Assistant for Foreign Policy in August 2000. He was appointed Deputy Chairman of the Cabinet and Minister of Foreign Affairs on 27 November 2000. In a drastic cabinet resizing on 24 September 2001, following President Lukashenka's re-election, he was stripped of the deputy chairmanship but retained his position at the Ministry of Foreign Affairs. Among his chief concerns has been closer integration with the **Russian Federation**.

Mikhail Khvastow is married and has two children. He speaks fluent English and French.

Address: Ministry of Foreign Affairs, 19 Lenin St, 220030 Minsk.
Telephone: (17) 2272922.
Fax: (17) 2274521.
Internet: www.mfa.gov.by

Kiev

The capital city of **Ukraine,** situated on the Dnieper river in the northern central region of the country. *Population*: 2.7m. (2001 estimate). The city has, on and off, been an important administrative and commercial centre since the establishment of the Kievan Rus, the first **Slavic** state, in the 9th century. Kiev benefited, then as now, from its position on the north-south Dnieper, which serves as a transport link between the Black and Baltic Seas. Despite being destroyed by Mongol invaders in 1240, the city regained its importance in the 16th century as a key trading port and the centre of **Orthodox** Slavic resistance to the power of Polish Catholicism. Between 1667 and 1793 Kiev became a ward of the expanding **Russian** Empire.

Under Russian suzerainty Kiev became a flourishing cultural centre and was the focus of aspiring **Ukrainian** nationalists. Russian industrialization in the 19th century connected the city to the rest of the empire and further boosted its economy. During the 1917 revolution Kiev became, briefly, the capital of a self-declared independent Ukraine under the Menshevik rather than the Bolshevik faction. On the front line of, successively, the First World War, the Russian Civil War and the Russo-Polish War, the city was ravaged by sieges, occupation and ultimately by devastating famine. Ukrainian nationalism was then strongly suppressed by the new **Soviet** authorities and between 1920 and 1934 the Ukrainian capital was shifted to Kharkov. However, industrialization continued apace and the city's economy grew substantially under the rolling five-year plans.

During the Second World War Kiev was once again occupied by German forces. Within days of its fall in September 1941 over 30,000 **Jews**, Soviet soldiers and 'partisans' were massacred in the nearby Babi Yar ravine. Thousands more were killed in the following two years. During its capture and liberation by Soviet forces in 1943 much of the city was destroyed, and there was massive industrial reconstruction after the war ended, while Kiev was also politically rehabilitated, receiving the accolade of the Order of Lenin.

Kiev became the capital of an independent Ukraine once again in 1991. As such it is home to the **Parliament** and other central administrative institutions. Economic activity is dominated by heavy metal engineering. Other manufacturing includes machinery and engineering parts and tools. Chemical processing is also important.

Kinakh, Anatoliy

Prime Minister of **Ukraine**. Anatoliy Kyrylovych Kinakh is a supporter of President Leonid **Kuchma** and head of the pro-market Union of Industrialists and Entrepreneurs (UIE). Twice a Deputy Prime Minister in the 1990s, he was appointed Prime Minister on 29 May 2001.

Born in the northern Moldovan village of Bratushany on 4 August 1954, he graduated from the Leningrad Shipbuilding Institute in 1978. He worked as an engineer at military ship repair plants first in **Tallinn** (Estonia) and then at the Mikolaiv plant in Ukraine, where he had risen to production manager by the time he left in 1990. For two years he was a member of the **Parliament**, and was then appointed in 1992 as the President's Representative in the Mikolaiv region, heading the Regional Council from 1994. In 1995 he was appointed Deputy Prime Minister for industrial policy. His close working relationship with President Kuchma was reinforced in 1996, when he was appointed as a presidential adviser and headed a number of economic committees and councils. He re-entered the Supreme Council in March 1998 and was appointed First Deputy Prime Minister in August 1999. He served in this post until that December, during which time he also headed the pro-Kuchma **People's Democratic Party of Ukraine**. He joined the influential UIE in April 2000 and became its Chairman, a position previously held by Kuchma. His long support for the President was rewarded when he was appointed Prime Minister in May 2001.

Address: Office of the Prime Minister, M.Grushevskogo St 12/2, 252008 Kiev.
Telephone: (44) 2262289.
Fax: (44) 2932093.
E-mail: web@kmu.gov.ua
Internet: www.kmu.gov.ua

KKP *see* **Conservative Christian Party**.

Klaipeda

A port in the centre of **Lithuania**'s **Baltic** coast, formerly the East Prussian city of Memel. *Population*: 199,000 (1997 estimate). The original **Lithuanian** settlement was occupied by the Germanic Teutonic Knights in 1252 and became the base for their colonization of the Baltic region. Developed as a vitally important ice-free port, the city of Memel was inherited by the **Prussian** state and ultimately the newly-formed German state in 1871. After Germany's defeat in the First World War the region was made a ward of the League of Nations before being handed to the new state of Lithuania and renamed Klaipeda in 1923.

The city's German history made it a prime target for the irredentism of the Nazi regime and between 1939 and 1945 it was returned to German rule. Since the end of the Second World War it has been an integral part of Lithuania (under **Soviet** control until 1991). The redrawing of the European map after 1945, and the mass expulsion of **Germans** from **eastern Europe**, ensured that German claims to the city have been reduced to the fanciful dreams of the extreme right.

The port provides major shipbuilding yards and is the base for a large deep-sea fishing fleet. The city is also a centre for light industries including electrical equipment and papermaking. It is fairly well connected to the Lithuanian interior and **Latvia** to the north.

Klaus, Václav

Former Finance Minister in post-communist **Czechoslovakia** and then first Prime Minister (1993–97) of the independent **Czech Republic**; leading advocate of a rapid and comprehensive transition to a free-market economy. Born in **Prague** in 1941, he identified with the 1968 reformists as a young economist, but took a low profile under the subsequent repressive regime, working in the state bank. He joined **Civic Forum** in December 1989 and was Czechoslovak Finance Minister from December 1989 until June 1992. Describing himself as a 'Thatcherite', he earned a reputation for ruthless efficiency, with achievements including, in particular, masterminding the mass privatization scheme. Klaus's views on economic policy hastened the split in Civic Forum, of which he became Chairman in October 1990. He cofounded the right-wing liberal **Civic Democratic Party** (ODS) in February 1991 and became its leader. The ODS scored a striking success in the Czech Republic in the 1992 elections. Klaus became Czech Prime Minister in July 1992 and, grasping that the Czechoslovak Federation was doomed, he resolved to end it on terms as favourable as possible to the Czechs. On this and other issues, his relations with President Václav **Havel** thereafter became sensitive. The new Czech Constitution passed in autumn 1992 gave the presidency a limited, mainly ceremonial role, making the Prime Minister the dominant political figure in what became from 1 January 1993 the independent Czech Republic. As its Prime Minister Klaus continued to concentrate on transforming the economy. Elections in mid-1996 left his ODS-led coalition short of an absolute majority, but he remained as Prime Minister, with 'external' support from the **Czech Social Democratic Party** (ČSSD), until the defection of two minor coalition parties brought down his Government in November 1997. The ODS (of which Klaus remains Chairman) lost further ground at the June 1998 elections, since which time it has been out of government, although giving qualified external support to a ČSSD-led minority Government.

KNK see **Confederation of the Peoples of the Caucasus**.

KNSB see **Confederation of Independent Trade Unions of Bulgaria**.

KNSS-Neodvisnost
see **Independence Confederation of New Trade Unions of Slovenia**.

Kocharian, Robert

President of **Armenia**.

Robert Kocharian's success has been largely based on his support for the rights of his homeland, the Armenian enclave of **Nagorno-Karabakh**, of which he was the first 'President' (1994–97). However, he now faces stiff popular opposition. He was brought into the mainstream Armenian Government as Prime Minister on 19 March 1997, and replaced Levon Ter-Petrossian as President on 9 April 1998.

Born on 31 August 1954 in the Nagorno-Karabakh capital Stepanakert (now known as Xankändi), he joined the Soviet army in 1972 before going on to study technology at the Yerevan Polytechnic Institute. In 1987 he joined the communist party in Stepanakert, but the following year he began actively campaigning for the Armenian nationalist movement. He founded the ostensibly apolitical group *Miatsum* (Unification), which became the leading faction in the Karabakh movement. In 1989 he left the communist party and became a deputy in the Armenian Supreme Council. On 2 September 1991 Nagorno-Karanakh declared itself a separate republic and Kocharian was elected a deputy to its Supreme Council. In December 1994 he was elected the first 'President' of the 'Nagorno-Karabakh Republic' (NKR).

His high-profile position attracted the attention of Armenian President Ter-Petrossian who appointed him Prime Minister of Armenia on 19 March 1997 in a populist gesture to try and increase the Government's wavering support among the nationalist movement. Kocharian's switch to the Armenian Cabinet meant he was forced to give up the presidency of the NKR. He increasingly came into conflict with Ter-Petrossian over the latter's apparent willingness to make concessions over the status of Nagorno-Karabakh in the search for a lasting peace with **Azerbaijan**. This rivalry ended in Kocharian's favour when the now deeply unpopular Ter-Petrossian unexpectedly resigned in February 1998, leaving Kocharian in a prime position to succeed him. He was inaugurated as President on 9 April that year. As Head of State he has found himself repeating Ter-Petrossian's conciliatory tone, although to a somewhat lesser extent, over Nagorno-Karabakh, and has attracted similar public criticism as a result.

Kocharian is married to Bella and has three children.

Address: Office of the President, Marshal Baghramian St 26, 375077 Yerevan.
Telephone: (1) 520204.
Fax: (1) 521551.
E-mail: web@president.am
Internet: www.president.am

Kodori Gorge

A volatile and largely lawless mountain region making up the northern section of the border between **Abkhazia** and **Georgia** proper, and home to the pro-Georgian Svan minority. The Kodori river goes on to flow into the Black Sea via the centre of Abkhaz territory. Officially within the borders of the Abkhaz state, the gorge remains partially under Georgian control, although in reality it forms a contiguous lawless zone along the Abkhaz-Georgian border with the southern Gali district.

Brief kidnappings of UN observers in the region raised tensions in 1999 and 2000, and Abkhaz-Georgian relations were pushed to a low ebb in 2001 with the arrival in the gorge of ethnic **Chechen** and renegade Georgian fighters. The destruction of a UN observer helicopter on 8 October 2001 led to a rapid renewal of tensions and precipitated violent clashes between the renegades and Abkhaz forces in the gorge.

KOK *see* **Christian Labour Confederation**.

Kola peninsula

A thick finger of land in the far north of **European Russia,** just north of the Arctic Circle, jutting away from **Karelia** and surrounded by the icy waters of the Barents Sea to the north and the White Sea to the south. Kola is sparsely populated owing to its harsh climate, although the sizeable port of Murmansk lies at its western extreme. The rest of the population live mainly in small mining towns, and around 2,000 **Sami** live in the interior. The peninsula, which contains the world's largest known deposit of apatite (used in fertilizers) and considerable quantities of zirconium and columbium, has become a byword for appalling toxic waste pollution.

Komi Republic

The largest non-**Russian** republic of the **Russian Federation** in **European Russia**. *Population*: 1.25m. (1997 estimate). The tundra-covered Komi Republic is situated at the far north of the western Ural mountains. Under the authority of the **Moscow** principality from the 14th century it became a centre for fur-trading until overhunting exhausted supplies. The region's fortunes were restored after the foundation of the capital, Syktyvkar, in the 18th century which prompted a wave of ethnic Russian migration. It was established as an autonomous *oblast* (region) within Bolshevik Russia in 1921, and raised to a **Soviet** republic in 1936. It gained recognition as a sovereign republic, after the collapse of the Soviet Union, in March 1992. Its Government has sought to retain control of the considerable coal deposits and the great natural resource of the Arctic forest. It also aspires to incorporate the adjoining Komi-Permiak autonomous *okrug* (district). Vladimir Torlopov was elected President of the Komi Republic on 16 December 2001.

The **Finno-Ugric** Komi, who make up only about 23% of the republic's population (Russians are the majority), profess **Orthodox Christianity**. They are most closely related to the **Mari**, further south. Geographic isolation from the rest of Russia did not prevent russification, especially after the Second World War.

Korbut, Nikolay

Minister of Finance, **Belarus**. Nikolay Petrovich Korbut, a political independent, was head of the **National Bank of Belarus** from 15 January 1997 before joining the Cabinet as Finance Minister later the same year.
Address: Ministry of Finance, vul. Savetskaya 7, 220010 Minsk.
Telephone: (17) 2226137.
Fax: (17) 2226640.
E-mail: mofb@office.un.minsk.by
Internet: www.ncpi.gov.by/minfin

Kosovo

A province in the south-western corner of **Serbia (Yugoslavia)**, with **Albania** to the west and **Macedonia** to the south, which is populated mainly by ethnic **Albanians** (90% of the population), and is currently under UN administration following conflict in 1998–99. *Population*: 1.8m. (2000 estimate). *Capital*: Priština.

Kosovo was historically an integral part of Serbia, and the loss of the province to the invading Ottomans at the Battle of Kosovo in 1389 forms a cornerstone of **Serb** nationalism, which has laid the foundations for centuries of ethnic tensions. Albanians began to arrive in the region following its incorporation into the **Muslim** Ottoman Empire but did not become the dominant population until the mid-20th century, when it was already a part of the **Socialist Federal Republic of Yugoslavia** (SFRY).

Kosovo acquired a degree of autonomy within the Serbian republic under the SFRY framework, but calls for greater rights for the ethnic Albanian community created a backlash among Serb nationalists, who felt their position increasingly beleaguered within what they regarded as the heartland of their national identity. The aspiring Serbian leader Slobodan **Milošević** exploited these feelings in building a nationalist platform for himself, and in 1989 the autonomous statuses of both Kosovo and **Vojvodina** were withdrawn. Repression and discrimination against the Albanian community gathered pace under Milošević's later Government. Full-scale fighting between Serbian paramilitary police and the **Kosovo Liberation Army** (UCK) nationalist militia broke out in 1998. The Yugoslav police, soon backed by the regular Yugoslav army, implemented a brutal policy of '**ethnic cleansing**', prompting worldwide condemnation and the threat of international intervention. Hundreds of thousands of Kosovar Albanians were forced from their homes and found shelter in neighbouring countries. A US-led bombing campaign under the aegis of the **North Atlantic Treaty Organization** (NATO) began in March 1999, and Serb forces were finally withdrawn in June.

The province was divided into sectors to be patrolled by UK, US, French, German, Italian and later **Russian** troops as part of the international **KFOR** peacekeeping force. Albanian refugees began returning to their homes and plans were laid for a multi-ethnic police force, and later a full domestic administration. In the interim, Kosovo was placed under the UN Interim Administration Mission in Kosovo (UNMIK), which was established as the supreme legal and executive authority, overseeing civilian administration and reconstruction as an autonomous province.

Tensions between the ethnic Albanian and remaining minority Serb communities remain high, particularly in the heavily divided town of Mitrovica where a number of clashes have taken place since 1999 (*see also* **Presevo Valley**). Ethnic Serbs have frequently condemned the alleged bias of the UN administration in favour of Albanians and have repeatedly withdrawn their support for the UN administration. On the other hand ethnic Albanians have continued to press for the province's full independence. Elections for a UN-sponsored Assembly, held in November 2001, resulted in the moderate Democratic League of Kosovo (LDK), headed by Ibrahim Rugova, becoming the largest party. Former Danish Defence Minister Hans Haekkerup was the UN Special Representative heading UNMIK from December 2000, but did not renew his contract at the end of 2001.

Kosovo Force *see* **KFOR**.

Kosovo Liberation Army
Ushtria Clirimtare e Kosovës (UCK)

The principal armed movement of ethnic **Albanians** in **Kosovo**, seeking the province's independence from **Serbia/Yugoslavia**. The UCK came to prominence in 1998 as the focus of ethnic Albanian resistance to a ruthless assertion of Serbian authority by government forces, mounting a well-armed and well-financed military campaign which established effective control over substantial areas of Kosovo. UCK representatives participated in the Rambouillet talks on Kosovo in early 1999 but failed to secure Western support for independence, whereupon the UCK announced that its leader, Hashim Thaci, had become 'Prime Minister' of a provisional Kosovo Government.

The withdrawal of Serbian forces from Kosovo in June 1999 accentuated divisions between UCK 'moderates' prepared to co-operate with the succeeding UN administration and hardliners advocating continued struggle for independence and eventual union with **Albania** (*see* **Greater Albania**). Although UCK representatives joined the UN-appointed Kosovo Transitional Council, little real progress was made on disarming the UCK, some elements of which created more militant organizations which in early 2001 became involved in an insurgency in ethnic Albanian areas of neighbouring **Macedonia**.

Meanwhile, the UCK 'moderate' wing had signalled its willingness to participate in the political process by presenting candidates in municipal elections in October 2000, in which Thaci led the Democratic Party of Kosovo (*Partia Demokratike e Kosovës*—PDK) to a 27% vote share, which gave it control of six of

the 30 municipalities at issue. Its popularity remained stable the following year when it won 26% of the vote (and 26 seats) in the November 2001 elections for the UN-sponsored Assembly.
Leadership: Hashim Thaci (Political Leader).

Koštunica, Vojislav

President of the Federal Republic of **Yugoslavia**.

Vojislav Koštunica heads the small nationalist **Democratic Party of Serbia** (DSS) within the ruling **Democratic Opposition of Serbia** (DOS). A consistent and vocal opponent of Yugoslav Governments since the 1970s, he was chosen as presidential candidate for the DOS largely because he was free from connections with the disgraced **Milošević** regime. He was inaugurated as President on 8 October 2000.

Born in **Belgrade** on 24 April 1944, he graduated from the University of Belgrade's Faculty of Law, achieving a master's degree in 1970 and a doctorate in 1974. His firm nationalist politics jarred with the communist regime and his support of prominent critics of Marshal **Tito**'s 1974 Federal Constitution, which ensured autonomy within **Serbia** for **Kosovo** and **Vojvodina**, led to his dismissal from the faculty. When offered a professorship at the same faculty in 1989 he famously refused. From 1974 he worked at the Institute for Social Sciences in Belgrade and was briefly its Director in the mid-1980s. During this period he also edited several well-respected political and legal journals and had his own writings on law and politics published. He mixed **Serbian** nationalism with advocacy of human rights and was prominent on the Board for the Protection of the Freedom of Thought and Expression. In 1989 he cofounded the **Democratic Party** (DS). In elections in 1990 he won a seat in the lower house which he held through consecutive elections (and the break-up of Yugoslavia) until 1997.

Koštunica left the DS in 1992 because he considered its stance during the Yugoslav Civil War to be insufficiently nationalistic. Instead he created the DSS, of which he has been President ever since. By 1993 the DSS was on the very fringe of Serbian politics, becoming known derisively as the 'van party' on the basis that all of its supporters could fit in one van. He earned the dubious honour of being lumped among the 'war party' in the **Federal Assembly** for his continual attacks on the various Western-proposed peace plans, and his support for the extreme nationalist Radovan **Karadžić** and the rebellious Serbs in **Bosnia and Herzegovina**—although he condemned the excessive violence of the various paramilitary groups. His belligerent policies kept him out of popular politics until the Kosovo conflict in 1999 when hostility to Milošević grew in strength. The disparate opposition parties turned to him in July 2000 as a unifying candidate who was utterly free from the taint of the corrupt regime. After the electoral commission admitted to having been ordered to falsify the results of the 24 September elections, a wave of mass demonstrations on 5 October forced Milošević to resign. The October revolution brought offers for Yugoslavia to rejoin the international community and Koštunica was universally hailed as a champion of democracy. However, he proved to be as consistent as ever and continued to condemn outside interference while warning of a future conflict with ethnic Albanian guerrillas in southern Serbia. In January 2001 he sent shock waves through the DOS when he met with Milošević to discuss the issues of the day, and he has openly condemned the **International Criminal Tribunal for the former Yugoslavia** as a 'monstrous institution'.

Vojislav Koštunica is married to Zorica Radović, who is also a lawyer. He famously eschews the trappings of power, living in a modest Belgrade apartment and being seen driving through the streets of the capital in his battered old Yugo car.

Address: Office of the Federal Presidency, Lenjinov Bulevar 2, 11070 Belgrade.
Telephone: (11) 636466.

KOZSR *see* **Confederation of Trade Unions of the Slovak Republic.**

KPB *see* **Communist Party of Belarus.**

KPRF *see* **Communist Party of the Russian Federation.**

KPSS *see* **Communist Party of the Soviet Union.**

KPU *see* **Communist Party of Ukraine.**

Krajina

The collected border territories, literally 'border lands', of **Croatia**. The regions, forming a broad bulge along the central and southern Croatia–**Bosnia and Herzegovina** border and the far eastern edge of **Slavonia**, were populated by Orthodox **Serbs** fleeing the occupation of Bosnia by the Ottomans in 1463. Relations between them and the (Catholic) **Croats** were characterized by repeated acts of brutality. During the Second World War the fascist Croat Government persecuted the Serb population with mass killings. As **Yugoslavia** collapsed and Croats asserted their nationalist identity the ethnic Serbs, fuelled by the territorial ambitions of the proponents of **Greater Serbia,** voted in a referendum on 12 May 1991 to secede from Croatia and remain part of Yugoslavia. Exactly a week later the rest of Croatia voted for independence. The contrasting decisions led within two months to open conflict between ethnic Serbs, backed by the regular Yugoslav army, and Croat forces—effectively heralding the beginning of war.

The Republic of Serbian Krajina (RSK) was declared during a hiatus in the conflict on 4 April 1992 and was led by self-styled President Milan Babić. A call for the RSK to be amalgamated with the **Serb Republic** in neighbouring Bosnia and other Serb lands (*see* Greater Serbia) in June 1993 led to a continuing low-level offensive against the Krajina by Croat troops. Ethnic Serbs became themselves the victims of a concerted policy of '**ethnic cleansing**' wherever settlements in the Krajina came under Croat military domination. The RSK was eventually destroyed in the decisive Operation Storm mounted by Croat forces in August 1995, although the border region of eastern Slavonia remained under Serb control. Eastern Slavonia was eventually returned to Croatia under the terms of the **Dayton Agreement** of November 1995, averting further bloodshed.

Hundreds of thousands of Serbs fled the advancing Croat forces during Operation Storm, arriving for the most part in the Serbian-controlled areas of Bosnia and in Yugoslavia itself. This demographic shift in the Krajina helped to settle relations between Croatia and Yugoslavia after the war. Following the collapse of the overtly nationalist regimes in Croatia and Yugoslavia, after the death of **Tudjman** and the downfall of **Milošević** respectively, the Krajina is no longer a focus of cross-border tension.

Kremlin

The triangular walled city (literally 'citadel') in **Moscow** which became synonymous with the Government of the **Soviet Union,** and which remains an important office complex and residence for Government Ministers of the **Russian Federation**. It is now also a tourist attraction boasting many fine cathedrals, churches and a theatre. First founded as a fortified settlement overlooking the Moskva and Neglina rivers in the 12th century, it rose to prominence as a political centre distinct from the rest of Moscow in the mid-14th century. Its importance declined after the **Romanov dynasty** switched the Russian capital to **St Petersburg**, but was revived when the Bolsheviks reversed that change and returned central government to Moscow in 1918. From then the Kremlin became a secretive walled citadel, housing all the major organs of the Soviet state machinery, including the infamous secret service, the KGB (*see* **Federal Security Service**). With the collapse of the Soviet Union the Kremlin was opened up once more but retained its links with Government. Since 1992 it has been home to the President of the Russian Federation and his administration.

Križanović, Jozo

Member of the Presidency (Croat), **Bosnia and Herzegovina**, and its current Chairman. Jozo Križanović, born in 1944, is a member of the multi-ethnic, pro-Western **Socialist Democratic Party of Bosnia and Herzegovina** (SDPBiH) and represented the central canton of Travnik, in the **Muslim-Croat Federation**. A businessman from the region, he was appointed to the tripartite Presidency on 30 March 2001 and took over as Chairman of the body on 14 June.

Address: Office of the Presidency, Musala 5, 71000 Sarajevo.
Telephone: (33) 664941.
Fax: (33) 472491.

Kryashen

A sizeable community of **Tatars** who practise **Orthodox Christianity**, having been converted by Russian missionaries in the 18th century. The word Kryashen means 'the baptized'. Found mostly in **Tatarstan** and neighbouring regions of the **Russian Federation**, the 320,000 or so Kryashen have pressed for recognition as a separate ethnic group in time for the Russian census due in October 2002. They were last separately designated in the 1926 Soviet census. Their initiative faces opposition from Tatar nationalists who see it as an attempt to dilute Tatar unity.

KSČM *see* **Communist Party of Bohemia and Moravia**.

KSSh *see* **Confederation of Albanian Trade Unions**.

KTR *see* **Confederation of Labour of Russia**.

Kučan, Milan

President of **Slovenia**.

Milan Kučan first became President of the Slovene Republic in the communist era. Known as a reformist, he retained the presidency when Slovenia declared its independence from the **Socialist Federal Republic of Yugoslavia,** winning the first post-independence presidential elections as a non-party candidate in December 1992 and re-election five years later.

Born on 14 January 1941, in the Prekomurje village of Krizevci near the Slovene-Hungarian border, he graduated in law from Ljubljana University in 1963. He became involved in politics in 1964, leading the youth wing of the League of Communists of Slovenia (ZKS), and was a member of the ZKS Secretariat from 1969 to 1973. He was elected in 1978 as President of the Slovene Assembly. Between 1982 and 1986, he was the Slovenian representative on the Central Committee of the **League of Communists of Yugoslavia** in **Belgrade**, returning to Slovenia in 1986 to become leader of the ZKS. He worked to turn the organization into a social democratic party and in 1989 it was renamed the ZKS Party of Democratic Reform. He was elected President of Slovenia in April 1990 and was instrumental in preparing the country for independence in June 1991. He deliberately stood aside from party politics and renounced his party membership in time to stand as a non-party candidate in the country's first presidential election after independence, on 6 December 1992, with the backing of the newly-created **United List of Social**

Democrats (ZLSD). He won a decisive 64% of the vote in the first round and was re-elected, again in the first round, on 23 November 1997. His popularity is attributed to a combination of his diplomatic skill, his image as a moderate, and the relative smoothness of Slovenia's adaptation to the free market in the post-communist period.

Address: Office of the President, Erjavčeva 17, 1000 Ljubljana.
Telephone: (1) 4781205.
Fax: (1) 4781357.
Internet: www.gov.si/up-rs

Kuchma, Leonid

President of **Ukraine**.

Leonid Danilovich Kuchma is constitutionally an independent but receives key support from right-of-centre parties in the **Parliament**. As a leading advocate of a rapid transition to a free-market economy he was appointed Prime Minister in 1992. He was first elected President in July 1994.

Born on 9 August 1938 in the village of Chaikino, in the Chernihiv region, he graduated as a Mechanical Engineer from the University of Dnipropetrovsk in 1960. He spent the next 32 years working at the Pivdenmash machine-building factory, the **Soviet Union**'s largest weapons manufacturer, rising to become Managing Director in 1986. From 1966 to 1975 he was also the Technical Manager at Baikonur Cosmodrome in Kazakhstan, the centre of the Soviet space programme. He had joined the **Communist Party of the Soviet Union** (KPSS) in 1960, and was Party Secretary at the Pivdenmash factory from 1975 until 1982. He was a member of the Central Committee of the **Communist Party of Ukraine** from 1981 to 1991 and was elected to the Ukrainian Supreme Soviet in March 1990. He resigned from the party as it went out of existence in the wake of the abortive **August coup** in **Moscow** in 1991 and the ensuing rapid disintegration of the Soviet Union. The following year he retired from his Directorship of the Pivdenmash factory, and was appointed as Ukraine's second post-independence Prime Minister on 27 October.

Kuchma resigned as Prime Minister in September 1993 after resistance from leftist parties to his radical economic reforms and use of emergency powers. In December he became President of the pro-market Union of Industrialists and Entrepreneurs (UIE), and the following year won election as Ukraine's President, supported by the centre-right Inter-regional Bloc for Reform (MBR) and, in the second round on 10 July, backed also by the now reformed Communist Party of Ukraine and ethnic **Russians**.

As President he sought to reform the **Ukrainian economy** and increase his own constitutional powers. Obtaining in June 1996 the right to issue legislative decrees, he has used his powers to centralize the Executive, thus retaining for himself the authority to make both appointments and policy. His authoritarian stance has provoked strong opposition from the left but has been endorsed by dubious referendums and election results. He was re-elected on 31 October 1999. Suggestions of his involvement in the disappearance of outspoken journalist Georgiy Gongadze provoked mass demonstrations against his rule in December 2000 and March 2001. He has also faced stiffening opposition in the Parliament.

Leonid Kuchma is married to Ludmila Mikolayovna; they have one daughter.
Address: Office of the President, vul. Bankova 11, 252220 Kiev.
Telephone: (44) 2263265.
Fax: (44) 2931001.

Kudrin, Aleksei

Deputy Chairman and Minister of Finance, **Russian Federation**.

Aleksei Leonidovich Kudrin is a political independent but a key supporter of President Vladimir **Putin**, with whom he served in the Leningrad (now **St Petersburg**) city administration in the early 1990s. He was appointed to President Boris **Yeltsin**'s Office in 1996 and was moved into the Council of Ministers proper under Putin on 18 May 2000.

Born on 12 October 1960 to a military family serving in Dobel, Latvia, he graduated in economics from the Leningrad State University in 1983. For seven years he worked as a researcher at the Soviet Academy of Sciences, where Anatolii Chubais was lecturer. He followed Chubais into the Leningrad city administration in 1990 and worked under him in the municipal Committee on Economic Reform. He became First Deputy Mayor of the city under Putin's political mentor, Anatoly Sobchak, in 1994. During his six years in the city's Government he worked with Putin and others to introduce much needed reforms to bring a turnaround in the city's dire finances.

In August 1996 Kudrin was brought into Yeltsin's presidential administration as a Deputy Chief and Head of the Control Department. He was appointed First Deputy Minister of Finance in 1997. He reconnected with Chubais in January 1999 when he was appointed First Deputy Chairman of the Unified Power Grids of Russia (UPGR) under his former colleague. He has tried to distance himself from the oligarchic image of Chubais since his departure from UPGR in June 1999, when he was reappointed First Deputy Minister of Finance. He was elevated in May 2000 to full Minister, and Deputy Chairman of the Government, in Putin's new Cabinet in May 2000, where he has worked with Chairman Mikhail **Kasyanov** on the revival of the Russian economy.

Address: Ministry of Finance, ul. Ilinka 9, 103097 Moscow.
Telephone: (095) 2062171.
Fax: (095) 9246989.

Kukan, Eduard

Minister of Foreign Affairs, **Slovakia**.

Eduard Kukan is a member of the centrist Slovak Democratic and Christian Union (SDKU), which is yet to compete in elections and is still a part of the ruling **Slovak Democratic Coalition** (SDK). A seasoned diplomat, he was first appointed Foreign Minister in 1994, and was reappointed on 30 October 1998.

Born on 26 December 1939 in Trnovca nad Váhom in western Slovakia, he studied at the Moscow Institute of International Affairs, and received a doctorate in law from the Charles University in Prague. He joined the sub-Saharan Africa Department of the Czechoslovak Foreign Service in 1964 and divided the next 30 years between **Czechoslovakia** and its Embassies in Zambia, the USA, and Ethiopia (where he was Czechoslovak Ambassador in 1985–88). Within the Ministry he headed regional departments covering sub-Saharan Africa and Latin America. His final diplomatic posting was as Permanent Representative to the UN in New York, first for Czechoslovakia and then, as Czechoslovakia separated into two halves, as Permanent Representative for the newly independent Slovakia in 1993. He transferred from diplomacy to mainstream politics in 1994 when he was elected to the **National Council** on behalf of the Democratic Union of Slovakia (DÚS) (which later joined the SDK) and held the post of Foreign Minister from March to December that year. He chaired the DÚS from 1997 until taking up the post of Vice-Chairman of the SDK coalition in 1998, when he was also reappointed Foreign Minister. He joined the SDKU on its formation in 2000, giving up his post within the SDK.

Address: Ministry of Foreign Affairs, Hlboká 2, 83336 Bratislava.
Telephone: (2) 59781111.
Fax: (2) 59782213.
Internet: www.foreign.gov.sk

Kuliyev, Vilayat Mukhtar

Minister of Foreign Affairs, **Azerbaijan**.

Vilayat Mukhtar oglu Kuliyev is a member of the **Azerbaijan National Independence Party** (AMIP) and has represented the party in the **National Assembly** since 1996. He was appointed Foreign Minister on 26 October 1999.

Born on 5 November 1952 in the central town of Agjabadi, he had a long career at the Azerbaijan State University's Faculty of Philology where he eventually became a professor. He was first elected to the National Assembly in February 1996, in run-off elections left over from the November 1995 poll, and was subsequently re-elected in 2000. Despite his lack of obvious experience in international diplomacy, he was appointed Foreign Minister in October 1999.

Vilayat Mukhtar Kuliyev is married and has two children; he speaks Persian and English.

Address: Ministry of Foreign Affairs, Ghanjlar meydani 3, 370004 Baku.
Telephone: (12) 926856.
Fax: (12) 988480.
E-mail: mfazer@azerin.com

Kumyks

A **Turkic** people whose language and culture has become dominant as a *lingua franca* among the diverse peoples of the north **Caucasus**. Around 220,000 Kumyks live in the interior regions of the **Russian** republic of **Dagestan**, making them the fourth-largest single group (12%) in this ethnically-varied state. Their cultural dominance has led to the assimilation into the Kumyk population of some Caucasian neighbours, particularly from among the **Avars** and **Dargins**. Kumyk nationalists, led by the *Tenglik* (Equality) movement, have spearheaded calls for greater autonomy within Dagestan, and even for a mini-federal system of ethnic republics. Tensions engendered by these views have led to clashes, particularly with the Dargins. Like most other Dagestanis, the Kumyks are Sunni **Muslim**.

Kurds

A Caucasian people spread across the north of the Middle East with sizeable populations in **Armenia**, **Azerbaijan**, **Georgia**, Iran, Iraq, Turkey and Turkmenistan. The area of Kurdish settlement straddles international borders to an extent which leaves the Kurds unusually vulnerable to cultural fragmentation and political and social discrimination. Thousands attempt to illegally migrate to western Europe every year.

Kurdish is most closely related to Iranian and there are several distinct dialects. Kurds living in the **Caucasus region** have had a separate script based on **Cyrillic** since 1944. They arrived in the Caucasus to escape persecution in their homeland (known as Kurdistan) in the 19th century. Economic activity is traditionally agricultural, focusing on livestock, although many Kurds have migrated to urban centres in the 20th century.

While most Kurds are **Muslim** the Yezidis of Armenia, Georgia and Iraq practise a hybrid religion based largely on ancient Persian beliefs with borrowings from Christianity and Judaism. According to this faith the Yezidis are descended from Adam but not from Eve, making them separate from the rest of humanity. They are also prohibited from cultivation, restricting economic activity. Consequently Yezidis are often regarded as a separate ethnic group, especially by Christian and Muslim Kurds.

The largest Kurdish population in eastern Europe—around 200,000—is in the west of Azerbaijan. Azeri attempts to assimilate the country's various ethnic groups prompted a backlash among Kurds who have called for the resurrection of the

1920s autonomous Kurdish region. Almost all the 60,000 Kurds now in Armenia are Yezidis, since many Muslim Kurds were expelled from Armenia along with resident **Azeris** in the early 1990s. The Armenian authorities have been unusually accommodating towards the Kurdish minority, establishing Kurdish-language broadcasts and a Kurdish newspaper as early as 1987. In Georgia the Kurdish minority is small and intermixed with the **Meskhetians**.

Kursk

A **Russian** nuclear submarine, named after the western city, which sank to the bottom of the Barents Sea on 13 August 2000 with the loss of all 118 sailors aboard. Having raised the craft, investigators finally concluded in November 2001 that the explosion of one of its own torpedoes was the main cause of the vessel's sinking, although the reason for this explosion remained unclear. The sinking highlighted endemic weaknesses in the colossal Russian military system, showing the dangers of attempting to retain its capabilities when vital maintenance was impossibly expensive. One consequence of the tragedy was the end of Russian President Vladimir **Putin**'s political honeymoon (although his popularity remains high). His handling of the affair, initially refusing international help and failing to respond in kind to the strong emotional reaction in the country, led to the beginning of popular criticism of his newly-elected regime.

Kuvendi Popullor *see* **People's Assembly (Albania)**.

Kwaśniewski, Aleksander

The President of **Poland** from 1995, elected as the candidate of the **Democratic Left Alliance** (SLD) within which he led the erstwhile ruling communist party (restyled as Social Democracy of the Polish Republic—SdRP) as representative of a younger generation of pragmatic reformers. Born in November 1954, he graduated from the University of Gdańsk with a degree in transport economics, and joined the ruling Polish United Workers' Party (PZPR) in 1977, having been an energetic political activist in the student socialist youth union. He moved on from editing party newspapers to a post in the Council of Ministers in 1985, with special responsibility for youth affairs. In 1989 he took part in the historic round-table debates on the creation of a pluralist system, which opened the way for partially free elections. After the PZPR had entered a **Solidarity**-led coalition Government, the party held an extraordinary congress in January 1990 and reconstituted itself as the social democratic SdRP, with the youthful Kwaśniewski a forward-looking choice as its first Chairman.

Elected in 1991 to sit as a Deputy in the *Sejm*, the lower chamber in what had become a bicameral **National Assembly**, Kwaśniewski chaired the Parliamentary

Constitutional Committee for two years from November 1993, and gained a reputation for seeking consensus in the interests of political unity. This even extended to giving his initial support to the conclusion of a concordat between Poland and the Vatican, to which many in his party were openly hostile. In the 1995 presidential election, Kwaśniewski narrowly defeated the incumbent Lech **Wałęsa** on the second round. He was sworn in on 22 December, after the constitutional tribunal had ruled against Wałęsa's attempt to have him disqualified for allegedly misleading the voters about his electoral qualifications by claiming a postgraduate degree. As President, Kwaśniewski committed himself to promoting national consensus—a promise sorely tested the following year by the issue of abortion. He also expressed his support for continuing economic reforms and concluding the formulation of a democratic constitution (which finally took effect in October 1997), as well as backing Poland's applications for membership of the **European Union** and the **North Atlantic Treaty Organization** (NATO). His re-election for a second presidential term in October 2000, again as candidate of the SLD, was achieved convincingly on the first round with 54% of the vote.

Address: Office of the President, ul. Wiejska 10, 00902 Warsaw.
Telephone: (22) 6952060.
Fax: (22) 6952257.
E-mail: listy@prezydent.pl
Internet: www.prezydent.pl

Kyiv *see* **Kiev**.

L

Laar, Mart

Prime Minister of **Estonia**.

Mart Laar heads a three-party coalition led by his own centre-right **Fatherland Union** (IL). He was the country's first post-Soviet Prime Minister from 1992 to 1994, when his pro-market policies were credited with making Estonia one of the most successful former Soviet states. He was appointed Prime Minister for his second term on 25 March 1999.

Born in the central town of Viljandi on 22 April 1960, he graduated from Tartu University with a degree in history in 1983 and went straight to work as a history teacher in **Tallinn**. He left teaching to combine history with politics in 1987 when he became the Chairman of the Historical Heritage Department of the Ministry of Culture. He manoeuvred into the political forefront as the **Soviet Union** disintegrated and joined the Estonian Christian Democratic Union in 1990. After democratic elections in 1992 he was appointed Prime Minister at the head of the Pro Patria Coalition (RKI). He was named as Young Politician of the World in 1993, as his youthful Cabinet thrust Estonia into the full rigours of the free market. His extreme radical approach proved less popular domestically, however, and he left office in 1994. In opposition he oversaw the merging of his RKI with the Estonian National Independence Party to form the IL in December 1995, and he has chaired the party since 1998. After success in legislative elections in March 1999 he was appointed Prime Minister for a second term. He faced calls for his resignation in February 2001 after reports that he had used a picture of **Estonia Centre Party** (EKe) leader Edgar Savisaar for shooting practice in 1999. By the end of the year dissension within the ruling coalition prompted Laar to announce his resignation in December, to take effect in January 2002.

Address: Office of the Prime Minister, Stenbock House, Rahukohtu 3, Tallinn 15161.
Telephone: 6935860.
Fax: 6935914.
E-mail: valitsus@rk.ee
Internet: www.peaminister.ee

Labour Union
Unia Pracy (UP)

A small leftist political party in **Poland**. Formed in 1993, the UP remained on the sidelines of Polish politics until it allied with the **Democratic Left Alliance** (SLD) for the September 2001 elections. Through this alliance the party won a share of the SLD-UP's 216 seats in the **National Assembly**. After the election it was welcomed into the governing alliance along with the SLD and the **Polish Peasant Party**. UP Leader Marek Pol was appointed Deputy Prime Minister, with responsibility for Infrastructure in the initial Cabinet of Prime Minister Leszek **Miller**.
Leadership: Marek Pol (Leader).
Address: Nowogrodzka 4, 00513 Warsaw.
Telephone: (22) 6285859.
Fax: (22) 6256776.
E-mail: biuro@uniapracy.org.pl
Internet: www.uniapracy.org.pl

Lagumdžija, Zlatko

Prime Minister and Minister of Foreign Affairs, **Bosnia and Herzegovina**.

The US-educated Zlatko Lagumdžija, who heads the **Social Democratic Party of Bosnia and Herzegovina** (SDPBiH), was first elected to the **Parliamentary Assembly** in 1996. He has helped to lead the SDPBiH into a controlling position in the non-partisan middle ground of Bosnian politics, taking support away from the traditional ethnically-based parties. He was appointed Prime Minister on 18 July 2001, having entered the Cabinet in January.

Born on 26 December 1955 in **Sarajevo**, where his father was Mayor, he was educated in the USA but returned to study at the University of Sarajevo in 1976. He received his doctorate in electrical engineering in 1988 and became a professor at the university the following year. In 1990 he cofounded the SDPBiH from the ashes of the communist party. In 1993 he was seriously injured during an attack on Sarajevo and was flown to Stockholm to receive medical treatment. He returned to Bosnia after his rehabilitation and was made Director of the Centre for Management and Computer Technology in 1995. He entered the Parliamentary Assembly in 1996 and became President of his party the following year. The SDPBiH contested the November 2000 elections as part of the multi-ethnic Alliance for Change, and the following July, after the incumbent Prime Minister Bozidar Matić had resigned following the failure of some key electoral legislation, Lagumdžija was appointed in his place.

Zlatko Lagumdžija is married and has two children.
Address: Office of the Prime Minister, Zmaja od Bosne 3, 71000 Sarajevo.
Telephone: (33) 213777.
Fax: (33) 272877.

Lapps see **Sami**.

Latvia
Latvijas Republika

An independent **Baltic State** located in north-eastern Europe bounded to the north by Estonia, to the south by Lithuania and Belarus, to the east by the Russian Federation and to the west by the Baltic Sea. Administratively, the country is divided into 26 counties (rajoni) and seven municipalities.

Area: 64,100 sq km; *capital*: **Riga**; *population*: 2.4m. (2001 estimate), comprising **Latvians** 57.7%, **Russians** 29.6%, **Belarusians** 4.1%, **Ukrainians** 2.7%, **Poles** 2.5%, others 3.4%; *official language*: Latvian (Lettish); *religion*: Lutheran, **Roman Catholic, Russian Orthodox**.

Legislative authority is vested in a unicameral **Saeima** (Parliament), which has 100 deputies directly elected for a four-year term by a system of proportional representation, subject to thresholds of 5% for individual parties and 7% for alliances. The Head of State is the President, who is elected for a four-year term (once renewable) by the Saeima. Executive authority is vested in the Prime Minister, who is appointed by the President.

History: Settled by the Balts in ancient times, Latvia was conquered by the **German** Teutonic Knights during the 13th century and became part of the state of **Livonia** for the next 200 years. During the religious wars of the 16th century Livonia was partitioned and Latvia came successively under Polish and Lithuanian, and then Swedish, rule. The 1721 Treaty of Nystad between **Russia** and Sweden, concluding the Great Northern War, brought much of Livonia, with **Estonia**, under Russian rule. Latvia was fully integrated by the late 18th century and remained part of the Russian Empire until the 1917 revolution. By this time nationalist groups had developed into a political force and Latvia declared its independence in 1918, although this was only fully achieved once Bolsheviks forces had been expelled and the 1920 **Riga Treaty** had been signed with the **Soviet Union**. A coup in 1934 replaced the democratic Government with a right-wing authoritarian regime.

In 1940, after the start of the Second World War, Soviet forces occupied Latvia, along with neighbouring Estonia and **Lithuania** (as agreed under the 1939 **Nazi-Soviet Pact**), and all three countries were incorporated into the USSR as Soviet Socialist Republics. German forces then invaded and occupied Latvia from 1941 until 1944, when the Soviet Union regained control and continued the process of 'Sovietization' begun in 1940. Neither the USA nor the UK ever formally recognized the Soviet absorption of Latvia and the other two Baltic republics.

In the late 1980s, influenced by the **Solidarity** movement in **Poland** and the *glasnost* (openness) initiative in the Soviet Union, the growing opposition movements in Latvia united in a political force—the Latvian Popular Front (LPF)—to campaign for sovereignty and democracy. At the same time, close links were established with popular fronts in Estonia and Lithuania. Official status was given to the Latvian language, and the 1989 elections to the Latvian Supreme Soviet returned the LPF with a majority of seats, so bringing to an end the communist monopoly of power.

The initial declaration of Latvian independence in May 1990 (subject to a transitional period for negotiation) caused violent clashes between independence supporters and communists. President **Gorbachev** of the Soviet Union annulled the declaration and in early 1991 Soviet forces briefly went into Riga. Latvia boycotted an all-Union referendum on the future of the USSR and instead held a referendum in March 1991 on outright Latvian independence, which received a 73% vote in favour. Following the failure of the attempted **August coup** against Gorbachev, Latvia declared itself an independent republic, gaining recognition from the Soviet Government the following month.

Latvia has had unstable, often minority, ruling coalitions since leaving the Soviet Union, averaging almost one Government per year. In the first post-independence legislative and presidential elections, held in 1993, the LPF lost huge popular support and was replaced as the governing party by a centre-right coalition led by Valdis Birkavs, of the newly-formed **Latvia's Way** (LC), and the Latvian Farmers' Union (LZS). Guntis Ulmanis, leader of the LZS, was elected as the first President. Maris Gailis (the Deputy Prime Minister) replaced Birkavs in a new coalition formed following the withdrawal of LZS support in 1994.

After the 1995 general elections had produced a hung parliament, President Ulmanis opposed a coalition of two of the largest parties—the Democratic Party Saimnieks (the Master) and the radical right-wing Popular Movement for Latvia–Zigerists (TKL–ZP). The result was that a broad centre-right coalition was formed, headed by a non-party Prime Minister, Andris Škele. Ulmanis was re-elected to the presidency in 1996. When Škele resigned as Prime Minister in July 1997 (because of opposition to his authoritarian style and conflicts of interest over ministerial appointments), Guntars Krasts of the right-wing **Fatherland and Freedom–Latvian National Conservative Party** (TB–LNNK) formed a new coalition administration in August.

Latest elections: In the legislative elections held in October 1998, the newly-established **People's Party** (TP) led by former Prime Minister Škele was returned as the largest single party with 24 seats and 21.2% of the vote, followed by the LC with 21 (18.1%), the TB–LNNK with 17 (14.7%), the centre-left **National Harmony Party** (TSP) with 16 (14.1%), the Latvian Social Democratic Union (LSDA) with 14 (12.8%) and the New Party (JP) with 8 (7.3%). Despite the TP's success, however, Vilis Krištopans of the LC formed a minority coalition in November with the TB–LNNK and the JP, and in February 1999 signed a co-operation agreement under which the LSDA pledged qualified external support. The LSDA subsequently became the **Latvian Social Democratic Workers' Party** (LSDSP) and the JP became the **New Christian Party** (JKP).

Latvia

Recent developments: At the same time as the legislative polling in October 1998, a referendum was held on controversial amendments to Latvia's citizenship laws as introduced in 1991 and requiring residents who were not citizens of the pre-1940 republic (or their descendants) to apply for naturalization, qualification for which included 16 years' residence and knowledge of the Latvian language. In the referendum just over 50% of voters approved the amendments, which ended naturalization quotas, granted citizenship to those children born in Latvia after independence if their parents requested it, and provided for simpler language tests for older residents. The amendments would therefore make it easier for (mainly Russian) non-citizens currently resident in Latvia to obtain Latvian citizenship, and for that reason were welcomed by the **Organization for Security and Co-operation in Europe** (OSCE) and the **European Union** (EU). In a further adaptation to European norms, the Saeima in April 1999 overcame its earlier reluctance to abolish the death penalty in Latvia.

In presidential elections in the Saeima in June 1999 the political neutral Vaira **Vike-Freiberga** was elected Latvia's first female President after seven rounds of voting. She received a slim majority of 53 votes, against 20 for Birkavs (LC) and nine for Ingrida Udre (JP).

The Krištopans Government lasted until July 1999, when the LC surrendered the premiership to Škele of the TP, who formed a majority centre-right coalition including the LC and the TB–LNNK. However, the Government collapsed in April 2000 amidst political infighting and as Škele and other senior officials were implicated in a paedophilia scandal (from which they were later cleared). The outcome in May 2000 was the formation of a four-party coalition headed by Andris **Berzinš** of the LC and including the TP, the TB–LNNK and the JP (renamed as the JKP in 2001).

International relations and defence: Upon its recognition as an independent state, Latvia was admitted to the United Nations in 1991 and became a member of the OSCE; it also joined the **World Trade Organization** (in 1999). Pursuing closer links with Western institutions, Latvia was admitted to the **Council of Europe** in 1993 and joined NATO's **Partnership for Peace** programme in 1994. In December 1999 Latvia was accorded official candidate status by the EU, formal negotiations beginning in February 2000. The **Russian Federation** has opposed Latvia's application for full **NATO** membership, and a treaty delimiting the Latvian–Russian border (based on the 1920 Treaty of Riga) has not yet been implemented, amidst continuing unhappiness in Moscow over the effect of Latvian citizenship laws on Latvia's ethnic Russian minority.

Notwithstanding an unresolved boundary dispute with Lithuania, Latvia maintains close co-operation with its Baltic and Nordic neighbours, and is a member of the **Council of Baltic Sea States**. In January 1998 the Presidents of Latvia, Estonia and Lithuania and the USA signed a **US-Baltic Partnership** charter.

Latvia's defence budget for 2000 amounted to some US $72m., equivalent to about 1% of GDP. The size of the armed forces at the end of 2000 was some 5,000 personnel, including those serving under compulsory conscription of 12 months, while reservists numbered an estimated 14,500.

Latvia, economy

In transition from state control to a free-market system, assisted by links with the Nordic region. Latvia is a maritime **Baltic State**, with limited natural resources.

GNP: US $7,165m. (2000); *GNP per capita*: $2,860 (2000); *GDP at PPP*: $9,800m. (1999); *GDP per capita at PPP*: $4,200 (1999); *exports*: $1,865m. (2000); *imports*: $2,895m. (2000); *currency*: lats (plural: lats; US $1=L0.63 at the end of December 2001).

In 1999 industry accounted for 28% of GDP, agriculture for 4% and services for 68%. Some 27% of the land is arable, 13% permanent pasture and 46% forests and woodland. The main crops are grain, sugar beet and vegetables. Dairy farming and pig breeding are a more important element of agriculture than arable farming. Latvia has a developed fishing fleet, and forest resources are exploited. Mineral resources include small reserves of amber, peat, limestone and dolomite. Some petroleum reserves have, however, been identified and exploration has begun with foreign partners. The main industries are food products, textiles and clothing, wood products and transport equipment. Latvia is heavily dependent on imports to meet its energy requirements, notably electrical energy from **Estonia** and **Lithuania** and petroleum products from the **Russian Federation** and Lithuania.

Latvia's main exports by value in 2000 were timber and timber products (37% of the total), textiles (14%), metals and metalwork (13%), food products and live animals (11%) and chemical products (6%). Principal imports in 2000 were machinery and electrical equipment (21%), mineral products (13%), chemical industry products (11%), foodstuffs (10%) and metals and metalwork (8%). Germany and the UK both took 17% of Latvia's exports in 2000, followed by Sweden (11%). Germany was the supplier of 16% of Latvia's imports in 2000, while the Russian Federation provided 12% and Finland 9%. The **European Union** (EU) accounted in 1998 for 50% of Latvia's exports and 55% of its imports.

After regaining independence in 1991, Latvia experienced considerable difficulties as regards trading patterns with the other former Soviet republics, notably in respect of fuels and other raw materials. Agricultural output dropped sharply, many manufacturing sectors suffered extreme difficulties in securing supplies, manufacturing output fell drastically and inflation rose to around 1,000% in 1992. However, as economic reform measures introduced in 1992 began to take effect, buttressed by the introduction of the lats as the currency in 1993, gradual improvements were experienced from 1994. Real GDP growth of 3.3% in 1996 was followed by rapid expansion of 8.6% in 1997, during which the inflation rate was brought down to single figures and unemployment to 7% of the labour force. By 1997 almost all prices had been freed, most subsidies had been removed and a new competition law had been enacted.

The Russian financial crisis of mid-1998 (*see* **Russian Federation, economy**) caused serious repercussions, aggravated by disputes over the rights of ethnic **Russians** in Latvia. GDP growth fell back to under 4% in 1998 and to only 0.1% in 1999, while unemployment rose to nearly 10% by the end of 1999. Strong recovery began in 2000, with real GDP growth of 6.6% and a reduction in unemployment to under 8%, while inflation was only slightly higher at 2.6%. The Government reported in December 2000 that tax collection and social insurance payment rates had risen to over 70% of sums due and that the size of the 'black' economy was declining, although its share of economic activity remained worrying high at over 40%. The Government's budget for 2001 provided for expenditure of L1,500m. and revenue of L1,440m., the projected deficit being equivalent to 1.7% of GDP. GDP growth of 4.4% was projected for 2001, while inflation was expected to increase to 3.5%.

Latvia became a full member of the **World Trade Organization** in February 1999 and in December 1999 secured acceptance as a designated candidate for EU membership, on which formal negotiations opened in February 2000. The key determinant of domestic economic policy therefore became the perceived need to adapt Latvian laws and procedures to EU requirements and to ensure that Latvian economic indicators were brought within the EU's Maastricht criteria.

Land reform and the process of land privatization, which had already begun before independence, was accelerated in 1992 with the division of collectivized land into individual plots, although some of the resultant private farms were uneconomically small. The privatization of state-owned enterprises was launched in 1994, but considerable difficulties were met owing to strong political and trade union opposition to the sell-off of the larger entities. In 1996 all state-owned enterprises were transferred to the **Latvian Privatization Agency** (established in 1994) and by the end of 2000 the disposal of the small and medium-sized sectors had been largely completed. However, moves to privatize certain large shipping, energy and other enterprises continued to be dogged by problems of domestic opposition and failure to find suitable buyers.

Latvia's Way
Latvijas Celš (LC)

A pivotal centrist political party in **Latvia**, affiliated to the **Liberal International**. Originally a loose grouping of well-known pro-independence personalities of the Soviet era, the LC became the largest parliamentary party in the 1993 elections, winning 34 of the 100 seats with a 32.4% vote share, and becoming the leading party in the succeeding coalition Government, first under Valdis Birkavs and from September 1994 under Maris Gailis. Paying the democratic penalty for government incumbency in difficult economic times, the LC slumped to 17 seats and 14.6% in the 1995 elections, although it continued in government in a broad centre-right coalition in which Gailis became a Deputy Prime Minister.

In the October 1998 elections the LC recovered somewhat to 21 seats and 18.1% of the vote, and the LC's Vilis Krištopans became Prime Minister of a new centre-right coalition Government. In July 1999 the LC surrendered the premiership to the **People's Party** but recovered it in April 2000 in the person of Andris **Berzinš**, the Mayor of **Riga**, who became head of Latvia's ninth Government in a decade of independence.

Leadership: Andris Berzinš (political leader); Andrejs Pantelejevs (Chair.).
Address: 25–29 Jauniela, Riga 1050.
Telephone: 7224162.
Fax: 7821121.
E-mail: lc@lc.lv
Internet: www.lc.lv

Latvian Chamber of Commerce and Industry
Latvijas Tirdzniecibas un Rupniecibas Kamera

The principal organization in **Latvia** for promoting business contacts, both internally and externally, in the post-communist era. Originally founded in 1934.

President: Viktors Kulbergs.
Address: K. Valdemara iela 35, Riga.
Telephone: 7225595.
Fax: 7820092.
E-mail: info@chamber.lv
Internet: www.chamber.lv

Latvian Development Agency

Promotes foreign investment and exports in **Latvia**. Founded in 1993.

Director-General: Maris Elerts.
Address: Perses iela 2, Riga 1442.
Telephone: 7283425.
Fax: 7820458.
E-mail: invest@lda.gov.lv
Internet: www.lda.gov.lv

Latvian Free Trade Union Confederation
Latvijas Brivo Arodbiedribu Savieniba (LBAS)

Latvia's main trade union centre, directly descended from the Soviet-era structure, which was reorganized at independence in 1990. The LBAS has seen its influence decline, as trade union membership fell in the 1990s from around 80% in the Soviet-era to under 30% of the labour force by 2000. Affiliated to the

International Confederation of Free Trade Unions (ICFTU), LBAS has 26 affiliated unions representing about 200,000 workers.
Chair.: Juris Radzevics.
Address: 29–31 Bruninieku St, Riga 1001.
Telephone: 7270351.
Fax: 7276649.
E-mail: lbas@com.latnet.lv

Latvian Privatization Agency
Latvijas Privatizacijas Agentura (LPA)

The agency in **Latvia** established in April 1994, which was charged with the privatization of all state assets by the Andris Škele Government in 1996. Although more than 300 entities were privatized by 1997, the process was inhibited by political differences which caused several Economic Ministers to resign. In May 1999, Prime Minister Vilis Krištopans was appointed Minister for the LPA (a new portfolio) and the 'state proxy', previously held by the dismissed Minister of Economics Ainars Slesers.
Director-General: Janis Naglis.
Address: K. Valdemara iela 31, Riga 1887.
Telephone: 7021358.
Fax: 7830363.
E-mail: info@mail.lpa.bkc.lv
Internet: www.lpa.bkc.lv

Latvian Social Democratic Workers' Party
Latvijas Socialdemokratiska Stradnieku Partija (LSDSP)

Latvia's leading party in the 1920s but much less influential after independence was regained in 1990, despite having the imprimatur of **Socialist International** membership. Re-established in 1989 after 50 years in exile, the LSDSP performed poorly in early post-independence elections, not least because social democratic forces were split.

In October 1997 it joined with the (ex-communist) Latvian Social Democratic Party (LSDP) to launch the Latvian Social Democratic Union (LSDA), which in the October 1998 elections advanced strongly to 14 seats on a 12.8% vote share. In February 1999 the LSDA undertook to give qualified support to the incumbent centre-right coalition headed by **Latvia's Way**. In May 1999 the LSDA components opted for collective reversion to the historic LSDSP designation.
Leadership: Prof. Juris Bojars (Chair.).
Address: Ranka dambis 1, Riga 1048.
Telephone: 7614099.

Fax: 7614600.
E-mail: lsdsp@liv.lv
Internet: www.lsdsp.lv

Latvians

An Indo-European people. The name 'Latviji' is thought to have derived from a river 'Latve' and was modified to 'Latvis' by **Finno-Ugric** settlers. German rulers changed the name to Lette and renamed the state Livonia. Closely related to Lithuanian, the Latvian language belongs to the Baltic group, a highly inflective language written in the Latin script. It replaced Russian as the official language in **Latvia** in 1988. The earliest written forms are from 16th-century catechisms. The proportion of ethnic Latvians fell significantly following the policy of 'Sovietization' and a substantial number moved abroad, notably to the USA. Western Latvia retains the cultural and religious ties of German and Scandinavian rule, while eastern Latvia (Latgale) retains more Polish and Russian influences.

Law and Justice
Prawo i Sprawiedliwość (PiS)

A right-wing anti-crime political party in **Poland** which was among a trio of rightist parties to achieve surprising success in elections in 2001. The PiS was originally a faction within the **Solidarity Electoral Action** (AWS) party led by Lech Kaczyński, who was appointed Justice Minister in the AWS Government of Prime Minister Jerzy **Buzek** in mid-2000. He led a hugely popular anti-crime drive from the Ministry and was regularly cited as the second-most popular politician in Poland after President Aleksander **Kwaśniewski**. However, his crusade against organized crime and corruption ran into conflict with the State Prosecutor's Office, prompting tensions with Buzek. Kaczyński was finally dismissed from the Cabinet on 4 July 2001 and immediately set about transforming the PiS group into a fully-fledged political party with the help of his brother Jarosław Kaczyński, the former leader of the right-wing minority Centrum Alliance. In the September 2001 elections the PiS won a sizeable 9.5% of the vote and was awarded 44 seats in the lower house of the **National Assembly**.

Leadership: Lech Kaczyński and Jarosław Kaczyński.
Address: ul. Wiejska 4/6/8, 00902 Warsaw.
Telephone: (22) 6942181.
Fax: (22) 6942057.
E-mail: kp.pis@sejm.org.pl
Internet: www.kp.pis.org.pl

LBAS *see* **Latvian Free Trade Union Confederation.**

League of Communists of Yugoslavia

LC *see* **Latvia's Way**.

LCS *see* **Lithuanian Centre Union**.

LCY *see* **League of Communists of Yugoslavia**.

LDF *see* **Lithuanian Federation of Labour**.

LDK *see* **Democratic League of Kosovo**.

LDPB *see* **Liberal Democratic Party of Belarus**.

LDPR *see* **Liberal Democratic Party of Russia**.

LDS *see* **Liberal Democracy of Slovenia**.

LDS *see* **Lithuanian Workers' Union**.

League of Communists of Yugoslavia
Savez Komunista Jugoslavije (SKJ)

The single ruling party of the **Socialist Federal Republic of Yugoslavia** (SFRY) until 1990. Founded in 1919 as the Communist Party of Yugoslavia (KPJ), the party supported the communist partisan resistance during the Second World War and came to power in 1945. The KPJ stuck closely to the format of the **Communist Party of the Soviet Union** (KPSS) until 1952, when at the KPJ's sixth party congress it broke its ties to the KPSS and renamed itself the SKJ. The various republican branches of the party were named in turn as the Serbian League of Communists and so on. Under the leadership of **Tito**, the SKJ was the centre of political power in the SFRY and membership was seen as the main route to influence and power. However, from 1952 to Tito's death in 1980 the party underwent moves to reduce its grip on the State, particularly on the economy. Despite attempts by Tito to reassert its position every now and then, by the 1980s its membership and influence had decreased considerably. Under the reformist 1974 Constitution other political parties were tolerated as appendages of the SKJ, leading to the erosion of its central power. The defining moment in the party's demise came at the 14th party congress, in 1990. The single-party State was abandoned and multi-party elections were agreed in principle. However, attempts to formalize the process of decentralization and reverse the growing influence of the Serbian League were floated and blocked, prompting the **Slovenian** delegation to stage a walk out of the conference which effectively engendered the collapse of the SFRY.

The republican divisions of the SKJ reorganized themselves as new parties, ranging from left-of-centre to nationalist. In **Serbia** the successor **Socialist Party** of **Serbia** (SPS), headed by Slobodan **Milošević**, took on the role as **Yugoslavia**'s ruling party.

League of Polish Families

Liga Polskich Rodzin (LPR)

An 'ultra-conservative' religious political party in **Poland**. The LPR was established in February 2001 and has very close relations with the **Roman Catholic Church**. It advocates 'family values' and is vehemently against the country's accession to the **European Union** (EU). Party officials have even described the EU as a pagan institution, and accuse it of attempting to abrogate Poland's sovereignty. As an opposing stance it has called for much closer ties to the USA. It has accordingly received particular support among expatriate **Poles** in the USA. The LPR was one of a handful of radical parties to fare surprisingly well at the polls in September 2001, winning 7.9% of the vote and 38 seats in the lower house of the **National Assembly**.
Leadership: Antoni Macierewicz.
Address: ul. Wiejska 4/6/8, 00902 Warsaw.
Telephone: (22) 6941497.
Fax: (22) 6941548.
E-mail: klub-parlament@lpr.pl
Internet: www.lpr.pl

LETA
(Latvian Telegraph Agency)

The main news agency in **Latvia** which was founded as the state service in 1919 by the provisional Latvian Government under the name Latopress. It was transformed into the Latvian Telegraph Agency (LETA) in 1920. Under Soviet rule it was 'subordinated' to the Telegraph Agency of the Soviet Union (TASS—*see* **ITAR-TASS**), and renamed Latinform in 1971. On independence LETA was reformed as the state news agency. It was privatized in 1997 but remains the country's 'national' news agency.
Chair.: Martinš Barkans.
Address: Palasta iela 10, Riga 1502.
Telephone: 7222509.
Fax: 7223850.
E-mail: leta.marketing@leta.lv
Internet: www.leta2000.com

Lezghins

A Caucasian and Sunni **Muslim** people found in the north of **Azerbaijan** and in the south of the **Russian** republic of **Dagestan** in a region historically known as Lezghistan. The Caucasian Lezghins were divided between the Russian imperial administrative regions around the cities of **Baku** in Azerbaijan and Derbent in Dagestan. Since the collapse of the **Soviet Union** in 1991 this has meant the first international division of the Lezghin people.

Officially numbering around 290,000 in Azerbaijan, Lezghins have faced attempts to assimilate them into the **Azeri** population there. Discrimination in the workplace and a lack of education in the Lezghin language is thought to lead many Lezghins to deny their ethnicity in censuses. Estimates suggest that the real number of Lezghins in Azerbaijan may be as high as one million. Tensions with Azeris were fuelled by the conflict with **Armenia**. Azeris evicted from the Armenian enclave of **Nagorno-Karabakh** were resettled in Lezghistan, and the Lezghin community resented conscription to fight in the war. The *Sadual* (Unity) movement was established to promote Lezghin rights.

The 250,000 Lezghins living in Dagestan have much greater political and cultural freedom. The Unity movement, known in Dagestan as *Sadval*, has led calls for the reunification of Lezghistan. A Lezghin National Council was created in December 1991 to promote the idea to the regional governments. The closure of the Russia-Azerbaijan border in 1994 during the war in **Chechnya** provoked strong reactions from the Lezghin community on both sides of the new divide.

Liberal Alliance of Montenegro
Liberalni Savez Crne Gore (LSCG)

A political party which has been consistently and strongly in favour of the withdrawal of **Montenegro** from federation with **Serbia** within **Yugoslavia**. Having taken third place by winning 13 seats in the December 1992 Montenegrin Assembly elections, the LSCG contested the November 1996 elections within the People's Unity alliance, which won 19 Montenegrin seats and eight in the **Federal Assembly** lower house. Reverting to independent status for the next Montenegrin elections in May 1998, it won five seats on a platform of secession from the Yugoslav Federation.

Following the exit of the **Milošević** regime in **Belgrade** in late 2000, the LSCG contested the April 2001 Montenegrin Assembly elections outside the pro-independence alliance led by the **Democratic Party of Socialists of Montenegro** (DPSCG), fearing that the DPSCG was not deeply committed to separation. The narrowness of the result between the pro-independence and pro-Federation sides left the LSCG, which won six seats, able to give the DPSCG-led bloc an overall majority. However, coalition talks foundered on the LSCG's demand for additional seats in the Assembly, whereupon the party pledged external support to a DPSCG-

led minority Government which promised to hold an early independence referendum.
Leadership: Slavko Perović (Chair.).
Address: c/o Skupština Crne Gore, Podgorica.
E-mail: lscginfo@lscg.crnagora.com
Internet: www.lscg.crnagora.com

Liberal Democracy of Slovenia
Liberalna Demokracija Slovenije (LDS)

The centre-left party which has dominated political life in **Slovenia** in the post-independence period. It is a secular party affiliated to the **Liberal International**. The present LDS was founded in 1994 as a merger of the then ruling Liberal Democratic Party, itself derived from the communist-era Federation of Socialist Youth of Slovenia (ZSMS), and three small formations, including the Slovenian Greens. The Liberal Democrats had come to power in April 1992 at the head of a centre-left coalition under Janez **Drnovšek** (a former member of the collective presidency of the **SFRY**) and had become the largest party in the first post-independence elections in December 1992, winning 22 seats on a 21.4% vote share. A third of the deputies in the **National Assembly** joined the new LDS, which advocated the decentralization of power and rapid transition to a market economy.

Despite losing two of its coalition partners in the interim, the LDS retained power until the November 1996 Assembly elections, in which it remained the largest single party but with only 25 seats on a 27% vote share. The following month Drnovšek narrowly secured re-election as Prime Minister on the basis of a disparate coalition which included the left-wing **United List of Social Democrats** (ZLSD), the far-right **Slovenian National Party** (SNS) and the **Democratic Party of Slovenian Pensioners** (DeSUS). In February 1997, however, he succeeded in forming a more stable coalition which included the **Slovenian People's Party** (SLS) and the DeSUS.

In presidential elections in November 1997 the LDS candidate, Bogomir Kovač, came a distant seventh with only 2.7% of the vote. Thereafter, increasing strains in the coalition culminated in the withdrawal of the SLS in April 2000 and Drnovšek's resignation after he had lost a confidence vote, whereupon an SLS-led coalition took office in June. Drnovšek obtained revenge in parliamentary elections in October 2000, when the LDS advanced to 34 of the 90 seats on a vote share of 36.3%. He proceeded to form a broad-based centre-left coalition which included what had become the SLS+SKD, the ZLSD and the DeSUS.

Leadership: Janez Drnovšek (Chair.).
Address: Trg Republike 3, Ljubljana 1000.
Telephone: (1) 2312659.
Fax: (1) 4256150.

E-mail: lds@lds.si
Internet: www.lds.si

Liberal Democratic Party of Belarus
Liberalna-Demokratychnaya Partiya Belarusi (LDPB)

A right-wing **pan-Slavic** formation, the **Belarus** fraternal party of Vladimir Zhirinovskii's **Liberal Democratic Party of Russia**. In September 1998 the LDPB was a founder member of the pro-**Lukashenka Belarusian People's Patriotic Union** (BNPS), grouping some 30 conservative parties which backed the **Belarus-Russia Union** treaty, including the **Communist Party of Belarus**. In elections to the House of Representatives (the lower house of the **National Assembly**) in October 2000 the BNPS and its allies obtained near-total ascendancy, amidst opposition and external claims of electoral manipulation and fraud.

Leadership: Syargey Gaydukevich (Chair.).
Address: 22 Platonava Street, Minsk 220056.
Telephone: (17) 2695909.
Fax: (17) 2477257.
E-mail: ldpb@infonet.by

Liberal Democratic Party of Russia
Liberalno-Demokraticheskaya Partiya Rossii (LDPR)

A populist ultra-nationalist formation in the **Russian Federation** which rose to prominence in the early 1990s but lost support thereafter. The LDPR was founded in 1990 under the leadership of Vladimir Zhirinovskii, who attracted attention for his xenophobic views tinged with antisemitism, his more extravagant proposals including one for a Russian reconquest of Finland. He obtained 7.8% of the vote in the 1991 presidential poll, following which the party was technically banned in August 1992 for falsifying its membership records. It was allowed to contest the December 1993 elections to the State Duma (lower house of the **Federal Assembly**), in which it became the second-strongest party with 64 seats and headed the proportional voting with a 22.8% share.

Although forming the main parliamentary opposition to the **Yeltsin** administration in 1993–95, the LDPR gradually lost momentum as Zhirinovskii attracted much international opprobrium for his increasingly controversial statements and conduct. In the December 1995 State Duma elections, the LDPR again took second place with 51 seats, but fell back to 11.4% of the proportional vote. In the 1996 presidential elections, moreover, Zhirinovskii came no better than a poor fifth in the first round, with only 5.7% of the vote.

Having called for the banning of all communist formations, Zhirinovskii led the LDPR to a further major setback in the December 1999 State Duma elections, in which the party slumped to 17 seats and 6% of the proportional vote. Even worse followed in the March 2000 presidential elections, in which the LDPR leader obtained only 2.7% of the vote. The party's 12th congress in May 2001 called for an alliance of ex-Soviet republics as a counterweight to **NATO**, the adoption of Tsarist territorial divisions in the Russian Federation, greater state control of the economy and the reactivation of the death penalty.

Leadership: Vladimir Zhirinovskii (Chair.).
Address: Lukov per. 9, Moscow 103045.
Telephone: (095) 2610033.
Fax: (095) 9282444.
E-mail: pressldpr@duma.gov.ru
Internet: www.ldpr.ru

Liberal Democratic Union
Bashkimi Liberal Demokrat (BLD)

A small centrist political party in **Albania**. The BLD joined the **Union for Victory** electoral coalition, headed by the major opposition **Democratic Party of Albania**, in time for the June 2001 election. The coalition won 46 seats in the 140-seat **People's Assembly** but denounced the results of the election, which was won by the **Socialist Party of Albania**, and boycotted the chamber for three months from its opening in September.

Leadership: Teodor Laço.

Liberal International

The world union of 83 liberal parties in 58 countries, founded in 1947.
Leadership: Annemie Neyts-Uyttebroek (President);
Jan Weijers (Secretary-General).
Address: 1 Whitehall Place, London, SW1A 2HD, United Kingdom.
Telephone: (20) 78395905.
Fax: (20) 79252685.
E-mail: all@liberal-international.org
Internet: www.liberal-international.org

Liberal Party
Liberalna Stranka (LS)

A centrist party in **Croatia** which joined the Government coalition in January 2000. The LS was launched in January 1998 by 1997 presidential contender Vlado Gotovać after he had lost the leadership of the **Croatian Social-Liberal Party** (HSLS). In the January 2000 elections to the lower house of the **Assembly** the party was part of the United List (ZL) alliance headed by the **Croatian Peasants' Party**, winning two seats in its own right and obtaining one portfolio in the resultant six-party coalition Government headed by the **Social Democratic Party of Croatia** (SPH). At the party's second congress in October 2000, Zlatko Kramarić was elected LS Chairman in succession to Gotovać, who died two months later.

Leadership: Zlatko Kramarić (President).
Address: 16/I Ilica, 10000 Zagreb.
Telephone: (1) 4833798.
Fax: (1) 4833799.
Internet: www.liberali.hr

Lithuania
Lietuvos Respublika

An independent **Baltic State** in north-eastern Europe, bounded to the north by Latvia, to the east and south-east by Belarus, to the south-west by Poland, and to the west by the Baltic Sea and by the **Kaliningrad** enclave of the Russian Federation. Administratively, the country is divided into 11 cities and 44 regions (rajonai).

Area: 65,200 sq km; *capital*: **Vilnius**; *population*: 3.7m. (2001 estimate), comprising **Lithuanians** 80.6%, **Russians** 8.7%, **Poles** 7%, **Belarusians** 1.6%, others 2.1%; *official language*: Lithuanian; *religion*: mainly **Roman Catholic**, with **Russian Orthodox** and Lutheran minorities.

Legislative authority is vested in the unicameral **Parliament** (Seimas). It has 141 deputies elected for a four-year term, of whom 71 are returned from single-member constituencies by majority voting and 70 by proportional representation subject to a 5% threshold. The Head of State is the President, who is elected for a five-year term (renewable once) by universal suffrage. Executive power is held by the Prime Minister, who is appointed by the President, and by the Council of Ministers.

History: The kingdom of Lithuania emerged in the mid-13th century, as the Lithuanian tribes united to resist the repeated invasions of the German Teutonic Knights. A dynastic union with **Poland** in 1386 enabled Vytataus the Great to win a decisive victory over the Knights at Tannenberg in 1410, following which the dual monarchy became Europe's largest state, stretching from the Baltic to the Black Sea. Under the 1569 Union of Lublin Lithuania became a principality of the unified Polish kingdom, as part of which it was annexed by the Russian Empire in the partitions of Poland in 1772–95.

Occupied by Germany at the outbreak of the First World War, Lithuania declared its independence in 1918, although this was only fully achieved once German and Soviet troops were expelled and a peace treaty was signed with the **Soviet Union** in Moscow in 1920. The fact that Vilnius, the historic Lithuanian capital, was taken by revived independent Poland fuelled inter-war nationalist sentiment in Lithuania, where an authoritarian regime seized power in 1926. Following the outbreak of the Second World War in 1939, Vilnius was recovered in the German–Soviet repartition of Poland, but at the speedy expense in 1940 of incorporation into the USSR as the Lithuanian Soviet Socialist Republic. Germany invaded and then occupied Lithuania from 1941 (many thousands of Lithuanian **Jews** being murdered), but Soviet forces regained control in 1944. The 'Sovietization' of Lithuania followed, including agricultural collectivization and mass deportations, despite Lithuanian guerrilla resistance. Neither the USA nor the UK ever formally recognized the Soviet absorption of Lithuania and the other two Baltic republics.

In the late 1980s, encouraged by the Polish **Solidarity** movement and the *glasnost* (openness) initiative in the Soviet Union, dissident movements of Roman Catholics (*see* **Roman Catholic Church**) and anti-communist intellectuals united to form the **Sąjudis** popular front to campaign for Lithuanian independence. Links with popular fronts in **Estonia** and **Latvia** were also established. The 1990 elections to the Lithuanian Supreme Soviet returned pro-independence Sąjudis candidates with a majority of seats, so abolishing the communist monopoly of power, while the majority wing of the Lithuanian Communist Party severed its Soviet ties and became the Lithuanian Democratic Labour Party (LDDP). The new legislature declared the independent Republic of Lithuania and elected Vytautas Landsbergis, the Sąjudis Chairman, as Head of State. In retaliation, the Soviet Union imposed an economic blockade. This was lifted when the legislature agreed to suspend the independence declaration, but in early 1991, after Soviet troops had fired on civilians in Vilnius, Lithuanian voters gave overwhelming support in a national referendum (90%) for outright independence. Following the failure of the attempted coup to remove Soviet President Mikhail **Gorbachev** in August 1991 (*see* **August coup**), Lithuania achieved its independence the following month.

Legislative and presidential elections were held in 1992 and 1993 respectively, following the approval of a new Constitution by referendum. The parliamentary elections resulted in a heavy defeat for the increasingly right-wing Sąjudis and the unexpected return to power of the LDDP on a platform of gradual transition to a free-market economy. In the presidential contest in early 1993, LDDP candidate Algirdas **Brazauskas** (former First Secretary of the Lithuanian Communist Party) was directly elected with 60% of the vote.

Appointed as Prime Minister in 1993, Adolfas Šleževičius (LDDP) had nearly completed a full term when disclosures of alleged corruption forced him to resign in February 1996. In a general election in October–November of that year the Sąjudis successor party, the **Homeland Union–Lithuanian Conservatives** (TS–LK), won a large majority (70 seats) but opted to form a centre-right coalition with the **Lithuanian Christian Democratic Party** (LKDP) and the **Lithuanian Centre Union** (LCS) under the premiership of Gediminas Vagnorius. In presidential elections in late 1996 and early 1997, TS–LK-backed independent candidate Valdas **Adamkus** narrowly-defeated former prosecutor Arturas Paulauskas, who was supported by the left, by 50.3% to 49.7% in the second round. Adamkus had emigrated to the USA in 1944, after fighting against Nazi and Soviet occupation during

Lithuania

the Second World War, and had obtained US citizenship, which he relinquished in order to contest the election.

In one of a series of adaptations to European norms, the Seimas in December 1998 approved the abolition of the death penalty in Lithuania.

An escalating conflict between Adamkus and Vagnorius, highlighting differences of government style, forced the latter out of office in April 1999, whereupon the premiership was entrusted to Rolandas Paksas, the conservative Mayor of Vilnius. Growing divisions between the coalition parties compelled Paksas to resign in October 1999, the new Prime Minister being Andrius Kubilius (TS–LK). Paksas and his supporters promptly defected to the opposition **Lithuanian Liberal Union** (LLS), of which Paksas became Chairman.

Latest elections: Parliamentary elections in October 2000 resulted in the left-wing 'A. Brazauskas Social Democratic Coalition', including the LDDP and the **Lithuanian Social Democratic Party** (LSDP), winning 51 of the 141 seats with 31.1% of the vote. In second place came the reinvigorated LLS with 34 seats (17.3%), followed by the **New Union (Social Liberals)** (NS) with 29 (19.6%), the TS–LK with 9 (8.6%), the **Lithuanian Farmers' Party** (LVP) with 4 (4.1%), the LKDP with 2 (3.1%), the LCS with 2 (3.1%) and the **Lithuanian Poles' Electoral Action** (LLRA) with 2 (1.9%). Five other parties won one seat each and three independents were elected.

Recent developments: Despite having become substantially the largest parliamentary group in the October 2000 elections, the Social Democratic Coalition was outmanoeuvred in subsequent inter-party negotiations on a new Government by the ascendant centrist parties. The outcome was a three-party majority coalition headed by Paksas of the LLS and including the NS and the LCS, committed to accelerated liberalization of the economy and to achieving speedy accession to the **European Union** (EU) and the **North Atlantic Treaty Organization** (NATO).

However, divisions within the coalition over the pace of Paksas's privatization drive led to the departure of the NS on 18 June 2001 and Paksas's resignation two days later. In the meantime, the LDDP and the LSDP had responded to their continued opposition status by formally merging in January 2001 under the historic LSDP party name and under the leadership of former President Brazauskas. Now the largest single party in the Seimas, the LSDP could not be ignored and, in a coalition with the NS, it formed a new Government with Brazauskas as Prime Minister in early July.

International relations and defence: Lithuania was admitted to the United Nations in 1991 and also joined the **Organization for Security and Co-operation in Europe**. In 1993 it became a full member of the **Council of Europe**. Following the completion in 1993 of the Russian military withdrawal from its territory, Lithuania joined NATO's **Partnership for Peace** programme in 1994. A Treaty of Friendship and Co-operation with Poland, stressing the two countries' strong historical ties, was signed in 1994, guaranteeing the rights of ethnic minorities and recognizing the existing borders. In 1997 Lithuania signed a treaty with the **Russian**

Federation delimiting the common border and guaranteeing Russian access to its Kaliningrad enclave, although the Russian Federation remained hostile to Lithuania's aim of becoming a full NATO member. In December 1999 Lithuania was accorded official candidate status by the EU, formal negotiations beginning in February 2000. In May 2001 Lithuania's membership of the **World Trade Organization** (WTO) was formally approved.

Independent Lithuania has pursued close co-operation with the other two Baltic states, while membership of the **Council of Baltic Sea States** provides an organizational basis for political, economic and other co-operation between Lithuania and other littoral and adjacent countries. In January 1998 the Presidents of Lithuania, Latvia, Estonia and the USA signed a **US-Baltic Partnership** charter.

Lithuania's defence budget for 2000 amounted to some US $157m., equivalent to about 1.5% of GDP. The size of the armed forces at the end of 2000 was some 12,500 personnel, including those serving under compulsory conscription of 12 months, while first-line reservists numbered an estimated 28,000.

Lithuania, economy

In transition from state control to a free-market system. Lithuania is a maritime **Baltic State**, with few natural resources.

GNP: US $11,039m. (2000); *GNP per capita*: $2,900 (2000); *GDP at PPP*: $17,300m. (1999); *GDP per capita at PPP*: $4,800 (1999); *exports*: $3,808m. (2000); *imports*: $5,418m. (2000); *currency*: litas (plural: litai; US $1=L4.00 at the end of December 2001).

In 1999 industry accounted for 32% of GDP, agriculture for 9% and services for 59%. The main crops are grain, vegetables, and sugar beet; animal husbandry declined sharply after independence in 1991, with the dismantling of the large collective and state farms which had supplied the **Soviet Union**. Lithuania has hardly any mineral resources, although there are reserves of peat and various construction materials; small-scale oil production began in 1990. The main industries include peat and construction material extraction, the refining of imported oil, food products and textiles. Over 80% of electricity production comes from nuclear generation (although concern has been expressed that the main reactors are of the same type as in the Ukrainian **Chernobyl** plant), and Lithuania exports considerable quantities of electricity, including to **Latvia**.

Lithuania's main exports are machinery and electrical equipment (19% of the 1998 total), mineral products (19%), textiles and clothing (19%), chemical products (10%) and foodstuffs (10%). Principal imports include machinery and transport equipment (30% of the 1998 total), crude oil and other mineral products (16%), chemical products (9%) and textiles and clothing (9%). In 2000 Latvia was the main purchaser of Lithuania's exports (15% of the total), followed by Germany (14%) and the UK (8%), while the **Russian Federation** was the main supplier of

Lithuania's imports (28%), with 15% coming from Germany and 5% each from **Poland** and the UK.

During the Soviet era the Lithuanian economy was transformed away from agriculture and into industry. Over 90% of Lithuania's trade was with Russia and other Soviet republics by the 1980s. Following the regaining of independence in 1991, Soviet-era trading patterns continued to be important, but the ending of the direct link and difficulties in adjusting to the global marketplace resulted in a sharp contraction in real GDP, by over 20% in 1992 alone, while inflation spiralled to over 1,000% in 1992. Although hampered by a financial crisis affecting two major banks in late 1995, recovery to GDP growth of 3.3% in 1995 gathered pace in 1996 with growth of 4.7%, while Lithuania's 7.3% GDP expansion in 1997 was one of the highest rates in the region. Over the same period, new currency board arrangements and fiscal stringency brought the inflation rate down to 8% in 1997 and to 2.4% in 1998.

The Russian financial crisis (*see* **Russian Federation, economy**) in mid-1998 impacted adversely on Lithuania, where slower GDP growth of 5.1% in 1998 was followed by contraction of 4% in 1999, in which aggregate import and exports volumes declined, the inflation rate fell to 0.3% and the budget deficit rose to 8.6% of GDP. The Government therefore launched a new IMF-approved stabilization and restructuring programme, geared in particular to preparing Lithuania for membership of the **European Union** (EU), on which formal negotiations began in February 2000. The result was renewed growth of around 3% in 2000 and a partial recovery in external trade, while the budget deficit was reduced to 3.3% of GDP. The Government's budget for 2001 as approved in December 2000 provided for expenditure of L7,100m. and revenue of L6,200m., the projected deficit being equivalent to 1.5% of GDP excluding debt repayment. An adverse consequence of the programme was sharply rising unemployment, to a record level of 13% in January 2001.

In June 2001 the **Bank of Lithuania** announced that the litas would switch from its peg to the US dollar to a peg to the euro as from February 2002 (the month after the EU currency went into circulation in the eurozone).

Legislation was adopted in 1991 for the restitution of land to former owners or their heirs and for the privatization of state-owned farms and the reorganization of collective farms. The privatization of industry was also embarked upon, initially through the voucher system and from 1997 mostly by direct sale. Although the process was complicated by the sharp post-independence economic downturn, over 80% of state assets had been privatized by the end of 1995 and the share of GDP generated by the private sector rose to 70% by 1998. In that year substantial stakes were sold to foreign companies in the main oil refining, telecommunications and dockyards enterprises, with much of the proceeds to be devoted to recompensing those who had lost savings in the 1992 hyper-inflation and the 1995–96 banking crisis. The new restructuring programme launched in 2000 included privatization of the remaining two large state-owned banks, the natural gas company and the power distribution network.

Lithuanian Centre Union
Lietuvos Centro Sajunga (LCS)

A small pro-market centrist party in **Lithuania** influential in the late 1990s, affiliated to the **Liberal International**. Dating from 1992, the LCS won two seats in the 1992 parliamentary elections and advanced strongly to 13 seats in 1996, becoming a junior partner in a centre-right coalition headed by the **Homeland Union–Lithuanian Conservatives** (TS–LK). It paid the penalty for the Government's unpopularity in the October 2000 elections, falling back to two seats and 2.9% of the vote, but nevertheless became part of the post-election centre-right coalition Government headed by the **Lithuanian Liberal Union** (LLS). However, divisions in the Government over the pace of the privatization programme led to its collapse in June 2001, and the LCS was left out of a new centre-left coalition headed by the **Lithuanian Social Democratic Party**.
Leadership: Kestutis Glaveckas (Chair.).
Address: Literatu 8, Vilnius 2001.
Telephone: (521) 24095.
Fax: (521) 23790.
E-mail: info@lcs.lt
Internet: www.lcs.lt

Lithuanian Christian Democratic Party
Lietuvos Krikščioniu Demokratu Partija (LKDP)

A party in **Lithuania** affiliated to the **Christian Democrat International**, launched in 1989 as the revival of a pre-Soviet party dating from 1905. The LKDP's political importance declined through the 1990s. It adopted a Christian democratic programme on the west European model, favouring Lithuania's integration into Western institutions.

The party's third-place vote share of 12.2% and 18 seats in the 1992 parliamentary elections was achieved in co-operation with other groups, notably the **Sąjudis** reform movement, which later became the **Homeland Union–Lithuanian Conservatives** (TS–LK). It was nevertheless in opposition until the 1996 elections. Although it slipped to 16 seats and 10% of the vote in that poll, it became the second-largest party, and joined a centre-right coalition Government headed by the TS–LK.

Serious strains in coalition relations from mid-1999 were accompanied by factional strife in LKDP ranks and the formation of alternative Christian democratic groupings. In the October 2000 parliamentary elections the rump LKDP slumped

to only two seats and 3.1% of the vote, going into opposition. In late 2000 the LKDP initiated talks with other Christian democratic factions on reunifying the historic party. The first stage of this was achieved in April 2001 when the LKDP merged with the Christian Democratic Union.
Leadership: Kazys Bobelis (Chair.).
Address: Pylimo 36/2, Vilnius 2001.
Telephone: (26) 26128 [(526) 26128 from September 2002].
Fax: (521) 27387.
E-mail: lkdp@takas.lt
Internet: www.lkdp.lt

Lithuanian Development Agency
Lietuvos Ekonomines Pletros Agentura (LEPA)

A state body acting as a local partner for foreign businesses interested in investing in **Lithuania** or sourcing products. The agency provides information about investment opportunities, conditions and procedures, as well as facilitating business partnerships and assisting in contacts with Lithuanian authorities and business organizations.
Director-General: Vytas E. Gruodis.
Address: Sv. Jono St 3, Vilnius 2600.
Telephone: (26) 27438 [(526) 27438 from September 2002].
Fax: (521) 20160.
E-mail: lda@lda.lt
Internet: www.lda.lt

Lithuanian Farmers' Party
Lietuvos Valstiečiu Partija (LVP)

An agrarian political formation in **Lithuania** dating from 1905, revived in 1990, which adopted its present name in 1994. Having won one seat in the 1996 national balloting, the party polled strongly in local elections in March 2000, before advancing to four national seats (with 4.1% of the vote) in the October 2000 parliamentary elections.
Leadership: Ramunas Karbauskis (Chair.).
Address: Blindžiu 17, Vilnius 2000.
Telephone: (27) 25268 [(527) 25268 from September 2002].

Lithuanian Federation of Labour (LDF)

One of several competing union centres in **Lithuania**, founded in 1991. Claiming descent from a pre-Soviet organization founded in 1919, the LDF is of Christian orientation and is affiliated to the World Confederation of Labour.
Chair.: Kazimieras Kuzminskas.
Address: 5/140 V. Mykolaičio-Putino, Vilnius 2026.
Telephone: (23) 12029 [(523) 12029 from September 2002].
Fax: (521) 27153.
E-mail: df@lietuva.net

Lithuanian Liberal Union
Lietuvos Liberalu Sajunga (LLS)

A centrist political party in **Lithuania** which gained a leading government role in 2000. The LLS was founded in November 1990 by pro-independence activists of Vilnius University and elsewhere. It failed to gain representation in the 1992 elections and won only one seat in 1996, but it polled strongly in the March 1997 local elections. In December 1999 it was greatly strengthened by the adhesion of a breakaway faction of the **Homeland Union–Lithuanian Conservatives** (TS–LK) led by former Prime Minister Rolandas Paksas, who became LLS Chairman.

In the October 2000 parliamentary elections the LLS achieved a major advance, to 34 seats on a 17.3% vote share. Paksas was therefore able to form a centrist majority coalition Government embracing the LLS, the **New Union (Social Liberals)** (NS) and the **Lithuanian Centre Union** (LCS). However, divisions between the parties over the Government's privatization programme led to its collapse in June 2001 with the departure of the NS. Paksas and the LLS were forced into opposition to a new coalition headed by the **Lithuanian Social Democratic Party** and including the NS.
Leadership: Rolandas Paksas (Chair.).
Address: A. Jakšto 9, Vilnius 2001.
Telephone: (23) 13264 [(523) 13264 from September 2002].
Fax: (27) 91910 [(527) 91910 from September 2002].
E-mail: lls@lls.lt
Internet: www.lls.lt

Lithuanian Poles' Electoral Action
Lietuvos lenku rinkimu akcija (LLRA)

A party founded in 1994 in **Lithuania** in succession to the Lithuanian Polish Union (LLS). The LLS had been formed in 1992 to represent the country's ethnic **Poles** (7% of the total population). The LLS won four parliamentary seats in 1992 on a platform calling for the 'national rebirth' of Lithuanian Poles, through the

promotion of Polish education within the context of a commitment to the Lithuanian State. It contested subsequent elections as the LLRA, which won only one seat in 1996 but improved to two in October 2000 on a 1.9% vote share.
Leadership: Valdemar Tomaszevski (Chair.).
Address: Didžioji 40, Vilnius 2601.
Telephone: (521) 23388.

Lithuanian Reform Movement
Sąjudis

The pro-democracy movement formed in **Lithuania** on 3 June 1988 which led the country to full independence two years later. Founded by around 500 activists, Sąjudis went on to organize anti-communist demonstrations, gaining rapid support. In free elections held in 1990 the movement won a clear majority in the Lithuanian **Parliament** and declared the country's independence on 11 March 1990. However, the arrival of independence exposed the internal divisions within the movement and it was ousted from power in elections held in October–November 1992. Following this defeat Sąjudis transformed itself into the right-wing **Homeland Union–Lithuanian Conservatives** (TS-LK) in May 1993.

Lithuanian Social Democratic Party
Lietuvos Socialdemokratu Partija (LSDP)

A member of the **Socialist International**, directly descended from the original LSDP founded in 1896 and since January 2001 uniting democratic socialist forces in **Lithuania**.

Prominent in the inter-war period of independence and maintained in exile under Soviet communist rule, the LSDP was revived in Lithuania in 1989 and formed part of the broad pro-independence movement under the umbrella of **Sąjudis**. The party contested the 1992 parliamentary elections independently, winning 5.9% of the vote and eight seats. It subsequently formed part of the parliamentary opposition to a Government of the Lithuanian Democratic Labour Party (LDDP, the relaunched pro-reform successor to the Communist Party of Lithuania), led by Algirdas **Brazauskas**.

In the October 1996 parliamentary elections, which represented a serious reverse for the LDDP, the LSDP by contrast advanced to 12 seats and 7% of the vote. The LSDP candidate, Vytenis Andriukaitis, came a disappointing fourth, with 5.7% of the vote, in the presidential elections of late 1997 and early 1998. However, the LSDP and the LDDP mounted increasingly effective joint opposition to the post-1996 centre-right Government headed by the **Homeland Union–Lithuanian Conservatives** (TS–LK).

The October 2000 parliamentary elections were contested jointly by the LSDP and the LDDP within the 'A. Brazauskas Social Democratic Coalition', which also included the small New Democratic Party (NDP) and the Lithuanian Russians' Union (LRS). The Coalition became substantially the largest group, winning 51 of the 141 seats with 31.1% of the vote. However, its leaders were outmanoeuvred in the subsequent party negotiations, which resulted in the formation of a centrist coalition Government headed by the **Lithuanian Liberal Union** (LLS).

Continuing in opposition, the LSDP and the LDDP formally merged at a **Vilnius** congress in January 2001. Brazauskas was elected Chairman of the unified party, which adopted the historic LSDP name to signify the reunification of the Lithuanian left after 80 years of division. In June when the coalition Government collapsed amidst divisions over its own privatization programme, the reinvigorated LSDP could not be overlooked. It formed a coalition with the **New Union (Social Liberals)** (NS), and Brazauskas was appointed Prime Minister on 3 July.

Leadership: Algirdas Brazauskas (Chair.).
Address: B. Radvilaites 1, Vilnius 2000.
Telephone: (26) 13907 [(526) 13907 from September 2002].
Fax: (26) 15420 [(526) 15420 from September 2002].
E-mail: info@lsdp.lt
Internet: www.lsdp.lt

Lithuanian State Privatization Agency

Government agency in **Lithuania**, founded in 1995. Its main functions are: to form a list of the enterprises to be privatized and to submit it for confirmation to the Government; to prepare privatization programmes; to determine the method of privatization; to publish a Privatization Information Bulletin; to look for potential investors; and to conclude the privatization transactions.

Director: Vytis Atkočiunas.
Address: Gedimino pr. 38/2, Vilnius 2600.
Telephone: (26) 24671 [(526) 24671 from September 2002].
Fax: (26) 23510 [(526) 23510 from September 2002].
E-mail: kpc@is.lt

Lithuanian Trade Union Unification
Lietuvos Profesiniu Sąjungu Susivienijimas (LPSS)

One of several competing union centres in **Lithuania**, founded in 1992. It is one of two Lithuanian affiliates to the International Confederation of Free Trade Unions (ICFTU) and has 12 member unions representing 42,300 workers.

Lithuanian Workers' Union (LDS)

Chair.: Algirdas Sysas.
Address: 9/213 J. Jasinskio, Vilnius 2600.
Telephone: (26) 10921 [(526) 10921 from September 2002].
Fax: (26) 19078 [(526) 19078 from September 2002].
E-mail: lpss@takas.lt

Lithuanian Workers' Union (LDS)

One of several trade union centres in **Lithuania**. It was founded under Soviet rule in 1988 as part of the **Sąjudis** pro-independence movement and became organizationally independent in 1989. Affiliated to the International Confederation of Free Trade Unions since 1994 and enjoying close links with the AFL-CIO (American Federation of Labor and Congress of Industrial Organizations) in the USA, the LDS links some 10 individual union organizations.
President: Aldona Balsiene.
Address: 5 V. Mykolaičio-Putino, Vilnius 2026.
Telephone: (26) 21743 [(526) 21743 from September 2002].
Fax: (26) 15253 [(526) 15253 from September 2002].

Lithuanians

A **Baltic** people dominant in modern **Lithuania**. The Baltic tribes have long been associated with the territory on the eastern bank of the Baltic Sea (from where their collective name is derived). The Lithuanian language is most closely related to Latvian and is similarly transcribed using the Latin script. The distinct history of the Lithuanians has set them culturally apart from their northern neighbours. Long connected since the later mediaeval period with the **Poles**, the Lithuanians adopted **Roman Catholicism**. They successfully managed to avoid russification after the incorporation of Lithuania into the **Soviet Union** in 1940.

Livonia

A historic term for an area in the hinterland of the **Baltic** coast comprising territory now in modern **Estonia, Latvia** and the **Russian Federation**. After the conquest of the region by the German Teutonic Knights in the early 13th century it was given the name Livland (Livonia in Latin) after the Livs, a **Finno-Ugric** tribe native to the area but later replaced by **Latvians** and **Estonians**. After centuries of rule the area was divided and redivided by conquest and war until in the 18th century when Livonia was occupied by Russia and split into the administrative districts of Estonia (to the north), Livonia (in the centre: modern-day southern Estonia and northern Latvia) and Courland (modern-day southern Latvia). The concept of Livonia was effectively lost in 1917 when Estonia and Latvia claimed their independence, dividing historic Livonia once again. These territorial boundaries were passed down to the present day.

Ljubljana

The capital of **Slovenia** situated in the centre of the country's mountainous terrain. *Population*: 258,960 (1998 estimate). After centuries of destruction and reconstruction, the city became an important regional centre under Austrian suzerainty in the 15th century (known in German as Laibach). Its role as a base for Slovene and south **Slavic** autonomy began when it was designated as the capital of Napoleon I's Illyrian provinces. Agitation for an autonomous south Slav union was also based in Ljubljana in the late 19th century. On Slovenia's inclusion in the Kingdom of Serbs, Croats and Slovenes in 1918 the city maintained its role as the Slovene capital and developed its transport links with the rest of the **Balkans**. Economic activity is varied including metalwork, textiles and general consumer goods.

Ljubljana Stock Exchange (LjSE)
Ljubljanska borza vrednostnih papirjev

The stock exchange in **Slovenia**, established in December 1989. Trading began in March 1990. Market capitalization at the end of 2000 totalled US $5,000m. At 1 December 2001 there were 33 members trading on the LjSE.
   President and Chief Executive: Dr Draško Veselinovič.
   Address: Slovenska cesta 56, 1000 Ljubljana.
   Telephone: (1) 4710211.
   Fax: (1) 4710213.
   E-mail: info@ljse.si
   Internet: www.ljse.si

LKDP *see* **Lithuanian Christian Democratic Party**.

LLRA *see* **Lithuanian Poles' Electoral Action**.

LLS *see* **Lithuanian Liberal Union**.

LPR *see* **League of Polish Families**.

LPSS *see* **Lithuanian Trade Union Unification**.

LS *see* **Liberal Party**.

LSCG *see* **Liberal Alliance of Montenegro**.

LSDP *see* **Lithuanian Social Democratic Party**.

LSDSP *see* **Latvian Social Democratic Workers' Party**.

Lukashenka, Alyaksandr

President of **Belarus** since 1994 and leading proponent of a **Belarus-Russia Union**.

Alyaksandr Grigorjevich Lukashenka was born on 30 August 1954 in the village of Alyaksandryna in the Mogilev region. After doing a history degree at the local pedagogical institute, he worked as a political propagandist in the army and in Komsomol, the Communist Youth League. He then did a degree in economics and was a manager on a collective farm in Shklov, then of a construction materials factory in the same town, before becoming head of the Harazdiec farm in his home region of Mogilev between 1987 and 1994.

First elected in July 1990 as a Deputy to the Supreme Soviet of the Belarus Soviet Socialist Republic, he founded a 'Communists for Democracy' deputies' group, and in the attempted **August coup** in Moscow in 1991 he supported the hardline communist 'national emergency committee' which briefly seized power in the **Kremlin**. In December 1991 he was the only Deputy in the Belarus Supreme Soviet to vote against the dissolution of the Soviet Union and formation of the **Commonwealth of Independent States** (CIS).

As Chairman of the newly independent Belarus's Supreme Soviet Commission for the Struggle against Corruption, a post to which he was appointed in April 1993, he played a key role in ousting the reformist Stanislau Shushkevich as Chairman of the Supreme Soviet in January 1994. A new Constitution providing for a presidential form of government opened the way for direct presidential elections held in two rounds in June and July 1994. In an unexpected result, Lukashenka was elected President for a five-year term, polling 44.8% of the vote in the first round and 80.1% in the second.

Lukashenka promoted increasingly close political relations with the **Russian Federation** as the centrepiece of his political platform. Domestically he came frequently into conflict with the legislature, the judiciary, the media and the wider public, as he strengthened his hold on power. In a nationwide referendum on proposals to change the 1994 Constitution, on 24 November 1996, the results were recorded as an 84% turnout and a 70.4% 'yes' vote for establishing a bicameral Parliamentary Assembly and extending Lukashenka's term of office to the year 2001 (a term extended further to 2002 in June 1997). The opposition denounced the vote as a 'farce' designed to legitimize a dictatorship. Domestic and more particularly international pressure eventually led him to hold a fresh election in September 2001, which he won by a convincing margin.

Address: Office of the President, Dom Urada, vul. K. Marksa 38, 220016 Minsk.
Telephone: (17) 2226006.
Fax: (17) 2260610.
E-mail: contact@president.gov.by
Internet: www.president.gov.by

LUKoil

The largest private oil-producing and exporting company in the **Russian Federation**. LUKoil was founded in 1991 through the merger of three of the biggest oil concerns in western **Siberia**: Langepasneftegaz, Uraineftegaz and Kogalymneftegaz. Since then it has expanded operations to other areas of the Russian Federation and particularly oil fields in Kazakhstan. LUKoil absorbed the KomiTEK company in 1999. LUKoil operates in 25 different countries and controls one of the biggest oil reserves in private hands, accounting for 24% of all oil produced in the Russian Federation and employing 120,000 people worldwide.
President: Vagit Yusufovich Alekperov.
Address: 11 Sretenski Boulevard, 101000 Moscow.
Telephone: (095) 9274444.
Fax: (095) 9289841.
E-mail: pr@lukoil.com
Internet: www.lukoil.com

Lustration laws

Post-communist **Czechoslovakia**'s controversial process of identifying and purging those found to have collaborated in the past with the **StB** (the secret police) under the communist regime. Lustration (or 'purification') was regarded by some as a key part of the decommunization process. The first significant act of lustration took place in March 1991, when several parliamentary deputies were publicly denounced as former collaborators by a Parliamentary Commission on the basis of evidence in the StB archive. In June 1991 a screening law was passed, allowing the dismissal of state employees found to have collaborated with the StB. Critics of lustration argued that the StB archive was unreliable and incomplete; that although many had been forced to collaborate under duress, there was no formal legal means of refuting allegations; and that the process would be manipulated by unscrupulous politicians keen to discredit their rivals.

LVP *see* **Lithuanian Farmers' Party**.

M

Macedonia
(Former Yugoslav Republic of Macedonia, FYROM)
Republika Makedonija

An independent landlocked republic in south-eastern Europe, bounded by Albania to the west, the Federal Republic of Yugoslavia (Serbia) to the north, Bulgaria to the east and Greece to the south. Administratively, the country is divided into 34 counties (opstinas).

Area: 25,300 sq km; *capital*: **Skopje**; *population*: 2m. (2001 estimate), comprising ethnic **Macedonians** 65%, **Albanians** 22%, **Turks** 4%, **Roma** 3%, **Serbs** 2%, others 4%; *official language*: Macedonian; *religion*: Eastern **Orthodox** 67%, **Muslim** 30%, other 3%.

Under the 1991 Constitution, legislative power rests with a unicameral **Assembly of the Republic** (Sobranie), which has 120 members elected by universal suffrage for a four-year term, 85 in single-member constituencies and 35 by proportional representation. The executive President is directly elected for a five-year term. The Cabinet, headed by a Prime Minister, is accountable to the legislature.

History: The present-day republic occupies the western part of the ancient kingdom of Macedon, dating from the 6th century BC and from 338 BC the ruler of the Greek Hellenistic world. A Roman province from 148 BC, Macedon came under the authority of the Byzantine Emperor after the Roman Empire was divided in 395 AD. In the 6th century **Slavic peoples** settled the region, which subsequently fell under intermittent **Bulgarian** and Byzantine influence until it became a part of the Ottoman Empire in the 14th century. Turkish rule lasted for the next 500 years, up to the Balkan wars of 1912–13, when the geographical area of Macedonia was divided between **Serbia** (which took the territory of the present-day republic), **Bulgaria** and Greece. After the First World War Serbian Macedonia became part of the Kingdom of Serbs, Croats and Slovenes (renamed **Yugoslavia** in 1929). During the Second World War it was occupied by Bulgaria (which was allied with Nazi Germany), before becoming at the end of the war a separate republic within a reconstituted (and communist-ruled) Yugoslav federal state under **Tito**.

Following President Tito's death in 1980, Yugoslavia's federal structure became increasingly unable to contain ethnic and nationalist rivalries between the constituent republics. Macedonia's aspirations towards independence were complicated by the presence of a large Albanian minority in the territory and by Greek objections to the name 'Macedonia' (also a province in northern Greece) being used in the official title of another State. Following the collapse of communist rule, multi-party elections to the Sobranie were held in late 1990, although with inconclusive results. No single party won an overall majority, the largest number of seats being won by the nationalist **Internal Macedonian Revolutionary Organization–Democratic Party for Macedonian National Unity** (VMRO–DPMNE), which formed the core of the resultant 'Government of experts'.

In a referendum in September 1991, some 95% of the two-thirds of eligible voters who participated—ethnic Albanians having boycotted the poll—backed an independent and sovereign Macedonia. A new Constitution was promulgated in November 1991 and Macedonia achieved its secession from the Yugoslav federation without violence, although inter-ethnic tensions and an increase in unrest necessitated the deployment of a United Nations peacekeeping contingent in the country from late 1992 until early 1999 (see below). The international controversy over the country's official name was partially resolved in September 1995 when Greece agreed to the formula 'Former Yugoslav Republic of Macedonia' (FYROM) and the two countries signed an agreement to establish diplomatic relations.

Presidential elections in late 1994 were won by the incumbent, Kiro **Gligorov** (in office since January 1991), standing as the candidate of the Union of Macedonia (SM), comprising the (ex-communist) **Social Democratic Union of Macedonia** (SDSM), the Liberal Party of Macedonia (LPM) and the Socialist Party of Macedonia (SPM). In simultaneous legislative elections the SM won 95 of the 120 seats (the SDSM taking 58, the LPM 29 and the SPM 8). A coalition Government was subsequently formed between the SM and the (Albanian) **Party for Democratic Prosperity** (PDP). In February 1996, following discord within the SM, a new Government was formed under incumbent Prime Minister Branko Crvenkovski, including the SDSM, SPM and PDP but excluding the Liberals.

Latest elections: Macedonia's third democratic legislative elections were held in October and November 1998, against a regional backdrop of escalating conflict between Serbian security forces and the majority Albanian population in the neighbouring Yugoslav province of **Kosovo**. The VMRO–DPMNE, in coalition with the recently-formed **Democratic Alternative** (DA), won 59 of the 120 seats with 38.8% of the proportional vote, the SDSM 29 (25.1%), and an alliance of the PDP and the **Democratic Party of Albanians** (DPA) 14 and 11 respectively (19.3%), the Liberals—reconstituted as the Liberal-Democratic Party—4 (7.0%) and an alliance of the SPM and the Roma Union of Macedonia 2 and 1 respectively (4.7%). A coalition Government of the VMRO–DPMNE, the DA and the DPA was formed in December 1998, with the VMRO–DPMNE leader, Ljubčo **Georgievski**, as Prime Minister.

Presidential elections were held in October–November 1999, with partial rerun of the second round being required in December because of irregularities in the main polling. The outcome was that Boris **Trajkovski** of the VMRO–DPMNE was elected in the second round with 52.9% of the vote against 45.9% for Tito Petkovski of the SDSM.

Recent developments: Increasing strains between the VMRO–DPMNE and the DA resulted in the latter's withdrawal from the Government in November 2000, whereupon Georgievski formed a new coalition between the VMRO–DPMNE and the DPA, dependent for a parliamentary majority on Liberal and dissident DA deputies. The reconstituted Government faced its greatest challenge, however, from an insurgency launched in February 2001 by ethnic Albanian rebels seeking greater rights for the Albanian community. The so-called National Liberation Army (UCK) fought government troops for six months, prompting fears in the international community of a recurrence of the bloody conflicts which had engulfed other former Yugoslav states in the 1990s. Under intense international pressure a Government of National Unity was established in May comprising parties from all sides of the Assembly, including the opposition PDP and SDSM. The coalition was volatile as the struggle for greater Albanian autonomy was largely backed by the Albanian parties and had prompted a powerful nationalist backlash among their ethnic Macedonian counterparts. However, peace initiatives gradually gained ground in July and a final agreement was signed between the Government and the UCK at Ohrid on 13 August 2001. A **North Atlantic Treaty Organization** (NATO) peace mission, dubbed 'Operation Essential Harvest', moved in to disarm the rebels and oversee the implementation of the accord. By September 3,875 weapons had been collected, and the UCK disbanded itself.

The process of approving the various key elements of the peace deal—providing limited autonomy and social equalization for the Albanian community—was complex and frequently delayed. At its conclusion in November, the SDSM and the Liberals withdrew from the grand coalition. **New Democracy** (ND), which had been formed in March from a small splinter of the DA, was drafted in to take their place.

International relations and defence: Following independence and the adoption of the interim FYROM designation as its official title, the new state of Macedonia was admitted to the United Nations in April 1993. After Greece had accepted the FYROM formula in September 1995 subject to further negotiations on a definitive name, Macedonia was admitted to the **Council of Europe** and to the **Organization for Security and Co-operation in Europe**. In April 1996 Macedonia and the Federal Republic of Yugoslavia (comprising Serbia and **Montenegro**) established full diplomatic relations, recognizing each other's sovereignty, independence and territorial integrity. A friendship and co-operation agreement was signed with the **Russian Federation** in February 1998.

In a controversial move in January 1999, the Macedonian Government established full diplomatic relations with Taiwan, joining the Vatican as the only European states to recognize the Taipei regime. An infuriated China responded in February by using its veto in the UN Security Council to block the renewal of the mandate of the UN Preventive Deployment Force (UNPREDEP) in Macedonia, which therefore wound up its operations in March. Taiwan subsequently denied that it had promised Macedonia US $1,000m. in aid in return for recognition. Some Taiwanese aid did arrive, but during the ethnic conflict in 2001 (see above) Macedonia, feeling the need for China's support for international intervention, formerly revoked its recognition of Taiwan on 18 June.

In February 1999 Bulgaria and Macedonia signed a declaration settling a longstanding language dispute involving Bulgaria's refusal to recognize Macedonian as a language separate from Bulgarian. The agreement also resolved potential territorial disputes and provided for the finalization of 20 bilateral accords that had remained unsigned since Macedonia's independence.

Macedonia's limited resources were stretched severely by the refugee and humanitarian crisis arising from the repression of Kosovar Albanians by the Serb authorities which provoked punitive military action against Serbia by NATO in the first half of 1999. Macedonia was therefore allocated substantial **European Union** and other Western reconstruction aid within the framework of the South-East European Co-operation Process (SEECP). NATO forces were called directly into Macedonia itself in August 2001 following the signing of a peace accord between the Government and ethnic Albanian rebels.

Macedonia's defence budget for 2000 amounted to some US $77m., equivalent to about 2% of GDP. The size of the armed forces at the end of 2000 was some 16,000 personnel, including those serving under compulsory conscription of nine months, while reservists numbered an estimated 60,000. The Government announced plans in December 2001 to overhaul the military in light of its unimpressive performance against Albanian irregulars earlier in the year. Plans included a smaller 'rapid-reaction' force.

Macedonia, economy

An economy seeking to emerge from communist-era neglect, but impeded in its transition to a market economy by regional conflict and internal ethnic divisions.

GNP: US $3,252m. (2000); *GNP per capita*: $1,710 (2000); *GDP at PPP*: $7,600m. (1999); *GDP per capita at PPP*: $3,800 (1999); *exports*: $1,319m. (2000); *imports*: $2,085m. (2000); *currency*: denar (plural: denars; US $1=D69.17 at the end of December 2001).

In 1999 industry accounted for 33% of GDP, agriculture for 11% and services for 56%. Some 24% of the land is arable, 2% under permanent crops, 25% permanent pastures and 39% forests and woodland. The main crops are rice, grain, sugar beet, vegetables and grapes (for wine), and there is an important dairy industry. The main mineral resource is brown coal (lignite), although there are other broadly-unexploited mineral deposits. The main industries are metallurgy, chemicals, textiles and the production of tobacco. There is the potential for the development of the tourism industry, but this has been halted by the security situation. The main energy sources are hydroelectric power and coal-fired plants, while natural gas is now imported from the **Russian Federation** via **Bulgaria**.

Macedonia's main exports by value are food, beverages and tobacco (19% in 1998), iron and steel (15%), non-ferrous metals (8%) and machinery and transport equipment (8%). Principal imports include machinery and transport equipment, especially road vehicles (17%), food and live animals (14%), fuel products (11%) and chemical products (11%). **Yugoslavia** was the main purchaser of Macedonia's exports in 2000 (25%), followed by Germany (19%) and the USA (13%). Imports in that year came mainly from Germany (12%) and **Ukraine** and Greece (10% each).

As the poorest of the republics within the former **Socialist Federal Republic of Yugoslavia**, Macedonia immediately encountered external threats to its economy when it declared full independence in November 1991. It was heavily dependent on its relations with the rest of the former Yugoslavia (especially **Serbia** and **Montenegro**) and suffered from the international sanctions placed on that country to 1995. Moreover, in 1994–95 Greece acted on its objections to the new state being called Macedonia by imposing an economic blockade which cut off much of its oil and other essential imports. However, GDP stabilized in 1996, having fallen by an average of 5.5% a year in the period 1990–95, and increased modestly in 1997 by 1.5% and by 3% in 1998. Severe post-independence inflation, rising to nearly 2,000% in 1992, was brought down to around zero by the end of 1996 and remained at a low level thereafter.

The economic situation in Macedonia was thrown into some disarray in the spring of 1999, when the unrest in **Kosovo** (the Serbian province of Yugoslavia to the north of Macedonia) erupted into warfare, causing the massive exodus to Macedonia of ethnic **Albanian** refugees and **NATO** air-strikes against Serbia. However, IMF credits and other aid from Western Governments enabled Macedonia to cope with the crisis sufficiently well that GDP growth fell back only slightly to 2.5% in 1999, followed by a return to 3% expansion in 2000 as a panoply of economic restructuring and liberalization measures began to take effect. On the other hand, unemployment remained very high at around 35% officially in the late 1990s and in reality even higher (partly masked by the existence of a huge 'black' economy).

A privatization programme introduced in 1992 made little headway during the initial post-independence years of external pressure, consisting mainly of management buy-outs ('**nomenklatura** privatization'). After the lifting of the sanctions on Yugoslavia and of the Greek blockade, however, the programme made real progress, special attention being paid to the privatization of the banking sector. The situation was further complicated by the collapse in early 1997 of a fraudulent **'pyramid' investment scheme** which led to an overall lack of economic confidence. Nevertheless, by mid-1998 around 95% of industrial, commercial and mining enterprises had been privatized, as had about half of state-owned farms. A landmark privatization in 1999 was that of the OKTA oil refinery, the sale of which to a Greek company resulted in a Macedonian-Greek agreement to build a US $90m. pipeline from **Skopje** to Thessaloniki. The sale of Macedonia's largest bank to Greek and other interests followed in April 2000, in which month further legislation was approved providing for the return to former owners or their heirs of property and land confiscated since 1945.

Macedonian question

A territorial and diplomatic dispute based on the division of historical **Macedonia** and the emergence of a separate Macedonian state. A powerful country in ancient times, Macedonia was absorbed by the **Turkic** Ottoman Empire in the 14th century. When that Empire's last remaining **Balkan** possessions were finally partitioned in the Balkan Wars of 1912–13, the Macedonian elements were carved up under the Treaty of London in 1913 between the three Balkan allies, **Bulgaria**, **Serbia** and Greece.

Although Bulgaria was allocated one of the larger shares, the **Bulgarian royal family** of the time aspired to sovereignty over all of Macedonia—based on the ethnic similarity between **Macedonians** and **Bulgarians**, and on the state's brief annexation of Macedonia under the 1878 Treaty of San Stefano. Late in 1913 Bulgaria turned on its erstwhile allies and attempted to seize historic Macedonia for itself. It was easily defeated. Under the resultant Treaty of Bucharest, Macedonia was finally divided along the modern borders it has today. The territory known as Vardar Macedonia, after the river of the same name, forms the basis of the modern Macedonian state and was awarded to Serbia. A small chunk to the east, known as Pirin Macedonia, was left in Bulgarian hands and the final southern belt (Aegean Macedonia) became a part of Greece.

Tensions persist between Macedonia (the heir to the Serbian cession) and its eastern and southern neighbours. Bulgarian, and even some Macedonian, nationalists still call for greater ties if not full reunification with Bulgaria, while Greece's reluctance to recognize a 'Macedonian' state in the 1990s reflected Greek fears of possible Macedonian irredentism.

Macedonian Stock Exchange (MSE)
Makedonska Berza

The first organized stock exchange in **Macedonia**. The MSE was founded in September 1995 and trading began in March 1996. Market capitalization of trading in 142 companies in 1999 totalled US $7.7m. As of December 2001 there were 10 members.

Chair.: Evgeni Zografski.
Address: Mito Hadživasilev Jasmin 20, 1000 Skopje.
Telephone: (2) 122055.

Fax: (2) 122069.
E-mail: mse@mse.org.mk
Internet: www.mse.org.mk

Macedonians

A south **Slavic people** who had established themselves in north and central (geographical) Macedonia (*see* **Macedonian question**) by the 8th century. They now constitute around 67% of the population of modern (political) **Macedonia**. The conquest of the area by the **Bulgarians** to the east in the 9th century resulted in the merging of the two peoples. Consequently there is dispute as to whether Macedonian is even a separate language or merely a dialect of Bulgarian, which it closely resembles. The issue is a cause for tension between Macedonia and **Bulgaria**.

The separate identity of the Macedonians was denied by the royal **Yugoslav** authorities in the inter-war years but was resurrected by the communist regime which founded the Socialist Republic of Macedonia in 1943. In the following years Macedonian grammar was established as part of an effort to reduce Bulgarian influence in the region.

The Macedonians converted to **Orthodox Christianity** while under the yoke of the Serbian Empire in the early second millennium. A separate Macedonian Orthodox Church was established by the communist authorities in 1967. Although it is not officially recognized by other Orthodox Patriarchates it receives much support within Macedonia. However, some Macedonians converted to Islam under Ottoman rule and their descendants, known as **Pomaks**, number around 50–60,000.

Communities of ethnic Macedonians live in neighbouring countries. Over 10,000 live in south-western Bulgaria although their identity and number are contested by both Macedonian and Bulgarian authorities. Around 50,000 live in the rump Yugoslav state. Upwards of 4,500 live in the east of **Albania**. Most Macedonians living in Aegean Macedonia in Greece emigrated north after the First World War. A small community remains and are known as Slavomacedonians. They are subject to general discrimination and many have assimilated with the Greek population.

Mádl, Ferenc

President of the Republic, **Hungary**.

Ferenc Mádl, an independent with links to the centre-right, was a lawyer and university lecturer until joining the Cabinet as Minister without Portfolio in 1990. He was elected President on 6 June 2000.

Born on 29 January 1931 to a poor peasant family in the small western village of Bánd, he graduated in law from the Eötvös Loránd University in 1955. From the late 1960s he worked at the Institute of State and Legal Sciences at the Hungarian

Academy of Sciences, until he returned to the Eötvös Loránd University in 1971 to begin a 29-year academic career. He was appointed Minister without Portfolio in the conservative-dominated Cabinet elected after the first post-Soviet elections in 1990. Despite the defeat of the conservatives in 1993 he remained in the Cabinet, as Minister of Culture and Education until 1994. He stood as a nominal candidate for centrist parties against the popular incumbent President Árpád **Göncz** in 1995. The following year he took up the chairmanship of the centrist Hungarian Civic Co-operation Association. He returned to political activity in 1999 under the conservative administration of Prime Minister Viktor **Orbán**, to whose Government he became a scientific adviser. He was nominated by the right-wing **Independent Smallholders' and Civic Party** (FKgP) as a consensus candidate for presidential elections in 2000 and was finally elected to the post in June.

Ferenc Mádl married his wife Dalma in 1955 and they have one son and one granddaughter. He is known affectionately in the **National Assembly** as 'Mr Professor' as he had taught many parliamentarians in his time as a university lecturer.

Address: Office of the Prime Minister, Kossuth Lajos tér 1–3, 1055 Budapest.
Telephone: (1) 4414000.
Fax: (1) 2683050.
Internet: www.kancellaria.gov.hu

Magyar Koalíció Pártja (MKP) *see* **Hungarian Coalition Party**.

Magyars *see* **Hungarians**.

Makfax

The main private news agency in **Macedonia**. Founded in 1992, Makfax began services the following year and promotes itself as a major regional source of independent and objective reporting. It has only seven permanent employees but ranks major European news agencies among its subscribers.

Address: 11 Oktomvri 36/3, POB 738, 1000 Skopje.
Telephone: (2) 110125.
Fax: (2) 110184.
E-mail: makfax@unet.com.mk
Internet: www.makfax.com.mk

Manoli, Mihail

Minister of Finance, **Moldova**.

Mihail (or Mihai) Manoli was an academic before being drafted into the Cabinet as Deputy Minister of Finance in 1995. He was appointed full Finance Minister on 21 December 1999.

Born on 20 September 1954 in Valea Mare, in the west of Moldova, he studied economics at the Chişinau Polytechnic Institute and later at the M. V. Lomonosov State University in Moscow. After graduating he worked as an economist for the Central Committee of the Moldovan Communist Party. After pursuing his academic career at the Moldovan State University and the M. V. Lomonosov State University, he began an eight-year relationship with the College of Finance at the Moldovan State University. He moved to the Moldovan Academy for Economic Studies in 1991. He joined the Government in 1995 as Deputy Finance Minister and was promoted to full Minister in December 1999. He was reconfirmed in the post under the new communist Government of President Vladimir **Voronin** on 19 April 2001.

Mihail Manoli is married and has one child.
Address: Ministry of Finance, Cosmonauţilor 7, 277005 Chişinau.
Telephone: (2) 233575.
Fax: (2) 228610.

Mari El Republic

A republic within the **Russian Federation**, some 500 km east of Moscow. Absorbed into the Russian Empire in the 15th–16th centuries, the **Finno-Ugric** Mari people (formerly Cheremis) were granted an Autonomous Soviet Socialist Republic (ASSR) in December 1936. Today they constitute around 43% of the 750,000-strong Mari El population. Long contact with the **Russians** brought the Mari to an urban lifestyle and they adopted the **Cyrillic alphabet** to transcribe their language. However, the Mari are unusual among the regional Finns for resisting the spread of **Orthodox Christianity** and still retain elements of the original Finnish animist religion and culture. A crackdown on Mari identity under the **Soviet Union** served to strengthen the connection between Mari nationalism and efforts to preserve the Mari language and culture.

Situated on marshy land extending north from the River Volga, the republic is heavily forested and has a continental climate. Economic activity is centred on the forest and associated products. Raw wood is floated down the Volga to processing plants in the capital Ioshkar-Ola and other cities. Only a third of the republic's population live in rural areas. Mari El receives little in the way of foreign investment or aid. Leonid Igorevich Markelov has been President of Mari El since January 2001.

Markarian, Andranik

Prime Minister of **Armenia**.

Andranik Naapetovich Markarian is the leader of the **Republican Party of Armenia** (HHK), and heads the large Unity Bloc (Miasnutiun) in the **National**

Assembly. However, he relies on smaller factions and non-partisans to establish a working majority. He was briefly detained for seditious nationalism under **Soviet** rule and is now seen as a close ally of President Robert **Kocharian**. He was appointed Prime Minister on 13 May 2000.

Born on 12 June 1951 in **Yerevan**, in what was then the Soviet Socialist Republic of Armenia, he became involved with nationalist activists from an early age. In 1968 he joined the banned National United Party and was arrested by the Soviet authorities in 1974. After two years in a penitential gulag he returned to Armenia. His prisoner-of-conscience past is renowned in Armenia where he insists it does not equate to modern-day anti-Russian sentiment. He joined the HHK in 1992 and became its Chairman in 1999. President Kocharian appointed Markarian as his Premier in May 2000. He soon got rid of dissident Ministers from within the Unity Bloc. One of his main concerns is to end the conflict between the Government and Kocharian. However, popular opposition to the nationalist Head of State remains very strong.

Address: Office of the Prime Minister, Government House, Republic Sq. 1, 375010 Yerevan.
Telephone: (1) 520360.
Fax: (1) 151035.

Martonyi, János

Minister for Foreign Affairs, **Hungary**.

János Martonyi is a member of the right-of-centre **Federation of Young Democrats–Hungarian Civic Party** (FIDESz–MPP). After training as a lawyer he first entered government service in 1979 with the Ministry of Trade. He joined the Cabinet as Minister of International Economic Relations in 1990 and was appointed Foreign Minister for the second time in July 1998.

Born on 5 April 1944 in Kolozsvár (now Cluj Napoca in Romania), he graduated from the Law School of Attila József University in Szeged in 1967. He completed his studies in international law in London and The Hague, gaining a doctorate in 1979. In the same year he turned his occasional work as an in-house counsel for the Government into an official post at the country's Trade Office in Belgium. He returned to Hungary in 1984 to be a Head of Department at the Trade Ministry. He was appointed Minister of International Economic Relations in 1990 in the first post-communist Government, and transferred to the Foreign Ministry the following year. After the Government's defeat in elections in 1994 he practised private law before returning to the Government in July 1998 as Foreign Minister.

János Martonyi is married and has one daughter and one son.

Address: Ministry of Foreign Affairs, Bem rkp. 47, 1027 Budapest.
Telephone: (1) 4581000.
Fax: (1) 2125918.

E-mail: titkarsag.kabinet@kum.hu
Internet: www.mfa.gov.hu

Mass Privatization Programme (Poland)

Responsible for the divestment of various state-owned enterprises in **Poland**.
Address: c/o Department of National Investment Funds, Ministry of the Treasury, ul. Krucza 36, 00522 Warsaw.
Telephone: (22) 6958453.
Fax: (22) 6958701.

MDF see **Hungarian Democratic Forum**.

Mečiar, Vladimír

Former Prime Minister of **Slovakia**, its leader through the '**velvet divorce**' from the **Czech Republic** at the end of 1992.

Born in Zvolen, north-east of **Bratislava**, on 26 July 1942, he held a post in local government after completing secondary school, then did military service, and began rising rapidly within the communist youth movement. In 1969, however, at the all-Slovakia conference of the Youth Union, Mečiar expounded progressive and reformist ideas which resulted in his expulsion from the communist party. During the period of 'normalization' following the 1968 '**Prague Spring**', Mečiar was offered high rank in the Slovak Central Committee of the Youth Union on the condition that he retract his statements but he refused to do so. Initially unable to find employment because of his political views, he eventually began work six months later as an assistant smelter at the heavy engineering works, Dubnica nad Váhom. During this time he enrolled for an external course at the Comenius University of Bratislava, graduating with a law degree in 1974. From 1974 until 1990 he worked at the Skloobal concern in Nemšová, quickly rising to the position of company lawyer.

In 1989 Mečiar joined the **Public Against Violence** (VPN) movement which, together with its Czech counterpart **Civic Forum**, was instrumental in bringing down the communist regime in December 1989. In the non-communist Government which was then formed on an interim basis, he held the post of Slovak Minister of the Interior and the Environment. In the June 1990 legislative elections to the Federal and Republican Assemblies, Mečiar was elected to the Federal Assembly and was appointed Prime Minister of a Slovak coalition Government dominated by the VPN.

Increasingly overt in his advocacy of full autonomy for Slovakia, and accused of abusing his access to secret information, he was obliged to resign in March 1991. He left the VPN to form the nationalist **Movement for a Democratic Slovakia**

(HZDS) and was elected as its Chairman later the same year. In the federal and republican elections, which were held in June 1992, the HZDS became the strongest Slovak party in both the Federal Assembly and the Slovak National Council. Mečiar was accordingly again appointed Slovak Prime Minister and proceeded to negotiate the dissolution of **Czechoslovakia** with the then Czech Premier, Václav **Klaus**.

The ensuing period was marked by growing tensions between Mečiar and Michal Kováč, elected President of the newly independent Slovakia in February 1993. A series of government resignations and the formation of a breakaway party eventually led to the fall of Mečiar's Government in March 1994 after he lost a parliamentary vote of confidence. However, after the September–October 1994 general election Mečiar was again able to form a Government in December, this time comprising his HZDS, the **Slovak National Party** and the Association of Workers of Slovakia. Upon his return to power Mečiar used his party's majority in the **National Council** to repeal privatization legislation approved under Jozef Moravčík, while the animosity between Mečiar and Kováč continued to paralyse the process of government. Differences culminated in May 1997 over the holding of a referendum on Slovakia's proposed membership of the **North Atlantic Treaty Organization** (NATO) and the nature of the Slovak presidency, with both sides accusing the other of acting undemocratically. In the event the referendum was boycotted by 90% of the electorate in protest at the Government's decision to omit the question on presidential elections and was thus declared invalid. Elections in 1998 saw Mečiar ousted and a new Government formed by the former opposition grouping, the **Slovak Democratic Coalition**.

Medved *see* **Unity Inter-regional Movement**.

Meidani, Rexhep

President of the Republic, **Albania**.

Rexhep Meidani was a distinguished physicist before becoming Secretary-General of the **Socialist Party of Albania** (PSS), the reformed communist Party of Labour, in 1996. He directed the party away from its Stalinist past towards pragmatic social democratic policies. He was elected President of Albania on 24 July 1997.

Born on 17 August 1944 in **Tirana**, he graduated in physics from Tirana University in 1966. He received his doctorate after 10 years of research in Paris and returned to Albania in 1976 to lecture in his subject. As Albania began to move towards multi-party democracy in 1990 he became Chairman of the State Electoral Commission, participating in many commissions and organizations seeking to promote the democratization of the education system, while also remaining a physics professor at the University. He also chaired the board of the Centre of Human

Rights Documentation from November 1994, campaigning for the strengthening of non-governmental organizations. He joined the PSS in July 1996 and was elected Secretary-General that September. Following the country's descent into lawlessness after economic collapse at the end of that year, the PSS won an overall majority in the **People's Assembly** in 1997 and Meidani, having won a seat, was elected President on 24 July. He immediately resigned all his duties and functions within the PSS.

Rexhep Meidani is married to a mathematician and they have two children.
Address: Office of the President, Tirana.
Telephone: (4) 228313.
Fax: (4) 233761.
E-mail: presec@presec.tirana.al
Internet: presidenca.gov.al

Memel see **Klaipeda**.

Menagharishvili, Irakli

Minister of Foreign Affairs, **Georgia**.

Irakli Menagharishvili is an independent. He trained as a medical therapist but has pursued a career in government since 1980. He first entered the Cabinet as Deputy Minister for Health in 1982 and was appointed Foreign Minister on 15 December 1995.

Born on 18 May 1951 in **Tbilisi**, he graduated from the Tbilisi Medical Institute in 1974 as a therapist. He was appointed Head of the Office for Public Health in the city in 1980 and was promoted to the Cabinet of the Soviet Georgian republic in 1982 as Deputy Minister for Health. He was made Health Minister in 1986 and remained in the post until Georgian independence in 1991. After a brief spell as Director of the Strategic Research Centre in Tbilisi, he was reappointed Health Minister in December 1992. He made his first break from the Ministry of Health in September 1993 when he was nominated Deputy Prime Minister. He was appointed Foreign Minister in December 1995.

Irakli Menagharishvili married Manana Mikaberidze in 1975 and they have two sons.
Address: Ministry of Foreign Affairs, Tskhra Aprilis 4, 380018 Tbilisi.
Telephone: (32) 989377.
Fax: (32) 997248.
E-mail: public@mfa.gov.ge
Internet: www.mfa.gov.ge

Menatep SPb (St Petersburg)

One of the largest commercial banks in the **Russian Federation**, founded in 1995. It has capital of 1,370m. roubles and a network of 57 branches.
Chair. of the Executive: Dmitry A. Lebedev.
Address: 1 Nevsky Avenue, 191186 St Petersburg.
Telephone: (812) 3263901.
Fax: (812) 3263940.
E-mail: entrance@menatepspb.com
Internet: www.menatepspb.com

Meri, Lennart

The first freely-elected President of **Estonia** after the country regained its independence from **Soviet** rule, and Head of State for two terms from 1992 to 2000. A diplomat's son, he was born on 29 March 1929 in **Tallinn** and spent his early school years partly in Paris and Berlin, but within a year of the Soviet annexation of Estonia in 1940 he was deported with his family to **Siberia**, returning only in 1946. He graduated in history from Tartu University in 1953 and then made his name as an author on Estonian cultural issues and an award-winning filmmaker. Never a member of the communist party, he entered politics only in 1990, the year of Estonia's declaration of independence. In April 1990 he became Minister of Foreign Affairs, in which post he gave particular emphasis to promoting co-operation in the Baltic region and Scandinavia. After a six-month spell in 1992 as Ambassador to Finland, he returned to contest the presidential elections that October. He trailed the incumbent President, former communist Arnold **Rüütel**, in the popular vote, but the outcome was left to be decided in the **State Assembly** because Rüütel had failed to win an absolute majority. This greatly strengthened Meri's prospects of victory, since his right-wing Pro Patria group (Isamaa) was the largest faction, and on 5 October 1992 he was elected by 59 votes to 31.

Perhaps ironically, given his nationalist credentials and pro-Western orientation, the charismatic, witty and legendarily well-informed President Meri lost some of his support during his first term because he was seen as too conciliatory towards Russian concerns on two major issues. These were the position of ethnic **Russians** under new citizenship laws, and Estonia's Western-oriented stance as an aspiring member of the **European Union** and the **North Atlantic Treaty Organization**. His personal popularity and advantage as the incumbent were finally enough to allow him to defeat Rüütel for the second time, in October 1996, on the fifth round of voting in the electoral college (which had been widened after three inconclusive rounds to include local council representatives as well as members of the State Assembly). In his second term Meri's popularity rose once again, due in part to the country's continuing successes in switching over to a free-market economy, and in part to the perception that he adhered to high ethical standards, dispensing strong criticism of politicians guilty of self-enrichment. Nevertheless, his arch rival Rüütel ultimately managed to win the presidency in the 2001 elections, held in August–September, when Meri could not be a candidate because of the constitutional ban on a third presidential term.

Mesić, Stipe

President of the Republic, **Croatia**.

Stjepan (Stipe) Mesić is a moderate nationalist heading the **Croatian People's Party** (HNS). He first entered the Croatian **Assembly** in 1970 while the country was still a constituent republic of the **Socialist Federal Republic of Yugoslavia** (SFRY). He was elected to the joint presidency of the SFRY in 1990, and was that country's last Head of State before Croatian independence in 1991. Increasingly critical of Croatian President Franjo **Tudjman** in the ensuing decade, he was elected President himself in February 2000 following Tudjman's death.

Born in the eastern town of Orahovica on 24 December 1934, he graduated in law from Zagreb University in the late 1950s. He was forced from the Croatian Assembly in 1971 and was jailed for one year for his involvement in the anti-Belgrade agitation known as the 'Croatian Spring'. He joined Tudjman's right-wing nationalist **Croatian Democratic Union** (HDZ) and was appointed President of the Executive Council—effectively Croatian Prime Minister—of the non-communist Government in 1990. Taking the nationalist struggle to the federal level, he was elected to be the Croat representative on the federal Collective State Presidency later that year, simultaneously becoming SFRY Vice-President under the rotation system in October 1990. He was proclaimed President of the SFRY on 30 June 1991, but it was a short-lived tenure as Croatia officially pronounced itself independent on 8 October. He resigned as SFRY President on 5 December, famously declaring, 'Yugoslavia no longer exists'.

As Speaker of the Assembly in the newly independent Croatia, he became a leading opposition voice to the HDZ's authoritarianism and especially the rising cult of personality surrounding President Tudjman. He was ousted from the Assembly after forming the Croatian Independent Democrats and later switched to the HNS, becoming that party's Vice-President in 1997. His election as President of Croatia in the wake of Tudjman's death was largely owing to the stark contrast between his relaxed approach and the authoritarian stance of Tudjman. He has sought to reduce the presidency's power within the Croatian political system, handing over many of his constitutional duties to the Head of Government. He has come under the greatest criticism for his outspoken support for the **International Criminal Tribunal for the former Yugoslavia** in its prosecution of Croatian war criminals.

Stipe Mesić is married with two daughters and two grandchildren.

Address: Office of the President, Pantovčak 241, Zagreb.
Telephone: (1) 4565191.
Fax: (1) 4565299.

E-mail: office@president.hr
Internet: www.predsjednik.hr

Meskhetians

A people of undetermined **Turkic/Kurdish** origin who were deported *en masse* from their homeland in southern **Georgia** in 1944. During the final stages of the Second World War, Stalin's paranoia reached such heights that whole ethnic groups around the **Soviet Union** were uprooted and exiled to **Siberia** and central Asia. The Meskhetians were one such unfortunate group and in 1944 around 200,000 were relocated to the steppes of central Asia. Many thousands died on the way. The Meskhetians are significant among the **deported nationalities** as for them the 1950s did not bring rehabilitation and they have largely remained a refugee population ever since. Some 20,000 managed to return to the **Caucasus region**, settling in Georgia and **Azerbaijan**, but the rest were barred re-entry. Demands for their repatriation to Meskheti increased after bloody attacks on the Meskhetians in the Fergana Valley region of Uzbekistan in 1989.

The collapse of the Soviet Union in 1991 transferred the Meskhetian refugee problem from Moscow to Tbilisi. The Georgian authorities, soon occupied with ethnic separatism themselves, were not keen to establish a new non-Georgian region, especially next to the (so far peaceful) **Armenian** enclave of **Javakheti**. Arguing that the Meskhetian homeland was not in Georgia but ultimately in Turkey, they finally agreed in 1996 to accept 5,000 Meskhetians over the following four years. However, very few have arrived in Meskheti and some have faced immediate deportation from Georgia despite the decree.

Meta, Ilir

Prime Minister of **Albania**.

Ilir Meta was a prominent student activist in the final days of Albanian communism, and went on to work within the ruling **Socialist Party of Albania** (PSS)—the reformed communists—as a leading figure in its Foreign Relations Department before becoming Deputy Prime Minister in 1998. He was appointed Prime Minister on 27 October 1999—the first handover of power since 1991 which did not result in riots—and was reappointed for a second term on 20 August 2001.

Born in 1969 in the mountainous southern border region of Skrapar, he graduated with a degree in economics in 1990. He joined the PSS in 1991 and was first elected to the **People's Assembly** and appointed as a Deputy Chairman of the party the following year. After re-election to the Assembly in 1996 he was appointed as a Ministerial Secretary for Foreign Affairs. Throughout the turbulent year of 1997 he served as Secretary of State for Euro-Atlantic Integration and in 1998 he was promoted to Deputy Prime Minister. His conduct as the Government's international representative during the **Kosovo** conflict in 1999 won him international praise. He succeeded as Prime Minister in October 1999, heralding an unprecedented compromise between the PSS's warring factions. Although it faced increasingly popular opposition protests in its first term, the PSS was re-elected in July 2001, and Meta was reappointed as Prime Minister on 20 August. However, the PSS Government soon ran into internal party difficulties. Party Chairman Fatos **Nano** blocked the appointment of Cabinet Ministers in a reshuffle in late 2001, accusing Meta and his team of corruption and ultimately forcing the resignation of four Ministers in December. Tensions between Meta and Nano remained high.

Ilir Meta is married to Monika Kryemadhi, a former Vice-President of the International Union of Socialist Youth.

Address: Office of the Prime Minister, Tirana.
Telephone: (4) 228210.
Fax: (4) 227888.
Internet: www.albgovt.gov.al

MIEP *see* **Hungarian Justice and Life Party**.

Miller, Leszek

Prime Minister of **Poland** from October 2001 and Chairman of the **Democratic Left Alliance** (SLD). Briefly a Politburo Member in the ruling Polish United Workers' Party (PZPR) at the very end of the communist era, and holder of various ministerial posts since then, he is renowned for standing up for the record of the former communist Government, and for his intention to put some distance between the Polish State and the Catholic Church. However, he has softened his tone in recent years, and is a strong advocate of free-market economics and European integration.

Leszek Miller was born on 3 July 1946 in Żyrardów, just west of **Warsaw**. He left school at 17 and worked for seven years as an electrician in the linen industry in his home town, then held various administrative posts within the PZPR (which he joined in 1969), while also studying political science at the Higher School of Social Sciences in Warsaw. He rose within the party to be a member of the Politburo by 1989 and was a founder member in 1990 of the reformed-communist Social Democracy of the Republic of Poland, which became part of the SLD alliance. He was elected to the **National Assembly** in 1991 and was appointed Minister of Labour and Social Policy in 1993. He switched to the post of Minister-Head of the Office of the Council of Ministers in 1996 before becoming Interior Minister in 1997. Following the SLD's electoral defeat that year he served on various Assembly committees, and was nominated as a goodwill ambassador for UNICEF in 2000. He led the rejuvenated SLD in legislative elections in 2001 against a deeply

unpopular conservative Government, and was appointed Prime Minister in October that year after a sweeping electoral victory for his party.
Address: Office of the Prime Minister, Al. Ujazdowskie 1/3, 00567 Warsaw.
Telephone: (22) 6946000.
Fax: (22) 6252637.
E-mail: cirinfo@kprm.gov.pl
Internet: www.kprm.gov.pl

Milli Majlis

Common term used in Islamic states for a representative assembly, as used in **Azerbaijan** for the **National Assembly**.

Milošević, Slobodan

President of **Yugoslavia** in 1997–2000, and before that the President of **Serbia** from 1989. His ruthless pursuit of a **Serb** nationalist agenda contributed significantly to inflaming the violent conflicts which accompanied the disintegration of the **Socialist Federal Republic of Yugoslavia** (SFRY). He is the first ex-Head of State ever to face charges for war crimes in an international court.

Slobodan Milošević was born in Požaravec, near **Belgrade**, on 20 August 1941. His father was an **Orthodox Christian** priest of Montenegrin descent, who left home soon after Slobodan's birth, and later committed suicide, as did his mother in 1973. Milošević met his future wife Mirjana Marković, who came from a leading Serb communist family, while at secondary school in Požaravec. She subsequently became a university professor and a significant political figure in her own right as head of the nationalist **Yugoslav United Left**. They have one son, Marko Milošević, and one daughter, Marija.

Milošević joined the ruling **League of Communists of Yugoslavia** (SKJ) when he was 18, graduated in law from the University of Belgrade in 1964, and worked at the national gas extraction company, Tehnogas, rising to become its Director-General in 1973. Meanwhile he held several party posts in Belgrade, became a member of the Presidium of the SKJ Central Committee in 1984 and two years later took over the leadership of the party in Serbia. In April 1987 he famously told **Kosovo**'s Serbs (who had been in a violent confrontation with police whilst demonstrating against greater autonomy for the province's ethnic **Albanians**): 'No one has the right to beat you. No one will ever beat you again.' His words struck a chord and he returned to Belgrade as the hero of the Serb nationalists, using this to strengthen his position in the party hierarchy and, in May 1989, to win election by the Republican Parliament as President of Serbia. Within months the autonomous status of Kosovo and **Vojvodina** within Serbia had been revoked.

Milošević, Slobodan

Dominating Serbia's first multi-party presidential elections in December 1990, Milošević won 65% of the vote, as the candidate of the **Socialist Party of Serbia** (SPS), the renamed communist party. He was re-elected two years later, by which time Serbia was no longer one of six Republics under the old Yugoslav structure, but the larger of two (with **Montenegro**) in a 'rump' State, formed in April 1992 as the Federal Republic of **Yugoslavia** (FRY).

During the bloody break-up of Yugoslavia, Milošević initially gave full backing to the idea of a '**Greater Serbia**', but he has consistently denied conniving at providing military support from the regular Yugoslav army for Bosnian Serb militias (who attempted to advance the Greater Serbia cause by '**ethnic cleansing**' of non-Serbs in **Bosnia and Herzegovina**). In the later stages of the Bosnian war it became expedient for the international community to deal directly with Milošević, rather than with Bosnian Serbs, in negotiating what became the **Dayton Agreement** to end the conflict. This initially boosted his regime in Serbia, but mass demonstrations over the manipulation of municipal elections in 1996 highlighted growing domestic dissatisfaction with his Government, at least in Belgrade. Seeking to maintain his position of power beyond the end of his second and final term as Serbian President, he switched to the Federal Presidency in July 1997 and worked to transform what was effectively a figurehead position into a powerful executive position, without ever altering the constitutional role. Opposition within the FRY was severely repressed, in a climate of fear carefully managed by Milošević's powerful state machine.

The 1999 **NATO** bombing campaign, prompted by the actions of Serb security forces against ethnic Albanians in Kosovo, laid the seeds for Milošević's eventual downfall. Despite public outrage at the NATO 'aggression', the humiliation of having to retreat from Kosovo, the cradle of Serb nationalism, made him politically vulnerable. This was compounded by his indictment for war crimes by the **International Criminal Tribunal for the former Yugoslavia** (ICTY), and by the imposition of crippling economic sanctions which would only be rescinded on his own removal. Rival forces came together in the **Democratic Opposition of Serbia** (DOS) coalition in time for simultaneous presidential and legislative elections called for 24 September 2000, Milošević having gambled by changing the Constitution to allow him to seek a fresh term as Federal President by introducing direct elections to that post. It was not obvious at the time if he considered his support to be sufficiently strong, or the resolve of the opposition sufficiently weak in the face of his own ability and willingness to control results. Either way, it was a miscalculation. The DOS claimed victory, and a massive public outcry greeted his initial attempts to have the first round of the presidential contest declared inconclusive. When it was made known that he himself had ordered the results doctored in his favour, the protestors took over the streets on 5 October, demanding his resignation. Milošević conceded defeat and DOS candidate Vojislav **Koštunica** was inaugurated in his place two days later.

Koštunica himself regarded Milošević as having a legitimate political role, and strongly maintained that he should never be extradited to the ICTY in The Hague. Many still saw him as a defender of Serb national pride against Western aggression. However, the new Serbian Prime Minister elected in December 2000, Zoran **Djindjić**, was keenly aware that Yugoslavia's international rehabilitation, and particularly the return of international aid, depended on bringing Milošević to justice. On 1 April 2001 Milošević was arrested after a dramatic police siege of his Belgrade home; and on 28 June, contrary to initial promises that he would only be tried in Yugoslavia, he was extradited to the ICTY. At the pre-trial in October 2001 he took a typically combative stance, denying the legitimacy of the Tribunal and refusing either to appoint legal representation or to enter pleas.

Milutinović, Milan

President of the Republic, **Serbia**.

A staunch ally of ousted dictator Slobodan **Milošević**, and his successor as Serbian President from 21 December 1997, Milan Milutinović was a leading member of the far-right **Socialist Party of Serbia** (SPS) before the party's internal disputes in mid-2001. He is wanted by the **International Criminal Tribunal for the former Yugoslavia** in The Hague over atrocities committed by Serbian troops in **Kosovo** in 1999.

Born on 12 December 1942 in **Belgrade**, he graduated from the city's university with a degree in law. He became a leading member of the Socialist Youth Union of Yugoslavia in 1969 and represented the ruling **League of Communists of Yugoslavia** (SKJ) in the Federal Parliament. He rose rapidly through the party's ranks and was appointed Serbian Minister of Science and Education in 1977. After five years in the Republic's Cabinet he left to become Director of the Serbian National Library in 1983, then head of sector for Press in the Ministry of Foreign Affairs. During the crucial years surrounding the bloody disintegration of the **Socialist Federal Republic of Yugoslavia** (SFRY), he served as Ambassador to Greece. He was appointed Foreign Minister in 1995 as the war in **Bosnia and Herzegovina** came to a conclusion, and earned a reputation as a tough negotiator during talks for the **Dayton Agreement**. He was nominated as Milošević's successor as Serbian President in 1997 and was elected only after a fourth round of voting, which was described by international observers as 'fundamentally flawed'. Milošević retained his previous power as Federal President, despite that position's relatively constitutional weakness, leaving Milutinović as little more than a key ally. The dictator's fall in October 2000 did little to change the situation, with the new Serbian Prime Minister Zoran **Djindjić** regularly circumventing the Serbian presidency. Milutinović has since attempted to distance himself from the previous regime, of which he was the only member to remain in a position of political power. The Government refuses to extradite him to The Hague.

Address: Office of the President, Andričev venac 1, 11000 Belgrade.

Minsk

The historic capital city of **Belarus**. *Population*: 1.6m. (1991 estimate). The settlement was first mentioned in 1067. The centre of a White Russian principality, the city with its surrounding territory was absorbed by **Lithuania** in the 14th century and later by **Poland**. In the second partition of Poland in 1793 Minsk was made a regional administrative centre of the **Russian** Empire. Economic activity increased after the completion of a rail link from the Baltic coast to **Ukraine** via Minsk in the 1870s, and its regional importance made it the capital of the emergent Belarusian republic in 1919. However, its position between eastern Europe and **European Russia** has led to repeated and damaging military occupation during major campaigns. The city was destroyed by French troops in 1812, by German soldiers in 1918, by Polish conquerors between 1919 and 1920, and by the Germans again in 1941, but the greatest damage occurred during the **Soviet** advance in 1944. The city's large **Jewish** population of around 80,000 had been almost entirely wiped out during the Nazi occupation.

Post-war development produced wide streets and large apartment blocks. The population grew faster than any other Soviet city, tripling from 500,000 in 1959 to 1.6 million by 1989. Minsk became the capital of Belarus and the administrative centre of the **Commonwealth of Independent States** (CIS) in 1991. Its main economic activity today is the production of heavy machinery. As the Belarusian capital it is also home to the **National Assembly** and other government offices.

Minsk Group

A group established in 1992 as an offshoot of the **Organization for Security and Co-operation in Europe** (OSCE) to oversee the peace process in **Nagorno-Karabakh**. The intention was to convene a peace conference on Nagorno-Karabakh, to take place in **Minsk**. Although it has not to this date been possible to hold the conference, the so-called Minsk Group spearheads the OSCE effort to find a political solution to this conflict. In December 1994 the OSCE decided to establish a co-chairmanship for the process, and expressed the political will to deploy multinational peacekeeping forces as an essential part of the overall settlement of the conflict.

> *Members*: **Armenia**, Austria, **Azerbaijan**, **Belarus**, France, Germany, Italy, Portugal, **Romania**, **Russian Federation**, Sweden, Turkey and the USA.
> *Leadership*: Carey Cavanaugh (USA), Jean-Jacques Gaillarde (France) and Nikolay Gribkov (Russian Federation) (Co-Chairs).

Mir space station

The world's first permanently-manned space station. Mir (literally 'commune' or 'village', from the Russian word for peace) was launched by the **Soviet Union** in

February 1986 and finally brought back to Earth on 23 March 2001, crashing into the Pacific Ocean. Its 15-year history coincided with the end of the **Cold War** and the transition of Russia from communism to democracy. Its launch demonstrated the Soviet Union's ability to out-perform the USA, in a year that the US Space Shuttle programme saw its darkest hour with the Challenger disaster. However, the station was not fully completed until 1996, having been given an extension to its original seven-year lifespan, and the final module was attached at a time when US-Russian relations had entered a new co-operative phase. The joint Shuttle-Mir programme saw Russian cosmonauts and US astronauts take part in the two countries' space programmes from 1995 onwards. Cosmonauts aboard Mir performed experiments on the effects of long-term weightlessness, and made many scientific observations of Earth. The increasing cost of maintaining Mir proved too great for the economically-weakened **Russian Federation**, and the station was commercialized in 2000. However, despite the insistence of MirCorp., the new operators, that the station should be maintained as a potential tourist attraction, the Russian Government agreed to destroy the spacecraft to clear the scientific budget for its involvement in the new International Space Station, for which Mir had acted as an important base for construction.

Mission
Arakelutun

A political party in **Armenia** established shortly before the May 1999 **National Assembly** elections, in which it won only 0.8% of the proportional vote but secured one constituency seat.
Leadership: Artush Papoyan (Chair.).
Address: 15 Njdeh Street, Gyumri.
Telephone: (41) 34350.

Mityukov, Ihor

Minister of Finance, **Ukraine**.

Ihor Oleksandrovich Mityukov is an independent. A career economist, he first entered government as Deputy Prime Minister in September 1994 and was appointed Finance Minister on 25 February 1997.

Born on 27 September 1952 in **Kiev**, he graduated in economics from the Kiev State University in 1975. For the next 15 years he worked at the Soviet Academy of Sciences, then transferred to the Ukraina commercial bank, where in 1992 he was appointed Deputy Head of the Board of Directors.

He entered the Government of Ukraine under newly-elected President Leonid **Kuchma** in September 1994 as Deputy Prime Minister with responsibility for finance and banking. In July 1995 he went to Brussels as the Ukraine's Special

Representative to the **European Union**. In a cabinet reshuffle in February 1997 he was appointed Finance Minister, and was reappointed to the post on 30 December 1999.
Address: Ministry of Finance, M. Grushevskogo St 12/2, 252008 Kiev.
Telephone: (44) 2262044.
Fax: (44) 2937466.

Mkhedrioni

A right-wing political faction in **Georgia** formed in September 1998 from the remains of the outlawed paramilitary group of the same name (literally 'warriors'). The original Mkhedrioni was set up in 1988 by bank-robber-turned-playwright Dzhaba Ioseliani as a nationalist pro-democracy group. Its violent activities in 1992 against supporters of the former President Zviad Gamsakhurdia (the **Zviadists**) are well documented, included beatings and torture. By the time of the war with **Abkhazia** in 1993 it had been legalized by the Georgian Government and had attracted around 3,000 young volunteers, many of whom fought with the regular Georgian forces in the conflict. Relations between the Mkhedrioni and the Georgian Government deteriorated thereafter, however, and the group was banned in 1995. Ioseliani, who at his height had been described by visiting journalists as the second most powerful man in Georgia, was sentenced to 11 years in prison in November 1998 for the group's various crimes, and more specifically, for his involvement in the August 1995 assassination attempt on Georgian President Eduard **Shevardnadze**. Ioseliani was released in May 2000, and elected Chairman of the Mkhedrioni, which had been reformed as a non-violent right-wing political movement calling among other things for an end to the present presidential system.

MKP (Magyar Koalíció Pártja) *see* **Hungarian Coalition Party**.

Moderates
Moodukad

A progressive political party in **Estonia**, affiliated to the **Socialist International**. The Moderates was launched in 1990 as an electoral alliance of the Estonian Rural Centre Party (EMK) and the Estonian Social Democratic Party (ESDP), the latter descended from the historic ESDP founded in 1905 when Estonia was part of the **Russian** Empire. The alliance won 12 seats in the 1992 **State Assembly** elections and was a member of the resultant Government headed by what became the **Fatherland Union** (IL). In the March 1995 elections the Moderates slumped to six seats, despite receiving endorsement from the then Prime Minister, Andres Tarand (EMK), who in April 1996 became Chairman of the combined party.

In the March 1999 parliamentary elections the Moderates advanced strongly to 17 seats on a 15.2% vote share, becoming the progressive end of a new centre-right coalition Government headed by the IL and also including the **Estonian Reform Party**. Having missed out on the premiership, Tarand had some consolation in becoming Chairman of the coalition's co-ordinating council. In May 1999 the Moderates absorbed the People's Party, which had been formed in 1998 as a merger of the Estonian Farmers' Party and the right-wing Republican and Conservative People's Party.

Internal dissent within the coalition led to the announcement by Prime Minister Mart **Laar** in December 2001 that he would resign in January, casting doubt over the future of the IL-led coalition itself.

Leadership: Andres Tarand (Chair.).
Address: Valli 4, Tallinn 10148; POB 3437, Tallinn 19090.
Telephone: 6207980.
Fax: 6207988.
E-mail: kirjod@moodukad.ee
Internet: www.moodukad.ee

Moldova
Republica Moldova

A landlocked independent republic in eastern Europe, bounded to the north, east and south by Ukraine, and to the west by Romania. Administratively, the country is divided into 40 districts.

Area: 33,700 sq km; *capital*: **Chişinau**; *population*: 4.3m. (2001 estimate), comprising ethnic **Moldovans** 64.5%, **Ukrainians** 13.8%, **Russians** 13%, Gagauz 3.5%, **Jews** 1.5%, **Bulgarians** 2%, others 1.7%; *official language*: Moldovan (very close to Romanian); *religion*: Eastern **Orthodox** 98.5%, **Jewish** 1.5%.

Under amendments to the 1994 Constitution adopted in 2000, Moldova is a 'Parliamentary Republic' in which supreme authority is vested in the unicameral **Parliament** (Parlamentul), which has 101 members directly elected for a four-year term by proportional representation of parties which obtain at least 6% of the national vote. The Head of State is the President, who is elected by the Parliament for a four-year term (having before 2000 been directly elected). Executive authority is vested in the Prime Minister and Council of Ministers, subject to approval by the Parliament.

History: Once a Roman province, Moldova became an independent principality in the mid-14th century and was a powerful state under Stefan the Great. A period of decline followed his death, and by the mid-16th century Moldova had become an Ottoman principality. It was then caught up in the struggles between the **Russian** and Ottoman Empires before being partitioned under the Treaty of Bucharest in 1812, by which Tsarist Russia annexed the territory, east of the River Prut and stretching to the River Dnester, naming it Bessarabia, and the Ottoman Turks retained the region west of the River Prut. The latter region became part of the independent state of **Romania** under the 1878 Treaty of Berlin, while Bessarabia was incorporated into a **greater Romania** following the First World War.

In 1924 the new Bolshevik regime in Moscow established the Moldovan Autonomous Soviet Socialist Republic (ASSR) on the eastern bank of the Dnestr to signify its non-acceptance of the post-1918 territorial settlement. Soon after the start of the Second World War, Romania was forced to cede Bessarabia to the **Soviet Union**, as agreed under the 1939 **Nazi-Soviet Pact**. The major part of the province was united with the ASSR to form the Moldovan Soviet Socialist Republic, while the southernmost parts were joined to Soviet **Ukraine**. Allied with Nazi Germany, Romanian forces occupied the lost territory from 1941 until the Red Army regained control in 1944, Soviet sovereignty being confirmed by the 1947 Treaty of Paris. The subsequent 'Sovietization' of Moldova included the collectivization of agriculture, the imposition of a **Cyrillic alphabet** to separate the Moldovan and Romanian languages, and immigration of ethnic Russians and Ukrainians.

In the late 1980s the influence of the *glasnost* ('openness') initiative in the Soviet Union encouraged the growth of a pro-Romanian popular movement in Moldova, whose demands focused on the language issue. A law was passed in 1989 returning Moldovan from the Cyrillic to the Latin alphabet. The following year the communist monopoly of power ceased, the nationalist Moldovan Popular Front securing a majority of seats in the February 1990 elections to the Moldovan Supreme Soviet. The Government declared the sovereignty of the republic and denounced the 1940 Soviet annexation of Bessarabia as illegal. Following the failure of the attempted **August coup** in the Soviet Union to remove President **Gorbachev**, Moldova declared its independence in August 1991. In December, in the first popular presidential election, Mircea Snegur (formerly the Supreme Soviet Presidium Chairman) was elected unopposed.

In parallel developments among Moldova's ethnic minorities, the **Slavs** of **Transdnestria** in the east and the Turkish-speaking people in **Gagauzia** in the south declared breakaway republics in September 1990, with their capitals in Tiraspol and Komrat respectively. Fearing a resurgence of Romanian nationalism, Slav guerrillas waged war with government forces in Transdnestria, before a Russian-Moldovan peacekeeping force was deployed in July 1992 and a cease-fire declared in August.

The Moldovan Popular Front Government fell in July 1992 and was replaced by a Government of national consensus. In Moldova's first multi-party parliamentary elections in February 1994, the Agrarian Democratic Party of Moldova (PDAM) led by Andrei Sangheli won an overall majority of seats in the new Parliament, the defeat of parties advocating union with Romania being followed by a referendum in March which returned a 95% vote in favour of Moldova's independence. The new Constitution adopted in July 1994 proclaimed the country's neutrality and granted special autonomous status to Gagauzia and Transdnestria within Moldova.

In the second round of presidential elections in December 1996, Petru Lucinschi, the PDAM-backed Speaker of the Parliament, defeated Snegur, who had earlier launched the rival Party of Revival and Accord of Moldova (PRCM) with a cautious leaning towards unification with Romania. In January 1997 President Lucinschi appointed free-market reformer Ion Ciubuc as Prime Minister and announced measures to grant special status to Transdnestria, whose leader, Igor Smirnov, had meanwhile called a number of referendums which favoured ultimate independence. A memorandum of understanding was signed in May 1997 committing the two sides to further negotiations, pending which Russian troops remained deployed in the breakaway republic (see below).

In the March 1998 parliamentary elections the revived **Communist Party of the Moldovan Republic** (PCRM) led by Vladimir **Voronin** became the largest party but failed to win a majority. The various centre-right formations, headed by Snegur's right-wing Democratic Convention of Moldova (CDM) alliance and including pan-Romanian parties, were therefore able to form a majority coalition under the continued premiership of Ciubuc. He was replaced in February 1999 by Ion Sturza, previously Deputy Prime Minister and a member of the Movement for a Democratic and Prosperous Moldova. Before the year was out, however, Sturza had lost a vote of confidence and had been succeeded by Dumitru **Braghis** (then non-party), who formed a mainly technocratic Government backed by most of the centre-right parties.

Changes secured by the Braghis Government in 2000 included the abolition of the death penalty and the adoption by Parliament of constitutional amendments which curtailed the executive powers of the President, who would henceforth be elected by Parliament rather than by the people (see above). Unsuccessfully resisted by President Lucinschi, the changes meant that Parliament was called upon to elect a new Head of State in December. Amidst increasing disarray on the centre-right, the deputies failed to produce the required majority for any candidate, so that Lucinschi was able to dissolve Parliament and call early elections. Following the dissolution, Prime Minister Braghis launched the **Braghis Alliance** (AB) electoral bloc of assorted centrist and left-wing parties.

Latest elections: The February 2001 parliamentary elections yielded a landslide victory for the PCRM, which won 71 of the 101 seats with 49.9% of the vote. Only two other formations gained representation, namely the AB with 19 seats (13.4% of the vote) and the **Christian Democratic People's Party** with 11 seats (8.3%). In early April Moldova became the first former communist country to democratically elect a communist as Head of State, when Voronin was elected President by the new Parliament, while Vasile **Tarlev** became Prime Minister of a PCRM Government committed to a strong state role in the economy and the re-establishment of close ties with the Russian Federation.

International relations and defence: Independent Moldova joined the **Commonwealth of Independent States** (CIS) in 1991 and was admitted to the **Organization for Security and Co-operation in Europe** (OSCE) and the United

Nations in 1992. It became a member of NATO's **Partnership for Peace** programme in 1994 and of the **Council of Europe** in 1995. It is also a member of the **Organization of the Black Sea Economic Co-operation** and the **Central European Initiative**. To counter Russian regional influence, Moldova was a founder member in 1998 of what became the **GUUAM group** (with **Georgia**, Ukraine, **Uzbekistan** and **Azerbaijan**) and in August 1998 concluded a border delineation agreement with the Ukraine (to allow for the construction of a Moldovan oil terminal on the Danube river); but Moldova has opted out of GUUAM military co-operation on grounds of its neutrality and for the same reason effectively withdrew from the CIS Collective Security Treaty in 1999. Following the PCRM's election victory in February 2001, however, the Moldovan Parliament speedily ratified a military co-operation agreement signed with the Russian Federation in 1997, as the new Government signalled its desire to take Moldova into the **Belarus-Russia Union**.

The May 1997 memorandum of understanding between Moldova and Transdnestria was brokered by the Russian Federation and Ukraine, which also, with the OSCE, sponsored protocols signed by the two sides in February 1998. The following month the 'Odessa accords' concluded with the Russian Federation and Ukraine provided that a reduced peacekeeping force would remain in Transdnestria until a political solution was achieved. Thereafter the Chişinau and Tiraspol Governments continued to differ fundamentally on the terms of 'special status' for Transdnestria. A new Russian plan for a 'common state' tabled in September 2000 found little immediate favour in Chişinau, even though President **Putin** had in July pledged that Russian forces would be withdrawn from the region by the end of 2002. However, the change of Government in Moldova in February 2001 opened the prospect that a new Chişinau-Moscow axis would produce a resolution of the problem. Indeed the last Russian troops pulled out of the breakaway republic in November 2001, a year ahead of schedule.

Moldova's defence budget for 2000 amounted to some US $5m., equivalent to about 0.5% of GDP. The size of the armed forces at the end of 2000 was some 10,000 personnel, including those serving under compulsory conscription of 18 months, while reservists numbered an estimated 66,000.

Moldova, economy

One of the poorest in Europe, in slow and difficult transition from Soviet-era central control. One of the smallest former Soviet republics, Moldova is landlocked but has river access to the Black Sea, and the land is very fertile.

GNP: US $1,343m. (2000); *GNP per capita*: $400 (2000); *GDP at PPP*: $9,700m. (1999); *GDP per capita at PPP*: $2,200 (1999); *exports*: $805m. (2000); *imports*: $1,347m. (2000); *currency*: leu (plural: lei; US $1=L13.09 at the end of December 2001).

In 1999 agriculture accounted for 25% of GDP, industry for 22% and services for 53%. Some 53% of the land is arable, 14% under permanent crops, 13% permanent pasture and 13% forests and woodland. The main crops are vegetables, fruit (notably grapes for wine), sugar beet, sunflowers and tobacco, and there is animal husbandry and dairy farming. There are few substantial mineral reserves, although some oil and natural gas fields have been identified. The industrial sector is dominated by food processing and by wine and tobacco production. As there is no domestic exploitation of fuel reserves, all energy sources are imported, notably as oil and natural gas from the **Russian Federation** and **Ukraine** and in the form of electricity from Ukraine.

Moldova's main exports are wine, tobacco and other prepared foodstuffs (56% of the total in 1998) and vegetable products, live animals and animal products (an aggregate of 16%). The principal imports are mineral products and fuel (31%), machinery and mechanical appliances and transport equipment (18%), food products and live animals (11%) and chemical products (7%). The Russian Federation was the principal purchaser of Moldovan exports in 2000 (37% of the total), followed by the USA (14%) and Germany (7%). The principal suppliers of Moldova's imports were the Russian Federation (17%), Ukraine (14%), **Romania** (12%) and Germany (11%).

Within the **Soviet Union**, Moldova had been an important supplier of industrial goods to the other republics, but such activity is concentrated in the eastern **Transdnestria** region, which declared a breakaway republic in 1990. Since then the economies of the two parts of Moldova have functioned largely separately and economic restructuring efforts by the Moldovan Government have been concerned principally with small and medium-sized industries. Independence and the security situation, as well as a severe drought in 1992, combined to cause huge inflation (of some 1,800% in 1993), until the introduction of a new currency in 1993 and a tightening of monetary and fiscal policy resulted in a progressive reduction to about 11% in 1997. However, financial stabilization did not result in improved living standards, as GDP fell sharply following independence, before showing modest growth of 1.6% in 1997. Officially registered unemployment remained low at around 2% in 1997–98, but underemployment was believed to be very high.

Moldova was particularly hard hit by the financial crisis in the Russian Federation (*see* **Russian Federation, economy**) in mid-1998, the sudden collapse of its main export market resulting in a contraction in real GDP of 8.6% in 1998, while the inflation rate rose to over 18% and the national currency lost some 60% of its external value between July 1998 and May 1999. Further GDP contraction of 4.4% was experienced in 1999, in which inflation climbed to over 40%, and Moldova continued to suffer difficulties in its trade position, notably in paying for its large imports of natural gas from the Russian Federation. Some signs of recovery were apparent in 2000, in which GDP growth of 1.9% was provisionally recorded and inflation was reduced to around 20%. The Government's budget for 2001 provided for expenditure of L3,646m. and revenue of L3,363m.

An economic reform plan adopted in 1991 anticipated a programme of privatization, largely through the issue of vouchers (*see* **voucher privatization**), but this was slow in taking off and was replaced by a new scheme in 1994. By 1996 privatized enterprises were estimated to account for some two-thirds of Moldova's industrial base. In December 1998 parliamentary approval was given to the privatization of the monopoly provider of telecommunications services and the sale of certain power companies, while in 2000 the privatization of agricultural land was accelerated. In April 2000, however, the **Parliament**'s rejection of proposals for the privatization of the state-owned wine and tobacco industries resulted in the suspension of **IMF** credits and **World Bank** lending.

The successful conclusion in February 2001 of negotiations for Moldova to join the **World Trade Organization** (WTO) boosted confidence in longer-term economic prospects. On the other hand, major doubts about Moldova's commitment to a free-market economy were raised by the election the same month of a communist Government pledged to maintaining a strong state role and even to reintroducing state monopolies in some sectors.

Moldovan Stock Exchange (MSE)

The stock exchange in **Chişinau**, **Moldova**, established in December 1994. Trading began in June 1995 and with US assistance the MSE was upgraded to a 'modern exchange' by October that year. By 31 December 1999, 58 companies were listed on the MSE and trading was conducted in shares of over 900 unlisted firms. Trade volume in 1999 reached US $35.6m.

Chair.: Ion Gangura.
Address: Blvd Ştefan cel Mare 73, Chişinau.
Telephone: (2) 277594.
Fax: (2) 277368.
Internet: www.moldse.md

Moldovans

A Romance people dominant in **Moldova** and ethnically identical to the neighbouring **Romanians**. Like the Romanians they are descended from ancient **Vlach** communities, and largely follow the Eastern **Orthodox Christian** faith. Moldovans can be distinguished from Romanians by the use of the **Cyrillic alphabet** to transcribe their form of the shared Romanian language. Separated from the rest of **Romania** by imperial **Russian** occupation in 1812 the Moldovans have since been strongly russified, particularly during the Soviet era.

Calls for reunification with **Romania** followed the collapse of the **Soviet Union** in 1991. Any chance of realizing this idea was dispelled, however, by regional separatism in Moldova's non-Moldovan enclaves, particularly the struggle of the mixed Moldovan/Russian population of **Transdnestria**. Since then there has been more focus on closer ties with **Ukraine** and the Russian Federation. The dire economic plight of Moldova has forced a great many Moldovans to seek seasonal employment in neighbouring countries.

Moldpres *see* **National News Agency**.

Molotov-Ribbentrop Pact *see* **Nazi-Soviet Pact**.

Montenegro

The smaller of the two constituent republics of **Yugoslavia**, measuring 5,332 square miles (13,812 sq km), bounded by the Adriatic Sea to the south-west, Bosnia and Herzegovina to the north-west, Serbia to the north-east and Albania to the southeast. Historically, Montenegro had long held on to its independence in the impenetrable Black Mountain region (from which the country derives its name) against the encroaching power of the Ottomans. Although nominally controlled by the Ottoman Empire the province was never really dominated and was internationally recognized as an independent state in the 1878 Treaty of Berlin. The newly-emerged Montenegro was also enlarged to include border areas in **Albania** and the plains around **Podgorica**, and to give it access to the Adriatic. Montenegro was eventually absorbed into the Kingdom of the Serbs, Croats and Slovenes (Yugoslavia) in 1918 but reappeared as a separate state during the Second World War. Once more it disappeared into the Yugoslav State in 1945.

During the collapse of the post-communist Yugoslavia, Montenegro's pro-Serbian Government sided with the Belgrade authorities and joined **Serbia** in the 'third Yugoslavia'. However, criticism of Serbian strategies ultimately led to the removal of Montenegrin forces from the Yugoslav army. A split in the ruling **Democratic Party of Socialists of Montenegro** (DPSCG) in 1997 led to the election of the outwardly anti-**Milošević** Milo **Djukanović** as Montenegrin President. Tensions with Belgrade, strained since the disintegration of the **Socialist Federal Republic of Yugoslavia**, have increased dramatically. Djukanović has steadily argued the case for greater autonomy for Montenegro, and if necessary independence, despite strong opposition from Serbia, the international community and within Montenegro among the 'White Montenegrins' (those in favour of closer connection with Serbia).

By the end of Slobodan Milošević's rule as Federal President, the republic had cut almost all ties with the central regime and ordered a boycott of federal elections in 2000, protesting at the alteration in the Yugoslav Constitution which downgraded Montenegro's position in the Federation. The boycott allowed pro-Milošević parties to represent the Republic at federal level.

Moravia

The narrowness of the result of the 2001 Montenegrin Assembly elections between the pro-independence and pro-Federation sides took away some of the momentum for an independence referendum, but the DPSCG suggested that it could be held in 2002.

The Montenegrin people, ethnically similar to the neighbouring **Serbs** and **Croats**, arrived in the area during the south **Slav** migration into the region in the 7th century. Strongly **Orthodox Christian** in faith, the Montenegrins follow the Serbs in using the **Cyrillic alphabet** to transcribe their common language. Despite small-scale industries, introduced during the communist era, the Republic consumes a considerable amount of aid to sustain its agricultural population. Sentiment towards the union with Serbia divides the country. Pro-union 'White Montenegrins' stress the ethnic, linguistic and religious similarities between the two peoples, while the 'Green' faction instead champion the idea of a distinct Montenegrin identity.

Moravia

One of the two ancient states which in combination form the modern **Czech Republic**, the other being **Bohemia**. Moravia, now the south-eastern third of the republic, was an important early mediaeval **central European** kingdom. At its maximum expansion, the Great Moravian kingdom occupied all of neighbouring Bohemia, southern **Poland** and the western Pannonian plain of modern **Hungary**, as well as the **Slovak** lands in between. King Rostislav greatly influenced the future of the region when he invited the renowned Byzantine missionaries, Saints Cyril and Methodius, to convert his people to Christianity in 864. The resulting Slavic liturgy won the enthusiastic approval of the Pope in Rome, encouraging the Moravians to adopt **Roman Catholicism** and to introduce the Latin script to transcribe their language—somewhat ironically, since it was the other great achievement of the mission to create the modified Greek script known as **Cyrillic**, which was adopted by the south **Slavs** of Byzantium.

Moravia was absorbed into the kingdom of Bohemia from 1029 and has remained tied to its western neighbour ever since, though it retained a distinct relationship with the Habsburg Austrian overlords who dominated the region from 1526 onwards. It ceased to exist as a separate administrative region in 1949 under the communist regime. On the disintegration of **Czechoslovakia** in 1993 Moravia was included in the Czech Republic without question.

Mordova

A constituent and impoverished republic of the **Russian Federation** situated in the centre of **European Russia**. *Population*: 963,504 (1997 estimate). The **Finno-Ugric** Mordvin constitute a third of the republic's population and are divided into two distinct groups—the Erzya and the Moksha—with mutually unintelligible languages. They first encountered ethnic **Russians** as early as the 12th century and came under direct Russian rule after the fall of the Kazan khanate in 1552. This long contact with Russian culture has somewhat diluted Mordvin identity, a process speeded up during the Soviet era. Mordova (also known as Mordvinia) was made an autonomous *oblast* (region) in 1930 and a full republic from 1934. Nikolay Ivanovich Merkushkin has been President of the Republic since September 1995.

Unlike the other Volga-Ural republics Mordova was not heavily industrialized and agriculture remains the main economic activity. Most crops are grains, but some tobacco and hemp are also harvested. The Mordvin are renowned as expert beekeepers, and also raise livestock including horses. Light industries focus on agricultural and timber products. Peat is burned as fuel at the capital Saransk.

Moscow

The capital and largest city of the **Russian Federation**, situated in the west of **European Russia** on the Moskva river. *Population*: 9.3m. (1999 estimate). The foundation of the city is generally ascribed to the Russian Prince, Yuri Dolgoruky, who held a feast in Moscow in 1147. The site of the contemporary wooden settlement corresponds to the modern citadel, or **Kremlin**. The location of the town, near important riverine trade routes, led to its growing importance under the suzerainty of the **Tatar** Golden Horde from 1237. Having become a separate Principality in its own right, Moscow ceased paying tribute to the Horde under the reign of Ivan III (the Great) in the 15th century. Despite being briefly captured by Polish forces in the 1570s, the Muscovite State spread rapidly into the surrounding Russian lands and formed the basis of the future Russian Empire over the course of the following centuries and under the rule of the **Romanov dynasty** from 1613. At this time it was one of the largest cities in the world with over 200,000 occupants. Its international importance was founded on its position as the foremost **Slavic** State in Europe and the home of the **Orthodox Christian** Church—earning it the title 'the Third Rome'.

Despite the removal of the Russian capital from Moscow to **St Petersburg** in 1712, the city remained an important political, cultural and economic centre, situated as it was near to the geographic middle of the Empire. All Russian Tsars continued to be crowned in the city and the invading armies of Napoleon Bonaparte sought its capture as the key to taking the entire Empire. Following the defeat of Russian forces at the 1812 Battle of Borodino, Napoleon's army entered a deserted city which was burned to the ground that night, forcing the invading army to begin its disastrous retreat from Russian territory. The city was rapidly rebuilt as the heart of the modernizing State. In 1851 it was connected to the capital by one of the country's first railways and became the terminus of the famous **Trans-Siberian Railway** in 1891. By the opening of the 20th century the city's population passed one million. During the October Revolution of 1917, Moscow was the scene of some of the worst street violence across the country. It was restored to its status as the capital of Russia in 1918 as German forces encroached on St Petersburg (recently renamed Petrograd).

As capital of the **Soviet Union**, Moscow was developed as the centre of the vast bureaucracy and remodelled along Stalinist lines in a comprehensive and ambitious development plan. The underground rail system was completed in 1935. Unlike St Petersburg (by now renamed Leningrad), Moscow did not suffer direct attack during the Second World War, although German forces came within 40 km of the capital in December 1941. Development continued after the war with many highrise buildings and housing developments spreading across the old city. The urban sprawl advanced on the surrounding region and the earlier charm of the city was overshadowed by concrete and glass. As the political heart of the Soviet Union, Moscow was also home to the pro-democracy movement in the 1980s. Boris **Yeltsin**, the head of the city's municipal branch of the **Communist Party of the Soviet Union**, purged the city administration of the **nomenklatura** and gave permission for open demonstrations on the streets. His personal popularity in the city secured mass support for his stand against communist hardliners during the 1991 **August coup**, and ultimately his election as President. Moscow remained the Russian capital after the collapse of the Soviet Union on 31 December 1991. The post-Soviet city has faced similar problems to other urban areas in the Russian Federation: economic instability and rising crime. Its fortunes have reflected those of the country at large.

Moscow is home to a variety of industries and is the main transport hub for the entire country. The Federal Government is based there, in the Kremlin and the **White House**, as are the headquarters of major financial and cultural institutions.

Moscow Central Stock Exchange (MCSE)

One of two main stock exchanges in the **Russian Federation**, the other being the **Moscow International Stock Exchange** (MISE). There are in addition a number of regional exchanges and an active electronic trading system, the Russian Trading System (RTS), which was set up in October 1995 and acquired a stock exchange licence in January 2000. The MCSE itself was the first of the exchanges to come into existence, being founded and registered on 21 November 1990. It began regular trading sessions in August 1991. Since 1996 it has operated under a regulatory framework overseen by the Russian Federation Commission on Securities and the Capital Market (FCSM).

Address: ul. Ilinka 3/8, Moscow.
Telephone: (095) 9212551.
Fax: (095) 9214364.

Moscow International Stock Exchange (MISE)

One of two main stock exchanges in the **Russian Federation**, the other being the **Moscow Central Stock Exchange** (MCSE). There are in addition a number of regional exchanges and an active electronic trading system, the Russian Trading System (RTS), which was set up in October 1995 and acquired a stock exchange licence in January 2000. The MISE was established in 1990 and started regular trading sessions on 30 October 1991. Since 1996 it has operated under a regulatory framework overseen by the Russian Federation Commission on Securities and the Capital Market (FCSM).

President: Viktor Sakharov.
Address: Prosvirin per. 4, 103045 Moscow.
Telephone and Fax: (095) 9233339.

Mostar

A historic town in south-eastern **Bosnia and Herzegovina**, traditionally the capital of **Herzegovina** and now in the **Croat**-dominated canton of **Herceg-Bosna**. The town's single span stone bridge, after which it was named (from the Serbo-Croat word *most* meaning bridge), was constructed over the River Neretva in 1566 by Ottoman engineers, and was one of the former **Yugoslavia**'s most celebrated historic monuments. The bridge was destroyed during heavy bombardment by Croat forces during the Bosnian war in November 1993. Its destruction, after months of brutal fighting between local Muslims and Croats in a town formerly famed for its multi-culturalism, was a heavy symbolic blow to the ideal of inter-ethnic harmony. The city became the base of a revived separate Croat state during 2001.

MOSz *see* **National Federation of Workers' Councils**.

Movement for a Democratic Slovakia
Hnutie za Demokratické Slovensko (HZDS)

The populist party which has dominated the politics of **Slovakia** since independence, both in government and in opposition. The HZDS was launched in May 1991 a month after Vladimír **Mečiar** (a former communist) had been ousted from the premiership of Slovakia (then still part of **Czechoslovakia**) after coming into conflict with the mainstream leadership of the pro-democracy **Public Against Violence** (VPN). The HZDS quickly confirmed that it was Slovakia's leading political formation, winning 74 of the 150 Slovak Council seats in the June 1992 elections. Restored to the premiership, Mečiar led Slovakia to sovereignty from the beginning of 1993 and formed a governing coalition with the radical right-wing **Slovak National Party** (SNS).

The Mečiar Government quickly came under criticism for its authoritarian tendencies and the entrenched position of former communists in the state bureaucracy. Policy and personal clashes precipitated a series of defections from the HZDS in 1993–94, while the appointment of a former communist as Defence Minister in March 1993 caused the SNS to leave the Government, which was thus reduced to minority status. Having failed to persuade the (ex-communist) **Party of the Democratic Left** (SDĽ) to join the Government, Mečiar restored the coalition with the SNS in October 1993. However, chronic divisions within the HZDS led to the Prime Minister's defeat in a no-confidence motion and reluctant resignation in March 1994. The HZDS went into opposition to a centrist coalition, but remained the country's strongest formation with its combination of economic conservatism and strident nationalism.

Allied in the autumn 1994 elections with the small Agrarian Party of Slovakia, the HZDS won a decisive plurality of 61 seats in the **National Council** (on a 34.9% vote share) and became the lead partner in a 'red-brown' coalition with the SNS and the left-wing Association of Workers of Slovakia. Public commitments notwithstanding, the return of the HZDS to power meant a slow-down in the pace of transition to a market economy. It also revived earlier political conflict between Mečiar and President Michal Kováč, who had been elected by the legislature in February 1993 as candidate of the HZDS but who had subsequently distanced himself from the movement. The tension flared up in March 1995 when the President refused at first to sign a bill transferring overall control of the security services from the Head of State to the Government. Although he signed the measure the following month when the National Council had readopted it, the HZDS executive called for his resignation and expulsion from the party.

The confrontation between Mečiar and President Kováč rumbled on in 1996–97, with the HZDS Government blocking opposition moves for a referendum on a proposal that the President should be directly elected. As Kováč's five-year term came to an end, the legislature failed to produce the required three-fifths majority for a successor, so that in March 1998 Mečiar, as Prime Minister, assumed key presidential functions. HZDS deputies thereafter blocked further attempts to elect a President, with damaging effects on the party's public standing. In National Council elections in September 1998 the HZDS narrowly remained the largest party, but slumped to 43 seats on a 27% vote share and went into opposition to a centre-left coalition.

Following the adoption of a constitutional amendment by the new legislature in January 1999 providing for direct presidential elections, Mečiar emerged from post-election seclusion to become the HZDS presidential candidate. However, in the elections in May 1999 he was defeated in the second round by the centre-left nominee on a 57% to 43% split. In March 2000 Mečiar was re-elected HZDS Chairman by a party congress which also approved the conversion of the HZDS into a formal political party with the suffix 'People's Party', signifying a shift to a less nationalistic stance, while the party declared its full support for membership of the **European Union** (EU) and the **North Atlantic Treaty Organization** (NATO).

In April 2000 Mečiar suffered the indignity of being arrested and fined for refusing to testify on the murky affair of the kidnapping of President Kováč's son in 1995 at the height of Mečiar's confrontation with the President. The HZDS then succeeded in collecting sufficient signatures to force a referendum on its proposal that early parliamentary elections should be held. However, only 20% of the electorate voted when the consultation was held in November 2000, so that the result had no validity.

Leadership: Vladimír **Mečiar** (Chair.).
Address: Tomášikova 32/A, POB 49, Bratislava 83000.
Telephone: (2) 43293800.
Fax: (2) 43410225.
E-mail: webmaster@hzds.sk
Internet: www.hzds.sk

Movement for Rights and Freedoms
Dvizhenie za Prava i Svobodi (DPS)

The main political formation in **Bulgaria** representing the **Muslim** ethnic **Bulgarian Turks**. The policies of compulsory assimilation practised in the 1980s by the communist regime, resulting in the flight of many ethnic Turks to Turkey and elsewhere, formed the background to the DPS's aims on its creation in January 1990, which included full political, cultural and religious rights, but excluded any fundamentalist or separatist objectives. In the June 1990 **National Assembly** elections the DPS won 23 of the 400 seats at issue with 6% of the national vote. From December 1990 it participated in a national unity coalition under a non-party Prime Minister, together with the dominant **Bulgarian Socialist Party** (BSP) and the **Union of Democratic Forces** (SDS). In further elections in October 1991 the DPS improved its position, winning 24 of 240 seats with 7.6% of the vote.

From November 1991 the DPS gave crucial parliamentary backing to a minority SDS administration, being rewarded with the lifting of a ban on optional Turkish-language instruction in secondary schools. But the SDS Government's subsequent pro-market policies were described as 'blue fascism' by the DPS, which withdrew its support in September 1992, thereby precipitating the Government's fall in October. After the BSP had failed to fill the political vacuum, the DPS successfully nominated a non-party Prime Minister (Lyuben Berov) to head a 'Government of experts' which included semi-official DPS representation. In 1993 the DPS backed the Berov Government but was weakened by internal dissension and by continuing emigration of ethnic Turks. Since this time the party has attempted to broaden its support base among Bulgaria's other non-**Slavic** minority groups, principally the Muslim **Pomaks**. In March 1994, after Berov had suffered a heart attack, DPS Deputy Premier Evgeni Matinchev (an ethnic **Bulgarian**) briefly became Acting Prime Minister.

Weakened by the launching of the breakaway Party of Democratic Change (PDP) in 1994, the DPS slipped to 5.4% of the vote and 15 seats out of 240 in the December elections, therefore reverting to opposition status. It recovered to 8.2% of the vote nationally in municipal elections in October 1995, thereafter backing the successful candidacy of Petar **Stoyanov** of the SDS in the autumn 1996 presidential elections. Prior to the April 1997 legislative elections, the DPS's decision not to join the SDS-led United Democratic Forces (ODS) caused a pro-SDS faction to form the breakaway National Movement for Rights and Freedoms. For the elections the rump DPS headed the Union for National Salvation (ONS), including the Green Party and the New Choice Union, which won 19 seats on a 7.6% vote share. In opposition, the DPS in July 1998 participated in the launching of the four-party Liberal Democratic Alliance, while in January 2000 the PDP rejoined the DPS.

At the head of an alliance with the Liberal Union and Euroroma, the DPS retained a 7.5% share of the vote in legislative elections in June 2001, and was again allocated 19 seats in the Assembly. When the ODS refused to take part in a coalition with the overwhelming victors of the poll, the newly-formed **National Movement Simeon II**, the Prime Minister-designate Simeon **Saxecoburggotski** turned to the DPS to provide the overall majority his movement needed in the Assembly. For the first time in its history the DPS was directly part of the Government, gaining two seats in the initial Cabinet.

Leadership: Ahmed Dogan (President).
Address: Tzarigradsko St 47/1, Ivan Vazov, 1408 Sofia.
Telephone: (2) 881823.

Movement for the Reconstruction of Poland
Ruch Odbudowy Polski (ROP)

A small right-wing political party in **Poland**. The ROP was launched by Jan Olszewski as a radical pro-market and nationalist formation on the strength of his respectable fourth place (with 6.9% of the vote) in the first round of the November 1995 presidential election. Then identified with the Centre Alliance (PC), Olszewski had become Prime Minister in the wake of the 1991 parliamentary elections, heading a centre-right coalition which had eventually fallen in June 1992 in acrimonious circumstances related to the Government's proposal to publish lists of communist-era collaborators. In the September 1997 **National Assembly** elections, the ROP won 5.6% of the vote and six seats in the *Sejm* (lower house). However, the party's support suffered greatly from its alliance in June 2001 with the ruling **Solidarity Electoral Action** (AWS). In elections in September 2001 the so-called AWS-Right bloc failed to receive sufficient votes to qualify for any seats in the Sejm while newer, more radical right-wing parties scored much higher. The ROP contested seats for the *Senat* (upper house) as part of the Blok Senat 2001 coalition

(which included the **Citizens' Platform**, **Law and Justice**, the AWS and the **Freedom Union**), which won 15 seats.
Leadership: Jan Olszewski (Chair.).
Address: c/o Zgromadzenie Narodowe, ul. Wiejska 6/8, Warsaw 00902.
Telephone: (22) 6941497.
Fax: (22) 6941598.
Internet: www.rop-jo.com

Movement of Legality Party
Partia Lëvizja e Legalitetit (PLL)

The political wing of the monarchist movement in **Albania**. Founded in 1943 to back the unsuccessful attempt of King Zog to regain the throne, the PLL was relaunched in February 1991 to back the restoration aspirations of the exiled **Albanian royal family** now headed by Zog's son, Leka Zogu. A referendum on whether the monarchy should be restored was held simultaneously with the second round of **People's Assembly** elections in July 1997. The PLL dismissed the official result, showing a 'no' vote of 66.7%, as fraudulent. The PLL won two seats in the Assembly at this time. It joined the **Union for Victory**, headed by the main opposition **Democratic Party of Albania**, for the 2001 elections. The coalition won 46 seats but staged a four-month boycott of the Assembly in protest at the 'farcical' poll.
Leadership: Ekrem Spahiu (Chair.).
Address: Rr. P. Shkurti pall. 5/1, Tirana.

Mrkonjič Grad

A town in the western half of what is now the **Serb Republic**, in west-central **Bosnia and Herzegovina**, the site of mass killings of ethnic **Serbs** at the hands of **Croat** forces during the Bosnian War. The town is an important administrative centre in the region of **Banja Luka** and is of such strategic value that it was 'liberated' 39 times during the Second World War.

The town fell to Croatian forces on 10 October 1995 during the successful 'Operation Storm'. Although most of the Serbian population fled, around 220 people were killed by Croat forces and buried in a mass grave.

MSzOSz *see* **National Confederation of Hungarian Trade Unions**.

MSzP *see* **Hungarian Socialist Party**.

MTI *see* **Hungarian News Agency**.

Musavat *see* **New Muslim Democratic Party**.

Muslim-Croat Federation

The autonomous **Bosniak** and Bosnian **Croat** entity within **Bosnia and Herzegovina**. It is formally, if confusingly, known simply as the Federation of Bosnia and Herzegovina. Bordered to the north and east by the **Serb Republic** and to the south along the **Dalmatian** coast by **Croatia,** it forms a rough triangle of land with its north-eastern point near the town of **Brčko**. The Federation was established during the Bosnian conflict of 1992–95, by the Washington Accords agreed on 18 March 1994, sealing an alliance between Bosniak and Croat forces. Under the **Dayton Agreement** of December 1995 the Federation was formalized alongside the Serb Republic in the current loose confederal arrangement. The Federation is a loose framework of eight cantons—four Bosniak, two Croat **(Herzegovina)** and two multi-ethnic—with its capital at **Sarajevo** on its eastern edge. The strength of the Federation was tested in 2001 when Bosnian Croats in Herzegovina briefly established a separate state.

Muslim peoples

People who have embraced Islam, including over 20 ethnic groups in **eastern Europe**. Islam is the second largest religion in the world with around 1,300 million adherents. It is divided into two main denominations, the majority Sunni and the smaller Shi'ite sect. The biggest populations of Muslims in Europe can be found in the **Balkans**, in southern **European Russia** and the **Caucasus**. Islam was brought to these regions by the invading **Turkic peoples** in the 14th century and, although their political power was shattered by the early 20th century, their religious legacy has been the source of ethnic tensions into the 21st century, and a significant element in conflicts in **Bosnia and Herzegovina, Chechnya, Dagestan** and most recently **Macedonia**. The wide variety of languages, and intermingling of Muslim with non-Muslim peoples, particularly in the **Russian Federation**, dilutes pan-Islamic sentiment among European Muslims, but such sentiment is nevertheless significant, notably in the Caucasus, where it was heightened after the commencement of war in Muslim Afghanistan in 2001.

The only majority Muslim independent states in Europe (not including Turkey which lies mostly in Asia) are **Azerbaijan** (93% Muslim) and **Albania** (70%). Other majority Muslim republics lie within the **Russian Federation**. Ethnic groups in eastern Europe with a majority of Muslim followers are the **Abaza**, Abkhaz (*see* **Abkhazia**), Adygei (*see* **Adygeya**), Adzharians (*see* **Adzharia**), **Albanians, Azeris,** Balkars (*see* **Kabardino-Balkaria**), Bashkirs (*see* **Bashkortostan**), **Bosniaks, Bulgarian Turks**, Chechens, **Cherkess,** Ingush (*see* **Ingushetia**), Kabards, Karachai (*see* **Karachai**-Cherkessia), **Kazakhs, Kumyks, Kurds, Meskhetians,** Ossetes (*see* **Ossetia question**), **Pomaks** and the **Tatars**, together with the majority of peoples in the ethnically-mixed republic of Dagestan.

N

NACC

The North Atlantic Co-operation Council, replaced in 1997 by the **Euro-Atlantic Partnership Council**.

Nagorno-Karabakh

An effectively autonomous **Armenian**-populated enclave in western **Azerbaijan**. *Population*: 130,000 (1998 estimate). *Capital*: Xankändi (formerly Stepanakert). Tensions between the predominantly Armenian (and Christian) population and the **Azeri (Muslim)** authorities led to a protracted war between **Armenia** and Azerbaijan in 1988–94, and a final peace accord remains elusive.

Between 1920 and 1923 Nagorno-Karabakh was officially an autonomous Armenian region within the Transcaucasian Republic, but this status was revoked by Stalin in his role as the then **Soviet** Commissar for nationalities, and it was instead ceded to the Azeri republic. Both Armenia and Azerbaijan now lay claim to the mountainous district, centred on Xankändi. Attempts by the 75% Armenian community to assert Nagorno-Karabakh's independence from Azerbaijan in 1988 led to a series of armed clashes with Azeri forces. The move was popularly supported in Armenia although the Government there has never officially admitted any military involvement in the ensuing war.

The Soviet military was deployed in the region but failed to calm tensions. A period of direct rule from Moscow was dropped in November 1989 and the Armenian Government declared that Nagorno-Karabakh should become a part of the Armenian republic, which became independant in 1991. The situation escalated into all-out war in 1992, when a Karabakh legislature was created and independence for the Nagorno-Karabakh Republic (NKR) was approved through referendum. In the following two years Karabakh forces successfully beat back their Azeri opponents. They claimed control both of the enclave and of the Lechin corridor joining it to neighbouring Armenia—a total area equal to about 15% of Azeri territory. Ethnic Armenians living in the rest of Azerbaijan, facing a series of bloody pogroms, migrated to the enclave and Armenia proper in their thousands.

For Azeris in the NKR the situation was similar the other way around. The land of evicted Azeris was given over to arriving Armenians. An effective Azeri counter-offensive in early 1994 prompted moves to secure a cease-fire, which has held ever since. Peace talks, however, have been mired in nationalist rhetoric, unable to deal with the intractable problem of evicted nationals from both sides, while the Karabakh authorities became increasingly resistant to any form of accommodation which would leave the enclave still part of Azerbaijan. Renewed efforts to bring the two sides together in Key West, Florida, in 2001 proved fruitless, with an outline proposal being rejected on closer inspection. Some suggestions for a compromise have included territory-swaps involving the Lechin corridor and land in southern Armenia adjacent to the Azeri **Nakhichevan** exclave.

The NKR effectively administers itself as an independent republic, even issuing its own car licence plates. It uses the Armenian dram as currency. Its army, largely funded by covert donations from Armenia and the Armenian diaspora, is considered one of the most efficient in the **Commonwealth of Independent States**. Arkadii Ghukasian is President of the NKR.

Nagy, Imre

Hungarian reformist premier during the 1956 revolution. Born in 1896, Nagy was in **Russia** as a prisoner of war at the time of the 1917 revolution there. He fought in the Russian civil war as a communist party member, returning to Hungary in the 1920s but then going back to the **Soviet Union**, and working there until the Red Army liberated his native country in 1944. He was briefly Agriculture Minister, then Interior Minister (until February 1946), but became a critic of the agricultural collectivization programme, and was expelled from the Politburo in 1949. Nagy escaped further punishment in the purges, however; he returned to government in 1951, and was made Prime Minister in July 1953 at the urging of the Soviet leadership, charged with improving living standards in an attempt to mitigate the unpopularity of the regime of Mátyás Rákosi. Ousted in April 1955, he retired to write and then advocate a 'revisionist' alternative to the Stalinism of Rákosi. In the dramatic conditions of October 1956 he was recalled to office by a hardline leadership hoping to harness his popularity. His declaration of Hungarian neutrality hastened the Soviet invasion which crushed the attempted Hungarian uprising. Nagy's arrest, secret trial and June 1958 execution made him a potent martyr figure. His ceremonial reburial in June 1989 was attended by some 200,000 mourners.

Nakhichevan

An autonomous **Azeri** exclave sandwiched between **Armenia**, Iran and Turkey on the north bank of the Aras river. It is 30 km at nearest approach to the rest of

Azerbaijan, of which it is part. *Population*: 305,000 (1991 estimate). Like the rest of Azerbaijan, Nakhichevan and its similarly-titled capital city, has had a long history of conquest and reconquest. It finally passed to the **Russian** Empire in 1828. Having a predominantly Azeri population it became an autonomous region under the **Soviet** authorities from 1924, and maintained strong links with Azerbaijan. When the Soviet Union collapsed in 1991 Nakhichevan became a part of Azerbaijan.

The conflict in 1992–94 with Armenia over the **Armenian**-dominated **Nagorno-Karabakh** enclave in Azerbaijan raised tensions in Nakhichevan. With Armenian troops making successful gains across the border in the main part of Azerbaijan, it was feared that the exclave could be targeted next. However, the proximity of Azerbaijan's ally Turkey effectively guaranteed the area's security. Ongoing discussions on the Nagorno-Karabakh issue have included Armenian claims to the area of Nakhichevan, and some have even suggested a 'population-swap' for the two regions, with Azerbaijan ceding its sovereignty over Nakhichevan.

NAM *see* **Non-Aligned Movement.**

Nano, Fatos

Socialist leader and former Prime Minister of **Albania**. Fatos Nano headed three Governments in all in the 1990s: twice for brief periods either side of the country's first multi-party elections in 1991, and then again from July 1997 to September 1998, after his **Socialist Party of Albania** (PSS) had won that year's elections.

Born in 1952, Nano was a lecturer in economics under the communist-era regime, and became one of its few critics from a reform communist perspective in the late 1980s. When the regime took the gamble in December 1990 of opening up the political system and abandoning the one-party state, Nano entered a transitional Government, as Secretary-General of the Council of Ministers, and in March 1991 he assumed the leadership of a provisional Government formed in advance of the country's first multi-party elections. After the elections (held on 31 March) he was again appointed as Prime Minister, in May, and on 12 June became Chairman of the newly-formed PSS, the successor party to the former ruling communist Party of Labour of Albania (PPS).

Although Nano committed his Government to creating a free-market economy, a wave of anti-communist strikes forced it from office within a month. Nano continued to sit as a Deputy in the **People's Assembly**, but was arrested on 30 July 1993 and stripped of his parliamentary immunity from prosecution to face charges of embezzlement. In April 1994 he was convicted of mishandling US $8m. of aid from the Italian Government, of dereliction of duty and of falsifying state documents, although no evidence was presented to indicate that he had himself benefited from the alleged fraud. His detention and the arrest of several other Ministers prompted protests against alleged gross violations of legal procedure. He was kept in prison for over three years, during which time he was re-elected to the PSS leadership and remained the main political opponent (as well as bitter personal rival) of the then President, Sali Berisha.

Released and formally pardoned in March 1997, as rebellion precipitated by economic collapse transformed the political landscape, Nano was Prime Minister within four months, in the wake of a PSS election victory, while PSS Secretary-General Rexhep **Meidani** replaced Berisha as President. Nano's Government took office on 25 July 1997, committed to restoring order in the country and to seeking membership of both the **European Union** and the **North Atlantic Treaty Organization**. Although a resurgence of unrest and rioting damaged his Government, his own resignation as Prime Minister on 28 September 1998 was somewhat unexpected. It left a question of where real authority lay, with the PSS remaining in power, but Nano winning re-election as Party Chairman (defeating the PSS reformist wing led by the then Prime Minister) in October 1999 after a brief flirtation with the idea of launching his own separate political movement. By the end of 2001 there was an open rift once again between Nano and the Prime Minister (in this case Ilir **Meta**) over policy and the composition of the Government.

NAP *see* **National Agency for Privatization (Albania)**.

Národná Rada *see* **National Council (Slovakia)**.

Narodna Sobranie *see* **National Assembly (Bulgaria)**.

Narva

A town in the far north-east of **Estonia** on the border with the **Russian Federation**. *Population*: 73,000 (1998 estimate). As with much of the industrialized northeast of Estonia, Narva is home to a large ethnic **Russian** population. The town is of major importance to the regional economy, providing access to the Gulf of Finland for the Russian hinterland. As such it has been dominated through the centuries by Swedish and Russian Empires, and was secured for the latter by Peter the Great in 1704. The River Narva came to form the border between the Russian Federation and Estonia in the 20th century, placing most of the town in the Estonian republic, but leaving the **Jaanilinn** district in the Leningrad (**St Petersburg**) *oblast*. On Estonia's independence in 1991 the majority Russian inhabitants of Narva voted for regional autonomy in a ballot deemed illegal by the Estonian authorities. Since the mid-19th century the town has been a major centre for cotton textiles.

Nastase, Adrian

Prime Minister of **Romania**. Adrian Nastase is Chairman of the left-wing **Social Democrat Party** (PSD). He first entered **Parliament** in 1990 and is seen as a key figure of the moderate left. He was appointed Prime Minister on 28 December 2000.

Born on 22 June 1950 in **Bucharest**, he graduated from the city's university with a degree in law in 1973 and began a 17-year academic career which brought him into contact with many institutions outside communist Romania. Among others he worked with UNESCO and the International Institute of Human Rights in Strasbourg. He was made a full professor of international law in 1990. Maintaining his links to the West, he has been a Member of the Board at the Institute for East–West Studies in New York since 1991, and an associate of international law at the Sorbonne since 1994. He first entered Parliament in 1990 as a representative of the leftist National Salvation Front (NSF), which had won a majority of seats. He was appointed to the Council of Ministers by President Ion **Iliescu** as Foreign Minister in June 1990, and became Parliamentary Chairman in 1992, at the beginning of Iliescu's second term. He followed the President into the Executive of the Social Democracy Party of Romania (PDSR) in 1993 following the collapse of the NSF. As PDSR Vice-President he helped to reform the party after its electoral defeat in 1996.

He was appointed Prime Minister, and elected President of the party, after Iliescu's, and the party's, electoral success in November 2000. When the PDSR merged with the Romanian Social Democratic Party in June 2001 Nastase became President of the resulting new party, the PSD.

Address: Office of the Prime Minister, Piaţa Victoriei 1, 71201 Bucharest.
Telephone: (1) 6143400.
Fax: (1) 2225814.
E-mail: prim.ministru@guv.ro
Internet: www.guv.ro

National Agency for Privatization (Albania)
Agjencia Kombetare e Privatizimit

The agency in **Albania** established in 1992 under the Council of Ministers, charged with proposing and preparing the legal framework for the privatization of state-owned assets (*see* **Albania, economy**).

Director: Qirjako Theodhori.
Address: c/o Këshilli i Ministrave, Bul. Dëshmorët e Kombit, Tirana.
Telephone: (4) 257457.
Fax: (4) 227933.
Internet: www.akp.gov.al

National Assembly (Armenia)
Azgayin Joghov

The unicameral legislature of **Armenia**. It has 131 members, directly elected for a four-year term. The last elections were held on 30 May 1999.
   Address: Azgayin Joghov, 19 Marshal Baghramian Ave, 375095 Yerevan.
   Telephone: (1) 588225.
   Fax: (1) 529826.
   E-mail: miba@parliament.am
   Internet: www.parliament.am

National Assembly (Azerbaijan)
Milli Majlis

The unicameral legislature of **Azerbaijan**. It has 125 members, directly elected for a five-year term. The last elections were held on 5 November 2000. However, the poll was heavily criticized, and repeat elections were held in 11 districts on 7 January 2001.
   Address: Milli Majlis, 1 Parliamentary Avenue, 370152 Baku.
   Telephone: (12) 399750.
   Fax: (12) 934943.
   E-mail: azmm@meclis.gov.az
   Internet: www.meclis.gov.az

National Assembly (Belarus)
Natsionalnoye Sobranie

The bicameral legislature of **Belarus**, comprising the House of Representatives (Palata Predstaviteley) and the Council of the Republic (Soviet Respubliki). The lower House of Representatives has 110 members, directly elected for a maximum of four years. It met for the first time on 17 December 1996, and consisted of members of the previous legislature, the Supreme Council. The upper Council of the Republic has 56 members elected by regional Soviets, and eight members appointed by the President. It first met on 13 January 1997. The last elections were held between 15 and 29 October 2000 (House of Representatives) and 21 November 2000 (Council of the Republic). Repeat elections were held in 13 of the 110 constituencies of the House of Representatives on 13–18 March 2001, with a further round on 1 April.
   Address of lower house: Palata Predstaviteley, Natsionalnoye Sobranie, Sovetskaya St 11, 220010 Minsk.
   Telephone: (17) 2272514.
   Fax: (17) 2223178.
   E-mail: vasko@belarus.minsk.by

Address of upper house: Soviet Respubliki, ul Krasnoarmeiskaya 4, 220016 Minsk.
Telephone: (17) 2891181.
Fax: (17) 2272318.
E-mail: chrnsh@sovrep.gov.by
Internet: president.gov.by/eng/nationsobr/index.htm

National Assembly (Bulgaria)
Narodno Sobranie

The unicameral legislature of **Bulgaria**. It has 240 members, directly elected for a four-year term. The last elections were held on 17 June 2001.
Address: Narodno Sobranie, 1 Aleksandur Battenberg Sq., 1169 Sofia.
Telephone: (2) 9804034.
Fax: (2) 9808916.
E-mail: protokol@nt14.parliament.bg
Internet: www.parliament.bg

National Assembly (Hungary)
Országgyűlés

The unicameral legislature of **Hungary**. It has 386 members, directly elected for a four-year term. The last elections were held on 10–24 May 1998.
Address: Országgyűlés, Kossuth tér 1–3, 1357 Budapest.
Telephone: (1) 4414344.
Fax: (1) 4415972.
E-mail: struve.gabriella@mkogy.hu
Internet: www.mkogy.hu

National Assembly (Poland)
Zgromadzenie Narodowe

The bicameral legislature of **Poland**, comprising the Diet (Sejm) and the Senate (Senat). The lower Diet has 460 members, directly elected for a four-year term. The upper Senate has 100 members, elected for a four-year term. The last elections were held on 23 September 2001.
Address of lower house: Sejm, ul. Wiejska 4/6/8, 00902 Warsaw.
Telephone: (22) 6942500.
Fax: (22) 6941863.
Internet: www.sejm.gov.pl
Address of upper house: Senat, ul. Wiejska 4/6/8, 00902 Warsaw.
Telephone: (22) 6942410.

National Assembly (Slovenia)

Fax: (22) 6942224.
Internet: www.senat.gov.pl

National Assembly (Slovenia)
Državni Zbor

The unicameral legislature of **Slovenia**. It has 90 members, directly elected for a four-year term. A National Council (Državni Svet), with 40 indirectly-elected members, has an advisory role and its nature and status are under discussion.
Address: Državni Zbor, Šubičeva 4, 1000 Ljubljana.
Telephone: (1) 4789400.
Fax: (1) 4789845.
E-mail: Jozica.Veliscek@dz-rs.si
Internet: www.sigov.si/dz

National Bank of Azerbaijan

The Central Bank of **Azerbaijan**. Established in 1992, the Bank is an arm of the state which attempts to regulate the national currency, the manat (which replaced the rouble and became sole legal tender in 1994). The Bank also regulates banking in Azerbaijan and deals in the securities market as well as foreign currencies.
Governor: Elman Roustamov.
Address: R. Bebutov St 32, 370070 Baku.
Telephone: (12) 931122.
Fax: (12) 935541.

National Bank of Belarus

The Central Bank of **Belarus**. A Belarusian branch of the Soviet State Bank was established in **Minsk** in 1922 and acted as a Central Bank for the Belarusian republic within the **Soviet Union**. It was temporarily rehoused during the Nazi invasion of the Soviet Union in the Second World War, and at one time was based in Kazakhstan. The bank returned to Minsk in 1944. It was transformed into the National Bank of Belarus in December 1990 and took on the role of regulating the country's currency and banking industry. The Belarusian rouble was introduced in 1992 and suffered massive hyperinflation until 1994, the year in which it fully replaced the old Soviet rouble. In a reversal of fortune the Russian rouble is set to be reintroduced in Belarus in 2005 as a precursor to the introduction of a joint currency in 2008. The Belarusian rouble was readjusted in December 2000. As of December 1997 the bank had reserves of 5,517,686m. Belarusian roubles.
Governor: Pyotr Prakapovich.
Address: pr. F. Skaryny 20, Minsk 220008.

Telephone: (17) 2276431.
Fax: (17) 2274879.
E-mail: nbrb@nbrb.belpak.minsk.by
Internet: www.nbrb.by

National Bank of Georgia (NBG)

The Central Bank of **Georgia**. The NBG was founded in 1991 from the Georgian branches of the State bank of the **Soviet Union**. It is the 'bank of banks', overseeing currency policy and supervising and regulating the banking industry. Although it is independent it is the banker of the Government. The NBG has issued the lari from December 1995, although the notes are printed in France. As at December 1998 the NBG had reserves of 9.3m. lari.

President and Chair. of Board: Irakli Managadze.
Address: 3/5 Leonidze St, Tbilisi 380005.
Telephone: (32) 996505.
Fax: (32) 999885.
E-mail: webmaster@nbg.gov.ge
Internet: www.nbg.gov.ge

National Bank of Hungary
Magyar Nemzeti Bank (MNB)

The Central Bank of **Hungary**. The first Hungarian Central Bank was formed in 1848–49 during a brief period of revolutionary autonomy from the Habsburg Empire. It was resurrected at the end of the First World War after the collapse of the Empire, and the Royal Hungarian State Bank was transformed into the National Bank of Hungary in June 1924. The national currency, the forint, was introduced by the MNB in August 1946. Under communist rule the country's banking system was effectively nationalized, but a two-tier system was reintroduced in January 1987, with commercial banks being separated off from the MNB. The political independence of the Bank was reasserted in October 1991. The MNB's role as a supervisor of the banking sector was restricted by new legislation in 1997, leaving it mainly in control of only monetary policy. As at December 1999 the bank had reserves of 56,216m. forint.

President: Zsigmond Járai.
Address: Szabadság tér 8–9, 1850 Budapest.
Telephone: (1) 3023000.
Fax: (1) 3323913.
Internet: www.mnb.hu

National Bank of Macedonia
Narodna banka na Republika Makedonija

Established as a Central Bank in April 1992, following **Macedonia**'s secession from the **Socialist Federal Republic of Yugoslavia**. The Bank is charged with maintaining the stability of the domestic currency (the denar), ensuring liquidity in the economy, and supervising the functioning of the banking system. Although the National Bank is independent of the Government, it is the latter which sets the nation's major economic objectives, such as inflation and growth targets. However, the Bank is free to undertake monetary measures and determine the monetary instruments necessary to achieve these goals.
Governor: Ljube Trpeski.
Address: POB 401, Kompleks banki b.b., 1000 Skopje.
Telephone: (2) 108108.
Fax (2) 108357.
Internet: www.nbrm.gov.mk

National Bank of Moldova
Banca Naţionala a Moldovei (BNM)

The Central Bank of **Moldova**. A two-tier banking system was established in 1991 creating the BNM from the remains of the Soviet State Bank. Its main concern is overseeing monetary policy. The Moldovan leu was introduced by the bank in November 1993 and helped to control rampant inflation, bringing it down from 2705.7% in that year to just 11.2% in 1998. Although the Bank is independent of the Government it is answerable to **Parliament**. From 1995 the BNM has also been responsible for regulating the country's banking system.
Governor: Leonid Talmaci.
Address: Blvd Renaşterii 7, 2006 Chişinau.
Telephone: (2) 221679.
Fax: (2) 221591.
E-mail: official@bnm.org
Internet: www.bnm.org

National Bank of Poland
Narodowy Bank Polski (NBP)

The Central Bank of **Poland**. A centralized bank for Poland first came into being under Russian rule in 1828 in that part of the country which **Russia** had incorporated in recent partitions. This Bank of Poland began issuing złotys in 1830. Between 1885 and the First World War the Bank was subsumed into the Russian State Bank but it was reborn in the independent Poland of the inter-war period. The eventual National Bank of Poland was constituted in January 1945 from the various institutions created by the puppet Governments of the Second World War, and złotys were reintroduced that year. From the beginning the Bank was subordinate to the Government and from 1948 it oversaw the country's transition to a planned economy. A two-tier, market-economy banking system did not reappear until the late 1980s. A revalued new złoty was introduced in 1995. The role of the Bank was last revised in the Act on the NBP adopted in August 1997. In its new role it governs monetary policy and regulates the banking industry. As at December 1998 the Bank had reserves totalling 24,845m. złotys.

President: Leszek **Balcerowicz**.
Address: ul. Świętokrzyska 11/21, POB 1011, 00919 Warsaw.
Telephone: (22) 6531000.
Fax: (22) 6208518.
E-mail: nbp@nbp.pl
Internet: www.nbp.pl

National Bank of Romania
Banca Naţionala a României (BNR)

The Central Bank of **Romania**. The BNR predates Romanian independence and was first established in 1880. On its creation it took over the running of the national currency, the leu, whose regulation remains a primary function for the Bank. After 1945 the Bank operated within a single-tier system but was released and charged with steering the country to a market economy in 1990. The BNR enjoys a large amount of autonomy but works closely with the **Parliament of Romania**. As at December 1997 the Bank held reserves of 364,300m. lei.

Governor: Emil Iota Ghizari.
Address: Str. Lipscani 25, 70421 Bucharest.
Telephone: (1) 6130410.
Fax: (1) 3123831.
Internet: www.bnro.ro

National Bank of Slovakia
Národná banka Slovenska (NBS)

The Central Bank of **Slovakia**. The NBS was founded on 1 January 1993 following the dissolution of **Czechoslovakia** and the emergence of a separate Slovakian state. Its main functions are to supervise monetary policy and regulate the country's banking industry. It is independent of the Government although the Bank's Governor is appointed by the President. The koruna was introduced in August 1993. As at December 1998 the bank had reserves of 9,730m. koruny.

Governor: Marián Jusko.
Address: Štúrova 2, 81325 Bratislava.

Telephone: (2) 59531111.
Fax: (2) 54131167.
E-mail: webmaster@nbs.sk
Internet: www.nbs.sk

National Bank of Ukraine

The Central Bank of **Ukraine**. An office of the **Russian** imperial State Bank in **Kiev** was first opened in 1839 and the building remains the home of the National Bank which emerged in March 1991. The Bank controls monetary policy and regulates the banking sector. It began issuing the karbovanets in November 1992 to replace the Russian rouble but was forced to supersede the currency with the hryvna in September 1996 as part of widespread banking reforms. As at December 2001 the bank had a total capitalization of 49,499m. hryvnas.

Governor: Volodymyr Stelmach.
Address: vul. Institutska 9, 252007 Kiev.
Telephone: (44) 2936921.
Fax: (44) 2934204.
E-mail: cmail@bank.gov.ua
Internet: www.bank.gov.ua

National Bank of Yugoslavia
Narodna banka Jugoslavije (NBJ)

The Central Bank of **Yugoslavia**. A Central Bank for the newly independent Kingdom of **Serbia** was first founded in **Belgrade** in 1884. It was transformed in to a central financial institution for the 'Kingdom of Serbs, Croats and Slovenes' in 1920. Freeing itself from reliance on foreign printers the Bank began printing dinars in 1927. During the Second World War the Bank operated in exile in London but returned to Belgrade in 1944. It became the NBJ in 1945 and it was nationalized the following year with the creation of the **Socialist Federal Republic of Yugoslavia**. Reconstituted as an independent Central Bank in 1992, it controls monetary policy and regulates the banking sector. However, the **Federal Assembly** appoints the Governor and sets the exchange rate of the dinar. Separate Central Banks operate in Serbia, **Montenegro** and **Kosovo**. As at December 1998 the NBJ had reserves totalling 1,861m. dinars.

Governor: Dušan Vlatković.
Address: Revolucije 15, POB 1010, 11000 Belgrade.
Telephone: (11) 3248841.
Internet: www.nbj.yu

National Confederation of Hungarian Trade Unions
Magyar Szakszervezetek Országos Szövetsége (MSzOSz)

Hungary's principal trade union centre, founded in March 1990 as successor to the communist-era union organization. Partly because of its communist antecedents and its links with the (ex-communist) **Hungarian Socialist Party**, the MSzOSz has faced competition from several other federations, notably the **Democratic League of Independent Trade Unions**, although in 1992 it accepted that they were entitled to a share of the assets of the communist-era organization. It has remained the largest trade union centre, supporting privatization of the economy with safeguards for the rights of workers as well as Hungary's application for membership of the **European Union**. Following the election victory of a centre-right coalition in 1998, the MSzOSz accused the new Government of abandoning social dialogue with trade union representatives and of being prepared to sacrifice workers' rights in order to attract foreign investment. Claiming a total membership of 700,000 (including pensioners) in 43 affiliated unions, the MSzOSz is one of three Hungarian members of the International Confederation of Free Trade Unions (ICFTU).

President: Dr László Sándor.
Address: 84B út Dózsa György, Budapest 1068.
Telephone: (1) 4785266.
Fax: (1) 3421799.

National Council (Slovakia)
Národná Rada

The unicameral legislature of **Slovakia**. It has 150 members, directly elected for a four-year term. The last elections were held on 25–26 September 1998.
Address: Národná Rada, Nám. Alexander Dubčeka 1, 81280 Bratislava.
Telephone: (2) 59341111.
Fax: (2) 54415324.
E-mail: valdpete@mail.ncsr.sk
Internet: www.nrsr.sk

National Democratic Party of Belarus
Natsyianalna-Demokratychnaya Partiya Belarusi (NDPB)

A pro-market, nationalist formation founded in 1990 seeking the political, economic and cultural revival of an independent **Belarus** oriented towards the West. The NDPB became a constituent party of the **Belarusian Popular Front–Renaissance** (NFB–A) and opposed the **Belarus-Russia Union** treaty. The NFB–A boycotted the October 2000 legislative elections on the grounds that there was no prospect of their being free and fair.

Leadership: Viktar Navumenka (Chair.).
Address: 97/140 Labanka Street, Minsk.
Telephone: (17) 2719516.
Fax: (17) 2369972.

National Democratic Union of Armenia
Azgayin Zhoghorvrdavarakan Miutyun (AZhM)

A centre-right political party formed by Vazgen Manukian following his resignation as Prime Minister in September 1991, when he left the then ruling **Pan-Armenian National Movement** (HHSh).

Having staged demonstrations against the HHSh Government, the party won 7.5% of the vote and five seats in the 1995 **National Assembly** elections. In the September 1996 presidential contest Manukian was runner-up with 41.3% of the vote, subsequently claiming that the result had been rigged.

Manukian stood again in the March 1998 presidential elections, but was eliminated in the first round with 12.2% of the vote. Having failed to find alliance partners for the May 1999 Assembly elections, the AZhM slipped to 5.2% of the vote but increased its representation to six seats. Although critical of the presidency of Robert **Kocharian** (non-party), the party accepted a ministerial post in February 2000. Manukian ruled out an alliance with the main ruling **Republican Party of Armenia**, or any other formation, at an AZhM congress in December, but favoured qualified co-operation with the Kocharian presidency. He was therefore attacked by party members who advocated a return to outright opposition.

Leadership: Vazgen Manukian (Chair.).
Address: 12 Abovian Street, Yerevan.
Telephone: (1) 523412.
Fax: (1) 563188.
E-mail: adjm@arminco.com

National Federation of Workers' Councils
Munkástanácsok Országos Szövetsége (MOSz)

One of the smaller trade union federations in **Hungary**, dating from 1989 but descended from workers' councils established during the 1956 Hungarian Uprising. The MOSz is affiliated to the Christian Democratic World Confederation of Labour (WCL) and claims a membership of some 60,000.

Chair.: Imre Palkovics.
Address: 2–4 Tárogáto St, Budapest 1021.
Telephone: (1) 2751445.
Fax: (1) 3942802.
E-mail: mosz.int.dept@pronet.hu

National Front
Balli Kombëtar (BK)

A right-wing political party in **Albania** with minimal electoral support.

Claiming descent from the anti-communist wing of the Second World War resistance, the BK was revived following the collapse of communist rule in 1990–91. BK leader Abaz Ermenji returned to Albania in October 1995 after 49 years in exile and led the party into an alliance with other nationalist parties for the 1997 **People's Assembly** elections, in which the BK won three seats with 2.3% of the vote. The party was weakened in August 1998 by the formation of the breakaway Right National Front by former leading BK official Hysen Selfo. It was returned to the Assembly in June 2001 as part of the rightist '**Union for Victory**' coalition, headed by the **Democratic Party of Albania,** which won 46 seats but boycotted the chamber for three months in protest at the 'farcical' elections. BK is now led by Shpetim Rroqi.

Leadership: Shpetim Rroqi (Chair.).
Address: c/o Kuvendi Popullor, Tirana.

National Harmony Party
Tautas Saskanas Partija (TSP)

A centre-left party in **Latvia** advocating reconciliation between **Latvians** and non-Latvians with guaranteed rights for minorities. The TSP consists of the residue of the Harmony for Latvia–Rebirth grouping which split in 1994. It won only six of the 100 seats in the autumn 1995 elections and was reduced to four seats by a further split in July 1996, although it was strengthened in September 1997 by a parliamentary alliance with the five-strong Latvian Socialist Party (LSP) group led by Alfreds Rubiks, who had been leader of the Soviet-era Latvian Communist Party.

For the October 1998 elections the TSP created an alliance called 'For Equal Rights in a United Latvia', which included the LSP and two ethnic **Russian** groupings, but failed to secure registration in time to run under that label. The alliance's candidates therefore stood under the TSP banner, winning 16 seats on a 14.1% vote share. The formation thus became the largest component of the opposition to the succeeding centre-right coalition. By late 2000, however, serious divisions had developed within the TSP-led alliance over the LSP's advocacy of civil disobedience by ethnic Russians against language law regulations.

Leadership: Janis Jurkans (Chair.).
Address: 60 Lačpleša iela, Riga 1010.
Telephone: 7289913.
Fax: 7281619.

National Liberal Party
Partidul Național Liberal (PNL)

A centre-right political formation in **Romania** with roots in 19th-century liberalism, which favours the restoration of the **Romanian royal family** deposed in 1947. Dating from 1848 and founded as a party in 1875, the PNL ceased to function in 1947 following the communist takeover and was revived in January 1990 after the fall of the **Ceaușescu** regime. The party came third in the May 1990 **Parliament** elections, winning 29 Chamber of Deputies seats on a 6.4% vote share, and in 1992 was briefly a member of the broad centre-right Democratic Convention of Romania (CDR) before most of the PNL withdrew because of policy differences. In the same year the exiled King Michael declined nomination as the PNL presidential candidate.

In 1993–94 the party went through a lengthy leadership struggle from which Mircea Ionescu-Quintus emerged as Chairman, following which some dissident PNL elements rejoined the party. The PNL re-entered the CDR for the November 1996 elections, backing the successful presidential candidacy of Emil Constantinescu (CDR) and winning 25 Chamber seats under the CDR banner. The party became a component of the resultant CDR-led coalition Government, although frequent strains with other CDR components were accompanied by internal divisions and defections, notably over the choice of a presidential candidate for 2000.

In the event, the PNL contested the November–December 2000 elections outside the CDR and therefore escaped the obliteration of the latter by an electorate experiencing economic and social deterioration. The party's presidential candidate, Teodor Dumitru Stolojan, came third in the first round with 11.8% of the vote, while in the parliamentary contest the PNL advanced to 30 Chamber seats on a vote share of 6.9%. It thereafter gave qualified external support to a minority Government of the **Social Democratic Pole of Romania**, although without great enthusiasm within the party. In February 2001 a PNL congress elected former Justice Minister Valeriu Stoica as Party Chairman in succession to Ionescu-Quintus.

Leadership: Valeriu Stoica (Chair.).
Address: Blvd Nicolae Balcescu 21, Bucharest 71112.
Telephone: (1) 6143235.
Fax: (1) 3239508.
Internet: www.pnl.ro

National Movement Simeon II
Nacionalno Dvizhenie Simeon Vtori (NDS II)

The centrist political movement in **Bulgaria** established by ex-King Simeon II (Simeon **Saxecoburggotski**), which stormed to victory in the June 2001 elections, taking over 42% of the vote and half the seats in the **National Assembly**.

Essentially a personalist movement based on the non-party image of Simeon II, NDS II was created on 28 April 2001 with the co-operation of the Party of Bulgarian Women and the National Revival Movement. It advocates a free market and encouragement of private investment while seeking to guarantee personal rights. Among its stated aims is to continue the path of economic and social reforms instigated by previous, post-communist Governments. Closer European integration and future membership of the **North Atlantic Treaty Organization** remain top priorities.

Barred from running himself in presidential elections, Saxecoburggotski used the movement to champion his particular vision of a liberal Bulgaria and received almost instant support from many disaffected followers of the incumbent **Union of Democratic Forces** (SDS) Government. Following its electoral success, it seemed at first that Saxecoburggotski would shun the office of Prime Minister to remain instead behind the scenes—and effectively keep alive his goal of running for President in the later presidential contest. When it appeared unlikely that this would be allowed, and in the face of massive popular demand, he eventually agreed to head the new Government, in which NDS II went into a coalition with the ethnic Turkish **Movement for Rights and Freedoms**.

Saxecoburggotski lent his support to incumbent SDS President Petar **Stoyanov** in the November 2001 poll, instead of fielding a separate NDS II candidate, but Stoyanov was nevertheless defeated.

Leadership: Simeon **Saxecoburggotski** (Chair.).
Address: 30 'Tzar Shishman' St, Sofia 1000.
Telephone: (2) 9871956.
Fax: (2) 9812695.
E-mail: nds2@nds2.orbitel.bg
Internet: www.ndsimeon2.org

National News Agency (Moldova)
Moldpres

The state news agency of **Moldova**. Separated from the state broadcasting monopoly in 1997, Moldpres continues to provide news from Moldova to other regional news agencies, chiefly **ITAR-TASS**. As the state agency it also specializes in official statements and releases.

Address: str. Puşkin 22, 2012 Chişinau.
Telephone: (2) 233428.
Fax: (2) 234371.
E-mail: inform@moldpres.md
Internet: www.moldpres.md

National Property Fund (Czech Republic)

Responsible for state property and state-owned companies in the **Czech Republic** in the period up to their privatization.
Chair.: Jan Stiess.
Address: Rašínovo nábřeží 42, 12800 Prague 2.
Telephone: (2) 24991285.
Fax: (2) 24991379.

National Property Fund (Slovakia)

Supervises the privatization process in **Slovakia**. Founded in 1993.
President: Jozef Kojda.
Address: Drieňová 27, 82101 Bratislava.
Telephone: (2) 48271448.
Fax: (2) 48271484.

National Stock Exchange (Lithuania)
Nacionaline vertybiniu popieriu birža

The stock exchange in **Lithuania**, founded in September 1993. In 1999 a memorandum of understanding was signed with the **Riga Stock Exchange** and the **Tallinn Stock Exchange** with a view to increasing co-operation. As of 1 December 2001 there were 20 brokerage companies operating on the bourse.
President: Rimantas Busila.
Address: Ukmerges 41, Vilnius 2600.
Telephone: (27) 23871 [(527) 23871 from September 2002].
Fax: (27) 24894 [(527) 24894 from September 2002].
E-mail: office@nse.lt
Internet: www.nse.lt

National Trade Union Bloc
Blocul Naţional Sindical (BNS)

One of many competing union centres in post-communist **Romania**. Founded in 1991, the BNS is affiliated to the International Confederation of Free Trade Unions (ICFTU) and claims to represent 150,000 members in 40 professional federations and 36 regional organizations (as at the end of 2000).
President: Dumitru Costin.
Address: 202A Splaiul Independentei, Floor 4, Bucharest 77208.
Telephone and Fax: (1) 3123886.

National Unity Party
Partia e Unitetit Kombëtar (PUK or UNIKOMB)

An ultra-nationalist political party in **Albania** with minimal electoral support.

Founded in mid-1991, the PUK cultivated links with the ethnic **Albanians** of **Kosovo** in pursuit of its goal of a **Greater Albania**. It declined to put up candidates in the 1992 **People's Assembly** elections in protest against what it regarded as an 'anti-democratic' electoral law, and in July 1993 party leader Idajet Beqiri received a six-month prison sentence for claiming that President Berisha wanted to create a fascist dictatorship. In January 1996 Beqiri was again charged, this time with crimes allegedly committed as a state prosecutor during the communist era. The PUK contested the 1997 Assembly elections as part of the Union for Democracy headed by the **Democratic Party of Albania** (PDS), winning one seat, but by the time of the 2001 elections the party lacked any significant political presence.

Leadership: Idajet Beqiri (Chair. of the Steering Committee).
Address: Rr. Alqi Kondi, Tirana.
Telephone: (4) 227498.
Fax: (4) 223929.

NATO *see* **North Atlantic Treaty Organization**.

Natsionalnoye Sobranie *see* **National Assembly (Belarus)**.

Nazi-Soviet Pact

A non-aggression pact signed between Nazi Germany and the **Soviet Union** on 23 August 1939 which enabled Germany to invade **Poland** unopposed on 1 September, effectively beginning the Second World War. Red army troops crossed the Polish border on 17 September, dividing the briefly independent state between the two aggressors. The pact also included the division of the **Baltic States** into German and Soviet zones of influence, with the Soviet Union gaining access to Finland, **Estonia** and **Latvia** and leaving Germany with proposed control of **Lithuania**. Also known as the Molotov-Ribbentrop pact, after the Foreign Ministers of the Soviet Union and Germany respectively, it came as a severe shock to the international community which had hitherto witnessed the two countries engaging in a vicious war of rhetoric against one another. Collaboration with Germany ended abruptly in June 1941 when Adolf Hitler tore up the non-aggression pact and launched Operation Barbarossa—the Nazi invasion of the Soviet Union.

ND *see* **New Democracy (Macedonia)**.

ND *see* New Democracy (Yugoslavia).

NDPB *see* National Democratic Party of Belarus.

NDPU *see* People's Democratic Party of Ukraine.

NDS II *see* National Movement Simeon II

Near abroad

A phrase used in **Russia** to denote neighbouring states of the former **Soviet Union** in which Russia retains a special interest (for economic, military-strategic or nationalistic reasons). The phrase has been criticized as implying that these states are somehow less than fully sovereign and are liable to be included within a newly-imposed Russian sphere of influence, particularly through the institution of the **Commonwealth of Independent States** (CIS).

Neman question

A question of the border between southern **Lithuania** and the **Russian** enclave of **Kaliningrad** along the River Neman (Nemunas in Lithuanian). At the end of the Second World War the borders of the **Baltic States** were redrawn by the Soviet authorities to create ethnic republics and guarantee direct Russian access to an ice-free port on the Baltic Sea at Kaliningrad. Following the disintegration of the **Soviet Union** in 1991 and the resurrection of an independent Lithuania the issue of this somewhat arbitrary border was raised. Elements on the far right of Lithuanian politics called for the total annexation of the Kaliningrad enclave (home to a mixed Russian-**German** population) in light of its geographic separation from the rest of the **Russian Federation** by around 750 km. However, the debate has been negated by the immediate agreement by members of the **Commonwealth of Independent States** (CIS) to set their Soviet borders as inviolable.

Neuilly, Treaty of

A treaty signed on 27 November 1919 at the Paris Peace Conference, convened following the conclusion of the First World War, concerning the territorial restructuring of **Bulgaria** which had allied itself during the war with the defeated Central Powers. The treaty fixed Bulgaria's borders, significantly ceding the coastal region of Western Thrace to Greece, and the agriculturally important region of southern **Dobruja** to **Romania**. *See also* Treaties of **Trianon** and **Versailles**.

New Azerbaijan Party
Yeni Azerbaycan Partiyasi (YAP)

Azerbaijan's ruling party from 1993 onwards, headed by President Heydar **Aliyev**, and was founded in September 1992 as an alternative to the then ruling **Azerbaijan Popular Front** (AKC).

Aliyev's initiative in founding the YAP followed his exclusion from the June 1992 presidential election because he was over a newly-decreed age limit of 65. A former Politburo member of the Soviet Communist Party, and First Secretary of the party in Azerbaijan from 1969, Aliyev was at this time President of the Azerbaijani enclave of **Nakhichevan**, and had conducted an independent foreign policy for the enclave, signing a cease-fire with **Armenia** and developing relations with the **Russian Federation**, Turkey and Iran.

Aliyev used the YAP to rally opposition to the AKC Government of Abulfaz Elchibey, who was deposed in June 1993. Elected interim Head of State, Aliyev received popular endorsement of a kind in a presidential election in October 1993 (for which the 65-year age limit was rescinded), being credited with 98.8% of the vote against two other candidates, neither of whom represented major opposition parties. Meanwhile, at Aliyev's urging, in September long-delayed parliamentary approval had been given to Azerbaijan's membership of the **Commonwealth of Independent States**. The new Government launched a crackdown against the AKC, while Aliyev moved to improve Azerbaijan's regional relations and sought a settlement of the **Nagorno-Karabakh** conflict with Armenia, involving the return of a limited Russian military presence to Azerbaijan proper.

In the November 1995 **National Assembly** elections (completed in February 1996), the YAP formed a front with three minor parties and was credited with 62% of the national vote in its own right. It therefore held an overwhelming majority of Assembly seats when pro-Government independents were included in the tally. Firmly entrenched in power, Aliyev secured a predictable victory in the October 1998 presidential elections as the YAP candidate, winning 76.1% of the vote against five other contenders. International bodies criticized widespread irregularities in the polling, the official result of which was rejected by the opposition parties. Aliyev nevertheless reappointed Artur **Rasizade** as Prime Minister of a YAP-dominated Government.

In December 1999 Aliyev was re-elected YAP Chairman at the party's first congress, which also elected the President's son, Ilham Aliyev, as one of five Deputy Chairmen. Ilham Aliyev headed the YAP list for the proportional section of Assembly elections held in November 2000 and early January 2001. Amidst opposition claims of widespread fraud, the ruling party won another overwhelming victory, taking 75 seats out of 124 filled and also having the backing of most of the 29 'independents' elected.

In November 2001 the party voted to give its backing to Ilham Aliyev as his father's eventual successor.

Leadership: Heydar Aliyev (Chair.).
Address: 6 Landau Street, Baku 370073.
Telephone: (12) 393875.

New Christian Party
Jauna Kristigo Partija (JKP)

A centre-left political formation in **Latvia** founded as the New Party (JP) in March 1998 and renamed in January 2001. Popular composer Raimond Pauls was prime mover in setting up the JP and first Chairman of the party, which drew support from the upwardly-mobile young for its pro-market, pro-Western policies combined with an inclusive approach to ethnic **Russians** (provided they learnt Latvian). In the October 1998 parliamentary elections, however, the JP won only eight of the 100 seats (with 7.3% of the vote), losing out badly to the even newer **People's Party** (TP). It nevertheless became the most junior partner in a centre-right coalition Government and in early 2001 transformed itself into the JKP, with clergyman Guntis Dislers as Chairman, in what was seen as a move to attract support from existing Christian Democratic parties.

Leadership: Guntis Dislers (Chair.).
Address: 18 Stabii iela, Riga.
Telephone: 7312742.
Fax: 7312743.

New Croatian Initiative
Nova Hrvatska Inicijativa (NHI)

A moderate **Croat** political party in **Bosnia and Herzegovina**. The NHI was established in June 1998 by Kresimir Zubak, then the Croat member of the Bosnian collective presidency, who had broken with the dominant **Croatian Democratic Union** (HDZ) after hardliner Ante Jelavić had replaced him as HDZ leader the previous month. In the September 1998 elections to the collective presidency, Zubak managed only third place in the Croat section with 11.4% of the vote (and 2.5% nationally), while joints lists of the NHI and the Croatian Christian Democratic Union won one seat in the union lower house and two in the **Muslim-Croat Federation** lower house. In the November 2000 legislative elections, the NHI achieved the same representation standing on its own.

Leadership: Kresimir Zubak (Chair.).
Address: 2/II Sime Milutinovića, Sarajevo.
Telephone: (33) 214602.
Fax: (33) 214603.
E-mail: nhi@nhi.ba

New Democracy (Macedonia)

A small recently-formed right-wing party in **Macedonia** which aims to promote human rights alongside nationalism. Although it opposed the peace agreement signed between the Government and the ethnic **Albanian** UCK rebels in August 2001, it has maintained that it is essentially a multi-ethnic party and encourages membership among 'patriotic' Albanians. When New Democracy (ND) was formed as a splinter to the **Democratic Alternative** (DA) on 1 March 2001 it attracted only four deputies in the **Assembly of the Republic** to join it. However, it was invited into government in November 2001 following the collapse of the Government of National Unity with the withdrawal of the **Social Democratic Union of Macedonia** (SDSM) and the Liberal Party of Macedonia (LPM). The ND's Deputy Chairman, Slobodan **Casule**, was appointed Foreign Minister.

Leadership: Cedo Petrov (Chair.).

New Democracy (Yugoslavia)
Nova Demokratija (ND)

A political party in **Yugoslavia** within the **Democratic Opposition of Serbia** (DOS), which came to power in late 2000. The ND was established in 1990 as the successor to the communist-era official youth organization, subsequently attracting support in the business community. Claiming to be both social democratic and liberal, the party contested the 1992 **Federal Assembly** elections and 1993 Serbian Assembly elections as part of the DEPOS opposition alliance, but in February 1994 deserted DEPOS to join the Serbian Government led by the **Socialist Party of Serbia** (SPS) of Slobodan **Milošević**. It remained allied with the SPS in the 1996 federal and 1997 Serbian elections (winning five seats in the latter contest), but later joined what became the DOS anti-Milošević alliance. It therefore participated in the DOS victories in the elections of late 2000, ND leader Dušan Mihajlović becoming a Deputy Prime Minister in the new Serbian Government appointed in January 2001.

Leadership: Dušan Mihajlović (Chair.).
Address: Krunska 76, Belgrade 11000.
Telephone: (11) 4449932.
Fax: (11) 4449778.
E-mail: savetnici@novademokratija.org.yu
Internet: www.novademokratija.org.yu

New Muslim Democratic Party
Yeni Musavat Partiyasi (YMP-Musavat)

A moderate **Islamic**, **pan-Turkic** political formation in **Azerbaijan**. Indirectly descended from the pre-**Soviet** Musavat nationalists, the present-day party was founded in June 1992. It was closely allied with the **Azerbaijan Popular Front** (AKC) under the 1992–93 Government, when Musavat leader Isa Gambar was Chairman of the interim National Assembly.

The party came into sharp conflict with the post-1993 Government of Heydar Aliyev of the **New Azerbaijan Party** (YAP) and won only one seat in the **National Assembly** elections held in November 1995 and February 1996. Musavat boycotted the October 1998 presidential election but participated in local elections in December 1999, winning 618 of some 10,000 seats at issue.

Initially refused registration for the November 2000 Assembly elections, the party was in the event allowed to present candidates and won two constituency seats, having achieved only 4.9% in the proportional section. Musavat subsequently joined with other opposition formations in condemning the ballot as fraudulent.

Leadership: Isa Gambar (Chair.); Vurgun Eyyub (Secretary-General).
Address: 37 Azerbaijan Prospekt, Baku 370001.
Telephone: (12) 981870.
Fax: (12) 983166.

New Slovenia–Christian People's Party
Nova Slovenija–Krščanska Ljudska Stranka (NSi)

A centrist formation in **Slovenia** launched as a prime ministerial vehicle before the 2000 elections, in which it failed to make the hoped-for impact. Following the fall of the Government headed by **Liberal Democracy of Slovenia** (LDS) in April 2000, the successor administration formed in June was led by Andrej Bajuk, Deputy Chairman of the **Slovenian People's Party** (SLS+SKD), who had lived most of his life in Argentina. The following month Bajuk reacted to the **National Assembly**'s rejection of his proposal for the abandonment of proportional representation by resigning from the SLS+SKD, which had voted against any change, and announcing the creation of the NSi (the preferred abbreviation despite the party's longer official title).

The new formation attracted support from some prominent centrists, especially members of the Slovenian Christian Democrats (SKD) opposed to the SKD's merger with the SLS. However, in the October 2000 parliamentary elections it obtained only eight seats and 8.6% of the vote, whereupon Bajuk resigned as Prime Minister and took his new party into opposition, having headed the shortest-lived Government since independence.

Leadership: Andrej Bajuk (Chair.).
Address: Državni Zbor, Šubičeva 4, 1000 Ljubljana.
E-mail: webmaster@nsi.si
Internet: www.nsi.si

New Union (Social Liberals)
Naujoji Sąjunga (Socialliberalai) (NS)

A recently-created progressive centrist party in **Lithuania**.

The NS was launched in April 1998 by Arturas Paulauskas, a former public prosecutor who, standing as an independent, had narrowly lost the presidential election in late 1997 and early 1998, winning 49.7% of the vote in the second round. The new formation polled strongly in its first election in October 2000, winning 29 seats on a 19.6% vote share and becoming a leading component of the resultant centrist coalition headed by the **Lithuanian Liberal Union** (LLS). Splits in this coalition over the pace of the Government's efforts to privatize state industries prompted the NS to leave the coalition in June 2001, signalling the end of the LLS Government. The NS then joined a left-of-centre coalition headed by the **Lithuanian Social Democratic Party**.

Leadership: Arturas Paulauskas (Chair.).
Address: Mickevičiaus g. 14, Vilnius 2004.
Telephone: (27) 91664 [(527) 91664 from September 2002].
Fax: (27) 91653 [(527) 91653 from September 2002].
E-mail: centras@nsajunga.lt
Internet: www.nsajunga.lt

News Agency of the Slovak Republic
Tlačová agentúra Slovenskej republiky (TASR)

The partially state-funded news agency in **Slovakia**. Established in 1992, TASR collects and compiles news from Slovakia under the guidance of the 1996 statute demanding objectivity. The General Director is responsible to the Government.

General Director: Ivan Ćeredejev.
Address: Pribinova 23, 819 28 Bratislava.
Telephone: (2) 59210152.
Fax: (2) 52962468.
E-mail: market@tasr.sk
Internet: www.tasr.sk

Nezavisnost *see* **Independence Trade Union Confederation**.

NFB–A *see* **Belarusian Popular Front–Renaissance**.

NHI *see* **New Croatian Initiative**.

NKOS *see* **Independent Christian Trade Union of Slovakia**.

Noghaideli, Zurab

Minister of Finance, **Georgia**.

Zurab Noghaideli is a member of the right-of-centre **Citizens' Union of Georgia** (SMK). He has been a member of the **Parliament of Georgia** since 1992 and was appointed Finance Minister in May 2000.

Born in the Adzharian town of Kobuleti in 1964, he graduated in physics from the Moscow Lomonosov University in 1988. He returned to Georgia and worked as a Senior Science Worker, and eventually Head of the Laboratory, at the Batumi Scientific Research Institute. Following Georgian independence he was elected to the new Parliament in 1992, 1995 and 1999, and has headed parliamentary committees on the environment and tax. From 1996 to 1997 he was also a member of the Supreme Council of **Adzharia**. He had joined the SMK in 1995 and was appointed Finance Minister under President Eduard **Shevardnadze** in May 2000.

Zurab Noghaideli is married and has one daughter.
Address: Ministry of Finance, Abashidze 70, 380062 Tbilisi.
Telephone: (32) 226805.
Fax: (32) 292368.

Nomenklatura

(Russian, 'list of names and offices') The system of appointments in the **Soviet Union**, co-ordinated by the security police (the KGB or its precursor the NKVD—*see* **Federal Security Service**) and the Cadres Department of the Central Committee of the **Communist Party of the Soviet Union**, which together assigned 'suitable' candidates to a range of state offices. The nomenklatura system ensured discipline and deference to the party. Those rewarded by the nomenklatura came to be regarded as an elite and were treated preferentially in the distribution of resources such as apartments, cars and holidays. In the early post-communist period, well-placed officials were sometimes able to re-invent themselves as business leaders and secure the choicest assets when state industries were being sold—a process described derisively as 'nomenklatura privatization'.

Non-Aligned Movement (NAM)

An international grouping of countries professing not to be aligned with either side in the **Cold War**, and therefore not including any of the socialist states of **eastern Europe** which were part of the **Warsaw Pact** military structure. **Yugoslavia**, however, was an active member of the Non-Aligned Movement, which was founded as an organized entity in 1961 when it held its first summit conference in **Belgrade**. Yugoslavia's membership was suspended in 1992. The only other east European country among the 115 members is **Belarus**, which joined as a mark of its independence (having previously been part of the **Soviet Union**) after 1991.

Address: c/o Permanent Representative of South Africa to the UN, 333 East 38th St, 9th Floor, New York, NY 10016, USA.
Telephone: (212) 2135583.
Fax: (212) 6922498.
Internet: www.nam.gov.za

North Atlantic Co-operation Council (NACC)

Replaced in 1997 by the **Euro-Atlantic Partnership Council**.

North Atlantic Treaty Organization (NATO)

The key institution of the Atlantic Alliance, which after the end of the **Cold War** underwent a reappraisal of its identity and purpose, seeking ways of co-operating with, instead of confronting, the countries of **eastern Europe** which had hitherto been members of the **Warsaw Pact**. The original 1949 North Atlantic Treaty was a defensive and political military alliance of a group of European states (then numbering 10) and the USA and Canada. Its objectives were (and remain) to provide common security for its members through co-operation and consultation in political, military and economic fields, as well as scientific, environmental and other non-military aspects. Since January 1994, NATO's **Partnership for Peace** programme has provided a loose framework for wider co-operation.

A Founding Act on Mutual Relations, Co-operation and Security was signed between the **Russian Federation** and NATO in May 1997. This addressed some Russian concerns about the implications of an eastward expansion of NATO itself, for which a number of countries were pressing. The **Czech Republic**, **Hungary** and **Poland** were the first three such countries to join NATO, on 12 March 1999.

NATO's Heads of State and Government committed themselves at that time to considering further enlargement by no later than 2002, at the summit due in **Prague** in November of that year. The official candidates are **Albania**, **Bulgaria**, **Estonia**, **Latvia**, **Lithuania**, **Macedonia**, **Romania**, **Slovakia** and **Slovenia**. Also seen as a potential member is **Croatia**, while **Azerbaijan** and **Georgia** have expressed their desire to join. **Ukraine** seeks as close a relationship as possible, but not membership.

Leadership: Lord Robertson of Port Ellen (Secretary-General).
Address: blvd Léopold III, 1110 Brussels, Belgium.
Telephone: (2) 7074111.
Fax: (2) 7074579.
E-mail: nato-doc@hq.nato.int
Internet: www.nato.int

North Ossetia *see* **Ossetia question**.

Northern Bukovina *see* Bukovina question.

Northern Dobruja *see* Dobruja question.

Northern Epirus *see* Epirus question.

Northern Transylvania *see* Transylvania.

Novitski, Gennadz

Chairman of the Government (Prime Minister), **Belarus**.

Gennadz Vasilevich Novitski is an independent. He first entered the Cabinet as Minister of Architecture and Construction in 1994 and was appointed Chairman on 10 October 2001 as a compromise candidate.

Born on 2 January 1949 in Mogilev, he graduated from the Belarusian Polytechnic Institute in 1971 as an engineer. His career at the Mogilev Construction Trust, in the construction department of the Mogilev regional committee of the Communist Party of Belarus (then Byelorussia), and at the region's Interkolkhoz (collective farms) Construction Trust, led to his becoming Chairman of the Rural Construction Trust in 1988 after completing a course at the Soviet Academy of Sciences. He remained in this position until summoned to the Cabinet to be Minister of Architecture and Construction in 1994, and was promoted to Deputy Chairman in 1997. His appointment as Prime Minister in October 2001 surprised everyone, including himself. President Alyaksandr **Lukashenka** explained that, besides his qualities as a 'team man', he valued his experience in construction.

Address: Office of the Prime Minister, pl. Nezalezhnasti, Dom Urada, 220010 Minsk.
Telephone: (17) 2226905.
Fax: (17) 2226665.
E-mail: contact@udsm.belpak.minsk.by
Internet: www.president.gov.by

Novosti
Rossiiskoye Informatsionnoye Agentstvo–Novosti/Vesti
(Russian Information Agency (RIA)–Novosti/Vesti)

The main state news agency in the **Russian Federation**, focusing originally on supplying information to foreign countries, as opposed to handling domestic markets (*see* **ITAR-TASS**). Novosti was created in 1991 but dates back to the creation in 1941 of the Soviet Information Bureau (Sovinformburo), which was transformed into the Novosti Press Agency (APN) in 1961. APN acted as a tool to spread the Soviet authorities' official line on life in Russia to the outside world, and to keep the Russian people 'informed' about life beyond the **Soviet Union**. Over 120 APN

offices were established abroad. It launched the *Moscow News*, which became independent in 1990, and was responsible for publishing more than 200 books. The agency branched into television in 1989 with the launch of TV Novosti. APN was transformed into the RIA in 1991 and was subordinated to the Foreign Ministry in the newly democratic Russian Federation. In 1998 RIA was officially renamed RIA–Vesti (guide), but retained the 'Novosti' suffix in general use.
Chair.: Alexei V. Zhidakov.
Address: Zubovskii blvd 4, 119021 Moscow.
Telephone: (095) 2018445.
Fax: (095) 2014060.
Internet: www.rian.ru

NPT *see* **Nuclear Non-Proliferation Treaty**.

NS *see* **New Union (Social Liberals)**.

NSi *see* **New Slovenia–Christian People's Party**.

NSZZ *see* **Solidarity**.

Nuclear Non-Proliferation Treaty (NPT)

The 1968 Treaty on the Non-Proliferation of Nuclear Weapons (known as the Non-Proliferation Treaty—NPT), which entered into force in 1970, attempts to maintain a clear distinction between countries which have nuclear weapons, and the wider group which have nuclear power. All non-nuclear-weapon states party to the treaty (i.e. states which had not manufactured and exploded a nuclear weapon or other nuclear explosive device prior to 1 January 1967) were required to conclude an agreement with the **International Atomic Energy Agency** (IAEA) undertaking to accept IAEA safeguards on all nuclear material in all their peaceful nuclear activities for the purpose of verifying that such material is not diverted to nuclear weapons or other nuclear explosive devices. The five nuclear-weapon states at the time the treaty was concluded—the People's Republic of China, France, **Russia**, the UK and the USA—have concluded safeguards agreements with the IAEA that permit the application of IAEA safeguards to all their nuclear activities, excluding those with 'direct national significance'. By January 2000 the only countries which had not ratified and acceded to the treaty were Cuba, Israel, India, Pakistan and Taiwan, although not all of the non-nuclear-weapon states had concluded their safeguards agreements.

Nuclear Suppliers' Group (NSG)

A group formed in the 1970s, at US instigation and spurred by India's nuclear test in 1974, to create common guidelines among the countries supplying nuclear material and technology so as to prevent their being used by non-nuclear-weapon states for weapons development. The NSG included France, which was not party to the 1968 **Nuclear Non-proliferation Treaty** (NPT), and had 15 member countries by early 1978 when its guidelines and control list were published.

The NSG did not meet throughout the 1980s, but resumed annual meetings beginning in The Hague in March 1991, its membership expanding to 34 (including most recently **Ukraine**, as well as **Bulgaria, Czech Republic, Hungary, Poland, Romania, Russian Federation** and **Slovakia**). It also holds two consultations annually on its arrangement to control nuclear-related 'dual-use' exports, of material and technology which could be used both for nuclear weapons and fuel-cycle activities and for other, non-nuclear purposes.

Nuclear Test Ban Treaty

A term usually referring to the Partial Test Ban Treaty (PTBT) of 1963, signed by the USA, the **Soviet Union** and the UK but not by the other two known nuclear-weapon states of that time, France and China. It banned nuclear tests in the atmosphere, under water and in space, but not underground. The treaty was intended to address concern both about the nuclear arms race and about nuclear fallout from atmospheric testing. On the former issue it was reinforced by the **Nuclear Non-proliferation Treaty** (NPT) in 1968, prohibiting non-nuclear-weapon states from possessing, manufacturing or acquiring nuclear weapons.

In 1991 the parties to the PTBT met to discuss converting it into a ban on all nuclear-weapon tests. Negotiations for a Comprehensive Nuclear-Test-Ban Treaty (CTBT) began in 1993 and culminated in the Treaty's conclusion on 10 September 1996 by the UN General Assembly in New York. Opened for signature on 24 September, it was signed immediately by 71 states, including the five declared nuclear-weapon states of that time, but not by India or Pakistan.

O

Oder-Neisse line

The border between eastern Germany and **Poland** formed from the Oder-Neisse river system and extending from the Baltic Sea to the **Czech Republic**. In the closing stages of the Second World War, as the Allied Powers debated the future make-up of a post-Nazi Europe, the reconstruction of Poland, and therefore also of Germany, became of central importance. Poland was liberated by Soviet forces that went on to occupy Berlin in 1945, putting the **Soviet Union** in a commanding position in negotiations over Poland's future. Since the country was losing substantial eastern territories to the Soviet Union itself, the new communist authorities in Poland pressed for territory in the west at the expense of defeated Germany. The Soviet leadership consequently proposed the course of the lower Oder river, and its tributary the Neisse, as a natural frontier, pushing the new Poland far into historically German lands. Initially the idea was opposed by the Western allies, seeking to limit the consequent population movements and national upheaval for Germany. However, the presence of Soviet troops on the ground, and the desire of the Western leaders to be accommodating towards Stalin on this issue, led the Allies to agree to the Oder-Neisse proposal in the **Yalta** and **Potsdam Agreements**. Millions of Germans were forcibly deported from the annexed territory.

The post-1945 borders were recognized by the newly-established East German state in 1950. West Germany, however, continued to regard them as no more than a temporary administrative border until 1971, when a change in stance on policy towards the East was marked by recognition of the enduring status of the Oder-Neisse line. At the time of German reunification in 1990, the Federal Republic of Germany moved quickly to attest the legitimacy of the Oder-Neisse line as Poland's inviolable western border. This was confirmed in the German-Polish Treaty signed in Warsaw on 14 November 1990.

ODS *see* **Civic Democratic Party**.

OE *see* **Country of Law Party**.

OECD *see* **Organization for Economic Co-operation and Development**.

OF *see* **Civic Forum**.

Office of the High Representative (OHR)

The highest civilian authority in **Bosnia and Herzegovina**. The OHR was created, under the terms of the 1995 **Dayton Agreement** signed at the end of the Bosnian civil war, to oversee all civilian aspects of the peace treaty. The Representative is nominated by the international Peace Implementation Council (PIC) and then endorsed by the UN. He or she does not have authority over the military aspects of the peace accord, specifically the **Stabilization Force** of the **North Atlantic Treaty Organization**. Wolfgang **Petritsch** has been High Representative since August 1999.
    Address: Emerika Bluma 1, 71000 Sarajevo.
    Telephone: (33) 283500.
    Fax: (33) 283501.
    Internet: www.ohr.int

OIC *see* **Organization of the Islamic Conference**.

Omonia *see* **Democratic Union of the Greek Minority–Concord**.

Open Society Institute *see* **Soros Foundations network**.

OPZZ *see* **All-Poland Alliance of Trade Unions**.

Orbán, Viktor

Prime Minister of **Hungary** since July 1998 and youthful leading light of the radical liberal Young Democrats since the dying days of the communist regime. Born in May 1963, Orbán gained a reputation as an activist and outspoken critic of the communist system during his time as a law student in **Budapest** in the mid-1980s. He continued in this vein with the **Federation of Young Democrats** (Fidesz), launched formally in March 1988, and attracted wide attention in July 1989, in a speech at the state reburial of Hungarian national hero Imre **Nagy**, calling for multi-party elections and the full withdrawal of **Russian** troops. In September of that year he won a scholarship to Pembroke College in Oxford, UK, to study the philosophy of English liberal politics, but returned to Hungary after the announcement that multi-party elections were to be held in 1990.

    In April 1990, in the first free elections to be held since 1947, Orbán was elected to the **National Assembly** and led Fidesz's small parliamentary group. The party's profile was raised in the international arena in 1992 when it joined the **Liberal International** (LI) and Orbán was elected to be Vice-President of that organization. The following year he became a member of the LI's Executive and was also elected as Fidesz's first Chairman.

Once he was officially leader of the movement, Orbán began the transformation of Fidesz in 1993, away from its radical image as a youth movement to make it a more widely acceptable, and electable, political force. He was unable to turn around its fortunes in time for the elections held in May 1994, when its proportion of seats in the Assembly actually fell. In 1995 the party added the suffix 'Hungarian Civic Party' (MPP) to its name, stressing the traditionally conservative civic qualities of respect and fairness. In legislative elections held in May 1998, Fidesz–MPP increased its share of seats in the National Assembly from just 20 to 148 out of 386, and the following month Orbán was asked by the President to form a new Government. In July his three-party coalition was sworn in.

As part of Hungary's drive to be accepted into the **European Union**, and in an effort to elevate its international image as a serious and independent political contender, Orbán made a point of breaking with tradition to make France, and not Germany, his first foreign visit as Prime Minister. He also oversaw the country's popular accession to membership of the **North Atlantic Treaty Organization** (NATO) in March 1999. The immediate afterglow of this diplomatic coup was quickly eroded when NATO launched military action in neighbouring **Serbia** by the end of the same month. Genuine fears of physical retaliation from **Yugoslavia** forced Orbán to agree to Hungary's involvement being limited to allowing its larger NATO allies the use of Hungarian military bases and airspace during their airstrikes. Following an internal Fidesz–MPP vote in December 1999 it was agreed that party and governmental roles should be clearly separated and Orbán duly stepped down as Chairman in January 2000.

Organization for Economic Co-operation and Development
(OECD)

An influential grouping within which the Governments of industrialized countries discuss, develop and attempt to co-ordinate their economic and social policies. Founded in 1961, it replaced the Organization for European Economic Co-operation (OEEC) which had been established in 1948 in connection with the Marshall Plan for post-war reconstruction. The OECD's officially-stated aims are to promote policies designed to achieve the highest level of sustainable economic growth, employment and increase in the standard of living while maintaining financial stability, and to contribute to economic expansion in member and non-member states and to the expansion of world trade.

Members: 30 including the **Czech Republic, Hungary, Poland** and **Slovakia**.
Leadership: Donald J. Johnston (Secretary-General).
Address: 2 rue André-Pascal, 75775 Paris Cédex 16, France.

Organization for Security and Co-operation in Europe (OSCE)

Telephone: (1) 45248200.
Fax: (1) 45248500.
E-mail: webmaster@oecd.org
Internet: www.oecd.org

Organization for Security and Co-operation in Europe (OSCE)

The Organization for Security and Co-operation in Europe was established in 1972 as the Conference on Security and Co-operation in Europe (CSCE), providing a multilateral forum for dialogue and negotiation. The areas of competence of the CSCE were expanded by the **Charter of Paris for a New Europe** (1990)—which transformed the CSCE from an *ad hoc* forum to an organization with permanent institutions—and the Helsinki Document 1992. CSCE membership had reached 52 by 1994, as it sought to encompass all recognized states in Europe and the former **Soviet Union**, together with Canada and the USA.

The CSCE's role included securing the observance of human rights, and providing a forum for settling disputes among member countries. Some member countries, notably the **Russian Federation**, advocated its development as the principal organization for managing the responses of European countries on a range of continent-wide concerns. Its initial impact, however, was principally in promoting East-West détente, bringing together 35 countries including the rival **North Atlantic Treaty Organization** and **Warsaw Pact** alliances for the Helsinki CSCE conference which began in July 1973 and culminated in the 1975 **Helsinki Final Act**.

In December 1994 the summit conference adopted the new name of OSCE, in order to reflect the organization's changing political role and strengthened Secretariat. The OSCE's main decision-making body, the Permanent Council, convenes weekly in Vienna to discuss and make decisions on current developments in the OSCE area. Also meeting weekly in Vienna is the Forum for Security Co-operation, which is concerned with military aspects of security in the OSCE area, in particular confidence- and security-building measures. The OSCE's Senior Council/Economic Forum convenes once a year in **Prague** to focus on economic and environmental issues.

The OSCE also has: a Parliamentary Assembly; an Office for Democratic Institutions and Human Rights (ODIHR), based in **Warsaw** and originally created (in 1990) as the Office for Free Elections, concerned to promote human rights and democracy; a High Commissioner on National Minorities and a Representative on Freedom of the Media; and a Court of Conciliation and Arbitration overseeing its disputes settlement procedures.

Members: 55 participating states, comprising all the recognized countries of Europe and the former Soviet republics, Canada and the USA. (The Federal Republic of **Yugoslavia**, suspended from the CSCE in July 1992, was admitted to the OSCE in November 2000.)

The position of Chairman-in-Office is held by a Minister of Foreign Affairs of a member state for a one-year term; the post was held in 2001 by Mircea Dan **Geoana** of **Romania**. In January 2002 the Portuguese Foreign Minister Jaime Matos da Gama became OSCE Chairman-in-Office, when Portugal succeeded to the one-year chairmanship of the organization.

Leadership: Ján Kubiš (Secretary-General).
Address: Kärntner Ring 5–7, 1010 Vienna, Austria.
Telephone: (1) 514360.
Fax: (1) 51436105.
E-mail: info@osce.org
Internet: www.osce.org

Organization of the Black Sea Economic Co-operation (BSEC)

An organization derived from the Black Sea Economic Co-operation (BSEC) grouping formed in 1992 to strengthen regional co-operation, particularly on economic development. In June 1998, at a summit meeting held in Yalta, **Ukraine**, participating countries signed the BSEC Charter, thereby officially elevating the BSEC to regional organization status. The Charter entered into force on 1 May 1999, at which time the BSEC formally became the Organization of the Black Sea Economic Co-operation, retaining the same acronym.

Members: **Albania, Armenia, Azerbaijan, Bulgaria, Georgia**, Greece, **Moldova, Romania, Russian Federation**, Turkey and Ukraine.
Leadership: Valeri Chechelashvili (Secretary-General).
Address: Istinye Cad. Müşir Fuad Paşa Yalisi, Eski Tersane 80860, Istinye-Istanbul, Turkey.
Telephone: (212) 2296330.
Fax: (212) 2296336.
E-mail: bsec@turk.net
Internet: www.bsec.gov.tr

Organization of the Islamic Conference (OIC)

An organization which groups 57 countries, principally in the Middle East, Africa and Asia, to promote Islamic solidarity and co-operation. **Azerbaijan** and **Albania**, its only **eastern European** members, joined in 1991 and 1992 respectively. The organization had formally been established in May 1971, when its Secretariat became operational. The impetus for the creation of the organization had come from the summit meeting of **Muslim** Heads of State at Rabat, Morocco, in September 1969, followed up by conferences at foreign ministerial level in Jeddah and Karachi during 1970.

Leadership: Dr Abdelouahed Belkeziz (Secretary-General).

Address: Kilo 6, Mecca Road, POB 178, Jeddah 21411, Saudi Arabia.
Telephone: (2) 6800800.
Fax: (2) 6873568.
E-mail: info@oic-oci.org
Internet: www.oic-oci.org

Országgyűlés *see* **National Assembly (Hungary)**.

Orthodox Christianity

The form of Christianity most widespread in south-eastern Europe. Separated from **Roman Catholicism** by the 'Great Schism' which was completed in 1054, the so-called 'Orthodox Catholic Church' was championed by the Byzantine Empire centred on Constantinople, and was spread to the pagan tribes north and east of that city. This geographical spread, and conversely the success of Roman Catholicism in the western world has given Orthodox Christianity a distinctly 'eastern' feel. Its practices are dominated by the belief that the form of worship has not changed since the days of Jesus Christ. The tradition of iconic art is strong.

Unlike the Roman Catholic Church with its Pope, the Orthodox Church does not have a single head, but rather is divided into separate *autocephalous* (independent) Churches, or Patriarchates. These Churches are headed by a local Patriarch or Metropolitan. The original branch, the Autocephalous Church of Constantinople (Istanbul), is deemed the 'first among equals' and the Patriarch of Constantinople is considered 'ecumenical', but theoretically does not have any actual powers over the other Churches. Ecumenical Patriarch Bartholomew ascended the 'throne' of the Constantinople Church on 2 November 1991. The **Russian Orthodox Church** also carries great weight within the religion, having by far the largest single congregation. (see below).

Estimates of the number of Orthodox Christians worldwide range from 100 million to 300 million. The biggest congregations are in the **Russian Federation** (up to 100 million) and **Romania** (c.15 million—*see* **Romanian Orthodox Church**). Orthodox Christians were persecuted by the communist authorities; 98% of churches in the **Soviet Union** were closed and many priests executed. However, a general revival in religious activity since the late 1980s has seen a resurgence in the size of congregations and the social influence of the Church hierarchy.

Eastern European countries with autocephalous Churches are: **Albania**, **Bulgaria**, **Georgia**, **Poland**, Romania, Russian Federation and **Serbia**. The autonomous Churches of **Moldova** (*see also* **Bessarabian Church**) and **Ukraine** are subordinated to the Russian Church. Small congregations in other countries are subordinate to various neighbouring Churches. 'Lesser' or 'Oriental' Churches related to the Orthodox faith include the **Armenian Apostolic Church**. The symbol of the Orthodox Church is the three-barred cross (representing the crucifix upon which Jesus Christ was executed, and including the nameplate above his head and the footplate).

OSCE *see* **Organization for Security and Co-operation in Europe**.

Oskanian, Vartan

Minister of Foreign Affairs, **Armenia**.

Vartan Oskanian is an Armenian-American who came to prominence as Armenia's chief negotiator after the 1994 cease-fire in the **Nagorno-Karabakh** conflict while he was Deputy Foreign Minister. He has been full Foreign Minister since the inauguration of President Robert **Kocharian** in April 1998.

Born on 7 February 1955 in Syria, he was educated there and at the Yerevan Polytechnic Institute before travelling to the USA where he studied at Tufts University and at Harvard. He became actively involved in the Armenian-American community, editing the *Armenian International Magazine*, and became a naturalized citizen of the USA. He returned to Armenia in 1992 after independence and began work at the Ministry of Foreign Affairs. As the Azeri-Armenian conflict over Nagorno-Karabakh came to a tentative cease-fire in 1994, Oskanian was appointed principal negotiator at the **OSCE** dialogue in **Minsk**. His promotion to full Minister was assured in April 1998 on the election of President Kocharian and represented a key continuity with the previous peace process.

Vartan Oskanian is married and has two sons.

Address: Ministry of Foreign Affairs, Government House 2, Republic Sq. 1, 375010 Yerevan.
Telephone: (1) 506167.
Fax: (1) 562543.
Internet: www.armeniaforeignministry.com

Ossetia question

A territorial dispute arising from the division of the territory of the ethnic Iranian Ossetes between the **Russian Federation** and **Georgia**. The region first came under the Russian Empire in 1774 and control from Moscow was confirmed with the establishment of a fortress at Vladikavkaz (literally 'rule of the **Caucasus**') in 1784. It was briefly united in a single ethnic territory from 1905, but was ultimately divided into the present two halves by the **Soviet** Commissar for Nationalities, Josef Stalin, in the 1920s. North Ossetia, now known locally as Alania, was expanded slightly during the Soviet era at the expense of neighbouring **Ingushetia**, leading to ethnic tensions which were further exacerbated by the influx of southern Ossetes after 1990. Russian troops were deployed there in 1993.

Ossetia question

In the face of growing Georgian nationalism, the *oblast* (region) of South Ossetia in Georgia pressed in 1989 for an upgrade to full autonomous republic status (as enjoyed by **Adzharia**) as a precursor to unification with North Ossetia. The calls were led by the nationalist South Ossetia Popular Front (*Adaemon Nykhas*). In response the Georgian authorities voted in 1990 to abolish South Ossetia's regional autonomy altogether. This vote in turn prompted the South Ossetian authorities to proclaim the region's independence from Georgia in September. The ensuing tensions quickly spilled over into clashes between Ossete and Georgian paramilitaries and prompted the migration of nearly 40,000 of South Ossetia's 60,000 Ossetes into North Ossetia.

A concerted effort in 1992 by newly-appointed Georgian leader Eduard **Shevardnadze** and the then Russian President Boris **Yeltsin** brought a joint Russian-Georgian peacekeeping force into the region and calmed the violence. However, no final solution to the Ossetia question was reached and the South Ossetian Republic, declared in 1990, remains essentially a separate state (with its capital at Tskhinvali), reliant on aid donations from the Russian Federation and the lucrative oil smuggling industry. The economic inability/unwillingness of Georgia to uphold its pledges to invest in the region has turned South Ossetia even further towards its northern neighbour. However, unpaid power bills led to the temporary termination of energy supplies from the Russian Federation and from Georgia in 1999 and calls for the resignation of South Ossetian President Lyudvig Chibirov. Although this particular problem was overcome it highlighted the economic vulnerability of the republic.

North Ossetian President Aleksandr Dzasokhov has, since his election in January 1998, pressed for a rapprochement between all sides in the dispute. In 2001 he added calls for the eventual unification of the Ossetias. He is particularly keen to repatriate the 40,000 South Ossetian refugees and to develop the economic potential of the poorer southern neighbour. He facilitated talks in late 2000 on increasing Georgia's actual financial commitment to South Ossetia.

Russian citizen Eduard Kokoyev was elected President of South Ossetia in November–December 2001. He declared during the campaign that he would insist on the region becoming a part of the Russian Federation.

OVR *see* **Fatherland–All Russia.**

P

PAIZ *see* Polish Agency for Foreign Investment.

Palata Predstaviteley
(House of Representatives)

The lower house of the **National Assembly** of **Belarus**.

Pamyat—National Patriotic Front

An extremist antisemitic group in the **Russian Federation** which aims to return the country to an autocratic **Orthodox Christian** monarchy. Formed from a collection of far-right groups in the 1970s, Pamyat (literally 'memory') was one of the founding parties of the far-right political movement in Russia. However, its electoral popularity is minimal and it has been undermined by continual discord and new splinter movements. Dmitri Vasiliev has been Chairman of Pamyat since 1985.

Pan-Armenian National Movement
Haiots Hamazgaien Sharzhoum (HHSh)

The political formation established in late 1989 which led **Armenia** to independence in 1990–91 but gradually lost influence thereafter.

The HHSh originally brought together the pro-independence elements of the then ruling **Communist Party of Armenia** (HKK). It won a landslide victory in the May 1990 legislative elections. Following the temporary dissolution of the HKK, the then HHSh leader Levon Ter-Petrossian was directly elected President in October 1991 with 83% of the vote. In the 1995 **National Assembly** elections the party headed the victorious Republican Bloc (Hanrapetoutioun), which also included the **Republican Party of Armenia**, the **Armenian Christian Democratic Union** and the **Social Democratic Hunchakian Party**. As the governing party, the HHSh sought a successful outcome of the **Nagorno-Karabakh** conflict with

Azerbaijan involving territorial adjustments to make it contiguous with Armenia proper.

The election of Mayor of **Yerevan** and former Interior Minister Vano Siradeghian as HHSh Chairman in July 1997 precipitated internal divisions culminating in the formation in September 1997 of the breakaway Homeland movement. The resignation of Ter-Petrossian as President in February 1998 increased the party's difficulties. Although it backed the successful candidacy of Robert **Kocharian** (non-party) in the March 1998 presidential elections and was included in the new Government, by the end of 1998 the HHSh had become an opposition party. It was also damaged by strong criticism of Siradeghian's record as Interior Minister in 1992–96. Accused of instigating political assassinations in that period, Siradeghian fled abroad in January 1999 two weeks before the Assembly voted to strip him of parliamentary immunity from prosecution.

Siradeghian was nevertheless re-elected as HHSh Chairman in March 1999 at the party's 11th congress, which launched a fierce attack on the creation of a 'military-police system' by the Kocharian presidency. Siradeghian returned shortly before the May 1999 Assembly elections and was promptly arrested. The elections demonstrated the marginalization of the HHSh, which was reduced to a single seat (won by Siradeghian in a constituency contest) and only 1.2% of the proportional vote. Siradeghian again fled abroad in April 2000 and was replaced as HHSh Chairman by former Foreign Minister Aleksandr Arzumanian, who was confirmed in the leadership by the party's 12th congress in December 2000.

Leadership: Aleksandr Arzumanian (Chair.).
Address: 27 Khanjian Street, Yerevan.
Telephone: (1) 557982.
Fax: (1) 570470.

Pan-Germanism

An internationalist concept promoting the closer integration and unity of ethnic **German** people across Europe. Significant numbers of ethnic Germans have been spread across **eastern Europe** since mediaeval times, but are now only loosely connected. The notion of unifying them under a single state was partially realized with the unification of Germany in 1871 under the dominance of **Prussia**, although this did not include other German communities more widely distributed across the region, mostly under the suzerainity of the German-speaking Austrian Empire. Later 20th-century attempts to press ideas of pan-Germanism were of course hijacked by Nazism and the expansion of Hitler's Third Reich. The failure of the Nazi German Empire prompted mass movements of German people into the rump German state (*see* **Yalta** and **Potsdam Agreements**). Another mass migration followed the collapse of the **Soviet Union** and other communist states in eastern Europe in 1989–91. The resettlement of ethnic Germans in Germany has consequently stripped pan-Germanism of much of its potency.

Pan-Slavism

The idea that promotes the closer integration and possible unification of all **Slavic peoples** based on their shared ethnic and linguistic background. There are two major pan-Slavic movements that have achieved concrete results. The agitation of **Croat** and **Slovene** pan-Slavists for a union of south Slavs, or **Yugoslavs**, was the basis for the creation in 1918 of the Kingdom of Serbs, Croats and Slovenes (*see* **Yugoslavia**). More recently, the close ethnic similarities of the east Slavs have been the foundation for the **Belarus-Russia Union** and for closer links between these two countries and **Ukraine**. However, the deep religious divide and historical animosity between the south Slavs violently undid the Yugoslav experiment in the 1990s, and the pace of the Belarus-Russia Union has been significantly slowed in the face of economic realities and the eagerness of the **Russian Federation** to maintain its separate, internationalist role.

Pan-Turkism

The idea that promotes the closer integration and possible unification of all **Turkic peoples** based on their shared ethnic and linguistic background. The Turks are spread across the far east of Europe, mostly in the constituent republics of the **Russian Federation**, and in Asia. Their language and culture are similar, although regional differences can be great. The concept of uniting these territories under a single Turkish State has had little strength and is often viewed with suspicion by Turkic people outside modern Turkey who are wary of Turkey's own international ambitions. However, the idea of pan-Turkism does encourage greater co-operation between these States, for example Turkey's support for **Azerbaijan** during its conflict with neighbouring **Armenia**. Within the Russian Federation the **Tatars** of **Tartarstan** have led efforts to increase pan-Turkic ties (*see* **Idel-Ural**).

Pankisi Gorge

An area of north-eastern **Georgia** bordering the Russian federal republic of **Chechnya** and with an estimated Chechen minority population of around 7,000. The open conflict since 1994 between Chechen separatists and the Russian army across the border has made the gorge a diplomatic tinderbox. Determined to maintain good relations with the **Russian Federation**, the Georgian authorities have attempted to clamp down on the movement of ethnic Chechens in the region and prevent the trafficking of troops and arms. However, thousands of Chechens have arrived in Pankisi since the renewed Russian offensive in 1999 and 2000. The possibility of the destabilization of the area and its already-troubled neighbour South **Ossetia,** and suggestions in some circles of proclaiming an autonomous Chechen republic in the gorge have led to Georgian calls to repatriate around 7,500 Chechens. The Georgian Government has steadfastly refused requests to

Parliament (Czech Republic)

allow the Russian army into the gorge, and maintains that the migrating Chechens are merely refugees and not soldiers. The issue threatened to widen considerably in late 2001 with the alleged arrival in the region of Islamic extremists fleeing the US bombing campaign in Afghanistan.

PAP *see* **Polish Press Agency.**

Paris Charter *see* **Charter of Paris for a New Europe.**

Parlamentul *see* **Parliament (Moldova).**

Parlamentul României *see* **Parliament of Romania.**

Parliament (Czech Republic)
Parlament

The bicameral legislature of the **Czech Republic**, comprising the Chamber of Deputies (Poslanecká Sněmovna) and the Senate (Senát). The lower Chamber of Deputies has 200 members, directly elected for a four-year term. The upper Senate has 81 directly-elected members. All members of the Senate were first elected in November 1996; one-third of the seats come up for re-election every two years, and Senators will then serve six-year terms. The last elections were held on 19–20 June 1998 (Chamber of Deputies) and 12–19 November 2000 (Senate).

Address of lower house: Poslanecká Sněmovna, Sněmovní 4, 11829 Prague 1.
Telephone: (2) 57175111.
Fax: (2) 57532361.
E-mail: petrickova@psp.cz
Internet: www.psp.cz
Address of upper house: Senát, Valdstejnské námesti 4, 11811 Prague 1.
Telephone: (2) 57071111.
Fax: (2) 57534499.
E-mail: bartonovae@senat.cz
Internet: www.senat.cz

Parliament (Latvia)
Saeima

The unicameral legislature of **Latvia**. It has 100 members, directly elected for a term extended from three to four years on 4 December 1997. The last elections were held on 3 October 1998.

Address: Saeima, Jekaba iela 11, 1811 Riga.
Telephone: 7087129.

Fax: 7087348.
E-mail: saeima@saeima.lv
Internet: www.saeima.lv

Parliament (Lithuania)
Seimas

The unicameral legislature of **Lithuania**. It has 141 members, directly elected for a four-year term. The last elections were held on 8 October 2000.
  Address: Seimas, Gedimino pr. 53, 2002 Vilnius.
  Telephone: (23) 96008 [(523) 96008 from September 2002].
  Fax: (23) 96460 [(523) 96460 from September 2002].
  E-mail: rivait@lrs.lt
  Internet: www.lrs.lt

Parliament (Moldova)
Parlamentul

The unicameral legislature of **Moldova**. It has 101 members, directly elected for a four-year term. The last elections were held on 25 February 2001.
  Address: Parlamentul, Blvd Ștefan cel Mare 105, 2073 Chișinau.
  Telephone: (2) 237009.
  Fax: (2) 233210.
  E-mail: info@parlament.md
  Internet: www.parlament.md

Parliament (Ukraine)
Verkhovna Rada

The unicameral legislature of **Ukraine**. It has 450 members, directly elected for a four-year term, one-half by simple majority, and one-half by party list. Future elections were set to be entirely by party list, according to an election law passed in November 1999, but President Leonid **Kuchma** overturned this clause by decree in 2001. The last elections were held on 29 March 1998, and the next are scheduled for 31 March 2002.
  Address: Verkhovna Rada, M. Grushevskogo St 5, 01008 Kiev.
  Telephone: (44) 2930486.
  Fax: (44) 2933217.
  E-mail: vidmz@alpha.rada.kiev.ua
  Internet: www.rada.kiev.ua

Parliament of Georgia
Sakartvelos Parlamenti

The unicameral legislature of **Georgia**, which is to become bicameral 'following the creation of appropriate conditions', according to the 1995 Constitution. The Parliament has 235 members, 85 elected in single-member constituencies and the rest from party lists, for a four-year term. The last elections were held between 31 October and 14 November 1999.
   Address: Sakartvelos Parlamenti, 8 Rustaveli Ave, 380018 Tbilisi.
   Telephone: (32) 935113.
   Fax: (32) 999594.
   E-mail: ccppd@parliament.ge
   Internet: www.parliament.ge

Parliament of Romania
Parlamentul României

The bicameral legislature of **Romania**, comprising the Chamber of Deputies (Camera Deputaţilor) and the Senate (Senatul). The lower Chamber of Deputies has 345 members (with 18 seats reserved for minorities), directly elected for a four-year term. The upper Senate has 140 members, directly elected for a four-year term. The last elections were held on 26 November 2000.
   Internet: diasan.vsat.ro
   Address of lower house: Camera Deputaţilor, Palatul Parlamentului, St Izvor 2–4, Sector 5, 70647 Bucharest.
   Telephone: (1) 4021444.
   Fax: (1) 3126600.
   E-mail: secretar.general@cdep.ro
   Internet: www.cdep.ro
   Address of upper house: Senatul, Piaţa Revoluţiei 1, Bucharest.
   Telephone: (1) 3150200.
   Fax: (1) 3121184.
   E-mail: gsterea@unix1.senat.ro
   Internet: www.senat.ro

Parliamentary Assembly (Bosnia and Herzegovina)
Skupština

The bicameral legislature of **Bosnia and Herzegovina**, comprising the House of Representatives (Predstavnički Dom) and the House of Peoples (Dom Naroda). The lower House of Representatives has 42 members who are directly elected to the two constituent chambers: the Chamber of Deputies of the **Muslim-Croat Federation** (known as the Federation), with 28 members, and the Chamber of

Deputies of the **Serb Republic** (Republika Srpska), with 14 members. The upper House of Peoples has 15 members, 10 of them appointed from the Federation and five from the Serb Republic. Both Houses have two-year terms.

The Federation also has a House of Representatives, with 140 directly-elected members, and an indirectly-elected 74-member House of Peoples, which has one-half Bosniak and one-half Croat representation. The Serb Republic has a People's Assembly with 83 directly-elected members.

The last elections were held on 11 November 2000 for the House of Representatives, and the Federation and Serb Republic legislatures.

Address: Skupština, Hamdije Kresevljakovica 3, 71000 Sarajevo.
Telephone: (33) 667977.
Fax: (33) 472188.

Partnership for Peace (PfP)

The **North Atlantic Treaty Organization**'s Partnership for Peace programme was established in January 1994 within the framework of the North Atlantic Co-operation Council (NACC—*see* **Euro-Atlantic Partnership Council**). It has provided a mechanism for a rapprochement between NATO and the countries of central and eastern Europe since the end of the **Cold War**.The PfP incorporated practical military and defence-related co-operation activities that had originally been part of the NACC Work Plan. Participation in the PfP requires an initial signature of a framework agreement, establishing the common principles and objectives of the partnership, the submission of a presentation document, indicating the political and military aspects of the partnership and the nature of the future co-operation activities, and finally, the development of individual partnership programmes establishing country-specific objectives.

Participating states: 27 countries. **Albania**, **Armenia**, Austria, **Azerbaijan**, **Belarus**, **Bulgaria**, **Croatia**, **Estonia**, Finland, **Georgia**, Kazakhstan, Kyrgyzstan, **Latvia**, **Lithuania**, **Macedonia**, Malta, **Moldova**, **Romania**, **Russian Federation**, **Slovakia**, **Slovenia**, Sweden, Switzerland, Tajikistan, Turkmenistan, **Ukraine** and Uzbekistan.

Party for Bosnia and Herzegovina
Stranka za Bosne i Hercegovine (SBiH)

A moderate non-sectarian formation in **Bosnia and Herzegovina** which has sought to challenge the dominance of the ethnic nationalist parties. The SBiH was founded in April 1996 by Haris Silajdžić, who had resigned as Prime Minister of the Bosnian Government in January in opposition to apparent Islamic fundamentalist tendencies in the dominant **Party of Democratic Action** (SDA). In the first post-**Dayton** elections in September 1996, Silajdžić came second in the contest for the **Muslim** member of the collective presidency, winning 13.5% of the Muslim vote, while the SBiH took two seats in the union lower house and 11 in the **Muslim-Croat Federation** lower house. In December 1996 Silajdžić was appointed as one of the two union Co-Prime Ministers, continuing in the post until the move to a single Prime Minister in June 2000.

The SBiH contested the September 1998 elections within the SDA-led Coalition for a Single and Democratic Bosnia and Herzegovina (KCD). Standing alone in the November 2000 elections, the SBiH won five union lower house seats with 11.4% of the vote and 21 in the Federation lower house.

The party joined the Alliance for Change grouping of moderate parties in early 2001, and Beriz **Belkić** of the SBiH was appointed as the Bosniak member of the union presidency, replacing Halid Genjac of the SDA.

Leadership: Haris Silajdžić (President).
Address: 7A Maršala Tita, Sarajevo.
Telephone and Fax: (33) 214417.

Party for Democratic Prosperity
Partija za Demokratski Prosperitet (PDP)

A political formation in **Macedonia**, one of several representing ethnic **Albanians**, who constitute about a quarter of the country's population. Formed in 1990, the PDP won 25 seats in the **Assembly of the Republic** elections that year and in 1992 opted to join a coalition Government headed by what became the **Social Democratic Union of Macedonia** (SDSM). Such participation resulted in the breakaway of militant factions, while from mid-1994 the rump PDP came into sharp conflict with its coalition partners over the conviction of a group of alleged Albanian separatists on subversion charges. The party fell back sharply to 10 seats in the 1994 Assembly elections but continued to be a member of the coalition Government headed by the SDSM.

From February to July 1995 PDP deputies boycotted the Assembly in protest against a new law banning the use of Albanian in official identity documentation; but such action failed to prevent the defection of another anti-Government PDP faction and the formation in mid-1997 of the **Democratic Party of Albanians** (DPA) as a merger of anti-PDP ethnic Albanian groupings. Nevertheless, the PDP contested the autumn 1998 Assembly elections in partial alliance with the PDA, winning 14 seats (against 11 for the PDA), thereafter going into opposition, whereas the PDA opted to join the new Government.

In the presidential elections of late 1999, PDP candidate Muhamet Halili won only 4.4% of the first-round vote (while the PDA nominee obtained 14.9%). The PDP's pre-1998 status as the leading ethnic Albanian party was further eroded by the onset of ethnic strife in Macedonia in early 2001 and by the formation in March 2001 of the National Democratic Party (PDK) by militant ethnic

Albanians. The PDP briefly joined a Government of National Unity, which brought together parties from all sides of the Assembly in a show of consensus while a peace deal was brokered, but withdrew from this unity Government in November.

Leadership: Dr Ymer Ymeri (Chair.).
Address: 62 Karaorman, Tetovo 94000.
Telephone: (44) 25709.

Party of Civic Understanding
Strana Občianskeho Porozumenia (SOP)

A small social liberal party in **Slovakia**, whose founder won election as state President in 1999. The SOP was launched in April 1998 under the leadership of Rudolf **Schuster**, the ethnic German Mayor of Košice, and included Pavol Hamzik, who had served as non-party Foreign Minister in 1996–97 in the Government headed by the **Movement for a Democratic Slovakia** (HZDS).

In its first **National Council** elections in September 1998, the SOP won 13 seats on a vote share of 8% and opted to join a centre-left coalition headed by the **Slovak Democratic Coalition** (SDK) and also including the **Party of the Democratic Left** (SDĽ) and the **Hungarian Coalition Party** (SMK).

After the new Government had quickly enacted constitutional amendments providing for direct presidential elections, Schuster was chosen as the candidate of all four ruling parties. In the polling in May 1999, Schuster was the comfortable victor, heading the first-round vote with 47.4% and defeating HZDS leader Vladimír **Mečiar** in the second by 57.2% to 42.8%.

Leadership: Pavol Hamzik (Chair.).
Address: Ružová dolina 6, Bratislava 82108.
Telephone: (2) 50221161.
Fax: (2) 50221121.
E-mail: rk@sop.sk
Internet: www.sop.sk

Party of Democratic Action (Bosnia and Herzegovina)
Stranka Demokratske Akcije (SDA)

The dominant political formation of the majority **Muslim** population in **Bosnia and Herzegovina**. Founded in May 1990, the SDA became the largest Assembly party in elections in late 1990 and also won three seats on the then seven-member collegial presidency, with SDA leader Alija **Izetbegović** becoming its Chairman. Under Izetbegović's presidency, Bosnia and Herzegovina moved to full independence in March 1992; but the intention that the new state's Government should be a coalition of the SDA, the **Serbian Democratic Party** (SDS) and the **Croatian Democratic Union** (HDZ) proved unattainable, as deepening hostilities between the communities resulted in the effective breakdown of inter-party co-operation by late 1992. In the mid-1990s the SDA was weakened by splits, resulting in the creation of the breakaway **Democratic People's Union** and the **Party for Bosnia and Herzegovina** (SBiH).

Nevertheless, in the first post-**Dayton** elections in September 1996 the SDA maintained its hold on the Muslim vote. Izetbegović was elected as the Muslim representative on the new three-member collective presidency, with over 80% of the Muslim vote, while the SDA won 19 of the 42 seats in the lower house of the union legislature and 78 of 140 seats in the **Muslim-Croat Federation** lower house. In the September 1998 elections, Izetbegović was candidate of the SDA-led Coalition for a Single and Democratic Bosnia and Herzegovina (KCD), which included the non-sectarian SBiH, and was re-elected with 86.8% of the Muslim vote (and about 32% nationally). However, the KCD won only 17 seats in the union lower house and 68 in the Federation lower house.

Having succeeded to the rotating presidency of the Muslim-Croat Federation from the beginning of 2000, Ejup Ganić of the SDA was expelled from the party in May for refusing to resign over the SDA's poor showing in local elections the previous month. Standing on its own in the November 2000 legislative elections, the SDA won only eight of the union lower house seats and only 38 in the Federation lower house, being challenged in both legislatures by the multi-ethnic **Social Democratic Party of Bosnia and Herzegovina**. Prior to the elections, Izetbegović had finally retired as a member of the union collective presidency (being succeeded by Halid Genjac of the SDA), although he continued as SDA Chairman until October 2001, when Sulejman Tihic was appointed to replace him.

Leadership: Sulejman Tihic (Chair.).
Address: 14 Mehmeda Spahe, Sarajevo.
Telephone: (33) 667274.
Fax: (33) 650429.
E-mail: sda@bih.net.ba
Internet: www.sda.ba

Party of Democratic Action (Yugoslavia)
Stranka Demokratske Akcije (SDA)

A moderate ethnic **Albanian/Muslim** formation in **Yugoslavia** linked to the ruling party of the same name in **Bosnia and Herzegovina**. Distinct SDA factions have operated in **Kosovo**, **Montenegro** and other Yugoslav regions with significant ethnic Albanian/Muslim populations, winning three seats in the Montenegrin Assembly and one **Federal Assembly** lower house seat in 1996 and three seats in the Serbian Assembly in 1997. In 1998 SDA factions took the five Montenegrin Assembly seats reserved for ethnic Albanians under a new electoral law but were split on whether to co-operate with the new reformist Government of the **Democratic Party of Socialists of Montenegro**. Under the new leadership of Rasim Ljajić, the

SDA joined the anti-**Milošević Democratic Opposition of Serbia** (DOS) alliance and therefore participated in the DOS victories in the elections of late 2000, Ljajić becoming Minister of National and Ethnic Communities in the new Federal Government.
Leadership: Rasim Ljajić (Chair.).
Address: Poštanskifah 101, Novi Pazar 36300.
Telephone: (20) 311454.

Party of Democratic Progress
Partija Demokratskog Progresa (PDP)

A centrist **Serb** political formation in the **Serb Republic** (RS). The PDP was launched in September 1999 by Mladen **Ivanić**, a well-known economist who had come second in the Serb section of the elections for the union collective presidency in September 1996 as a moderate non-party candidate, with 30% of the vote. In the November 2000 elections the PDP won 11 of the 83 seats in the RS Assembly. Ivanić become RS Prime Minister in January 2001 at the head of a loose coalition which included the **Socialist Party of the Serb Republic**, one **Muslim** and one member of the nationalist **Serbian Democratic Party**.
Leadership: Mladen Ivanić (Chair.).
Address: 66 Voyvode Momchela, Banja Luka.
Telephone: (51) 218078.
Fax: (51) 218115.

Party of Independent Social Democrats
Stranka Nezavisnih Socijaldemokrata (SNSD)

A centre-left political formation in **Bosnia and Herzegovina** commanding a significant level of support in the **Serb** community. Founded in March 1996, the SNSD contested the post-**Dayton** elections in September 1996 as part of the moderate People's Alliance for Peace and Progress. It won two **Serb Republic** (RS) Assembly seats in November 1997, following which party leader Milorad Dodik became RS Prime Minister in January 1998, heading a non-partisan administration. In the September 1998 elections the SNSD backed the successful **Socialist Party of the Serb Republic** (SPRS) candidate for the Serb seat on the union collective presidency, while the party increased its representation in the RS Assembly to six seats. In early 1999 Dodik, with Western support, resisted efforts by RS President Nikola Poplasen of the ultra-nationalist **Serbian Radical Party** (SRS) to replace him as Prime Minister, withdrawing his resignation when the UN **High Representative** dismissed Poplasen. In the November 2000 elections, however, Dodik came a poor second in the contest for the RS presidency, winning only 26% of the vote and being defeated by hardliner Mirko **Sarović** of the SRS. Although

the SNSD improved its representation in the RS Assembly to 11 seats (and also won one in the **Muslim-Croat Federation** lower house), Dodik was succeeded as RS Prime Minister by Mladen **Ivanić** of the **Party of Democratic Progress** (PDP).
Leadership: Milorad Dodik (Chair.).
Address: 5 Petra Kocića, Banja Luka 51000.
Telephone: (51) 218936.
Fax: (51) 218937.
E-mail: snsd@inecco.net
Internet: snsd.tripod.com

Party of Slovenian Youth
Stranka Mladih Slovenije (SMS)

An ecologically-oriented formation contending that the established parties do not adequately represent young people. In its first **National Assembly** elections in October 2000, the SMS unexpectedly surmounted the 3% barrier to representation, winning 4.3% of the vote and being allocated four seats.
Leadership: Dominik S. Černjak (Chair.).
Address: Tržaška 2, Ljubljana 1000.
Telephone: (1) 4254014.
Fax: (1) 4252821.
E-mail: info@sms.si
Internet: www.sms.si

Party of the Democratic Left
Strana Demokratickej Ľavice (SDĽ)

The political party in **Slovakia** which is the direct descendant of the Slovak Communist Party, but which is now affiliated to the **Socialist International**. Re-established as an autonomous formation following the collapse of communist rule in **Czechoslovakia** in late 1989, the Slovak Communist Party adopted the SDĽ title in 1990. In the June 1992 elections, the SDĽ became the second-largest party in the Slovak **National Council**, winning 29 seats on a 14.7% vote share and thereafter overcoming its initial reservations about the creation of an independent Slovakia from 1 January 1993.

After the Government of the **Movement for a Democratic Slovakia** (HZDS) had been reduced to minority status in March 1993, the SDĽ declined to join a coalition with the HZDS and instead became the leading party in the Common Choice (SV) centre-left opposition alliance which also included the Social Democratic Party of Slovakia, the Slovak Green Party and the Farmers' Movement of Slovakia. In the autumn 1994 elections, however, the SV won only 18 seats (the SDĽ itself falling back to 13), as voters preferred the incumbent HZDS as the real 'party of continuity'. In 1995–96 the SDĽ became increasingly divided over whether to accept further HZDS offers of coalition status, the election of the relatively unknown Jozef Migaš as leader in April 1996 being a compromise between the contending factions.

Standing on its own in the September 1998 National Council elections, the SDĽ advanced to 23 seats on a 14.7% vote share and opted to join a centre-left coalition headed by the centrist **Slovak Democratic Coalition** (SDK) and also including the **Party of Civic Understanding** (SOP) and the **Hungarian Coalition Party** (SMK). The SDĽ obtained six portfolios in the new Government, which was committed to accession to both the **European Union** and the **North Atlantic Treaty Organization**, and Migaš became Speaker of the National Council. In the May 1999 direct presidential elections, the SDĽ backed the successful candidacy of Rudolf **Schuster** of the SOP.

Leadership: Pavel Koncoš (Chair.).
Address: 12 Gunduličova 12, Bratislava 81105.
Telephone: (2) 54435475.
Fax: (2) 54433574.
E-mail: international@sdl.sk
Internet: www.sdl.sk

PAS *see* **Albanian Agrarian Party**.

Passy, Solomon

Minister of Foreign Affairs, **Bulgaria**.

Solomon Isak Passy is a renowned mathematician and a one-time member of the right-of-centre **Union of Democratic Forces** (SDS), but now has no party affiliation. He is famous for founding and leading the pro-Western Atlantic Club since 1991. He was appointed Foreign Minister on 24 July 2001.

Born on 22 December 1956 in Plovdiv, he studied maths at the St Kliment Ohridski University in **Sofia** from the mid-1970s. He received his doctorate in the subject in 1985 and continued to teach at the university until 1994. He was active in the pro-democracy **Ecoglasnost** movement from 1989, and from 1990 to 1991 he sat in the **National Assembly** as a member of the SDS before founding and heading the Atlantic Club to promote stronger ties between Bulgaria and the West, particularly with the **North Atlantic Treaty Organization** (NATO). Between 1991 and 2001 he worked with a number of liberal non-governmental organizations. He also joined the country's scientific expeditions to Antarctica between 1993 and 1996. Prime Minister Simeon **Saxecoburggotski** appointed him Foreign Minister in July 2001 in an overt gesture to promote Bulgaria's ties with the West.

Solomon Passy is married with three children.

Address: Ministry of Foreign Affairs, Alexander Zhendov St 2, 1113 Sofia.
Telephone: (2) 737997.
Fax: (2) 703041.
E-mail: mfabg@mb.bia-bg.com
Internet: www.mfa.government.bg

PBDNj *see* **Human Rights Union Party**.

PCA *see* **Permanent Court of Arbitration**.

PCRM *see* **Communist Party of the Moldovan Republic**.

PD (Albania) *see* **Democrat Party**.

PD (Romania) *see* **Democratic Party**.

PDK (Democratic Party of Kosovo) *see* **Kosovo Liberation Army**.

PDP (Bosnia and Herzegovina) *see* **Party of Democratic Progress**.

PDP (Macedonia) *see* **Party for Democratic Prosperity**.

PDS *see* **Democratic Party of Albania**.

PDSR (Social Democracy Party of Romania) *see* **Social Democrat Party**.

Peasants' Party of Ukraine
Selianska Partiya Ukrainy (SelPU)

The largest of the various peasant parties in **Ukraine**, favouring the retention of Soviet-era collectivization.

Supported by collective farm chairmen and agro-industry heads, the SelPU was founded in January 1992 as the party of rural organizations of the state-run agricultural system and has striven, with considerable success, to ensure the continuation of large subsidies to farming and to obstruct plans for land privatization. In alliance with the **Communist Party of Ukraine** (KPU) and the **Socialist Party of Ukraine** (SPU) in the 1994 **Parliament** elections, the SelPU polled strongly in conservative rural areas, winning 19 seats and becoming the leading component of the Rural Ukraine faction in the new legislature.

The SelPU contested the 1998 parliamentary elections in an alliance with the SPU called 'For the Truth, For the People, For Ukraine' (Za Pravdu, Za Narod, Za Ukrainu'), winning 12 of the joint list's 28 seats (with 6.3% of the vote). Leading

SelPU member Oleksandr Tkachenko was elected President of the new Parliament and became a prospective candidate in the 1999 presidential elections, until withdrawing in favour of KPU leader Petro Symonenko (who was defeated in the second round by incumbent Leonid **Kuchma**). In a lengthy political crisis in early 2000, the centre-right majority ousted Tkachenko as President of the Parliament.
Leadership: Serhiy Dovhan (Chair.).
Address: Maiakovskogo 6/29, Kherson 35200.
Telephone: (55) 2224452.

Pentagonale

A sub-regional co-operation initiative in **central** and **eastern Europe**, which was formed in 1989 and included Austria, **Czechoslovakia**, Italy, **Hungary** and the **Socialist Federal Republic of Yugoslavia**. The Pentagonale was expanded in July 1991 with the inclusion of **Poland**, becoming known as the Hexagonale, and went on to form the basis of the **Central European Initiative** in 1992.

People's Assembly (Albania)
Kuvendi Popullor

The unicameral legislature of **Albania**. It has at least 140 members under the 1998 Constitution, directly elected for a maximum of four years, 100 in single-member consituencies and at least 40 by proportional representation. The last elections were held between 24 June and 29 July 2001.
Address: Kuvendi Popullor, Tirana.
Telephone: (4) 232003.
Fax: (4) 227949.
E-mail: Ishestani@parliament.tirana.al
Internet: www.parlament.al

People's Democratic Party of Ukraine
Narodne-Demokratychna Partiya Ukrainy (NDPU)

A pro-market centrist political formation in **Ukraine**. The NDPU was formed in mid-1996 as a merger of several small centrist groupings, notably the Democratic Revival Party of Ukraine (PDVU), which had won four parliamentary seats in 1994, and New Wave (NK), which had also won four. From July 1997 the NDPU provided the Prime Minister in the person of Valeriy Pustovoytenko.

In the March 1998 **Parliament** elections the NDPU advanced to 28 seats on a proportional vote share of 6.3% and became part of the centre-right parliamentary majority, giving qualified backing to Governments appointed by President Leonid **Kuchma**, whom the party also supported in his successful re-election bid in 1999.

In September 2000 NDPU parliamentary leader Oleksandr Karpov was elected head of the centre-right pro-Government majority in Parliament.
Leadership: Anatoliy Matviyenko (Chair.).
Address: Saksaganskogo 37/122, Kiev.
Telephone: (44) 2528418.
Fax: (44) 2168333.
E-mail: postmaster@ndp.org.ua
Internet: ndp.org.ua

People's Party
Tautas Partija (TP)

Since 1998 the leading centre-right party in **Latvia**, advocating family values and national regeneration. The TP was officially launched in May 1998 by Andris Škele, a former businessman who had been non-party Prime Minister in 1995–97 attempting to lead a series of fractious centre-right coalitions. In the October 1998 parliamentary elections the TP emerged as narrowly the largest party, winning 24 of the 100 seats on a 21.2% vote share. It nevertheless went into opposition to a coalition headed by **Latvia's Way** (LC) until July 1999, when Škele returned to the premiership at the head of a majority centre-right coalition. Škele was forced to resign in April 2000 over a paedophilia scandal (later being cleared of allegations against him personally), whereupon the TP again became a junior partner in a coalition headed by the LC.
Leadership: Andris Škele (political leader).
Address: 68 Dzirnavu iela, Riga.
Telephone: 7286441 *Fax*: 7286405
E-mail: koord1@tautas.lv
Internet: www.tautaspartija.lv

People's Party of Armenia
Hayastani Zhoghovrdakan Kusaktsutyun (HZhK)

A party in **Armenia** founded in February 1999 on a platform of 'democratic and popular socialism' and calling for the reversal of post-**Soviet** 'deindustrialization'.

The first HZhK leader was Karen Demirchian, who had been runner-up to Robert **Kocharian** (non-party) in the March 1998 presidential elections, winning 30.7% in the first round and 40.5% in the second. He had been First Secretary of the then ruling **Communist Party of Armenia** from 1974 until his dismissal in 1988 for failing to curb Armenian nationalism.

The HZhK contested the May 1999 **National Assembly** elections in an alliance with the **Republican Party of Armenia** (HHK) called the Unity Bloc (Miasnutiun), which dominated the contest by winning 55 of the 131 seats and 41.7% of the proportional vote. While the then HHK leader became Prime Minister, Karen Demirchian was elected Speaker of the new Assembly. However, in October 1999 he was one of eight political leaders, including the Prime Minister, shot dead by gunmen during an Assembly debate. He was succeeded as HZhK Chairman in December by his younger son, Stepan Demirchian, while Armen Khachatrian of the HZhK became Speaker.

Although Stepan Demirchian initially pledged the HZhK's continued participation in the Unity Bloc, his criticism of the Government's policies intensified following the appointment of HHK Chairman Andranik **Markarian** as Prime Minister in May 2000. The divisions sharpened in September when HHK deputies led an attempt to oust Khachatrian from the speakership, following which Demirchian in October refused to commit the HZhK to supporting the Markarian Government and withdrew the party from Miasnutiun altogether in September 2001.

Leadership: Stepan Demirchian (Chair.).
Address: 24 Moskovian Street, Yerevan.
Telephone: (1) 581577.

Perestroika

The slogan, meaning 'restructuring' in Russian, adopted by Soviet leader Mikhail **Gorbachev** in late 1986 to denote his policies of pragmatic reform, particularly in the economic sphere. Perestroika's themes were efficiency (as reflected in decentralization, the limited introduction of market mechanisms, and campaigns against alcohol abuse) and equality of opportunity (an emphasis on ending corruption, nepotism and excessive party privilege). Perestroika, however, failed to galvanize a moribund command economy, and Gorbachev's liberal critics attacked it as timid and directionless.

Permanent Court of Arbitration (PCA)
(also known as *Cour permanente d'arbitrage*, CPA)

An international court based in The Hague, Netherlands, designed to provide a peaceful forum for the solution of international disputes. The PCA was established by the Convention on Pacific Settlement of International Disputes, which was signed in 1899 during the first Hague Peace Conference—convened by Russian Tsar Nicholas II as an attempt to prevent future international conflict and to de-escalate the arms race of the time. The Convention was revised at the second Conference in 1907 and 95 countries had, as of 31 December 2001, signed up to either one or both of the conventions, giving them access to the PCA. These included Belarus, Bulgaria, Croatia, Czech Republic, Hungary, Latvia, Macedonia, Poland, Romania, Russian Federation, Slovakia, Ukraine and Yugoslavia. The court also now

hears case of international commercial arbitration in a specially-convened Council. The court uses two official languages, English and French.
Secretary-General: Tjaco van den Hout.
Address: International Bureau, Peace Palace, Camegieplein 2, 2517 KJ, The Hague, The Netherlands.
Telephone: (70) 3024165.
Fax: (70) 3024167.
Email: bureau@pca-cpa.org
Internet: pca-cpa.org

Pesić, Dragiša

Prime Minister of **Yugoslavia**.

Dragiša Pesić is a leading member of the nationalist **Socialist People's Party of Montenegro** (SNPCG). He was first elected to the **Federal Assembly** in 1996 and was appointed Federal Prime Minister in mid-July 2001.

Born in Danilovgrad, central Montenegro, on 8 August 1954, he graduated in economics from the University of Sarajevo in 1977. He remained in **Bosnia and Herzegovina** for five years, working as a financial expert for the private company, Vatrostalna, but returned to Montenegro in 1982 to work in a similar capacity for the **Podgorica**-based company, Industriaimport. He began his political career in 1989 as President of the Municipal Government in the Montenegrin capital, representing the **Democratic Party of Socialists of Montenegro** (DPSCG). He was elected to the Yugoslav Federal Assembly in 1996 and was appointed Federal Finance Minister in 1998 after he sided with the pro-Yugoslav faction of the DPSCG, which went on to become the SNPCG. The position of Federal Prime Minister became vacant in mid-2001 after the incumbent Zoran Zizić resigned over the extradition of former dictator Slobodan **Milošević**. Pešic was appointed in his place after the SNPCG leader Momir Bulatović rejected the post.

Address: Office of the Prime Minister, Lenjinov Bulevar 2, 11070 Belgrade.
Telephone: (11) 334281.
Fax: (11) 659682.

Petritsch, Wolfgang

An experienced Austrian diplomat, appointed as the UN's **High Representative** to **Bosnia and Herzegovina** in August 1999. Born on 26 August 1947 in Klagenfurt, southern Austria (near the border with **Slovenia**), and raised bilingually in German and Slovenian, he received a doctorate in eastern European history from the University of Vienna in 1972. He served as an adviser and Press Secretary to the then Austrian Chancellor Bruno Kreisky from 1977 to 1983. After a year working for the **Organization for Economic Co-operation and Development** (OECD) in

Paris he went to the USA in 1984 to take up the position of head of the Austrian Press and Information Service in New York. Between 1992 and 1997 he served in various diplomatic roles based in Austria before being appointed Ambassador to **Yugoslavia** in September 1997.

As tensions increased in the **Albanian**-dominated province of **Kosovo** he was appointed as the **European Union**'s Special Envoy there in October 1998 and acted as chief negotiator at the Kosovo peace talks held in France between February and March 1999. Transferring his focus of attention to Bosnia and Herzegovina with his appointment in August 1999 as UN High Representative, he heads efforts to implement civilian aspects of the **Dayton Agreement**.

Petsamo question

A dispute between Finland and the **Russian Federation** over the far northern Petsamo border district. The district with its mainly ethnically Finnish population was incorporated, along with southern **Karelia**, into the newly independent Finland in 1920 under the second Treaty of **Tartu**. Hostilities between the two countries during the Second World War saw the region occupied by Soviet forces in 1944 and permanently absorbed into the **Soviet Union**. Until the collapse of communist power in 1991 the question of sovereignty over the Petsamo region was firmly locked away with both sides claiming the new border inviolable. However, in the early 1990s the disintegration of the Soviet Union sparked calls among irredentist Finns for the recovery of the ceded territories as the basis for better cross-border relations. The Finnish Government has not supported these calls.

Petseri question

A dormant territorial dispute between **Estonia** and the **Russian Federation** over the Petseri county area, which lies south-east of **Narva**. The county was ceded to Estonia under the first Treaty of **Tartu** in 1920 along with other **Russian**-dominated areas, but the Soviet authorities reannexed Petseri in 1944. The collapse of the **Soviet Union** in 1991 and the creation of an independent Estonia raised calls for a return to the borders agreed in 1920. However, Petseri has a predominantly Russian community, a fact which did not leave the Estonian claim with much weight, and in November 1995 Estonia agreed to drop its claims to the county.

PfP *see* **Partnership for Peace**.

PHARE programme

The programme in the early 1990s for **European Union** aid initially to **Poland** and **Hungary**, and thereafter extended to the rest of **central** and **eastern Europe**. The name Phare, meaning 'lighthouse' in French, comes from the French acronym for 'Poland and Hungary; economic reconstruction assistance'.

Picula, Tonino

Minister of Foreign Affairs, **Croatia**.

Tonino Picula is one of the younger faces in the ruling **Social Democratic Party of Croatia** (SPH). He was appointed Foreign Minister on 27 January 2000.

Born on 31 August 1961 on the island of Lošinj, he graduated from the University of Zagreb in 1987 with a degree in philosophy, and then spent two years as Executive Secretary of the editorial board for *Kulturni Radnik*, a well-established sociological and current affairs periodical. In 1990 he joined the reformed communist party (which became the SPH in 1991), and since 1993 he has been its Secretary for International Relations. He worked extensively for the party at the local level until his election to the **Assembly** in January 2000. He is also Secretary of the non-governmental Croatian-Bosnian Friendship Society.

Address: Ministry of Foreign Affairs, Trg N. Š. Zrinskog 7–8, 10000 Zagreb.
Telephone: (1) 4569964.
Fax: (1) 4569988.
E-mail: mvp@mvp.hr
Internet: www.mvp.hr

Pirin Macedonia *see* **Macedonian question**.

PiS *see* **Law and Justice**.

PKE *see* **Ecoglasnost Political Club**.

PKK *see* **National Unity Party**.

PLL *see* **Movement of Legality Party**.

PNL *see* **National Liberal Party**.

PNŢCD *see* **Christian Democratic National Peasants' Party**.

PO *see* **Citizens' Platform**.

Podgorica

A city in the south-west of **Yugoslavia** and the capital, and main urban centre, of **Montenegro**. *Population*: 130,290 (2001 estimate). Founded by the ancient Illyrians and adopted by the Romans, the city of Podgorica lies at the confluence of the Morača and Ribnica rivers. It was given its modern name in 1326, having previously been known as Ribnica while it served, briefly, as the capital of **Serbia**. Through most of the long Ottoman rule in the region the city was beyond the pale of the fiercely independent Montenegrin rulers. Podgorica became the Montenegrin capital for the first time when *de facto* independence was finally recognized by the international community in 1878. It remained in this capacity when the Republic was absorbed in 1918 into the Kingdom of Serbs, Croats and Slovenes (which would later become Yugoslavia), and indeed the 'Great People's Council' at which Montenegro was voluntarily united with Serbia, was held in Podgorica on 26 November 1918. Much of the old city was destroyed during the Second World War and socialist reconstruction has left a thoroughly 'modern' city in its place. From 1946 until the collapse of the **Socialist Federal Republic of Yugoslavia** in 1992, Podgorica was known as Titograd in honour of the Yugoslav leader Marshal **Tito**.

As the capital of the all-but-independent Montenegro, Podgorica is the centre of the Republic's economy and home to a wide variety of light industries. It is a key transport hub for Montenegro and contains the Republic's main airport, which is still known internationally by the ex-Titograd code TGD.

Podkrepa Confederation of Labour

An independent trade union centre in **Bulgaria** seeking to challenge the dominance of the **Confederation of Independent Trade Unions of Bulgaria** (KNSB). Podkrepa ('Support') was founded by intellectuals in February 1989, becoming part of the pro-democracy movement which brought about the collapse of communist rule. In the 1990s the organization became increasingly critical of the slow progress towards a market economy, corruption in ruling circles and government moves to limit trade union negotiating rights. Affiliated to the International Confederation of Free Trade Unions (ICFTU), Podkrepa embraces about 50 union bodies with a combined membership of some 500,000.

President: Konstantin Trentchev.
Address: 2 Angel Kanchev St, Sofia 1000.
Telephone: (2) 9814551.
Fax: (2) 9812928.
E-mail: encho.bg@bulinfo.net

Poland
Rzeczpospolita Polska

An independent republic situated in northern central Europe, bordered to the west by Germany, to the south-west by the Czech Republic, to the south by Slovakia, to the north by Lithuania, the Baltic Sea and the Kaliningrad territory of the Russian Federation, and to the east by Belarus and Ukraine. Administratively, the country is divided into 16 provinces (voivodships).

Area: 312,683 sq km; *capital*: **Warsaw**; *population*: 38.6m (2001 estimate), comprising **Poles** 97.6%, **Germans** 1.3%, **Ukrainians** 0.6%, **Belarusians** 0.5%; *language*: Polish; *religion*: **Roman Catholic** 95%, other 5%.

Under the Constitution approved by referendum in 1997, legislative authority is vested in the bicameral **National Assembly**, which consists of a 460-member Diet (Sejm) and a 100-member Senate (Senat). Sejm members are elected for a four-year term by a complex system of proportional representation subject to a 5% threshold; the Senate is directly elected for a four-year term by a majority vote on a provincial basis. Executive authority is vested in the President (Head of State) and Prime Minister. The President is elected for a five-year term by popular vote and appoints the Prime Minister.

History: Slavic tribes united under Prince Mieszko I of the Piast dynasty in the late 10th century to form the first Polish state. After subsequent feudal fragmentation, Poland was reunited and royal authority restored in the 14th century. Existing close dynastic links with **Lithuania** led in 1569 to the formation of a powerful confederation under the Union of Lublin. However, after 200 years of elective monarchy marked by wars and territorial losses, **Russia**, **Prussia** and Austria partitioned Poland in three stages between 1772 and 1795. At the Congress of Vienna in 1815, Poland remained partitioned and the Napoleonic Duchy of Warsaw (created by the Treaty of Tilsit in 1807) became the puppet kingdom of Poland under Tsarist Russian domination.

Polish nationalists led by Marshal Jozef Piłsudski declared Poland's independence in 1918 following the collapse of Germany and Tsarist Russia during the First World War. Independence was guaranteed by the 1919 **Versailles** settlements, but was only fully achieved after Soviet troops had been expelled and the 1921 Treaty of **Riga** signed with the new **Soviet Union**. After a period of crisis-ridden democratic politics, Marshal Piłsudski became virtual dictator of Poland in 1926. In September 1939, despite Anglo-French guarantees, Germany and the Soviet Union invaded and divided Poland (as had been secretly agreed under the 1939 **Nazi-Soviet Pact**). Following the German attack on the Soviet Union in 1941, all of Poland was occupied by German forces.

In 1944 the Soviet-backed 'Lublin Committee' declared itself the provisional Polish Government, as the Red Army drove out German forces. At the Allies' **Potsdam** conference in 1945 Poland's borders were redrawn westwards to include former German territory up to the **Oder-Neisse line**, in partial compensation for the cession of a larger area of eastern Poland to the Soviet Union. Having ruthlessly suppressed its opponents, the communist Polish Workers' Party engineered a victory for itself and allied parties in the 1947 elections, following which it declared a people's republic and renamed itself the Polish United Workers' Party (PUWP). In 1952 Poland adopted a Soviet-style Constitution and in 1955 joined the **Warsaw Pact** military alliance.

In 1980, following a visit by the Polish Pope **John Paul II** the previous year, workers' strikes in **Gdańsk** led to the birth of **Solidarity**, a free trade union led by Lech **Wałęsa**. Martial law was imposed in 1981 and Solidarity was outlawed, but by the late 1980s the influence of the *glasnost* ('openness') initiative in the Soviet Union had rekindled public unrest. Unable to contain the political challenge, the PUWP regime agreed to a measure of power-sharing and representation for the opposition. In elections in 1989 Solidarity candidates won all the unreserved seats in the Sejm (around two-thirds being reserved for approved organizations, particularly the PUWP) and all but one seat in the Senate. Tadeusz Mazowiecki, a Solidarity activist, was appointed Prime Minister, leading a coalition Government with a non-communist majority. The PUWP voted to disband, re-forming as Social Democracy of the Polish Republic in early 1990 and later becoming the dominant component of the **Democratic Left Alliance** (SLD). In December 1990 Wałęsa was overwhelmingly elected as Poland's first post-communist President, his first Prime Minister being pro-marketeer Jan Bielecki.

Political instability followed the first fully democratic parliamentary elections in October 1991, which gave 29 parties representation in the Sejm. A fragile centre-right coalition Government led by Jan Olszewski, then a centrist, resigned after seven months and was succeeded in July 1992 by a seven-party coalition headed by Hanna Suchocka of the Democratic Union. In May 1993 the President dissolved the Sejm and new electoral rules were enacted to exclude parties which won less than 5% of the vote. The September 1993 elections returned the SLD as the largest party with 171 lower house seats, followed by the **Polish Peasant Party** (PSL) with 132. The SLD and PSL formed a left-wing coalition Government under PSL leader Waldemar Pawlak, but he was replaced by Józef Oleksy of the SLD in early 1995 following serious tensions between the Government and the President. Wałęsa narrowly failed to secure a second term in the November–December 1995 presidential elections, being defeated in the second round by Aleksander **Kwaśniewski** of the SLD. In early 1996 he appointed Włodzimierz **Cimoszewicz** (the SLD Deputy Prime Minister) to replace Oleksy, who had resigned over spying allegations. Thereafter, amidst economic and social difficulties associated with transition to a market economy, the SLD-PSL coalition became increasingly unpopular.

Parliamentary elections in September 1997 were won by the centre-right **Solidarity Electoral Action** (AWS), a multi-party Christian-oriented alliance which took 201 seats in the Sejm. The SLD was pushed into opposition as Jerzy **Buzek** of the AWS was appointed Prime Minister and formed a centre-right coalition Government with the liberal **Freedom Union** (UW). The new Government went on to secure the ratification in January 1998 of a concordat with the Vatican, signed in

1993 but shelved by the SLD-PSL Government, providing *inter alia* for the legalization of church marriages. It also ensured the abolition of capital punishment under a new penal code introduced in September 1998. However, increasing strains in the ruling coalition culminated in the withdrawal of the UW in June 2000, leaving Buzek as head of a minority AWS Government with diminishing parliamentary and popular support.

Presidential elections in October 2000 were won in the first round by SLD incumbent Kwaśniewski, who took 53.9% of the vote, while AWS nominee Marian Krzaklewski, leader of the Solidarity trade union wing, came a poor third with only 15.6%. The popularity of the Government slipped even further as the Solidarity movement withdrew its support for AWS altogether in May 2001 and the party became mired in corruption scandals. Buzek became the first Prime Minister to complete a term in office in post-communist Poland but had the indignity of seeing the AWS wiped out of the Assembly entirely in elections in September. The poll saw a great success for more radical right-wing parties on the political fringe.

Latest elections: The SLD, in alliance with the **Labour Union** (UP), secured 216 seats in the September 2001 Sejm elections, based on 41% of the vote. The centrist **Citizens' Platform** (PO) won 65 seats (12.7% of the vote), the rightist and agrarian **Self-Defence of the Polish Republic** (Samoobrona) 53 (10.2%), **Law and Justice** (PiS) 44 (9.5%), PSL 42 (9%), the nationalist **League of Polish Families** (LPR) 38 (7.9%). AWS received only 5.6% of the vote and was denied any seats in the Sejm, as were the UW (which won 3.1% of the vote) and the conservative **Movement for the Reconstruction of Poland** (ROP). Two seats were reserved for the German Minority of Lower Silesia (MNSO).

The 100-seat Senat was also renewed. The SLD/UP alliance secured 75 seats, Blok Senat 2001 (which included the PO, PiS, AWS and ROP) 15, PSL 4 and 2 each for Samoobrona, the LPR and non-partisans.

Leszek **Miller** of the SLD formed a coalition Government with the UP and PSL.

International relations and defence: Post-communist Poland signed a Treaty of Friendship and Co-operation with reunified Germany in 1991, giving legal recognition to the Oder-Neisse border and the rights of the German minority in Poland. A similarly-named treaty was signed with the Russian Federation in 1992. In the early 1990s Poland joined the **Organization for Security and Co-operation in Europe**, the **Council of Europe**, the **Central European Initiative** and the **Central European Free Trade Area**, later becoming a member of the **Organization for Economic Co-operation and Development** and the **World Trade Organization**. Having acceded to **NATO**'s **Partnership for Peace** programme in 1994, Poland formally joined the NATO Alliance (together with the **Czech Republic** and **Hungary**) in March 1999. Following its 1994 application for membership of the **European Union** (EU), Poland opened formal accession negotiations with the EU in March 1998.

Poland's defence budget for 2000 amounted to some US $3,200m., equivalent to about 2% of GDP. The size of the armed forces at the end of 2000 was some

217,000 personnel, including those serving under compulsory conscription of 12 months, while reservists numbered an estimated 400,000. In March 2001 the Government approved a six-year $26,000m. programme to upgrade the armed forces to NATO standards and to reduce their number to 150,000 by 2006.

Poland, economy

One of the largest economies in central-eastern Europe, along with the **Russian Federation** and **Ukraine**, in transition from communist-era central control.

GNP: US $157,812m. (2000); *GNP per capita*: $4,200 (2000); *GDP at PPP*: $276,500m. (1999); *GDP per capita at PPP*: $7,200 (1999); *exports*: $31,609m. (2000); *imports*: $48,940m. (2000); *currency*: złoty (plural: złotys; US $1=Z3.952 at the end of December 2001).

In 1999 industry accounted for 37% of GDP, agriculture for 4% and services for 59%. Some 47% of the land is arable, 1% under permanent crops, 13% permanent pasture and 29% forests and woodland. The main crops are vegetables, grain and sugar beet; there is a significant animal husbandry sector (which in monetary terms accounted for nearly half of agricultural output in the mid-1990s), including dairy farming. The main mineral resources are hard and brown coal, some oil and natural gas, and various non-ferrous metal ores, including copper, zinc, lead and silver, together with sulphur reserves. The principal industries are machine building, iron and steel, coal mining, chemicals, shipbuilding, food processing, textiles and beverages. Coal is by far the greatest energy source, although petroleum is imported to supplement the indigenous coal; there are no plans for nuclear-sourced electricity.

Poland's main exports are manufactured goods (46% in 1999), machinery and transport equipment (30%), food and live animals (8%), chemical products (6%) and mineral fuels (5%). Principal imports are machinery and transport equipment (38% in 1999), manufactured goods (30%), chemical products (14%), mineral fuels and lubricants (7%) and food and live animals (6%). In 2000 Germany was by far the greatest purchaser of Polish exports (35%), followed by Italy (6%) and France and the Netherlands (5% each). Germany is also the biggest provider of Polish imports (24% in 2000), followed by the Russian Federation (9%) and Italy (8%). The **European Union** (EU) accounted in 1998 for about two-thirds of Poland's exports and imports.

Poland avoided the protracted slump in output experienced by most other post-communist countries, becoming in 1994 the first to improve on its 1989 GDP and achieving average annual GDP growth of 5% in the period 1993–98, including increases of between 6% and 7% in 1996–98. Within this framework, the share of the industrial sector dropped sharply as the old, centralized economy with a concentration on heavy industry was replaced by a more modern service-oriented market economy in which the relative importance of the agricultural sector also declined as Poland became more integrated into the wider European market.

Annual inflation dropped from around 30% in 1994 to 13.2% in 1997 and to 8.6% at the end of 1998, while unemployment fell from 14% in 1996 to 10% in 1998.

GDP growth slowed to around 4% in 1998 and 1999, as Poland was adversely affected by the mid-1998 financial crisis in the Russian Federation—still an important trading partner (see **Russian Federation, economy**), by rising world oil prices and by the slow-down in EU countries. In late 1998 and early 1999 there were a number of strikes and other expressions of industrial unrest as some workers resisted certain of the Government's reform measures. The inflation rate rose to 10% and unemployment to 12% in 1999, during which time both the trade balance and the current account balance showed a deterioration to 9% and 7% of GDP respectively. The annualized GDP growth rate picked up in the first half of 2000 to 6% but fell back in the second half, resulting in 4.1% expansion over the full year, while inflation remained stable at 10% and unemployment increased to over 15% by year's end. The Government's budget for 2001 provided for expenditure of Z181,600m. and revenue of Z161,100m., projecting a deficit of 3% of GDP, GDP growth of 4.5%, an inflation rate of 7% and a further rise in unemployment to 16%.

Economic policy in recent years has been wholly geared to the aim of joining the EU, Poland being one of the five original 'fast-track' entry candidates among the former communist states with which accession negotiations opened in 1998. As a major step towards eventual membership of the EU's economic and monetary union, the złoty was floated from April 2000 and became freely convertible against the euro. Poland was a founder member of the **Central European Free Trade Area** (CEFTA) in 1993 and the third post-communist state to join the **Organization for Economic Co-operation and Development** (in 1996), having also become a founder member of the **World Trade Organization** in 1995.

Because the role of the state was less dominant in Poland than in other communist states, especially in that the agricultural sector was mostly under private ownership, the privatization process in the 1990s has been less disruptive, although it has consistently been controversial. After initial concentration on eliminating subsidies and liquidating uneconomic concerns, legislation was enacted in 1990 providing for the privatization of over 7,500 enterprises, the first sales taking place later that year. The first mass privatization programme, as announced in 1991, was initiated from 1993. Later stages, which were finally implemented after procedural delays, involved also the 'commercialization' rather than necessarily the full privatization of enterprises, and the issue of vouchers to citizens (see **voucher privatization**). The new Constitution which entered into force in October 1997 committed Poland to a social market economy based on freedom of economic activity and private ownership.

The centre-right Government elected in 1997 announced proposals for the eventual privatization of the coal and steel industries, the national telecommunications company, the largest insurance company, the national airline, the state railways, various state banks and the arms manufacturing industry. By mid-2000 the number of state-owned concerns had been reduced by half to less than 2,800, but these included over 400 larger enterprises in highly-unionized sectors such as mining and heavy industry in which union opposition to privatization was strong. In July–August 2000 the Government secured narrow parliamentary approval for a complex 'enfranchisement' bill under which all adult Poles would receive vouchers entitling them to a stake in the shares resulting from the planned mass privatization of remaining state-owned enterprises and property. In September, however, the bill was vetoed by President **Kwaśniewski** (of the **Democratic Left Alliance**) and the *Sejm*, the lower house of the **National Assembly**, failed to override the veto in October, a week after Kwaśniewski's re-election.

Poles

A west **Slavic people** overwhelmingly dominant in modern **Poland** with sizeable minority populations in **Belarus**, Germany and **Lithuania**. The Polish language is very similar to Czech and Slovak. The ancestors of the Poles were dominant in the east of the north European plain by the 10th century when the northern Polanie united with the southern Wislanie to create a single Polish state. Despite their proximity to their east Slavic relations the Poles followed a westward-leaning path through history after accepting **Roman Catholicism** and the Latin script from the **Czechs** of **Bohemia** in 966. In the modern period the decline of Polish power was mirrored by the growing importance of **Prussia** (originally based on Königsberg, now called **Kaliningrad**), as a focal point of German unification, and by the westward extension of **Russian** power. The Poles' ethnic homogeneity was greatly challenged as their territory was swallowed up by the neighbouring powers, the Polish state disappearing entirely in the late 18th century. The influx of non-Polish people was accompanied by attempts to germanize and russify the population, with most Poles reduced to little better than the status of serfs. However, the preservation throughout this period of a sense of Polish identity, enhanced by the brief existence of the Napoleonic Duchy of **Warsaw**, provided a basis for nationalism in the independent state established in 1918. The devastation of the country under Nazi domination after 1939, the obliteration of its minority population of **Jews**, the mass deportations, and then the displacement of ethnic **Germans** (and redrawing of boundaries) in 1945, left modern Poland with an almost entirely ethnic Polish population.

Polish Agency for Foreign Investment (PAIZ)

Government agency supervising the search for and administration of inward investment in **Poland**'s privatization and economic development programmes.
President: Adam Pawłowicz.
Address: Al. Róz 2, 00599 Warsaw.

Polish Chamber of Commerce

Telephone: (22) 6210706.
Fax: (22) 6226169.
E-mail: post@paiz.gov.pl
Internet: www.paiz.gov.pl

Polish Chamber of Commerce
Krajowa Izba Gospodarcza

The principal organization in **Poland** for promoting business contacts, both internally and externally, in the post-communist era. Founded in 1990.
President: Andrzej Arendarski.
Chair.: Kazimierz Pazgan.
Address: Head Office, Trębacka 4, POB 361, 00074 Warsaw.
Telephone: (22) 8260143.
Fax: (22) 8279478.

Polish Peasant Party
Polskie Stronnictwo Ludowe (PSL)

A traditional political formation of **Poland**'s large agricultural population. The PSL is descended from the historic Peasant Party founded in **Galicia** in 1895, and more precisely from the group led by Stanisław Mikolajczyk, which in 1945 rejected the party leadership's decision to enter into close co-operation with the communists. In November 1949, after Mikolajczyk had been ousted by leftist PSL members, the two groups merged as the United Peasant Party (ZSL), which became part of the communist-dominated 'unity front'. The ZSL was thus committed to the goal of transforming Poland into a socialist society, although private peasant ownership of land was guaranteed from 1956.

As communist rule collapsed, the PSL was revived in August 1989 and reconstituted in May 1990 at a congress which unified various strands of the peasant movement. The then PSL leader, Roman Bartoszcze, received only 7.2% of the vote in the first round of presidential elections in November 1990 and was replaced in June 1991 by Waldemar Pawlak. Pawlak restored unity to the party and led it to a respectable 8.7% of the vote and 48 seats in the October 1991 **National Assembly** elections. Although it broadly supported the subsequent centre-right Olszewski Government, the PSL opposed its proposal to release secret police files to expose informers of the communist era. This issue brought down the Government in June 1992, whereupon Pawlak was endorsed by the *Sejm* (lower house) as the new Prime Minister, but was unable to form a Government.

Benefiting from rural disenchantment with economic **'shock therapy'**, the PSL polled strongly in the September 1993 parliamentary elections, becoming the second-largest party with 132 seats on an overall vote share of 15.4% (and a historically high 46% of the peasant vote). It then opted to join a coalition Government with the **Democratic Left Alliance** (SLD), the largest formation. In the light of lingering doubts about the SLD's pro-communist ancestry, the SLD agreed that Pawlak should become Prime Minister. The new coalition quickly displayed internal tensions, while the PSL also came into conflict with President **Wałęsa** because of its objections to what it regarded as precipitate moves to a free-market economy. The outcome was Pawlak's resignation in February 1995 and the appointment of an SLD Prime Minister, although the coalition was maintained. In the November 1995 presidential elections Pawlak received only 4.3% of the first-round vote.

The PSL's stint in government came to an end at the September 1997 parliamentary elections, in which its vote share slumped to 7.3% and its Sejm representation to 27 seats. The following month Pawlak gave way as Party Chairman to former Agriculture Minister Jarosław Kalinowski, a representative of the PSL's conservative Christian democratic wing which favoured tariff protection for Polish agriculture. In February 1998 the PSL was weakened by the formation of the breakaway Peasant Democratic Party (PLD) by former Deputy Prime Minister Roman Jagieliński, while in January 2000 radical farmers' groups launched the National Peasant Bloc. In the October 2000 presidential election Kalinowski came fourth with 6% of the vote.

In the September 2001 legislative elections the PSL improved to 9% of the vote, gaining 42 seats in the Sejm and 4 in the *Senat* (upper house). It re-entered government in a SLD-led coalition (together with the **Labour Union**) which was headed by Leszek **Miller**.

Leadership: Jarosław Kalinowski (Chair.).
Address: ul. Grzybowska 4, Warsaw 00131.
Telephone: (22) 6206020.
Fax: (22) 6543583.
E-mail: biuronkw@nkw.psl.org.pl
Internet: www.psl.org.pl

Polish Press Agency
Polska Agencja Prasowa (PAP)

The state news agency in **Poland**. Established by the **Soviet** authorities in 1944 to replace the pre-war Polish Telegraph Agency, the PAP is now the major news provider in Poland with branches in 28 Polish towns and 22 foreign capitals. Made a joint stock company in 1998, it was partly privatized in 2001.

President: Robert Bogdański.
Address: ul. Pawia 55, 00950 Warsaw.
Telephone: (22) 6280001.
Fax: (22) 6213439.
E-mail: webmaster@pap.com.pl
Internet: www.pap.com.pl

Pomaks

A widely-used name for Muslim **Slavs** living in the southern **Balkans**. Around 250,000 Pomaks live in **Bulgaria**, and around 50,000 in **Macedonia**. Ethnically identical to their Slavic neighbours, the Pomaks embraced **Islam** during the 500 years of Ottoman rule.

The Pomaks in Bulgaria came under severe pressure to abandon their faith and culture under the repressive communist regime. They suffered from policies to Bulgarianize the population and the use of Muslim and Arabic names was forbidden. Aligning themselves with the similarly-treated **Bulgarian Turks**, some Pomaks were forcibly dispersed across the country. Unlike the Turks, the Pomaks were denied the option of emigrating to Turkey. The Pomak population is in a crisis of self-identity, often claiming either Bulgarian or Turkish ethnicity. Pomaks do not have official political representation, as ethnically-based political parties are banned in Bulgaria, but the **Movement for Rights and Freedoms** has increasingly wooed the Pomak vote as its own traditional support base among the Bulgarian Turks has dwindled.

Some Pomak communities living in Macedonia complain of deliberate campaigns to assimilate them into the **Albanian** community, with whom they are mistakenly lumped together because of their common Muslim identity. However, the existence of the substantial Albanian minority in Macedonia has meant greater cultural and religious freedom in that country, from which the Pomaks also benefit.

Pontic Greeks

An ethnic Greek minority found in **Georgia** and originally concentrated in the breakaway republic of **Abkhazia**. The Pontic Greeks are ultimately descended from Greek colonists of the **Caucasus region** (who named the Black Sea the Pontic Sea). Practising **Orthodox Christianity**, they were easily assimilated into the mixed-faith Abkhaz population despite a prevalence of Islam. However, the Greeks felt a stronger kinship with the **Georgian** majority in Abkhazia and were exiled along with them after the Abkhaz victory in the 1992–94 separatist war in the region. Most of the 15,000 Pontic Greeks were forced to seek refuge in Georgia proper and their homes and land were confiscated by the Abkhaz authorities. In the early 21st century the Pontic Greek community in Georgia expressed concern that efforts to repatriate war migrants were focusing almost exclusively on ethnic Georgians.

Popular Movement of Ukraine
Narodniy Rukh Ukrainy (Rukh)

A moderate nationalist party in **Ukraine** derived from the pro-independence anti-communist opposition to Soviet rule. Modelled on similar movements in the

Baltic States, the original Rukh emerged from an opposition movement which was crushed by the authorities in the summer of 1988 but re-established during the winter of 1988–89 as a broad alliance which included pro-reformists from the **Communist Party of Ukraine** (KPU). In partially free republican elections in March 1990, the Rukh front organization, the Democratic Bloc, won 27% of the legislative seats, but thereafter other opposition groups also took up the cause and Rukh fell increasingly under the control of its nationalist wing. The various elections and referendums of 1991 brought no advance for Rukh, which split at its third congress in early 1992, with the more nationalist wing breaking away. Vyacheslav Chornovil was left as leader of a rump Rukh, which formally became a political party in December 1992.

Under Chornovil's leadership, Rukh pursued a centrist/moderate nationalist line, supporting market reforms and a liberal democratic state united around territorial rather than ethnic patriotism, but also advocating strong national defence and Ukraine's withdrawal from the **Commonwealth of Independent States** (CIS). It won only 20 seats in the 1994 **Parliament** elections, subsequently strongly opposing the successful KPU-backed presidential candidacy of Leonid **Kuchma**, whom Chornovil described as Ukraine's 'most dangerous enemy'.

Declaring itself to be in favour of Ukrainian membership of the **European Union** and the **North Atlantic Treaty Organization**, Rukh sought to rally anti-left forces for the March 1998 parliamentary elections. Benefiting from its extensive support in western Ukraine, Rukh emerged from that contest as the second-largest party (though far behind the KPU), winning 42 seats on a vote share of 9.5%. It then became part of a highly fluid parliamentary majority defined by its opposition to the left and broadly supportive of Kuchma-appointed Governments, although without any enthusiasm for Kuchma himself.

Divisions within Rukh came to a head in January 1999 when Chornovil was replaced as Party Chairman by Yuriy Kostenko, whereupon Chornovil and his supporters formed another version of Rukh. On Chornovil's death in a car crash in March 1999, he was succeeded as leader of the breakaway Rukh by Hennadiy Udovenko. Both Kostenko and Udovenko were candidates in the autumn 1999 presidential elections, but won only 2.2% and 1.2% of the first-round vote respectively. With antipathy between the two factions growing, a third Rukh faction was formed in November 2000 under the leadership of Bohdan Boyko with the aim of reuniting the other two.

Leadership: Yuriy Kostenko, Hennadiy Udovenko, Bohdan Boyko (Chairs of different Rukh factions)
Address: Shevchenko 37/122, Kiev.
Telephone: (44) 2249151.
Fax: (44) 2168333.
E-mail: mail@rukhpress-center.kiev.ua
Internet: www.rukhpress-center.kiev.ua

Porkkala peninsula

A small promontory just south-west of the Finnish capital Helsinki which was leased as a military base to the **Soviet Union** until 1956. At the conclusion of the 1944 'Winter War' between Finland and the Soviet Union the use of the Porkkala peninsula as a military base was established in the harsh peace accords, along with the loss of 10% of Finnish territory. As post-war relations between the two countries stabilized and a mutual assistance pact was secured the need for a permanent Soviet naval base in the Gulf of Finland became less tenable. Soviet troops began to withdraw in 1955 and Porkkala was returned to Finnish use the following year.

Posavina Corridor *see* **Brčko**.

Poslanecká Sněmovna
(Chamber of Deputies)

The lower house of **Parliament** of the **Czech Republic**.

Potsdam Agreements

The conclusion of the Potsdam Conference on 17 July 1945 between the Heads of Government of the UK, the USA and the **Soviet Union**, held at Potsdam in Germany following the conclusion of the war in Europe. The Potsdam meeting essentially endorsed the conclusions of the previous summit held in **Yalta**, placing **eastern Europe** effectively within the Soviet sphere of influence. It also established the principle of an international tribunal for war criminals (which became the basis for the Nuremburg trials, and more recently the **International Criminal Tribunal for the former Yugoslavia**), and agreed a framework for the mass repatriation of ethnic **Germans** from all over eastern Europe.

PPCD *see* **Christian Democratic People's Party**.

Prague

The capital city of the **Czech Republic**, situated in the centre of **Bohemia**.

Population: 1.2m. (1996 estimate). The city has been the administrative centre of Bohemia since it was a kingdom in the Holy Roman Empire (Prague was the imperial capital under Charles IV in the 14th century), through its incorporation into the Habsburg Empire. Its long history has left an array of intriguing architecture making the city the republic's major tourist attraction and sparing it some of the worst excesses of communist planning. It was also spared the damage experienced elsewhere during Europe's many wars. Even the city's **Jewish** quarter was saved from the devastation wreaked elsewhere, although only as Hitler intended to preserve it as a monument to the Jewish people. As capital of the **Czechoslovak** state from 1919 to 1993, Prague was the centre of the country's cultural and political life and as such played a significant role in the major events of the last 50 years. In 1968 it saw the brief blossoming of liberal culture during the **Prague Spring**, and in 1989 it was the centre stage for the dramatic '**velvet revolution**'.

Prague Spring

Communist **Czechoslovakia**'s brief experiment in 1968 with socialism with a human face. An 'action programme' in April set out plans to extend democracy and civil rights, and the newly-freed press radicalized the political climate, although communist party leader Alexander **Dubček** never questioned the leading role of the communist party while in office. The **Prague Spring** was crushed by an invasion by **Warsaw Pact** tanks and troops in September 1968.

The brief rise of **Croatian** reform communism and moderate nationalism in 1969–71, under the **Tito** regime in communist **Yugoslavia**, was sometimes referred to, by analogy, as the Croatian Spring.

Prague Stock Exchange
Burza cenných papírů Praha

The stock exchange in the **Czech Republic** originally founded in 1871, which reopened after the communist period in November 1992. Trading began again in April 1993. As at 1 December 2001 it had 36 members.
General Secretary: Pavel Hollman.
Address: Rybná 14, 11005 Prague 1.
Telephone: (2) 21832411.
Fax: (2) 21833040.
E-mail: info@pse.cz
Internet: www.pse.cz

Predstavnički Dom
(House of Representatives)

The lower house of the **Parliamentary Assembly** of **Bosnia and Herzegovina**.

Presevo Valley

The disputed border region between eastern **Kosovo** and south-western **Serbia**. Although never a part of mainly **Albanian**-populated Kosovo, the Presevo Valley is home to a significant ethnic Albanian community, particularly in the towns of Bujanovac, Medvedja and Presevo. Militant Albanians there were prompted to take up arms during the conflict over control of Kosovo in 2000, with the Liberation Army of Presevo, Medvedja and Bujanovac (known by its Albanian initials UCPMB) attacking **Serb** police. Benefiting from the protection of the UN buffer zone established to keep Serb security forces out of Kosovo, they subsequently sought to have the Presevo Valley included in the UN administration of Kosovo. However, neither the post-**Milošević** authorities in **Yugoslavia**, nor the international community were sympathetic to this. In May 2001 Serb paramilitary police were given permission to re-enter the buffer zone and by the end of the month the UCPMB had agreed to disarm.

Prevlaka peninsula

A strategic spit of land forming the southernmost extreme of **Croatia** and jutting out into the Bay of Kotor, effectively controlling access to the south-western **Montenegrin** ports. The area was overrun by Yugoslav forces, particularly Montenegrins, in 1991–92 but control was handed back to Croatia at the end of the war under the **Dayton Agreement** of November 1995 despite initial attempts by **Yugoslavia** to demand control of the area. Sovereignty over the region remains in dispute between the two countries, although relatively good regional relations in the early 21st century took some of the heat out of the argument. It remains a demilitarized zone, monitored by a UN observer mission.

Pripet Marshes

Europe's largest marshland, lying across some 104,000 square miles of north-western **Ukraine** and southern **Belarus**. The heavily-wooded and impenetrable region is filled from water from the Pripet and Dnieper rivers and from heavy rainfall. Since 1872 reclamation projects have provided a vast amount of land for agricultural use. The process has been accelerated owing to economic pressures in the late 20th century.

Privatization Agency (Bulgaria)

Organizes the privatization of state-owned enterprises whose assets exceed 70m. leva. Founded in 1992.
  Executive Director: Levon Hampartsumian.
  Address: Aksakov St 29, 1000 Sofia.
  Telephone: (2) 8977579.
  Fax: (2) 9816201.

E-mail: bgpriv@mbox.digsys.bg
Internet: www.privatization.bg

Privatization Agency of the Federation of Bosnia and Herzegovina

Government agency in the **Muslim-Croat Federation**.
Director: Adnad Mujagić.
Address: Alipašina 41, Sarajevo.
Telephone: (33) 212884.
Fax: (33) 212883.
E-mail: apfbih@bih.net.ba
Internet: www.apf.com.ba

Privatization Agency of the Republic of Macedonia

Government agency in **Macedonia**.
Director: Marina Nakeva-Kavrakova.
Address: POB 410, Nikola Vapcarov 7, 1000 Skopje.
Telephone: (2) 117564.
Fax: (2) 126022.
E-mail: agency@mpa.org.mk
Internet: www.mpa.org.mk

PRM *see* **Greater Romania Party**.

Progressive Socialist Party
Prohresyvna Sotsialistychna Partiya (PSP)

A political formation in **Ukraine** regarded as the most left-wing party in the **Parliament** elected in 1998. The PSP was launched in 1996 by a dissident faction of the **Socialist Party of Ukraine** (SPU). Under the leadership of Nataliya Vitrenko, the party called for a return to 'the radiant past' of the Soviet era, opposed privatization, particularly of 'national security enterprises', and advocated closer links with the **Russian Federation** and **Belarus**. The PSP obtained 11 seats in the March 1998 parliamentary elections and became part of the left-wing parliamentary opposition headed by the **Communist Party of Ukraine** (KPU). Standing for the PSP in the 1999 presidential elections, Vitrenko came a creditable fourth, with 11% of the first-round vote.

Leadership: Nataliya Vitrenko (Chair.).
Address: c/o Verkhovna Rada, M. Grushevskogo St 5, Kiev 01008.

Promyana National Trade Union

One of the smaller competing trade union centres in **Bulgaria**. Of Christian orientation, it has been affiliated to the World Confederation of Labour since 1999.
 Chair.: Pancho Mutafchiev.
 Address: 10A Graf Ignatiev St, Sofia 1000.
 Telephone: (2) 9863209.
 Fax: (2) 9866605.
 E-mail: npspromiana@intech.bg

Protestantism

Any Christian denomination founded on the principles of the 16th-century reformers who rejected the hierarchy and supremacy of the **Roman Catholic Church**. Started in Germany by Martin Luther, the Reformation, the adherents of which 'protested' against the Catholic Church, spread across western and northern Europe. Protestantism represented a two-pronged attack on mediaeval society, on the one hand affirming the political independence of European states from Rome, and on the other attempting to democratize and personalize Christianity for the laity. It served as both a revolutionary movement for greater democracy and at the same time as a means to increase the power of local rulers. The establishment of Protestant states in northern Europe and the rationalist development of the enlightenment stripped mainstream Protestantism of its antagonistic vein and pushed it firmly into the religious mainstream. It is now represented by many different denominations, the major ones of which in **eastern Europe** are Lutheranism and Calvinism. Eastern European countries with significant Protestant populations are **Estonia** (56% Lutheran), **Latvia** (55% Lutheran) and **Hungary** (20% Calvinist). Elsewhere in the region it is greatly overshadowed by Roman Catholicism and **Orthodox Christianity**.

PRS *see* **Albanian Republican Party**.

Prussia

Historically, the ethnically **German** state whose original centre was around Königsberg (now **Kaliningrad**) and the southern Baltic coast. The Kingdom of Prussia was a key player in European and **pan-German** politics from the 17th century and a key driving force in shaping the German unification process, culminating in 1870–71. Prussia's growth during this period saw it stretch across the economically important regions of Pomerania (along the Baltic coast) and Silesia, both of which are now integral parts of modern **Poland**. Prussia was effectively reintroduced into the European story in 1919 with the territorial changes imposed on Germany under the Treaty of **Versailles**. Parts of Pomerania were ceded to Poland, leaving the isolated German exclave of East Prussia as a focus for German nationalism and regional tensions. Following the mass resettlement of populations after the Second World War, most of what was Prussia is now indisputably Polish, with the remainder forming the **Russian** enclave of Kaliningrad.

PSD *and* **PSDR** *see* **Social Democrat Party**.

PSDS *see* **Social Democratic Party of Albania**.

PSL *see* **Polish Peasant Party**.

PSP *see* **Progressive Socialist Party**.

PSS *see* **Socialist Party of Albania**.

PSU *see* **Serbian Unity Party**.

Public Against Violence
Verejnosť proti násiliu (VPN)

Slovakia's sister party to the Czech **Civic Forum**, founded in November 1989 during the '**velvet revolution**'. Public Against Violence was a popular front drawing together various disparate political forces in opposition to the communist regime, to demand free elections. It fragmented after elections in 1990.

Purvanov, Georgi

President-elect of **Bulgaria**, the unexpected winner of presidential elections in November 2001 as candidate of the former communist **Bulgarian Socialist Party** (BSP), of which he had been Chairman for the preceding five years.

Georgi Sedefchov Purvanov was born in Sirishtnik in western Bulgaria on 28 June 1957. He served two years in the army from 1975 before studying history at Sofia University. After graduating in 1981 he joined the Bulgarian Communist Party (BKP) and worked as a researcher in the party's Institute of History, specializing in the emergence of the modern Bulgarian state at the turn of the 20th century.

He was elected to the recently-renamed BSP's Supreme Council in 1991 and championed the realignment of the party towards a more centrist approach in the newly democratic Bulgaria. The BSP was returned to power in elections in 1994, but faced increasing political and economic problems. Although his faction within the party gained the ascendancy and he was elected Party Chairman in December

1996, Purvanov realized how untenable the Government's position had become, and he and the new Prime Minister, Nikolai Dobrev, refused a further mandate, instead leading the BSP into opposition. From here he worked to transform the party in line with other social democratic parties elsewhere in Europe. Although he led the party's opposition to **NATO** bombing in **Yugoslavia** in 1999, the following year he pledged its support for Bulgaria's campaigns to join both NATO and the **European Union** (EU).

The personal prestige of the incumbent President Petar **Stoyanov**, who also had the full backing of the hugely popular and newly-elected Prime Minister Simeon **Saxecoburggotski**, made Purvanov's electoral victory in presidential elections in November 2001 all the more surprising. He is to be inaugurated as President on 22 January 2002. He has vowed to pursue his predecessor's policies of promoting Bulgaria's ties to the West, and has also expressed a desire to deepen relations with former allies to the east.

Address: Office of the President, 2 Dondukov Blvd, Sofia 1000.
Telephone: (2) 9833839.
E-mail: president@president.bg
Internet: www.president.bg

Putin, Vladimir

President of the **Russian Federation**.

Having spent the majority of his career away from the political limelight working as a KGB agent, Vladimir Putin was thrust to the forefront by the decision of the then President Boris **Yeltsin** in 1999 to make him Prime Minister. Initially in that role, and then as successor to Yeltsin in the presidency (to which he was elected on 26 March 2000), he has won guarded applause from the international community for his recentralization of the unwieldy Russian state. He is also closely identified with the ruthless prosecution of the war in **Chechnya**. This brought him considerable domestic popularity, but heavy international criticism on human rights grounds, at least until the re-evaluation of his regime in the light of its supportive attitude towards the US-led 'war on terrorism' in 2001.

Vladimir Vladimirovich Putin was born on 7 October 1952 in Leningrad (now **St Petersburg**). His grandfather had once been Lenin's cook, and from an early age Putin expressed a desire to serve the state by working as a spy. In 1975 he graduated from the law department of Leningrad's State University and was immediately recruited by the KGB. Little is known of the details of his secret service career other than that he spent most of his time in East Germany following his transfer there in 1984. By the time he left active service in 1990 he had reached the rank of Colonel. He became a reservist and returned to Leningrad where he began work as an adviser on international affairs to the State University and the City Council. He quickly made his name in city politics under his old law professor and mentor, the reformist Mayor Anatoly Sobchak. Putin became a Deputy Mayor and worked as the Chair of the Committee on Foreign Relations from 1994 to 1996. He instigated a series of successful export quotas designed to generate funds to tackle the city's acute shortages.

After Sobchak was defeated in mayoral elections in 1996, Putin moved to **Moscow**. The following year he was appointed Head of the Control Department, Deputy Manager of Property and Deputy Administrator for the Presidential Department; in the latter role he was an influential adviser to President Yeltsin on matters concerning Russia's regional policy. In July 1998 Yeltsin promoted him to head the KGB's successor agency, the **Federal Security Service** (FSB). As Director of the FSB, Putin's mandate was economic espionage and cracking down on illegal foreign trading. By March 1999 he was diversifying with the role of Secretary of the Security Council and was heavily involved in the dispute with the **North Atlantic Treaty Organization** over its military action over **Kosovo**. He was unexpectedly named as Chairman of the Government (Prime Minister) and endorsed as Yeltsin's preferred presidential heir that August. On his first day he set the tone of his political method: a hard line on separatism, no matter how critical the international response, with as little domestic upheaval as possible. **Muslim** rebels in **Dagestan** were crushed with remorseless swiftness while the economic policies of the previous Government were left largely untouched. The subsequent Russian military invasion of Chechnya proved extremely popular in Russia, despite initial media cynicism, and he was soon hailed as a national hero. Politically he was building an impressive support base. Although an independent himself, he could count on support in the Duma from the pro-Putin parties which recorded significant victories in the elections of late December 1999.

As part of Yeltsin's dramatic resignation announcement on New Year's Eve at the end of 1999, Putin was appointed Acting Head of State. His new position made him personally responsible for the Chechen war, which was signally failing to reach its apparently 'imminent' conclusion. A swift PR campaign to soften his public image was enough to repair any damage done in time for presidential elections in March 2000. He received just over 50% of the vote in the first round, leaving his nearest rival, **Communist Party** leader Gennadii **Zyuganov**, with less than 30%. Vladimir Putin was sworn in on 7 May 2000.

The Putin presidency, played out against a background of increasingly-improved prospects for the struggling Russian economy, has been notable for the consolidation of power at the central government level. Confronting the regional Governors and the business 'oligarchs', the power-brokers of the Yeltsin era, Putin has lived up to his reputation as a ruthlessly efficient political operator. On the other hand, his slowness in responding to the national mood over the *Kursk* submarine tragedy in August 2000, when he exposed himself to the charge of being cold and unfeeling, underlined that he has no special aptitude for winning public affection.

Vladimir Putin is married to the media-shy Lyudmila; they have two children.
Address: Office of the President, Kremlin, Moscow.
Telephone: (095) 2062511.

Fax: (095) 2065173.
E-mail: president@gov.ru
Internet: president.kremlin.ru

'Pyramid' investment schemes

Essentially fraudulent savings schemes offering very high interest rates, the collapse of which in **Albania** reduced the country to anarchy in 1997. A feature of several post-communist countries, 'pyramid' schemes became especially popular in Albania in the 1990s as a means of supplementing meagre salaries and pensions and as an alternative to the suspect banking system. Also providing a channel for money-laundering by corrupt elements, the schemes offered substantially higher interest rates (25% in some cases) than were obtainable elsewhere, but interest payments were in reality made from new deposits rather than from investment income.

The inevitable collapse of the Albanian schemes from late 1996, with losses totalling an estimated US $1,500m., impelled the **People's Assembly** in January 1997 to freeze their assets and to ban new schemes. However, faced with the loss of their life savings, tens of thousands of people took to the streets, fuelling an open insurrection and bringing about the effective demise of central government authority by March, particularly in the south. A central complaint of the protesters was that the Government of the **Democratic Party of Albania** (PDS) under President Sali Berisha had connived with the 'pyramid' scheme operators, notably Vefa Holdings, which had become Albania's largest private company.

Although the Berisha regime responded with a plan under which investors were supposed to recover 50–60% of their savings over time, the crisis led to the installation of a new Government headed by the **Socialist Party of Albania** (PSS) and to the resignation of Berisha in July 1997. In November 1997 a new PSS-dominated Assembly adopted constitutional amendments allowing the Government to audit and administer private companies whose activities were deemed to threaten the 'the economic interests of citizens'. In December 1999 the official liquidator of the schemes said that only about 6% of savings would be recovered by about 150,000 investors, whereas hundreds of thousands would recover nothing at all.

Pytalovo *see* **Abrene question**.

PZU *see* **Green Party of Ukraine**.

R

Račan, Ivica

Prime Minister of **Croatia**.

Ivica Račan heads the reformed communist **Social Democratic Party of Croatia** (SPH). A communist from his youth, he was elected President of the League of Communists of Croatia (SKH) in 1989. He transformed the SKH into the more moderate SPH in 1991, after Croatia's secession from the **Socialist Federal Republic of Yugoslavia** (SFRY). He has held a seat in the **Assembly** since 1990 and was appointed Prime Minister on 4 January 2000.

Born on 24 February 1944 in a Nazi labour camp in Germany, he was taken home to Croatia in 1945 and became actively involved as a teenager with the ruling **League of Communists of Yugoslavia** (SKJ) at the republican level. He graduated in law from Zagreb University in 1970, was on the Croatian SKH's Central Committee by 1974, and was part of the collective presidency of the SKJ at federal level from 1986 to 1989. In that year, having been elected President of the SKH, he led a walkout of regional delegates at the SKJ's 14th party congress in Belgrade—one of the decisive events in precipitating the collapse of the SFRY.

As a *de facto* leader of Croatia, he oversaw the holding of democratic elections in 1990 and won a seat as part of the opposition to the victorious **Croatian Democratic Union** (HDZ). He transformed the SKH into the SPH in 1991 and built a solid support base in opposition to the authoritarian HDZ. He was re-elected to the Assembly in 1995, 1997 and 2000, with the SPH becoming the largest single party in the Assembly in the 2000 poll. He was appointed Prime Minister on 4 January 2000. He has worked with President Stipe **Mesić** to curb the powers of the executive and complete the democratic transformation of Croatia. On 15 July 2001 he successfully defeated a vote of no confidence which had been prompted by his support for the UN's prosecution of Croatian war criminals (*see* **International Criminal Tribunal for the former Yugoslavia**).

Address: Office of the Prime Minister, Trg sv. Marka 2, 10000 Zagreb.
Telephone: (1) 4569201.
Fax: (1) 6303019.
Internet: www.vlada.hr

Radišić, Zivko

Member of the Presidency (Serb), **Bosnia and Herzegovina**.

Zivko Radišić is the leader of the **Socialist Party of the Serb Republic** (SPRS), which is directly linked to the Serb nationalist movement in **Yugoslavia**. Regarded as a relative moderate, he held government office in the Bosnian republic in the early 1980s, while it was still part of the **Socialist Federal Republic of Yugoslavia** (SFRY), but then devoted himself mainly to business interests throughout the next 10 turbulent years. He was elected as the Serb member of the tripartite Presidency on 13 September 1998 and has been its Chair twice.

Born on 15 August 1937 in Malo Palančište, near Prijedor in north-western Bosnia, he spent two and a half months with his family in a concentration camp run by the Croatian fascist Ustaša in 1942. From 1977 to 1982 he was Mayor of **Banja Luka**, then spent four years in the Bosnian republican Government, notably as Defence Minister. In the latter part of the 1980s, and through the break-up of the SFRY and the 1992–1995 Bosnian War, he headed the Čajavec holding company. In the first elections following the **Dayton Agreement**, held in September 1996, he stood for the presidency of the **Serb Republic** as the candidate of the People's Alliance for Peace and Progress, a grouping dominated by the SPRS, and finished in third place. His party's performance as part of a new alliance in the parliamentary election of September 1998 was strong enough to secure him the post of Serb member of the Bosnian presidency later that month, replacing archnationalist Momčilo Krajišnik. He was appointed Chair of the Presidency on 13 October 1998 under the rotation system. Replaced in his turn on 15 June 1999, he returned as Chair on 14 October 2000. His second term as effective Head of State ended on 14 June 2001.

Both of Zivko Radišić's sons fought in the Bosnian War, and one was injured.

Address: Office of the Presidency, Musala 5, 71000 Sarajevo.
Telephone: (33) 664941.
Fax: (33) 472491.

Ranković, Jovan

Federal Minister of Finance, **Yugoslavia**.

Jovan Ranković is a member of the nationalist **Democratic Party of Serbia** (DSS), headed by Federal President Vojislav **Koštunica**. A career economist, he was appointed Finance Minister on 24 July 2001.

Born in 1930, Ranković graduated in economics from the University of Belgrade. During a long academic career he taught at the universities of Belgrade, Kragujevac, Podgorica, Sarajevo and Zagreb. He is President of the Serbian Economists' Association. He was appointed to the Federal Cabinet as Finance Minister in July 2001.

Address: Federal Ministry of Finance, Nemanjina 22–26, 11000 Belgrade.

Telephone: (11) 658883.
Fax: (11) 646436.

Rasizade, Artur

Prime Minister of **Azerbaijan**.

Artur Tahir oglu Rasizade is a member of the post-communist **New Azerbaijan Party** (YAP) and was a Deputy Prime Minister at republican level before Azeri independence. He worked in the communist Azeri Government from 1978, becoming First Deputy Prime Minister in 1986. He was appointed Prime Minister in November 1996 after spending four years in opposition.

Born on 26 February 1935 in Gyanja, western Azerbaijan, he trained at the Azerbaijan Institute of Industry. He joined the Azerbaijan Institute of Oil Machine Construction in 1957 and had risen to the post of Director by 1973. In 1978 he became Deputy Head of the Azerbaijan State Planning Committee before joining the Central Committee of the Communist Party of Azerbaijan in 1981. He was appointed to the Cabinet as First Deputy Prime Minister in 1986 and retained this position until 1992—a year after the independence of Azerbaijan.

He spent four years in opposition after multi-party elections that year and joined the newly-formed YAP. Following the party's electoral success in 1995 he was appointed assistant to President Heydar **Aliyev** in the following year and reinstated as First Deputy Prime Minister in May 1996. After the fall of the incumbent Premier in July, Rasizade was appointed Acting Prime Minister, and was confirmed in the post on 26 November 1996. Real power is wielded by the President.

Artur Rasizade is married with one child.

Address: Office of the Prime Minister, Lermontov St 63, 370066 Baku.
Telephone: (12) 913165.
Fax: (12) 989786.

Republican Party of Armenia
Hayastani Hanrapetakan Kusaktsutyun (HHK)

A centre-right formation which became the main ruling party in **Armenia** in 1999.

The current HHK party was launched in mid-1998 as the result of a merger between the Yerkrapah Union of Veterans (of the **Nagorno-Karabakh** war) and the original HHK, which had been founded in May 1991 and had been part of the victorious Republican Bloc in the 1995 **National Assembly** elections. The Yerkrapah leader and then Defence Minister Vazgen Sarkissian was elected Chairman of the new HHK, which espoused free-market economic policies.

The HHK stood in the May 1999 Assembly elections in an alliance with the left-leaning **People's Party of Armenia** (HZhK) called the Unity Bloc (Miasnutiun), which won 55 of the 131 seats and 41.7% of the proportional vote. As leader of the

Riga

stronger partner, the HHK's Vazgen Sarkissian became Prime Minister of a Government in which smaller parties were also represented. However, in October 1999 he was one of eight political leaders assassinated by gunmen who invaded an Assembly debate. He was succeeded as Prime Minister by his younger brother, Aram Sarkissian, and as HHK Chairman by Andranik **Markarian**.

In May 2000 Aram Sarkissian was dismissed by President **Kocharian** and replaced by Markarian, who quickly faced opposition from the HHK's Yerkrapah wing, which formed a separate Assembly group strongly critical of the President. In August 2000 Aram Sarkissian announced his intention to form a new party with Yerkrapah members as its nucleus. Also undermining the Miasnutiun alliance in late 2000 was the increasing disaffection of the HZhK.

Leadership: Andranik Markarian (Chair.).
Address: 23 Tumanian Street, Yerevan.
Telephone: (1) 580031.
Fax: (1) 581259.

Republika Srpska *see* **Serb Republic**.

Riga

Capital city of **Latvia** and a major Baltic port situated near the mouth of the River Daugava on the northern coast. *Population*: 815,851 (1997 estimate).

An ancient Liv settlement, Riga was founded by the Bishop of **Livonia** in 1201 and was converted to Christianity. The privileges of the bishopric granted some freedom to the city, which joined the Hanseatic League in 1282. In the 1520s the country converted to Lutheranism (*see* **Protestantism**). Under Polish rule from 1581, and Swedish rule from 1621, Riga was granted self-government until ceded to **Russia** by the Treaty of Nystad in 1721. Riga was the capital city of independent Latvia from 1918 until its Soviet occupation in 1940. Under German occupation from 1941, much of the old town centre was destroyed before it was reoccupied by the **Soviet Union** as the capital of the Latvian Soviet Socialist Republic from 1944 until independence was regained in 1991.

Riga Stock Exchange
Rigas fondu birža (RFB)

The exchange in **Latvia** founded originally in 1816, which was reopened after the communist period in December 1993. Trading began in July 1995. The RFB has been intimately involved in the privatization process and most of the 70 companies listed have emerged from this process. In 1999 a memorandum of understanding was signed with the **National Stock Exchange** of **Lithuania** and the **Tallinn Stock Exchange** with a view to increasing co-operation.

President: Guntars Kokorevics.
Address: Doma Lauk. 6, Riga 1885.
Telephone: 7212431.
Fax: 7229411.
E-mail: rfb@rfb.lv
Internet: www.rfb.lv

Riga, Treaties of

Two peace treaties signed by the **Soviet Union** with neighbouring countries. The first, signed with **Latvia** on 11 August 1920 at the conclusion of the brief war between the two countries, included the recognition of Latvian independence by the Soviet Government (later revoked) and the cession of the **Abrene** region to Latvia. The second was signed with **Poland** on 18 March 1921 after the defeat of a Polish invasion of **Russia**. It fixed the two countries' border mid-way between the mediaeval Polish border far to the east and its modern edge to the west. The second treaty was revoked with the division of Poland between Soviet and Nazi forces in 1939 (*see* **Nazi-Soviet Pact**). *See also* Treaties of **Tartu**.

Riigikogu *see* **State Assembly (Estonia)**.

Roma

A nomadic people of traditionally-mixed ethnicity who arrived in Europe from the Indian sub-continent in waves of migration beginning in the 9th century. They are also known in English as the Gypsies, a name generally considered to be derogatory and which is derived from the misconception that they originated in Egypt. As a nomadic people they spread across the European continent and have been subject to serious discrimination and outright abuse ever since. As a language Romani is most closely related to Punjabi (Hindi) and three main dialects exist in Europe: Romani in the west, Lomarven in **central Europe** and Domari in the east. There is no official written form. The language is in decline, as a large proportion of Roma have adopted the language of fellow minorities in their home countries. The Roma are divided into four main tribes or 'nations'—the Kalderash, Machavaya, Lovari and Churari—and various sub-tribes. Romani culture has been generally eroded owing to assimilation into the fringe of other European cultures. Loyalty to the extended family remains its cornerstone.

Throughout history the Roma have been subject to violent discrimination. They were often enslaved in feudal societies. Following the end of Romani slavery in the mid-19th century, great numbers joined other disfavoured groups of European society in emigrating to the New World. One of the most systematic persecutions of

Roma was in the Nazi Holocaust when an estimated half a million were liquidated in death camps across occupied territories.

Persecution continued after the Second World War on a local level, with many regional authorities reflecting popular prejudice in open discrimination. Often Roma have been forced to take on a settled lifestyle so as to participate in the industrialization of the European economies. To this day the Roma are seriously maligned as a minority across **eastern Europe**, with poor access to education and employment, and are targeted in violent attacks by the extreme right. Attempts to organize better collective representation resulted in a resolution to press for greater rights at the most recent of the (infrequent) World Romani Congresses, held in **Prague** in 2001. However, the division of Romani society into sub-tribes has greatly hindered collective action.

Of the roughly 12 million Roma living worldwide, around 34% (4 million) reside in eastern Europe, although their exact number is hard to pin down, owing to fear of persecution and wholesale integration with other minorities. Of these populations the most significant are the 1.8 million Roma resident in **Romania**, where they are officially known as Rroma to distinguish from Romanians (official census information put the figure at only 409,723 in 1992). Up to half of adult Rroma are unemployed and 40% of their children fail to attend the first years of schooling. They are also subject to frequent and poorly-investigated violence.

Other major populations are 500,000 in **Hungary**, and communities of 300,000 in **Slovakia**, **Bulgaria** and the **Czech Republic**. In all cases official discrimination stopped after the fall of communism in 1989 but continues in entrenched public and local government attitudes.

Roman Catholic Church

The dominant Christian denomination centred on the Vatican City in Rome. Roman Catholicism (often just called Catholicism, taking its name from catholic, meaning 'universal') is the largest single religious denomination in the world and is prevalent over much of Europe, particularly in western and **central Europe**. It chiefly differs from other Christian Churches in its belief in the primacy of the Bishop of Rome (Pope) as the 'Vicar of Christ'. It was divided from **Orthodox Christianity** in the 'Great Schism' of 1054 (a split which, more than 900 years later, formed the basis of one of the principal divisions in **Yugoslavia**), and from **Protestantism** during the 16th-century Reformation. The cult of the Saints and particularly the Virgin Mary are very strong. The role of priests is central to the religion. Unlike in most other Christian denominations, Roman Catholic priests (only men) take a vow of celibacy. The election of the Polish Cardinal Karol Wojtyła as Pope **John Paul II** in 1978 (the first Polish Pope ever, and the first non-Italian pontiff for over 400 years) brought Catholicism closer to the communist-dominated east and helped link it to pro-democracy movements such as Poland's

Solidarity. Pope John Paul II has also attempted to breach the divide between Catholicism and Orthodoxy, making historic visits to Greece and **Ukraine** in 2001.

The connection between spiritual and temporal power and the Church's inherent conservatism have led to the formation of Catholic-oriented right-of-centre political parties in many central European countries, often called Christian Democrats or People's parties. Catholic political activity and influence often attracted repression under communist rule, although the Church's popularity in some countries led to efforts to integrate it into the political mainstream.

Despite the close association of much of **eastern Europe** with Orthodoxy, there are some 62 million Catholics in the region with the largest congregations in **Poland** (36 million—94% of the population), **Hungary** (6 million—64%) and the **Czech Republic** (4 million—39%). Countries with majority Catholic populations are **Croatia**, Hungary, **Lithuania**, Poland, **Slovakia** and **Slovenia**. All Roman Catholic Churches are subordinate to the papacy, as is the **Uniate Church**.

Romania

An independent republic in south-eastern Europe, bounded by Ukraine to the north, Moldova to the north-east, Bulgaria to the south, the Federal Republic of Yugoslavia (Serbia) to the south-west, Hungary to the north-west, and the Black Sea on its south-eastern coastline. Administratively, the country is divided into 40 counties and one municipality.

Area: 237,500 sq km; *capital*: **Bucharest**; *population*: 22.4m (2001 estimate), comprising **Romanians** 89.1%, **Hungarians** 8.9%, **Germans** 0.4%, **Ukrainians Serbs**, **Croats**, **Russians**, Turks and **Roma** 1.6% (although the Roma probably comprise a significantly larger percentage of the population—possibly even as high as 8%—as their numbers are frequently underestimated in censuses owing to the method of designation and the high proportion of this group which do not register); *official language*: Romanian; *religion*: **Romanian Orthodox** 70%, **Roman Catholic** 6%, **Protestant** 6%, unaffiliated 18%.

Legislative authority is vested in the bicameral **Parliament** (Parlamentul), which consists of the upper 140-member Senate (Senatul) and the lower 345-member Chamber of Deputies (Camera Deputatilor), which includes 18 seats reserved for minorities. Members of both houses are directly elected for a four-year term by a system of proportional representation subject to a 5% threshold and are barred from holding ministerial office (following the French system of executive–legislative separation, which provides for a strong presidency). Executive power is vested in the President, who is directly elected for a four-year term and who appoints the Prime Minister.

History: Once part of the Roman province of Dacia, and then subjected to successive waves of invasions and foreign domination, present-day Romania evolved from the union of the two Danubian principalities of **Wallachia** and Moldavia in the 1850s. These principalities had emerged in the 14th century and subsequently came under nominal Ottoman rule from the 1500s. Romania was recognized as an independent state in 1878 (by the Treaty of Berlin) and became a kingdom under the Hohenzollern dynasty in 1881. After Romania had fought with the Western powers in the First World War, it was rewarded under the post-war settlement by the creation of a **Greater Romania** which included **Bessarabia** (formerly under **Russian** rule) and **Bukovina** and **Transylvania** (from the dismembered Austro-Hungarian Empire). In 1938 King Carol II established a royal dictatorship, abolishing the democratic Constitution of 1923.

Having been forced in 1940, under the second of the so-called **Vienna Awards** (and as agreed in the 1939 **Nazi-Soviet Pact**), to cede Bessarabia and northern Bukovina to the **Soviet Union** and northern Transylvania to **Hungary**, Romania then sided with Nazi Germany during the Second World War until 1944, when the fascist regime of Ion Antonescu was ousted prior to Soviet occupation. Under the post-war treaties Romania recovered northern Transylvania (so that ethnic **Hungarians** in Romania formed post-war Europe's largest single minority group), but lost Bessarabia and northern Bukovina to the Soviet Union and southern **Dobruja** to **Bulgaria**. A communist-led Government won elections in 1946 and the Romanian People's Republic was declared in 1947, following the abdication of King Michael. Having adopted a Soviet-style Constitution, Romania joined the **Warsaw Pact** in 1955. Nicolae **Ceauşescu** became First Secretary of the Romanian Communist Party (PCR) in 1965 (replacing Gheorghe Gheorghiu-Dej) and was made President of the Republic in 1974. Under Ceauşescu, Romania adopted an independent foreign policy (refusing, for example, to participate in the Warsaw Pact invasion of **Czechoslovakia** in 1968), while maintaining a repressive and rigid orthodox line at home.

In 1989 internal opposition to economic austerity and human rights abuses led to the violent overthrow and execution of Ceauşescu (along with his wife) in December. A National Salvation Front (FSN) formed a provisional Government, which abolished the communist monopoly of power and dissolved the feared Securitate secret police, proceeding to win about two-thirds of the vote in free elections in May 1990. Its leader, Ion **Iliescu** (a former communist official), was elected President with over 85% of the vote and Petre Roman was appointed Prime Minister. Roman resigned the premiership in September 1991 following serious civil unrest, and a national referendum the following December endorsed a new Constitution providing for political pluralism, guaranteed human rights and a commitment to a market economy.

In 1992 the FSN split, with the pro-Iliescu wing of the party (opposed to the rapid economic change) forming the Democratic National Salvation Front, which quickly became the Social Democracy Party of Romania (PDSR). Iliescu was re-elected to the presidency in September 1992, and concurrent parliamentary elections returned a PDSR-led minority Government under Nicolae Vacaroiu. In 1994 the ultra-nationalist Romanian National Unity Party (PUNR) was brought into the ruling coalition, with support from the extreme right-wing **Greater Romania Party**

(PRM) and the neo-communist Socialist Party of Labour (PSM). However, serious differences between the parties developed, resulting in the collapse of the coalition arrangement by September 1996.

A dramatic change in the political landscape took place in November 1996 as the opposition Democratic Convention of Romania (CDR), a centre-right alliance headed by the **Christian Democratic National Peasants' Party** (PNȚCD), successfully contested concurrent presidential and parliamentary elections. The CDR leader, Emil Constantinescu, won a clear second-round victory over President Iliescu, and the alliance secured nearly 30% of the vote in the legislative polling. A new administration was formed, led by Victor Ciorbea of the PNȚCD and including representatives of the **National Liberal Party** (PNL), the **Hungarian Democratic Union of Romania** (UDMR) and the Social Democratic Union (USD), consisting of the **Democratic Party** (PD) and the Romanian Social Democratic Party (PSDR).

A radical economic reform programme and anti-corruption drive were introduced in 1997, but in February 1998 the USD withdrew from the coalition, precipitating the resignation of Ciorbea the following month and his replacement as Prime Minister by Radu Vasile of the PNȚCD. The reconstituted centre-right coalition, despite persistent internal divisions, subsequently survived political challenges from left-wing and nationalist parties but became deeply unpopular against a background of deteriorating economic and social conditions and extreme industrial unrest. Vasile resigned in December 1999 and was succeeded by Mugur Isarescu (non-party), hitherto Governor of the **National Bank of Romania**.

Latest elections: The political pendulum again swung sharply in the November–December 2000 presidential and parliamentary elections, as the centre-right was heavily defeated by the new **Social Democratic Pole of Romania**, an alliance of the PDSR, the PSDR and the small Humanist Party of Romania (PUR). Iliescu regained the presidency for the PDSR, winning 36.4% in the first round and 66.8% in the second, in which his opponent was Corneliu Vadim Tudor of the far-right PRM, who had taken second place in the first round with 28.3%, benefiting from a strong vein of popular disenchantment with both the left and the centre-right.

In the parliamentary contest, the Pole became substantially the largest formation, winning a total of 155 seats (PDSR 142, PSDR 7, PUR 6) with 36.6% of the vote, while the PRM took 84 (19.5%), the PD 31 (7.0%), the PNL 30 (6.9%), the UDMR 27 (6.8%) and 18 ethnic minority parties one seat each. In the simultaneous Senate elections, the Pole parties won 65 seats (PDSR 60, PUR 4, PSDR 1), the PRM 37, the PD 13, the PNL 13 and the UDMR 12.

Recent developments: In December 2000 the Pole alliance formed a minority Government under the premiership of Adrian **Nastase**, who secured qualified pledges of external support from the PD, the PNL and the UDMR, with the particular aim of excluding the ascendant PRM from any policy-making role. The new administration undertook to continue the pro-market economic reforms of its predecessor, with an admixture of greater concern for their social consequences, and to pursue Romania's aspiration to join the **European Union** (EU). It introduced new legislation to strengthen the language rights of ethnic Hungarians and other minorities, thereby triggering a national campaign of opposition by the PRM, while strains quickly appeared in the Government's fragile understanding with the PD and the PNL. In June 2001 the PDSR and the PSDR merged to form the **Social Democrat Party**, with Nastase at its head. In the same month the Government, despite the potential for public controversy, moved to bring Romania in line with western Europe in lifting the longstanding ban on homosexuality (Article 200 of the penal code). At the close of the year Nastase overcame a vote of no confidence in his Government brought by opposition parties, claiming it was obstructing economic reform.

International relations and defence: Romania is a member of the United Nations, the **Organization for Security and Co-operation in Europe**, the **Council of Europe** and the **Danube Commission**, also becoming a founder member of the **Organization of the Black Sea Economic Co-operation** in 1992 and joining the **Central European Initiative** in 1996 and the **Central European Free Trade Area** in 1997. Successive Governments have sought closer integration with the West, actively pursuing membership of the **North Atlantic Treaty Organization** (with which Romania co-operates in the **Partnership for Peace** programme) and more urgently of the EU. Having applied for EU membership in 1995, Romania was accepted as an official candidate in December 1999 and formal negotiations opened in February 2000, although Romania remained the most economically backward of the ex-communist applicants (*see* **Romania, economy**).

In 1996 Romania signed a treaty of reconciliation with Hungary, under which the latter formally renounced any claim to parts of Transylvania, while Romania guaranteed rights to its ethnic Hungarian population. Economic and military co-operation accords were reached with **Ukraine** in 1997 and a treaty was signed agreeing to try to settle differences over territorial issues and minority rights. Attempts to sign a new Romanian-Russian treaty have made little progress since the end of communist rule in Moscow. A basic treaty initialled with neighbouring **Moldova** in 2000 remained unratified by 2002, in part because of its ambiguity about the goal espoused by some Romanian parties of reunification with the ethnic **Romanian** majority of Moldova.

Romania's defence budget for 1999 amounted to some US $600m., equivalent to about 1.8% of GDP. The armed forces at the end of 2000 numbered about 207,000 personnel, including those serving under compulsory conscription of 12 months, while reservists totalled an estimated 470,000.

Romania, economy

A formerly centrally-planned economy making a slow and difficult transition to a free-market system.

GNP: US $36,355m. (2000); *GNP per capita*: $1,670 (2000); *GDP at PPP*: $287,400m. (1999); *GDP per capita at PPP*: $3,900 (1999); *exports*: $10,367m.

(2000); *imports*: $11,868m. (2000); *currency*: leu (plural: lei; US $1=L31,745 at the end of December 2001).

In 1999 industry accounted for 31% of GDP, agriculture for 16% and services for 53%. About 41% of the land is arable, 3% under permanent crops, 21% permanent pasture and 29% forests and woodland. The main crops are grain, grapes for wine, sugar beet, sunflowers and vegetables, and there is important animal husbandry and also timber extraction. The main mineral resources are petroleum, natural gas, hard coal and brown coal (lignite), iron ore and bauxite. Onshore oil production was severely affected by a huge earthquake in the main producing area in 1977, but there has more recently been increasing offshore exploitation. Among the main industries are mining, petroleum production and refining, metal-working, timber extraction, machine-building and food processing. The main energy sources have been petroleum, natural gas and coal and hydroelectricity, with important imports of petroleum for electricity generation. Romania's first nuclear power station unit was opened in December 1996, and the nuclear sector currently provides some 10% of the country's energy production.

Romania's main exports by value are textiles and footwear (33% in 1998), metals and metal products (19%), machinery and equipment (9%), mineral and fuels (6%). Principal imports include machinery and transport equipment (23% in 1998), fuels and minerals (14%), chemicals (9%) and food and agricultural goods (8%). Italy took about 22% of Romania's exports in 2000, followed by Germany (16%) and France (7%). Italy was the supplier of 19% of Romania's imports in 2000, with Germany providing 15% and the **Russian Federation** 9%.

With the overthrow of **Ceauşescu** at the end of 1989, the inefficiencies and corruption of the former regime meant that the new administration was faced with severe problems in seeking to restore order, while external support was difficult to secure. The change of Government accelerated the decline of the heavy industrial sector created by Ceauşescu, largely at the expense of traditional agriculture, in an abortive effort to make Romania a key industrial nation. Simmering social problems and deteriorating living standards stimulated massive strike actions, particularly by coal miners fearful of the contraction of their inefficient industry and consequential job losses. The post-communist Governments introduced successive programmes to reform the economy, but for the first six years these were relatively cautious and not fully implemented.

GDP fell sharply in the early 1990s but incomes were allowed to rise, so that inflation in the 1991–93 period was at or above 200% per annum. Government measures brought the inflation rate down to 28% in 1995, in which substantial real GDP growth of 7% was achieved, followed by 4% expansion in 1996, although inflation doubled to 57%. The situation deteriorated under the centre-right Government elected in late 1996, with GDP contracting by 6.1% in 1997, 5.4% in 1998 and 3.2% in 1999, as inflation rose to over 150% in 1997 before being only partially curbed to a rate of 55% in 1999. Officially-recorded unemployment also rose, from 6.5% at the end of 1996 to 11.5% at the end of 1999. The appointment of the Central Bank Governor as Prime Minister in December 1999 resulted in some improvement in 2000, in which GDP growth of about 2% was achieved and exports increased by 25% in dollar terms, although inflation remained high at 41% and about a third of the population were living below the poverty line.

Although the left-wing Government elected in late 2000 pledged that it would pursue the pro-market economic reform programme, its collateral promise that every effort would be made to minimize adverse social consequences raised doubts internationally about whether it would display the necessary rigour. In February 2001 the **International Monetary Fund** confirmed that Romania would receive no further credits under a standby facility negotiated in mid-1999 until real progress had been made on the economic reform programme. The Government's budget for 2001 provided for a fiscal deficit of 3.8% of GDP and projected GDP growth of 4% and an inflation rate of 25%.

Romania in mid-1997 became the 6th member of the **Central European Free Trade Area** (CEFTA), as a stepping-stone to its goal of membership of the **European Union** (EU), for which it had applied in 1995. In December 1999 Romania was accepted as an official candidate for EU membership, on which formal negotiations opened in February 2000. In November 2000, however, the European Commission identified Romania as the least advanced of the ex-communist applicants towards meeting EU accession requirements.

In the early post-communist years some initiatives were announced on privatization of state-owned enterprises, but little actual progress was made. Among the factors inhibiting industrial disposals were continuing bureaucratic lethargy and government reluctance to antagonize key elements of the workforce. New efforts towards 'realistic' privatization and industrial restructuring were announced in 1998 but again were subject to change and delay in the face of overall economic deterioration.

Although by 2000 some 4,000 small and medium-sized enterprises had been privatized (and the private sector accounted for 60% of GDP), the heavy industrial sector, textiles, utilities and communications remained largely under state ownership. In February 2001, therefore, the incoming Government announced an extensive new privatization programme under which over 60 larger concerns would be sold off as quickly as possible, although in such a way as not to damage 'social equilibrium'.

Also in February 2001, a controversial new restitution law was promulgated under which properties nationalized between 1945 and 1989 could be recovered by their former owners. However, fierce criticism of the law both from former owners and from present-day occupants suggested that it was unlikely to be any more effective than a 1995 restitution law under which only about 1% of an estimated 300,000 eligible properties had been recovered by former owners.

Romanian Development Agency
Agenţia Româna de Dezvoltare

Promotes foreign investment in **Romania**'s industry. Founded in 1991.
President: Sorin Fodoreanu.
Address: Blvd Magheru 7, 70161 Bucharest.
Telephone: (1) 3122886.
Fax: (1) 3120371.

Romanian Orthodox Church

An autocephalous branch of the **Orthodox Christian** Church based in **Romania**. By tradition Christianity was first brought to the modern Romanian region by the Apostle St Andrew in the 1st century, and from then the religion was spread, initially in **Dobruja**, by the occupying Romans and later by the Byzantines. By the 6th century Dobruja, known as Scythia Minor, was designated as a semi-autonomous metropolitan province within the Byzantine Church. Although political control of Romania has changed hands over the centuries, Christianity remained the main religion. Links with neighbouring **Slavic** Churches were reinforced by the use of Church Slavonic from the 10th to the 17th century. The Romanian states of **Wallachia** and Moldavia were recognized as autocephalous metropolitan sees in 1359 and 1401 respectively, while the Church in the **Hungarian**-dominated provinces of **Transylvania** achieved recognition from the 16th century. The three Churches remained close, despite the conversion of many Transylvanian Romanians to the **Uniate Church** under Habsburg rule. The Wallachian and Moldavian Churches were unified into a single Romanian Church in the late 19th century, recognized as a full Patriarchate in 1925. Under communist rule over 1,000 priests were arrested or deported and the Church was labelled a 'cult'. The majority of Uniate Church followers returned to the Orthodox congregation after 1948. The Church has regained some of its social importance in the last few decades.

Patriarch Teoctist was elected in November 1986.

Romanian royal family—Hohenzollern-Sigmaringen dynasty

The family which gave rise to the hereditary monarchs of **Romania** from 1881 to 1947. The current claimant to the Romanian throne is Mihai (Michael) Hohenzollern-Sigmaringen, who has spent most of his life as a businessman based in the UK and Switzerland. The dynasty was founded by the German Prince Karl of Hohenzollern-Sigmaringen who was proclaimed King Carol in 1881. The last reigning monarch was Michael himself. Having been proclaimed King as a small child in 1927, he was deposed by his own father in 1930, but became King for the second time at the age of 19 when his father (Carol II) abdicated in 1940. In 1944 Michael headed the coup which overthrew the pro-Nazi regime of Gen. Ion

Antonescu. The communist regime established in the post-war period forced him to abdicate in December 1947 and he fled to the West, initially to the UK. Following the overthrow of the **Ceauşescu** Government, he attempted to return to the post-communist Romania, but was initially deported and faced hostility from the leftist regime of President Ion **Iliescu**. However, he returned in 1992, had his citizenship and passport restored in 1997, and was granted the same rights as other former Heads of State in mid-2001. In recent years he has lobbied for the return of royal property confiscated by the State. His heir apparent is his eldest daughter Princess Margareta.

Romanian Social Democratic Party see **Social Democrat Party**.

Romanians

An Indo-European people indigenous to the fertile banks of the eastern end of the Danube and now comprising the majority of people in the modern state of **Romania**. Very few Romanians live abroad, with around 300,000 (divided between Romanians and **Moldovans**) in **Ukraine**, 35,000 in northern **Serbia** and 10,000 in **Hungary**. Romanians are ethnically and linguistically identical to the neighbouring Moldovans, differing only in that they use the Latin alphabet rather than the **Cyrillic alphabet**. Both are descended from ancient **Vlach** communities.

The Romanian language is derived ultimately from Latin and is not dissimilar to modern Italian. The region converted to Christianity at the time of the Roman Empire. A majority of modern Romanians practise **Orthodox Christianity**. Despite their shared creed the Romanians foster a sense of cultural isolation amidst the predominantly Slavic countries around them (see **Slavic peoples**).

Romanov dynasty

The royal dynasty which ruled **Russia** from 1613 until the first Russian Revolution of March 1917. Key members of the dynasty include: its founder Michael Romanov, Peter the Great who transformed the Kingdom into an Empire in 1721, Alexander II who abolished serfdom in 1861 and the final Tsar, Nicholas II, who abdicated in 1917 and was infamously murdered, along with his entire family and retinue, in Yekaterinburg on 17 July 1918. The Bolshevik Government maintained that the execution had never been officially sanctioned, and was treated as a crime. Remains which were generally accepted to be the bones of the Romanov family, exhumed from their unmarked forest grave in 1991, were reinterred in July 1998.

ROMPRES
(Romanian National News Agency)

The official state news agency of **Romania**. Rompres was created in 1990 but traces its lineage back to the Romanian Telegraph Agency (Ruomagence) which was founded as a government mouthpiece in 1889. Rompres was reorganized under state control after the emergence of democracy in Romania but prides itself on its constitutional independence.
General Manager: Constantin Badea.
Address: Piaţa Presei Libere 1, 71341 Bucharest.
Telephone: (1) 2228340.
Fax: (1) 2220089.
E-mail: webmaster@rompres.ro
Internet: www.rompres.ro

ROP *see* **Movement for the Reconstruction of Poland**.

Rop, Anton

Minister of Finance, **Slovenia**.

Anton Rop is an independent. A member of the Cabinet between February 1996 and June 2000, he returned to government as Finance Minister on 1 December 2000.

Born in **Ljubljana** on 27 December 1960, he graduated in Economics from the University of Ljubljana in 1984. He became an Assistant Director of the Slovene Institute for Macroeconomic Analysis and Development in 1985. From 1992 he advised the newly independent Government on economic policy and was appointed State Secretary for Privatization at the Ministry of Economic Relations and Development in 1993. He was appointed as Minister of Labour, Family and Social Affairs on 7 February 1996, holding this post until 7 June 2000. He was reappointed to the new Government in December 2000.
Address: Ministry of Finance, Župančičeva 3, 1000 Ljubljana.
Telephone: (1) 4785211.
Fax: (1) 4785655.
Internet: www.gov.si/mf

Rosoboronexport

The state-run arms-exporting monopoly which accounts for almost 90% of defence-related exports from the **Russian Federation**. Rosoboronexport was created from the amalgamation of the two leading state-run arms exporters, Rosvooruzenie and Promexport, in November 2000. It has built on previous

experience in marketing and selling complete defence systems around the world. Exports include everything from tanks and warships, to fighter planes and space rockets and even general purpose vehicles and handheld weapons.
Address: 27/3 Stromynka Street, Moscow 107076.
Telephone: (095) 9646140.
Fax: (095) 9632613.
Internet: www.rusarm.ru

Rosspirtprom

The state-run brewery and management company established to centralize and regulate the production of alcohol, principally vodka, in the **Russian Federation**. Rosspirtprom, often referred to as the 'alcohol ministry', was created within months of President Vladimir **Putin**'s inauguration in mid-2000, and by December 2001 had taken control of many regional distilleries and vodka producers. However, a majority of producers remain independent and the entire industry has become riddled with illegal producers. Rosspirtprom is headed by Putin loyalist Sergei Zivenko.
Director-General: Sergei Zivenko.
Telephone: (095) 2494308.
E-mail: rsp@rosspirtprom.ru
Internet: www.rosspirtprom.ru

Rouble zone

The zone, originally comprising all 15 countries of the former **Soviet Union**, within which the rouble continued to operate as a single currency for the initial period after the break-up of the Soviet Union in December 1991. This was initially a *de facto* arrangement, there being no other currency arrangements in place in the countries concerned. The **Central Bank of the Russian Federation** was the sole issuer of cash roubles, and the Central Banks of the new States issued money substitutes tied to the rouble's value at 1:1 parity. All countries were also entitled to issue credit within prescribed limits, and in practice did so without observing those limits.

Fundamental disagreements between the 15 countries about the desirable pace of economic reform, together with their need to make radical changes in the pattern of economic activity, undermined the case for retaining a single currency. Payments and settlements in roubles effectively meant that large price increases for fuel and raw materials fed through directly in the form of cost inflation in the various post-Soviet economies. The **Baltic States**, led by **Estonia** in June 1992, were the first to leave the rouble zone and establish their own currencies. In October 1992, eight **Commonwealth of Independent States** (CIS) participants—**Armenia, Belarus,** Kazakhstan, Kyrgyzstan, **Moldova, Russian Federation,**

Uzbekistan and **Ukraine**—signed an agreement on a single currency system and co-ordinated monetary policy. However, this idea was not implemented, and more countries issued their own national currencies. Ukraine in November 1992 took this step by way of the intermediate stage of issuing coupons, moving subsequently to a full national currency, a route also followed by others such as **Georgia** and Uzbekistan. Also, by mid-1993, the Russian Federation was increasingly concerned that its own ability to control monetary policy was weakened by the fact that the rouble remained the currency of other CIS States.

The rouble zone had thus become to a large extent defunct by mid-1993. In July of that year, following the Russian Federation's own currency reform, six countries—Armenia, Belarus, Kazakhstan, Russian Federation, Tajikistan and Uzbekistan—signed an agreement on setting up a new-style rouble zone, but this was never implemented, the Russians alienating the other potential participants by insisting that all gold and convertible currency reserves from rouble zone countries should be held in **Moscow**.

Attempts to use the CIS structure as a route to monetary union, with a Central Bank set up in 1993 and a payments union created nominally in 1994, have flown in the face of the increasing insistence on national-level control of the economy. Tajikistan, the last country to introduce its own currency, used the Tajik rouble from May 1995 until 30 October 2000 when its new currency, the somoni, was introduced. The rouble remained legal tender until 1 April 2001.

In Belarus under President **Lukashenka**, however, the trend has been in the other direction, towards reunification with the Russian Federation, and a treaty on the creation of a rouble zone involving the two countries was ratified by the Belarus **National Assembly** in 2001.

RS see **Serb Republic.**

Rukh see **Popular Movement of Ukraine.**

Rupel, Dimitrij

Minister of Foreign Affairs, **Slovenia**.

Dimitrij Rupel is a member of the centre-left **Liberal Democracy of Slovenia** (LDS). A prominent member of the intellectual opposition to the communist-era Government, he was branded a dissident, spending 12 years abroad, teaching at universities in Canada and the USA, before returning in 1990 to join the campaign for Slovenia's independence from the **Socialist Federal Republic of Yugoslavia** (SFRY). Foreign Minister in Slovenia's first post-communist Government in 1991–93, he was most recently reappointed to the post on 1 December 2000.

Born on 7 April 1946 in **Ljubljana**, he graduated in world literature and sociology from the University of Ljubljana in 1970. He went on to pursue his education in various universities in the West, including a doctorate in sociology in 1976 from Brandeis University, USA. Having come to the attention of the communist authorities for dissent during his compulsory service in the Yugoslav army, he was banned from teaching in the SFRY and travelled instead to Canada where he taught at Queen's University from 1977. He moved south to the USA to teach at the New York New School for Social Research in 1985, and across to Cleveland State University in 1989. He was a prolific writer of anti-communist articles and texts and cofounded the opposition *Nova Revija* magazine which published the 'Slovene National Programme' in 1987—the basis of the popular pro-democracy May Declaration of 1989. In 1990 he returned to his native land and helped form the Democratic Opposition of Slovenia. Foreign Minister at independence in 1991, he left the Cabinet to sit in the **National Assembly** from 1993, and then became Mayor of Ljubljana at the end of 1994 following the first direct elections to that office. After three years as Ambassador to the USA from 1997, he returned to Slovenia to rejoin the Government as Foreign Minister in February 2000, and has remained in the post with a two-month hiatus during October–December 2000.

Address: Ministry of Foreign Affairs, Prešernova cesta 25, 1000 Ljubljana.
Telephone: (1) 4782000.
Fax: (1) 4782340.
E-mail: info.mzz@gov.si
Internet: www.gov.si/mzz

RusAl *see* **Russian Aluminium**.

Rusnok, Jiří

Minister of Finance, **Czech Republic**.

Jiří Rusnok is a member of the leftist **Czech Social Democratic Party** (ČSSD). He is a career politician and has worked in various government economic departments. He was appointed Finance Minister on 14 April 2001.

Born on 16 October 1960 in Ostrava-Vítkovice, he graduated from the Prague School of Economics in 1984 and went straight to work at the Central Planning Commission. By 1992 he had progressed to Head of Department of Social Strategy at the Ministry of Social Planning. From 1992 to 1998 he acted as adviser and Head of the Social and Economic Section of the **Czech-Moravian Confederation of Trade Unions**. He joined the ČSSD in January 1998 and was appointed to the Cabinet as Deputy Minister of Labour and Social Affairs in August. He was promoted to Minister of Finance in a reshuffle in April 2001.

Jiří Rusnok is married and has two children.

Address: Ministry of Finance, Lětenská 15, 11810 Prague 1.
Telephone: (2) 57041111.
Fax: (2) 57042788.

E-mail: podatelna@mfcr.cz
Internet: www.mfcr.cz

Russian Aluminium (RusAl)

A large private company based in the **Russian Federation** which produces and exports aluminium products.

Founded in March 2000 through the merger of the Sibirsky Aluminium and Sibneft, RusAl has operations across the world, most recently purchasing a 25-year contract to operate a bauxite mine in Guinea from 2001. It is now the world's second-largest producer of primary aluminium products.

General Director: Oleg V. Deripaska.
Address: 13/1 Nikoloyamskaya Street, Moscow 109240.
Telephone: (095) 7205170.
Fax: (095) 7284912.
E-mail: press-center@rusal.ru
Internet: www.rusal.com

Russian Federal Property Fund

Founded in 1997 to ensure consistency in the privatization process and to implement privatization legislation.

Address: Nikolskii per. 9, Moscow.
Telephone: (095) 2061525.
Fax: (095) 9238877.

Russian Federation
Rossiyskaya Federatsiya

The Russian federal state, in existence in its current sovereign form since the demise in 1991 of the **Soviet Union**, of which the previous Russian Soviet Federative Socialist Republic (RSFSR) had been the largest element.

The Russian Federation, whose territory is identical with that of the former RSFSR, spans north-eastern Europe and northern Asia. **European Russia** is bounded to the west by Norway, Finland, Estonia, Latvia, Belarus and Ukraine, and to the south by Georgia, Azerbaijan and Kazakhstan. There is a short coastline in the north-west, near **St Petersburg**, where the country has access to the Baltic Sea. Towards the **Caucasus region**, European Russia has a coastline on the Black Sea in the south-west and on the Caspian Sea to the east. East of the Ural Mountains, the Russian Federation has southern frontiers with Kazakhstan, the People's Republic of China, Mongolia and, in the south-east, the People's Democratic Republic of (North) Korea. The eastern coastline straddles the Sea of Japan, the Sea of Okhotsk, the north Pacific Ocean and the Bering Sea. The northern coastline is on the Arctic Ocean and the Barents Sea. The Russian enclave of **Kaliningrad** (former German Königsberg) on the Baltic coast is separated from the rest of the Federation by Lithuania and Belarus (and also borders Poland).

Administratively, the country consists of 89 federal units, which were grouped into seven federal districts under a presidential decree of May 2000.

Area: 17,075,200 sq km; capital: **Moscow** (Moskva); *population*: 145m. (2001 estimate), comprising **Russians** 81.5%, **Tatars** 3.8%, **Ukrainians** 3%, **Chavash** 1.2%, Bashkirs (*see* **Bashkortostan**) 0.9%, **Belarusians** 0.8%, **Romanians** 0.7%, others 8.1%; *official language*: Russian; *religion*: **Russian Orthodox**, also **Muslim** and others.

Under the Constitution approved in 1993, executive authority is vested in the President, who is directly elected for a maximum of two four-year terms. The President appoints the Prime Minister (who takes over from the President in the event that he cannot carry out his duties), subject to approval by the legislature. Legislative authority rests with the bicameral **Federal Assembly** (Federalnoye Sobraniye), consisting of (i) the upper 178-member Council of the Federation (Soviet Federatsii), to which each of the 89 federal administrative units returns two representatives; and (ii) the lower State Duma (Gossoudarstvennaya Duma), half of whose 450 members are directly elected for a four-year term from single-member constituencies and half by proportional representation from party lists. If the State Duma rejects three presidential nominations to the office of Prime Minister, the President is required to dissolve the Duma and order fresh elections.

History: The first unified state of Eastern **Slavs**, Kievan Rus, was founded around **Kiev** (Kyiv) in the late 9th century, converting to Orthodox Christianity in about 988. Invaded by the Mongol Tatars in the 1200s, Russia was ruled by the Khanate of the Golden Horde until the Muscovite prince Ivan III unified the Russian principalities in the late 15th century and formed a centralized independent state. In the 16th century Ivan IV ('the Terrible'), who was crowned 'Tsar of Muscovy and all Russia' in 1547 and ruled until 1584, began the eastern expansion of Russian territory. Peter the Great, who reigned from 1682 to 1725, established Russia as a European power, modernizing the civil and military institutions of the state and founding **St Petersburg** as the new capital and centre for Russia's first navy. By the end of his reign Sweden had ceded the Baltic territories of present-day **Estonia** and **Latvia** to Russia. Catherine the Great, who ruled in 1762–96, continued to expand the Russian Empire, southwards in wars with the Ottoman Turks and westwards as a result of the partitions of **Poland**, in which Russia absorbed what are now **Belarus**, **Lithuania** and **Ukraine**.

During the reign of Alexander I (1801–25), Russia seized Finland from Sweden and **Bessarabia** from Turkey, and repelled the invading French forces of Napoleon Bonaparte. Under Tsars Nicholas I (1825–55) and Alexander II (1855–81), Russia's frontiers were extended into the **Caucasus**, central Asia and the Far East. Meanwhile, British and French mistrust of Russian territorial ambitions led to the

Crimean War of 1853–56. Having abolished serfdom in 1861, Alexander II was assassinated in 1881, as internal opposition mounted to autocratic rule and general economic deprivation. Russia's humiliating defeat in its 1904–05 war with Japan provoked insurrection at home, the last Tsar, Nicholas II, being forced to introduce limited political reforms, including elections to a Parliament (Duma).

Russian military reverses in the First World War, coupled with domestic economic and social chaos, left the Tsarist regime so weakened and vulnerable that it was overthrown in 1917. The first of the two revolutions of that year, the February Revolution, forced the Tsar to abdicate in favour of a provisional Government, which forfeited popular support by opting to remain in the war. In the October Revolution the anti-war Bolsheviks (the communist majority wing of the Russian Social Democratic Labour Party) led by Vladimir Ilyich Lenin seized power and proclaimed the Russian Soviet Federative Socialist Republic (RSFSR) with **Moscow** as its capital. The Treaty of Brest-Litovsk of March 1918 ended the war with Germany and the other Central Powers on draconian territorial terms for Russia. The Tsar and his family were executed in July, as civil war erupted between the Bolshevik Red Army and 'White' anti-communist forces supported by Britain and France. By 1922 the Red Army had defeated the 'White' challenge and regained control of Belarus, eastern Ukraine, **Transcaucasia** and the central Asian republics. These territories were united with the RSFSR to form the Union of Soviet Socialist Republics (USSR or **Soviet Union**).

Following Lenin's death in 1924, power passed to Josef Stalin as General Secretary of what became the All-Union Communist Party (Bolsheviks) in 1925. Creating a highly-centralized regime, Stalin instituted a programme of accelerated industrialization under a series of five-year plans, as well as the forcible collectivization of agriculture (at the cost of widespread famine). To maintain his leadership position, Stalin initiated a campaign of internal repression and political purges, resulting in mass arrests and executions in the 1930s.

Despite the signing of the **Nazi-Soviet Pact** shortly before the outbreak of the Second World War in 1939 and consequent Russian territorial gains, collaboration with Hitler's regime ended abruptly in June 1941 when German forces invaded the Soviet Union. An estimated 20 million Soviet citizens died in the subsequent 'Great Patriotic War' before Germany surrendered to the Allied Powers (principally the Soviet Union, UK and USA) in 1945, with the Red Army in control of most of central and eastern Europe. Under the post-war settlement, the Soviet Union not only recovered all the Russian territories lost in 1918 but also annexed eastern Poland, eastern **Prussia** (from Germany), substantial Finnish territory, **Ruthenia** (from **Czechoslovakia**) and northern **Bukovina** (from **Romania**), as well as the southern Kurile Islands (from Japan). Stalin proceeded to install communist regimes in the countries of what became known as the Soviet bloc, bringing down a so-called 'Iron Curtain' across Europe. Tensions with the Western powers deteriorated into the **Cold War** after the Soviet Union became a nuclear power in 1949.

After Stalin's death in 1953, Nikita Khrushchev eventually established undisputed power as leader of what had become the **Communist Party of the Soviet Union** (KPSS). At the 20th KPSS congress in 1956 Khrushchev stunned the world by denouncing Stalin's dictatorship and cult of personality, but his domestic bombshell had little effect on East-West tensions. Having formed the **Warsaw Pact** military alliance with its satellite states in 1955, the Soviet Union developed an inter-continental ballistic missile capability (by 1956) and inaugurated manned space flight (in 1961). At the same time, a serious ideological rift developed with communist-ruled China, while in 1962 the country came to the brink of nuclear war with the USA in the Cuban missile crisis.

The increasingly erratic Khrushchev was deposed in 1964 and replaced by Leonid Brezhnev, who maintained rigid communist orthodoxy. During the Brezhnev era the Soviet Union appeared to have established itself as a military and political superpower, recognition of which status facilitated an improvement in Soviet-US relations in the 1970s. However, East-West détente and disarmament initiatives were undermined by the Soviet invasion of Afghanistan in 1979, while the ultimate failure of the intervention not only revealed the serious limitations of Soviet military power but also stimulated the first popular criticism of the KPSS regime.

Brezhnev's death in November 1982 was followed by a 30-month interregnum, during which first Yurii Andropov and then Konstantin Chernenko died in office as Soviet leader. In March 1985 the 54-year-old Mikhail **Gorbachev**, a reformist, became KPSS leader (and in 1988 also Head of State), initiating radical economic and political change under the *glasnost* (openness) and *perestroika* (restructuring) initiatives and a new détente in international relations. The major nuclear accident at **Chernobyl** in 1986 heightened awareness of the need for fundamental reform in the Soviet polity. Events accelerated in 1989 as the European satellite communist regimes collapsed one after another, while some of the Soviet Union republics declared independence. Seeking to preserve the Soviet Union, Gorbachev proposed a new voluntary Union federation, before an attempted coup in Moscow in August 1991 (*see* **August coup**) sought to reinstate hardline communist government. The failure of the coup attempt was due in large measure to determined resistance by democratic forces led by Boris **Yeltsin**, the recently-elected President of the Russian Federation.

The failed coup accelerated the break-up of the Soviet system, in that most of the republican parties withdrew from the KPSS while it was in progress, and were subsequently banned or suspended as the republics moved to independence. In the Russian Federation both the KPSS and its Russian wing were banned in November 1991 by presidential decree, their assets being declared state property. On 21 December 1991 the Russian Federation and 10 other Soviet republics signed up to the **Commonwealth of Independent States** (CIS), thereby effectively dissolving the Soviet Union, of which Gorbachev resigned as President four days later.

In the newly independent Russian Federation, a power struggle ensued between President Yeltsin, backed by reformist political groups, and the legislative structure left over from the Soviet era. In September 1993 Yeltsin dissolved the Congress of People's Deputies and announced elections to a new bicameral Federal Assembly. At an emergency session of the Congress, however, Vice-President Aleksandr Rutskoi was appointed acting President and led a revolt against Yeltsin. A siege of the parliament building followed, until troops loyal to Yeltsin stormed it in October, with over 100 fatalities and the arrest of the leaders of the revolt.

A referendum on a new constitution granting the President substantial authority to govern by decree was held in December 1993, together with the first post-Soviet parliamentary elections. The approval of the Constitution by 58.4% of the vote was a victory for Yeltsin. However, the Federal Assembly elections, while resulting in the emergence of the pro-reform Russia's Democratic Choice (DVR) as the largest bloc in the State Duma, also saw the unexpected rise of the right-wing nationalist **Liberal Democratic Party of Russia** (LDPR) and the achievement of significant representation by the revived **Communist Party of the Russian Federation** (KPRF).

In 1994 civil war broke out in predominantly Muslim **Chechnya**, which had declared its independence in 1991 after a nationalist coup and had refused to sign the Russian Federation Treaty the following year. Russian military intervention in the face of fierce Chechen resistance resulted in a high civilian death toll and increasing international concern. Opposition to the Government's handling of the crisis and concerns about Yeltsin's faltering health were reflected in the results of further State Duma elections in December 1995, when the KPRF became substantially the largest parliamentary group with 157 seats and the DVR retained only nine deputies.

Yeltsin responded to the conservative left's electoral advance by dropping prominent reformists from the Government. He nevertheless faced a strong challenge in presidential elections in mid-1996, obtaining only a marginal first-round lead over KPRF leader Gennadii **Zyuganov**. Yeltsin therefore speedily appointed the third-placed candidate, ex-Gen. Aleksandr Lebed of the nationalist Congress of Russian Communities, as National Security Adviser, this alliance enabling him to win the second ballot against Zyuganov with 54% of the vote. Lebed resumed negotiations with the Chechen rebel leadership in August 1996, concluding a cease-fire and withdrawal agreement which deferred a final decision on Chechen sovereignty for five years.

Facing the opposition of a KPRF-dominated State Duma, Yeltsin used his strong presidential powers to make frequent and increasingly unpredictable government changes, dismissing four Prime Minsters (Viktor Chernomyrdin, Sergei Kiriyenko, Yevgenii Primakov and Sergei Stepashin) between March 1998 and August 1999, as his deteriorating health and drinking habits gave increasing cause for concern. Stepashin's successor was Vladimir **Putin**, a former **KGB** official and then politically unknown, who was also nominated as Yeltsin's preferred candidate for the next presidential elections due in 2000.

Concurrently with the political turmoil in Moscow, Muslim insurgents declared an independent Islamic state in the southern republic of **Dagestan** in August 1999, while the following month further political violence linked to Chechen Islamic separatism led to renewed Russian military intervention in the republic. Russian forces besieged the rebel-held Chechen capital of Grozny, finally capturing it in February 2000 after a ferocious assault which, although popular with the Russian public, attracted widespread international criticism.

Latest elections: Elections to the State Duma in December 1999 resulted in the conservative left and the ultra-nationalists losing ground to more liberal formations. The KPRF declined to 113 seats (with a party list vote share of 24.3%), while the new pro-Putin **Unity Inter-regional Movement** (Medved) won 72 seats (23.3%), the **Fatherland–All Russia** (OVR) bloc 67 (13.3%), the **Union of Right Forces** (SPS) 29 (8.5%), Yavlinskii–Boldyrev–Lukin Bloc (**Yabloko**) 21 (5.9%), the LDPR 17 (5.9%), Our Home is Russia (NDR) 7 (1.2%), seven other parties 9, independents 106. The NDR subsequently merged into Medved, which also attracted a number of independents. (Eight constituency seats where majorities had been cast against all candidates were subsequently filled in by-elections in March 2000 and the Chechnya seat in August 2000.)

In a surprise announcement on 31 December 1999, President Yeltsin resigned from office, Putin becoming Acting President pending fresh presidential elections. These were held in March 2000 and resulted in Putin, running without party affiliation but backed by most of the centre-right formations, achieving a comfortable first-round victory with 52.9% of the vote against 29.2% for Zyuganov of the KPRF.

Recent developments: On being inaugurated in May 2000, President Putin appointed Mikhail **Kasyanov** (First Deputy Prime Minister and Finance Minister under Yeltsin) as Prime Minister, heading a Government which included some reformists in economic ministries but showed continuity with the previous administration in the 'power' ministries covering national security. Putin's first legislative initiative was aimed at curtailing the powers of the elected Governors of the Russian Federation's 89 constituent regions, who had often resisted central policy decisions. Seven 'super-regions' were created to encompass the 89 federal units, with presidential envoys being appointed to each to ensure compliance with federal legislation.

Putin also ended the automatic right of leaders of the 89 federal units to sit in the Council of the Federation (the upper chamber of the federal legislature), creating as an alternative a new advisory State Council as a forum in which the Presidents and Governors of the federal entities would advise on regional issues. In the State Duma, Putin could normally rely on majority support from the groups of the centre-right led by Medved, although these continued in apparently endless flux, in contrast to the constancy of the KPRF on the conservative left.

Putin's high post-election standing was badly dented in August 2000 when the Russian nuclear submarine *Kursk* sank in the Barents Sea with the loss of all 118 personnel on board. The President was strongly criticized for being slow to react to the disaster, which was seen as highlighting the deterioration in Russian capabilities and the unchanged official inclination to withhold information. Also in

August 2000, the latest in a series of bomb attacks attributed to Chechen militants and a fire in a Moscow television tower, which deprived the capital of reception for more than a month, stimulated further criticism of the Government. In September 2000, moreover, claims were made that Putin's election victory had been gained on the strength of electoral malpractice by his supporters.

At the end of 2000 the Russian Federation adopted a new national anthem restoring the Soviet-era tune (with new words), as well as state insignia based on those of the Tsarist era. Early in 2001 the Federal Government was confronted with a major winter energy supply crisis in **Siberia**, where familiar charges were made that incompetence and corruption in Moscow were the root cause. In March 2001 the Interior and Defence Ministers were replaced in changes described by Putin as 'the demilitarization of public life'. Later in the year proposals to formalize the party system were finalized with a law on party formation passed on 29 June: parties now require a certain threshold of support across the country to be officially registered.

International relations and defence: On the demise of the Soviet Union at the end of 1991 and the creation of the CIS, the Russian Federation succeeded to the Soviet Union's seat in the UN Security Council and its membership of the **Organization for Security and Co-operation in Europe**, also assuming the Soviet Union's obligations under international and bilateral arms control treaties. It subsequently became a member of the **Council of Europe**, the **Organization of the Black Sea Economic Co-operation** and the **Arctic Council**.

A participant in **NATO**'s **Partnership for Peace** programme since 1994, the Russian Federation signed a further important co-operation agreement with the alliance in May 1997. However, relations cooled during 1999 over Russian opposition to NATO's enlargement into **eastern Europe** and the alliance's bombing campaign against **Serbia** over the conflict in **Kosovo**. Russian troops joined the subsequent UN-approved peacekeeping force in Kosovo, however, and relations with the USA in particular received a major boost as a consequence of the Russian Federation's supportive stance in the immediate aftermath of the September 2001 terrorist attacks on New York and Washington D.C. A partnership and co-operation agreement with the **European Union** entered into force in 1997, since when Russian Presidents have regularly conferred with EU leaders during EU summits. The Russian Federation is also a member of the **Group of Eight** (whose other members are the Group of Seven leading industrialized countries).

A lengthy dispute with Ukraine over ownership of the Black Sea naval fleet was resolved under a framework agreement concluded in 1997. In the same year the Russian Federation and Belarus concluded agreements establishing a structure for the co-ordination of their joint affairs, leading to the signature in December 1999 of the **Belarus-Russia Union** treaty.

The Russian Federation and China agreed in 1997 to end a long-running frontier dispute and allow for the implementation of a 1991 demarcation accord (although two disputed sections of the boundary remain to be settled). An unresolved territorial dispute with Japan over the southern Kurile Islands, annexed by the Soviet Union at the end of the Second World War, has prevented the two sides from signing a formal peace treaty, while Caspian Sea boundaries have yet to be determined between the Russian Federation and the other littoral states of **Azerbaijan**, Iran, Kazakhstan and Turkmenistan.

The Russian Federation's defence budget for 2000 amounted to some US $29,000m., equivalent to about 2.6% of GDP. The size of the armed forces at the end of 2000 was some 1.1 million personnel, including those serving under compulsory conscription of 18–24 months, while reservists numbered an estimated 20 million. The Russian Federation's large strategic defence capability is believed to include some 5,000 nuclear missiles of various types.

Under a new military doctrine approved by Putin in April 2000, the existing stipulation that the Russian Federation would not initiate a nuclear war was supplemented by a clause permitting the use of nuclear weapons in the event of a threat to the 'very existence' of the country. In early 2001 the Putin administration announced that the size of Defence Ministry forces would be reduced by 365,000 over five years.

Russian Federation, economy

A huge economy with diverse resources, which was vastly the largest economic component of the former **Soviet Union**, but has since been engaged in a difficult and contentious transition from a centrally-planned to a market-oriented system. The Russian Federation is in geographical size more than three times the combined area of the other 14 former Soviet republics, and it has about the same aggregate population as those 14. As of 1999 its GNP was more than double that of the other 14 republics combined.

GNP: US $240,026m. (2000); *GNP per capita*: $1,660 (2000); *GDP at PPP*: $620,300m. (1999); *GDP per capita at PPP*: $4,200 (1999); *exports*: $102,998m. (2000); *imports*: $33,853m. (2000); *currency*: rouble (plural: roubles; US $1=R30.50 at the end of December 2001).

In 1999 industry accounted for 38% of GDP, agriculture for 7% and services for 55%. Of the 66 million workforce, about 35% are engaged in manufacturing and construction, 16% in agriculture, forestry and fishing and 49% in services and other sectors. Some 8% of the land is arable, 4% permanent pasture and 46% forests and woodland, while 42% is described as 'other'. The main crops are grain and vegetables, and animal husbandry is an important agricultural sector. The Russian Federation has huge reserves of oil, natural gas and coal (both hard coal and lignite), and large amounts of many strategic minerals, but climatic and other conditions make some of these difficult to exploit. There is a wide range of industrial activity, including mining and extractive industries, machine-building and transport equipment, textiles and foodstuffs. The Russian Federation's electricity requirements are met from coal-fuelled stations (26%), nuclear power plants (13%), gas- and oil-fuelled stations and hydroelectricity.

The Russian Federation's main exports by value are petroleum and gas (47%), ferrous and non-ferrous metals and derivatives (21%), machinery and transport equipment (10%) and chemical products (8%). Principal imports are machinery and transport equipment (35%), foodstuffs and live animals (26%), chemical products (15%) and ferrous and non-ferrous metals and derivatives (7%). The largest markets for Russian exports in 2000 were Germany (9%), the USA (8%) and Italy (7%), while the principal suppliers of imports were Germany (12%) and **Belarus** and **Ukraine** (11% each). The Russian Federation has consistently recorded substantial trade surpluses, achieved principally from its exports of petroleum and gas.

The dissolution of the Soviet Union at the end of 1991 brought to the forefront many of the economic problems of the unified state, including significant uncompetitiveness in the industrial sector. With the development of *perestroika* and *glasnost* in the 1980s and the effective end of the **Cold War**, it became clear that much of Soviet industry had become obsolete and this weakness was in fact hindering these initiatives. The emergence of an independent Russian Federation paved the way for dramatic moves to liberalize the economy, to reduce the prime role of state ownership, to cut central government expenditure and to end the remaining aspects of the command economy. However, as in other post-communist states, there was initially very high inflation (especially in 1992–93) and declining GDP in the first few years. Over the period from 1989 to 1997 industrial output fell by about a half, with even higher reductions in sectors such as light industry and engineering, while agricultural output dropped by 40%. In terms of GDP there was in 1990–96 an annual average fall of 9.0% compared with an annual average growth of 2.8% in 1980–90.

From 1995 the Russian Federation's economy was assisted by a series of measures agreed with the **International Monetary Fund** (IMF), which it had joined in June 1992. In April 1995 the IMF agreed a 12-month US $6,800m. standby loan for the Russian Federation to assist the current 'bold and imaginative' economic and stabilization programme. This was followed in March 1996 by a three-year $10,200m. extended fund facility credit to support the Government's medium-term macroeconomic programme. As a result, the economic situation appeared to stabilize in 1997: real GDP growth (of 1%) was achieved for the first time since independence and inflation fell to around 15%.

In July 1998 the IMF increased the extended fund facility credit by US $8,300m. to support the Government's economic programme for 1998 and also agreed a $2,900m. compensatory and contingency funding facility in respect of an export shortfall related mainly to lower prices of crude oil in 1998. However, the situation was thrown into turmoil in August 1998 when a banking and financial crisis hit the country and led to a huge devaluation of the rouble and a moratorium on certain categories of debt service. As a result the IMF suspended further releases of credit. The economic crisis was aggravated by political turmoil, with President Boris **Yeltsin** making constant appointments to ministerial and other posts amidst a seeming inability on the part of the authorities to institute necessary economic changes. The result was a contraction in GDP of 4.9% in 1998, during which the rouble depreciated from 5.96 to the US dollar to 20.65 and the year-on-year inflation rate spiralled to 85% by December 1998.

A new US $4,500m. IMF standby credit granted in July 1999 underpinned a return to relative financial stability in 1999, assisted by the tripling of world oil prices in the second half of the year. Real GDP expanded by 3.2% in 1999 (and industrial production by 8%), while the year-on-year inflation rate was brought down to under 40% by December 1999. The recovery gathered strength in 2000, during which inflation fell to 20% and real GDP grew by 8.3% (and industrial production by 9%), so that overall output was officially stated to have returned to its 1994 level. At the same time, official figures showed that over 25% of incomes were below the official 'survival minimum' in the last quarter of 2000, real unemployment was estimated at over 10% of the active population, the 'black' economy was believed to account for some 45% of activity and large sectors of industry remained essentially uncompetitive. There was also increasing evidence that much of the financial assistance received by the Russian Federation was being siphoned off by profiteers and criminals and laundered into foreign bank accounts. The Government's budget for 2001 provided for a balance between revenue and expenditure at R1,190,00m., based on projected GDP growth of 4% and an inflation rate of around 14%.

Privatization of state and municipal assets started in 1992 with the issue of **vouchers**, while from July 1994 provision was made for the auction of state companies. Disposal of state farms was instituted, so by mid-1996 some 60% of the Russian Federation's agricultural land was in private ownership, although most field crops such as grain and sugar beet were produced on unreconstructed former state and collective farms. By 1997 some 125,000 enterprises had been privatized, of which a third were in manufacturing, construction, transport and communications, just over 2% in agriculture and the rest in services and other sectors. Around 70% of the Russian Federation's GDP was generated in the private sector in 1998, while restrictions limiting foreign participation in petroleum companies were lifted.

In the last period of the Yeltsin presidency, however, the privatization process stagnated and foreign investors were scared off by the unstable financial situation, widespread corruption among officials and endemic organized crime. Also of concern was the increasing economic and political influence exercised by the 'oligarchs', the prominent businessmen who now controlled major former state enterprises, some of them with criminal connections. In co-operation with the IMF, the new administration of Vladimir **Putin** which came to power early in 2000 included a new commitment to privatization in its economic reform programme, envisaging that some 11,000 remaining state-owned enterprises would be sold off by 2004. However, although receipts from disposals rose sharply in 2000 to the equivalent of US $1,600m., uncertainty persisted about the Government's willingness and ability to complete the privatization programme in the face of political opposition led by the powerful **Communist Party of the Russian Federation**.

Russian Information Agency–Novosti *see* Novosti.

Russian nationalist group *see* Pamyat—National Patriotic Front.

Russian Orthodox Church

An autocephalous branch of the **Orthodox Christian** Church based in the **Russian Federation**. By tradition Christianity was first brought to modern Russian territory by the Apostle St Andrew in the 1st century, but it was not until 988 that a Russian ruler, Prince Vladimir of Kiev, officially adopted the religion. From then until 1448 the Russian Church was subordinated to the Constantinople Patriarchate, but achieved full independence just before the collapse of the Byzantine Empire. The Patriarchate of **Moscow** then took on the mantle as the champion of Orthodox Christianity in Europe, adopting the unofficial title of the Third Rome (Byzantium having become the Second Rome after the Schism of 1054). Under the reforms of Peter the Great, the Russian Church abandoned its traditional hierarchical model in 1721, and switched from a single Patriarch to a collective Holy Synod. However, the primacy of the Moscow Patriarch was restored in 1917. For the first three decades of communist rule the Church was pitted as a direct enemy of the atheist state. Thousands of priests, monks and nuns were imprisoned or even executed and 98% of churches were closed down across the country. A convenient rapprochement between Church and State was encouraged by the needs of the latter during the Second World War, and the Church even sponsored a tank and a naval division. Relations remained tense, however, into the late 20th century until the collapse of the **Soviet Union** in 1991. Since then the Church has grown rapidly, with churches and monasteries restored across the country. Patriarch Aleksiy II was elected in 1990.

Russians

An east **Slavic people** dominant throughout the constituent republics of the **Russian Federation** and with sizeable minorities in most of the former **Soviet** states. Arriving in **European Russia** in the 5th century the Russians established themselves in the thick forests of the north. Political and economic power was brought to the Slavic tribes by the Viking *Rus* (from whom the name Russian is derived) who developed the riverine trade routes between the Baltic and the Black Seas. The first ever ethnic Slavic state was thus created around the modern Ukrainian capital of **Kiev** in the 9th century. A century later the Russians adopted

Christianity from the west, adhering to **Orthodox Christianity** after the 11th century schism (*see* **Russian Orthodox Church**).

During the steady expansion of the emerging Russian Empire, from the 15th to the 20th century, Russians colonized the farthest reaches of modern Russia, soon coming to outnumber the resident populations. Russian language and culture became the *lingua franca* of the Empire. A strong sense of nationalism built on these beginnings survives today.

Russians account for over 85% of the Russian Federation's population, totalling around 125 million. Russian migrations to the former Soviet states fall into two distinct phases: pre-20th century (historic) migrations and the larger Soviet-era movement of workers. These migrations have been greatly countered by post-1991 repatriations to Russia owing to economic conditions and social discrimination. Despite this growing trend a large number of Russians—around 24 million—live outside the Federation.

The largest of these Russian minorities is the 11 million-strong community in **Ukraine**. In some areas, notably the **Crimea**, Russians form a majority and a large number of Ukrainians consider themselves bilingual, with Russian often dominating business. Fears of separatist movements arising after independence in 1991 proved largely unfounded, and Ukrainian Russians have pushed instead for limited regional autonomy and protection of their language. The plan to unite **Belarus** and the Russian Federation, and the success of the Communist Party in **Moldova** in 2001, increased calls to draw Ukraine closer to the Moscow sphere.

The second-largest group of Russians in eastern Europe, outside the Federation—1.3 million—reside in Belarus, where their strong east Slavic affiliation with the local Belarusians has mitigated any major tension. Relations between ethnic Russians and their hosts are not so cordial in the **Baltic States** where the influx of over 1.5 million Russians in the Soviet era greatly undermined the countries' ethnic balances, particularly in **Estonia** and **Latvia** where they formed almost a third of the populations. In this region Russians are almost exclusively urbanized and generally live in regions close to the Russian Federation or Belarus, in areas subject to simmering border disputes. The question of language has dominated these countries with Russian downgraded in the latter two to an unofficial tongue. This discrimination has encouraged a large exodus of Russians back across the border since 1991.

A similar story is also true for the 8.9 million Russians living in the five central Asian states (5.8 million live in Kazakhstan). Smaller communities range from 562,000 in Moldova (particularly in **Transdnestria**), 440,000 in **Azerbaijan** and 300,000 in **Georgia**, to just around 20,000 in **Armenia**, **Bulgaria**, Finland and **Romania** (where they are known as Lipovans). In all cases, voluntary returns to the Russian Federation after 1991 have reduced these communities considerably, although levels of discrimination vary greatly. Modern migrations are also to be found within the Federation, with the north **Caucasus** region suffering particularly badly from a loss of ethnic Russians.

Ruthenia *see* Transcarpathia.

Ruthenians

An east **Slavic people**, dominant in western **Ukraine** (*see* **Transcarpathia**). Historically, the term Ruthenian was applied to all ethnic **Ukrainians**. A distinction arose in the 16th and 17th centuries when the **Orthodox Church** of western 'Ruthenia' recognized the supremacy of the **Roman Catholic Church**, while under Polish sovereignty (*see* **Uniate Church**). These people, who were later brought into the Austro-Hungarian Empire, are the inheritors of the designation 'Ruthenian'.

Rüütel, Arnold

President of **Estonia**.

Arnold Rüütel heads the right-of-centre **Estonian People's Union** (ERL) and became President on 21 September 2001. He is a respected agronomist and was formerly a senior member of the communist hierarchy, retaining his office to be briefly (until 1992) Estonia's first post-communist Head of State.

Born on 10 May 1928 on the island of Saaremaa during Estonia's brief period of inter-war independence, he graduated from an agricultural college in 1949 and began a long career in the Soviet agricultural sector. His positions included Head of the Agronomic Department on Saaremaa, Head Zootechnician at the Estonian Institute of Cattle Breeding, and Director of the Tartu Model State Farm. From 1977 he began combining his scientific and administrative work with politics, and in 1983 he was elected Chairman of the Supreme Soviet of the Estonian SSR. In this capacity he played a vital role in the emergence of a separate Estonian state in the late 1980s and was re-elected to the position in 1990 as the country began the process of separating itself from the **Soviet Union**. He acted as the *de facto* Head of State until 1992, when he failed to win presidential elections. In the **State Assembly** he headed the Estonian Rural People's Party (later to become the ERL) from 1994, was elected Vice-Speaker of the house in 1995 and headed the regional Baltic Assembly. He continued to promote agricultural issues and established a number of agricultural and environmental bodies, including the Estonian Society for Nature Protection and the Estonian Green Cross. The State Assembly elected him President of Estonia on 21 September 2001.

Arnold Rüütel married Ingrid in 1958 and they have two daughters.

Address: Office of the President, Weizenbergi 39, Tallinn 15050.
Telephone: 6316202.
Fax: 6316250.
E-mail: sekretar@vpk.ee
Internet: www.president.ee

S

Sabor *see* Assembly (Croatia).

Saeima *see* Parliament (Latvia).

St Petersburg

The second city of the **Russian Federation** and formerly the imperial capital, situated in the far west of the country at the confluence of the River Neva and the Gulf of Finland. *Population*: 4.7m. (2000 estimate). The Neva region, an integral part of Russian states from the 9th century, was annexed to the Swedish Empire in 1617 but won back in the early stages of the Northern War (1700–21) under the **Romanov** Tsar Peter the Great. Despite the widely-acknowledged unsuitability of the site, with its damp climate and persistent flooding, its strategic significance led Peter to found the city of St Petersburg there in May 1703. Construction of the fortified encampment was hazardous in the extreme and scores of soldiers and peasants were killed. Peter employed European architects to create a distinctly European city. By 1712 his 'Venice of the North' had become sufficiently prosperous and important to become the new capital of the Russian Empire, indicating its westward orientation.

St Petersburg was to be the economic and cultural heart of the expanding Empire. In 1837 it became one terminus of the country's first railway and in 1851 it was connected by track to **Moscow** deep in the interior. As the centre of political life, it was also the focus of popular dissent. The emancipation of the serfs in 1861 prompted an influx of migrant labour, creating overcrowding and the basis for mass unrest. The 'Bloody Sunday' massacre of pro-reform supporters in the city's Palace Square in January 1905 launched a revolution leading to the introduction of broad, if poorly-backed, political liberalization. The legislative Duma was based in the city from 1906.

Following the outbreak of war with Germany in 1914 the city's name was changed in a gesture of Russian patriotism to the less Germanic form Petrograd. The severe impact of the First World War on the city and the country at large prompted further discontent. The scene in early 1917 of the March Revolution, Petrograd then became the base for the meetings of the Soviets and the cradle for the burgeoning Bolshevik party, which organized the celebrated siege of the governmental headquarters in the Winter Palace—the start of the October Revolution. The establishment of a Bolshevik state prompted a civil war and saw the city once again threatened by hostile forces. In early 1918 the new authorities removed their capital to Moscow. This loss of status was compounded by the massive loss of population inflicted by the war. From a 1917 high of 2.3 million, the city's population had fallen to 722,000 at the end of 1920. In 1924, on the death of Lenin, the city was renamed once again as Leningrad to honour the founding father of the **Soviet Union**.

Reconstruction and the renewed expansion of the city began under Stalin. By 1939 it had a population of three million and was the source of 11% of the Soviet Union's industrial output. Progress was devastatingly interrupted in 1941, however, when the invading Nazi forces began the 900-day Siege of Leningrad. From 8 September 1941 until 27 January 1944 the city was blockaded, leaving 641,000 people dead. Most of the victims were buried in mass graves. After the conclusion of the siege, and later of the Second World War itself, Leningrad quickly returned to relative prosperity. Cheap housing became a central issue, but unlike other war-ravaged Soviet cities, Leningrad was reconstructed largely along its pre-war lines, rather than rebuilt in Stalinist sobriety. The city gathered momentum as an economic dynamo into the second half of the 20th century, regaining its pre-war population levels in the 1960s.

In 1991 a referendum popularly endorsed the reversion to the original name of St Petersburg and the city faced the collapse of the Soviet Union with falling wages and a sudden rise in crime levels. Nevertheless, foreign investment flooded in and the city once again became Russia's main portal to the West. As the country's economy wobbled towards stability in the 21st century, so the city took on a renewed sense of calm and prosperity. The election of Vladimir **Putin** as President in May 2000 did much to bring St Petersburg back into the political limelight. Putin had spent the first five years after the collapse of the Soviet Union in the city's administration and continues to promote the careers of fellow former members of the city's Government. Vladimir Anatolyevich Yakovlev has been Governor (Mayor) of St Petersburg since 2 June 1996.

St Petersburg's economic importance is based on its large size and its position as the country's only Baltic port, giving it unique access to northern and western European markets. It is also a hub for the regional transport network, particularly for the many waterways of northern **European Russia**, making it the centre of systems linking the Baltic and White Seas with the **Volga** river, and the Caspian and Black Seas beyond. Its Soviet legacy is a preponderance of heavy engineering.

Sąjudis *see* **Lithuanian Reform Movement.**

Sakartvelos Parlamenti *see* **Parliament of Georgia.**

Sakinform

The main news agency in **Georgia**. Sakinform is the heir to the Soviet-era, **Russian**-dominated Telegraph Agency of the Soviet Union (TASS—*see* **ITAR-TASS**), whose Georgian branch (SAKDES) was established in 1921. It prides itself on its role as the main official mouthpiece in the **Caucasus region** during the Soviet-era.
Director: Kakha Imnadze.
Address: Rustaveli 42, 380008 Tbilisi.
Telephone: (32) 931920.
Fax: (32) 999200.
E-mail: gha@lberiapac.ge
Internet: www.sakinform.ge

SALT

The Strategic Arms Limitation Talks, held between the USA and the **Soviet Union** between 1969 and 1979. The first round, SALT I, in 1969–72, produced the important 1972 treaty limiting anti-ballistic missile systems, and another accord on limiting each side's overall number of ballistic missiles. The second phase, SALT II, began with the Washington summit of 1973, when the two sides set out an agenda for moving from arms control—the stage involving weapons classifications and ceilings—on to the actual **START** arms reduction process. Although the talks became bogged down in complexities over multiple warheads, the climate of détente was restored by the new US President Jimmy Carter in 1977 and his decision to halt development of the neutron bomb and long-range B-1 bomber. A SALT II treaty was concluded and signed in Vienna on 18 June 1979 (after which the SALT talks were renamed START), but the Soviet intervention in the Afghan War destroyed any prospect of its being ratified by the US Senate. Carter's successor Ronald Reagan never resubmitted it for ratification, although both the USA and the **Soviet Union** agreed informally to comply with its provisions. The US plan for a National Missile Defence system, pursued in 2001 by new President George W. Bush, was especially controversial in that it marked an apparent US readiness to set aside the landmark SALT I agreement.

Sami

A **Finno-Ugric people** (formerly widely called Lapps) living across the Arctic tundra of Scandinavia and the **Kola peninsula**. Present in the region from 1500 BC, the normadic Sami developed separately from the Finns. Until very recently the herding of reindeer was central to their way of life. Only a small number of Sami now live in their traditional manner, however, as there has been great pressure for them to adopt a more sedentary lifestyle and so contribute to the economic dynamics of their respective countries.

The language of the Sami divided from Finnish around 3,000 years ago and bears little real relation to modern Finnish. Indeed the isolation of their traditional nomadic lifestyle has created several strongly distinct, and sometimes mutually unintelligible, dialects.

Around 2,000 Sami live in northern **Russia.** Their small number means that they have not been represented as a distinct group in the Russian Federation, but since 1992 they have sent representatives to the Sami Council. They are joined on the council by members from the much larger communities living in Norway (100,000), Sweden (15,000) and Finland (7,000).

Samoobrona *see* **Self-Defence of the Polish Republic**.

Sandzak

A region lying on the border between **Serbia** and **Montenegro** in **Yugoslavia** with a sizeable Muslim population. The area was the site of bitter inter-ethnic conflict during the Second World War. A considerable number of the Sandzak's Muslims fled the area during the conflicts which followed the collapse of the **Socialist Federal Republic of Yugoslavia**, reducing the chance of conflict in the region itself in the 1990s. The major urban centre in the Sandzak is the town of Novi Pazar.

Sarajevo

The capital of **Bosnia and Herzegovina,** situated in the heart of the country and the seat of the federal institutions. It has long been home to a **Bosniak** majority and has developed a distinctly **Muslim** identity. *Population*: 451,631 (1991 census). The ancient city was established as the capital of the Ottoman province of Bosnia and Herzegovina in 1850 and retained that role after the region was ceded to the Habsburg Empire in 1878. It was perhaps most famous for the assassination of Austrian Archduke Ferdinand in 1914, which sparked the First World War. A second claim to fame came 70 years later when the city, by then the capital of the Bosnian republic within communist **Yugoslavia**, hosted the 1984 Winter Olympics in an unusual display of international harmony between east and west.

Sarajevo's designation as a UN 'safe haven' in May 1993 during the Bosnian War failed to protect it and the surrounding area from heavy Bosnian **Serb** bombardment. The city became internationally renowned once more, this time for the plight of its inhabitants facing sniper fire and incessant shelling. In the final phase of the war Sarajevo was linked to the rest of the Muslim-Croat territory. With peace restored the work to rebuild the shattered city began.

Sarović, Mirko

President of the **Serb Republic**.

Mirko Sarović is a member of the ultra-nationalist **Serbian Democratic Party** (SDS). A prominent politician in **Sarajevo**'s municipal institutions, he first entered the Serb Republic's Government as Vice-President in 1998. He was inaugurated as President on 16 December 2000.

Born on 16 September in Rogatica, south-eastern **Bosnia**, he graduated in law from the University of Sarajevo in 1979. He worked for 10 years for the commercial companies Famos and Unis before beginning a political career in the Sarajevo Municipal Assembly in 1989. He was elected to the Federal **Parliamentary Assembly** in 1996 and appointed Vice-President of the Serb Republic in 1998. He was elected full President for a brief term on 26 January 2000 but was never officially recognized by the UN **High Representative**, and was forced from office on 2 February. He returned to the post, for the second time, in December 2000.

Savezna Skupština see Federal Assembly (Yugoslavia).

Saxecoburggotski, Simeon

Prime Minister and ex-King of **Bulgaria**.

Simeon Borisov Saxecoburggotski, the former King Simeon II of Bulgaria, returned to a lead role in the country's public life in 2001 when he headed a newly-formed centrist **National Movement Simeon II** (NDS II) at the June elections and swept the incumbent right-of-centre Government from power. The party, with no specific stated political leanings, promised to steer Bulgaria out of its economic malaise. Although Saxecoburggotski has never officially renounced his claim to the Bulgarian throne (which he held from 1943 to 1946) he has effectively rejected its restitution by swearing allegiance to the Republic. He was proclaimed Prime Minister on 15 July 2001 and formed a coalition Government with the minority-based **Movement for Rights and Freedoms** (DPS).

Born Prince Simeon Saxe-Coburg-Gotha in **Sofia** on 16 June 1937, he was immediately named Prince of Tirnovo and next in line to the throne. He was proclaimed King Simeon II on the death of his father, King Boris III, on 28 August 1943. The monarchy was rejected in a stage-managed referendum organized by the post-war communist Government on 6 September 1946, and Simeon and his remaining family were exiled. After studying at the British Victoria College in Alexandria, Egypt, he was offered asylum in Spain in 1951. He graduated from the Lycée Français in Madrid in 1956 and then attended the Valley Forge Military Academy in Pennsylvania, USA, until 1959. For the next 40 years he worked in various business ventures based mainly in Spain and Morocco, including the Omnium holding company, the Casablanca-based Consumar sugar producer and the

Eurobuilding hotel chain. He travelled extensively around the Mediterranean, and claims proficiency in eight languages.

He returned to Bulgaria in 1996 to massive popular acclaim, but maintained his professional career in Madrid. Having been barred from running in presidential elections, he returned again to Bulgaria in April 2001 and announced the formation of a new political party, the NDS II, which gained rapidly in opinion polls. The NDS II won 43% of the vote in the June elections and claimed exactly half of the seats in the **National Assembly**. Despite initially signalling that he would not seek the premiership, Simeon was given a mandate to form a new Government by President Petar **Stoyanov** on 15 July, and took the name Simeon Saxecoburggotski. He has appointed a distinctly pro-Western technocratic Cabinet.

Simeon Saxecoburggotski married Margarita Gomez y Acebo in 1962 and they have five children. The eldest, Kardam, bears the title Prince of Tirnovo as heir to the throne.

Address: Office of the Prime Minister, 1 Dondukov Blvd, Sofia 1000.
Telephone: (2) 9402770.
Fax: (2) 9802056.
E-mail: iprd@government.bg
Internet: www.government.bg

SBiH *see* **Party for Bosnia and Herzegovina**.

SBS-Agro

A large bank in the **Russian Federation** which collapsed with disastrous effects on the **Russian economy** in 1998. The former Stolichny Savings Bank merged with the remnants of the Soviet-era Agroprombank in 1995 to create SBS-Agro which soon became the main agent of the Ministry of Agriculture and built up a network of investments in the Russian media under the stewardship of Russian 'oligarch' Aleksandr Smolensky. As the global financial crisis of 1998 began to impact on the Russian Federation, SBS-Agro was quickly proved to have very few actual financial reserves, prompting its rapid descent into bankruptcy. It had the inglorious commendation of being the first Russian bank to have its licence revoked by the new **Central Bank**. Its assets, and debts, were redivided, but not before the Russian economy had faltered, prompting a devaluation of the rouble.

Schmögnerová, Brigita

Minister of Finance, **Slovakia**.

Brigita Schmögnerová is a prominent member of the reformed communist **Party of the Democratic Left** (SDĽ) and a former Deputy Premier. She was appointed Finance Minister on 30 October 1998.

Born in **Bratislava** on 17 November 1947, she graduated from the Economic University of Bratislava in 1973. She received her doctorate in 1979, then worked at the Slovak Academy of Sciences. She was appointed as an adviser on economic policy at the Czechoslovak Prime Minister's Office for a brief period in 1990, and acted as adviser to the Privatization Ministry until 1992. From 1993 to 1994 she advised the President of the newly independent Slovakia and was Head of the Economic Policy Department at the Presidential Office. In an interim Slovak Government formed in 1994 she held the post of Deputy Prime Minister with responsibility for economic policy. Elected to the **National Council** in December that year as a representative of the SDĽ, she was the party's Vice-Chair from 1995 to 1998 and stood as its candidate in presidential elections in 1998. She was appointed Finance Minister in a new leftist coalition Government in October 1998.

Address: Ministry of Finance, Štefanovičova 5, 81005 Bratislava 15.
Telephone: (2) 59581112.
Fax: (2) 52493531.
E-mail: inform@mfsr.sk
Internet: www.finance.gov.sk

Schuster, Rudolf

President of the Republic, **Slovakia**.

The country's first directly-elected President, in office since 15 June 1999, Rudolf Schuster is a former Mayor of the eastern city of Košice, who founded the centrist Party of Civic Understanding (SOP) in 1998 but resigned as its leader on his election as President, in line with the Constitution. He is also a prolific writer and documentary film maker.

Born in Medzev on 4 January 1934, Schuster graduated from the Slovak Technical University in **Bratislava** in 1959. After two years working as a designer at the city's Regional Agricultural Planning Institute, he spent 12 years at the Eastern Slovakia Iron Works (VSZ). Having joined the Slovak Communist Party (CPS) in 1964, he was appointed to the City Council in Košice in 1974, became Mayor in 1983, and sat on the CPS Central Committee from 1986. Schuster remained prominent within the (reformed) communist party after the '**velvet revolution**' of 1989, holding the post of Speaker of Slovakia's **National Council**. He was posted to Canada as Ambassador for the new democratic Czechoslovakia in 1990. He returned as the country fragmented into its two constituent republics at the end of 1992, and was appointed to the Ministry of Foreign Affairs in the independent Slovakian Government in 1993.

Re-elected mayor of Košice in 1994, he founded the pro-market SOP in 1998, taking it into government after elections in October of that year in a new administration headed by the **Slovak Democratic Coalition** (SDK). Schuster was backed by the SDK as a suitably pro-Western candidate in the first direct presidential elections in May 1999. As President, his relationship with the National Council has been marked by clashes over his derogatory remarks about the country's **Roma** minority, and his continued pride in the country's communist past. The most significant of his battles has been over the assumption of presidential powers by the Government during his serious illness in 2000.

Address: Office of the President of the Republic, Štefánikova ul. 1, 81104 Bratislava - Hrad.
Telephone: (2) 54417121.
Fax: (2) 54430683.
E-mail: vkpsr@prezident.sk
Internet: www.prezident.sk

SDA (Bosnia and Herzegovina)
see **Party of Democratic Action (Bosnia and Herzegovina)**.

SDA (Yugoslavia) *see* **Party of Democratic Action (Yugoslavia)**.

SDHP *see* **Social Democratic Hunchakian Party**.

SDK *see* **Slovak Democratic Coalition**.

SDĽ *see* **Party of the Democratic Left**.

SDPB *see* **Belarusian Social Democratic Party**.

SDPBiH *see* **Social Democratic Party of Bosnia and Herzegovina**.

SDPNZ *see* **Social Democratic Party of Popular Accord**.

SDPU–O *see* **Social Democratic Party of Ukraine–United**.

SDS (Bosnia and Herzegovina) *see* **Serbian Democratic Party**.

SDS (Bulgaria) *see* **Union of Democratic Forces**.

SDS (Slovenia) *see* **Social Democratic Party of Slovenia**.

SDSM *see* **Social Democratic Union of Macedonia**.

Seimas *see* **Parliament (Lithuania)**.

Sejm
(Diet)

The lower house of the **National Assembly** of **Poland**.

Self-Defence of the Polish Republic
Samoobrona Rzeczypospolitej Polskiej (Samoobrona)

A right-wing agrarian-based political party in **Poland**. Samoobrona was formed in 2000 from the radical farmers' union of the same name and is headed by the union's leader Andrzej Lepper. As a union leader Lepper was outspoken in his opposition to the agricultural policies of the **European Union** and organized numerous demonstrations in rural areas, including roadblocks. These demonstrations often descended into violent clashes with police. As popularity for the ruling rightist **Solidarity Electoral Action** (AWS) waned, Samoobrona converted itself into a political party in order to champion the cause of the rural community, which it felt was being neglected by the traditional peasants' party, the **Polish Peasant Party**. Although Lepper's rhetorical style is regarded by the international community as somewhat comical, he gained domestic public notice by raising accusations of high-level corruption while serving as President of the *Sejm* (lower house of the **National Assembly**) between October 2000 and November 2001. Samoobrona was the most successful of a number of extreme right-wing parties to benefit from the collapse of the mainstream right in elections in September 2001 and gained 53 seats in the Sejm, having garnered 10.2% of the popular vote. It became the third-largest party in the Sejm.

Leadership: Andrzej Lepper.
Address: Al. Jerozolimskie 30, 00024 Warsaw.
Telephone: (22) 6250472.
Fax: (22) 6250477.
E-mail: samoobrona@samoobrona.org.pl
Internet: www.samoobrona.org.pl

SelPU *see* **Peasants' Party of Ukraine**.

Senate (Czech Republic)
Senát

The upper house of **Parliament** of the **Czech Republic**.

Senate (Poland)
Senat

The upper house of the **National Assembly of Poland**.

Senate (Romania)
Senatul

The upper house of the **Parliament of Romania**.

Serb Republic
Republika Srpska (RS)

The autonomous Bosnian **Serb** entity which constitutes around 49% of **Bosnia and Herzegovina**. The republic is divided into a northern half, running along the northern border with **Croatia** (which contains the capital, **Banja Luka**), and an eastern half, bordering **Yugoslavia**. The two halves are linked by a tight land corridor which passes through the disputed town of **Brčko**. It was established as the Serb Republic of Bosnia and Herzegovina on 9 January 1992 initially in an attempt to maintain links with Yugoslavia in the face of calls for Bosnian independence. The original multi-ethnic population of the republic was transformed into Serbian dominance through a determined policy of **'ethnic cleansing'** led by the ultra-nationalist Tigers militia.

The assistance of the regular Yugoslav army ensured the Bosnian Serbs significant successes in their campaigns during the Bosnian Civil War until the formation of a Muslim-Croat alliance shifted the balance in 1994. The **Dayton Agreement** of November 1995 formalized the existence of the republic, and of the **Muslim-Croat Federation**, in a loose confederal arrangement within the Bosnian state.

Serbia

The larger constituent republic of **Yugoslavia**, measuring 34,116 square miles (88,360 square kilometres), bounded by the plains of Hungary to the north, the River Danube to the east, the highlands of Macedonia to the south, and Montenegro, Herzegovina and Bosnia to the west. The extent and centre of gravity of Serbian territory has shifted considerably. Historically, it included **Herzegovina**, now in the modern state of **Bosnia and Herzegovina**, but did not extend to the **Hungarian**-dominated region of **Vojvodina**. It has also traditionally incorporated the (now **Albanian**-dominated) area of **Kosovo**.

Inhabited by **Serbs** since their arrival in the 7th century, Serbia was under Roman and then Byzantine rule but became increasingly independent, under the Serbian Princes from 1180 onwards. The brief Serbian Empire, carved out by Stephen

Dushan (1331–55), set the tone for later territorial ambitions. A major landmark in Serbian national history was their defeat in 1389 at the hands of the Ottoman Turks at the Battle of Kosovo—a defining moment also for other independent countries of the **Balkans**. An independent Serbia reappeared in 1878 and was extended to include **Macedonia** in 1913 (*see* **Macedonian question**).

The dominant position of Serbia within the newly-created Yugoslavia was sealed in 1919 when the initial monarchy was handed to the Serbian royal house. The authoritarian rule instigated from **Belgrade** between 1929 and 1939 laid the foundations for resentment amongst the other elements within Yugoslavia. The postwar communist Yugoslav regime of Marshal **Tito** sought to achieve a better balance among the nationalities, although the Constitution he introduced in 1974 devolved greater power to the individual republics, thereby contributing to a resurgence of rival nationalisms in the next decade which led to the collapse of Yugoslavia in the 1990s. The rump **Yugoslav** state after 1992 consisted only of Serbia (incorporating Vojvodina and Kosovo whose autonomous status was suppressed in 1989) and the much smaller republic of **Montenegro**.

Economic development under communist rule fostered the growth of a series of industrial centres down Serbia's north–south axis, from Novi Sad to Niš, along the fertile Morava Valley. Serbian agricultural production is based on dairy, fruit and livestock, while industry focuses on finished metallic and textile products.

Serbia's bicameral republican parliament is based in Belgrade, as are the federal Yugoslav chambers (*see* **Federal Assembly**).

Serbian Democratic Party
Srpska Demokratska Stranka (SDS)

The dominant **Serb** nationalist political formation in **Bosnia and Herzegovina**, formerly led by Radovan **Karadžić**. Launched in July 1990, the SDS secured most of the ethnic Serb vote in the November–December 1990 elections, winning the two guaranteed Serb seats on the then seven-member collegial presidency with about 25% of the popular vote. It joined a post-election coalition with the (**Muslim**) **Party of Democratic Action** (SDA) and the **Croatian Democratic Union** (HDZ), arguing that Bosnia and Herzegovina should remain within a federal **Yugoslavia**. When the Government opted for independence, the SDS withdrew from the Assembly in **Sarajevo** and in March 1992 led the proclamation of the **Serb Republic** (RS) of Bosnia and Herzegovina in Serb-controlled territory, with its own Assembly at Pale. Thereafter the SDS was closely identified with the Bosnian Serbs' military struggle and was technically banned by the central Government in June 1992.

Karadžić and the SDS secured the Bosnian Serbs' rejection of successive international peace plans, on the grounds that they did not guarantee sovereignty for a Bosnian Serb entity. The party therefore came into political conflict with the leadership of rump Yugoslavia, which came to favour a settlement with the aim of securing the lifting of UN sanctions. The SDS also condemned the US-inspired creation of the **Muslim-Croat Federation** in March 1994. Increasing Yugoslav and international pressure on the Bosnian Serbs in 1995 caused divisions in the SDS, especially after Karadžić was named as a suspected war criminal by the **International Criminal Tribunal for the Former Yugoslavia** at The Hague. Under the US-brokered peace agreement concluded at **Dayton**, Ohio, in November 1995, indicted war criminals were specifically excluded from standing for office in post-settlement political structures. Bowing to international pressure, Karadžić relinquished the RS presidency to the more moderate Biljana Plavšić in mid-1996, but remained very much in control behind the scenes.

The SDS maintained its hold on the Serb vote in the first post-Dayton elections in September 1996. Hardliner Momčilo Krajišnik was elected as the Serb member of the new collective presidency of Bosnia and Herzegovina, with 67% of the Serb vote, while Plavšić was returned as RS President with 64% support. In the simultaneous legislative elections, the SDS won an overall majority of 45 seats in the RS People's Assembly as well as nine in the union lower house. Plavšić quickly came into conflict with Karadžić and the hardliners and was expelled by the SDS in July 1997, subsequently forming what became the **Serbian People's Union–Biljana Plavšić** (SNS–BP). In further RS elections in November 1997, the SDS was reduced to 24 seats, with the result that Gojko Klicković (SDS) was succeeded as RS Prime Minister by Western-backed moderate Milorad Dodik of the **Party of Independent Social Democrats** (SNSD).

In June 1998 hardliner Dragan Kalinić, having been ousted as RS People's Assembly President, replaced Aleksa Buha as SDS President. In the September 1998 elections for the RS presidency the SDS backed Nikola Poplasen of the ultra-nationalist **Serbian Radical Party** (SRS), ensuring his easy victory over Plavšić. However, the SDS declined further in the RS People's Assembly to only 19 seats (and to four in the union lower house), while Krajišnik failed to secure re-election as the Serb member of the union collective presidency, winning only 44.9% of the Serb vote. The SDS staged a recovery in the November 2000 elections, securing the election of hardline RS Vice-President Mirko **Sarović** of the SRS as RS President with 50.1% of the vote and advancing to 31 seats in the RS People's Assembly with 36.1% (and to six seats in the union lower house). From its restored dominance, the SDS agreed in January 2001 to support a new RS Government headed by Mladen **Ivanić** of the **Party of Democratic Progress**, who appointed one SDS Minister to his 'non-partisan' administration despite Western opposition to SDS participation.

Leadership: Dragan Kalinić (Chair.).
Address: 13/1 Kralia Alfoesa, Banja Luka.
Telephone: (51) 212738.
Fax: (51) 217640.

Serbian Orthodox Church

An autocephalous branch of the **Orthodox Christian** Church based in **Serbia**. The first mass conversion of the **Serbs** was in the 7th century. A Serbian Patriarchate was established unilaterally by the Serbian King (Tsar) Stephen Dushan in 1346. The Church featured prominently in the defining symbolic event of Serbia's national identity, the defeat of its Princes at the Battle of **Kosovo** in 1389 at the hands of the Ottoman Empire. Orthodox Christians were persecuted under Ottoman rule and many fled to neighbouring Christian states under Habsburg rule (*see* **Krajina**). The Serbian Patriarchate, abolished in September 1766, was resurrected in 1919 after the creation of the Kingdom of Serbs, Croats and Slovenes (*see* **Yugoslavia**). The link between the Serbian Church and Serbian nationalism was strengthened further when ethnic **Serbs** were victimized by the fascist puppet Croat (and **Roman Catholic**) state during the Second World War.

Patriarch Pavle was 'enthroned' in **Belgrade** in December 1990.

Serbian People's Alliance–Biljana Plavšić
Srpski Narodni Savez–Biljana Plavšić (SNS–BP)

A moderate **Serb** political party in **Bosnia and Herzegovina**. The **Banja Luka**-based SNS was launched in September 1997 by Biljana Plavšić, then President of the **Serb Republic** (RS), who had been elected in September 1996 as candidate of the nationalist **Serbian Democratic Party** (SDS) but had come into conflict with the SDS hardline wing led by Radovan **Karadžić** and based in Pale. Her move to dissolve the SDS-dominated RS People's Assembly in July 1997 had resulted in her speedy expulsion from the SDS, following which she needed physical and political protection from **NATO** troops and the UN **Office of the High Representative** to ensure her survival. Under a UN-brokered agreement, new RS Assembly elections were held in November 1997 and resulted in the SNS winning 15 of the 83 seats, mainly at the expense of the SDS. Plavšić was therefore able to appoint a 'non-partisan' RS Government headed by Milorad Dodik of the **Party of Independent Social Democrats** (SNSD) and to move the seat of Government from Pale to Banja Luka.

For the September 1998 elections the SNS was part of the moderate Sloga ('Unity') alliance, which included the SNSD and the **Socialist Party of the Serb Republic** (SPRS). Although the alliance secured a victory for the SPRS candidate in the election of the Serb member of the union collective presidency, Plavšić was defeated in the RS presidential contest, winning 47% of the vote against 53% for Nikola Poplasen of the ultra-nationalist **Serbian Radical Party** (SRS), who was backed by the SDS. In the RS Assembly elections, for which Plavšić's name was added to the party title, SNS representation was reduced to 12 seats.

In early 1999 the SNS–BP supported Dodik in his successful resistance to Poplasen's efforts to replace him as RS Prime Minister. However, growing divisions between the Sloga parties contributed to SNS–BP internal strife, which resulted in Plavšić tendering her resignation as leader in May 2000. The following month the party's assembly adopted a vote of no confidence in her and elected Dragan Kostić as Chairman. However, Plavšić speedily obtained a Banja Luka court judgement that her ejection had been illegal and that she and her supporters could retain the party's title. She then convened a special party conference which confirmed her leadership, which was backed by Dodik even though all seven Ministers from the party supported Kostić (who renamed his part of the former SNS the **Democratic People's Alliance**).

In the November 2000 elections the SNS–BP backed the unsuccessful RS presidential candidacy of Dodik and was reduced to two seats in the RS Assembly with only 2.3% of the vote (and won one seat in the union lower house).

Leadership: Biljana Plavšić (Chair.).
Address: 4 Srpski Yunaka, Banja Luka.
Telephone: (51) 218339.
Fax: (51) 218213.

Serbian Radical Party (Bosnia and Herzegovina)
Srpska Radikalna Stranka (SRS)

The powerful ultra-nationalist **Serb** party in **Bosnia and Herzegovina**. The SRS originated as the Bosnian Serb wing of the **Serbian Radical Party of Yugoslavia** and has operated in the **Serb Republic** (RS) as the even more hardline wing of the dominant **Serbian Democratic Party** (SDS). It won seven RS People's Assembly seats in the first post-**Dayton** elections in September 1996, increasing to 15 seats in the further balloting in November 1997, when it drew support from former SDS voters. In the September 1998 elections, SRS leader Nikola Poplasen, to Western dismay, comfortably defeated incumbent Biljana Plavšić of the **Serbian People's Alliance** (SNS) for the RS presidency, winning 53% of the vote with SDS backing, although SRS representation in the RS Assembly fell to 11 seats.

In early 1999 Poplasen was unsuccessful in his efforts to install a new RS Prime Minister in place of Milorad Dodik of the moderate **Party of Independent Social Democrats** (SNSD), his conduct impelling the UN **High Representative** to dismiss him as President in March for 'abuse of power'. Poplasen's unwillingness to depart produced a political impasse, notably in that his Vice-President, Mirko Sarović, was equally unacceptable. However, Sarović gained revenge for the party in the November 2000 elections by winning the RS presidency with 53% of the vote, benefiting from SDS backing to defeat Dodik. In return, the SRS supported SDS candidates in the RS Assembly elections, enabling the latter party to recover its numerical dominance. In January 2001 Sarović appointed Mladen Ivanić of the **Party of Democratic Progress** as RS Prime Minister, heading a 'non-partisan' Government which included an SDS representative.

Serbian Radical Party (Yugoslavia)

Leadership: Mirko Blagojević(Chair. of Executive Committee).
Address: Svetozara Markovića, Banja Luka.
Telephone and Fax: (51) 308886.
Internet: www.srpskastranka-rs.org

Serbian Radical Party (Yugoslavia)
Srpska Radikalna Stranka (SRS)

An ultra-nationalist party in **Yugoslavia** and a leading political advocate of a **Greater Serbia** stretching from the Adriatic to the Aegean. Founded in 1991, the SRS won 34 **Federal Assembly** lower house seats in December 1992 and subsequently co-operated with the dominant **Socialist Party of Serbia** (SPS) until September 1993. Its representation in the Serbian Assembly was almost halved to 39 seats in December 1993, following which the party disbanded its paramilitary wing (named after the Second World War resistance **Chetniks**), which had been accused of atrocities in **Serb** separatist campaigns elsewhere in former Yugoslavia. In the November 1996 federal elections the party's lower house representation fell to 16 seats on a 17.9% vote share. In the September 1997 Serbian Assembly elections, however, the SRS advanced strongly to 82 seats and 29.3% of the vote and in March 1998 was included in a Serbian coalition Government headed by the SPS. Meanwhile, SRS leader Vojislav Šešelj had stood in the protracted Serbian presidential elections in late 1997, his victory in the first contest being annulled because of a low turnout, following which his losing vote share against the SPS candidate in the second was 40%.

The SRS strongly backed President **Milošević**'s intransigence in the 1998–99 **Kosovo** crisis, and was correspondingly critical of the withdrawal of Serbian forces in June 1999, although it remained part of the ruling coalition. The party opted to run a candidate, Tomislav Nikolić, in the September 2000 federal presidential elections, but he was believed to have obtained only 6% of the first-round vote. In the post-election crisis surrounding Milošević's reluctance to accept his defeat by Vojislav **Koštunica** of the **Democratic Opposition of Serbia** (DOS), a crucial factor in his belated concession was Šešelj's declaration of support for Koštunica. Having won only five lower house seats in the simultaneous federal parliamentary elections, the SRS slumped to 23 seats (and 8.5% of the vote) in Serbian Assembly elections in December 2000.

Leadership: Vojislav Šešelj (President).
Address: Ohridska 1, Belgrade 11000.
Telephone: (11) 457745.

Serbian Renewal Movement
Srpski Pokret Obnove (SPO)

A moderate nationalist **Serb** party in **Yugoslavia** reliant on the personal following of its leader Vuk Drašković. Formed in 1990 as a merger of four previous groups, the party became the lynchpin of the DEPOS opposition alliance in the 1992 and 1993 elections, in which the DEPOS parties won 20 **Federal Assembly** lower house seats and 45 seats in the Serbian Assembly. It subsequently joined the Zajedno (Together) alliance with the **Democratic Party** (DS), the **Democratic Party of Serbia** (DSS) and the **Civic Alliance of Serbia** (GSS), which won 22 lower house seats in the November 1996 federal elections. In late 1997 the SPO was the only moderate opposition party to contest the Serbian presidential and parliamentary elections, Drašković coming third in the former contest with 15.4% of the first-round vote and the party winning 45 seats and 20% of the vote in the latter.

In January 1999 Drašković took the SPO into the Federal Government headed by the **Socialist Party of Serbia** (SPS), becoming a Deputy Prime Minister, but the party withdrew three months later after objecting to President **Milošević**'s hardline policy on **Kosovo**. In the September 2000 federal presidential elections which ousted Milošević from power, SPO candidate Vojislav Mihailović obtained only about 3% of the vote, while the party failed to win representation in either the federal lower house or the Serbian Assembly.

Leadership: Vuk Drašković (Chair.).
Address: Knez Mihajlova 48, Belgrade 11000.
Telephone: (11) 635281.
Fax: (11) 628170.
E-mail: info@spo.org.yu
Internet: www.spo.org.yu

Serbian Unity Party
Partija Srpskog Ujedinjenja (PSU)

An ultra-nationalist grouping in **Yugoslavia**, led by notorious **Serb** warlord Arkan until his assassination in January 2000. The PSU was founded in 1992 with support from the then ruling **Socialist Party of Serbia** (SPS) led by Slobodan **Milošević**, who reportedly saw the party's paramilitary provenance as a counterweight to the Serbian Radical Party (SRS) and its paramilitary wing. The PSU leader Zeljko Raznjatović, known universally by his nom de guerre Arkan, had previously created the Tigers paramilitary group, which had been linked with many of the worst atrocities and '**ethnic cleansing**' in the regional conflicts then raging.

The PSU won five seats in the December 1992 elections for the Serbian Assembly, receiving strong support from ethnic Serbs in **Kosovo**. It failed to win representation in the December 1993 Serbian elections and made little impact in subsequent contests in the 1990s, as relations between Arkan and the ruling elite cooled. In March 1999 the **International Criminal Tribunal for the former Yugoslavia** (ICTY) at The Hague disclosed that it had indicted Arkan and sent a warrant for his arrest to the **Belgrade** Government (which took no action). The assassination of Arkan by unknown gunmen in a Belgrade hotel in January 2000 provoked a torrent of speculation about responsibility, much of it centring on Arkan's reported readiness to give evidence against Milošević to the ICTY.

Under the new leadership of fellow paramilitary Borislav Pelević, the PSU unexpectedly made a political comeback in the post-Milošević Serbian Assembly elections in December 2000, winning 14 seats (and 5.3% of the vote).

Leadership: Borislav Pelević.
Address: c/o Skupština Srbije, Belgrade 11000.

Serbs

A south **Slavic people** dominant in modern **Serbia** and forming significant minorities in neighbouring **Bosnia and Herzegovina** and **Croatia**. Their ancestors, who settled in the eastern **Herzegovina** area in the 7th century, converted to **Orthodox Christianity** under Byzantine suzerainty in the early middle ages, distinguishing them from the western **Croats** who adopted **Roman Catholicism**. The Serbian tribes were spread throughout the western **Balkans** during this period and reached their zenith under the Serbian Empire of Stephen Dushan (1331–55). The occupation of Serbian lands by the Ottomans from the 15th century led to the migration of many Serbs, perhaps as many as 25% in total, into neighbouring lands (which came under the sway of the Habsburgs), notably modern-day **Vojvodina** and Croatia.

Very much in the political ascendancy in the royalist **Yugoslav** state in the period before the Second World War, the Serbs were not overtly privileged in the same way under the subsequent communist regime set up by Marshal **Tito**, although Serbia was the largest of its constituent republics and the federal army in particular was heavily Serb-dominated. The disintegration of the **Socialist Federal Republic of Yugoslavia** in the 1990s gave free rein once again to a revived Serbian nationalism. However, the flight of many Croatia-based Serbs during the wars of the early 1990s, and the eventual Bosnian settlement giving local Serbs an autonomous status within the **Serb Republic**, moved the nationalist idea of **Greater Serbia** further down the political agenda. The failure of nationalist politics in Serbia itself in 2000 further dampened nationalist ardour.

The Serbian language is almost identical to Croatian and Bosnian but can be distinguished by its use of the **Cyrillic alphabet**.

Serpents' Island

A small island opposite the delta of the Danube river in the Black Sea, which is the subject of a territorial dispute between **Romania** and **Ukraine**. The island was ceded to Romania in 1878 but control was handed to the authorities of the **Soviet Union** in 1948 in a clandestine agreement. It remains unclear who has the legal claim to the island. The matter is of significance, not only because of the question of the movement and stationing of the post-Soviet **Black Sea Fleet**, but also because of the sea's deposits of oil and natural gas. In 1999 the two countries agreed to put the question 'on hold' for two years.

Sevastopol

A strategically important port on the **Crimean** peninsula in southern **Ukraine**. *Population*: 366,200 (1991 estimate). The impressive natural harbour has served the people of the peninsula since the Greeks established the colony of Chersonesus at the site. Despite years of neglect under the Turkish Ottoman Empire the city was rapidly developed as a major strategic port by **Russia** after it annexed the Crimea in 1783. Severe damage sustained during the crucial Crimean War siege of Sevastopol between 1854 and 1855 was repaired in the late 19th century. However, commercial activity was shifted to the port of Feodosiya, while Sevastopol took on its present role as a principal naval base for the imperial **Black Sea Fleet**. Further destruction during the Second World War was again repaired, by the **Soviet** authorities. The Russian navy still maintains a significant presence in the city.

SFOR *see* **Stabilization Force**.

SFRY *see* **Socialist Federal Republic of Yugoslavia**.

Shamiran Women's Party (SWP)

A women-only party in **Armenia** which took as its title the Armenian version of the name of the legendary Queen Semiramis of Assyria, reputed to have built the Hanging Gardens of Babylon. The party won an impressive 17% of the vote and eight seats in the 1995 **National Assembly** elections, to become the largest single opposition party. It slumped to 0.2% of the proportional vote and no seats in the 1999 elections.
 Leadership: Gayane Saroukhian (Chair.).

Shanghai Co-operation Organization (SCO)

An organization founded in June 2001 to promote regional security and co-operation between China, the **Russian Federation** and four of the former Soviet central Asian Republics. The SCO has specifically pledged to work to combat terrorism and to promote regional stability. Its Declaration to this effect was signed on 15 June 2001 by the Presidents of its six member states—China, Russian Federation, Kazakhstan, Kyrgyzstan, Tajikistan and Uzbekistan. The SCO is based on the 'Shanghai Five' group (not at that time including Uzbekistan) brought together at the invitation of the Chinese in Shanghai in 1996.

Shevardnadze, Eduard

President of **Georgia**, its dominant political figure and Head of State since 1992, and a former high-ranking communist who, as Soviet Foreign Minister under Mikhail **Gorbachev** in 1985–90, helped to engineer the **Soviet Union**'s withdrawal from the **Cold War** arms race and from regional hegemony in **eastern Europe**.

Eduard Amvrosiyevich Shevardnadze was born on 25 January 1928, the son of a teacher in the Georgian village of Mamat. Heavily involved as a teacher and activist in Komsomol, the communist youth league, he became its First Secretary in Georgia in 1957. Two years later he was elected to the Supreme Soviet in the Republic, and also in 1959 completed a correspondence degree in history. Drafted into the civilian police (MVD), Shevardnadze began to make a name for himself as Head of Georgia's Ministry of Public Order from 1965 onwards, tackling both unrest and corruption, and clamping down on self-enrichment by government and party officials. He was promoted to be the Republic's Minister of the Interior and, from 1972, First Secretary of the Georgian Communist Party. His sudden emergence within the top leadership at Soviet level in 1985, when he became a member of the Politburo of the **Communist Party of the Soviet Union** (KPSS) and simultaneously Foreign Minister, was mainly owing to his political association and growing personal friendship with new KPSS General Secretary Gorbachev. The crowds who welcomed the collapse of communism across the countries of central and eastern Europe in 1989 hailed Shevardnadze, like Gorbachev, as a hero of democratization.

Shevardnadze felt the growing danger, however, of a Soviet military and hardline backlash. Resigning as Foreign Minister in December 1990, he warned that 'dictatorship is coming', a fear which was later vindicated by the 1991 **August coup** attempt in Moscow. Joining in efforts to rally support for Gorbachev, he returned briefly to the post of Soviet Foreign Minister as the Soviet Union was disintegrating in 1991.

He returned in March 1992 to a newly independent Georgia, where open conflict between nationalist factions was threatening to destroy a country already in serious economic disarray. Appointed within four days as Chairman of a military-dominated State Council, he was pitched into a period of overt conflict with the ousted former President Zviad Gamsakhurdia and more seriously with secessionists in **Abkhazia**. On 11 October 1992, he was elected Chairman of the **Parliament of Georgia**, and a referendum endorsed him as Head of State and Commander-in-Chief of the Armed Forces. In February 1994 he and **Russian** President Boris **Yeltsin** signed a treaty of friendship and co-operation, controversially allowing the extended presence of Russian military bases on Georgian soil. He also took Georgia into the Russian-dominated **Commonwealth of Independent States** (CIS), recognizing how vulnerable Georgia's isolated position had become, especially after rebel forces gained the upper hand in Abkhazia (where he himself came under heavy shelling during one visit).

The country faced economic problems so severe that Shevardnadze was forced to announce unpopular food rationing measures. Over the next few years, however, he began to be able to claim some success in tackling chronic instability, although there were renewed flare-ups in the conflict with Abkhazia, and other separatist struggles in different parts of the country. Shevardnadze's own life came under threat, his regime having struggled to control the private armies of various nationalist leaders. He survived a car bombing in **Tbilisi** in August 1995, and another assassination attempt in February 1998.

Under a new Constitution in 1995, the office of President was reintroduced, with executive powers, and Shevardnadze was elected for a five-year term in a nationwide ballot on 5 November 1995, winning more than three-quarters of the votes cast. He was re-elected overwhelmingly in April 2000 for a further five-year term commencing on 1 May. Shevardnadze also chairs the **Citizens' Union of Georgia**, which he founded in 1993 as a pro-democracy and free-market-oriented alliance and which won a large majority in the 1995 and 1999 legislative elections.

Address: Office of the President, Ingorokva 7, 380007 Tbilisi.
Telephone: (32) 999653.
Fax: (32) 990879.
E-mail: office@presidpress.gov.ge
Internet: www.presidpress.gov.ge

Shock therapy

A policy of rapid transition from a command economy to a market-based economy, which in the short term imposes economic and social hardship in pursuit of medium- to long-term gains. **Poland**'s Balcerowicz plan was the most notable example of shock therapy. Introduced by the country's first post-communist Finance Minister, Leszek **Balcerowicz**, in January 1990, it was the first and most radical market-oriented economic reform package in any post-communist State. It abolished price controls and state subsidies but, in an attempt to reduce inflation, it retained wage controls. State spending was to be held down and state-owned enterprises to be privatized. The Balcerowicz plan succeeded in reducing the inflation rate and brought goods into shops, ending the queues of the communist era. However, industrial production declined rapidly and unemployment grew, and the plan proved politically unpopular.

Siberia

The vast, empty steppe and tundra stretching to the east of the Ural mountains. Siberia constitutes the major part of Asiatic **Russia**. It is perhaps most famous as the final destination of many of Stalin's **deported nationalities** and the setting for the many gulag prison camps. The Arctic Circle passes across almost half of Siberia and the climate is unforgiving all year round. A particularly harsh winter struck the region in 2000/01, but there are also real concerns about the effect of global warming on the permafrost of the north. Heavy industry is concentrated in cities such as Magnitogorsk at the south-western edge near the Ural mountains and in equally isolated settlements scattered throughout. Industrial output from Siberia in 1999 accounted for around 25% of the country's total.

The indigenous people of Siberia were first conquered by the Mongols in the 13th century under the rule of the Golden Horde. Russian dominance came quickly between the 1590s and the 1640s and has remained ever since. Annexation by the Russian Empire brought waves of ethnic **Russian** colonists and permanently altered the ethnic make-up of Siberia. Population is most dense along the region's southern edge. Industrialization supplemented fur trading in the Arctic wastes and was speeded up greatly following the construction of the celebrated **Trans-Siberian Railway** (TSR), which eventually linked **Moscow** with Vladivostok (literally 'rule of the east') on the Amur Valley's Sea of Japan coast.

The principal non-Russian republics and regions of Siberia include Yakutia in the north-east, Buryatia on the eastern shores of Lake Baikal in the south-east and the Jewish Autonomous Region on the border with China.

SKJ *see* **League of Communists of Yugoslavia**.

Skopje

The capital of **Macedonia** situated on the River Vardar in the mountainous northern part of the country. *Population*: around 444,000. Skopje has had a long history as a regional centre and has undergone several different incarnations after natural disasters, purposeful destruction and political changes.

Founded in ancient times as an Illyrian settlement, the city became a regional administrative centre under the Romans. After near total destruction in an earthquake in 518 the city recovered towards the end of the first millennium. It first fell into **Slavic** hands when it was conquered by **Serbian** princes in 1189. However, a long period of Turkish domination followed conquest of the region by the

Ottomans in 1392. Skopje (Usküb) became the capital of the province of Macedonia but Austrian forces razed it to the ground in 1689 to combat a cholera epidemic. The region was revitalized in the late 19th century with the construction of the Belgrade–Thessaloniki railway line.

With the collapse of the Ottoman Empire in Europe, Skopje and Macedonia came once more under Serbian rule in 1913, beginning an 80-year political connection with **Belgrade**. Named as the capital of the Macedonian republic within **Yugoslavia** in 1945, Skopje has since been the republic's political and cultural centre. A massive earthquake in 1963 ruined 80% of the city and international assistance in reconstruction efforts earned it the name of 'City of International Solidarity'. The post-quake city has been designed to resist future geological upheavals. It is fortunate that it also retains a Roman aqueduct and a handful of mediaeval buildings.

In its latest incarnation as capital of an independent Macedonia, Skopje is home to governmental institutions (on the left bank of the Vardar) and has become a centre for light industry (on the river's right bank).

Skupština *see* **Parliamentary Assembly (Bosnia and Herzegovina)**.

Slavic peoples

The largest single ethnic family in Europe. The Slavs are an Indo-European ethnic group whose area of settlement spreads from the far-eastern shores of Asiatic **Russia** to the heart of central Europe and across the **Balkans**. Slavs are divided into three main branches: the east Slavs (**Belarusians, Russians** and **Ukrainians**), west Slavs (**Czechs, Poles, Slovaks** and the minority Sorbs, or Wends, in eastern Germany), and south Slavs (**Bosniaks, Croatians, Montenegrins, Serbs** and **Slovenes—Yugoslavs**). The **Bulgarians** and **Macedonians** are also considered south Slavs and they speak a Slavic language, although their origin is generally accepted to have been from a mixing of Slavs and **Tatars**.

Arising from Asian origins in the 3rd or 2nd millennium BC, the Slavs historically settled north of the Carpathian mountains. The divide into the three major groups occurred from the 5th century AD as **German** tribes migrated westward into central Europe. The resultant geographic division encouraged separate linguistic and cultural differences.

The most potent of these differences is the split between **Roman Catholicism** (west Slavs, Croats, Slovenes, and some Belarusians and Ukrainians) and **Orthodox Christianity** (remaining east Slavs, Bulgarians, Macedonians, Montenegrins and Serbs). Along this fault line can also be found the use of the Latin and **Cyrillic alphabets** respectively (although all Belarusians and Ukrainians use Cyrillic). Pan-Slavic movements, usually inspired by Russian imperialism, have generally failed owing to this religious/cultural difference, among others.

Slavonia

The most recent experiment, uniting the majority of south Slavs in **Yugoslavia**, proved a notable disaster—the religious differences there being further complicated by the existence of two groups of south Slavs which follow the Islamic faith, the Bosniaks (who use the Latin script), and the **Pomaks** in **Macedonia** (who use Cyrillic).

Slavic languages are similar enough for rudimentary understanding between all Slavic peoples. In some cases, particularly within the former Yugoslav states, the differences between languages are small and distinctions are inspired more by nationalism than by linguistics.

The development of the various Slavic countries today has been largely due to the political divisions of the 20th century. The west and the south Slavs now generally aspire to greater integration with western Europe (*see* **central Europe**) whereas the east Slavs, the most homogenous group, tentatively seek closer regional integration between themselves, based around the economic dominance of the **Russian Federation**.

Slavonia

The north-eastern portion of **Croatia**, geographically incorporating the south-western corner of the Pannonian plain. Historically the centre of **Croatian** settlement, literally 'land of the **Slavs**', the region was dominated by the Catholic **Hungarian** kingdom until the establishment of the Kingdom of the Serbs, Croats and Slovenes in 1918. The region contained a large proportion of Croatia's **Serbian** population in the **Krajina** areas in its south and far east. These communities were devastated by the intense fighting in the area in the mid-1990s, and the flight of hundreds of thousands of Serb refugees in the face of a successful Croat military offensive launched in August 1995.

SLD *see* **Democratic Left Alliance**.

Slovak Chamber of Commerce and Industry
Slovenská obchodná a priemyselná komora

The principal organization in **Slovakia** for promoting business contacts, both internally and externally, in the post-communist era.
President: Peter Mihók.
Address: Gorkého 9, 81603 Bratislava.
Telephone: (2) 54433291.
Fax: (2) 54131159.
E-mail: sopkurad@scci.sk

Slovak Democratic Coalition
Slovenská Demokratická Koalícia (SDK)

An alliance of centre-left parties in **Slovakia** which came to power in 1998. The SDK had been launched in April that year as an electoral alliance of five parties then in opposition, namely (i) the Christian Democratic Movement (KDH), which had been founded in February 1990 under the leadership of communist-era Catholic dissident Ján Carnogurský and which had won 17 seats in the 1994 **National Council** elections; (ii) the Democratic Union of Slovakia (DÚS), which had been founded in 1994 as a merger of two centrist parties and which had won 15 seats in that year's elections; (iii) the Social Democratic Party of Slovakia (SDSS), which had won two seats in 1994 in alliance with the **Party of the Democratic Left** (SDĽ); (iv) the Slovak Green Party (SZS), which had also won two seats in 1994 in alliance with the SDĽ; and (v) the unrepresented Democratic Party (DS).

Under the leadership of former KDH Minister Mikuláš **Dzurinda**, the SDK in July 1998 registered as a single party, in light of new electoral rules specifying that each component of an alliance must surmount the 5% threshold to obtain representation. In the September 1998 elections, the SDK narrowly failed to overtake the then ruling **Movement for a Democratic Slovakia** (HZDS), winning 42 of the 150 seats with 26.3% of the vote. Nevertheless, on the basis of a pre-election agreement, Dzurinda was able to form a majority coalition Government which included the SDĽ, the **Party of Civic Understanding** (SOP) and the **Hungarian Coalition Party** (SMK), on a programme of accelerated pro-market reform and accession to the **European Union** and the **North Atlantic Treaty Organization**.

In direct presidential elections in May 1999, the SDK officially backed the successful candidacy of Rudolf **Schuster** of the SOP; but the reluctance of some SDK components to abandon their individual party identities became increasingly apparent. In January 2000, therefore, Prime Minister Dzurinda announced the creation of the Slovak Democratic and Christian Union (SDKU) as the effective successor to the SDK, being elected SDKU Chairman at its founding conference in November. So as not to provoke open defections by SDK components, however, activation of the SDKU was deferred until the 2002 parliamentary elections, pending which the SDK would continue in being under Dzurinda's chairmanship.

Nevertheless, in December 2000 deputies associated with the KDH and the DS withdrew from the SDK parliamentary group, while the SDSS entered into 'parallel' talks for a possible merger with either the SDĽ or the SOP. Although all the SDK components said that they would continue to support the Government, Prime Minister Dzurinda expressed disappointment at the reaction to his SDKU concept.

Leadership: Mikuláš Dzurinda (Chair.).
Address: Nábrežie Ludvíka Svobodu 1, Bratislava 81101.
Telephone: (2) 54416207.
Fax: (2) 43414114.
E-mail: sdk@sdk.sk
Internet: www.sdk.sk

Slovak Investment and Trade Development Agency

Government agency in **Slovakia**. Founded in 1991.
General Director: Roman Minarović.
Address: Drieňová 3, 82102 Bratislava.
Telephone: (2) 43421851.
Fax: (2) 43421853.
E-mail: sario@sario.sk
Internet: www.sario.sk

Slovak National Party
Slovenská Národná Strana (SNS)

A nationalistic formation, part of ruling coalitions in **Slovakia** between 1992 and 1998, which has given overt political expression to hostility within Slovakia to the **Hungarian** minority and to **Roma** (Gypsies). The SNS was launched in December 1989 after the collapse of communism in **Czechoslovakia**, on a platform calling for the revival of Slovak national pride, the establishment of Slovak-language schools in every district (including those with ethnic Hungarian majorities) and exclusive use of Slovak at all official levels. It obtained 13.9% of the vote in the 1990 Slovak **National Council** elections, but only 7.9% (and nine seats) in the June 1992 contest, after which it joined a coalition with the dominant **Movement for a Democratic Slovakia** (HZDS). It continued to support the Government after the resignation of its sole Minister in March 1993, and in October resumed formal coalition status, obtaining several key Ministries.

In February 1994 the SNS was weakened by a split involving the defection of the party's 'moderate' wing led by its then Chairman Ľudovit Černák. The following month, on the fall of the HZDS Government, the rump SNS went into opposition, whereupon the SNS Central Council decided in May that only ethnic **Slovaks** were eligible to be members of the party. In the autumn 1994 elections the SNS took only 5.4% of the vote (and nine seats), being nevertheless awarded two portfolios in a new HZDS-led coalition. Thereafter the party resolutely opposed the granting of any form of autonomy to ethnic Hungarian areas of Slovakia under the March 1995 Slovak-Hungarian friendship treaty and also continued to oppose Slovakian membership of **NATO**, even though the goal of accession was official government policy.

In the September 1998 parliamentary elections, the SNS advanced to 14 seats with 9.1% of the vote but went into opposition to a centre-left coalition headed by the **Slovak Democratic Coalition** (SDK). In the May 1999 presidential elections, then SNS leader Ján Slota came a very poor fifth with only 2.5% of the first-round vote, having attracted much criticism for his anti-Hungarian tirades during the campaigning. In September 1999 Slota was ousted as SNS Chair by a party congress and succeeded the following month by Anna Malíková, hitherto Deputy Chair.

In October 2000 Malíková reaffirmed her party's opposition to NATO membership on grounds of cost and its support for an independent European security system. In January 2001 the SNS elaborated on its controversial plan for 'reservations' in which 'unadaptable' Roma would be educated to become good citizens.
Leadership: Anna Malíková (Chair.).
Address: Safárikovo nám. 3, Bratislava 81499.
Telephone: (2) 52924260.
Fax: (2) 52966188.
Internet: www.sns.sk

Slovakia
Slovenská Republika

A small landlocked republic in central Europe, bounded to the west by the Czech Republic, to the north by Poland, to the east by Ukraine, to the south by Hungary and to the south-west by Austria. Administratively, the country is divided into eight regions (kraje).

Area: 49,034 sq km; *capital*: **Bratislava**; *population*: 5.4m. (2001 estimate), comprising **Slovaks** 85.7%, **Hungarians** 10.7%, **Roma** 1.5%, **Czechs** 1%, **Ruthenians** 0.3%, **Ukrainians** 0.3%, **Germans** 0.1%, **Poles** 0.1%, others 0.3%; *official language*: Slovak; *religion*: **Roman Catholic** 60.3%, atheist 9.7%, **Protestant** 8.4%, **Orthodox** 4.1%, other 17.5%.

Supreme legislative authority is vested in the unicameral **National Council** (Národná Rada) composed of 150 deputies, who are elected for a four-year term by a system of proportional representation, subject to a 5% threshold for individual parties whether or not they run in alliances. The Head of State is the President, who is directly elected for a five-year term (renewable once only) and who appoints the Prime Minister.

History: The region was settled by **Slavic** tribes from the 5th century and, in the 9th century, the Great Moravian Empire (Slovakia, **Bohemia** and **Moravia**) was established. Slovakia was then conquered by the Magyars (Hungarians), however, and consolidated into the Hungarian kingdom in the 11th century. In 1526 the Austrian Habsburg dynasty inherited the Hungarian throne, retaining most of the Slovakian lands. The establishment of the Austro-Hungarian dual monarchy in 1867 restored Slovakia to separate Hungarian rule, under which a policy of 'Magyarization' was introduced and nascent Slovak nationalism suppressed. Following the collapse of the Hapsburg Empire in the First World War, Slovakia declared independence in 1918. Under the 1919 Treaty of **Versailles**, however, it became part of the new Republic of **Czechoslovakia**, together with Bohemia, Moravia and Ruthenia (*see* **Transcarpathia**).

During the first republic the Slovaks increasingly resented the political dominance of the Czechs and their unwillingness to allow internal self-government for Slovakia. Following the 1938 Munich Agreement, under which Czechoslovakia was forced to accept the annexation by Germany of its German-populated **Sudetenland** border territories, the main Slovak national party declared autonomy (and **Hungary** annexed Hungarian-speaking areas in south Slovakia). In 1939 Nazi Germany invaded Czechoslovakia and established Slovakia as a self-governing, albeit 'puppet', state under fascist leadership, while Bohemia and Moravia became a German protectorate.

Soviet forces liberated the country from German occupation in 1945, and Slovakia, with limited autonomy, was returned to the pre-war Czechoslovak state. The Hungarian-speaking south was also restored, although Ruthenia was ceded to the **Soviet Union**. In legislative elections in 1946, the Communist Party of Czechoslovakia won 38% of the vote and became the dominant political party. Two years later the communists gained full control and declared a 'People's Democracy' in the Soviet style of government. In 1968, following the repression of the post-war years, Communist Party leader Alexander **Dubček** (a Slovak) introduced a programme of political and economic liberalization known as the '**Prague Spring**'. This was perceived by the Soviet Union as a threat to its control of **eastern Europe**, with the result that **Warsaw Pact** forces invaded the country to restore orthodox communist rule. One of Dubček's reforms survived, however: in 1969, under a new federal system, Slovakia became the Slovak Socialist Republic, although with largely powerless institutions.

In 1989, encouraged by democratization movements elsewhere in eastern Europe, anti-Government demonstrations in Czechoslovakia forced the communists, in the so-called '**velvet revolution**', to relinquish their monopoly of power. By the end of that year, a new Government with a non-communist majority had been formed and Václav **Havel**, a prominent writer and former dissident, had replaced Gustáv **Husák** as state President. At the same time, a strong Slovak nationalist movement emerged. Led by Vladimír **Mečiar**, who assumed the premiership in Slovakia in 1990, the **Movement for a Democratic Slovakia** (HZDS) became the political platform for outright independence in the 1992 parliamentary elections. The creation of separate Slovak and Czech entities was agreed and took effect in January 1993 with the dissolution of the Czechoslovak federation (the so-called '**velvet divorce**'). Michal Kováč was subsequently elected President of the new Slovak Republic.

Having lost parliamentary support owing to defections, Mečiar's coalition Government was defeated on a vote of no confidence in March 1994 and obliged to resign. In the September–October 1994 general elections, however, the HZDS was returned as substantially the largest party with 61 seats, so that Mečiar formed a new coalition in alliance with the **Slovak National Party** (SNS) and the Association of Workers of Slovakia.

Over the next four years the authoritarian nature of Mečiar's regime slowed down Slovakia's transition to a free-market economy, generating political conflict and international concern about the observance of civil and constitutional rights. Tension between Mečiar and President Kováč led to a parliamentary vote of no confidence in Kováč in 1995, although without the three-fifths majority required to oust the President, so that a lengthy political confrontation ensued. When President Kováč's term expired in March 1998, the National Council was repeatedly unable to elect a successor because no candidate could win the necessary three-fifths majority. In the political vacuum, Mečiar assumed the presidential role but his seemingly undemocratic actions served to unite the political opposition.

Latest elections: In the September 1998 parliamentary elections, the HZDS narrowly retained the largest number of seats, winning 43 on a vote share of 27.0%. The new centre-left **Slovak Democratic Coalition** (SDK) came a close second with 42 seats (and 26.3% of the vote), followed by the **Party of the Democratic Left** (SDĽ) with 23 (14.7%), the **Hungarian Coalition Party** (SMK) with 15 (9.1%), the SNS with 14 (9.1%) and the **Party of Civic Understanding** (SOP) with 13 (8.0%). The outcome was the formation of a majority centre-left coalition under the premiership of Mikuláš **Dzurinda** (SDK) and also including the SDĽ, the SMK and the SOP.

The new Government speedily secured the enactment of constitutional amendments providing for direct elections for the presidency, the first such balloting taking place in May 1999. Nominated as the candidate of all four ruling parties, Rudolf **Schuster** of the SOP easily defeated Mečiar and four other candidates, winning 47.4% in the first round and 57.2% in the runoff against the HZDS leader.

Recent developments: Commanding a majority of 93 of the 150 National Council seats, the Dzurinda Government remained politically secure in 2000–01, as it injected greater urgency into pro-market reform after years of slow progress under the HZDS (*see* **Slovakia, economy**) and steered Slovakia more enthusiastically towards membership of the **European Union** (EU) and the **North Atlantic Treaty Organization** (NATO) (see below). In opposition, the HZDS attempted to reassert its previous dominance by forcing a referendum on its proposal that early parliamentary elections should be held, but the exercise failed dismally in November 2000 when the voter turnout was less than half of the 50% required for the result to be valid.

On the other hand, Dzurinda encountered difficulties in his attempt to weld the SDK into a unitary party, with the result that in January 2000 he announced the creation of a new party called the Slovak Democratic and Christian Union (SDKU). However, because of the reluctance of some SDK components to join a new party, the Prime Minister stated that the SDKU would not be activated until the start of campaigning for the 2002 parliamentary elections.

International relations and defence: In 1993 Slovakia, as a newly sovereign state, became a member of the United Nations, the **Council of Europe**, the **Organization for Security and Co-operation in Europe**, the **Central European Initiative**, the **Central European Free Trade Area** and the **Danube Commission**. The following year Slovakia acceded to NATO's **Partnership for Peace** programme with the aim of achieving full NATO membership (although it was not included in the first NATO enlargement to central Europe in 1999). Having applied for EU membership in 1995, Slovakia was accepted as an official candidate in December 1999 and formal negotiations opened in February 2000.

In 1995 Slovakia and Hungary signed a Treaty of Friendship and Co-operation, which guaranteed the rights of ethnic minorities in each country and confirmed existing borders. However, bilateral tensions continued over a controversial Slovak language law of 1995 which restricted the official use of any language other than Slovak and also over a dispute about the joint hydroelectric **Gabčíkovo-Nagymaros Dam** project on the Danube river. The centre-left Government elected in September 1998 enacted a new language law in 1999 which authorized the official use of Hungarian and other languages in towns with an ethnic minority population of over 20%. However, the law was criticized as inadequate in Hungary and by ethnic Hungarian groups in Slovakia.

Slovakia's defence budget for 2000 amounted to some US $350m., equivalent to about 1.7% of GDP. The size of the armed forces at the end of 2000 was some 38,500 personnel, including those serving under compulsory conscription of nine months, while trained reservists numbered an estimated 20,000.

Slovakia, economy

An economy whose transition from state control to a market system is closely tied to the aim of achieving **European Union** (EU) membership.

GNP: US $18,793m. (2000); *GNP per capita*: $3,700 (2000); *GDP at PPP*: $45,900m. (1999); *GDP per capita at PPP*: $8,500 (1999); *exports*: $11,869m. (2000); *imports*: $12,786m. (2000); *currency*: koruna (plural: koruny; US $1=K48.01 at the end of December 2001).

In 1999 industry accounted for 35% of GDP, agriculture for 5% and services for 60%. Some 31% of the land is arable, 3% under permanent crops, 17% permanent pasture and 41% forests and woodland. The main crops are grain, vegetables, sugar beet, hops and fruit, while there is significant animal husbandry. The main mineral resources are brown coal (lignite) and some iron, copper and manganese ore; there are largely-unexploited reserves of petroleum and natural gas. The principal industries are light manufacturing, iron and steel, chemicals, food and beverages, and transport equipment. In 1999 56% of domestic energy generation came from nuclear power stations, 24% from coal-based thermal stations (which are being increasingly withdrawn because of the pollution which they cause) and some 20% from hydroelectricity. Slovakia is also a net importer of electricity, mainly from the **Czech Republic**.

Slovakia's main exports by value are machinery and transport equipment (39% of the total in 1999), intermediate manufactured goods (27%), miscellaneous manufactured goods (13%), chemicals (8%) and raw materials (4%). Principal imports are machinery and transport equipment (38% in 1999), intermediate manufactured goods (18%), mineral fuels and lubricants (13%), chemicals (11%) and miscellaneous manufactured goods (9%). Germany took 27% of Slovakia's exports in

2000, the Czech Republic took 17% and Italy 9%. Germany was also the main supplier of Slovakia's imports in 2000 (25%), with the **Russian Federation** providing 17% and the Czech Republic 15%. In 1998 the EU accounted for 56% of Slovakia's exports and 50% of its imports.

The division of **Czechoslovakia** into the Czech Republic and Slovakia from the beginning of 1993 presented economic problems to each of the new countries in view of the separation of their respective economic bases. Under communism, Slovakia had concentrated on various energy-intensive heavy industries, mostly run on inefficient bureaucratic lines and with relatively low productivity. Within the **Council for Mutual Economic Assistance** (Comecon), it had specialized in armaments production for the **Warsaw Pact**, the end of which left much of this sector redundant. Following the division of Czechoslovakia, interchange between Slovakia and the Czech Republic became less readily available than hitherto, as the uncompetitive realities of the industrial sector became more exposed.

Despite these problems, Slovakia experienced a much lower immediate drop in output than other ex-communist countries, with GNP and GDP each falling by only about 1% per annum on average during the period 1990–94. There followed three years of strong GDP growth of over 6% annually, underpinned by high foreign investment, as inflation was curbed from 23% in 1993 to 6% in 1997. However, the absence of real structural reform under Governments of the populist **Movement for a Democratic Slovakia** (HZDS), combined with poor public and private economic governance, served to reveal underlying weaknesses from 1997, associated in particular with ill-advised or corrupt lending by unreformed state-owned banks. The budget deficit jumped to over 5% of GDP in 1997–98 and current-account deficits of over 10% were recorded, as GDP growth fell back to 4% in 1998 and unemployment increased to 14% of the registered labour force. A speculative attack on the koruna in the wake of the mid-1998 Russian financial crisis (*see* **Russian Federation, economy**) forced the **National Bank of Slovakia** to float the currency in October 1998, immediately devaluing it by 6%.

The centre-left Government elected in September 1998 moved quickly to stabilize the economy and to initiate new structural reform measures intended to accelerate transition to a market economy. The budget deficit was reduced to 3.6% of GDP in 1999 and the current-account deficit to 6% of GDP, although GDP expansion declined further to 1.9% and inflation rose to 11%. Signs of renewed progress were apparent in 2000, during which GDP growth of 2.2% was recorded, although unemployment rose to a record level of just under 20% by January 2001.

The Government's budget for 2001, as adopted by the **National Council**, provided for expenditure of K217,800m. and revenue of K180,600m., and therefore for a fiscal deficit of 3.9% of GDP. A basic aim of government economic policy is to qualify Slovakia for EU accession, on which formal negotiations opened in February 2000. In August 2000 Slovakia was formally invited to become a member of the **Organization for Economic Co-operation and Development**.

Privatization of state-owned enterprises was initiated in the early 1990s within the Czechoslovakia framework and was largely undertaken through the **voucher privatization** system. Following the 1993 separation, political differences in Slovakia delayed further disposals of state assets, despite the introduction in 1995 of direct sales through the **National Property Fund**. By early 1997 the private sector accounted for about three-quarters of Slovakia's GDP, industrial output and employment. However, the then HZDS-led Government earmarked some 30 major enterprises for retention within the public sector, with the state also retaining a holding in a further batch of large concerns.

The new Government appointed in late 1998 abandoned these reservations and undertook to expedite the privatization process, with priority being given to disposal of the state-owned banking sector, telecommunications and the gas and electricity utilities, although in the case of the utilities the state would retain majority stakes. The Government was boosted in its quest for economic stability by the signature in May 2000, after seven years of negotiation, of an agreement with the Czech Republic dividing the state assets of former Czechoslovakia between the two successor countries.

Slovaks

A west **Slavic people** dominant in modern **Slovakia** who arrived in the region during the 7th century. Ethnically they are almost identical to the neighbouring **Czechs**, with whom they shared the state of **Czechoslovakia** for much of the 20th century. Slovak as a language is very similar to the other west Slavic languages (Czech and Polish) and is transcribed using the Latin script. Most Slovaks, like the Czechs, practise **Roman Catholicism**, although a sizeable minority follow Protestant faiths, and around 10% consider themselves atheists. The connection with the Czech people was broken when the empire of **Moravia** was splintered in the 10th century and Slovakia was absorbed into the **Hungarian** monarchy for the next 800 years. This long separation engendered a distinct Slovak identity. In the 20th century, ideas of separate Slovak nationhood remained muted within the Czechoslovakia of the inter-war period, although after 1939 the Nazis sought to exploit them with the creation of a puppet Slovak state. After the fall of communism, nationalist politicians placed more emphasis on the divergence of Slovak interests from those of the Czech Lands, leading to the separation of the two in the so-called '**velvet divorce**'. Sizeable Slovak minorities exist in the **Czech Republic** and **Hungary**.

Slovene Press Agency
Slovenska Tiskovna Agencija (STA)

The main news agency in **Slovenia**. Established in June 1991, STA is the first Slovenian news agency. Its creation was mooted by pro-democracy activists in the

1980s and realized during the collapse of the **Socialist Federal Republic of Yugoslavia** in 1991. From its beginnings as a mouthpiece for the emerging Slovene democracy, STA has now developed to provide news items to the international as well as the domestic press.
Director-General: Tadej Labernik.
Editor-in-Chief: Vera Celcer.
Address: Cankarjeva 5, p.p. 145, 1101 Ljubljana.
Telephone: (1) 2410100.
Fax: (1) 4266050.
E-mail: desk@sta.si
Internet: www.sta.si

Slovenes

A south **Slavic people** dominant in modern **Slovenia**. Early Slovene settlement south of the eastern Alps first took place in the 6th century. The 'Alpine Slavs' came into close contact with the various local powerbrokers, from the Avars to the Austrians. Although ethnically and linguistically the Slovenes are closely related to the neighbouring **Bosniaks, Croats** and **Serbs**, a long historical connection with western European politics and culture, particularly that of Austria, has developed a more **central European** identity. Like the Croats, Slovenes largely practise **Roman Catholicism**, and use the Latin script to transcribe their version of south Slavic (which contains many German and Italian loanwords). They were subjugated as a rural peasantry under Austrian rule and those finding themselves in modern German- or Italian-speaking states have been under pressure to assimilate into those communities. Around 100,000 Slovenes live in the **Trieste** region of north-eastern Italy, with a further 24,000 in **Croatia** and about 15,000 in southern Austria.

Slovenia
Republika Slovenija

A small republic in south-eastern Europe whose successful bid for independence in 1989–91 marked the first stage in the break-up of the **Socialist Federal Republic of Yugoslavia** (SFRY). It is bounded by Austria to the north, Hungary to the east, Croatia to the south, Italy to the west, and by a short coastal strip on the Adriatic Sea to the south-west. Administratively, the country is divided into 148 local authorities and municipalities.

Area: 20,256 sq km; *capital*: **Ljubljana**; *population*: 2m. (2001 estimate), comprising ethnic **Slovenes** 91%, **Croats** 3%, **Serbs** 2%, **Muslims** 1%, others 3%; *official language*: Slovenian; *religion*: **Roman Catholic** 71%, Lutheran 1%, Muslim 1%, atheist 4%, other 23%.

Slovenia

Under the 1991 Constitution, executive authority is exercised by the Prime Minister and Cabinet of Ministers. The President, who is directly elected for a maximum of two five-year terms, has largely ceremonial powers. Legislative power is vested in a unicameral **National Assembly** (Državni Zbor), with 90 members elected for a four-year term, 40 directly by constituencies and 50 by a system of proportional representation subject to a 3% threshold (with one seat each reserved for the **Hungarian** and Italian ethnic minorities). There is also an advisory 40-member National Council (Državni Svet), whose members serve five-year terms, 18 being indirectly elected by socio-economic interest groups and 22 elected by communities to represent local interests.

History: Once part of the Roman province of Illyria, Slovenia was settled by **Slavic** tribes from the 6th century and came under feudal Bavarian and Frankish domination in the 8th century. By the late 10th century much of present-day Slovenia was within the Holy Roman Empire and eventually passed under Habsburg rule in the 14th century. France briefly ruled western Slovenia during the Napoleonic era, but Habsburg rule was restored in 1815 at the Congress of Vienna. In 1867 most of Slovenia was incorporated into the Austrian half of the Austro-Hungarian Empire. The collapse of this imperial structure followed defeat in the First World War. Slovenia in 1918 joined other south Slav territories within the newly-formed 'Kingdom of Serbs, Croats and Slovenes' (renamed **Yugoslavia** in 1929).

During the Second World War Slovenia was under Italian and German occupation from 1941 until 1945. Resistance was led by the Slovene Liberation Front in alliance with the communist-led Yugoslav Partisans under **Tito**. At the end of the war, Slovenia came under communist rule as one of the six constituent republics of the Socialist Federal Republic of Yugoslavia (together with **Serbia**, **Croatia**, **Bosnia and Herzegovina**, **Macedonia** and **Montenegro**).

Tito's death in 1980 ushered in a period of instability as Yugoslavia's political structure began to break down because of increasing nationalism and rivalry among the constituent republics and their populations. In 1989 the Slovenian Assembly declared the sovereignty of the republic and its right to secede from Yugoslavia. Multi-party elections were held for the first time in April 1990. The parliamentary contest resulted in the defeat of the successor to the erstwhile ruling communist party (although the former communist leader Milan **Kučan** won election as President with 59% of the second-round vote). A nationalist Government led by the Democratic Opposition of Slovenia (DEMOS) was installed under the premiership of Lojze Peterle of the Slovenian Christian Democrats (SKD), the largest DEMOS component.

Following an overwhelming referendum vote in favour of independence, Slovenia seceded from the Yugoslav federation in June 1991, provoking military conflict with the Serb-dominated Yugoslav army. After a brief period of hostilities, the **European Union** (EU) brokered a cease-fire in July under which Yugoslav forces withdrew and Slovenia's independence was accepted by default. A new

Constitution providing for a multi-party democratic system was adopted in December 1991, as the DEMOS coalition was dissolved.

Slovenia held its first post-independence parliamentary and presidential elections in December 1992. The Assembly elections returned a new centre-left coalition, mainly comprising what became **Liberal Democracy of Slovenia** (LDS), the SKD and the **United List of Social Democrats** (ZLSD), under the premiership of Janez **Drnovšek** of the LDS. In the presidential elections Kučan was re-elected in the first round with 64% of the vote.

Strains in the ruling coalition were underlined by the withdrawal of the ZLSD in January 1996 after Drnovšek had announced the dismissal of one of its Ministers. In the November 1996 Assembly elections, the LDS secured only 25 of the 90 seats, while a centre-right 'Slovenian Spring' (SP) opposition alliance of the SKD, the **Slovenian People's Party** (SLS) and the **Social Democratic Party of Slovenia** (SDS) won an aggregate of 45. Following protracted negotiations, Drnovšek narrowly secured re-election as Prime Minister on the basis of an unlikely coalition which included the ZLSD on the left, the **Slovenian National Party** (SNS) on the far right, as well as the **Democratic Party of Slovenian Pensioners** (DeSUS) and the two national minority deputies. By February 1997, however, Drnovšek had succeeded in detaching the SLS from the SP alliance, and so was able to form a more stable coalition Government with the SLS and the DeSUS. In November 1997 President Kučan was re-elected for a second term, winning outright in the first round with 55.6% of the vote, and a new National Council was elected for a five-year term.

Growing strains in the ruling coalition culminated in the withdrawal of the SLS in April 2000 and the consequential fall of the Drnovšek Government. A lengthy crisis ensued, resulting in June in the appointment, pending elections in October, of an administration headed by what had become the SLS+SKD (by a merger between the two erstwhile SP allies), with Andrej Bajuk of the SLS+SKD as Prime Minister. Bajuk quickly broke with the SLS+SKD when its deputies voted against his proposal that proportional representation should be abandoned and all Assembly seats filled in individual constituency contests. In August 2000 he launched the **New Slovenia–Christian People's Party** (NSi), which attracted several prominent centrists, especially members of the former SKD.

Latest elections: The October 2000 Assembly elections resulted in a major advance for the LDS, which won 34 of the 90 seats with a vote share of 36.3%. Second place was taken by the SDS with 14 seats (15.8% of the vote), followed by the ZLSD with 11 (12.1%), the SLS+SKD with 9 (9.6%), the NSi with only 8 (8.6%), the DeSUS with 4 (5.2%), the SNS with 4 (4.4%) and the **Party of Slovenian Youth** (SMS) with 4 (4.3%). The Hungarian and Italian minorities again returned one Assembly member each.

Recent developments: The election outcome resulted in the return of Drnovšek to the premiership in November 2000, at the head of a majority centre-left coalition of his LDS together with the ZLSD, the SLS+SKD and the DeSUS. The new

Government was approved by the Assembly by a 61–5 majority, with the SDS and NSi deputies abstaining in protest against the allocation of committee posts. Drnovšek said that the Government would avoid '**shock therapy**' but would concentrate on revision of legislation to prepare Slovenia for EU membership.

International relations and defence: Slovenia was recognized as an independent state by the EU in January 1992, by the **Russian Federation** in February, and by the USA in April, and was admitted to the United Nations in May. It became a member of the **Council of Europe**, the **Organization for Security and Co-operation in Europe** and the **Central European Initiative**. In 1994 it joined NATO's **Partnership for Peace** programme, although its application to be included in the first round of **NATO** enlargement (along with the **Czech Republic, Hungary** and **Poland**) was rejected. On the other hand, Slovenia became one of the first six 'fast-track' candidates for EU membership, formal negotiations on which began in 1998.

Bilaterally, Slovenia's relations with **Croatia** had been clouded by various unresolved issues, including demarcation of land and maritime borders and control of the jointly-owned nuclear power station at Krsko (in Slovenia). Although the two sides agreed in mid-1998 that they would seek to settle outstanding problems speedily, little substantive progress had been made by the end of 2001.

One area of agreement between Slovenia and Croatia was their joint opposition to any Italian irredentism in respect of territory lost in the Second World War, and to Italian demands for the return of confiscated Italian properties in Istria. The latter issue caused Italy to block the signing of an EU association agreement with Slovenia, until an agreement was concluded in February 1998 under which Slovenia undertook to meet more than half of the financial compensation which former Yugoslavia had agreed to pay in respect of appropriated Italian properties.

Slovenia and Yugoslavia recognized one another in 1995, but relations remained cool as Slovenia condemned Serbia's repression in **Kosovo** and supported NATO military action in 1999.

Slovenia's defence budget for 2000 amounted to some US $275m., equivalent to about 1.5% of GDP. The size of the armed forces at the end of 2000 was some 9,000 personnel, including those serving under compulsory conscription of seven months, while reservists numbered an estimated 60,000.

Slovenia, economy

Formerly the most prosperous economy among the republics of the **Socialist Federal Republic of Yugoslavia**, now in transition to a market system preparatory to **European Union** (EU) membership.

GNP: US $18,114m. (2000); *GNP per capita*: $10,070 (2000); *GDP at PPP*: $21,400m. (1999); *GDP per capita at PPP*: $10,900 (1999); *exports*: $8,728m. (2000); *imports*: $10,089m. (2000); *currency*: tolar (plural: tolars; US $1=T245.6 at the end of December 2001).

Slovenia, economy

In 1999 industry contributed 33% of GDP, agriculture 3% and services 64%. Some 12% of the land is arable, 3% under permanent crops, 28% permanent pastures and 51% forests and woodland. The main crops are grain, vegetables, fruit (including grapes for wine) and sugar beet; there is also an animal husbandry sector. The main mineral resource is brown coal (lignite). The principal industries include electrical equipment, chemicals, food processing, textiles, metal manufacture and the exploitation of forestry. Tourism is an important part of the economy, with most tourists coming from Italy, Germany and Austria. Nearly 40% of energy requirements are met from a nuclear power station (whose ownership and output is shared between Slovenia and **Croatia**), while hydroelectricity contributes 25%.

Slovenia's main exports in 1999 were machinery and transport equipment, particularly electrical machinery and road vehicles (36%), basic manufactures (26%), miscellaneous manufactured articles, including clothing (21%) and chemical products (11%). Principal imports in 1999 included machinery and transport equipment, notably road vehicles (37%), basic manufactures (22%), miscellaneous manufactured articles (12%), chemicals (12%), fuels and lubricants (6%) and food and live animals (5%). The main destinations for Slovenian exports in 2000 were Germany (27%), Italy (14%) and Austria and Croatia (8% each). Germany was also the principal supplier of Slovenia's imports in 2000 (19%), followed by Italy (17%) and France (10%). Over two-thirds of Slovenia's external trade is with EU countries.

Immediately prior to the dissolution of former Yugoslavia in 1991, Slovenia had less than 10% of the total federal population but produced around 20% of its social product, although it had shared in the general Yugoslav economic deterioration of the 1980s. Slovenia experienced only a brief period of pre-independence hostilities in 1991, so that the economy was able to develop without the devastation suffered in Croatia and in **Bosnia and Herzegovina**. Nevertheless, the general disruption of trade in the area resulted in a 17% fall in GDP in 1990–92 and a further contraction of 3% in 1993, as inflation rose to a massive 500% in 1990, before falling back to 32% in 1993. A new currency, the tolar, was introduced in 1991 and economic reform programmes were announced; but little real structural change was achieved in the early years of independence.

A new comprehensive reform programme launched in early 1993 with support from the international financial institutions yielded GDP growth of 5.3% in 1994 followed by expansion rates of around 4% in the period 1995–99. Inflation was brought further under control, to 9% at the end of 1997 and to 6.5% at the end of 1998, before rising to 8% in 1999 because of the introduction of value-added tax (VAT). This progress was achieved despite a 1996 agreement under which Slovenia assumed 18% of the debts of the former Yugoslavia (a far greater proportion than relative population size), while Slovenia was little affected by the mid-1998 Russian financial crisis (*see* **Russian Federation, economy**). Assisted from February 1999 by the activation of its association agreement with the EU (following the opening of formal accession negotiations in November 1998) and by the freeing of capital movement later that year, Slovenia recorded further GDP growth of 4% in 2000, during which time inflation was curbed to 4% and the budget deficit remained low at around 1% of GDP. Although unemployment remained at over 7% in the period from 1995 to 2000, Slovenia continued to have the highest per head GDP among ex-communist countries in transition.

Privatization was launched in 1992 under complex procedures for the disposal of equity in state-owned enterprises, but did not get properly under way until 1994, with the allocation of **vouchers** to employees of such businesses. Most of these privatizations were in effect management/employee buy-outs of co-operatives, and generally there was little inward investment from abroad. Whereas privatization was originally due to have been completed by 1995, in early 1998 the state sector still accounted for over half of Slovenian enterprises in terms of value added and employment. Accordingly, a new privatization programme was initiated in 1999 covering state-owned banks, telecommunications and public utilities, while plans were announced for the dismantling of the remaining restrictions on foreign investment. Progress was slow, however, so that the centre-left Government which took office in late 2000 made completion of the programme a key economic policy goal.

Slovenian National Party
Slovenska Nacionalna Stranka (SNS)

An extreme right-wing formation in **Slovenia** with some electoral support but little political influence. Founded in 1991, the SNS advocates a militarily strong Slovenia, revival of the **Slovenes**' cultural heritage and protection of the family as the basic unit of society. It is also strongly opposed to Italian and **Croatian** irredentist claims on Slovenian territory or property. The party won 9.9% of the vote and 12 **National Assembly** seats in December 1992 but experienced internal dissension in 1993 after party leader Zmago Jelinčič was named as a federal Yugoslav agent, while other leaders were reported to be listed in security service files as having been informers in the communist era.

As a result of these and other difficulties, over half of the SNS deputies left the party, which slumped to only four seats and 3.2% of the vote in the November 1996 parliamentary elections. The SNS was then briefly co-opted into a disparate coalition headed by **Liberal Democracy of Slovenia** (LDS), but reverted to opposition status when the LDS found a larger partner in February 1997. In the October 2000 parliamentary elections the SNS improved slightly to 4.4% of the vote but again won only four seats.

Leadership: Zmago Jelinčič (Chair.).
Address: Tivolska 13, Ljubljana 1000.
Telephone and Fax: (1) 4301595.
Internet: www.sns.si

Slovenian People's Party
Slovenska Ljudska Stranka (SLS+SKD)

A conservative peasant-based formation in **Slovenia** whose SLS+SKD abbreviation signifies that in mid-2000 it merged with the Slovenian Christian Democrats (SKD).

Descended from a pre-Second World War Catholic party of the same name, the SLS was founded in 1988 as the Slovene Peasant League (SKZ), which registered as a party in January 1990 and won 11 **National Assembly** seats in 1990 as a member of the victorious Democratic Opposition of Slovenia (DEMOS) alliance. Having adopted the SLS label in 1991, it retained 11 seats in the December 1992 elections with 9% of the vote.

Affiliated to both the **Christian Democrat International** and the **International Democrat Union**, the SKD also claims descent from a pre-war party and was re-established in March 1990 by a group of 'non-clerical Catholic intellectuals' advocating full sovereignty for Slovenia, gradual transition to a market economy and integration into European institutions, especially the **European Union**. In the 1990 elections it was the largest component of the DEMOS alliance, winning 11 Assembly seats in its own right, so that SKD leader Lojze Peterle became Prime Minister and led Slovenia to independence in 1991. He remained Prime Minister despite the break-up of DEMOS at the end of 1991 but was forced to resign in April 1992 by a successful no-confidence motion criticizing the slow pace of economic reform. In the December 1992 Assembly elections the SKD advanced to 15 seats (on a 13.9% vote share), thereafter joining a new coalition headed by **Liberal Democracy of Slovenia** (LDS), whereas the SLS was in opposition.

Strains in the SKD's relations with the LDS intensified in 1994, leading to Peterle's resignation as Deputy Prime Minister and Foreign Minister in September in protest against the induction of an LDS President of the National Assembly, although the SKD remained a government party.

The SLS and the SKD contested the November 1996 parliamentary elections within the 'Slovenian Spring' (SP) alliance, the former party advancing to 19 seats on 19.4% vote share, whereas the latter fell back to 10 seats and 9.6%. The SLS then deserted the SP and joined a coalition Government headed by the LDS, whereas the SKD went into opposition. In the November 1997 presidential elections, neither the SLS candidate nor the joint nominee of the SKD and the **Social Democratic Party of Slovenia** made much impact against the incumbent, Milan Kučan (non-party), who won outright in the first round.

Strains in the SLS's relations with the LDS culminated in April 2000 in the party's withdrawal from the Government, which fell and was replaced in June by an SLS-led coalition under the premiership of Andrej Bajuk. The new Prime Minister promptly left the SLS to launch **New Slovenia–Christian People's Party**, while the rump SLS joined forces with the SKD to contest the October 2000 parliamentary elections as the SLS+SKD Slovenian People's Party. The merged party obtained a disappointing nine seats with 9.6% of the vote, but was included in the

new government coalition headed by the LDS and also including the **United List of Social Democrats** (ZLSD) and the **Democratic Party of Slovenian Pensioners** (DeSUS).
Leadership: Frank Zagozen (Chair.).
Address: Zarnikova 3, Ljubljana 1000.
E-mail: janez.vertacnik@sls-skd.si
Internet: www.sls.si

SLS *see* **Slovenian People's Party**.

SMK (Georgia) *see* **Citizens' Union of Georgia**.

SMK (Slovakia) *see* **Hungarian Coalition Party**.

SMS *see* **Party of Slovenian Youth**.

SNPCG *see* **Socialist People's Party of Montenegro**.

SNS (Slovakia) *see* **Slovak National Party**.

SNS (Slovenia) *see* **Slovenian National Party**.

SNS–BP *see* **Serbian People's Alliance–Biljana Plavšić**.

SNSD *see* **Party of Independent Social Democrats**.

Sobranie *see* **Assembly of the Republic (Macedonia)**.

Social Democracy Party of Romania *see* **Social Democrat Party**.

Social Democrat Party
Partidul Social Democrat (PSD)

The ruling party in **Romania** formed by the merger in June 2001 of the Social Democracy Party of Romania (PDSR) and the Romanian Social Democratic Party (PSDR).

The PDSR, which defined itself as a social democratic, popular and national party supportive of transition to a market economy on the basis of social responsibility, had been launched in 1993 as a merger of the Democratic National Salvation Front (FSND), the Romanian Socialist Democratic Party and the Republican Party, essentially to provide a party political base for President Ion **Iliescu**, a former senior communist apparatchik. The FSND had come into being in March 1992, when a group of pro-Iliescu deputies of the National Salvation Front (FSN) opposed to rapid economic reform withdrew from the parent party. The FSND had won a relative majority of seats in both houses of **Parliament** in the September 1992 elections and had backed Iliescu's successful re-election bid in the concurrent presidential contest. Having formed a minority Government after the 1992 elections, the PDSR in August 1994 formed a coalition with the right-wing Romanian National Unity Party (PUNR), with external support from the even more right-wing **Greater Romania Party** (PRM) and from the neo-communist Socialist Party of Labour (PSM). By mid-1995, however, serious differences had developed between the government parties, with the result that the PRM and the PSM withdrew their support in late 1995, while the PUNR was finally ejected from the Government in September 1996.

The other component of the new PSD, the PSDR, is descended from the historic party founded in 1893, which had been forced to merge with the Communist Party in 1948 and had thereafter been maintained in exile. Revived in Romania after the overthrow of the **Ceaușescu** regime, the party won only one seat in the Chamber of Deputies (lower house) in the May 1990 elections, improving to 10 in 1992 as a component of the mainly centre-right Democratic Convention of Romania (CDR). In January 1996 it left the CDR, instead joining an alliance with the **Democratic Party** (PD), itself the anti-Iliescu rump of the original FSN.

In the November 1996 elections Iliescu failed to secure re-election as President, being defeated in the second round by 54.4% to 45.9% by CDR candidate Emil Constantinescu, while in the parliamentary contest the PDSR won only 91 Chamber seats with 21.5% of the vote. It therefore went into opposition to a CDR-led coalition which included the PSDR, whose Chamber representation had remained at 10 seats. The rapprochement between the two future PSD partner parties began in September 2000 when the PSDR withdrew from the CDR-led coalition Government, abandoning its alliance with the PD, to form the Social Democratic Pole with the PDSR and the Humanist Party of Romania (PUR). This new grouping triumphed in the November–December 2000 elections. Iliescu regained the presidency as the Pole candidate, winning 66.8% of the second-round vote against a serious challenge by the PRM leader, while in the parliamentary contest the Pole parties won 155 of the 346 Chamber seats (and 36.6% of the vote), of which the PDSR obtained 142, the PSDR a disappointing seven and the PUR four. The Pole parties therefore formed a minority Government under the premiership of Adrian **Nastase**, which obtained qualified pledges of support from the PD, the **National Liberal Party** and the **Hungarian Democratic Union of Romania**.

In January 2001 Nastase was elected Chairman of the PDSR in succession to Iliescu (who was disqualified from party affiliation during his presidential term). The party then embarked upon negotiations for a formal merger with the PSDR, one consequence of which would be that the unified party would inherit the PSDR's membership of the **Socialist International** (which had declined to admit the PDSR

because of doubts about its democratic credentials). The merger was completed, forming the PSD, on 16 June 2001.
Leadership: Adrian Nastase (Chair.).
Address: Str. Kiseleff 10, Bucharest 71271.
Telephone: (1) 2222955.
Fax: (1) 2222879.
E-mail: psd@psd.ro
Internet: www.psd.ro

Social Democratic Hunchakian Party
Sotsial Demokratakan Hunchakian Kusaktsutyun (SDHK)

A political formation dating from 1887, registered in modern **Armenia** in 1991. Part of the victorious Republican Bloc in the 1995 **National Assembly** elections, it made no impact in 1999 elections, in which it contested three constituencies.
Leadership: George Hakobian (Chair.).
Address: 70 Pushkin Street, Yerevan.
Telephone: (1) 251781.
Internet: www.hunchak.org.am

Social Democratic Party of Albania
Partia Social Demokratike e Shqipërisë (PSDS)

A small centre-left political party in **Albania** founded in March 1991 but descended from labour parties of the pre-communist era. The PSDS won seven **People's Assembly** seats in the March 1992 elections (with 4.4% of the vote) and joined a coalition Government headed by the **Democratic Party of Albania** (PDS). The party's decision to leave the Government in late 1994 was not accepted by its two Ministers, who retained their posts and founded a breakaway party. In the May–June 1996 Assembly elections the PSDS was part of the 'Pole of the Centre' alliance with dissident former PDS moderates of the **Democratic Alliance of Albania**, and joined the opposition boycott of the second round of voting in June. In the June–July 1997 elections the PSDS won eight of the 155 seats (with 2.5% of the vote) in alliance with the **Socialist Party of Albania** (PSS). It subsequently joined a new PSS-led coalition Government and secured the election of Party Chairman Skender Gjinushi as President of the People's Assembly. The PSDS stood alone in elections in June 2001 when an increased share of the vote to 3.6% won it only four seats in the new Assembly.
Leadership: Skender Gjinushi (Chair.).
Address: Rruga Asim Vokshi 26, Tirana.
Telephone: (4) 226540.
Fax: (4) 227485.

Social Democratic Party of Bosnia and Herzegovina
Socijaldemokratska Partija Bosne i Hercegovine (SDPBiH)

A moderate centre-left formation in **Bosnia and Herzegovina** which aims to be a social democratic party on the west European model and disavows any specific ethnic/national identification. The SDPBiH was created in February 1999 by a merger of the Social Democrats of Bosnia and Herzegovina (SDBiH) and the Democratic Party of Socialists (DSS), each descended from Bosnian sections of communist-era formations. Affiliated to the **Socialist International** (which had pressed for the merger), the SDPBiH favours a regulated market economy.

Social democratic forces had been marginalized during the Bosnian civil war, but the SDBiH won two seats in the union lower house and six in the **Muslim-Croat Federation** lower house in the September 1998 elections, while the DSS took four and 19 seats respectively as well as securing second place (with 31.9% of the Croat vote) for its candidate in the **Croat** section of the elections for the Bosnian collective presidency.

New impetus was provided by the creation of the SDPBiH, which polled strongly in local elections in April 2000 and then took first place in the November 2000 elections to the union lower house, winning nine of the 42 seats, and second place in the Federation lower house, with 37 of the 140 seats. The party also won four seats in the **Serb Republic** People's Assembly, thus demonstrating its cross-community appeal. As the leading component of a new Alliance for Change of moderate parties, the SDPBiH then led a challenge to the union Prime Minister, a member of the nationalist **Croatian Democratic Union** (HDZ). The outcome in February 2001 was the appointment of Bozidar Matić (a Croat member of the SDPBiH) as union Prime Minister, heading the first all-Bosnia Government not dominated by nationalists.

Following the dismissal of the Croat member of the union presidency in March, Jozo **Križanović** (SDPBiH) was appointed from the moderate Alliance for Change. He assumed the rotating chairmanship of the presidency in June, at which point Matić had to resign (since the two posts cannot be held simultaneously by the same ethnic group). Matić was replaced the following month by party leader and Foreign Minister Zlatko **Lagumdžija**.

Leadership: Zlatko Lagumdžija (Chair.).
Address: 41 Alipašina, Sarajevo 71000.
Telephone: (33) 664044.
Fax: (33) 664042.
E-mail: sdp@sdpbih-centar.com
Internet: www.sdpbih-centar.com

Social Democratic Party of Croatia
Socijaldemokratska Partija Hrvatske (SPH)

A left-of-centre party derived from the former ruling **League of Communists of Yugoslavia** (SKJ), and the principal party in the coalition Government formed in **Croatia** in January 2000. The party is descended from Croatian elements which had been prominent in attempts to liberalize and reform the SKJ regime from within. In the post-1989 move to independence and multi-partyism, the Croatian branch of the SKJ was sidelined by the nationalist **Croatian Democratic Union** (HDZ). It failed to stem the outflow of support by changing its name to Party of Democratic Reform (SDP) and committing itself to democratic socialism and a market economy. In the 1990 pre-independence elections, the SDP trailed a poor second to the HDZ. The SPH title was adopted in 1991 (although the SDP suffix was retained for some years) and the party deferred to pro-independence sentiment by acknowledging Croatia as the 'national state of the Croatian people'.

Advocating economic modernization combined with preservation of the welfare state, the SPH was reduced to 11 seats in the August 1992 elections to the lower house of the **Assembly** and failed to secure representation in its own right in the February 1993 upper house balloting. It performed better in the October 1995 lower house elections, winning nearly 9% of the vote and 10 seats, while in the June 1997 presidential elections SDP candidate Zdravko Tomać took second place with 21%.

Following the death of President Franjo **Tudjman** of the HDZ in December 1999, the SPH contested the January 2000 Assembly elections in tandem with the **Croatian Social-Liberal Party** (HSLS) and two small regional formations. It became the dominant party by winning 44 seats on its own account and formed a six-party centre-left coalition Government headed by SPH Chairman Ivica **Račan**. In immediately succeeding presidential elections, the SPH backed the HSLS candidate in both rounds of voting, but welcomed the eventual victory of Stipe **Mesić** of the **Croatian People's Party**, which was a member of the new ruling coalition.

Leadership: Ivica Račan (Chair.).
Address: 9 Trg Iblerov, 10000 Zagreb.
Telephone: (1) 4552055.
Fax: (1) 4552842.
E-mail: sdp@sdp.tel.hr
Internet: www.sdp.hr

Social Democratic Party of Popular Accord
Satsiyal-Demokratychnaya Partiya Narodnaya Zgody (SDPNZ)

A technocratic party in **Belarus** emphasizing the need for economic reform. It is derived from the Party of Popular Accord (PNZ), which was founded in 1992 and remained outside the competing pro-democracy and conservative alliances, although it backed the **Belarusian Popular Front–Renaissance** candidate in the 1994 presidential elections after its own leader at that time Gennadz Karpenka, had failed to meet the nomination requirements. The PNZ won eight of the declared seats in the 1995 legislative elections and joined a 15-strong parliamentary group which included the **Belarusian Social Democratic Party**. In 1997 the PNZ added the Social Democratic label to the party name. Unlike most of the opposition, the SDPNZ participated in the October 2000 legislative elections, but only won one seat.

Leadership: Leanid Sechka (Chair.).
Address: 10 Karl Marx Street, Minsk 220050.
Telephone: (17) 2480221.

Social Democratic Party of Slovenia
Socialdemokratska Stranka Slovenije (SDS)

A party of conservative leanings, despite its name. The SDS is not an affiliate of the **Socialist International**, whose member party in **Slovenia** is the **United List of Social Democrats** (ZLSD).

Founded in February 1989, the SDS was a component of the victorious Democratic Opposition of Slovenia (DEMOS) alliance in the 1990 elections. In December 1992 its presidential candidate took only 0.6% of the first-round vote, but the party won 3.1% and four seats in the simultaneous legislative elections, subsequently participating in the centre-left coalition Government headed by **Liberal Democracy of Slovenia** (LDS). In 1993 the SDS Defence Minister and Party Chairman, Janez Janša, became enmeshed in an arms-trading scandal, which led indirectly to his dismissal from the Cabinet in March 1994, whereupon the SDS joined the parliamentary opposition.

The SDS contested the November 1996 parliamentary elections as part of the 'Slovenian Spring' (SP) alliance with the **Slovenian People's Party** (SLS) and the Slovenian Christian Democrats (SKD), making a breakthrough by winning 16 seats on a 16.1% vote share. It continued in opposition, making little impact in the November 1997 presidential elections but contributing crucially to the fall of the LDS-led coalition in April 2000 and becoming part of the SLS-led coalition formed in June 2000. In the October 2000 parliamentary elections the SDS slipped to 14 seats and 15.8% of the vote and reverted to opposition status.

Leadership: Janez Janša (Chair.).
Address: Komenskega 11, Ljubljana 1000.
Telephone: (1) 2314086.
Fax: (1) 2301143.
Internet: www.sds.si

Social Democratic Party of Ukraine–United
Sotsial-Demokratychna Partiya Ukrainy–Obyednana (SDPU–O)

Of the various social democratic parties in **Ukraine**, the grouping with the largest presence in the post-1998 **Parliament**. Social democratic groups claiming descent from the historic party founded in 1890 first emerged in Ukraine in 1988 as part of an all-**Soviet Union** movement. A congress in May 1990 to found a Ukrainian social democratic party resulted in an immediate split. The moderates, who supported Ukrainian sovereignty and German-style social democracy, formed the Social Democratic Party of Ukraine (SDPU) while the more left-wing faction took the SDPU–O name. After a disastrous showing in the 1994 elections, when the SDPU won only two seats and the SDPU–O none, a reunification attempt was made but broke down in late 1997.

In the 1998 parliamentary elections, most social democratic forces, including former President Leonid Kravchuk and former Prime Minister Yevhen Marchuk, swung behind the SDPU–O, but the party won only 13 seats (later supplemented by the adhesion of independent deputies). In the 1999 presidential elections, SDPU–O candidate Vasyl Onopenko won only 0.5% of the first-round vote. Thereafter, the SDPU–O parliamentary group became part of a fluid pro-Government centre-right majority, of which Kravchuk was the leader until September 2000.

Leadership: Viktor Medvedchuk (Chair.).
Address: vul. Suvurova 4/6, Kiev.
Telephone: (44) 2351146.
Fax: (44) 2900421.
E-mail: sdpuo@ngplus.relc.com
Internet: www.sdpuo.org.ua

Social Democratic Pole of Romania
Polul Democrat Social din România

A left-wing alliance in **Romania** formed for, and victorious in, the elections of November–December 2000, prefiguring the subsequent merger of the ex-communist Social Democracy Party of Romania (PDSR) and the non-communist Romanian Social Democratic Party (PSDR) into the **Social Democrat Party** (PSD) in June 2001.

Social Democratic Union of Macedonia
Socijaldemokratski Sojuz na Makedonije (SDSM)

Directly descended from the **League of Communists of Yugoslavia**, but now a pro-market party affiliated to the **Socialist International**. As the League of Communists of Macedonia–Party of Democratic Change (SKM–PDP), the party came second in **Macedonia**'s 1990 **Assembly of the Republic** elections, with 31 seats.

In January 1991 its nominee, Kiro **Gligorov**, was elected Head of State by the Assembly, following which the party adopted its present SDSM name. In mid-1992 it became the leading component of a coalition Government. Heading the Union of Macedonia (SM) centre-left alliance, it was confirmed in power in 1994 in both presidential and Assembly elections (winning 58 seats), and SDSM leader Branko Crvenkovski was reappointed Prime Minister at the head of a coalition of the SM parties and an ethnic **Albanian** formation.

The SDSM lost power in the parliamentary elections of late 1998, retaining only 29 seats on a 25.1% vote share and going into opposition to a Government headed by the **Internal Macedonian Revolutionary Organization–Democratic Party for Macedonian National Unity** (VMRO–DPMNE). In the late 1999 presidential elections, moreover, SDSM candidate Tito Petkovski lost to the VMRO–DPMNE nominee in the second round. In May 2000 the SDSM formed an opposition alliance with the small Liberal-Democratic Party and other centrist elements.

An insurgency launched in February 2001 by ethnic Albanian rebels seeking greater rights for the Albanian community led to the establishment of a Government of National Unity in May comprising parties from all sides of the Assembly, including the SDSM, but still headed by the VMRO–DPMNE. However, following a peace deal, signed in August 2001 and put in place by November, the SDSM and the Liberals withdrew from the grand coalition.

Leadership: Branko Crvenkovski (Chair.).
Address: Bihačka 8, Skopje 91000.
Telephone: (2) 321371.
Fax: (2) 221071.
E-mail: contact@sdsm.org.mk
Internet: www.sdsm.org.mk

Socialist Federal Republic of Yugoslavia (SFRY)

The formal name, from 1963, for the socialist state created after the Second World War on the territory of what had been the Kingdom of **Yugoslavia**, which included the modern Republics of **Bosnia and Herzegovina**, **Croatia**, **Macedonia**, **Montenegro**, **Serbia** and **Slovenia**, and which collapsed in the early 1990s.

It was the victory in 1945 of the wartime resistance Partisans, against both the Nazi invaders and the **Serb** nationalist **Chetniks**, which put the Yugoslav communists led by **Tito** in a position of control in the formation of the new Yugoslav entity. A Federal People's Republic of Yugoslavia was declared on 29 November 1945 (the SFRY name coming into existence with the 1963 Constitution). The State that Tito masterminded was a relatively loose federation, with regional autonomy also extending to the nominally Serbian provinces of **Kosovo** and **Vojvodina**. It pursued a non-aligned foreign policy, Tito having broken as early as 1948 with the concept of a monolithic Soviet-led communist bloc. It was politically dominated by the **League of Communists of Yugoslavia**, with no multi-party elections until 1990.

Nationalist tensions between the major ethnic groups were contained until after Tito's death in 1980, but thereafter came increasingly to destabilize the SFRY, which was also badly weakened by economic problems. Autonomy for Serbia's provinces was revoked in 1989 and discontent at the increasing centralization of control in **Belgrade**, under the then Serbian President Slobodan **Milošević**, prompted the leaders of first Slovenia and then Croatia to declare their secession from the SFRY in June 1991. The declarations prompted armed invasions by the Yugoslav National Army (JNA) and the beginning of the violent wars in the former Yugoslavia which raged until 1995. Macedonia seceded after holding a referendum in September 1991 and Bosnia and Herzegovina declared its own independence shortly afterwards. The SFRY having been declared non-existent by its Federal President Stipe **Mesić** in December 1991, the two remaining republics (Serbia and Montenegro) formed the rump Federal Republic of Yugoslavia (FRY) on 27 April 1992.

Socialist International

The world's oldest and largest association of political parties, founded in 1864 and grouping democratic socialist, labour and social democratic parties from 85 countries, including many of the countries of **central** and **eastern Europe**. The Socialist International provides a forum for political action, policy discussion and the exchange of ideas.

Members: 66 full member parties, 25 consultative and eight observer parties.
Leadership: António Guterres (President).
Address: Maritime House, Clapham, London, SW4 0JW, United Kingdom.
Telephone: (20) 76274449.
Fax: (20) 77204448.
E-mail: socint@gn.apc.org
Internet: www.socialistinternational.org

Socialist Party of Albania
Partia Socialiste e Shqipërisë (PSS)

The strongest political party in **Albania**, descended from the former ruling Party of Labour of Albania (PPS), itself created in 1948 as successor to the Albanian Communist Party (founded 1941).

Having won multi-party elections in March–April 1991, the PPS switched to the PSS designation in June 1991 to signify its renunciation of Marxism-Leninism and espousal of democratic socialism and the market economy. Former Prime Minister Fatos **Nano** became PSS Chairman in succession to President Ramiz **Alia**, while Ylli Bufi of the PSS was appointed to head a 'non-partisan' coalition Government. Continuing social unrest forced the PSS to vacate the premiership in December 1991, and in the March 1992 **People's Assembly** elections the party was heavily defeated by the **Democratic Party of Albania** (PDS).

In 1993 the opposition PSS was weakened by the conviction of Alia, Nano and other leaders on charges of corruption and abuse of power during the communist period. Nano remained titular PSS Chairman despite being imprisoned, with Deputy Chairman Servet Pellumbi leading the party in his absence. In November 1995 the PSS led abortive opposition to a law requiring senior public officials to be investigated for their activities during the communist era. Many PSS candidates were barred from the May–June 1996 elections, the second round of which was boycotted by the party in protest against malpractice in the first. With only 10 Assembly seats, the PSS nevertheless led popular opposition to the subsequent PDS-led Government. In March 1997 the PSS joined a 'Government of Reconciliation' headed by Bashkim Fino and was boosted by the release of Nano on a presidential pardon. In further Assembly elections in June–July 1997 the PSS returned to power with 101 of the 155 seats and 52.8% of the vote. In July 1997 Rexhep **Meidani** of the PSS replaced Sali Berisha (PDS) as President, whereupon Nano was appointed to head a five-party coalition Government.

Further instability resulted in Nano being replaced as Prime Minister in September 1998, his successor being PSS Secretary-General Pandeli Majko, who at 31 became Europe's youngest Head of Government. Internal party strains caused Nano to announce in January 1999 that he would resign as PSS Chairman in order to launch 'an emancipating movement' to restore hope among the people. At a PSS congress in October 1999, however, Nano was re-elected Chairman by a narrow majority over Majko, who therefore resigned as Prime Minister. He was replaced by Deputy Premier Ilir **Meta**, who was also on the PSS' reformist or 'Euro-socialist' wing but was more dependent on Nano and his conservative PSS faction. In October 2000 the PSS registered substantial local election advances, winning over 50% of the popular vote and taking control of **Tirana**, hitherto a PDS stronghold.

The success continued into 2001 when the PSS garnered 42% of the national vote in legislative elections in June, gaining an absolute majority of 73 seats in the Assembly. The PDS contested the results and boycotted the new parliamentary session for its first three months. However, despite this lack of parliamentary opposition, the party's internal divisions provided all the turbulence the new Government needed. Nano again clashed with Meta who had been easily re-elected Prime Minister by the party in August. Nano accused Meta and his Cabinet of corruption and pressed for a reshuffle, prompting the resignation of four Cabinet members in December. Tensions between Nano and Meta continued.

Leadership: Fatos Nano (Chair.).
Address: Bul. Dëshmorët e Kombit, Tirana.
Telephone: (4) 223409.
Fax: (4) 227417.

Socialist Party of Serbia
Socijalistička Partija Srbije (SPS)

The principal ruling party in **Serbia** and **Yugoslavia** until the defeat of Slobodan **Milošević** in the 2000 federal presidential elections. The SPS was created in 1990 by the merging of the **Serbian** wings of the former ruling **League of Communists of Yugoslavia** (SKJ) and the associated Socialist Alliance of the Working People, with Milošević (who had become leader of the Serbian SKJ in 1986 and Serbian President in 1989) as its Chairman. While acknowledging its origins in the communist-era ruling structure, the SPS officially subscribes to democratic socialism, favouring a continuing state economic role and preservation of the social security system. In fact, the SPS became the political vehicle for the hardline pro-Serb policies of Milošević in the regional conflicts of the 1990s and for an increasingly repressive response to domestic opposition.

Having won an overwhelming majority in the Serbian Assembly in December 1990 (when Milošević was re-elected Serbian President with 65% of the vote), the SPS obtained a narrow lower house majority in the May 1992 **Federal Assembly** elections. The imposition of UN sanctions from mid-1992 resulted in reduced popular support for the SPS, which lost its overall majorities in the federal lower house and the Serbian Assembly in December 1992, although it remained the largest single party in both and Milošević was re-elected President of Serbia with 56% of the vote. In further Serbian elections in December 1993, the SPS increased its lower house representation from 101 to 123 seats out of 250, subsequently forming a Government with the **New Democracy** (ND) party.

Milošević's reluctant acceptance of the November 1995 **Dayton Agreement** for **Bosnia and Herzegovina** brought him into conflict with ultra-hardliners within the SPS, several of whom defected or were expelled. In federal elections in November 1996 a Joint List alliance of the SPS, the **Yugoslav United Left** (JUL) led by Milošević's wife, and the ND won 64 of the 138 lower house seats, so that the SPS continued to dominate the Federal Government. In simultaneous local elections, however, opposition parties captured **Belgrade** and most other Serbian cities—results which the Government-controlled courts tried to annul but which Milošević eventually accepted in the face of mass popular protests and strikes.

Being constitutionally barred from a third term as Serbian President, Milošević was in July 1997 elected as Federal President by the Federal Assembly, under the then prevailing system of indirect election. Serbian Assembly elections in September 1997 resulted in the SPS/JUL/ND alliance winning 110 seats, the eventual outcome being a coalition Government of the SPS, the JUL and the ultra-nationalist **Serbian Radical Party** (SRS) under the continued premiership of Mirko Marjanović. In protracted Serbian presidential elections in late 1997, SPS candidate Milan **Milutinović** was eventually returned with 59% of the vote, in balloting described as 'fundamentally flawed' by international observers.

The **Kosovo** crisis of 1998–99 and the eventual air bombardment of Serbia by the **North Atlantic Treaty Organization** initially appeared to strengthen Milošević and the SPS politically. However, following the withdrawal of Serbian forces from Kosovo in June 1999 and the indictment of Milošević for alleged war crimes, demands for a change of Government intensified from what became the **Democratic Opposition of Serbia** (DOS). Milošević and his coterie resisted the pressure, the President being re-elected as SPS Chairman unopposed in February 2000 and telling a party congress that the Kosovo conflict had been 'a struggle for freedom and independence'. In July 2000, moreover, Milošević secured the enactment of constitutional amendments providing for direct elections for the federal presidency and lifting the previous ban on second federal presidential terms.

However, the calling of federal elections in September 2000 proved to be a crucial political miscalculation by Milošević. Intimidation and vote-rigging by Milošević supporters in the presidential ballot failed to prevent what was widely seen as an outright first-round victory for the DOS candidate. Last-ditch attempts by the regime to sidestep the outcome provoked a massive popular uprising, and Milošević eventually surrendered the federal presidency in early October. In simultaneous federal parliamentary elections, themselves marred by irregularities, the SPS/JUL alliance declined to 44 lower house seats. Three months later, the Serbian Assembly elections in December 2000 revealed the true state of opinion by reducing the SPS/JUL to only 37 seats and 13.8% of the vote.

Milošević remained defiant after losing office, pledging that he would lead a revitalized SPS back to power in the near future. At the beginning of April, however, he was arrested at his home in Belgrade and charged with misappropriation of funds and other abuses as President. Despite the new Government's initial insistence that he should be tried in Yugoslavia, he was subsequently extradited to face the **International Criminal Tribunal for the former Yugoslavia** at The Hague. In his absence, Marjanović was elected as the party's new Chairman in December 2001.

Leadership: Mirko Marjanović (Chair.).
Address: Lenjinov Bulevar 6, Belgrade.
Telephone: (11) 634921.
Fax: (11) 626642.
E-mail: www@sps.org.yu
Internet: www.sps.org.yu

Socialist Party of the Serb Republic
Socijalistička Partija i Republika Srpska (SPRS)

A party founded in 1993 as effectively the Bosnian **Serb** wing of the then ruling Yugoslav **Socialist Party of Serbia** led by Slobodan **Milošević**. In the post-**Dayton** era the SPRS became a vigorous opponent of the dominant **Serbian Democratic Party** (SDS) then led by Radovan **Karadžić**, in line with Belgrade's increasing disenchantment with the latter's intransigence in the Bosnian civil war. For the first post-Dayton elections in September 1996, the SPRS was the principal organizer of the relatively moderate People's Alliance for Peace and Progress, which also included the **Party of Independent Social Democrats** (SNSD). Zivko **Radišić** of the SPRS was the Alliance candidate for the **Serb Republic** (RS) presidency, coming third with 17% of the vote, while the Alliance nominee for the Serb seat on the union collective presidency, Mladen **Ivanić** (later leader of the **Party of Democratic Progress**), came a creditable second with 30%. In the legislative contests the Alliance won 10 RS People's Assembly seats and two in the all-Bosnia lower house.

Standing on its own in new RS Assembly elections in November 1997, the SPRS won nine seat. In the September 1998 polls the SPRS was part of the moderate Sloga ('Unity') alliance, which included the SNSD and the **Serbian People's Alliance** (SNS) led by Biljana Plavšić, and secured the election of Radišić as the Serb member of the Bosnian collective presidency with 51.2% of the Serb vote (and 21.8% nationally). Although Plavšić was defeated in the RS presidential contest, the SPRS improved to 10 seats in the RS Assembly, while Sloga candidates took four seats in the union lower house.

In early 1999 the SPRS backed RS Prime Minister Milorad Dodik of the SNSD in his successful resistance to efforts by new RS President Nikola Poplasen of the ultra-nationalist **Serbian Radical Party** (SRS) to replace him as Prime Minister. But increasing strains in the Sloga alliance came to a head in January 2000 when Dodik dismissed SPRS Deputy Prime Minister Tihomir Gligorić for causing disunity, thus provoking the SPRS to announce its withdrawal from the ruling coalition, reportedly on the orders of President Milošević of **Yugoslavia**. However, the SPRS Ministers remained in Dodik's Government, and in March a dissident SPRS faction opposed to the withdrawal broke away to form the **Democratic Socialist Party** (DSP). In the November 2000 elections, the rump SPRS was damaged by the impact of the new DSP, its representation falling to four seats in the RS Assembly and to one in the all-Bosnia lower house.

Leadership: Zivko **Radišić** (Chair.).
Address: 1 Kralia Petra, 103 Karadgordgevedga, Banja Luka.
Telephone and Fax: (51) 215336.
E-mail: sprs@inecco.net

Socialist Party of Ukraine
Sotsialistychna Partiya Ukrainy (SPU)

A small but influential political formation in **Ukraine**, directly descended from the **Soviet**-era ruling party. The first self-proclaimed successor to the **Communist Party of Ukraine** (KPU), the SPU was launched two months after the **August coup** attempt by hardliners in Moscow in 1991. Under the leadership of Oleksandr Moroz, who had been Chairman of the Soviet-era Ukrainian legislature, the party attacked the growth of 'national-fascism' and called for the reintroduction of state direction of the economy, price controls, 'socially just privatization' and closer economic and political ties with the **Russian Federation** and the other members of the **Commonwealth of Independent States** (CIS).

In June 1993 the SPU formed an alliance called 'Working Ukraine' with the **Peasants' Party of Ukraine** (SelPU) and smaller left-wing groups, in close co-operation with the KPU, although the latter did not join and quickly superseded the SPU as the leading left-wing formation. The SPU emerged from the 1994 elections with a parliamentary group of only 27 members, although Moroz was elected President of the **Parliament** with KPU and other left-wing support. In early 1996 the SPU was weakened by a split resulting in the formation of the breakaway **Progressive Socialist Party** (PSP).

The SPU contested the 1998 parliamentary elections in an alliance with the SelPU called 'For the Truth, For the People, For Ukraine' (Za Pravdu, Za Narod, Za Ukrainu'), their joint list winning 44 seats with 8.5% of the proportional vote. Plans for a joint presidential candidate of the alliance and other left-leaning parties foundered in the run-up to the 1999 contest, with the result that Moroz stood for the SPU and received 11.3% of the first-round vote. In the second round the SPU supported KPU leader Petro Symonenko, who was defeated by incumbent Leonid **Kuchma**. In early 2000 the SPU was prominent in left-wing attempts to prevent the ousting of Parliament President Oleksandr Tkachenko (SelPU) by the centre-majority, whose action was described by Moroz as tantamount to a coup d'état.

Moroz and the SPU were also prominent in the further political crisis which developed from late 2000 over President Kuchma's alleged role in the murder of a journalist. After being sued for slander by Kuchma's chief of staff for revealing apparent presidential involvement in the affair, Moroz described the crisis as 'a turning-point' in Ukraine's national history. In early May 2001 the SPU initiated moves for a national referendum in which voters would be asked to approve the removal of the President.

Leadership: Oleksandr Moroz (Chair.).
Address: Malopidvalna 21/41, Kiev 242034.
Telephone: (44) 2916063.
Internet: www.ukrnet.net/~spu

Socialist People's Party of Montenegro
Socijalistička Narodna Partija Crne Gore (SNPCG)

A political formation in **Yugoslavia** which supports the maintenance of **Montenegro**'s Federation with **Serbia**. The SNPCG was launched early in 1998 by a breakaway faction of the **Democratic Party of Socialists of Montenegro** (DPSCG) led by Momir Bulatović, following his narrow and much-resented defeat by an anti-Federation DPSCG candidate in Montenegrin presidential elections of October 1997. The SNPCG drew on substantial pro-Federation opinion to take second place in the May 1998 Montenegrin Assembly elections, winning 29 of the 78 seats with 36% of the vote. Shortly before the elections, Bulatović had been appointed Federal Prime Minister by President Slobodan **Milošević** of the **Socialist Party of Serbia** (SPS), charged with maintaining the Federation at a time of national crisis over **Kosovo**.

The SNPCG maintained its pro-Federation line in the September 2000 federal elections in which Milošević and the SPS were defeated by the **Democratic Opposition of Serbia** (DOS). The dubious official results gave the SNPCG 28 of the 138 lower house seats, following which Bulatović resigned as Party Chairman. He was succeeded in February 2001 by Predrag Bulatović (no relation), who was aligned with the new Government in **Belgrade** and who established the 'Together for Yugoslavia' pro-Federation alliance for the April 2001 Montenegrin Assembly elections. The SNPCG-led alliance lost very narrowly and therefore contended that the resultant minority DPSCG Government had no mandate for independence.

Under the Federal Yugoslav Constitution, which stipulates that the President and Prime Minister must be from different republics, newly-elected Federal President Vojislav **Koštunica** of the DOS appointed Zoran Zizić of the SNPCG to be his Prime Minister. However, Zizić's opposition to the arrest and subsequent extradition of Milošević in June 2001 prompted him to resign, taking most of the SNPCG Cabinet members with him. Eventually Koštunica secured the co-operation of the relative moderate SNPCG candidate Dragiša **Pesić** as the new Prime Minister, after Party Chairman Bulatović had already rejected his overtures.

Leadership: Predrag Bulatović (Chair.).
Address: c/o Skupština Crne Gore, Podgorica.
E-mail: admin@snp.cg.yu
Internet: www.snp.cg.yu

Sofia

The capital city of **Bulgaria**, situated in the west of the country in the southern foothills of the Balkan Mountains. *Population*: around 1.25m. Originally named Serdica, after the Thracian Serdi community which founded the settlement, the city came into Greek hands around 29 BC. It flourished as an important Byzantine centre from the 4th century AD, and began its connection with the **Bulgarians** as early as the 9th century when it was absorbed into the First Bulgarian Empire. It gained the title Sofia, meaning wisdom and taken from the still surviving Church of St Sofia, under Byzantine administration in the 14th century. From 1382 to 1879 the city developed a distinctly eastern feel under the domination of the Ottoman Empire, but lost its regional significance until the rise of Bulgarian nationalism in the late 19th century.

1879 saw Sofia become the national capital of a newly-proclaimed, small autonomous Bulgarian principality. Full independence from Ottoman control in 1908 brought a vigorous building campaign, with city authorities keen to establish a modern European city. Sofia suffered severe damage in the Second World War, however, when it was firebombed by the Allies in 1944 before falling to the Red Army. Industrial development under the subsequent communist regime also left its mark on the city's architectural heritage. As the capital of present-day Bulgaria, Sofia is an important location for light industry, including engineering and metallurgy, as well as the country's cultural and political centre.

Solidaritate

A new small trade union confederation formed in 2000 from a splinter of the General Federation of Trade Unions of Moldova (FGSRM), previously the sole trade union centre in **Moldova**. The FGSRM was the reformed successor to the Soviet-era structure, whose assets it inherited. It benefited from almost universal union membership in the employed labour force.

In late 2000 the union broke into two separate unions—the **Confederation of Trade Unions of the Republic of Moldova** (CSRM) and Solidaritate. Solidaritate's members are from industry, transport, telecommunications, construction and social protection.

General Secretary: Nicolae Suruceanu.
Address: Chişinau.
Telephone: (2) 238287.
Fax: (2) 234508.

Solidarity
Solidarność

The principal trade union centre in **Poland**, responsible in the 1980s for instigating the collapse of communism in Europe. Its full official name is now the Independent and Self-Governing Trade Union Solidarity (Niezależny Samorzadny Zwiazek Zawodowy Solidarność). Its influence has declined in recent years.

Launched in 1980 to challenge the official trade union structure, Solidarity resulted from a strike at the **Gdańsk** shipyard which inspired massive countrywide stoppages and protests against economic conditions. Lech **Wałęsa** quickly emerged as the most prominent leader of Solidarity, which functioned both as an independent union and as a vehicle for national, religious and political aspirations, posing an increasing threat to the communist regime. Although Solidarity was initially granted official recognition, the possibility of a Soviet invasion impelled the Government to declare martial law in December 1981 and to ban Solidarity. At its height, Solidarity had 9.5 million members, while the Rural Solidarity peasants' counterpart had a further 2.4 million.

From 1982 a new official trade union structure was created, culminating in the establishment in November 1984 of the **All-Poland Alliance of Trade Unions** (OPZZ). However, Solidarity remained active underground and in the late 1980s re-emerged as a major force. In April 1989, amidst mounting political and economic crisis, the regime was forced to agree to the relegalization of Solidarity and also to partially free elections. Four months later the first Solidarity-backed Government was formed, setting the pattern of Solidarity's often conflicting twin identities as a political movement and a trade union.

After the collapse of communism and Wałęsa's election as Polish President in December 1990, Solidarity suffered from its identification with the new Government's austerity policies. Four consecutive years of falling real wages boosted support for the OPZZ, to which some dissident Solidarity elements defected, while others formed the breakaway 'Solidarity 80' movement. Roles were reversed when the (ex-communist) **Democratic Left Alliance** came to power in September 1993, following which Solidarity returned to opposition. The new Government continued the general approach of previous post-communist administrations, so that Solidarity obtained a new lease of life as it campaigned against the consequences of economic restructuring, including job losses and wage cuts.

After Wałęsa had narrowly failed to be re-elected President in December 1995, a Solidarity congress in June 1996 launched **Solidarity Electoral Action** (AWS) as an organizationally distinct political movement. Campaigning on a pro-market and pro-European platform in the September 1997 legislative elections, the AWS came to power in coalition with the centre-right **Freedom Union**, under the premiership of Jerzy **Buzek**, an early Solidarity leader. Solidarity trade union leader Marian Krzaklewski, who had been elected as an AWS member of the **National Assembly**, became Chairman of the AWS party caucus. The Solidarity trade union wing therefore again experienced the tensions caused by dual identity, as it frequently opposed the Buzek Government on economic and labour issues while distancing itself from the 'destabilizing' activities of the OPZZ and peasant groups. In October 2000 Krzaklewski was the AWS candidate in presidential elections but managed only third place with 15.6% of the vote. He subsequently faced renewed demands within Solidarity that he should choose between leading the union and his political ambitions. On 15 May 2001 the union members took the initiative and voted to withdraw Solidarity from the ruling coalition and to take the union out of active politics altogether. Under the new regulations union members can no longer head political parties, or work for their electoral committees.

As a union movement, Solidarity has lost members steadily in the post-communist era, as state industries have been privatized and the succeeding businesses have largely eschewed union organization. Nevertheless, at the end of 2001 Solidarity remained substantially the largest union movement in Poland, with over a million members in some 13,000 local enterprise branches and 16 industrially-based national branches. Solidarity is affiliated to both the International Confederation of Free Trade Unions (ICFTU) and, in view of its strong Catholic current, the World Confederation of Labour (WCL).

Chair.: Marian Krzaklewski.
Address: 24 Wały Piastowskie St, Gdańsk 80855.

Telephone: (58) 3084472.
Fax: (58) 3010143.
E-mail: zagr@solidarnosc.org.pl
Internet: www.solidarnosc.org.pl

Solidarity Electoral Action
Akcja Wyborcza Solidarność (AWS)

A centre-right multi-party formation in **Poland** descended indirectly from the **Solidarity** independent trade union movement.

The Solidarity political wing played a minor role in the early 1990s, having been disowned by Lech **Wałęsa** after his election as President of Poland in 1990 and having failed to win representation in the *Sejm* (lower house of the **National Assembly**) in 1993. Following Wałęsa's own failure to secure re-election to the Polish presidency in 1995, a Solidarity congress in June 1996 resolved to form the AWS for the 1997 National Assembly elections, the aim being to build a broad alliance of the centre-right to challenge the incumbent Government dominated by the **Democratic Left Alliance** (SLD). Chaired by Solidarity leader Marian Krzaklewski, the new grouping quickly attracted some 35 existing formations to its banner, notably the Christian National Union (ZChN), the Centre Alliance (PC), the Conservative Peasant Party (SKL), the Christian Democratic Labour Party (ChDSP) and the Christian Democratic Party (PChD).

Mobilizing substantial rural support, the AWS led the polling in the September 1997 elections, winning 201 of the 460 Sejm seats with 33.8% of the vote, well ahead of the SLD. It therefore formed a coalition Government with the liberal **Freedom Union** (UW) under the premiership of Jerzy **Buzek**, while Krzaklewski became Chairman of the AWS parliamentary group. At the end of 1997 about half of the AWS deputies formed the Social Movement–AWS (RS–AWS), also under Krzaklewski's chairmanship, in a move to create a unitary party. The other half, however, preferred to maintain their affiliation to AWS component parties. In September 1998 Krzaklewski was re-elected leader of the Solidarity trade union at a congress which resolved that senior union and party posts could not be held by the same person. Accordingly, Krzaklewski was succeeded by Buzek as RS–AWS leader in January 1999, although he remained Chairman of the AWS parliamentary group.

Increasing strains in the coalition Government culminated in the withdrawal of the UW in June 2000, so that Buzek now headed a minority AWS Government with eroding parliamentary and popular support. In the October 2000 presidential election Krzaklewski came a poor third with only 15.6% of the vote, the SLD candidate Aleksander **Kwaśniewski** being elected outright in the first round. By the end of the year defections had reduced the number of committed AWS deputies to 157, fewer than the 162-strong SLD contingent. In a bid to revive centre-right fortunes in advance of the autumn 2001 parliamentary elections, in January 2001 Buzek, as Chairman of the RS–AWS, took over the leadership of the overall AWS from Krzaklewski, who had been under further attack since his presidential election defeat. However, Buzek's efforts to create a more cohesive AWS bloc were rebuffed by the SKL, which in March 2001 withdrew from the AWS and aligned itself with the new **Citizens' Platform** (PO).

Relations between AWS and Solidarity reached breaking point in May 2001 when the union's members voted to withdraw from co-operation with the Government and from politics altogether. As the September poll approached it became clear that support for AWS was being eroded by other, much more radical, parties. Buzek became the first premier to complete a term in office since the fall of communism, but had the indignity of seeing AWS entirely wiped out of the Sejm. The party retained 15 seats in the *Senat* (upper house), but only within the Blok Senat 2001 in conjunction with the UW, the PO, **Law and Justice** and the **Movement for the Reconstruction of Poland**. Buzek resigned as leader of the party the following month and was replaced by Senator Mieczysław Janowski.

Leadership: Mieczysław Janowski (Chair.).
Address: c/o Zgromadzenie Narodowe, ul. Wiejska 6/8, Warsaw 00902.
Telephone: (22) 6941934.
Fax: (22) 6941943.

SOP *see* **Party of Civic Understanding**.

Soros Foundations network

A group of autonomous foundations across the world, but mostly in **eastern Europe**, founded by the **Hungarian**-born billionaire fund manager and philanthropist George Soros to promote the development of civil society and pluralist democracy. Its foundations include the New York-based Open Society Institute, established in 1993, which has been actively involved in making grants in central and eastern Europe. Latterly this has involved the creation of a Trust for Civil Society in Central and Eastern Europe, to support the long-term sustainable development of non-governmental organizations in the region. Another Soros Foundations initiative was the creation (initially in **Prague** and **Budapest** but increasingly concentrated in the latter city) of the Central European University (CEU), which established itself during the 1990s as an internationally-recognized institution of postgraduate education in social sciences and humanities.

Address: Open Society Institute, Oktober 6. ut. 12, 1051 Budapest, Hungary.
Telephone: (361) 3273100.
Fax: (361) 3273101.
Internet: www.soros.org

South Ossetia *see* **Ossetia question**.

Southern Bukovina *see* Bukovina question.

Southern Dobruja *see* Dobruja question.

Soviet Federatsii
(Council of the Federation)

The upper house of the **Federal Assembly** of the **Russian Federation**.

Soviet Respubliki
(Council of the Republic)

The upper house of the **National Assembly** of **Belarus**.

Soviet Union
(Union of Soviet Socialist Republics, USSR)

The historic communist state of 1922–91, which at its height was one of two global superpowers, and stretched from the Pacific coast of **Siberia** in the east to the borders of **eastern Europe** in the west, and from the Arctic Circle in the north to the edges of the Middle East in the south. The Soviet Union (known in Russian by its **Cyrillic** acronym *CCCP* [SSSR]) was the largest country in the world, and adhered closely to the borders of the old Russian Empire (the **Baltic States** and modern **Moldova** being added to the Union through military conquest in the Second World War). Its disintegration in 1991 left 15 independent successor states: **Armenia, Azerbaijan, Belarus, Estonia, Georgia,** Kazakhstan, Kyrgyzstan, **Latvia, Lithuania,** Moldova, the **Russian Federation,** Tajikistan, Turkmenistan, **Ukraine** and Uzbekistan. All but the three Baltic States then joined together to form the loose **Commonwealth of Independent States** (CIS).

Following the Bolshevik (communist) victory in the Russian Civil War (1918–22) the new authorities sought to spread socialist revolution but also to recentralize control of the far-flung Russian dominions. At first these were given the right to national determination, but very soon the 'ideal' of a communist revolution was enforced everywhere. Communist Governments were set up in the constituent republics, and the structure for the Soviet Union was drawn up under the guidance of the then Commissar for Nationalities, Josef Stalin. The new socialist state was based on the principle of rule by the *Soviets* (essentially councils representing trades unions and other collective groups). It was formally established on 30 December 1922.

The USSR brought together at the top level the Soviet Socialist Republics (SSRs), of which the Russian Soviet Federative Socialist Republic (RSFSR) was by far the largest. Within the SSRs were Autonomous Soviet Socialist Republics (ASSRs), based on smaller ethnic groups. (Within the Russian Federation of the post-Soviet era the ASSRs survive, for the most part, in the form of the various Republics. In the non-Russian successor states, however, the ASSRs have largely been subsumed into unitary structures, which has created tensions particularly in Georgia and Moldova.) Smaller subdivisions of SSRs and ASSRs were the autonomous *krai* (province), *oblast* (region), and *okrug* (district), as well as city, administrations.

Mikhail **Gorbachev** was the last President of the Soviet Union, which he dismantled formally on 25 December 1991 after it had been made effectively redundant through the declarations of independence of the SSRs.

SPB *see* **Belarusian Socialist Party.**

SPH *see* **Social Democratic Party of Croatia.**

Spitzbergen *see* **Svalbard.**

SPO *see* **Serbian Renewal Movement.**

SPRS *see* **Socialist Party of the Serb Republic.**

SPS (Bulgaria) *see* **Union of Right Forces.**

SPS (Yugoslavia) *see* **Socialist Party of Serbia.**

SPU *see* **Socialist Party of Ukraine.**

Srebrenica

A town deep in what is now the **Serb Republic** in north-eastern **Bosnia and Herzegovina**, the site of the mass execution of Muslim **Bosniaks** at the hands of Bosnian **Serb** forces in July 1995. Srebrenica, along with **Goražde** and **Sarajevo**, was an area with a clear Bosniak majority before the Bosnian War. It was declared a UN 'safe haven' on 6 May 1993. Dutch UN peacekeepers could do nothing to prevent the enclave falling to Bosnian Serb forces two years later on 11 July 1995, and were subsequently heavily criticized for their failure to take any effective action to try to protect its inhabitants. A total of 8,000 of the region's estimated 40,000 Bosniaks were executed in a deliberate campaign of **'ethnic cleansing'** in the town, the worst single atrocity of the entire war. International outrage over the massacre contributed to growing condemnations of Serb territorial aggression, and to a shift of opinion in favour of a less passive stance by international forces. Like many other previously cosmopolitan areas, Srebrenica now has a clear Serb majority.

SRS (Bosnia and Herzegovina) *see* Serbian Radical Party (Bosnia and Herzegovina).

SRS (Yugoslavia) *see* Serbian Radical Party (Yugoslavia).

SSAK *see* All-Georgian Union for Revival.

SSM *see* Confederation of Trade Unions of Macedonia

SSSH *see* Association of Autonomous Trade Unions of Croatia.

SSSJ *see* Confederation of Autonomous Trade Unions of Yugoslavia.

Stability Pact for South-Eastern Europe

A forum to promote co-operation and peaceful relations in the **Balkans**. Created in Cologne, Germany, under the initiative of the **European Union** (EU) in June 1999, the Pact strives to co-ordinate regional efforts in south-eastern Europe to secure lasting peace and economic prosperity. The Pact is headed by a Special Co-ordinator of the Regional Table, Erhard Busek. The Regional Table includes representatives from the Balkan countries, as well as neighbouring states, the EU, non-EU members of the **Group of Eight** industrialized countries and international financial institutions. Under the Regional Table are three Working Tables designed to construct and implement policy in the areas of: Democratization and Human Rights; Economic Reconstruction, Co-operation and Development; and Security Issues.

Perhaps the most significant relationships derived from the Pact are those with the EU. One of the Pact's stated aims is to encourage greater integration with other regional institutions, most notably the EU. Stabilization and Association Agreements have so far been signed between the Union and **Macedonia** (April 2001) and **Croatia** (October 2001). The EU is the largest single aid donor in the region, providing over 6,600m. euros in 2000 and 2001.

Leadership: Erhard Busek (Special Co-ordinator for the Round Table).
Address: rue Wiertz 50, B-1050 Brussels, Belgium.
Telephone: (2) 4018700.
Fax: (2) 4018712.
E-mail: scsp@stabilitypact.org
Internet: www.stabilitypact.org

Stabilization Force (SFOR)

The **NATO**-led peacekeeping force stationed in **Bosnia and Herzegovina** to assist in the implementation of the 1995 **Dayton Agreement**. SFOR is the legal successor to the Implementation Force (IFOR), which began overseeing the military aspects of Dayton from December 1995 with the full backing of the UN. It was the largest ever NATO operation, numbering around 60,000 personnel, and had a one-year mandate. In that year it secured the peace in the war-torn country and helped to rebuild the shattered infrastructure. At the end of its mandate and following the successful conduct of general elections in Bosnia and Herzegovina in September 1996, IFOR was replaced in December by the much smaller SFOR mission with responsibility for, literally, stabilizing the peace. Since then all NATO countries have provided troops to SFOR and so have a number of non-NATO countries, including many from **eastern Europe**. SFOR, now numbering around 20,000 troops, is controlled by NATO's Joint Force Commander, which was formed when control was widened from just the Supreme Allied Commander Europe, to include the Allied Forces Southern Europe command from February 2001. Lt-Gen. John B. Sylvester has been Commander of SFOR (COMSFOR) since September 2001.

Address: CPIC, Kasarna Maršala Tita, Zmaja od Bosne, 71000 Sarajevo.
Telephone: (33) 495000 ext. 5214.
E-mail: william.wood@sfor.nato.int
Internet: www.sfor.nato.int

START

The Strategic Arms Reduction Talks between the USA and the **Soviet Union**, which began in June 1982 despite the deadlock over **SALT** II. The US side began by pressing for major cuts in inter-continental ballistic missiles (land-based strategic missiles being much less significant in the US arsenal than in the Soviet one). The **NATO** decision, however, to go ahead with deployment of cruise and Pershing II missiles in Europe, prompted a Soviet walkout from the START talks in November 1982. When they reconvened in 1985 it was under an 'umbrella' framework linking strategic, intermediate and space-based systems. The talks, held in Geneva, moved towards separating the agenda on strategic weapons, creating a potential START I agreement and deferring more complex areas to START II. In the event, whereas START I took nearly a decade (and was signed in **Moscow** in July 1991), START II was agreed in principle in Washington in a completely different global context in June 1992, and signed only six months later by the **Russian Federation** and the USA in January 1993. START II went far beyond the cuts agreed in START I, committing both sides to cut two-thirds of their strategic arsenals. The collapse of the Soviet Union created complexities in the START I ratification process, particularly with **Ukraine**, but the promise of large-scale US aid eventually cleared the way for the accession by early 1994 of all four post-Soviet nuclear weapons states. The agreement involved three of them, **Belarus**, Kazakhstan and Ukraine, transferring ownership of all remaining weapons to the fourth, the Russian Federation.

State Assembly (Estonia)
Riigikogu

The unicameral legislature of **Estonia**. It has 101 members, directly elected for a four-year term. The last elections were held on 7 March 1999.
Address: Riigikogu, Lossi plats 1A, 15165 Tallinn.
Telephone: 6316331.
Fax: 6316334.
E-mail: riigikogu@riigikogu.ee
Internet: www.riigikogu.ee

State Duma (Russian Federation)
Gossoudarstvennaya Duma

The lower house of the **Federal Assembly** of the **Russian Federation**.

State Ownership Fund (Romania)
Fondul Proprietaţii de Stat

State property agency in **Romania**.
Chair.: Radu Sârbu.
General Director: Gabriel Mihut.
Address: Str. C. A. Rosetti 21, 70205 Bucharest.
Telephone: (1) 2118018.
Fax: (1) 2104459.

State Property Fund (Lithuania)
Valstybes Turto Fondas (VTF)

Created in 1997 and inaugurated in March 1998, incorporating the Lithuanian State Privatization Agency established in 1995. The Fund's principal tasks are to represent state interests in holding and disposing of state-owned property; to privatize state-owned property and administer privatization transactions; and to maintain documentation on state-owned property. The Fund may also represent municipalities in the privatization of municipal property.
Chair. of Board: G. Rainys.
Address: Vilnius St 16, Vilnius 2600.
Telephone: (26) 84999 [(526) 84999 from September 2002].
Fax: (26) 84997 [(526) 84997 from September 2002].
E-mail: info@vtf.lt
Internet: www.vtf.lt

State Property Fund (Ukraine)

Government agency in **Ukraine** responsible for the state's holdings in business.
Manager: Vitaliy Kryukov.
Address: vul. Kutuzova 18/9, 252133 Kiev.
Telephone: (44) 2951274.
Fax: (44) 2966572.

State Property Management Agency (Georgia)

Founded in 1992, the State Property Management Agency is responsible for the divestment of state-owned enterprises in **Georgia**.
Address: Tbilisi.

StB
Státní bezpečnost

The communist-era State Security Force (secret police) of the former **Czechoslovakia**. The StB was used to suppress dissent, sometimes violently, and to provide the authorities with information on security issues within the country. It was notably put to use in undermining the pro-democracy '**Prague Spring**' of 1968. Following its dissolution in February 1990 after the collapse of the communist Government, controversy over 'collaboration' with the Force prompted the drafting of so-called '**lustration laws**'.

Stoyanov, Petar

President of **Bulgaria** from January 1997 until January 2002.

Petar Stoyanov is a member of the right-of-centre **Union of Democratic Forces** (SDS). He first entered government as a Deputy Minister for Justice in 1992 but remained a political unknown until his surprise nomination as SDS presidential candidate in 1996. He was inaugurated as President on 20 January 1997.

Born in Plovdiv on 25 May 1952, he was educated at Sofia University, and graduated from the law faculty of the Kliment Ohridski University in **Sofia** in 1976. From 1978 to 1989 he practised as a lawyer. During this time he never joined the ruling Bulgarian Communist Party and only became politically active in 1989 as the democratic movement gathered pace. He joined the newly-formed SDS in June 1990 and entered government as Deputy Minister of Justice in 1992. After the SDS Government collapsed in 1993 he sat in the **National Assembly** as a member of the opposition and was elected Deputy Chair of the SDS in 1995. He was nominated as the presidential candidate of a broad alliance in 1996 in preference to incumbent President Zhelyu Zhelev, and went on to a convincing victory with 60% of the vote in the second round in November. After five months of 'cohabitation' with the incumbent **Bulgarian Socialist Party** (BSP) Government led by Prime Minister Zhan Videnov, the SDS returned to power. From May 1997 to July 2001 Stoyanov thus worked alongside the SDS Government of Prime Minister Ivan Kostov. His own popularity remained high, but that of his party plummeted as the Government implemented unwelcome **IMF**-backed reforms, in an effort to bring Bulgaria into the full glare of free-market economics.

The SDS defeat in the 2001 legislative elections brought the popular former King, Simeon **Saxecoburggotski,** into office as Prime Minister. He gave Stoyanov his full backing ahead of presidential elections in November 2001 but this was insufficient to save the SDS stalwart. Stoyanov was defeated in the second round by the BSP candidate, Georgi **Purvanov**, who garnered 54% of the vote against Stoyanov's 45.9%. Stoyanov remained in office until the inauguration of Purvanov in January 2002.

Petar Stoyanov is married to Antonina Stoyanova, who holds a doctorate in international law and is a former diplomat at the Bulgarian Embassy in London. They have two children.

Subcarpathia *see* **Transcarpathia**.

Sudetenland question

A flashpoint in the history of Europe in the 1930s, when Nazi Germany demanded the right to incorporate into the Third Reich the territory inhabited by a large **German** community within what was then **Czechoslovakia**. They were concentrated in the Sudetenland, the mountainous western border region which derives its name from the Sudeten mountains between **Bohemia** and Silesia (modern southwestern **Poland**). Under the Habsburg Empire, Austrian rule over Bohemia had enabled the Sudeten Germans to flourish, and representatives of the three million-strong German community protested strongly, but fruitlessly, when the whole of Bohemia was incorporated into the new Czechoslovak state under the 1919 Treaty of St Germain. Their stronger cultural connection with neighbouring Germany stimulated German nationalism in the area and encouraged Hitler's ambition to include the Sudeten Germans within his Third Reich. These aims were achieved at the Munich Conference in 1938, when the territorial integrity of Czechoslovakia was sacrificed to the Western desire to appease Hitler's demands. The entire Sudetenland area was ceded to the Nazi state, and this was followed by the expulsion of the region's **Czech** minority population.

At the end of the 1939–45 war, the restored Czechoslovak authorities not only reincorporated the territory of Sudetenland, but insisted that almost all its German inhabitants be forcibly 'repatriated' to Germany. The relatively small remaining minority community of some 165,000 had dwindled to just 50,000 by 1991 through voluntary emigration. Calls for compensation or the return of property taken from the fleeing Germans have largely been sidelined by good relations between Germany and the **Czech Republic**.

Svalbard

A group of islands deep in the Arctic Circle directly north of Norway. Its population of around 2,400 (2000 estimate) has had a small Norwegian majority since 1998, with the once majority ethnic **Russian** community forming the bulk of those leaving the islands in the 1990s. The Svalbard islands were ceded to Norway under the 1920 Spitsbergen Treaty which gave **Russia** access to the region's resources. A dispute between the two countries over the maritime border flared in 1977 when Norway declared an exclusive economic zone around its coast. The status of the Russian population of the islands was questioned in the late 1990s when the Russian Federation withdrew its state subsidies to the islanders.

Svilanović, Goran

Federal Minister of Foreign Affairs, **Yugoslavia**.

Goran Svilanović is Chairman of the radical liberal **Civic Alliance of Serbia** (GSS). A prominent member of the anti-war movement in Serbia throughout the 1990s, he was appointed Foreign Minister in November 2000.

Born in 1963 in Gnjilane, **Kosovo**, he graduated in law from Belgrade University and went on to study at the Institute of Law in Strasbourg and the European University of Peace in Austria. From 1986 to 1998 he worked as an Assistant Professor at Belgrade University before being discharged from the institution, along with many other colleagues, for his opposition to new authoritarian restrictions on education in the form of the 1998 University Act. Before joining the GSS he was a prominent advocate of human rights and was a member of the Yugoslav Forum for Human Rights, and the Centre for Anti-War Action during the conflicts of the 1990s. He also headed a telephone advice line for the victims of discrimination. He became GSS Spokesman in 1996, and was elected the party's Chairman in 1999. He was appointed Foreign Minister in late 2000 and is said to have been President Vojislav **Koštunica**'s personal choice for the role.

Address: Federal Ministry of Foreign Affairs, Kneza Miloša 24, 11000 Belgrade.
Telephone: (11) 682555.
Fax: (11) 682688.
E-mail: smip@smip.sv.gov.yu
Internet: www.smip.sv.gov.yu

SWP *see* **Shamiran Women's Party**.

SzDSz *see* Alliance of Free Democrats.

SzEF *see* Forum for the Co-operation of Trade Unions.

Szeklers

A **Finno-Ugric people** who arrived in **central Europe** some time in the late 10th century and ultimately settled in northern **Transylvania** under the encouragement of the mediaeval **Hungarian** Kingdom. The language of the Szeklers, known by the same name, is considered by Hungarian nationalists as the most pure form of their own language, and the Szeklers themselves are romanticized as embodying essential Hungarian traits. The modern Szeklers largely class themselves as Hungarian, making any estimate of their numbers very difficult.

T

Tabasarans

A Caucasian people largely resident in the southern **Russian** republic of **Dagestan**. Along with the closely-related **Lezghins** the Tabasarans are among the oldest-recorded inhabitants of the **Caucasus** region, first mentioned in the 5th century. Like most other Dagestanis they abandoned their animist beliefs and adopted **Islam** in the 8th and 9th centuries, although traditional practices are still widespread. The 80,000-strong Tabasaran community remains largely agriculturally based, with activity following the general Dagestani pattern—livestock in the highlands, cultivation in the few lower areas. Tabasaran is one of Dagestan's nine indigenous languages to have a literary tradition. It has been transcribed in **Cyrillic** since 1938.

Tallinn

Capital city of **Estonia** and a major Baltic port, situated on the northern Bay of Tallinn, on the Gulf of Finland. *Population*: 420,500 (1997 estimate).

In 1219 King Waldemar of Denmark conquered Toompea (Dome Hill), the hill fortress at what is now the centre of Tallinn. Sold to the Teutonic Knights of Germany in 1347, Tallinn prospered as a member of the Hanseatic League as the building of what is now the old town was completed. After two centuries of Swedish rule, Estonia was annexed in 1710 by **Russia**, which established Tallinn as a naval base for its Baltic fleet. It became a major industrial centre, a railway link to **St Petersburg** was established, and by 1917 the Tallinn population had increased to 160,000, largely due to the influx of Russian labourers.

Tallinn was the capital of independent Estonia from 1919 until its occupation by the **Soviet Union** in 1940. During German occupation from 1941 much of the old town architecture was destroyed. Tallinn was the Soviet capital of the Estonian Soviet Socialist Republic from 1944 until the country regained independence in 1991. Edgar Savisaar has been Mayor of Tallinn since 13 December 2001.

Tallinn Stock Exchange
Tallinna Börs

The exchange originally founded in 1920 during **Estonia**'s brief inter-war period of independence, which was re-launched in 1995 after the collapse of the **Soviet Union**. Trading began in May 1996. In April 2001 the Finnish HEX Group acquired strategic ownership of the TSE. In 1999 a memorandum of understanding was signed with the **National Stock Exchange** of **Lithuania** and the **Riga Stock Exchange** with a view to increasing co-operation. As at 1 December 2001 the TSE had nine members.
Chair.: Gert Tiivas.
Address: Pärnu St 12, 10148 Tallinn.
Telephone: 6408800.
Fax: 6408801.
E-mail: tse@tse.ee
Internet: www.tse.ee

Tanasescu, Mihai

Minister of Public Finance, **Romania**. A non-party technocrat, he worked within the Ministry of Public Finance for 14 years before a three-year stint at the **World Bank** in Washington D.C., from which he was recalled to take up his ministerial post in December 2000.

Mihai Nicolae Tanasescu was born on 11 January 1956 in **Bucharest**. He graduated from the city's Academy for Economic Studies in 1978. After graduation he worked for the state-owned real estate company, ICRAL, before joining the Public Finance Ministry in 1983. He continued his education alongside his career as a government official, with economic courses in Romania and abroad. Following the overthrow of **Ceauşescu**'s communist dictatorship in December 1989, Tanasescu moved into the executive of various departments within the Ministry, until in 1997 he was chosen as a World Bank Alternate Executive Chairman, representing 12 eastern European countries including Romania during his three years in this post.
Address: Ministry of Public Finance, Str. Apolodor 17, 70663 Bucharest.
Telephone: (1) 4103400.
Fax: (1) 3122077.
E-mail: presa@mail.mfinante.ro
Internet: www.mfinante.ro

Tanjug
Novinska Agencija Tanjug (Tanjug News Agency)

The main state news agency in **Yugoslavia**. Tanjug is a contraction of *Telegrafska agencija Nove Jugoslavije* (Telegraphic News Agency of New Yugoslavia). It was founded in 1943 at the height of the Second World War as a means of spreading information about the Yugoslav resistance to Nazi occupation. Under the **Socialist Federal Republic of Yugoslavia** Tanjug was one of the major international news agencies of its day, providing an alternative communist perspective against the might of the Soviet **Novosti** information machine, and particularly strong in international coverage of the **Non-Aligned Movement**. In the 1990s Tanjug was harnessed as a vital tool of Slobodan **Milošević**'s propaganda efforts. Following his downfall in 2000 it has been overhauled and purged of his supporters and its connections with the state. Tanjug is in the process of divorcing itself from government control altogether.

Director and Editor-in-Chief: Dušan Djordjević.
Address: Obilićev Venac 2, POB 439, 11001 Belgrade.
Telephone: (11) 3281608.
Fax: (11) 633550.
E-mail: agency@tanjug.co.yu
Internet: www.tanjug.co.yu

Taraclia

A semi-autonomous District in southern **Moldova** with a 64% majority **Bulgarian** population of some 48,000 (1999 estimate). Attempts by the Moldovan authorities to strip Taraclia of its distinct status in 1998–99 met stiff resistance from the Bulgarian community, which was supported by the Government of **Bulgaria**. Legislation drawn up in November 1998 proposed the incorporation of Taraclia into the greater Cahul County. Fearing loss of cultural rights in the new entity, where Bulgarians would become merely 16% of the population, an illegal referendum in Taraclia rejected the move by a sweeping 92% in January 1999. Eventually the Moldovan Government accepted their opposition and restored the District status of Taraclia in October 1999.

Tarlev, Vasile

Prime Minister of **Moldova**.

Vasile Tarlev is an independent and stands out conspicuously as a business executive within a communist Cabinet. He served on the Government's Supreme Economic Council from 1998 and was inaugurated as Prime Minister on 19 April 2001.

Born into the ethnic **Bulgarian** community in Bascalia in the extreme south of Soviet-controlled Moldova on 9 October 1963, he first worked as a driver of tractors and goods vehicles before being conscripted into the Soviet army in 1981. He returned to his earlier work in 1983 before enrolling with the Technology Faculty of the Chișinau Polytechnic Institute. On graduation he found employment with the confectionery giant, Bucuria. He rose swiftly through the company's hierarchy and was elected Director-General of the company and Chairman of the National Producers' Association in 1995. He was first awarded the accolade of 'Businessman of the Year' by the Chişinau City authorities in 1996 and held the title for four successive years. He was awarded a doctorate in technical studies in 1998 and entered government service as a member of President Petru Lucinschi's Supreme Economic Council. He was appointed Prime Minister by the newly-elected communist President Vladimir **Voronin** in April 2001 as a clear indication of the Government's intention to maintain a free-market economy.

Vasile Tarlev is married and has two children.

Address: Office of the Prime Minister, Piaţa Marii Adunari Nationale 1, 227033 Chişinau.
Telephone: (2) 233092.
Fax: (2) 242696.
Internet: www.moldova.md

Tartu, Treaties of

Treaties signed in 1920 by Soviet **Russia** securing peaceful relations and common borders with **Estonia** (2 February) and Finland (14 October). The first treaty guaranteed Russia's recognition of Estonia's independence (later revoked), while the second significantly included the cession of the **Petsamo** district to Finland.

See also **Riga**, Treaties of.

TASR *see* **News Agency of the Slovak Republic**.

Tatars

A **Turkic** and **Muslim** people, spread across the south of **European Russia** and into **Ukraine**. Tatars arrived in eastern Europe in the 13th century at the head of the Mongol invasion of Genghis Khan. From 1237 to 1552 the Tatar Golden Horde and its successor khanates dominated the **Russians**. With the collapse of the Kazan and **Astrakhan** khanates in 1552 these former masters fell under the dominion of the growing Russian Empire and have remained the second-largest ethnic group in Russia after the Russians. The Tatars were used as an administrative class to help subjugate the **Muslim peoples** of the north **Caucasus** and central Asia. However, the majority Tatar population fell victim to intense efforts to russify them and break links between the main communities in the southern Urals, **Crimea**, and the **Volga region**.

Tatar nationalism has long been a centre for anti-Russian protest. Stalin, and later Soviet leaders, crushed Tatar protests with characteristic severity. Many Tatars were deported to **Siberia** and central Asia to break up their communities. Since the end of the **Soviet Union** the Tatars of **Tatarstan** have pushed for high levels of autonomy within the **Russian Federation** and Tatar language and culture have flourished. The Tatars are most closely related to the **Bashkirs**.

Today 32% of the estimated 5.5 million Tatars live in Tatarstan, the only ethnic Tatar state in the world. The Volga and **Crimean Tatars** do not have autonomous representation.

Tatarstan

A heavily-industrialized constituent republic of the **Russian Federation** situated in the centre of the Volga-Ural region of **European Russia**. *Population*: 3.6m. (1997 estimate). **Tatar** nationalism flourished in the late 19th and early 20th centuries, centred in the main Tatar city of Kazan. During the Russian Civil War (1918–20) the Tatars sided with the anti-Bolshevik 'White' Russians and pressed for a Tatar-dominated **Idel-Ural** state. This aspiration was defeated, and when the Tatar-based republic of Tatarstan (known as Tataria in Russian) was formed in 1920 its borders were redrawn to place three-quarters of Russia's Tatars outside the republic.

During the Soviet era Tatarstan was heavily developed as an industrial centre. The first oil well opened in 1943. The main centre for oil is at Almetyevsk and natural gas production is based in Nizhnyaya Maktama. The petroleum chemical industry is based in the republic's capital, Kazan. The Volga river, which forms the republic's western border, is the main channel for the transport of exports to the rest of the Russian Federation. In 1999 Tatarstan accounted for 3.2% of the Federation's industrial output—more than half the amount produced in the **Moscow** region. Industrialization has brought high real wages and higher than average levels of crime.

Perestroika encouraged a resurgence in Tatar nationalism in the late 1980s and Tatarstan was at the forefront of calls for greater regional autonomy. A Sovereign Republic was declared on 30 August 1990. The new authorities refused at first to sign the 1992 Federation Treaty and actually declared independence after a successful referendum. However, complete separation from the Russian Federation was not internationally recognized and was never a tenable position, surrounded as the republic is by the Federation, and with a 43% **Russian** minority. A power-sharing agreement was concluded with the Russian authorities on 15 February 1994 and Tatarstan joined the Federation. Regional autonomy flourished under the *laissez faire* presidency of Boris **Yeltsin**. However, the efforts of Yeltsin's successor Vladimir **Putin** to recentralize the Federation brought Tatarstan into dispute with his administration. In April 2001 it was included in a list of four republics which maintained laws seriously contradicting the Federal Constitution. Tatar President Mintimer Sharipovich Shaimiev was elected for a third term in March 2001.

TB–LNNK
see **Fatherland and Freedom–Latvian National Conservative Party**.

Tbilisi

The capital city and main urban centre of **Georgia**, situated in the south-east of the country. Known in Russian as Tiflis. *Population*: 1.3m. (1990 estimate). Originally established as the capital of a Georgian kingdom in 458 AD, the city has fallen to numerous conquerors throughout its history—the Persians, Arabs, **Turks** and finally, in 1801, the **Russians**. As a frontier of the Russian Empire the city was developed as an administrative centre and military garrison. It was linked to Russia via the direct trans-Caucasian Georgian Military Highway from Vladikavkaz. East-west links were improved at the end of the 19th century with rail lines to Poti on the Black Sea coast and **Baku** on the Caspian. Tbilisi has since become a centre for railway products. As capital of Georgia it also has a diverse range of lighter industries including textiles and consumer goods.

Tetovo

The town in **Macedonia** that lies in the heart of the country's ethnic **Albanian**-dominated north-western region, and has been at the centre of support for greater autonomy. In 1995 the community established an illegal Albanian-language university in the city. The institution was finally recognized by the Macedonian authorities in July 2000 and formally opened later the following year, following the ending of months of armed conflict between Macedonian troops and the Albanian National Liberation Army (known by its Albanian initials UCK—*see* **Kosovo Liberation Army**), a conflict in which Tetovo was very much at the front line.

Tirana

Capital city of **Albania**, situated in the middle of the country, of which it is the political, economic and cultural centre. *Population*: 320,000.

The city is reputed to have been founded in 1614 by the Turkish feudal lord of the region, Sulejman Pasha Mulleti, who built a mosque and other facilities. It developed as an economic centre in the 18th century and was declared the capital of independent Albania in 1920.

Tirana Stock Exchange

Albania's only stock exchange. Officially opened on 2 May 1996 it is the first of its kind in Albania. It is run as an appendage of the **Bank of Albania** and currently

only trades in government bonds and treasury bills. There are plans to 'spin off' the exchange and allow greater trading.
Address: Sheshi Skënderbeu 1, Tirana.
Telephone: (4) 235568.
Fax: (4) 223558.
E-mail: emeka@bankofalbania.org
Internet: www.asc.gov.al/tiranastock.html

Tito

Communist **Yugoslavia**'s leader for 35 years until his death in 1980, and President from 1953 onwards.

Born Josip Broz in 1892, he was taken prisoner in the First World War when fighting as a soldier in the army of the Austro-Hungarian Empire, and was thus in **Russia** at the time of the 1917 revolution. He fought on the communist side in the Russian civil war. Returning to Yugoslavia, he established himself there as communist party leader and achieved heroic status under the adopted name of Tito as a leader of Partisan resistance to Nazi occupation from 1941.

A **Croat** himself, Tito achieved the remarkable feat of winning popularity with all Yugoslav nations, holding the tensions of the multi-ethnic State to some extent in abeyance throughout his period in power. Initially an orthodox Stalinist, he turned to his own brand of Marxism-Leninism as leader of post-1945 Yugoslavia, causing an irreparable rift with the Soviet authorities by the late 1940s. Titoism included Yugoslav neutrality, workers' self-management, economic decentralization and the concept of social ownership.

Tito showed great flexibility in adapting Yugoslav institutions in an attempt to solve the many structural problems which confronted the State. Under his stewardship, Yugoslavia did develop rapidly, as measured by both economic and educational indexes. His death in 1980 was immediately followed by predictions of the break-up of the **Socialist Federal Republic of Yugoslavia**, although almost a decade passed before this process entered its critical phase.

Titograd *see* **Podgorica**.

TP *see* **People's Party**.

TRACECA

The Transport Corridor Europe Caucasus Asia, a project assisted by the **European Union** to promote, co-ordinate and plan alternative transport links between **eastern Europe** and central Asia, via the **Caucasus**. Established in May 1993 as an extension of the existing transport corridor, TRACECA aims to increase regional trade and political ties between the EU and eastern Europe/central Asia.

Members: **Armenia**, **Azerbaijan**, **Georgia**, Kazakhstan, Kyrgyzstan, **Moldova**, Mongolia, Tajikistan, **Ukraine** and Uzbekistan.

Trajkovski, Boris

President of the Republic, **Macedonia**. Boris Trajkovski is a member of the centre-right **Internal Macedonian Revolutionary Organization–Democratic Party for Macedonian National Unity** (VMRO–DPMNE). Trained as a lawyer, he joined the Government as Deputy Foreign Minister in December 1998. He was finally confirmed as President on 6 December 1999, after a controversial election.

Born on 25 June 1956 in the eastern town of Strumica, he graduated from Skopje University with a law degree in 1980 and worked for a number of years as a lawyer for a construction company. He joined the VMRO–DPMNE in 1992 and from then until 1998 he was Chairman of the party's Foreign Relations Commission. From 1997 to 1998 he was an adviser to the Mayor of **Skopje**. His initial victory in presidential elections was dogged by accusations of fraud and he was only finally elected after a rerun in December. His opponents accused him of mobilizing gangs of ethnic Albanians to cast multiple votes and intimidate opposition supporters, while the **Organization for Security and Co-operation in Europe** (OSCE) announced 'serious concerns' about the result. His popularity was further dented by his 'concession' of a cease-fire with Albanian rebels in mid-2001.

Boris Trajkovski is married with a son and daughter. He is a committed Methodist Christian and for 12 years headed the Yugoslavian Methodist Youth organization. Since Macedonia's independence he has led the Executive Committee of the Methodist Church of Macedonia.

Address: Office of the President, 11 Oktomvri b.b., 91000 Skopje.
Telephone: (2) 113318.
Fax: (2) 112643.

Trans-Siberian Railway

The famous railway connecting **Moscow** in **European Russia** with Vladivostok on the Pacific Ocean. Construction of the railway began in 1891 at the behest of Tsar Alexander III and his industrialist-reformist Government, keen to exploit the vast mineral resources of **Siberia** and to definitively stamp **Russia**'s sovereignty on the far-eastern provinces of the Amur Valley. It was finally completed in 1905, and a new route bypassing Chinese-administered Manchuria made it conform to its present course from 1916. Since then the Trans-Siberian Railway (TSR or Transsib) has served as the main source of on-land shipment between the mines and factories of Siberia and the **Volga region**, the industrial heart of European

Russia. It is also now used as a lucrative tourist attraction. The complete 9310-km journey can take between five and seven days passing through the industrial cities of Yekaterinburg and Irkutsk and skimming past the scenic region around Lake Baikal.

Transcarpathia

A sliver of western **Ukraine** in the northern Carpathian mountains. The region forms the central edge of the historic region of Ruthenia (Little Russia, or more accurately, west Ukraine). Since its return to Ukraine in 1945 the territory has been known as the Zakarpatskaya *oblast* (region). It forms the modern border between Ukraine and (from north to south) **Poland**, **Slovakia**, **Hungary** and **Romania**. The ethnic **Ruthenian** peasantry was traditionally allowed access to its **Uniate Church** and developed a strongly pro-Russian culture after the 19th century.

The region was part of Hungary from 1015 until 1918, firmly establishing **Hungarian** claims to the region. However, with the collapse of the Habsburg Empire at the end of the First World War, the Hungarian lands were divided and Transcarpathia was incorporated into the new **Czechoslovak** state under the 1920 Treaty of **Trianon**. Between 1938 and 1945 Hungary reoccupied Transcarpathia under the supervision of the Nazi state. With the defeat of the Axis powers all of historic Ruthenia was absorbed as part of the victorious **Soviet Union** and ceded to the Ukrainian republic, including Transcarpathia. Although Transcarpathia is now accepted as an integral part of Ukraine, on the basis of its majority **Ukrainian** population, Hungarian nationalists still lay claim to the province, and aim to revise the borders set out by the Treaty of **Trianon**.

Economic activity is distinctly rural with the region's mountainous terrain precluding major industrial development. Timber and wood products dominate along with intensive agriculture on the small plains. Wine is produced in the Tisza valley area. The town of Chop in the western corner serves as the main entry point to Ukraine for traffic from Hungary and the surrounding region.

Transcaucasia or Transcaucasus

A geographical expression for the region and countries to the immediate south of the Greater **Caucasus** Mountains which effectively form the south-eastern border of Europe. The countries in question are **Armenia**, **Azerbaijan** and **Georgia**. These three countries were briefly united between 1922 and 1936 in the Transcaucasian Soviet Federal Socialist Republic before being divided into today's modern states.

Transdnestria
(Transdnester Moldovan Republic, PMR)

A small breakaway republic situated on the industrialized east bank of the Dnester river in **Moldova**. *Population*: 760,000 (1990 estimate). Designated the PMR in October 1991 it is ethnically divided between **Moldovans**, the largest group at around 39%, **Ukrainians** and **Russians**, but the Russian language is dominant. Open conflict with Moldovan forces in 1992 led to the intervention of Russian peacekeepers and was effectively resolved in June 1996 when Transdnestria was designated 'a republic within Moldova'. The bicameral regional government is based in Tiraspol and headed by self-styled President Igor Smirnov.

Politically dominated by Russia since absorption into the Russian Empire in 1791, Transdnestria was only briefly occupied by enemy forces during the two world wars. Its 200-year connection has led to a high degree of russification. Under Soviet rule the **Cyrillic alphabet** was introduced into the Moldovan Soviet Socialist Republic and Transdnestria in particular was developed as a regional centre for heavy industry, resulting in an influx of ethnic Russians. The Russian minority in Transdnestria and the Moldovan capital **Chişinau** came to dominate the Soviet bureaucracy. Calls for the unification of Moldova with **Romania** following the collapse of the **Soviet Union** spurred the declaration of sovereignty for the PMR through a referendum. Clashes between paramilitaries and the Moldovan army escalated into full conflict in the summer of 1992, leaving hundreds dead and leading to the intervention of the Russian army as peacekeepers. Despite the definitive failure in Moldova of the movement for unification with Romania, and the constitutional accommodation reached with the moderate pan-Moldovan Government in 1996, Transdnestria remains resolutely defensive of its autonomy. Hopes of a breakthrough in negotiations following the election of Moldovan President Vladimir **Voronin** in April 2001 had faded by the end of the year, but the Russian troops had withdrawn from the region by November, a year ahead of schedule.

Transylvania

A mountainous plateau situated in the corner of the eastern and southern Carpathians. Settled by **Hungarian** invaders (**Szeklers**) in the 10th century and by ethnic **Romanians** possibly from as early as the time of the Roman conquest of the area in the 2nd century. Under Hungarian rule the region also saw the arrival of ethnic **Germans**. It has been the centre of a prolonged territorial dispute between **Romania** and **Hungary** ever since its conquest at the hands of the Hungarian leader King (Saint) Stephen in the early 11th century.

Dominated by the Hungarians for centuries, Transylvania became an important part of Hungarian national aspirations under the Austro-Hungarian Empire, and was the centre of an anti-Austrian uprising in the mid-19th century. Following the break-up of the Empire at the end of the First World War, Transylvania was ceded to Romania on the basis that the majority of the population were by now ethnically Romanian. Tensions between the large Hungarian minority in Transylvania and the Romanian state were reinforced by the temporary annexation of northern Transylvania by the Nazi-supervised Hungarian Government during the Second World War. The dispute was successfully stifled during the **Cold War** era through the wholesale repression of Hungarian culture.

At the time of the collapse of communism in the late 1980s and early 1990s Transylvania played a key role in Romanian history. The overthrow of the hated **Ceauşescu** regime began with protests in the western Transylvanian city of Timişoara. Tensions between the ethnic communities have since then remained subdued. Political representation for the Transylvanian Hungarians (who include the **Szeklers**) is dominated by the sizeable **Hungarian Democratic Union of Romania**, and is offset by the racist nationalism espoused by the extreme right.

Trianon, Treaty of

A treaty signed on 4 June 1920 at the Paris Peace Conference, convened following the conclusion of the First World War. The Treaty of Trianon was concerned specifically with the territorial restructuring of the newly independent **Hungary**, and it established what are still that country's modern borders. It remains a source of resentment for Hungarian nationalists as it ceded much of historic Hungary to neighbouring countries, including south and eastern **Slovakia**, **Transylvania** and the **Vojvodina**. These areas are still home to significant ethnic **Hungarian** populations who retain very close links with Hungary and whose treatment is a source of regional tensions. *See also* Treaties of **Neuilly** and **Versailles**.

Trieste

An Italian city situated in the north-western corner of **Istria**. Developed as a major port by the Romans, Trieste flourished once again under Austrian control from 1891. The large Italian majority in the city prompted the Allies to grant it, along with the Istrian peninsula as a whole, to Italy after the First World War. As a frontier it has provided strong support for Italian nationalists ever since, while disputes over the adjoining territory continued.

Briefly held by **Yugoslav** communist forces from 1945 to 1947, Trieste was created a UN Free Territory with Allied and Yugoslav forces sharing control. Official claims to sovereignty over the city were not settled until a treaty in 1954 gave the eastern and northern hinterlands to **Yugoslavia**, and the city itself to Italy. The Italian Government did not drop its claims to the whole area until 1975.

TS–LK *see* **Homeland Union–Lithuanian Conservatives**.

TSP *see* **National Harmony Party**.

Tudjman, Franjo

Nationalist leader in **Croatia** and President from 1990 until his death in December 1999. Tudjman was born on 14 May 1922 in the village of Veliko Trgovišće. His father founded the wartime anti-fascist movement in his native region, but was nevertheless killed by the secret police after the war under the Tito regime. Franjo Tudjman himself also fought as a Partisan in north-west Croatia (as did his brother, killed in 1943). A military career after 1945 (he reached the rank of General in the Yugoslav National Army by 1960) gave way eventually to his interest in national history and political science. He resigned his commission in 1961 to pursue this research, and was expelled from the communist party in 1967 as his writing became increasingly controversial and his support for a specifically **Croat** identity more overt. His controversial *Wastelands of Historical Reality* claimed that the crimes of the wartime Ustaša regime (against which he had fought as a Partisan) were being grossly exaggerated by communist propagandists, and that the Ustaša should even be commended for achieving statehood for Croatia. He was imprisoned in 1972 and again between 1981 and 1984. Later that decade Tudjman travelled in North America and Europe, raising support among Croatian émigrés for the 1989 launch of his **Croatian Democratic Union** (HDZ).

In Croatia's first multi-party elections, in April–May 1990, the HDZ won a large majority and on 30 May the new Assembly elected Tudjman as President. Croatia declared itself independent in 1991, and bitter fighting followed as the **Serb**-dominated Federal Army moved in to support Croatian Serbs in resisting this secession, but by January 1992 the new state had won international recognition, albeit with a quarter of its former territory in Serb hands. As the hero of independence, Tudjman was returned to power with nearly 60% of the vote in presidential elections that August. Re-elected for another five-year term in June 1997, he was the dominant Croat nationalist figure throughout the period of conflict which followed the collapse of the **Socialist Federal Republic of Yugoslavia**. He was criticized internationally, however, both for his authoritarianism (in particular in restricting the press and broadcasting media) and for pursuing the temptation of a '**Greater Croatia**' by supporting ethnic Croat forces in the war which ravaged neighbouring **Bosnia and Herzegovina** between 1992 and 1995. Ultimately Tudjman became a firm supporter of alliance between Bosnian Croats and **Muslims**, and took the opportunity of recovering Serb-held areas of Croatia in a series of offensives in August and September 1995. Many thousands of Serb refugees were sent streaming eastwards, such '**ethnic cleansing**' having already become appallingly familiar in the region's four years of conflict. Tudjman was a signatory of the **Dayton Agreement** at the end of 1995, and also signed an accord with the rump **Yugoslavia** the following August. His narrowly nationalistic outlook, however, and lack of respect for democratic values, contributed to a loss of impetus in Croatia's bid for greater integration within a democratic and liberal free-market Europe. His death in December 1999 became the catalyst for a period of change and a more internationalist outlook in Croatian politics.

Turkic peoples

A large ethnic group encompassing nationalities spread across **eastern Europe** (particularly in **European Russia**) and central Asia. Historically the Turks are thought to have originated among the nomadic T'u-chüeh of western Mongolia. Through their 6th-century empire the Turks spread across the Russian steppe and established the first of their European colonies.

Turkic nationality groups in eastern Europe are the **Azeris**, Balkars (*see* **Kabardino-Balkaria**), Bashkirs (*see* **Bashkortostan**), **Bulgarian Turks**, **Chavash**, **Karachai**, **Kazakhs**, **Kumyks**, **Meskhetians** and **Tatars** (*see also* **Crimean Tatars**). All have mixed with local peoples over the centuries, often retaining only their language—which is of the Altaic group—by which they can be identified as Turkic, although they share similarities in culture and, apart from the Chavash, all embrace Islam. **Pan-Turkic** sentiment is strongest in **Tatarstan** but has found little popular support within the **Russian Federation**.

U

UCK *see* Kosovo Liberation Army.

UDMR *see* Hungarian Democratic Union of Romania.

Udmurtia

A heavily-industrialized constituent republic of the **Russian Federation** situated in the east of **European Russia**. *Population*: 1.6m. (1997 estimate).

Inhabited by the **Finno-Ugric** Udmurt people, the region came under the suzerainty of the Kazan khanate in the 14th century before being absorbed into the Russian Empire in 1552. Under the **Soviet Union,** Udmurtia was granted the status of an autonomous *oblast* (region) in 1920 (known as Votskaya until 1932) and became an autonomous republic in 1934. It was developed as a major industrial centre and now supplies around 1% of the Russian Federation's annual output. The republic declared its sovereignty on the collapse of the centralized Soviet state in September 1990.

The geography of Udmurtia displays strong differences between the largely marshy north and the drier, more fertile, south. Following these differences the republic's main industrial centres are in the north and produce a wide variety of goods including building materials, metal products, heavy industrial machines and textiles. The capital, Izhevsk, focuses on the construction of machinery.

The approximately 700,000 Udmurts are most closely related to the neighbouring **Mari** and **Komi** and constitute around 30% of Udmurtia and minority communities in the neighbouring republics. Aleksandr Volkov has been President of Udmurtia since 19 April 1995.

UIASM *see* Union of Independent and Autonomous Syndicates of Macedonia.

Ukraine
Ukraina

An independent republic in eastern Europe since 1991, formerly part of the **Soviet Union**. Ukraine is bounded to the west by Poland, Slovakia and Hungary, to the north by Belarus, to the north and east by the Russian Federation, and to the south by Romania, Moldova and the Black Sea. Administratively, the country is divided into 24 provinces (oblasti), one autonomous republic (**Crimea**) and two municipalities.

Area: 603,700 sq km; *capital*: **Kiev** (Kyiv); *population*: 49.1m. (2001 estimate), comprising **Ukrainians** 73%, **Russians** 22%, **Jews** 1%, others 4%; *official language*: Ukrainian; *religion*: **Orthodox, Roman Catholic**.

Under the Constitution adopted in June 1996, executive authority is vested in the President, who is directly elected for a five-year term and who nominates the Prime Minister and other members of the Government. Legislative authority is vested in the unicameral Parliament (Verkhovna Rada), which currently has 450 members serving for a four-year term. Under a 1997 constitutional amendment, the 1998 elections used a system where half of the members were elected by proportional representation from party lists, subject to a 4% threshold, while the other half were elected from single-seat constituencies. A legislative move to introduce proportional representation for all seats in the 2002 elections was vetoed by the President early in 2001 (see below).

History: The first unified state of Eastern **Slavs**, Kievan Rus, was founded in the late 9th century with Kiev at its centre. Christianity was adopted in 988. The Kievan state disintegrated into warring principalities and was destroyed by invading Mongol **Tatars** in the 1200s. By the mid-15th century most of Ukraine was ruled by **Lithuania**, subsequently coming under Polish influence in 1569. A **Cossack** revolt in 1648, fuelled by the imposition of serfdom and religious persecution, drove the **Poles** from central Ukraine. The eastern part of the territory became a **Russian** protectorate in 1654, and Ukraine was partitioned east-west between Russia and the Polish-Lithuanian confederation in 1667. The subsequent partitions of **Poland**, however, in the late 18th century, brought western Ukraine too under Russian rule except for the regions of **Galicia** and **Bukovina** (and the Crimea, which had been ruled by the Tatars, as the Crimean Khanate, since 1475). The country was then subject to intense 'russification', including the banning of the use of the Ukrainian language.

In the wake of the Russian Revolution of 1917 and the final defeat of German forces at the end of the First World War, a briefly independent Ukraine was embroiled in the Russian civil war and conflict with newly independent Poland. The eastern part was incorporated into the **Soviet Union** as a constituent republic in 1922, while western Ukraine became part of Poland. In the 1930s, forced collectivization of agriculture led to a severe famine which, coupled with the political purges under Stalinist rule, accounted for millions of deaths in Ukraine.

After the start of the Second World War, Soviet forces annexed western Ukraine from Poland and northern Bukovina from **Romania** (as agreed under the terms of the 1939 **Nazi-Soviet Pact**). German forces then occupied Ukraine from 1941 until 1944 (during which time millions more died) before the Soviet Union regained control of the territory. The post-war Ukrainian Soviet Socialist Republic, which (although part of the Soviet Union) was accorded membership of the United Nations in its own right, included not only former Polish territory but also Czechoslovak **Transcarpathia**, southern **Bessarabia** (a Romanian territory between the world wars) and parts of **Moldova**, while the Crimea was transferred from Russia in 1954. Although nationalist sentiment began to reassert itself among Ukrainians after Stalin's death in 1953, in the early 1970s an arch-conservative, Vladimir Shcherbitsky, assumed the leadership of the **Communist Party of Ukraine** (KPU) and initiated a widespread crackdown on political dissent.

In the late 1980s, encouraged by the *glasnost* (openness) initiative in the Soviet Union, opposition activity re-emerged, led by the **Popular Movement of Ukraine** (Rukh). In elections to the Ukrainian Supreme Soviet in March 1990, the Democratic Bloc (an electoral coalition including Rukh candidates) won about a quarter of the seats. The following July the new legislature declared Ukrainian sovereignty and elected Leonid Kravchuk as its Chairman.

In the aftermath of the abortive **August coup** by hardliners in **Moscow** in 1991, Ukraine declared full independence and outlawed the KPU (although the party was allowed to re-form in 1993). In December 1991 independence was approved by referendum (with 90% of the vote), Kravchuk was elected President and Ukraine joined the **Commonwealth of Independent States** (CIS). In May 1992 Ukraine granted the mainly Russian-speaking Crimea full autonomy, having revoked Crimea's earlier declaration of sovereignty.

The pursuit of market-led economic policies, the declared objective of post-independence Ukrainian Governments, was obstructed by a Parliament dominated by parties associated with the Soviet era. Leonid **Kuchma** was appointed Prime Minister in October 1992, entering into a long power struggle with President Kravchuk, who assumed Cabinet leadership in 1993. The following year the revived KPU, in alliance with the **Socialist Party of Ukraine** (SPU) and the **Peasants' Party of Ukraine** (SelPU), won the largest share of the seats in parliamentary elections. In the 1994 presidential elections, Kravchuk was defeated by Kuchma, who then appointed himself executive head of a reformist Government. In June 1995, having lost a no-confidence vote in the Parliament, Kuchma secured a constitutional agreement strengthening presidential powers, the changes being incorporated in the new Constitution adopted in 1996. Nevertheless, persistent conflict between Kuchma and the left-dominated legislature severely impeded the process of government, as Ukraine sank further into economic and social decline (*see* **Ukraine, economy**). A parallel crisis over Crimea, where a pro-Russian bloc in the Parliament had voted through a demand for Crimean sovereignty in 1994, led eventually to the introduction of a new Crimean Constitution in 1999 giving the autonomous republic greater budgetary powers.

Latest elections: Elections to the Parliament in March 1998 confirmed the dominance of the KPU, which won 115 of the 442 seats validly filled with 26.0% of the vote. Rukh came a poor second with 42 seats (and 9.5% of the vote), followed by a joint list of the SPU and SelPU with 28 (6.3%), the **People's Democratic Party of Ukraine** (NDPU) with 28 (6.3%), the **Hromada All-Ukrainian Association** with 20 (4.5%), the **Green Party of Ukraine** (PZU) with 19 (5.3%), the **Social Democratic Party of Ukraine–United** (SDPU–O) with 13 (2.9%), the **Progressive Socialist Party** (PSP) 11 (2.5%), the **Agrarian Party of Ukraine** (APU) with 8 (1.9%) and 11 other parties or alliances with 20, while 138 independent candidates were elected. Most of the independents joined parliamentary groups set up by the main parties, with the result that the centre-right factions commanded an overall majority of seats, although their precise composition was subject to a Byzantine process of endless flux.

Despite his unpopularity over Ukraine's economic difficulties, Kuchma retained office in presidential elections in October–November 1999, defeating KPU candidate Petro Symonenko by 56.3% to 37.8% in the second round. International observers reported that the polling had been flawed by many irregularities to the advantage of the incumbent.

Recent developments: President Kuchma's rediscovered commitment to economic reform was signalled by the appointment of the Governor of the **National Bank of Ukraine**, Viktor Yushchenko, as Prime Minister in December 1999. In another move welcomed in the West, in March 2000 the death penalty was formally abolished. However, the political process was again paralysed in early 2000 by the determination of the centre-right parties to oust Oleksandr Tkachenko (SelPU) as Chairman of the Parliament, which they achieved only after a protracted crisis in which two alternative legislatures were sitting at one stage.

President Kuchma then launched a campaign to correct the perceived deficiencies of the Parliament, securing overwhelming approval in a national referendum in April 2000 for proposed constitutional amendments providing for a bicameral legislature, a reduction in the size of the lower house from 450 to 300 members, reduced parliamentary immunity from prosecution and enhanced presidential powers of dissolution. None of these proposed changes secured the necessary parliamentary approval, however. Conversely, a new electoral law adopted by Parliament in January 2001, under which all seats would henceforth be allocated by proportional representation, was vetoed by Kuchma in March, and in May Parliament failed to muster the two-thirds majority needed to override the veto.

Meanwhile, another major political crisis had developed over the discovery in November 2000 of a headless body believed to be that of an opposition journalist, and the publication of tape transcripts appearing to show that Kuchma had been implicated in the murder. Amidst growing popular demands for his resignation, the President persisted with his denials of the authenticity of the tapes and resisted parliamentary moves to impeach him. His position was strengthened by the unwillingness of the KPU and its allies to support impeachment proceedings. In return, Kuchma in April 2001 bowed to a KPU-inspired vote of no confidence in the Government by dismissing Yushchenko as Prime Minister, to the general dismay of Western Governments.

International relations and defence: Following independence in 1991 and accession to the CIS, Ukraine became a member of the **Organization for Security and Co-operation in Europe**, the **Council of Europe**, the **Central European Initiative**, the **Organization of the Black Sea Economic Co-operation** and the **Danube Commission**. Ukraine was also a founder member in 1998 of what became the **GUUAM group** (with **Georgia**, Uzbekistan, **Azerbaijan** and Moldova) within the CIS.

Having acceded in 1994 to the **Partnership for Peace** programme of the **North Atlantic Treaty Organization** (NATO), Ukraine in 1997 signed an important co-operation agreement with NATO. A partnership and co-operation agreement with the **European Union** came into force in 1998, its provisions including one for EU financial assistance with the closure of the remaining reactors at the **Chernobyl** nuclear plant, site of the world's worst nuclear accident to date in 1986. Ukraine's longer-term aspirations to full membership of the EU and NATO were seen as dependent on the constellation of political forces within the country and the progress made in internal structural reform.

In 1994 Ukraine signed a trilateral agreement with the **Russian Federation** and the USA to dismantle its nuclear weapons in return for US economic aid, at the same time ratifying the **START**-I arms reduction treaty and the **Nuclear Non-Proliferation Treaty**. In May 1997 Ukraine and the **Russian Federation** signed a Treaty of Friendship and Co-operation, under which the two sides resolved a lengthy dispute on the division of the Soviet **Black Sea Fleet** and on the status of the **Sevastopol** naval base. Also in 1997 Ukraine signed accords with Romania agreeing to try to settle differences over territorial issues and minority rights. A border delineation with Moldova was concluded in mid-1998.

Ukraine's defence budget for 2000 amounted to some US $440m., equivalent to about 1% of GDP. The size of the armed forces at the end of 2000 was some 300,000 personnel, including those serving under compulsory conscription of 18 months, while reservists numbered an estimated one million. In late 2000 plans were approved to reduce the armed services to 285,000 uniformed personnel by 2005.

Ukraine, economy

An economy shaped by the central planning system of the Soviet era, which went into virtual free-fall following independence in 1991, until showing signs of limited recovery in 2000.

GNP: US $31,228m. (2000); *GNP per capita*: $700 (2000); *GDP at PPP*: $109,500m. (1999); *GDP per capita at PPP*: $2,200 (1999); *exports*: $14,579m. (2000); *imports*: $13,955m. (2000); *currency*: hryvna (plural: hryvnas; US $1=H5.314 at the end of December 2001).

In 1999 industry was estimated to account for 38% of GDP, agriculture for 13% and services and other sectors for 49%. About 58% of the land is arable, 2% under permanent crops, 13% permanent pastures and 18% forests and woodland. Ukraine is self-sufficient in most aspects of agricultural production, with large areas devoted to grain, as well as to sugar beet, potatoes and other vegetables; animal husbandry is also important, though in particular decline in the 1990s. Agricultural output was seriously affected by the 1986 **Chernobyl** nuclear reactor disaster, which made large areas of land unusable.

Ukraine has large resources of hard coal and iron ore as well as brown coal (lignite), titanium and manganese ore. There are also small reserves of petroleum (395m. barrels at the end of 1999) and of natural gas (40,000,000m. cu ft), but post-independence oil output has fallen steadily, and most petroleum and natural gas needs are met from imports, notably from the **Russian Federation** and Turkmenistan. The main industries are the extraction of coal, ferrous and non-ferrous metals, machinery and equipment, chemicals and food processing. In 1999 about 42% of Ukraine's electricity requirements were met through nuclear generation, but the future of the nuclear industry remains uncertain in the wake of the 1986 accident at the Chernobyl nuclear power station (where the remaining reactors were finally closed in December 2000).

Ukraine's main exports by value in 1999 were ferrous and non-ferrous metals (33% of the total), food items and raw materials (21%), chemicals (15%), machinery (14%) and fuel and energy products (9%). Principal imports in 1999 were fuel and energy products (52%), machinery (16%), chemicals (11%) and food items and raw materials (8%). Some 24% of Ukraine's exports in 2000 went to the Russian Federation, 6% to Turkey and 5% each to Germany and the USA. The main sources of imports in 2000 were the Russian Federation (42%), Germany (8%) and Turkmenistan (7%). In 1999 **European Union** countries accounted for 17% of exports and 23% of imports.

Prior to independence Ukraine was the 'bread-basket' of the **Soviet Union**, its rich agricultural land providing 25% of Soviet grain production, 20% of meat and dairy products and over 50% of sugar beet output. Soviet Ukraine also developed a substantial heavy industrial sector and was a principal producer of defence-related equipment. The disappearance of the Soviet framework exposed the chronic inefficiencies of both sectors, with the result that in the period 1991–96 GDP declined in real terms by an average rate of 14% a year, while consumer price inflation rose massively to over 1,000% in 1992 and to some 10,000% in 1993.

The election of Leonid **Kuchma** as President in mid-1994 heralded a serious attempt at economic reform. A comprehensive **IMF**-prescribed programme was introduced under which most price controls were lifted, a new currency (the hryvna) was launched in 1996 with a unified exchange rate, bread and utility subsidies were reduced and export quotas eliminated. The results were initially encouraging, in that the rate of GDP contraction was limited to about 3% in 1997, while inflation fell sharply to an annualized rate of about 10% at the end of 1997. Exports to Western markets also began to increase, more than offsetting a continuing fall in trade with the Russian Federation and other former Soviet republics.

The limited progress was halted by the mid-1998 Russian financial crisis (*see* **Russian Federation, economy**), which highlighted similar deficiencies in the Ukrainian economy. Although GDP contraction was reduced to 2% in 1998, inflation rose to 20% in 1998 and the hryvna lost more than half its external value in the latter part of year, being further devalued in early 1999. Although GDP contracted by only 0.4% in 1999, inflation remained high at around 20% and Ukraine experienced serious problems in funding essential oil and gas imports, while the **Kosovo** crisis restricted Ukraine's trade routes along the Danube river. The IMF noted in March 1999 that reform in the agricultural and energy sectors had been inadequate and delayed, that continued friction between **Parliament** and Government added uncertainty to the economic climate and that stronger fiscal adjustment was necessary to ensure progress towards macroeconomic stability. It also urged that higher priority should be accorded to structural reforms in the energy, coal and agricultural sectors, to a further downsizing in government and rationalization of the public sector, and to greater progress in deregulation and privatization. The appearance of evidence in early 2000 that IMF loans had been embezzled by Ukrainian officials caused the IMF to suspend further disbursements under a three-year facility agreed in 1998.

The re-election of Kuchma in November 1999 and the appointment of the Governor of the **National Bank of Ukraine**, Viktor Yushchenko, as Prime Minister signalled an apparent determination to step up reform efforts. A new five-year 'Reform for Prosperity' programme was quickly introduced, the hryvna was allowed to float from late February 2000 and the restructuring of foreign debt was agreed in April 2000. These efforts yielded speedy success to the extent that in 2000 Ukraine achieved real GDP growth, of 6%, for the first time since independence, while in December 2000 the IMF agreed to reactivate the 1998 financial support facility. However, inflation advanced to 26% in 2000, real unemployment was believed to be up to eight times higher than the official rate of around 5% and an estimated 60% of economic activity took place in the 'black' economy. Moreover, the major political crisis surrounding Kuchma in early 2001 and the dismissal of Yushchenko in April gave rise to renewed doubts about Ukraine's ability to pursue real economic reform. The Government's budget for 2001 provided for a balance between expenditure and revenue of H52,300m. under each head, based on projected GDP growth of 4% and an inflation rate of 13%.

Ambitious privatization plans announced in 1992 proved difficult to implement for political reasons, notably the strong opposition to them of the powerful **Communist Party of Ukraine** (KPU) and its parliamentary allies. After further partially-aborted efforts, fresh measures were introduced in March 1996 and had some success, especially with smaller enterprises, although the process was tarnished by pervasive corruption. By mid-2000 over 67,000 concerns had been privatized, including over 7,000 medium-sized and large industrial enterprises, and the decollectivization of agriculture was officially stated to have been completed by the restructuring of some 10,500 collective farms into 11,000 joint-stock companies and co-operatives.

New plans for the privatization of some 600 large and strategic enterprises still under state ownership, including the power supply sector and telecommunications, received parliamentary approval in May 2000, while in December 2000 the Government announced that all coal mines would be privatized in 2001. A pledge was also given that further disposals of state-owned assets would be more 'transparent' than the earlier privatization process.

Ukrainian Chamber of Commerce and Industry

The principal organization in **Ukraine** for promoting business contacts, both internally and externally, in the post-communist era. Originally founded in 1973.
Chair.: Oleksiy P. Mikhailichenko.
Address: vul. Velyka Zhitomirska 33, 254655 Kiev.
Telephone: (44) 2122911.
Fax: (44) 2123353.

Ukrainian Export–Import Bank
Ukreximbank

Founded as an independent entity in **Ukraine** in 1992, formerly a branch of the **Soviet Union** State Export-Import Bank. Capital: US $108m., 25 branches.
Chair.: Oleksandr Sorokin.
Address: vul. Gorkogo 127, 03150 Kiev.
Telephone: (44) 2262745.
Fax: (44) 2478082.
Internet: www.eximb.com

Ukrainian Stock Exchange (USE)

One of eight stock markets on which securities are traded in **Ukraine** (and one of three based in **Kiev**, the others being regional stock markets). Founded in 1992, the USE had nine companies officially listed as at the end of 2001 (three banks and six joint stock companies), while shares of 377 companies in all were traded on the non-official list. Total market capitalization was US $18.8m. In terms of volume of trading the USE has now been overtaken by the First Stock Trading System (PFTS).

Chair.: Valentin Oskolsky.
Address: 10 Rylsky Provulok, 01025 Kiev.
Telephone: (44) 2294158.
Fax: (44) 2285140.
E-mail: use@ukrse.kiev.ua
Internet: www.ukrse.kiev.ua

Ukrainians

An east **Slavic people** dominant in **Ukraine**, formerly known as **Ruthenians**. The Ukrainians are linguistically and culturally very close to the other east Slavs—**Belarusians** and **Russians**. Their language, like Belarusian, has a large number of Polish loan words. It is transcribed using the **Cyrillic alphabet**. The Ukrainians adopted Christianity in the 10th century and the majority now follow Eastern **Orthodoxy**. The autocephalous Ukrainian Church re-emerged in 1990 having spent over 200 years as part of the Russian Church.

Ukrainian nationalism and identity have traditionally been denied by the neighbouring Russians. The mediaeval Kievan Rus is seen as the cradle of east Slavic civilization and for many centuries Ukrainian was considered to be merely a dialect of Russian. Under the **Soviet** regime, the Ukrainian people bore the brunt of the famine in the early 1920s and civilian casualties during the Second World War. In all some 15 million people are estimated to have died between 1917 and 1945. Like many nationalities, Ukrainians were allowed a greater degree of cultural identity under Khrushchev in the 1950s. From the time of *glasnost* in the late 1980s, through independence in 1991, Ukrainian nationalism and culture flourished.

The largest community outside Ukraine is in the **Russian Federation** where there are 4.4 million Ukrainians, although, because they have their own established 'homeland' outside Russia, they receive little official aid there for cultural and linguistic programmes. Over 800,000 Ukrainians joined Russians and Belarusians in emigrating to Kazakhstan during the Soviet era, but many of them have returned since 1991. A further 600,000 live in **Moldova**, over half of them in **Transdnestria**. This group, heavily russified, has largely allied itself with Moldova's Russian community.

Ukreximbank *see* **Ukrainian Export–Import Bank**.

Ukrinform
Ukrainske Nationalne Informaziyine Agentstvo
(Ukrainian National News Agency)

The main independent news agency in **Ukraine**. Ukrinform was reorganized as an independent agency in 1990, when it was separated from the Telegraph Agency of

the Soviet Union (TASS—*see* **ITAR-TASS**), of which it had been the Ukrainian branch since 1918.
Director: Viktor Chamara.
Address: Bogdan Khmelnytsky St 8/16, Kiev.
Telephone: (44) 2298152.
E-mail: chiefadm@ukrinform.com
Internet: news.ukrinform.com.ua

UN War Crimes Tribunal for the former Yugoslavia
see **International Criminal Tribunal for the former Yugoslavia**.

Uniate Church

A denomination of Christianity significant mainly in **Ukraine**, which recognizes the primacy of the **Roman Catholic** Pope, but maintains traditional **Orthodox Christian** rites. Also known as Greek-Catholicism. The 'Uniate' Church was formed in 1596 when Orthodox Bishops in Ruthenia (*see* **Transcarpathia**) once more submitted to the authority of Rome but kept their Orthodox traditions, including allowing the clergy to marry. The Church has retained a strong sense of identification with ethnic **'Ruthenians' (Ukrainians)**. When Transcarpathia was integrated into the **Soviet Union** in 1946 the Uniate Church was persecuted and forced to reintegrate into the **Russian Orthodox Church**. However, the situation was reversed in 1989.

In **Belarus** the Church was abolished altogether by the occupying Tsarist Russian authorities in 1839 and was only restarted in the final days of communism in March 1990. The Uniate Church claims around 4.5 million followers in Ukraine but remains very much a minority religion elsewhere. Relations with the Roman Catholic Church remain close whereas the Orthodox Church is hostile to what it sees as a Catholic attempt to divide the Eastern Church.

Union for Victory
Bashkimi për Fitoren (BF)

A right-of-centre political coalition in **Albania** formed to contest the June 2001 legislative election and headed by the **Democratic Party of Albania** (PDS). The BF unites five parties including the PDS, the **Albanian Republican Party**, the **Liberal Democratic Union**, the **Movement of Legality Party** and the **National Front**. The coalition won 46 seats in the 140-seat **People's Assembly** but denounced the results of the election, which was won by the **Socialist Party of Albania**, and boycotted the chamber for three months from its opening in September.

Union of Chambers of Commerce and Industry of Albania

The principal organization in **Albania** for promoting business contacts, both internally and externally, in the post-communist era. Originally founded in 1958.
President: Anton Leka.
Address: Rruga Kavajes 6, Tirana.
Telephone and Fax: (4) 222934.

Union of Democratic Forces
Sayuz na Demokratichnite Sili (SDS)

The main centre-right political alliance in **Bulgaria**, a grouping which has held power during a substantial part of the post-communist era. The SDS was established in December 1989 under the chairmanship of Zhelyu Zhelev (a dissident philosophy professor of the communist era), its original 10 assorted pro-democracy member organizations being joined by half a dozen others in the run-up to the first multi-party **National Assembly** elections in June 1990. Although the elections were won by the **Bulgarian Socialist Party** (BSP), the new name of the Bulgarian Communist Party, the new Assembly elected Zhelev as President of Bulgaria in August 1990 following the resignation of the BSP incumbent. In December 1990 elements of the SDS joined a new coalition headed by a non-party Prime Minister and including the BSP.

The SDS gained political advantage from the BSP's ambiguous response to the abortive coup by hardliners in **Moscow** in August 1991 (*see* **August coup**) but dissension between moderate and radical elements resulted in the presentation of three distinct SDS lists in the new Assembly elections of October 1991, the main one being designated the SDS–Movement and the other two being the SDS–Centre and the SDS–Liberals. The outcome was a narrow plurality for the SDS–Movement, which won 110 of the 240 seats, just ahead of the BSP, whereas neither the SDS–Centre nor the SDS–Liberals obtained representation. The main SDS proceeded to form Bulgaria's first wholly non-communist Government since the Second World War, headed by Chairman Filip Dimitrov of the SDS environmentalist wing, with the parliamentary support of the (ethnic Turkish) **Movement for Rights and Freedoms** (DPS). In direct presidential elections in January 1992, Zhelev secured a popular mandate as the SDS candidate, winning 53% of the second-round vote.

The minority SDS Government quickly came into conflict with the trade unions, which opposed aspects of its pro-market economic programme. Serious strains also developed between the Government and President Zhelev, while the SDS Assembly group, harbouring over 20 distinct party groupings, became riven with dissension. The Dimitrov Government fell in October after the DPS had withdrawn its support and made common cause with the BSP in a no-confidence vote. The successor DPS-proposed 'Government of experts' under Lyuben Berov was approved by the Assembly in December 1992 with the support of most BSP and some 20 SDS deputies. Seen as increasingly conservative in orientation, the anti-Berov SDS in mid-1993 mounted demonstrations against President Zhelev for his alleged connivance in 're-communization'.

By early 1994 SDS numbers in the Assembly had fallen to some 90 deputies, less than the BSP's committed parliamentary strength, while the Berov team was widely credited with having restored political stability. Nevertheless, in April 1994 Zhelev sought to re-establish his SDS credentials by withdrawing political support from the Government, charging it with having delayed privatization and with failure to attract foreign investment. The Berov Government survived no-confidence votes in May and an SDS boycott of Assembly proceedings, but finally resigned in September 1994. New Assembly elections in December resulted in defeat for the SDS, which won only 24.2% of the vote and 69 of the 240 seats, and the installation of a new BSP-led coalition. Soon afterwards Dimitrov was replaced as SDS Chairman by Ivan Kostov, a former Finance Minister, who headed a party which, as the principal opposition formation, was now more cohesive by virtue of previous defections and which in 1996–97 moved to convert itself from a coalition into a single political party.

Public dissatisfaction with the BSP-led Government facilitated a comeback for the SDS in the autumn 1996 presidential elections, in which SDS candidate Petar **Stoyanov**, a relatively unknown lawyer, was elected with just under 60% of the vote in the second round. He eventually succeeded in calling early Assembly elections for April 1997, in which the SDS, heading an alliance called the United Democratic Forces (ODS), won 137 of the 240 seats. The ODS included the **Democratic Party** as well as two factions of the **Bulgarian Agrarian People's Union** and the **Bulgarian Social Democratic Party**. Kostov became the new Prime Minister, heading an SDS-led Government which survived for the four-year parliamentary term and was generally regarded as having overseen significant economic progress.

However, the benefits of this progress failed to buoy the party in the face of the overwhelmingly popular new political movement founded in April 2001 by ex-King Simeon II (now known as Simeon **Saxecoburggotski**). The **National Movement Simeon II** (NDS II) drew sizeable support from traditional right-of-centre sources, and even won over dissident members of the SDS and other ODS factions. NDS II won exactly half of the Assembly seats, pushing the ODS deep into opposition with only 18.2% of the vote and 51 seats. Kostov resigned the party chairmanship which passed to Ekaterina Mihaylova on 26 June. The party refused to join a broad coalition forged by NDS II with the BSP and DPS. Its humiliation was increased when Stoyanov was unexpectedly defeated in presidential polls in November by BSP Chairman Georgi **Purvanov**, despite receiving the personal backing of Prime Minister Saxecoburggotski, who himself had a very high rating in public opinion.

Leadership: Ekaterina Mihaylova (Chair.).
Address: 134 Rakovski Street, 1000 Sofia.
Telephone: (2) 9818035.
Fax: (2) 9810522.
E-mail: pr@sds.bg
Internet: www.sds.bg

Union of Independent and Autonomous Syndicates of Macedonia
(UIASM)

A small Christian-oriented trade union centre in **Macedonia**, affiliated to the World Confederation of Labour.
President: Slobodan Antovski.
Address: BB (bar. 2) Vasil Gorgov St, Skopje 91000.
Telephone and Fax: (2) 236313.
E-mail: darco321@yahoo.com

Union of Independent Trade Unions of Albania
Bashkimi i Sindikatave të Pavarura të Shqipërisë (BSPSh)

An independent trade union confederation founded in **Albania** in 1991 as an alternative to what became the **Confederation of Albanian Trade Unions**. Violent factionalism in the BSPSh included the assassination of two prominent union leaders in October 1997 and September 1998, amidst protracted legal disputes about leadership positions. The BSPSh has a membership of some 130,000, the mineworkers being its most important affiliate.
Address: Bul. Dëshmorët e Kombit, Pallati Ali Kelmendi, Tirana.
Telephone and Fax: (4) 241150.

Union of Right Forces
Soyuz Pravikh Sil (SPS)

A pro-market conservative political party in the **Russian Federation**. The SPS was created prior to the December 1999 elections to the State Duma (lower house of the **Federal Assembly**) as an alliance of parties and groups broadly descended, through many bewildering changes of name and alignment, from those which had supported the '**shock therapy**' economic policies of the early 1990s, notably Yegor Gaidar's Russia's Democratic Choice. These formations had lost influence in the more conservative later years of the presidency of Boris **Yeltsin**, with whom Gaidar broke irrevocably in 1996, and were widely blamed for the deterioration and corruption engendered by the early rush to a market economy.

The SPS won 29 State Duma seats in the December 1999 elections, with 8.5% of the proportional vote, and subsequently gave broad support to the new presidency of Vladimir **Putin**, while maintaining its distance from the main pro-Putin **Unity Inter-regional Movement** (Medved). In May 2000 the SPS alliance formally constituted itself as a national organization with former Prime Minister Boris Nemtsov being elected Chairman and Gaidar one of three Co-Chairmen. The following month plans were announced for an alliance between the SPS and **Yabloko**, providing initially for the presentation of joint candidates in forthcoming elections and possibly leading to a full merger. A splinter faction broke off in 2001 to form the Liberal Russia Party.

Leadership: Boris Nemtsov (Chair.).
Address: c/o Gossoudarstvennaya Duma, Okhotnyi Ryad 1, Moscow 103265.

Union of Soviet Socialist Republics (USSR) *see* **Soviet Union**.

United Civil Party of Belarus
Abyadnanaya Grazhdanskaya Partiya Belarusi (AGPB)

A pro-market liberal-conservative formation in **Belarus** founded in October 1995 as a merger of the United Democratic Party of Belarus (ADPB) and the Civil Party. The first leader of the AGPB, Stanislau Bahdankevich, had been dismissed as President of the **National Bank of Belarus** the previous month after disagreeing with President **Lukashenka**'s pro-Russian policies.

The ADPB had been founded in November 1990 as a merger of three recently-formed pro-democracy groupings, including Communists for **Perestroika** and the Democratic Party. Drawing its main support from the technical and scientific professional strata, it had become a member of the opposition **Belarusian Popular Front–Renaissance** (NFB–A), supporting the latter's unsuccessful candidate in the 1994 presidential elections. In the 1995 legislative elections the AGPB was credited with winning nine seats, and it later became the core of the Civil Action parliamentary group which by April 1996 had 18 members. In February 1996 the AGPB was joined by the Belarusian Christian Democratic Union (BKDZ) led by Petr Silko, an affiliate of **Christian Democrat International**. The NFB–A boycotted the October 2000 legislative elections on the grounds that there was no prospect of their being free and fair.

Leadership: Anatol Liabedzka (Chair.).
Address: 10–4 Sudmalisa Street, Minsk 220033.
Telephone: (17) 2290834.
Fax: (17) 2272912.
E-mail: ucp@ucp.minsk.by

United List of Social Democrats
Združena Lista Socialnih Demokratov (ZLSD)

The party in **Slovenia** which is directly descended from the former ruling **League of Communists of Yugoslavia** and its front organization. Now of social-democratic orientation, it is a member of the **Socialist International** (SI).

The ZLSD was established in 1992 as an alliance of formations deriving from the ruling structures of the Yugoslav era, which had backed the successful candidacy of former communist leader Milan **Kučan** in the pre-independence presidential elections in 1990. In post-independence elections in December 1992, the ZLSD gained third place in the new **National Assembly**, with 14 seats and 12.1% of the vote, while in the simultaneous presidential contest Kučan (now without party affiliation) was re-elected with 64% of the vote. The ZLSD opted to join a centre-left coalition Government headed by **Liberal Democracy of Slovenia** (LDS) and remained a coalition partner until January 1996, when the LDS Prime Minister's move to dismiss one of its four Ministers caused the party to withdraw from the Government. Later in 1996 the ZLSD was admitted to SI membership, replacing the conservative-leaning **Social Democratic Party of Slovenia**.

In the November 1996 parliamentary elections, the ZLSD declined to nine seats and 9% of the vote and continued in opposition. It improved to 11 seats and 12.1% in the October 2000 elections, opting thereafter to join a coalition Government headed by the LDS and also including the **Slovenian People's Party** (SLS+SKD) and the **Democratic Party of Slovenian Pensioners** (DeSUS).

Leadership: Borut Pahor (Chair.).
Address: Levstikova 15, Ljubljana 1000.
Telephone: (1) 1254222.
E-mail: office@zlsd.si
Internet: www.zlsd.si

United People's Party of Estonia
Eestimaa Ühendatud Rahvapartei (EÜR)

The principal party of the estimated 30% of **Estonia**'s population who were, or are descended from, Soviet-era settlers, mainly from **Russia**. For the 1995 **State Assembly** elections the EÜR joined with the Russian Party in Estonia (VEE) and the Russian Unity Party (RUP) in the 'Our Home is Estonia' alliance, which strongly opposed the 1993 Estonian citizenship law defining ethnic **Russians** and other Soviet-era settlers as foreigners and setting exacting conditions for their naturalization. The fact that only Estonian citizens were entitled to vote resulted in the alliance obtaining only 5.9% of the vote and six seats. The resultant parliamentary group was called the Russian Faction, which quickly split into at least two sub-factions and was dissolved in December 1996, before being revived in June 1998.

The EÜR contested the March 1999 parliamentary elections in a bloc with the RUP and the (ex-communist) Estonian Social-Democratic Labour Party (ESDT), the outcome again being six seats (on a 6.1% vote share). The personality clashes which had kept the VEE out of the bloc appeared to be resolved later in 1999. In May 2000 the EÜR parliamentary faction outraged most Estonian parties by signing a co-operation agreement with the **Fatherland–All Russia** group in the Russian **Duma**, covering *inter alia* joint opposition to Estonian membership of the **North Atlantic Treaty Organization** (NATO).

Leadership: Viktor Andreyev (Chair.).
Address: Estonia pst. 3/5, Tallinn 10141.
Telephone: 6455335.
Fax: 6455336.
E-mail: yhendatudfr@riigikogu.ee
Internet: www.stv.ee/~eurp

Unity Inter-regional Movement
Mezhregional'noye Dvizhenie Yedinstvo (Medved)

The main nationalist political party in the **Russian Federation** supporting the presidency of Vladimir **Putin**. Medved (meaning 'bear' in Russian) was launched in September 1999 by strategists associated with then President Boris **Yeltsin** concerned by the growing strength of the **Fatherland–All Russia** bloc. It became a political vehicle for the then Prime Minister Putin, although he did not formally join the party. It took second place in the December 1999 elections to the State Duma (lower house of the **Federal Assembly**), winning 72 seats with 23.3% of the proportional vote and subsequently attracting a number of independents to its parliamentary group, which thereby became of similar size to (and eventually larger than) the **Communist Party of the Russian Federation** (KPRF).

Medved formed the core support for Putin in the March 2000 presidential elections, his outright first-round victory with 52.9% of the vote being achieved with broad backing from 'moderate' nationalist and pro-market formations. In May 2000 Medved held a 'founding congress' in the **Kremlin**, declaring its aim of becoming the Russian Federation's governing party and re-electing Sergei Shoigu (Minister for Emergency Situations) as Party Chairman. In February 2001 it absorbed the Our Home is Russia (NDR) grouping led by former Prime Minister Viktor Chernomyrdin, which had been a key ruling party in the later years of the Yeltsin presidency but had won only seven State Duma seats in the December 1999 elections. Medved subsequently entered into negotiations for a merger with the Fatherland–All Russia (OVR) bloc.

Leadership: Vladimir Pekhtin (Chair.).
Address: c/o Gossoudarstvennaya Duma, Okhotnyi Ryad 1, Moscow 103265.

UP *see* **Labour Union**.

US *see* **Freedom Union (Czech Republic)**.

US-Baltic Partnership Committee

An inter-state co-ordinating group established in 1998 to promote the integration of the **Baltic states** into regional institutions—specifically the **European Union** and the **North Atlantic Treaty Organization**. In its founding Baltic Charter, signed on 16 January 1998, the partners 'declare that their shared goal is the full integration of **Estonia**, **Latvia** and **Lithuania** into European and trans-Atlantic political, economic, security and defence institutions'.

Members: Estonia, Latvia, Lithuania and the USA.

USSR *see* **Soviet Union**.

UW *see* **Freedom Union (Poland)**.

V

Valionis, Antanas

Minister of Foreign Affairs, **Lithuania**. Antanas Valionis is an independent, but was nominated to the Cabinet by the centre-left **New Union (Social Liberals)** (NS). He entered public service in 1990 in the Food Industry Department of the Ministry of Agriculture, and later became Lithuanian Ambassador to Bulgaria, Poland and Romania. He was appointed Foreign Minister on 30 October 2000.

Born on 21 September 1950 in the central Kedainiai region, he graduated in mechanics from the Kaunas Polytechnic Institute in 1974. He spent six years in the meat processing industry before joining a local committee of the Communist Party of Lithuania as head of its Industry and Transport Department in 1980. He was promoted to the Agriculture and Food Department of the party's national Central Committee in 1985. He maintained a similar position in the post-Soviet Agriculture Ministry from 1990 to 1994 before achieving a doctorate in political science from the University of Warsaw. He then took up the post of Lithuanian Ambassador to Poland. His role was expanded to include Bulgaria and Romania from 1996. He was appointed Foreign Minister on 30 October 2000 in the new Government of Prime Minister Rolandas Paksas, and retained the post under his successor, Prime Minister Algirdas **Brazauskas**, from 5 July 2001.

Antanas Valionis is married to Romualda and they have two sons.
Address: Ministry of Foreign Affairs, J. Tumo-Vaižganto 2, Vilnius 2600.
Telephone: (23) 62444 [(523) 62444 from September 2002].
Fax: (23) 13090 [(523) 13090 from September 2002].
E-mail: urm@urm.lt
Internet: www.urm.lt

Vardar Macedonia *see* **Macedonian question**.

Varga, Mihály

Minister of Finance, **Hungary**. Mihály Varga is a member of the right-of-centre **Federation of Young Democrats–Hungarian Civic Party** (FIDESz–MPP). He was elected to the **National Assembly** in 1990 and worked on various economic committees. He was appointed Finance Minister on 1 January 2001.

Born on 26 January 1965 in the eastern town of Karcag, he graduated from the Budapest University of Economics in 1989 and began work at the State Construction Company. He had joined FIDESz in 1988 and was elected to the National Assembly two years later. He has chaired a committee supervising debtors and bank consolidation, and the General Economics Committee. He was appointed State Secretary to the Ministry of Finance on 14 July 1998 and was promoted to the Cabinet as Finance Minister in January 2001.

Mihály Varga is married and has two children.
Address: Ministry of Finance, József Nádor tér 2–4, 1051 Budapest.
Telephone: (1) 3182066.
Fax: (1) 3182570.
Internet: www.meh.hu

VBP *see* **Civil Unity Party**.

Veće Gradjana
(Chamber of Citizens)

The lower house of the **Federal Assembly** of **Yugoslavia**.

Veće Republika
(Chamber of Republics)

The upper house of the **Federal Assembly** of **Yugoslavia**.

Velchev, Milen

Minister of Finance, **Bulgaria**.

Milen Emilov Velchev is a Western-educated economist and an independent. Having worked for two years for the Ministry of Foreign Affairs in the first post-communist Government from 1990, he was appointed Finance Minister in Prime Minister Simeon **Saxecoburggotski**'s technocratic Cabinet on 24 July 2001.

Born on 24 March 1966 in **Sofia**, he graduated from the city's University of National and World Economy in 1988. He spent two years at the Ministry of Foreign Affairs in the international organizations division before completing his education in business management and financial engineering in the USA, including two years at the renowned MIT from 1993 to 1995. On graduation from MIT he travelled to London to begin work with the Merrill Lynch investment company. From 1999 to 2001 he was Vice-President of the company's Emerging Markets department. He returned to Bulgaria following Saxecoburggotski's election and was appointed Finance Minister in July 2001.

Milen Velchev is married.

Address: Ministry of Finance, Rakovski St 102, 1000 Sofia.
Telephone: (2) 98591.
Fax: (2) 9806863.
E-mail: gudfk@bta.bg
Internet: www.minfin.government.bg

Velvet divorce

Czechoslovakia's relatively amicable dissolution and division into the **Czech Republic** and **Slovakia**, which was formally implemented on 1 January 1993. Despite economic growth and educational improvements, many **Slovaks** regarded the united Czechoslovakia created in 1918 as advantageous only to the more numerous **Czechs**. With the collapse of communism after the '**velvet revolution**' of 1989, Slovak nationalism revived. Elections in June 1992 revealed the extent of political polarization between the two Republics. The Czechs elected the neo-liberal **Civic Democratic Party** led by Václav **Klaus**, while the Slovaks elected the populist, social-democratic **Movement for a Democratic Slovakia** (HZDS) led by Vladimír **Mečiar**. Although the HZDS had sought no specific mandate for independence, the Slovak National Council declared its sovereignty in July 1992, and the same month negotiations on the dissolution of the Federation began. The Czechs perceived that a 'velvet divorce' would deliver them political and economic stability, and so acquiesced in the dissolution.

Velvet revolution

The near-bloodless overthrow of **Czechoslovakia**'s communist regime in November–December 1989. Despite moderate reforms in the **Soviet Union** and elsewhere in **eastern Europe**, the Communist Party of Czechoslovakia had remained highly orthodox. Tens of thousands of anti-Government demonstrators were prompted to rally in the capital, **Prague**, on 17 November 1989 by the collapse of hardline communist regimes in **Bulgaria** and East Germany in the preceding few weeks. Violent clashes with riot police at the demonstration left 140 demonstrators injured, spurring ever greater numbers of protestors to rally on Prague's streets over the next few days. Amidst the tumult, opposition forces combined to form the Czech **Civic Forum** and the Slovak **Public Against Violence**. On 24 November communist leader Miloš **Jakeš** resigned. A demoralized Communist Party agreed to the appointment on 10 December of a Government with a non-communist majority. On 29 December 1989, the former dissident playwright Václav **Havel** became interim President.

Verkhovna Rada *see* Parliament (Ukraine).

Versailles, Treaty of

The principal treaty signed on 28 June 1919 at the Paris Peace Conference following the conclusion of the First World War. The Versailles treaty itself deals with territorial, political and other matters relating to Germany, but the term is often used for the post-1918 settlement in Europe, the dismantling of the old imperial order and the creation of successor states based broadly on the nation-state principle. Among the treaty's relevant points was the restructuring of the border between Germany and the newly independent **Poland**. Shifted significantly to the west, Poland received a land corridor to the Baltic Sea—resulting in the separation of East **Prussia** from the rest of Germany—and areas adjacent to the economically vital region of Silesia. *See also* Treaties of **Neuilly** and **Trianon**.

Vienna Awards

Decisions made by the Foreign Ministers of Nazi Germany and Italy in 1938 and 1940 in favour of **Hungary**'s irredentist territorial demands to redress the loss of 'Hungarian' lands under the 1920 Treaty of **Trianon**. The First Vienna Award, made at the expense of **Czechoslovakia** in 1938, granted Hungary the portions of southern **Slovakia** which held significant **Hungarian** populations. The Second Vienna Award, in August 1940, gave Hungary northern **Transylvania**. In contrast to the first award, the lands handed over in the second had only a slim Hungarian majority. Both awards were nullified by the defeat of the Nazis and their Hungarian allies at the conclusion of the war in 1945.

Vike-Freiberga, Vaira

President of **Latvia**.

Vaira Vike-Freiberga is an independent and a political neutral. She was a prominent academic in Canada before returning to Latvia in 1998. She is the first female Head of State in any former Soviet country and has championed better relations with the **Russian Federation**. She was inaugurated as President on 8 July 1999.

She was born in **Riga** on 1 December 1937. Her family fled the Soviet advance at the end of the Second World War and she spent time in a refugee camp in Lübeck, Germany. Having moved on to Morocco in 1949, she attended college in Casablanca before emigrating to Canada in 1954. She graduated in English from Victoria College, University of Toronto, in 1958, and stayed at the university to pursue a postgraduate qualification in psychology. She was awarded a doctorate in experimental psychology from the McGill University in Montréal, Québec. In 1965 she was appointed as an assistant professor at the Université de Montréal and began a 33-year relationship with the university which was broken only by her return to Latvia in 1998. She gained full professorship in 1979. Her academic career included chairing a number of scientific and cultural organizations as well as a five-year term as Vice-Chair of the Canadian Science Council, from 1984 to 1989. She returned to Latvia in 1998 to serve as the Director of the Latvian Institute in Riga. Standing as a political neutral she was elected President after seven rounds of voting in **Parliament** in mid-1999.

Vaira Vike-Freiberga married Imants Freibergs in July 1960 and they have one son and one daughter.

Address: Office of the President, Pils Lauk. 3, Riga 1900.
Telephone: 7377548.
Fax: 7325800.
Internet: www.president.lv

Vilnius

The capital of **Lithuania** situated in the forested southern interior of the country's historic heartland. *Population*: 600,000 (2001 estimate). The city had a turbulent history throughout the 20th century. The ancient heart of the mediaeval Lithuanian state, it had developed as a thriving commercial and academic centre from the 14th century. From 1799 to 1938 Vilnius was the centre of east European **Jewish** cultural life, producing texts which are still standard and creating the first socialist and **Zionist** Jewish movements in the **Russian** sphere. Unlike other **Baltic** capitals it never came under direct Germanic or Scandinavian control, but rather served as the centre for a very much independent and powerful Lithuania—the largest country in Europe in the 15th century after its union with **Poland**. The city only came under foreign domination proper in the 18th century.

Under Russian occupation from 1795, Vilnius was occupied by Polish forces in 1919 during the Polish advance into the **Soviet Union** and became the focus of Polish–**Lithuanian** antagonism over the next decades. The Polish authorities made Vilnius the capital of their puppet Central Lithuanian state and drew it into union with Poland, prompting retaliation from Lithuanian forces and ultimately from the Soviet Union in 1939. The Nazi invasion in 1941 led to the almost total eradication of the 80,000-strong Jewish community and the destruction of much of the old city. Under renewed Soviet domination after the war the majority Lithuanian population of Vilnius was broken up and scattered throughout the Soviet Union and replaced with an influx of Russian workers. By 1959 Lithuanians constituted only 34% of its population.

As the capital of the socialist Lithuanian state the city was developed as an important industrial centre producing heavy machinery, electrical goods and textiles. It has retained this important role as the capital of an independent Lithuania. Its large ethnic Russian community is a source of underlying tension with the post-Soviet regime.

Visegrád Group

The organization of states in **central Europe**, initially **Poland**, **Hungary** and **Czechoslovakia** (later the **Czech Republic** and **Slovakia**), founded in the Hungarian town of Visegrád in February 1991. The group's initial purpose was to persuade the West that central Europe was better qualified for foreign investment and rapid accession to European institutions, including the **European Union**, than were the former communist states of **eastern Europe**. Its member countries also shared anxiety over rising **Russian** nationalism.

Internet: www.visegrad.org

VKT *see* **All-Russian Confederation of Labour**.

Vlachs
(also known as Aromani)

An Indo-European people of the Romance family, spread across the southern **Balkans** and ethnically similar to modern **Romanians/Moldovans**. Vlachs proudly claim descent from Romans who established the province of Dacia in what is now **Romania**.

They are thought to have stayed in the region since the third century AD, adopting a nomadic and pastoral way of life. A majority of Vlachs are still shepherds in remote regions of their host countries. Spreading around the region they gave their **Slavic** loan name, Vlach (they are generally known to themselves as Aromani), to the **Wallachia** region north of the lower Danube, and became dominant in **Bessarabia**. Their Romance language, which is divided into regional dialects, is most similar to Romanian. Most Vlachs, like Romanians, profess **Orthodox Christianity**.

In the 12th and 13th centuries an independent Vlach state is thought to have flourished around the Greek region of Pindus. It is in Greece that the greatest number of Vlachs reside, and where during the Second World War they established a fascist-inspired Principality of Pindus. Some 200,000 Vlachs are now well integrated into Greek culture. There are 50,000 Vlachs in the south-east of **Albania**, living mainly from animal husbandry, and 17,500 distributed throughout **Yugoslavia**. Smaller populations can also be found in **Bulgaria** and **Macedonia**, where they have established a League of Vlachs to promote their language and culture.

VMRO–DPMNE *see* **Internal Macedonian Revolutionary Organization–Democratic Party for Macedonian National Unity**.

Vneshtorgbank *see* **Bank for Foreign Trade**.

Vojvodina

The fertile district of **Serbia** lying north of **Belgrade**, in the southern Pannonian plain, with a sizeable **Hungarian** minority of around 20%. A conglomeration of local regions unified by the Habsburgs in 1848, it was named after the immigrant **Serb** leaders, or *vojvod*. Exceptional soil lends itself to the cultivation of wheat and cash crops. A part of **Hungary** throughout most of history, including the prolonged period of Ottoman rule, the Vojvodina did not emerge as a distinct political entity until the collapse of the Habsburg Empire at the end of the First World War, and its consequent inclusion in the newly-formed Kingdom of the Serbs, Croats and Slovenes (**Yugoslavia**) in 1918.

The shift in sovereignty over the area, and the later collapse of the **Socialist Federal Republic of Yugoslavia**, led to significant shifts in the region's ethnic make-up. Thousands of ethnic Hungarians fled north and ethnic Serbs re-established their position as the dominant population. Vojvodina achieved almost total autonomy within Serbia under communist Yugoslavia's 1974 Constitution owing to its distinction as an important agricultural area and the presence of the ethnic Hungarian minority population (now around 325,000 centred around the town of Subotica and the surrounding border region). This autonomy was removed in 1989. The fall of the Serbian dictator Slobodan **Milošević** in October 2000, however, raised hopes of its restitution, and the regional administration steadily strengthened its own voice over the course of 2001, upgrading the main administrative centre, Novi Sad, to the status of Vojvodina's official capital in October.

Vojvodina's economic importance led to the **North Atlantic Treaty Organization** alliance targeting many of its towns, factories and bridges during the 1999 air strikes against Yugoslavia. The region also suffers from pollution from poorly-maintained factories in neighbouring **Romania**.

Volga region

The region of **European Russia** defined by the Volga river, which flows south-east from east of **St Petersburg** to the north of the Caspian Sea at **Astrakhan**. The major cities of Yaroslavl, Nizhny Novgorod, Kazan, Ulyanovsk, Volgograd and Astrakhan mark the river's route. The Volga was used by the early **Russians** to colonize the region and to trade with Byzantium and the **Muslim** east. It came under the rule of the Russian Empire after the fall of the Kazan khanate in 1552 and then began the long process of settlement and economic exploitation.

The economically productive Volga-Ural region accounted for 11% of the total output of the **Russian Federation** in 1999 and drew 8.6% of total aid. Unemployment is a constant problem with around 11% of the Federation's nearly two million unemployed to be found in the Volga region.

The Volga region is home to a significant number of the Russian Federation's major ethnic groups. The various **Turkic** and **Finno-Ugric** peoples united briefly in 1918 in a loosely-conceived separate **Idel-Ural** state (Idel is the Turkic name for the Volga). As well as these long-established groups, there is a community of Volga **Germans** in the area, although most of the 800,000 Germans were deported to **Siberia** during the Second World War. The principal non-Russian republics of the Volga region are **Mari El** and **Tatarstan**.

Voronin, Vladimir

President of **Moldova**.

Vladimir Voronin leads the **Communist Party of the Moldovan Republic** (PCRM) and was elected President on 4 April 2001.

Born on 25 May 1941 in Corjova (Korzhevo), a village now within the breakaway republic of **Transdnestria**, he graduated from the Chişinău Consumer Co-operation College in 1961. He worked for 10 years as a manager in the bakery industry, staying close to home along the banks of the Dnester river. He retrained in 1971 as an economist at the Moscow Food Industry Institute and returned to Moldova to begin work within the Communist Party in the republic. He held office in various regional sections of the Moldovan party, and entered the Moldovan Supreme Soviet in 1980. He retrained once again as a political scientist at the **Communist Party of the Soviet Union**'s Academy of Social Sciences, graduating in 1983.

Voronin first entered the Moldovan Cabinet in the dying days of the **Soviet Union**, as Minister of Internal Affairs in 1989. He left the Government before it declared Moldovan independence in 1991 and retrained once more, this time in law, at the Academy of the Soviet Union's Ministry of the Interior: he remained a reservist in the Russian police force until 1993. He helped to co-ordinate the rebirth of the PCRM in 1993, and was elected its First Secretary in December 1994. He came third in presidential elections in 1996 and led the PCRM to increasing legislative success, campaigning against the weak presidential system and the country's painful economic reforms. He was elected President in April 2001 after the PCRM swept to power in legislative elections.

Vladimir Voronin is married and has two children and three grandchildren.

Address: Office of the President, Blvd Ştefan cel Mare 154, Chişinău.
Telephone: (2) 234793.
Fax: (2) 245089.
Internet: www.moldova.md/en/president/index.html

Voucher privatization

An innovative way of promoting a transition to free-market economics in post-communist countries, which involved moving companies from state to private ownership by 'selling' shares for vouchers which had been issued free of charge to all citizens. This had the apparent advantage that it theoretically gave everyone the opportunity of share ownership, but the disadvantage that the process brought neither capital nor management expertise into the firms concerned, many of which subsequently failed. The first voucher privatization initiative was implemented in **Czechoslovakia** in 1992, on a large scale, covering about 30% of the total value of all state-held assets scheduled to be privatized. All Czechoslovak citizens aged 18 and above received a booklet of vouchers, which they could use to bid for shares, either directly or (the more popular route) by investing in one of the Investment Privatization Funds. The two waves of Czechoslovak voucher privatization ultimately achieved the transfer into private ownership of 2,200 companies with an approximate book value of US $14,000m. In practice, however, the outcome was very rarely that ordinary citizens became long-term shareholders. Instead, they sold off their shares immediately, in many cases to foreign companies intent on asset stripping. A voucher privatization scheme was also implemented in the **Russian Federation** in the latter part of 1992 (with **Bosnia and Herzegovina** and **Montenegro** among those following this route later in the decade). Ostensibly the Russian scheme resulted in over 40 million individuals becoming shareholders, and the privatization of nearly 16,000 medium and large enterprises. Again, however, more than half the vouchers were either sold on, or used to buy into the investment funds, and a significant proportion were simply never used.

VPN *see* **Public Against Violence**.

Vujanović, Filip

Prime Minister, with responsibility for religious affairs, **Montenegro**.

Filip Vujanović is a moderate member of the centre-left **Democratic Party of Socialists of Montenegro** (DPSCG). He served in the Montenegrin Government as Justice Minister and Interior Minister before becoming Prime Minister in 1998 in succession to Milo **Djukanović**.

Born on 1 September 1954 in **Belgrade**, he graduated in law from the city's university in 1978. He began work in the District Attorney's Office in Belgrade before moving to **Podgorica**, the capital of his ancestral homeland, Montenegro, in 1981. He worked in the city's District Court before being registered as the youngest lawyer in the Attorney's Chamber in 1989. He became a well-known figure in 1992 when he represented the then President of Montenegro, Momir Bulatović, in his lawsuit against detractors. In March 1993 he was appointed to Djukanović's Cabinet as Justice Minister. He moved to the Interior Ministry and remained there in the next Djukanović Cabinet, inaugurated in 1996. Following Djukanović's electoral success as President, he was appointed Prime Minister of Montenegro on 5 February 1998. He was reconfirmed in the post on 2 July 2001.

Address: Office of the Prime Minister, Jovana Tomaševića bb, Podgorica.
Telephone: (81) 52833.
Fax: (81) 52246.

Vukovar

A town on the River Danube in the eastern **Slavonia** region of **Croatia**, and the scene of the first major incidence of '**ethnic cleansing**' accompanying the break-up of the former **Yugoslavia** in the early 1990s. The Yugoslav army, backing the ethnic **Serbs** of the **Krajina** who actively resisted Croatia's declaration of independence in 1991, mounted a particularly heavy artillery bombardment against **Croat**-held Vukovar. The town, which had a pre-war population of some 50,000, was effectively reduced to rubble. It finally fell to the Serbs after a three-month siege in November 1991. Its remaining Croat inhabitants were driven out, while over 2,000 Croat soldiers were massacred and buried in mass graves. The **Dayton Agreement** of November 1995 specified the return of Vukovar to Croatia along with the rest of eastern Slavonia.

W

Wałęsa, Lech

Leader of the **Solidarity** free trade union movement which dramatically challenged the communist regime in **Poland** in the 1980s, and the country's President in 1990–95.

Born in September 1943 near Lipno, he trained as an electrician and moved in 1967 to the Baltic port of Gdańsk, where he worked for nine years in the Lenin shipyard. Active in the worker protests there in December 1970, Wałęsa later won acclaim worldwide (and the 1983 Nobel prize for peace) as leader of the free trade union Solidarity, which was spawned by the shipyard strikes of 1980 and grew into a mass movement which rocked the communist system. He played a major role in negotiating the historic 'Gdańsk accords' signed at the end of August 1980, in which the Polish Government first conceded workers' demands on the right to form trade unions outside the official communist structure, and the following month he became Chairman of the National Co-ordinating Commission of the newly-formed Solidarność (Solidarity). Arrested as martial law was imposed in November 1981 and the movement was driven underground, he led its resurgence in 1988 and helped negotiate the dismantling of Poland's one-party State. When Tadeusz Mazowiecki was appointed Prime Minister, Wałęsa himself refused ministerial office and returned to trade union issues, but became increasingly critical of his erstwhile Solidarity allies as they introduced tough economic austerity measures. These differences became even more evident when Wałęsa stood against, and defeated, Mazowiecki in the 1990 presidential elections.

When the second-round result was declared in December, Wałęsa resigned as leader of Solidarity to emphasize that his new role stood above party politics. He used his international celebrity to help press his country's case for early inclusion within the **European Union** and the **North Atlantic Treaty Organization** (NATO). During his five years in office, however, his impatience, outspokenness and combative style appeared autocratic and divisive in a Head of State. Seeking to present himself as a national figure of historical significance, with echoes of the authoritarian inter-war dictator Piłsudski, he formed a Piłsudski-style Non-Party Bloc in Support of Reforms, but was unable to attract enough support for this bloc to avoid its defeat in the 1993 elections. His anti-communism made his relationship with the post-1993 Government of former communists especially problematic. He also angrily rejected allegations arising from the selective leaking of communist-era secret police records, suggesting that he had collaborated with the authorities in the early 1980s. In November 1995, seeking re-election, he was defeated in a bitterly fought campaign by the youthful former communist Aleksander **Kwaśniewski**.

Wałęsa returned to Gdańsk upon leaving office, re-emerging in the public eye at the time of the September 1997 legislative election, whose outcome gave the **Solidarity Electoral Action** the opportunity to return to government. He offered to broker a coalition deal between the winning parties, while denying any aspirations to the premiership himself. The following month, reflecting the extent to which the paths of different Solidarity figures had diverged, Wałęsa announced the formation of a new political party, Christian Democracy of Poland. Perhaps symbolically, the international media gave greater prominence to his subsequent announcement that he wanted his old job at the shipyard back, and stories of his apparent financial difficulties. Wałęsa was further embarrassed when, standing in the 2000 presidential elections, he finished in 7th place, with a humiliating 1.01% of the vote.

Wallachia

The fertile northern bank of the eastern end of the River Danube in **Romania**, bounded by the southern Carpathians to the north and the Danube to the south. Historically a Christian principality, it came under the suzerainty of **Hungary** in 1369 before beginning a long period of domination by the Ottomans from 1389 to 1878. Since 1859 it has been an integral part of a united Romania. Its main urban centre is **Bucharest**.

Warsaw

The capital city of **Poland**, situated in the east central part of the country on the River Vistula (Wisla). *Population*: 1.6m. (1998 estimate). The city has been destroyed by invading armies several times over the last 250 years, most recently by the German forces in 1944 after the failure of the Warsaw Uprising. The entire left bank of the city was systematically razed to the ground. However, Warsaw was re-established as the capital of communist Poland and resumed the role of the country's cultural and economic centre. Its destruction allowed a complete redesigning of the city including industrial developments in its suburbs, larger parks and wider streets. Some of the older buildings were reconstructed entirely. It was not only the city's architecture which was ravaged by the war. The previously multi-cultural population, with large numbers of **Jews**, **Germans** and **Russians**, was transformed into one almost entirely comprising **Poles**.

The local economy is dominated by the manufacture of electrical, metal and machine construction, along with lighter industries and food enterprises.

Warsaw Pact

A collective security agreement between the then communist states of **eastern Europe**, signed, and subsequently headquartered, in **Warsaw** on 1 May 1955 and dissolved in June 1991. Also known as the Warsaw Treaty Organization.

Members: **Albania** (excluded from 1962 and withdrew in 1968), **Bulgaria, Czechoslovakia**, East Germany, **Hungary, Poland, Romania** and the **Soviet Union**.

The Pact members agreed to place the control of their armed forces under a central military command based in **Moscow**.

The Warsaw Pact effectively served as a Soviet-led counterweight to the **North Atlantic Treaty Organization** (NATO). The signatories were bound together to provide mutual assistance against foreign aggressors, and, in practice, to a great extent surrendered control of their foreign policies to the Soviet Union. The Warsaw Pact–NATO rivalry formed the basis of the **Cold War**.

The most dramatic action undertaken by the Warsaw Pact was the suppression of the 1968 Czechoslovak liberal communist experiment, the so-called **Prague Spring**. Whereas the suppression of the Hungarian uprising 12 years earlier had been carried out by the Soviet army, the forces which entered Czechoslovakia on 20–21 August 1968, nominally at the invitation of hardline communists there, were explicitly identified as Warsaw Pact forces (excluding Romania which had refused to participate). The Prague Spring movement's leaders were arrested and taken to the Soviet Union where they were compelled to resign. A 'normalizing' occupation force remained in Czechoslovakia until 1988.

Warsaw Stock Exchange
Giełda Papierów Wartościowych (GPW)

The exchange, originally established in 1817, was one of seven operating in **Poland** before the Second World War, and was reopened in April 1991 after the communist period. Market capitalization for the 225 companies listed in 2000 totalled US $29,000m. Total turnover for that year equalled $55,000m. As at 1 December 2001 there were 30 members trading on the GPW.

President and Chief Executive: Dr Wiesław Rozłucki.
Address: Książęca 4, 00498 Warsaw.
Telephone: (22) 6283232.
Fax: (22) 6281754.
E-mail: gielda@wse.com.pl
Internet: www.wse.com.pl

Western European Union (WEU)

A defence co-operation organization whose future role was uncertain at the beginning of the 21st century. Based on the Brussels Treaty of 1948, the WEU was set up in 1955 as an inter-governmental organization for European co-operation in the field of security and defence. In the 1990s efforts were made to develop the WEU in parallel with the **European Union**, as a way of providing the EU indirectly with the defence component which it had not developed for itself, and thus as the means of strengthening the European pillar of the Atlantic Alliance under the **North Atlantic Treaty Organization**. However, from 1999 the EU committed itself directly to the formulation of a common European security and defence policy, incorporating the main crisis management responsibilities of WEU.

Members: Belgium, France, Germany, Greece, Italy, Luxembourg, Netherlands, Portugal, Spain, UK.

The status of associate partner was accorded in the 1990s to 10 **eastern European** countries: **Bulgaria, Czech Republic, Estonia, Hungary, Latvia, Lithuania, Poland, Romania, Slovakia** and **Slovenia**.

Leadership: Dr Javier Solana Madariaga (Secretary-General).
Address: 4 rue de la Régence, 1000 Brussels, Belgium.
Telephone: (2) 5004411.
Fax: (2) 5113519.
E-mail: ueo.presse@skynet.be
Internet: www.weu.int

White House

The name given to the building housing the Russian Federal Government in **Moscow**. Built with a white marble façade in the 1980s, the so-called White (or Government) House served as the home of the Russian Republic's Government until the dissolution of the **Soviet Union** in 1991 when it became the centre of power for the new Russian legislature. It came to international prominence as the scene of two dramatic attempted coups, in 1991 and 1993. In the first, Russian President Boris **Yeltsin** held out against Soviet hardliners from within the building (*see* **August coup**). In the second it was Yeltsin who had the White House surrounded. Elements of the Government opposed to his proposed political reforms—strengthening the presidency at the expense of parliament—refused to accept the Government's dissolution and the calling of fresh elections to a new **Federal Assembly**. Parliamentarians, led by Vice-President Aleksandr Rutskoi, barricaded themselves in the White House in September 1993 while their supporters attempted to seize other strategic buildings in the capital. Yeltsin forced the rebels to surrender in early October after ordering the bombardment of the parliament building by heavy artillery. The White House was badly damaged but was subsequently restored, and continues to house the offices of the Federal Assembly, along with those of the Prime Minister. Other government offices are found in the **Kremlin**.

White Rus Slavonic Council
Slavyanski Sabor Belaya Rus

A right-wing **pan-Slavic** political formation in **Belarus**. Founded in 1992, it advocates the union of Belarus, the **Russian Federation** and **Ukraine**, and is a member of the **Belarusian People's Patriotic Union** (BNPS). In elections to the House of Representatives (the lower house of the **National Assembly**) in October 2000 the BNPS and its allies obtained near-total ascendancy, amidst opposition and external claims of electoral manipulation and fraud.
Leadership: Mikalay Syargeeu (Chair.).
Address: 24/1/80 Pershamayskaya Street, Minsk 220088.
Telephone: (17) 2395232.
Fax: (17) 2700928.

White Russians

(1): The political term used for the anti-Bolsheviks/monarchists in the Russian Revolution, as opposed to the Bolshevik 'Reds', that was derived from the white banner of the Romanov dynasty.

(2): The literal translation of **Belarusians**, supposedly derived from the association in Russian culture of the colour white with the concept of freedom—relating to the fact that the region was never conquered by the Mongols.

World Bank

The UN's main multilateral lending agency. Established in December 1945, the World Bank was concerned initially with financing post-war reconstruction but it has broadened its objectives to promoting the overall economic development of member nations. Its role is to make loans where private capital is not available on reasonable terms to finance productive investments. Loans are made either directly to Governments, or to private enterprises with the guarantee of their Governments. The World Bank comprises the International Bank for Reconstruction and Development (IBRD) and the International Development Association (IDA).
Members: 183 countries. Only members of the **International Monetary Fund** are eligible, so in the case of most **east European** countries it was not until the 1990s that they were able to join. Those that are now members include Albania, Armenia, Azerbaijan, Belarus, Bosnia and Herzegovina, Bulgaria, Croatia, the Czech Republic, Estonia, Georgia, Hungary, Latvia, Lithuania, Macedonia,

Moldova, Poland, Romania, Russian Federation, Slovakia, Slovenia, Ukraine and Yugoslavia.
Leadership: James D. Wolfensohn (President and Chair. of Exec. Directors).
Address: 1818 H St, NW, Washington, DC 20433, USA.
Telephone: (202) 4771234.
Fax: (202) 4776391.
E-mail: pic@worldbank.org
Internet: www.worldbank.org

World Trade Organization (WTO)

The world body established on 1 January 1995 to give an institutional and legal foundation to the multilateral trading system. The successor to the General Agreement on Tariffs and Trade (GATT), it is intended to ensure that trading arrangements conform to an explicit set of rules. It provides procedures for the settlement of disputes, where WTO rulings are binding on member countries.

As of January 2002 the WTO had 144 members. Only four countries from **central** and **eastern Europe** (**Czech Republic**, **Hungary**, **Slovakia** and **Romania**) were members from the WTO's inception. Another 10 joined at different times in the course of the next seven years, namely (with dates of accession) **Albania** (8 September 2000), **Bulgaria** (1 December 1996), **Croatia** (30 November 2000), **Estonia** (13 November 1999), **Georgia** (14 June 2000), **Latvia** (10 February 1999), **Lithuania** (31 May 2001), **Moldova** (26 July 2001), **Poland** (1 July 1995) and **Slovenia** (1 July 1995). As of January 2002 there were also 28 countries in the process of applying for WTO membership. These included eight from eastern Europe, namely (with date of first establishment of a WTO working party on their application) **Armenia** (1993), **Azerbaijan** (1997), **Belarus** (1993), **Bosnia and Herzegovina** (1999), **Macedonia** (1994), **Russian Federation** (1993), **Ukraine** (1993) and **Yugoslavia** (2001).

Leadership: Michael Moore (Director-General); Supachai Panitchpakdi (Director-General designate, from September 2002).
Address: Centre William Rappard, rue de Lausanne 154, 1211 Geneva, Switzerland.
Telephone: (22) 7395111.
Fax: (22) 7314206.
E-mail: enquiries@wto.org
Internet: www.wto.org

Y

Yabloko
(Yavlinskii–Boldyrev–Lukin Bloc)

A centrist political party in the **Russian Federation** supporting gradual transition to a market economy. The formation was launched in 1993 as the Yavlinskii–Boldyrev–Lukin Bloc, named after its three founders, who were economist Grigorii Yavlinskii, scientist Yurii Boldyrev and former Ambassador Vladimir Lukin. It became generally known by its Yabloko acronym (meaning 'apple' in Russian) and Yavlinskii emerged as its leader. Opposing the **'shock therapy'** of the administration of Boris **Yeltsin** in pursuit of a market economy, Yabloko won 33 seats and 7.8% of the proportional vote in the December 1993 elections to the State Duma (lower house of the **Federal Assembly**). Having condemned the Russian military operation in **Chechnya** launched in December 1994, Yabloko took fourth place in the December 1995 State Duma elections by advancing to 45 seats, although its proportional vote share fell to 6.9%.

Yabloko's candidate in the mid-1996 presidential election was Yavlinskii, who came fourth in the first round with 7.3% of the vote and gave qualified support to Yeltsin in the second. The party nevertheless opposed many aspects of the Government's subsequent economic policy, drawing particular support from older professionals. In the December 1999 State Duma elections, Yabloko fell back to 21 seats with 5.9% of the proportional vote, while Yavlinskii obtained virtually the same percentage vote in the March 2000 presidential elections won by Vladimir **Putin**. Yabloko thereafter adopted a stance of 'constructive opposition' to the Putin administration.

Plans were announced in June 2000 for an alliance between Yabloko and the **Union of Right Forces** (SPS), providing initially for the presentation of joint candidates in forthcoming elections and possibly leading to a full merger. However, although the two formations had similar pro-market economic and social programmes, doubts about the viability of the alliance centred on whether it would follow Yabloko's line of opposing the Putin administration or the SPS line of giving it qualified support.

Leadership: Grigorii Yavlinskii (Chair.).
Address: Novy Arbat 36, Moscow.

Telephone: (095) 2928942.
E-mail: admin@yabloko.ru
Internet: www.yabloko.ru

Yalta Agreements

The conclusion of the famous summit between the Governments of the UK, the USA and the **Soviet Union** in the final stages of the Second World War. Meeting in Yalta (in modern-day **Ukraine**) in February 1945, the Allies unofficially parcelled up post-war Europe into spheres of influence, implicitly accepting that the Soviet Union would oversee the political future of the east. The conference also established the 1920 Curzon Line as the eastern frontier of **Poland**, granted international recognition, and support, to the Government of Marshal **Tito** in **Yugoslavia**, gave **Russia** its permanent seat on the United Nations Security Council and agreed to the mass repatriation of ethnic **German** and **Russian** populations across eastern Europe. *See also* **Potsdam Agreements**.

YAP *see* New Azerbaijan Party.

Yavlinsky–Boldyrev–Lukin Bloc *see* Yabloko.

Yeltsin, Boris

The **Russian Federation**'s first President of the post-communist era and dominant political figure of the 1990s.

Boris Nikolayevich Yeltsin was born on 1 February 1931 in Butka in Sverdlovsk *oblast* (region) in a working class family with a peasant farming background. Despite a youthful accident in which he lost two fingers playing with a grenade, he played professional volleyball for Sverdlovsk, one of the leading Soviet teams, during his student days. He completed his degree in construction engineering in 1955 and married a fellow graduate, Naina Iosifovna Girina (with whom he has had two daughters). Working initially as an industrial manager, he became increasingly involved in politics, joining the **Communist Party of the Soviet Union** (KPSS) in 1961, rising to chair the party's Regional Committee in Sverdlovsk, and in 1980 became a member of the KPSS Central Committee. The election of Mikhail **Gorbachev** as Party General Secretary in 1985 marked a turning point in Yeltsin's career. Moving to **Moscow**, he was made First Secretary of the KPSS in the city, joined the Central Committee's powerful Secretariat and became a candidate member of the Politburo.

His radical style and informal manner won him popularity in Moscow, where people identified with his willingness to criticize the failures of the Soviet system which condemned them to poor housing and empty shops. Apparently disillusioned with the pace of *perestroika* (restructuring), he became involved in open confrontation with leading conservatives in the party at the end of 1987, and was dropped from the Politburo and shunted from the Moscow leadership to a minor ministerial job.

The election of the **Soviet Union**'s newly-restyled Congress of People's Deputies in March 1989 gave him a chance to build a political support base. Representing a Moscow constituency, he became a founder member of the oppositional Inter-Regional Group, openly discussed multi-partyism, and called passionately for the transfer of more power from the centre to the Republics. He became a member of the Russian Federation Congress of People's Deputies, elected in March 1990, and in May that body chose him as Chairman of the Russian Federation Supreme Soviet—thus making him *de facto* Russian President. Deciding that this was incompatible with party membership, he threw his party card on the floor in front of Gorbachev at the party congress in July 1990, expressing disgust with the slow pace of reforms

Within the Russian Republic Yeltsin decided to go for more radical change with a 500-day 'dash to the market economy' package and a declaration of sovereignty. He also managed a temporary reconciliation with Gorbachev to ward off a conservative backlash. Yeltsin strengthened his own hand, as Gorbachev did not, by obtaining a popular mandate for his leadership, winning the first ever direct election for the Russian presidency with 57% of the vote in June 1991. Two months later, Yeltsin famously led the resistance to the hardline **August coup** in Moscow, rallying the crowds outside the Russian Parliament (the **White House**), and retaining the political initiative when the coup collapsed.

The dissolution of the Soviet Union in December 1991 left Yeltsin leading a newly independent Russian Federation, as its executive President. In the course of 1992, he moved to strengthen his own powers, but became locked in a struggle with the conservative forces in the Russian Parliament over economic reforms. Narrowly surviving an impeachment vote in March 1993, he won a vote of confidence in a popular referendum, but in September, when he issued a decree disbanding the Parliament, conservative communist and right-wing nationalist forces combined to resist him by force. The ensuing violent power struggle exposed Yeltsin's authoritarian intolerance of opposition. The shelling of the White House on his orders sent out a powerful negative image, from which his liberal democratic credentials never recovered. Elections to a new Parliament in December 1993 returned large numbers of communists and ultra-nationalists, although Yeltsin did get his way with the narrow endorsement of a new Constitution giving him stronger presidential powers.

Yeltsin's popularity touched a low point in 1995, as Russian troops fought a long and bloody war in **Chechnya** and the **Russian economy** languished in serious recession. A populist campaign nevertheless saw Yeltsin lead in the first-round poll of presidential elections in June 1996. He effectively disappeared from sight between the first and second rounds of voting and it was confirmed much later that he had had three heart attacks during the campaign. His support held up, however, and he defeated the communist leader Gennadii **Zyuganov** in the run-off on 3 July, with almost 54% of the vote.

Sworn in again on 9 August, Yeltsin suffered another collapse and needed quintuple coronary bypass surgery in November. His health became a major political factor, owing not only to his heart condition, but to pneumonia, stomach ulcers, 'high blood pressure and fatigue' and persistent evidence that he was unable to bring a longstanding drink problem under control. His domestic policy oscillated between commitment to economic reform, and periods of retreat in the face of unpopularity. Attempting to assert himself in 1998 and promising vigorous action on the economy, he sacked Prime Minister Viktor Chernomyrdin, then decided in August 1998 to reappoint him. The Parliament resisted the first change and blocked the second, stepping up its moves to impeach Yeltsin. An eventual compromise allowed him to continue until elections due in 2000, but not seek a further term, while giving the Prime Minister and Parliament greater power over ministerial appointments. New economic proposals were heavily influenced by the communist insistence on greater government intervention. In May 1999 he survived the impeachment votes, and the Parliament backed off from confrontations over his choice of successive new Prime Ministers, allowing him to see out the year before stepping down as President on 31 December 1999 and handing over power to his latest Prime Minister and chosen successor-designate, Vladimir **Putin**.

Yerevan

The capital city and main urban centre of **Armenia** situated near the country's southern border. *Population*: 1.2m. (1994 estimate). The city is built on extremely ancient foundations, with archaeological evidence suggesting settlement in the region as early as 8,000 years ago. From the 6th century BC it was a part of the Armenian Kingdom. In its long history it has fallen to a series of conquerors including Romans, Arabs, Mongols, **Turks** and eventually **Russians** in 1827. After the fall of the Russian Empire in 1917, Yerevan became the capital of the Armenian republic and has retained that role ever since.

Hydroelectric power from a plant on the nearby Hrazdan river fuelled Yerevan's industrialization under **Soviet** rule. Industry in the city is associated particularly with petroleum products, and there is also aluminium smelting.

Yerevan Stock Exchange

The principal stock exchange in **Armenia**, founded on 31 May 1993. It began trading shares on its floor in 1996 and by the beginning of 2000 there were 96 listed companies, with an overwhelming preponderance of industrial sector shares developing in recent years. The total volume of trade in 1999 came to US $1m.

President: Dr Sedrak Sedrakian.
Address: Hanrapetoutian St 5, 375010 Yerevan.
Telephone: (1) 523201.
Fax: (1) 151548.

Yezidis see Kurds.

YMP–Musavat see New Muslim Democratic Party.

Yugoslav Bank for International Economic Co-operation
Jugoslovenska Banka Za Medjunarodnu Ekonomsku Saradnju

Focuses on the financing of export-oriented and development projects in the Federal Republic of **Yugoslavia**. Founded in 1979. Total assets: US $61.3m. (2000).
President: Zoran Stanković.
Address: Srpskih vladara 5, POB 219, 11000 Belgrade.
Telephone: (11) 3239012.
Fax: (11) 3244114.
E-mail: jubmes@jubmes.co.yu

Yugoslav Chamber of Commerce and Industry
Privredna Komora Jugoslavije

The principal organization in **Yugoslavia** for promoting business contacts, both internally and externally, in the post-communist era. Founded in 1990.
President: Mihajlo Milojević.
Address: Terazije 23, POB 1003, 11000 Belgrade.
Telephone: (11) 3248123.
Fax: (11) 3248754.
E-mail: pkjdm@eunet.yu

Yugoslav United Left
Jugoslovenska Unianska Levica (JUL)

The political party led by the wife of ex-President Slobodan **Milošević**, closely aligned with her husband while he was in power. The JUL was launched in July 1995 under the leadership of Mirjana Marković—as Milošević's wife preferred to be known—as a Marxist-oriented alliance of over 20 groups mostly derived from the former ruling **League of Communists of Yugoslavia**. The formation's role was to rally unrepentant communists to the cause of the dominant **Socialist Party of**

Serbia (SPS); it later came to be accused of being the party of war profiteers and those corruptly benefiting from the disposal of state assets.

In **Federal Assembly** elections in November 1996 a Joint List alliance of the JUL, the SPS and **New Democracy** (ND) won 64 of the 138 lower house seats. Serbian Assembly elections in September 1997 resulted in the SPS/JUL/ND alliance winning 110 of the 250 seats, the eventual outcome being a coalition Government of the SPS, the JUL and the ultra-nationalist **Serbian Radical Party** (SRS).

In the controversial September 2000 elections which resulted in the downfall of Milošević, the JUL was allied only with the SPS in the contest for federal parliamentary seats, their joint list returning 44 members to the lower house. Serbian Assembly elections in December 2000 revealed the true state of opinion by reducing the SPS/JUL to only 37 seats and 13.8% of the vote.

Leadership: Mirjana Marković (Chair.).
Address: c/o Savezna Skupština, Trg Nikole Pašića 13, Belgrade 11000.
E-mail: jul@jul.org.yu
Internet: www.jul.org.yu

Yugoslavia
(Federal Republic of Yugoslavia, FRY)
Savezna Republika Jugoslavija (SRJ)

The so-called 'rump Yugoslav' state, comprising the republics of **Serbia** and **Montenegro**, situated in south-eastern Europe. It is bounded by Hungary to the north, Croatia, Bosnia and Herzegovina and the Adriatic Sea to the west, Romania and Bulgaria to the east, and Albania and the Former Yugoslav Republic of Macedonia (FYROM) to the south.

Area: 102,173 sq km; *Federal capital*: **Belgrade**; *Republic capitals*: Belgrade (Serbia), **Podgorica** (Montenegro); *population*: 10.5m. (2001 estimate), comprising **Serbs** 63%, **Albanians** 14%, Montenegrins 6%, **Hungarians** 4%, others 13%; *official language*: Serbo-Croat; *religion*: **Serbian Orthodox** 65%, **Muslim** 19%, **Roman Catholic** 4%, other 12%.

Under the 1992 Constitution as amended in 2000, executive authority is vested in the Federal President and in the Government headed by a Prime Minister. The Prime Minister is appointed by the President subject to parliamentary approval. The President is directly elected for a four-year term, renewable once. Legislative authority rests with the bicameral Federal Assembly (Savezna Skupština) consisting of (i) the Chamber of Citizens (Veće Gradjana) of 138 members, directly elected for a four-year term by a mixed constituency-based and proportional system (108 from Serbia and 30 from Montenegro); and (ii) the Chamber of Republics (Veće Republika) of 40 members (20 each for Serbia and Montenegro), who are also elected for a four-year term. The two constituent Republics have their own Presidents directly elected for four-year terms as well as unicameral Assemblies, namely the 250-member Serbian Assembly (Skupština Srbije) and the 78-member

Yugoslavia

Montenegrin Assembly (Skupština Republika Crne Gore), also elected for four-year terms.

History: **Slavic** tribes, including Serbs, settled in the **Balkan** peninsula from around the 6th century. In the 9th century the Serbs converted to **Orthodox Christianity**, later breaking free from Byzantine rule to form an independent Serbian kingdom by the 13th century. Military defeat by the Turks in 1389 led to the absorption of Serbia into the Ottoman Empire, although Montenegro in the southwest of the territory maintained semi-independence. Following popular uprisings against Turkish rule, Serbia and Montenegro secured autonomy in the early 19th century, full independence being achieved by both at the Congress of Berlin in 1878. In the Balkan wars of 1912–13 Serbia enlarged its territory at the expense of Turkey and **Bulgaria**, but remained embittered at Austria-Hungary's 1908 annexation of **Bosnia and Herzegovina** with its substantial Serb population. This hostility culminated in the assassination in **Sarajevo** in 1914 of the heir to the Austro-Hungarian throne by a Serb nationalist, precipitating the outbreak of the First World War, in which the Serbs fought bravely on what proved to be the winning side.

Following the defeat of the central powers in 1918, Serbia, Montenegro and other south Slav territories acceded to an uneasy union as the 'Kingdom of Serbs, Croats and Slovenes', which was renamed Yugoslavia in 1929. For most of the Second World War Yugoslavia was under occupation by Nazi Germany and its Axis allies. Resistance was led by Serbian-based **Chetniks** and by communist Partisans.

After the war Serbia came under communist rule as one of the six constituent republics, together with Bosnia and Herzegovina, **Croatia**, **Macedonia**, Montenegro and **Slovenia**, of a new **Yugoslav** Federal Republic led by Marshal **Tito** (which adopted the name **Socialist Federal Republic of Yugoslavia** in 1963). Despite the adoption of a Soviet-style Constitution, Yugoslavia maintained a largely independent stance in international affairs under Tito, who remained the dominating force in domestic politics until his death in 1980. Thereafter the country's federal structure was increasingly unable to contain ethnic and nationalist rivalries between, and within, the constituent republics. Political discontent during the 1980s, notably in the Serbian-ruled province of **Kosovo** with its overwhelmingly ethnic Albanian population, was exacerbated by economic deterioration and declining living standards.

The collapse of authority of the ruling **League of Communists of Yugoslavia** (SKJ) in 1990 was followed in 1991 by the failure of efforts to negotiate a new political structure for the country, heralding declarations of independence by most of the republics and subsequent military hostilities between several. Having by then abolished the autonomous status of Kosovo and Hungarian-populated **Vojvodina**, Serbia was firmly under the control of Slobodan **Milošević**. He had become leader of the republican SKJ in 1986 and Serbian President in 1989, before converting the SKJ into the **Socialist Party of Serbia** (SPS) in 1990.

In April 1992 Serbia and Montenegro adopted a new Constitution, proclaiming a new Federal Republic of Yugoslavia and effectively acknowledging the secession of the other republics, although Serbia continued to support violent nationalist resistance by Serb minorities in Croatia and Bosnia and Herzegovina. International pressure and mediation brought these conflicts to a negotiated if brittle conclusion by the end of 1995, but with a continuing legacy of political instability and inter-ethnic distrust (*see* **Dayton Agreement**).

Despite considerable internal opposition to Milošević's regime, the SPS emerged as the largest party in the legislative elections in November 1996, in alliance with the **Yugoslav United Left** (JUL) led by Milošević's wife Mirjana Marković and **New Democracy** (ND). At the same time, the then pro-Federation **Democratic Party of Socialists of Montenegro** (DPSCG) not only ensured an overall federal majority for the SPS but also won a majority of seats in the Montenegro Assembly. Milošević was constitutionally barred from a third term as Serbian President, but switched the institutional basis of his authority to the federal presidency instead, securing election by the Federal Assembly in July 1997 as President of Yugoslavia under the then prevailing system of indirect election. Serbian Assembly elections later that year resulted in a further SPS-led Government, although with reduced support, while in protracted Serbian presidential elections SPS candidate Milan **Milutinović** was eventually returned in balloting described as 'fundamentally flawed' by international observers. In Montenegro a reformist and anti-Milošević DPSCG candidate, Milo **Djukanović**, was elected as President in October 1997, while in May 1998 an electoral alliance led by the DPSCG won an outright majority of seats in the Montenegrin Assembly.

From early 1998 Serbia's attempts to maintain control over the province of Kosovo in the face of growing insurrection by the separatist **Kosovo Liberation Army** (UCK) had severe political and military repercussions. International efforts to deal with a serious escalation of violence between ethnic Albanians and Serbian security forces led eventually to military intervention from March 1999 by forces under the command of the **North Atlantic Treaty Organization** (NATO). Following an intensive NATO bombing campaign against the Belgrade regime, Serbian security forces withdrew from Kosovo in June 1999 and were replaced by UN-endorsed NATO and **Russian** peace-keeping contingents. The province was placed under UN administration (although remaining part of Yugoslavia) and efforts were initiated to reconcile the hostile ethnic communities.

Having been indicted for alleged war crimes by the **International Criminal Tribunal for the former Yugoslavia** at The Hague, President Milošević faced growing political opposition in Serbia in 2000, while in Montenegro pressure mounted for greater autonomy leading to outright independence. An assortment of 19 anti-Milošević parties and movements came together in the **Democratic Opposition of Serbia** (DOS) to demand early elections. These were called only after the enactment in July 2000 of federal constitutional amendments providing for direct presidential elections and thus enabling Milošević to stand for a further term. The amendments were strongly criticized by the Montenegrin Government.

Latest elections: Despite widespread intimidation and vote-rigging by Milošević supporters, elections for the federal presidency in September 2000 were widely believed to have produced an outright first-round victory for DOS candidate Vojislav **Koštunica**, leader of the nationalist **Democratic Party of Serbia** (DSS). Attempts by the regime first to insist that a second round of voting was necessary and then to annul the elections provoked a massive popular uprising, which forced Milošević to surrender the presidency to Koštunica in early October.

Simultaneous federal parliamentary elections were deemed to have been equally flawed. The official results showed that the DOS alliance had won 58 of the 138 seats in the Chamber of Citizens, the SPS/JUL 44, the **Socialist People's Party of Montenegro** (SNPCG) 28, the **Serbian Radical Party** (SRS) 5, the Serbian People's Party of Montenegro 2 and the Hungarian Union of Vojvodina 1. The ruling DPSCG in Montenegro boycotted both federal elections.

Following the ousting of Milošević, free and fair elections to the Serbian Assembly were held in December 2000, resulting in a landslide victory for the DOS alliance, which won 176 of the 250 seats with a 64.1% vote share, against 37 for the SPS/JUL (13.8%), 23 for the SRS (8.5%) and 14 for the **Serbian Unity Party** (5.3%).

Legislative elections in Montenegro in April 2001 resulted in a much tighter contest than had been expected. The pro-independence 'Victory is Montenegro's' coalition of Djukanović's DPSCG and the Social Democrats won 42% of the vote (36 seats in the 78-seat Montenegrin Assembly) against 41% (33 seats) won by the pro-Yugoslav 'Together for Yugoslavia' opposition, which was headed by the SNPCG. The **Liberal Alliance of Montenegro** (LSCG) won 7.8% (6 seats), the Democratic Union of Albanians 1.3% (2 seats) and the Democratic Alliance of Montenegro 1.1% (1 seat).

Recent developments: The inauguration of Koštunica was followed in November 2000 by the formation of a transitional Federal Government pending new elections, headed by Zoran Zizić of the Montenegrin SNPCG but consisting mainly of DOS representatives. A new Serbian Government appointed in January 2001 was headed by Zoran **Djindjić**, leader of the centre-right **Democratic Party** component of the DOS, whose prospects of being able to cohabit politically with incumbent President Milutinović (also an indicted war crimes suspect) were improved by the latter's resignation from the SPS leadership.

Uncertainty about the future of Milošević was partially resolved at the beginning of April 2001 when he was arrested in Belgrade on charges of misappropriation of state funds and abuse of his official position. President Koštunica insisted that the ex-President and other indicted war criminals would be tried in Yugoslavia rather than by the international tribunal at The Hague. However, Milošević was subsequently extradited to The Hague in June to face charges of war crimes there, the compliance of the Yugoslav Government with this course of action being secured (but a major political crisis over the extradition not being averted) by the promise of a very substantial Western aid package. In consequence Zizić resigned from his post as Federal Prime Minister, taking the SNPCG with him. However, he was replaced by SNPCG moderate Dragiša **Pesić** in July. The controversy over the fate of Milošević has had serious repercussions for the DOS coalition, exposing its inherent fragility and particularly the deep fault lines between the Government and the President.

Serbian security forces entered the last part of the demilitarized zone around Kosovo, with the blessing of the international community, in late May 2001 after a violent campaign in the **Presevo Valley** region by the ethnic Albanian Liberation Army of Presevo, Medvedja and Bujanovac (UCPMB).

Elections to the Montenegrin Assembly in April 2001 had meanwhile resulted in an extremely narrow victory for the pro-independence parties headed by the DPSCG. President Djukanović's declared intention to proceed quickly to a referendum on independence was therefore called into question, not only by the closeness of the election outcome but also by Western support for Koštunica's desire to preserve the Serbia-Montenegro federation. (President Koštunica also made it clear that his administration, while it acknowledged that Serbian forces had committed atrocities in Kosovo in 1999, regarded the province as inalienable Serbian territory.) The DPSCG was only able to form a minority Government because of the failure of negotiations with the pro-independence nationalist **Liberal Alliance of Montenegro**, which nonetheless agreed to offer parliamentary support to the new administration. Despite these setbacks Montenegrin Prime Minister Filip **Vujanović** pledged in July to convene a referendum on Montenegro's status as early as March 2002. No further announcements had been made by the end of 2001.

International relations and defence. The rump Federation of Serbia and Montenegro was recognized by most countries as the successor to the former Socialist Federal Republic of Yugoslavia, one important exception being the USA, which took the view that none of the successor republics represented a continuation of the former Yugoslavia. The rump Federation succeeded nonetheless to Yugoslavia's membership of the United Nations, the **Organization for Security and Co-operation in Europe** (OSCE) and other international organizations. Its support for ethnic Serb military action in other former Yugoslav republics in the early 1990s, however, resulted in its suspension from most international bodies and the imposition of comprehensive UN sanctions in May 1992. These were lifted in November 1995 under the Dayton peace agreement on Bosnia and Herzegovina, following which there was some progress towards normalization of Yugoslavia's regional and international relations. The onset of the 1998–99 Kosovo crisis returned Yugoslavia to international pariah status, which continued after the withdrawal of Yugoslav forces from Kosovo in June 1999 because Milošević remained in power. Not until Milošević ceased to be President in October 2000 was Yugoslavia restored to formal UN and OSCE membership, following which the new

Koštunica administration applied for membership of the **Council of Europe** and declared its aim of joining the **European Union** 'as soon as possible'.

Yugoslavia's defence budget for 2000 amounted to some US $1,300m., equivalent to about 10% of GDP. The size of the armed forces at the end of 2000 was some 97,000 personnel, including those serving under compulsory conscription of 12 months (to be reduced to 10 months in 2001), while reservists numbered an estimated 400,000.

Yugoslavia, economy

An economy whose transition from communist-era central control has been badly damaged by the regional and international conflicts in which it was involved in the 1990s. The rump Federal Republic of Yugoslavia (FRY) remaining after the secession of **Slovenia, Croatia, Bosnia and Herzegovina** and **Macedonia** in the course of 1991 has less than half of the land area and population of the former **Socialist Federal Republic of Yugoslavia** (SFRY). Within the FRY, **Serbia** (including **Kosovo** and **Vojvodina**) covers about 86% of the land area and contains some 95% of the FRY's population, with **Montenegro** accounting for only 14% and 5% respectively. The economy was severely damaged in the 1990s by the break-up of the SFRY, the application of UN sanctions and embargoes, the involvement of Serbia in the fighting in Croatia and in Bosnia and Herzegovina, and more especially the conflict over Kosovo and the 1999 **NATO** air-strikes on Serbia and the entry of NATO forces into Kosovo. The damage was compounded by the suspension of the FRY from the **International Monetary Fund** (IMF) and other international financial and development organs. Against this background, it was extremely difficult to determine realistic data on Yugoslavia's economic performance in the 1990s, especially in view of secrecy over economic indicators on the part of the Yugoslav and Serbian Governments themselves. Not until the fall of the **Milošević** regime in late 2000 and the readmittance of Yugoslavia to the IMF and other international bodies did normal transparency begin to apply.

No realistic figures for GNP are available. *GDP at PPP*: US $20,600m. (1999); *GDP per capita at PPP*: $1,800 (1999); *exports*: $1,025m. (2000); *imports*: $3,277m. (2000); *currencies*: new dinar in Serbia (plural: dinars; US $1=YD66.48 at the end of December 2001) and Deutsche Mark in Montenegro—replaced by euro in January 2002 (plural: marks; US $1=DM2.20=1.12 euros at the end of December 2001).

It is estimated that in 1998 industry (including mining, manufacturing, construction and power) accounted for 50% of GDP, agriculture for 20% and services for 30%. The main crops are maize, wheat, sugar beet, and vegetables and fruit. Mineral resources include coal, brown coal (lignite), copper ore and bauxite, together with iron ore, petroleum, natural gas and lead and zinc ore. Industries include machine-building, metallurgy, mining, chemical goods and consumer goods. The principal exports are manufactured goods, food and live animals, and raw material, the main imports being machinery and transport equipment, fuels and lubricants, manu-factured goods, chemicals, food and live animals, and raw materials. The main destinations of exports in 2000 were Italy (24%), Germany (18%) and Greece (8%), while the principal sources of imports were Italy (16%), Germany (15%) and **Bulgaria** (13%).

The dissolution of the SFRY in 1991 and the attendant regional hostilities resulted in output falling by 50% in Serbia and Montenegro in 1992–93 and inflation rising to very high levels in 1993. The introduction of a new currency (the new dinar) and other economic reforms in early 1994 produced a sharp reduction in inflation, but output did not recover until after the signature of the **Dayton Agreement** in 1995, following which GDP expanded by 8% in 1996 and by 10% in 1997. However, underlying weaknesses were highlighted by large fiscal deficits and by a 45% devaluation of the new dinar in April 1998, as evidence accumulated that the Milošević regime was more interested in retaining power than in reforming an increasingly inefficient economy still essentially under state control. An aggravating factor was the large proportion of government expenditure devoted to the defence and security sectors.

The economic framework was further disrupted by the increasing effect of renewed UN sanctions and embargoes imposed in 1998, and by the massive destruction of Serbia's infrastructure in March–June 1999 in the air bombardment carried out by NATO because of the Government's conduct in Kosovo. Although economic growth of 2% was recorded in 1998, GDP was estimated to have contracted by 20% in 1999, so that Yugoslavia emerged from the Kosovo crisis with output at about 40% of its 1989 level and unemployment of 50%, while inflation rose to 50% in 1999. Further depreciation of the new dinar impelled the Montenegrin Government to adopt the Deutsche Mark as the Republic's official currency in November 1999.

From a very low base, GDP growth of around 10% was officially recorded in 2000, but inflation rose to nearly 100% year-on-year. Not until the defeat of Milošević in the September 2000 elections and the resultant lifting of UN sanctions were conditions created for rebuilding the Yugoslav economic infrastructure after a decade of decline and containment. The new Government quickly gained admittance to the **European Bank for Reconstruction and Development** and the IMF and was granted the equivalent of US $150m. by the IMF in emergency post-conflict assistance in support of a programme to stabilize the FRY economy and to rebuild administrative capacities. At the same time, the **National Bank of Yugoslavia** announced in December 2000 that the fixed exchange rate for the dinar would be replaced by a managed float of the currency.

The new Government also declared its intention to launch a comprehensive privatization programme, the Milošević era having ended with around 80% of all companies, most of the large agricultural sector and over 90% of all assets still under state or social ownership. Although privatization measures had been announced in 1994 and again in 1997, the limited resultant disposals of state-owned enterprises had mostly benefited members of the ruling elite, often with connections in the criminal underworld.

Yugoslavs

Anyone from **Yugoslavia**. Literally 'south Slav', the term was first effectively coined for the creation of Yugoslavia in 1929 to legitimize the incorporation of all the south **Slavic peoples** in the western **Balkans** into one federation. Yugoslavism was championed by **Tito** and the communists in the Second World War as a non-nationalist ideal along socialist lines. However, by the early 21st century the collapse of the federation left the concept of Yugoslavia as effectively the ideal of **Serb** nationalists seeking to maintain the political dominance of **Belgrade**.

Z

Zagreb

The capital of **Croatia**, situated in the middle of the country's two forks of territory. *Population*: 706,770 (1991 census). The city was not effectively a single entity until the construction of new buildings in the 19th century joined the ancient fortress of Gradec with the religious town of Kaptol. By the end of that century Zagreb had grown into a thriving urban centre and served as the base of **Croatian** and south **Slavic (Yugoslav)** nationalism. The declaration of Croatian independence from the Austro-Hungarian Empire was made from Zagreb in 1918 and the city remained the administrative centre of Croatia within the Kingdom of Serbs, Croats and Slovenes (later **Yugoslavia**). In this role it ensured its position as the major industrial centre for Croatia with production focusing on chemicals but also consumer goods. It also gained good transport access to the rest of the **Balkans**.

Zagreb was home to a large **Serb** community before the mass migrations engendered by the region's fierce wars in the early 1990s. During the conflict the city itself was shelled by Croat Serb forces in May 1995.

Zagreb Stock Exchange (ZSE)
Zagrebačka Burza

The securities trading exchange founded in **Croatia** in 1991 as a joint stock company by leading banks and insurance companies. The ZSE has 34 shareholders who elect a nine-member Supervisory Board. Trading is carried out by 51 members and market capitalization in 1999 had totalled US $2,500m.

General Manager: Marinko Papuga.
Address: Ksaver 208, 10000 Zagreb.
Telephone: (1) 4677925.
Fax: (1) 4677680.
E-mail: public.relations@zse.hr
Internet: www.zse.hr

Zeman, Miloš

Prime Minister of the **Czech Republic**.

Miloš Zeman heads the left-wing **Czech Social Democratic Party** (ČSSD) in a minority Government supported in **Parliament** by the centre-right **Civic Democratic Party** (ODS). Having spent 21 years in the political wilderness after the '**Prague Spring**' of 1968, he was elected to the Czechoslovak Federal Assembly in 1990. He was appointed Prime Minister of the Czech Republic on 17 July 1998.

Born on 28 September 1944 in Kolín, just east of **Prague** in the newly-created **Czechoslovakia**, he was barred from attending university but nevertheless graduated from the Prague University of Economics in 1969, having taught himself at home. He had joined the ruling communist party in the liberalism of the 1968 'Prague Spring', but was expelled from its ranks two years later for his criticism of the reactionary Government installed after the Soviet invasion. His attempts at that time to resurrect the ČSSD, which had been forcibly subsumed into the communist party in 1948, were quashed by the new regime. Sacked from his job as a teacher in 1970, he eventually found work at the Prognostic Institution in Prague, forecasting models of economic and social systems. In 1984 the Government terminated Zeman's research at the Prognostics Institute because of his repeated criticism of the political regime and he restarted his forecasting career at a scientific research institute until the same chain of events unfolded and he was removed once more in five years later.

He became actively involved in the opposition **Civic Forum** (OF) during the '**velvet revolution**' of 1989, and represented its centre-left faction. In 1990 he was elected to the first democratic Federal Assembly of Czechoslovakia since 1946. He joined the re-formed ČSSD in 1992 and quickly came to dominate the party: he was elected Party Chairman in 1993. From 1996 the ČSSD supported a minority ODS Government until the situation was reversed in July 1998, and Zeman was appointed Prime Minister. The so-called 'stability pact' between the ČSSD and the ODS has made effective government arduous and has drawn criticism from all sides. Zeman was replaced as leader of the ČSSD on 7 April 2001 by Deputy Prime Minister Vladimir Špidla, but with the intention that he should remain as Prime Minister until legislative elections in June 2002.

Miloš Zeman has a daughter, from his marriage to his second wife Ivana Bednarčíková, and one son.

Address: Office of the Prime Minister, nábř. Eduarda Beneše 4, 11801 Prague 1.
Telephone: (2) 24002111.
Fax: (2) 24810231.
E-mail: posta@vlada.cz
Internet: www.vlada.cz

Zgromadzenie Naradowe *see* **National Assembly (Poland)**.

Zhivkov, Todor

Head of the Government and ruling party in communist-era **Bulgaria**, ousted in November 1989. Born in a peasant family in 1911, Zhivkov was apprenticed as a printer. He was a leading fighter in the communist Partisan resistance during the Second World War and helped organize the coup of September 1944 by which the Fatherland Front took power. He was brought into the top Bulgarian Communist Party leadership in 1954, and by 1962 was Prime Minister as well as the party's First Secretary. Skilled at playing off or cutting down possible rivals, he was at pains to remain always a loyal follower of the Moscow line, at least until the reform era initiated by Soviet leader Mikhail **Gorbachev** in the second half of the 1980s. With the Bulgarian economy deteriorating, Zhivkov clamped down on any domestic *glasnost* and launched in 1989 a fresh campaign against the **Bulgarian Turk** minority (already the target of 'Bulgarianization' in mid-decade). He was stunned when a 'palace coup' toppled him from power in November 1999 and his hope of an honourable retirement was dashed by the vehemence with which demonstrators denounced him. Zhivkov faced a wide range of charges brought in several installments from 1992. In September 1992 he was sentenced to seven years in prison for embezzlement (a charge overturned by the Supreme Court in 1996); he faced other charges relating to the labour camps in which hundreds of detainees died amidst extreme brutality, and to the anti-Turkish campaign, but was released from house arrest in September 1997 because of a limit on the length of time a defendant could be held without trial. He died on 5 August 1998.

Zionism

A movement founded in the 19th century to establish a Jewish homeland in Palestine, which gathered great momentum after the Holocaust and led to the creation of Israel in 1948. The migration of **Jews** to 'Israel' (known as making *aliyah*) was spearheaded by Jews from **eastern Europe** from the 1880s, and these *Ashkenazi* Jews had a profound impact on the culture and social hierarchy of the eventual Israeli State. Specific waves of migration followed pogroms and persecutions in eastern Europe, including those triggered by: the rise of nationalism in the late 19th century, the First World War, the spread of communism and, of course, the Second World War and Nazism. The latest migratory wave was triggered by the collapse of communism in 1989–91.

Zlenko, Anatoliy

Minister of Foreign Affairs, **Ukraine**.

Anatoliy Maksymovych Zlenko is an independent. His career has been mainly in Ukraine's Foreign Ministry, with long spells at the UN Educational, Scientific and Cultural Organization (UNESCO). He was Foreign Minister in 1990–94 and was reappointed to the post on 2 October 2000.

Born on 2 June 1938 in the **Kiev** region, he graduated from the Kiev State University in 1967 and began work as an attaché to the Department of International Organizations within the Ukrainian SSR's Foreign Ministry. First linked with UNESCO in March 1973, as a staff member of its Paris-based Secretariat, he returned to the Foreign Ministry in 1979 as a Counsellor in its UNESCO Division, and was appointed Ukraine's Permanent Representative to UNESCO in October 1983. He entered the Ukrainian republican Government in April 1987 as Deputy Foreign Minister and, as the country moved towards independence, became full Foreign Minister in July 1990. He left Ukraine in October 1994 to become its Permanent Representative at the UN in New York, and then spent three years as Ambassador to France before returning once more to Kiev in October 2000 to take up the post of Foreign Minister.

Address: Ministry of Foreign Affairs, Mykhaylivska pl. 1, 252018 Kiev.
Telephone: (44) 2263379.
Fax: (44) 2263169.
Internet: www.mfa.gov.ua

ZLSD *see* **United List of Social Democrats**.

ZSSS *see* **Association of Free Trade Unions of Slovenia**.

Zviadists

Supporters of former Georgian President Zviad Gamsakhurdia who formed a right-wing paramilitary organization to combat the regime of President Eduard **Shevardnadze** after 1991. Based largely in the western Samegrelo district, they were the subject of a ruthless campaign by the pro-Government **Mkhedrioni** militia in 1992, and their insurgency was effectively ended the following year. The regime has attempted to prosecute Zviadists, most of whom are in exile in the **Russian Federation**, but has recently edged towards reconciliation.

Zyuganov, Gennadii

Chairman of the **Communist Party of the Russian Federation** (KPRF).

Gennadii Andreyevich Zyuganov rose up the ranks of the Soviet-era Communist Party (KPSS) in the 1970s–1980s to become a champion of the party's more nationalist 'right wing', in opposition to reformist Head of State Mikhail **Gorbachev**. He has been Chairman of the KPRF since it was unbanned in 1993. He has twice been defeated in presidential elections, once by Boris **Yeltsin**, and most recently by the current President Vladimir **Putin** in 2000. Zyuganov's philosophies are a somewhat paradoxical mix of communism and overt nationalism—complete with a rejection of Marxist 'class struggle' in favour of racist rhetoric upholding the righteousness of the **Slavic people** in the face of Western capitalist imperialism. He opposes market reforms, but is in favour of a mixed economy and is also a champion of the voluntary restoration of a **Greater Russia**, while spouting invective against the **Commonwealth of Independent States** (CIS).

Born on 26 June 1944 in the village of Mymrino, near Orel in western **Russia**, he enrolled in 1962 as a student in the Department of Physics and Mathematics of the Orel Pedagogical Institute. Between 1963 and 1966 he served in Soviet military intelligence, but returned to his studies as soon as he was demobilized. He also joined the KPSS and entered the Communist Youth League (Komsomol) in 1966. He continued his education at the Institute, from where he graduated in 1969 and where he lectured until 1983, and also at the KPSS Academy of Social Sciences where he eventually received a doctorate in philosophy in 1995.

As a communist, Zyuganov advanced his career rapidly from positions within Komsomol, to a local Party Secretary from 1974, and finally into the 'Propaganda Department' of the central KPSS in 1983. By the time the **Soviet Union** was disintegrating in the late 1980s he had become a Deputy Head of Department and an outspoken critic of Gorbachev's *glasnost* (openness). In 1990 he was a founding member of the breakaway KPRF and a leader of its right-wing 'popular patriotic' faction. In opposition to the reformist authorities, Zyuganov was largely in accord with the various emerging nationalist and ultra-conservative movements. He was fortunate enough to be on holiday during the hardline Soviet **August coup** in 1991, which led to the banning of the Communist Party. Zyuganov was a key figure in the move to align opposition nationalist groups under the banner of the National Salvation Front in 1992 and was elected Chairman of the KPRF when the party was re-registered in 1993. Under his stewardship the party has had varying success, winning a consistently large share of the vote and remaining—until recent mergers—the largest single party in the **Federal Assembly**.

Zyuganov's personal standing has been damaged by his uncharismatic style. His controversial philosophies include suspicion of the **Jews** and an insistence that Slavs are not meant to be capitalists. His opposition to the popular war in **Chechnya** is seen as a political disadvantage, although it helps to distance the KPRF from the nationalist fringe. In his most recent presidential battle, in March 2000, he was easily defeated by Putin in the first round, receiving just 29.2% of the vote.

Country-by-Country Listing

Albania
Albanian Agrarian Party
Albanian Centre for Foreign
  Investment Promotion
Albanian Republican Party
Albanian royal family
Albanian Telegraphic Agency
Albanians
Alia, Ramiz
Angjeli, Anastas
Balkans
Bank of Albania
Confederation of Albanian
  Trade Unions
Dade, Arta
Democrat Party
Democratic Alliance of
  Albania
Democratic Party of Albania
Democratic Union of the Greek
  Minority–Concord
Enterprise Restructuring
  Agency
Epirus question
Greater Albania
Hoxha, Enver
Human Rights Union Party
Jews
Liberal Democratic Union
Meidani, Rexhep
Meta, Ilir
Movement of Legality Party
Muslim peoples
Nano, Fatos
National Agency for Privatization
National Front
National Unity Party
People's Assembly
'Pyramid' investment schemes
Social Democratic Party of
  Albania
Socialist Party of Albania
Tirana
Tirana Stock Exchange
Union for Victory
Union of Chambers of
  Commerce and Industry of
  Albania
Union of Independent Trade
  Unions of Albania
Vlachs

Armenia
Armenian Apostolic Church
Armenian Christian Democratic Union
Armenian question
Armenian Revolutionary
  Federation
Armenian State Foreign
  Economic and Trade
  Association
Armenians
Armenpress
Caucasus region
Central Bank of Armenia
Chamber of Commerce and
  Industry of the Republic of
  Armenia
Communist Party of Armenia
Country of Law Party
Democratic Party of Armenia
Deported Nationalities
General Confederation of
  Armenian Trade Unions
Jehovah's Witnesses
Justice and Accord Bloc
Khachatrian, Vartan
Kocharian, Robert
Kurds
Markarian, Andranik
Mission
Nagorno-Karabakh
National Assembly
National Democratic Union of
  Armenia
Oskanian, Vartan
Pan-Armenian National
  Movement
People's Party of Armenia
Republican Party of Armenia
Shamiran Women's Party
Social Democratic Hunchakian
  Party
Soviet Union
TRACECA
Transcaucasus
Yerevan
Yerevan Stock Exchange

Azerbaijan
AIDS
Alekperov, Avaz
Aliyev, Heydar
Armenians
Association of Independent
  Workers of Azerbaijan
Azerbaijan Communist Party
Azerbaijan National Independence Party
Azerbaijan Popular Front
Azerbintorg
Azeris
AzerTAJ
Baku
Baku Interbank Currency
  Exchange
Caucasus region
Caviar
Chamber of Commerce and
  Industry of Azerbaijan
Civil Unity Party
Confederation of Azerbaijan
  Trade Unions
Kuliyev, Vilayat Mukhtar
Kurds
Lezghins
Muslim peoples
Nagorno-Karabakh
Nakhichevan
National Assembly
National Bank of Azerbaijan
New Azerbaijan Party
New Muslim Democratic Party
Pan-Turkism
Rasizade, Artur
Russians
Soviet Union
TRACECA
Transcaucasus
Turkic peoples

Belarus

Agrarian Party of Belarus
Belarus-Russia Union
Belarusian Chamber of Commerce and Industry
Belarusian Congress of Democratic Trade Unions
Belarusian Currency and Stock Exchange
Belarusian Federation of Trade Unions
Belarusian Peasants' Party
Belarusian People's Patriotic Union
Belarusian Popular Front–Renaissance
Belarusian Social Democratic Party
Belarusian Socialist Party
Belarusians
BelTa
Chernobyl
Communist Party of Belarus
Conservative Christian Party
Cyrillic alphabet
Jehovah's Witnesses
Jews
Khvastow, Mikhail
Korbut, Nikolay
Liberal Democratic Party of Belarus
Lukashenka, Alyaksandr
Minsk
National Assembly
National Bank of Belarus
National Democratic Party of Belarus
Novitski, Gennadz
Poles
Pripet Marshes
Rouble zone
Russians
Slavic peoples
Social Democratic Party of Popular Accord
Soviet Union
START
United Civil Party of Belarus
White Rus Slavonic Council

Bosnia and Herzegovina

Balkans
Banja Luka
Behman, Alija
Belkić, Beriz
BH Press
Bosniaks
Bosnian-Herzegovinan Patriotic Party
Brčko
Central Bank of Bosnia and Herzegovina
Chamber of Economy of Bosnia and Herzegovina
Chetniks
Confederation of Trade Unions of the Serb Republic
Croatian Democratic Union
Croatian Peasants' Party
Croats
Cyrillic alphabet
Dayton Agreement
Democratic People's Alliance
Democratic People's Union
Democratic Socialist Party
Ethnic cleansing
Filipović, Karlo
Goražde
Grabovac, Nikola
Greater Croatia
Greater Serbia
Herceg-Bosna
Herzegovina
Independent Trade Union Association of Bosnia and Herzegovina
International Criminal Tribunal for the former Yugoslavia
Ivanić, Mladen
Izetbegović, Alija
Karadžić, Radovan
Križanović, Jozo
Lagumdžija, Zlatko
League of Communists of Yugoslavia
Mostar
Mrkonjič Grad
Muslim peoples
Muslim-Croat Federation
New Croatian Initiative
Office of the High Representative
Parliamentary Assembly
Party for Bosnia and Herzegovina
Party of Democratic Action
Party of Democratic Progress

Party of Independent Social Democrats
Petritsch, Wolfgang
Privatization Agency of the Federation of Bosnia and Herzegovina
Radišić, Zivko
Sarajevo
Sarović, Mirko
Serb Republic
Serbian Democratic Party
Serbian Orthodox Church
Serbian People's Alliance–Biljana Plavšić
Serbian Radical Party
Serbs
Slavic peoples
Social Democratic Party of Bosnia and Herzegovina
Socialist Federal Republic of Yugoslavia
Socialist Party of the Serb Republic
Srebrenica
Stabilization Force
Tito
Voucher privatization
Yugoslavs

Bulgaria

Balkans
Bulgarian Agrarian People's
  Union
Bulgarian Chamber of
  Commerce and Industry
Bulgarian Industrial Association
Bulgarian National Bank
Bulgarian News Agency
Bulgarian Orthodox Church
Bulgarian royal family—
  Saxe-Coburg-Gotha dynasty
Bulgarian Social Democratic
  Party
Bulgarian Socialist Party
Bulgarian Stock Exchange
Bulgarian Turks
Bulgarians
Confederation of Independent
  Trade Unions of Bulgaria
Cyrillic alphabet
Democratic Party
Dobruja question
Ecoglasnost Political Club
Edinstvo People's Trade Union
Euro-Left Coalition
Georgi Ganchev Bloc
Jews
Macedonian question
Macedonians
Movement for Rights and
  Freedoms
Muslim peoples
National Assembly
National Movement Simeon II
Neuilly, Treaty of
Passy, Solomon
Podkrepa Confederation of
  Labour
Pomaks
Privatization Agency
Promyana National Trade
  Union
Purvanov, Georgi
Roma
Saxecoburggotski, Simeon
Slavic peoples
Sofia
Stoyanov, Petar
Union of Democratic Forces
Velchev, Milen
Vlachs
Zhivkov, Todor

Croatia

Assembly
Association of Autonomous
  Trade Unions of Croatia
Balkans
Central Europe
Confederation of Independent
  Trade Unions of Croatia
Crkvenac, Mato
Croatian Association of Trade
  Unions
Croatian Chamber of Economy
Croatian Defence Force
Croatian Democratic Union
Croatian National Bank
Croatian Party of Rights
Croatian Peasants' Party
Croatian People's Party
Croatian Privatization Fund
Croatian Social-Liberal Party
Croats
Dalmatia
Dayton Agreement
Dubrovnik
Erdut Agreement
Ethnic cleansing
Greater Croatia
Greater Hungary
HINA news agency
International Criminal
  Tribunal for the former
  Yugoslavia
Istria
Istrian Democratic Assembly
Krajina
League of Communists of
  Yugoslavia
Liberal Party
Mesić, Stipe
Picula, Tonino
Prevlaka peninsula
Račan, Ivica
Roman Catholic Church
Serbs
Slavic peoples
Slavonia
Social Democratic Party of
  Croatia
Socialist Federal Republic of
  Yugoslavia
Tito
Tudjman, Franjo
United List
Vukovar
Yugoslavs
Zagreb
Zagreb Stock Exchange

Czech Republic

Bohemia
Central Europe
Charter 77
Christian Democratic Union–
  Czechoslovak People's Party
Christian Labour Confederation
Civic Democratic Party
Civic Forum
Communist Party of Bohemia
  and Moravia
Czech National Bank
Czech News Agency
Czech Social Democratic Party
Czech-Moravian Confederation of Trade Unions
CzechInvest
Czechoslovakia
Czechs
Dubček, Alexander
Economic Chamber of the
  Czech Republic
Freedom Union
Havel, Václav
Husák, Gustáv
Jakeš, Miloš
Kavan, Jan
Klaus, Václav
Lustration laws
Moravia
National Property Fund
Parliament
Prague
Prague Spring
Prague Stock Exchange
Roma
Roman Catholic Church
Rusnok, Jiří
Slavic peoples
Slovaks
StB
Sudetenland question
Velvet divorce
Velvet revolution
Voucher privatization
Zeman, Miloš

Estonia

Association of Estonian Trade
  Unions
Baltic States
Bank of Estonia
Central Europe
Estonian Centre Party
Estonian Chamber of
  Commerce and Industry
Estonian Coalition Party
Estonian Investment Agency
Estonian News Agency
Estonian People's Union
Estonian Privatization Agency
Estonian Reform Party
Estonians
Fatherland Union
Finno-Ugric peoples
Ilves, Toomas Hendrik
Jaanilinn question
Kallas, Siim
Laar, Mart
Livonia
Meri, Lennart
Moderates
Narva
Nazi-Soviet Pact
Petseri question
Protestantism
Russians
Rüütel, Arnold
Soviet Union
State Assembly
Tallinn
Tallinn Stock Exchange
Tartu, Treaties of
United People's Party of
  Estonia

Georgia

Abkhazia
Adzharia
All-Georgian Union for
  Revival
Armenians
Caucasus region
Chamber of Commerce and
  Industry of Georgia
Citizens' Union of Georgia
Confederation of the Peoples of
  the Caucasus
Deported Nationalities
Djorbenadze, Avtandil
Georgian Import Export
Georgian Orthodox Church
Georgian Stock Exchange
Georgian Trade Union
  Amalgamation
Georgians
Industry Will Save Georgia
Javakheti
Kodori Gorge
Kurds
Menagharishvili, Irakli
Meskhetians
Mkhedrioni
Muslim peoples
National Bank of Georgia
Noghaideli, Zurab
Ossetia question
Pankisi Gorge
Parliament of Georgia
Pontic Greeks
Russians
Sakinform
Shevardnadze, Eduard
Soviet Union
State Property Management
  Agency
Tbilisi
TRACECA
Transcaucasus
Zviadists

Hungary

Alliance of Free Democrats
Antall, József
Autonomous Trade Union
  Confederation
Budapest
Budapest Stock Exchange
Central Europe
Democratic League of
  Independent Trade Unions
Federation of Young Demo-
  crats–Hungarian Civic Party
Finno-Ugric peoples
Forum for the Co-operation of
  Trade Unions
Gabčíkovo-Nagymaros Dam
Germans
Göncz, Árpád
Greater Hungary
Horn, Gyula
Hungarian Chamber of
  Commerce and Industry
Hungarian Democratic Forum
Hungarian Justice and Life
  Party
Hungarian News Agency
Hungarian Privatization and
  State Holding Company
Hungarian Socialist Party
Hungarians
Independent Smallholders' and
  Civic Party
Kádár, János
Mádl, Ferenc
Martonyi, János
Nagy, Imre
National Assembly
National Bank of Hungary
National Confederation of
  Hungarian Trade Unions
National Federation of
  Workers' Councils
Orbán, Viktor
PHARE programme
Protestantism
Roma
Roman Catholic Church
Trianon, Treaty of
Varga, Mihály
Vienna Awards

Latvia

Abrene question
Baltic States
Bank of Latvia
Berzinš, Andris
Berzinš, Gundars
Berzinš, Indulis
Central Europe
Fatherland and Freedom—
  Latvian National Conservative Party
Interlatvija
Latvia's Way
Latvian Chamber of Commerce and Industry
Latvian Development Agency
Latvian Free Trade Union
  Confederation
Latvian Privatization Agency
Latvian Social Democratic
  Workers' Party
Latvians
LETA
Livonia
National Harmony Party
Nazi-Soviet Pact
New Christian Party
Parliament
People's Party
Protestantism
Riga
Riga Stock Exchange
Riga, Treaties of
Russians
Soviet Union
Vike-Freiberga, Vaira

Lithuania

Adamkus, Valdas
Association of Lithuanian
  Chambers of Commerce,
  Industry and Crafts
Baltic States
Bank of Lithuania
Brazauskas, Algirdas
Central Europe
ELTA
Grybauskaite, Dalia
Homeland Union–Lithuanian
  Conservatives
Klaipeda
Lithuanian Centre Union
Lithuanian Christian Democratic Party
Lithuanian Development
  Agency
Lithuanian Farmers' Party
Lithuanian Federation of
  Labour
Lithuanian Liberal Union
Lithuanian Poles' Electoral
  Action
Lithuanian Reform Movement
Lithuanian Social Democratic
  Party
Lithuanian State Privatization
  Agency
Lithuanian Trade Union
  Unification
Lithuanian Worker's Union
Lithuanians
National Stock Exchange
Nazi-Soviet Pact
Neman question
New Union (Social Liberals)
Parliament
Poles
Roman Catholic Church
Russians
Soviet Union
State Property Fund
Valionis, Antanas
Vilnius

Macedonia

Albanians
Assembly of the Republic
Balkans
Casule, Slobodan
Confederation of Trade Unions
  of Macedonia
Cyrillic alphabet
Democratic Alternative
Democratic Party of Albanians
Economic Chamber of
  Macedonia
Georgievski, Ljubčo
Gligorov, Kiro
Greater Albania
Greater Serbia
Gruevski, Nikola
Internal Macedonian Revolutionary Organization–
  Democratic Party for
  Macedonian National Unity
League of Communists of
  Yugoslavia
Macedonian question
Macedonian Stock Exchange
Macedonians
Makfax
Muslim peoples
National Bank of Macedonia
New Democracy
Party for Democratic
  Prosperity
Pomaks
Privatization Agency of the
  Republic of Macedonia
Skopje
Slavic peoples
Social Democratic Union of
  Macedonia
Socialist Federal Republic of
  Yugoslavia
Tetovo
Tito
Trajkovski, Boris
Union of Independent and
  Autonomous Syndicates of
  Macedonia
Vlachs
Yugoslavs

Moldova

AIDS
Balkans
Bessarabia question
Bessarabian Church
Braghis Alliance
Braghis, Dumitru
Bulgarians
Chamber of Commerce and Industry of the Republic of Moldova
Chișinău
Christian Democratic People's Party
Communist Party of the Moldovan Republic
Confederation of Trade Unions of the Republic of Moldova
Cyrillic alphabet
Dudau, Nicolae
Gagauzia
Greater Romania
Infotag News Agency
Manoli, Mihail
Moldovan Stock Exchange
Moldovans
National Bank of Moldova
National News Agency
Parliament
Russians
Solidaritate
Soviet Union
Taraclia
Tarlev, Vasile
TRACECA
Transdnestria
Ukrainians
Vlachs
Voronin, Vladimir

Poland

All-Poland Alliance of Trade Unions
Auschwitz-Birkenau
Balcerowicz, Leszek
Belka, Marek
Buzek, Jerzy
Central Europe
Chamber of Industry and Trade for Foreign Investors
Cimoszewicz, Włodzimierz
Citizens' Platform
Democratic Left Alliance
Freedom Union
Galicia
Gdańsk
Germans
Jaruzelski, Wojciech
Jehovah's Witnesses
Jews
John Paul II, Pope
Kwaśniewski, Aleksander
Labour Union
Law and Justice
League of Polish Families
Mass Privatization Programme
Miller, Leszek
Movement for the Reconstruction of Poland
National Assembly
National Bank of Poland
Nazi-Soviet Pact
Oder-Neisse line
PHARE programme
Poles
Polish Agency for Foreign Investment
Polish Chamber of Commerce
Polish Peasant Party
Polish Press Agency
Prussia
Riga, Treaties of
Roman Catholic Church
Self-Defence of the Polish Republic
Shock therapy
Slavic peoples
Solidarity
Solidarity Electoral Action
Versailles, Treaty of
Wałęsa, Lech
Warsaw
Warsaw Stock Exchange

Romania

Alpha Cartel National Trade Union Confederation
Balkans
Bessarabia question
Bucharest
Bucharest Stock Exchange
Bukovina question
Ceaușescu, Nicolae
Chamber of Commerce and Industry of Romania and the Municipality of Bucharest
Christian Democratic National Peasants' Party
Confederation of Democratic Trade Unions of Romania
Csángós
Democratic Party
Dobruja question
Fratia National Confederation of Free Trade Unions of Romania
Geoana, Mircea
Germans
Greater Hungary
Greater Romania
Greater Romania Party
Hungarian Democratic Union of Romania
Hungarians
Iliescu, Ion
Nastase, Adrian
National Bank of Romania
National Liberal Party
National Trade Union Bloc
Parliament of Romania
Roma
Romanian Development Agency
Romanian Orthodox Church
Romanian royal family
Romanians
ROMPRES
Serpents' Island
Social Democrat Party
Social Democratic Pole of Romania
State Ownership Fund
Szeklers
Tanasescu, Mihai
Transylvania
Vlachs
Wallachia

Russian Federation

Abaza
Abrene question
Adygeya
AIDS
Alfa-Bank
All-Russian Confederation of Labour
Archangel
Astrakhan
August coup
Aum Shinrikyo (or Aleph)
Avars
Bank for Foreign Trade
Bashkortostan
Belarus-Russia Union
Belarusians
Black Sea Fleet
Buddhism
Caucasus region
Caviar
Central Bank of the Russian Federation
Chamber of Commerce and Industry of the Russian Federation
Chavash Republic
Chechnya
Cherkess
Communist Party of the Russian Federation
Communist Party of the Soviet Union
Confederation of Labour of Russia
Confederation of the Peoples of the Caucasus
Cossacks
Cyrillic alphabet
Dagestan
Dargins
Deported Nationalities
Don Basin
Duma
European Russia
Fatherland-All Russia
Federal Assembly
Federal Security Service
Federation of Independent Trade Unions of Russia
Finno-Ugric peoples
Gazprom
Germans
Glasnost
Gorbachev, Mikhail
Greater Russia
Idel-Ural
Ingushetia
ITAR-TASS
Ivanov, Igor
Jaanilinn question
Jehovah's Witnesses
Jews
Kabardino-Balkaria
Kaliningrad
Kalmykia
Karachai-Cherkessia
Karelia question
Kasyanov, Mikhail
Kazakhs
Kola peninsula
Komi Republic
Kremlin
Kryashen
Kudrin, Aleksei
Kumyks
Kursk
Lezghins
Liberal Democratic Party of Russia
Livonia
LUKoil
Mari El Republic
Menatep SPb
Mir space station
Mordova
Moscow
Moscow Central Stock Exchange
Moscow International Stock Exchange
Muslim peoples
Nazi-Soviet Pact
Near abroad
Neman question
Novosti
Nuclear Test Ban Treaty
Ossetia question
Pamyat–National Patriotic Front
Pan-Turkism
Perestroika
Petsamo question
Petseri question
Prussia
Putin, Vladimir
Riga, Treaties of
Romanov dynasty
Rosoboronexport
Rosspirtprom
Rouble zone
Russian Aluminium
Russian Federal Property Fund
Russian Orthodox Church
Russians
St Petersburg
SALT
Sami
SBS-Agro
Siberia
Slavic peoples
Soviet Union
START
Svalbard
Tabasarans
Tartu, Treaties of
Tatars
Tatarstan
Trans-Siberian Railway
Turkic peoples
Udmurtia
Ukrainians
Union of Right Forces
Unity Inter-regional Movement
Volga region
Voucher privatization
White House
Yabloko
Yeltsin, Boris
Zyuganov, Gennadii

633

Slovakia

Bratislava
Bratislava Stock Exchange
Central Europe
Charter 77
Confederation of Trade Unions
  of the Slovak Republic
Czechoslovakia
Czechs
Dubček, Alexander
Dzurinda, Mikuláš
Gabčíkovo-Nagymaros Dam
Greater Hungary
Havel, Václav
Hungarian Coalition Party
Hungarians
Husák, Gustáv
Independent Christian Trade
  Union of Slovakia
Jakeš, Miloš
Klaus, Václav
Kukan, Eduard
Lustration laws
Mečiar, Vladimír
Movement for a Democratic
  Slovakia
National Bank of Slovakia
National Council
National Property Fund
News Agency of the Slovak
  Republic
Party of Civic Understanding
Party of the Democratic Left
Prague Spring
Public Against Violence
Roma
Roman Catholic Church
Schmögnerová, Brigita
Schuster, Rudolf
Slavic peoples
Slovak Chamber of Commerce
  and Industry
Slovak Democratic Coalition
Slovak Investment and Trade
  Development Agency
Slovak National Party
Slovaks
StB
Velvet divorce
Velvet revolution
Voucher privatization

Slovenia

Agency for Reconstruction and
  Privatization
Association of Free Trade
  Unions of Slovenia
Balkans
Bank of Slovenia
Central Europe
Chamber of Commerce and
  Industry of Slovenia
Democratic Party of Slovenian
  Pensioners
Development Corporation of
  Slovenia
Drnovšek, Janez
Independence–Confederation
  of New Trade Unions of
  Slovenia
Istria
Kučan, Milan
League of Communists of
  Yugoslavia
Liberal Democracy of Slovenia
Ljubljana
Ljubljana Stock Exchange
National Assembly
New Slovenia–Christian
  People's Party
Party of Slovenian Youth
Roman Catholic Church
Rop, Anton
Rupel, Dimitrij
Slavic peoples
Slovene Press Agency
Slovenes
Slovenian National Party
Slovenian People's Party
Social Democratic Party of
  Slovenia
Socialist Federal Republic of
  Yugoslavia
Tito
Trieste
United List of Social Demo-
  crats
Yugoslavs

Ukraine

Agrarian Party of Ukraine
AIDS
Black Sea Fleet
Bukovina question
Chernobyl
Communist Party of Ukraine
Confederation of Free Trade
  Unions of Ukraine
Crimea
Crimean Tatars
Cyrillic alphabet
Deported Nationalities
Donbass Russians
Fatherland
Federation of Trade Unions of
  Ukraine
Galicia
Germans
Green Party of Ukraine
Hromada All-Ukrainian
  Association
Jehovah's Witnesses
Jews
Kiev
Kinakh, Anatoliy
Kuchma, Leonid
Mityukov, Ihor
Muslim peoples
National Bank of Ukraine
Parliament
Peasants' Party of Ukraine
People's Democratic Party of
  Ukraine
Popular Movement of Ukraine
Pripet Marshes
Progressive Socialist Party
Romanians
Russians
Ruthenians
Serpents' Island
Sevastopol
Slavic peoples
Social Democratic Party of
  Ukraine–United
Socialist Party of Ukraine
Soviet Union
START
State Property Fund
Tatars
TRACECA
Transcarpathia
Turkic peoples
Ukrainian Chamber of
  Commerce and Industry
Ukrainian Export-Import Bank
Ukrainian Stock Exchange
Ukrainians
Ukrinform
Uniate Church
Zlenko, Anatoliy

Yugoslavia
Albanians
Balkans
Belgrade
Belgrade Stock Exchange
Chetniks
Civic Alliance of Serbia
Confederation of Autonomous
 Trade Unions of Yugoslavia
Cyrillic alphabet
Dayton Agreement
Democratic League of Kosovo
Democratic Opposition of
 Serbia
Democratic Party
Democratic Party of Serbia
Democratic Party of Socialists
 of Montenegro
Djindjić, Zoran
Djukanović, Milo
Ethnic cleansing
Federal Assembly
Foreign Trade Institute
Greater Albania
Greater Hungary
Greater Serbia
Hungarians
Independence Trade Union
 Confederation
International Criminal
 Tribunal for the former
 Yugoslavia
KFOR
Kosovo
Kosovo Liberation Army
Koštunica, Vojislav
League of Communists of
 Yugoslavia
Liberal Alliance of Montenegro
Macedonian question
Macedonians
Milošević, Slobodan
Milutinović, Milan
Montenegro
Muslim peoples
National Bank of Yugoslavia
New Democracy
Party of Democratic Action
Pesić, Dragiša
Podgorica
Presevo Valley
Prevlaka peninsula
Ranković, Jovan
Sandzak
Serbia
Serbian Orthodox Church
Serbian Radical Party
Serbian Renewal Movement
Serbian Unity Party
Serbs
Slavic peoples
Socialist Federal Republic of
 Yugoslavia
Socialist Party of Serbia
Socialist People's Party of
 Montenegro
Svilanović, Goran
Tanjug
Tito
Vlachs
Vojvodina
Voucher privatization
Vujanović, Filip
Yugoslav Bank for International Economic Co-
 operation
Yugoslav Chamber of
 Commerce and Industry
Yugoslav United Left
Yugoslavs

Index of Personal Names

A

Abashidze, Aslan 4, 16, 17
Abdić, Fikret 180, 284
Adamec, Ladislav 124
Adamkus, Valdas 3, 79, 253, 335
Agov, Petar 91
Ahmadov, Ramiz 38
Akhvlediani, Guram D. 105
Alekperov, Avaz 13
Alekperov, Vagit 347
Aleksejchik, Yakov 64
Aleksiy II, Patriarch 493
Alexa, Károly 260
Alia, Ramiz 7, 14, 542
Aliyev, Heydar 14, 15, 23, 34, 38, 39, 407, 408, 410, 467
Aliyev, Ilham 16, 35, 407
Alois, Anton 114
Andreyev, Viktor 590
Andriukaitis, Vytenis 342
Andropov, Yurii 126, 239, 486
Angjeli, Anastas 19
Antall, József 19, 258, 259
Antonescu, Ion 472, 477
Antovski, Slobodan 587
Apostolov, Apostol 95
Ardzinba, Vladislav 2
Arendarski, Andrzej 452
Arkan 511
Arsenishvili, Giorgi 116, 230
Arshakian, Azad 25
Arzumanian, Aleksandr 426
Atkočiunas, Vytis 343
Aushev, Ruslan 274
Aven, Petr 14
Aznar, José María 111

B

Babić, Milan 309
Baciu, Iacob 131
Badalian, Sergei 121
Badea, Constantin 479
Bagdasarian, Artur 137
Bahdankevich, Stanislau 588
Bajuk, Andrej 187, 410, 529, 533
Balcerowicz, Leszek 44, 221, 397, 515
Balsiene, Aldona 344
Bankja, Adriatik 194
el-Baradei, Mohammad 276
Barkans, Martinš 329

Bartholomew, Ecumenical Patriarch 422
Bartoszcze, Roman 452
Basescu, Traian 173
Bednarčíková, Ivana 622
Behman, Alija 51, 73
Belec, Berislav 145
Belka, Marek 63
Belkeziz, Abdelouahed 421
Belkić, Beriz 63, 73, 432
Beqiri, Idajet 405
Berisha, Sali 7, 47, 166, 167, 174, 176, 390, 405, 464, 543
Berov, Lyuben 83, 93, 383, 585
Berzinš, Andris 64, 65, 66, 322, 325
Berzinš, Gundars 65
Berzinš, Indulis 65
Bezhani, Theodhori 181
Bielecki, Jan 447
Birkavs, Valdis 321, 324
Blagojević, Mirko 510
Boban, Mate 146, 251
Bobelis, Kazys 340
Bogdański, Robert 453
Bojars, Juris 326
Bojinov, Bojidar 88
Boldyrev, Yurii 608
Bolfek, Mirko 252
Bonev, Ognyan 193
Bonner, Yelena 251
Bosić, Boro 71
Boyko, Bohdan 455
Braghis, Dumitru 76, 77, 373
Brazauskas, Algirdas 78, 247, 335, 342, 343, 592
Brezhnev, Leonid 126, 239, 486
Brojka, Albert 166
Broz, Josip see Tito
Budiša, Dražen 142, 152
Bufi, Ylli 543
Bugár, Béla 257
Bugayev, Aleksandr 17
Buha, Aleksa 507
Bulatović, Momir 178, 184, 442, 547, 600
Bulatović, Predrag 548
Bullock, Merry 270
Burdzhanadze, Nino 230
Busek, Erhard 555
Bush, George W. 498
Busila, Rimantas 404
Buzek, Jerzy 96, 327, 447, 550, 551

C

Čanak, Branislav 271
Cani, Shkëlqim 48
Carnogurský, Ján 519
Carter, Jimmy 498
Casule, Slobodan 98, 409
Cavanaugh, Carey 368
Ceauşescu, Nicolae 80, 100, 172, 259, 269, 402, 472, 475, 478, 535, 563, 572
Çeka, Neritan 167
Celcer, Vera 527
Ćeredejev, Ivan 411
Černák, Ľudovit 520
Černjak, Dominik S. 436
Chamara, Viktor 584
Chechelashvili, Valeri 421
Chernenko, Konstantin 126, 239, 486
Chernomyrdin, Viktor 68, 487, 590, 611
Chervenkov, Vulko 92
Chibirov, Lyudvig 424
Chiriac, Petru 133
Chornovil, Vyacheslav 455
Chubais, Anatolii 313
Churchill, Sir Winston 120
Chykin, Viktar 59, 122, 123
Cimoszewicz, Włodzimierz 115, 170, 447
Ciorbea, Victor 111, 112, 473
Ciubuc, Ion 373
Cojocaru, George 105
Constantinescu, Emil 111, 269, 402, 473, 535
Coposu, Corneliu 111
Costin, Dumitru 404
Crkvenac, Mato 140
Crockett, Andrew 47
Crvenkovski, Branko 349, 541
Csurka, István 258, 259, 260
Cucu, Gheorghe 106
Čuk, Jožko 105
Cupi, Frrok 12

D

Dade, Arta 163
Dalai Lama 294
Danev, Bojidar 89
Darbinian, Armen R. 27
Darbinian, Vladimir 121
Dávid, Ibolya 258
Demirchian, Karen 22, 440

637

Demirchian, Stepan 441
Demszky, Gábor 18
Denev, Panayot 90
Deripaska, Oleg V. 483
Dertliev, Petur 91
Diaconescu, Ion 111
Dimitrov, Filip 83, 192, 585
Dimitrov, Georgi 92
Dislers, Guntis 408
Djapić, Ante 149
Djelić, Bozidar 63
Djindjić, Zoran 171, 174, 177, 182, 367, 616
Djorbenadze, Avtandil 183, 230
Djordjević, Dušan 564
Djukanović, Milo 178, 179, 183, 377, 600, 615
Dobrev, Nikolai 462
Dodik, Milorad 71, 435, 436, 507, 508, 509, 546
Dogan, Ahmed 384
Domokos, Géza 259
Dovhan, Serhiy 439
Drašković, Vuk 511
Drnovšek, Janez 186, 331, 529
Dubček, Alexander 123, 156, 187, 267, 285, 457, 522
Dubko, Alyaksandr 58
Dudau, Nicolae 188
Dudayev, Dzhokhar 108
Dunal, Peter 257
Dzasokhov, Aleksandr 424
Dzemyantsei, Mikalay 122
Dzharimov, Aslan 4
Dzhughashvili, Yevgenii 16
Dzurinda, Mikuláš 189, 519, 523

E

Ehlers, Peter 45
Elchibey, Abulfaz 15, 35, 39, 407
Elerts, Maris 325
Ermenji, Abaz 401
Eyyub, Vurgun 410

F

Falbr, Richard 154
Fattayev, Murmahmud 41
Fernholm, Bo 279
Filipović, Karlo 72, 218
Fino, Bashkim 8, 543
Főcze, Lajos 33
Fodoreanu, Sorin 477

Forsts, Maris 274
Frasyniuk, Władysław 222
Freibergs, Imants 596
Frunda, György 259
Funar, Gheorghe 243
Für, Lajos 258
Fyedorov, Nikolay 108

G

Gaidar, Yegor 587
Gailis, Maris 321, 324
Gaillarde, Jean-Jacques 368
Gama, Jaime Matos da 421
Gambar, Isa 410
Gamsakhurdia, Zviad 16, 229, 234, 370, 515, 624
Gancharyk, Uladzimir 57, 58
Ganchev, Georgi 228
Gangura, Ion 376
Ganić, Ejup 434
Gansperger, Gyula 260
Gaskó, István 168
Gaspari, Mitja 49
Gavahi, Abdulrahim 193
Gavriyski, Svetoslav 89
Gaydukevich, Syargey 332
Gaziyev, Rakhim 40
Geghamian, Artashes 289
Genjac, Halid 72, 432, 434
Geoana, Mircea 227, 421
Georgievski, Ljubčo 98, 235, 275, 276, 349
Gerashchenko, Viktor 102
Geremek, Bronislaw 222
Gheorghiu-Dej, Gheorghe 100, 472
Ghizari, Emil Iota 397
Ghukasian, Arkadii 388
Gjinushi, Skender 536
Gjoka, Genc 11
Glaveckas, Kestutis 339
Gligorić, Tihomir 546
Gligorov, Kiro 237, 349, 541
Godo, Sabri 11
Gogoberidze, T. A. 233
Göncz, Árpád 18, 237, 263, 355
Gongadze, Georgiy 313
Gorbachev, Mikhail 15, 31, 34, 92, 120, 124, 126, 129, 198, 216, 229, 236, 238, 246, 321, 335, 372, 441, 486, 514, 554, 609, 623, 624
Gotovać, Vlado 152, 333
Gottwald, Klement 123
Grabovac, Nikola 240
Granić, Mate 142, 148
Grebeníček, Miroslav 125

Gribkov, Nikolay 368
Grinblats, Maris 213
Gromyko, Andrei 239
Gruevski, Nikola 246
Gruodis, Vytas E. 340
Gryb, Mechislau 52, 59, 122
Grybauskaite, Dalia 247
Guillaume, Gilbert 277
Gusinsky, Vladimir 226
Guterres, António 542

H

Haekkerup, Hans 307
Hajdari, Azem 175
Hakobian, George 536
Halili, Muhamet 432
Halilović, Safet 72, 218
Halilović, Sefer 76
Hampartsumian, Levon 458
Hamzik, Pavol 433
Haroutunian, Martin 227
Hasanov, Firudin 38
Havel, Václav 107, 118, 124, 156, 187, 249, 303, 522, 594
Hitler, Adolf 160, 236, 405, 426, 457, 485, 559
Hollman, Pavel 457
Horn, Gyula 254, 261, 264
Hossu, Bogdan 18
Hovhanissian, Vahan 27
Hoxha, Enver 7, 12, 14, 255
Hristov, Jeliazko 132
Hrle, Sulejman 273
Hureynov, E. M. 41
Husák, Gustáv 123, 156, 267, 285, 522

I

Ignatenko, Vitalii N. 281
Ilić, Radoslav 130
Iliescu, Ion 173, 244, 269, 391, 472, 478, 534
Iliev, Petko 88
Illya II, Cathilicos-Patriarch 233
Ilves, Toomas Hendrik 270
Ilyumzhinov, Kirsan 294
Imnadze, Kakha 498
Ionescu-Quintus, Mircea 402
Ioseliani, Dzhaba 370
Isarescu, Mugur 112, 473
Ivanić, Mladen 73, 282, 435, 436, 507, 509, 546
Ivanov, Igor 282
Izetbegović, Alija 71, 146, 180, 283, 433

J

Jafarov, Shahmerdan 40
Jagieliński, Roman 453
Jahn, Martin 161
Jakeš, Miloš 124, 267, 285, 594
Jakovčić, Ivan 281
Jankauskas, Kęstutis 194
Janowski, Mieczysław 552
Janša, Janez 539
Járai, Zsigmond 395
Jaruzelski, Wojciech 286
Jelavić, Ante 71, 146, 147, 408
Jelinčič, Zmago 532
John Paul II, Pope 288, 447, 470
Johnston, Donald J. 419
Jorda, Claude 277
Jurić, Davor 30
Jurkans, Janis 401
Jusko, Marián 397

K

Kaczyński, Jarosław 327
Kaczyński, Lech 327
Kádár, János 261, 263, 291
Kadyrov, Akhmed 109
Kalinić, Dragan 507
Kalinowski, Jarosław 453
Kallas, Siim 48, 204, 205, 292
Kandare, Boris 149
Karadžić, Radovan 70, 277, 295, 308, 506, 508, 545
Karbauskis, Ramunas 340
Karekin I, Supreme Patriarch and Catholicos 25
Karpenka, Henadz 539
Karpov, Oleksandr 440
Kartus, Kristi 293
Kasak, Vyacheslav A. 57
Kasal, Jan 114
Kasyanov, Mikhail 226, 297, 313, 488
Katanandov, Sergei 297
Kavaldzhiev, Todor 88
Kavan, Jan 298
Kebich, Vyacheslau 122
Kerimov, Ali 41
Khachatrian, Armen 441
Khachatrian, Vartan 299
Khrushchev, Nikita 108, 123, 126, 129, 182, 216, 255, 294, 486, 583
Khvastow, Mikhail 300
Kinakh, Anatoliy 301
Kiriyenko, Sergei 487
Klaus, Václav 117, 118, 119, 157, 221, 249, 303, 359, 594
Klicković, Gojko 507
Knastr, Aleksandr 14
Knaus, Gerald 209
Kocharian, Robert 22, 27, 36, 137, 177, 289, 303, 357, 400, 423, 426, 440, 468
Köhler, Horst 279
Kojda, Jozef 404
Kokorevics, Guntars 469
Kokov, Valery 291
Kokoyev, Eduard 424
Komsić, Ivo 150
Koncoš, Pavel 437
Kononov, Vitaliy 245
Konusenko, Vladimir 132
Kopriva, Jaroslav 114
Korbut, Nikolay 306
Kostenko, Yuriy 455
Kostić, Dragan 179, 509
Kostov, Ivan 84, 559, 586
Koštunica, Vojislav 171, 172, 174, 177, 182, 308, 366, 466, 510, 548, 560, 616
Kovač, Bogomir 331
Kováč, Michal 359, 382, 522
Kovács, László 261
Kövér, László 218
Kraft, Vahur 48
Krajišnik, Momčilo 71, 466, 507
Kramarić, Zlatko 334
Krasts, Guntars 213, 321
Kravchuk, Leonid 245, 540, 577
Kreid, Harald 103
Kreisky, Bruno 442
Krištopans, Vilis 321, 325, 326
Križanović, Jozo 73, 310, 537
Kryemadhi, Monika 364
Kryukov, Vitaliy 558
Krzaklewski, Marian 96, 448, 550, 551
Kubilius, Andrius 253, 336
Kubiš, Ján 421
Kubo, Märt 203
Kučan, Milan 311, 528, 533, 589
Kuchma, Leonid 5, 129, 212, 245, 256, 302, 312, 369, 429, 439, 455, 547, 577, 580
Kudrin, Aleksei 313
Kühnl, Karel 221
Kukan, Eduard 314
Kulbergs, Viktors 325
Kuliyev, Vilayat Mukhtar 314
Kuncze, Gabor 18
Kuron, Jacek 222
Kušar, Janko 178
Kuzminskas, Kazimieras 341
Kuznyatsow, Vyacheslau 61
Kwaśniewski, Aleksander 63, 170, 316, 327, 447, 451, 551, 603

L

Laar, Mart 198, 205, 214, 270, 293, 318, 371
Labernik, Tadej 527
Labovitjadhi, Jorgo 181
Laço, Teodor 333
Lagumdžija, Zlatko 319, 537
Landsbergis, Vytautas 253, 335
Lányi, Zsolt 272
Lazarenko, Pavlo 68, 212, 256
Lazový, Juraj 78
Lebed, Aleksandr 329, 487
Lebedev, Dmitry A. 361
Leka, Anton 585
Lemierre, Jean 208
Lepper, Andrzej 504
Lesun, Uladzimir K. 57
Lezsák, Sándor 258
Liabedzka, Anatol 588
Lilov, Aleksandur 92
Ljajić, Rasim 434, 435
Lőhmus, Tiit 203
Lokyan, Davit 27
Loladze, George 234
Lombar, Drago 271
Lucinschi, Petru 77, 125, 373, 565
Lugin, Yaugen 58
Lukashenka, Alyaksandr 5, 52, 55, 56, 58, 59, 61, 122, 134, 300, 332, 346, 414, 481,588
Lukin, Vladimir 608
Luman, Toomas 202
Lux, Josef 114
Luzhkov, Yurii 212, 213
Lysenka, Alyaksandr 57

M

Macierewicz, Antoni 329
McKinley, Brunson 279
Mádl, Ferenc 264, 354
Magomedov, Magomedali 164
Magyar, Bálint 18
Maiani, Luciano 208
Majko, Pandeli 8, 175, 543

639

Malíková, Anna 520, 521
Mamedov, Etibar 39
Managadze, Irakli 395
Manicki, Maciej 17
Manoli, Mihail 355
Manoyan, Giro 27
Manukian, Vazgen 400
Marazov, Ivan 94
Marchuk, Yevhen 540
Marga, Andrei 112
Margareta, Princess 478
Margaryan, Hrand 27
Marjanović, Mirko 544, 545
Markarian, Andranik 23, 356, 441, 468
Markelov, Leonid 356
Markó, Béla 259
Marković, Mirjana 365, 612, 613, 615
Marran, Mait 203
Martonyi, János 357
Maskhadov, Aslan 109
Matić, Bozidar 73, 319, 537
Matinchev, Evgeni 384
Matviyenko, Anatoliy 440
Maxim, Patriarch 90
May, Richard George 277
Mazowiecki, Tadeusz 221, 447, 602
Mečiar, Vladimír 249, 358, 381, 383, 433, 522, 594
Mediu, Fatmir 11, 12
Medvedchuk, Viktor 540
Mehbaliyev, Sattar 131
Meidani, Rexhep 8, 359, 390, 543
Meksi, Aleksander 7, 175
Melo, Vasil 257
Menagharishvili, Irakli 360
Meri, Lennart 198, 214, 361
Merkushkin, Nikolay 379
Mesić, Mladen 132
Mesić, Stipe 140, 142, 150, 151, 362, 465, 538, 542
Meta, Ilir 8, 363, 390, 543
Michael, King 402, 472, 477
Mićunović, Dragoljub 174
Migaš, Jozef 437
Mihailovic, Draza 110
Mihailović, Vojislav 511
Mihajlović, Dušan 409
Mihajlović, Svetozar 71
Mihaylova, Ekaterina 586, 587
Mihók, Peter 518
Mihut, Gabriel 557
Mikaberidze, Manana 361
Mikhailichenko, Oleksiy P. 582
Mikolajczyk, Stanisław 452
Miller, Alexei B. 226

Miller, Leszek 63, 170, 319, 364, 448, 453
Milojević, Mihajlo 612
Milošević, Slobodan 62, 117, 169, 170, 174, 177, 178, 182, 184, 271, 277, 295, 306, 308, 310, 329, 330, 365, 367, 377, 409, 435, 442, 458, 510, 511, 542, 544, 545, 548, 564, 598, 612, 614, 618
Milutinović, Milan 367, 544, 615
Minarović, Roman 520
Mityukov, Ihor 369
Mladenov, Petur 83, 92
Mock, Alois 254
Mollov, Valentin 227
Moore, Michael 607
Moravčík, Jozef 359
Moroz, Oleksandr 546, 547
Moser, Anastasia 88
Mrkša, Slobodan 219
Muço, Kastriot 130
Mujagić, Adnad 459
Mumba, Florence 277
Mutafchiev, Pancho 460
Mutalibov, Ayaz 35, 38, 40, 119

N

Naglis, Janis 326
Nagy, Imre 291, 388, 418
Nagy, Sándor 261
Nakeva-Kavrakova, Marina 459
Nano, Fatos 8, 15, 175, 364, 389, 542, 543
Nastase, Adrian 270, 391, 473, 535, 536
Navumenka, Viktar 400
Nazarbayev, Nursultan 207
Nemtsov, Boris 588
Nexipi, Muharem 176
Neyts-Uyttebroek, Annemie 333
Nicholl, Peter 102
Nihrizov, Yordan 91
Nikolić, Tomislav 510
Noghaideli, Zurab 412
Normington, Richard 278
Novikau, Vasil 122
Novitski, Gennadz 56, 414
Novotný, Antonín 123, 187
Novovesky, Peter 271

O

Olechowski, Andrzej 115, 116
Oleksy, Józef 170, 447
Olszewski, Jan 384, 385, 447
Onopenko, Vasyl 540
Oprescu, Sergiu 80
Orbán, Viktor 218, 264, 355, 418
Orlov, Yuri 251
Oskanian, Vartan 423
Oskolsky, Valentin 583

P

Padgainy, Michail 61
Pahor, Borut 589
Paksas, Rolandas 253, 336, 341, 592
Palkovics, Imre 400
Panakhli, Neymat 30
Panitchpakdi, Supachai 607
Pantelejevs, Andrejs 325
Papoyan, Artush 369
Papuga, Marinko 621
Paraga, Dobroslav 149
Parnits, Kadi 30
Parnoja, Mikhel 198
Passy, Solomon 437
Patiashvili, Dzhumber 16
Patrushev, Nikolai 109, 216
Paulauskas, Arturas 335, 411
Pauls, Raimond 408
Pavle, Patriarch 508
Pawlak, Waldemar 447, 452
Pawłowicz, Adam 451
Pazgan, Kazimierz 452
Paznyak, Zyanon 59, 134
Pekhtin, Vladimir 590
Pelević, Borislav 512
Pellumbi, Servet 543
Perović, Slavko 331
Pesić, Dragiša 442, 548, 617
Pešić, Vesna 117
Petcu, Marius 220
Peterle, Lojze 528, 533
Petkov, Nikola 87
Petkovski, Tito 350, 541
Peto, Iván 18
Petreski, Dušan 192
Petritsch, Wolfgang 418, 442
Petrov, Cedo 409
Petru Paduraru, Bishop 67
Picula, Tonino 444
Pirinski, Georgi 93
Plavšić, Biljana 71, 296, 507, 508, 509, 546
Plazyński, Maciej 115, 116
Pokorni, Zoltán 218
Pol, Marek 319

Pollo, Genc 166, 175
Ponomarev, Yurii V. 46
Poplasen, Nikola 71, 435, 507, 508, 509, 546
Prakapovich, Pyotr 394
Pramatarski, Aleksandur 172
Primakov, Yevgenii 487
Prlić, Jadranko 146
Puc, Mira 5
Puiu, Ion 111
Purvanov, Georgi 85, 94, 461, 559, 586
Pusić, Vesna 151
Pustovoytenko, Valeriy 439
Putin, Vladimir 56, 109, 127, 209, 212, 216, 226, 283, 297, 313, 316, 374, 462, 480, 487, 492, 497, 566, 588, 590, 608, 611, 624

R

Račan, Ivica 142, 465, 538
Radišić, Zivko 71, 146, 466, 546
Radmanović, Nebojsa 181
Radović, Zorica 309
Radzevics, Juris 326
Raguz, Martin 72, 146
Rainys, G. 557
Rajk, László 291
Rakhimov, Murtaza 50
Rákosi, Mátyás 388
Ranković, Jovan 466
Rasizade, Artur 35, 407, 467
Raznjatović, Zeljko see Arkan
Reagan, Ronald 498
Rekar, Marjan 182
Relve, Mart 202
Rimsevics, Ilmars 49
Rinpoche, Telo 294
Robertson of Port Ellen, Lord 413
Rohatinski, Zeljko 148
Roman, Petre 173, 472
Rop, Anton 479
Roşca, Iurie 112, 113
Roustamov, Elman 394
Rozłucki, Wiesław 604
Rroqi, Shpetim 401
Rubiks, Alfreds 401
Rugova, Ibrahim 169, 307
Ruml, Jan 221
Rupel, Dmitirij 481
Rusnok, Jiří 482
Rustamyan, Armen 27
Rutskoi, Aleksandr 487, 605
Rüütel, Arnold 198, 203, 204, 214, 361, 495

S

Sakharov, Viktor 381
Saktor, Ivan 134
Sanader, Ivo 148
Sándor, László 399
Sangheli, Andrei 372
Sârbu, Radu 557
Šarkinas, Reinoldijus 49
Sarkissian, Aram 23, 177, 468
Sarkissian, Ashot 105
Sarkissian, Tigran 101
Sarkissian, Vazgen 22, 467
Sarnet, Väino 204
Saroukhian, Gayane 513
Sarović, Mirko 72, 435, 500, 507, 509
Savisaar, Edgar 197, 201, 202, 318, 562
Savov, Stefan 172
Saxecoburggotski, Simeon 83, 90, 94, 384, 402, 403, 437, 462, 500, 559, 586, 593
Schmögnerová, Brigita 501
Schuster, Rudolf 189, 433, 437, 502, 519, 523
Schwimmer, Walter 137
Sechka, Leanid 539
Sedrakian, Sedrak 612
Selami, Eduard 175
Selfo, Hysen 401
Semolič, Dušan 30
Semyonev, Vladimir 294
Šešelj, Vojislav 510
Shahmammadov, Shamil Mammad oglu 42
Shaimiev, Mintimer 566
Sharetski, Syamyon 5
Shcharansky, Anatoly 251
Shcherbitsky, Vladimir 577
Shehu, Mehmet 14, 255
Shehu, Tritan 175
Shevardnadze, Eduard 16, 116, 183, 229, 234, 370, 412, 424, 514, 624
Shivarov, Svetoslav 88
Shmakov, Mikhail 217
Shoigu, Sergei 590
Shopov, Dragomir 88
Shushkevich, Stanislau 52, 122, 346
Siimann, Mart 198, 202
Silajdžić, Haris 71, 431, 432
Silko, Petr 588
Simeon II see Saxecoburggotski, Simeon
Simić, Ilija 150
Simor, András 81
Siradeghian, Vano 426
Škele, Andris 65, 66, 321, 326, 440

Slánský, Rudolf 123
Slesers, Ainars 326
Šleževičius, Adolfas 335
Slota, Ján 520
Smajlović, Mensur 106
Smirnov, Igor 373, 571
Smirnov, Stanislav A. 106
Smolensky, Aleksandr 501
Snegur, Mircea 112, 372
Sobchak, Anatoly 313, 462
Solana Madariaga, Javier 605
Soljić, Vladimir 146
Somr, Zdeněk 192
Sorokin, Oleksandr 582
Soros, George 552
Spahiu, Ekrem 385
Špidla, Vladimir 161, 622
Stalin, Josef 16, 34, 59, 81, 92, 99, 108, 122, 123, 126, 128, 135, 138, 139, 181, 185, 209, 236, 274, 290, 293, 294, 363, 387, 417, 423, 485, 497, 516, 553, 565, 577
Stamboliyski, Aleksandur 87
Stanishev, Sergei 94
Stanković, Zoran 612
Starosciak, Jacek 136
Statkevich, Nikolai 61
Stelmach, Volodymyr 398
Stepashin, Sergei 487
Stibral, Milan 155
Stiess, Jan 404
Stoica, Valeriu 402
Stolojan, Teodor Dumitru 402
Stoyan, Oleksandr 217
Stoyanov, Petar 84, 88, 91, 94, 172, 384, 403, 462, 501, 586
Stráský, Jan 117
Strasser, H. 165
Sturza, Ion 113, 373
Styraite, Julia 79
Suchocka, Hanna 222, 447
Sugarev, Edwin 192
Suruceanu, Nicolae 549
Svilanović, Goran 117, 560
Svoboda, Cyril 114
Svoboda, Jiří 124
Svoboda, Ludvík 123
Syargeeu, Mikalay 606
Sylvester, John B. 556
Symonenko, Petro 129, 130, 439, 547, 578
Sysas, Algirdas 344
Szabó, Endre 220
Szent-Iványi, István 18
Szili, Katalin 261

641

T

Taagepera, Rein 201
Talmaci, Leonid 396
Tanasescu, Mihai 563
Tanchev, Petur 87
Tarand, Andres 370, 371
Tarlev, Vasile 126, 373, 564
Tatliyev, Suleyman Bayram oglu 104
Teoctist, Patriarch 477
Ter-Petrossian, Levon 22, 27, 177, 304, 425
Thaci, Hashim 307, 308
Theodhori, Qirjako 391
Tihic, Sulejman 434
Tiivas, Gert 563
Tito 70, 110, 141, 237, 295, 308, 328, 348, 445, 457, 506, 512, 528, 541, 568, 573, 609, 614, 620
Tkachenko, Oleksandr 439, 547, 578
Tökés, Bishop László 259
Tolevski, Zhivko 133
Tolnay, Lajos 257
Tomać, Zdravko 538
Tomaszevski, Valdemar 342
Tomčić, Zlatko 150
Tomov, Aleksandur 207
Topadze, Giorgi 273
Torgyán, József 272
Torlopov, Vladimir 305
Trajkovski, Boris 275, 350, 569
Trentchev, Konstantin 445
Trpeski, Ljube 396
Tudjman, Franjo 141, 144, 147, 196, 242, 310, 362, 538, 573
Tudor, Corneliu Vadim 243, 244, 270, 473
Tugushi, Irakli 234
Tůma, Zdeněk 154
Tupurkovski, Vasil 167, 168
Turalić, Fuad 282
Tusevljak, Spasoje 72, 146
Tusk, Donald 115, 116, 222
Tymoshenko, Yuliya 131, 212

U

Udovenko, Hennadiy 455
Udre, Ingrida 322
Ulmanis, Guntis 321
Urbánek, Karel 124

V

Vaarja, Lauri 276
Vacaroiu, Nicolae 472
Vagnorius, Gediminas 253, 335
Vähi, Tiit 198, 202
Valentin, Marcel 299
Valionis, Antanas 592
van den Hout, Tjaco 442
Varga, Mihály 592
Varkulevičius, Rimas 31
Vashchuk, Kateryna 5
Vasile, Radu 112, 473
Vasiliev, Dmitri 425
Veidemann, Andra 201
Velchev, Milen 593
Vensel, Vello 48
Veselinovič, Draško 345
Videnov, Zhan 83, 93, 559
Vidošević, Nadan 145
Vike-Freiberga, Vaira 64, 322, 595
Vitrenko, Nataliya 459
Vlatković, Dušan 398
Vojković, Hrvoje 151
Volas, Cedo 133
Volkov, Aleksandr 575
Volynets, Mikhail 131
Voronin, Vladimir 125, 126, 356, 373, 565, 571, 599
Voskanian, Hrant 121
Vujanović, Filip 179, 600, 617
Vyachorka, Vintsuk 60
Vyakhirev, Rem I. 226

W

Wałęsa, Lech 115, 170, 226, 286, 317, 447, 453, 549, 551, 602
Weijers, Jan 333
Wellink, Nout 47
Wildhaber, Luzius 208
Wojtyła, Karol see John Paul II, Pope
Wolfensohn, James D. 607

X

Xhaferi, Arben 176
Xhuveli, Lufter 11

Y

Yakovlev, Vladimir 497
Yarov, Yurii 121
Yavlinskii, Grigorii 608
Yeltsin, Boris 31, 56, 108, 127, 129, 135, 212, 226, 240, 246, 282, 297, 313, 332, 380, 424, 462, 486, 492, 515, 566, 587, 590, 605, 608, 609, 624
Yeritssian, Sergo 137
Ymeri, Ymer 433
Yushchenko, Viktor 130, 578, 581

Z

Zagozen, Frank 534
Zeman, Miloš 157, 160, 298, 622
Zhelev, Zhelyu 83, 91, 93, 192, 558, 585
Zhidakov, Alexei V. 415
Zhirinovskii, Vladimir 332, 333
Zhivkov, Todor 83, 92, 192, 623
Zigerists, Joahims 213
Zivenko, Sergei 480
Zizić, Zoran 171, 442, 548, 616
Zlenko, Anatoliy 623
Zmejkovski, Boris 275
Zografski, Evgeni 353
Zogu, Leka 12, 385
Zoryan, Hrayr 28
Zubak, Kresimir 71, 146, 408
Zulfagarov, Tofik 35
Zyuganov, Gennadii 127, 128, 463, 487, 611, 624